Dear West Customer:

West Academic Publishing has changed the look of its American Casebook Series®.

In keeping with our efforts to promote sustainability, we have replaced our former covers with book covers that are more environmentally friendly. Our casebooks will now be covered in a 100% renewable natural fiber. In addition, we have migrated to an ink supplier that favors vegetable-based materials, such as soy.

Using soy inks and natural fibers to print our textbooks reduces VOC emissions. Moreover, our primary paper supplier is certified by the Forest Stewardship Council, which is testament to our commitment to conservation and responsible business management.

The new cover design has migrated from the long-standing brown cover to a contemporary charcoal fabric cover with silver-stamped lettering and black accents. Please know that inside the cover, our books continue to provide the same trusted content that you've come to expect from West.

We've retained the ample margins that you have told us you appreciate in our texts while moving to a new, larger font, improving readability. We hope that you will find these books a pleasing addition to your bookshelf.

Another visible change is that you will no longer see the brand name Thomson West on our print products. With the recent merger of Thomson and Reuters, I am pleased to announce that books published under the West Academic Publishing imprint will once again display the West brand.

It will likely be several years before all of our casebooks are published with the new cover and interior design. We ask for your patience as the new covers are rolled out on new and revised books knowing that behind both the new and old covers, you will find the finest in legal education materials for teaching and learning.

Thank you for your continued patronage of the West brand, which is both rooted in history and forward looking towards future innovations in legal education. We invite you to be a part of our next evolution.

Best regards,

Louis H. Higgins
Editor in Chief, West Academic Publishing

THE LAW AND ETHICS OF LAW PRACTICE

■ ■ ■

By

Margaret Raymond
Professor of Law
University of Iowa

AMERICAN CASEBOOK SERIES®

WEST®
A Thomson Reuters business

Mat #40590953

Thomson Reuters created this publication to provide you with accurate and authoritative information concerning the subject matter covered. However, this publication was not necessarily prepared by persons licensed to practice law in a particular jurisdiction. Thomson Reuters does not render legal or other professional advice, and this publication is not a substitute for the advice of an attorney. If you require legal or other expert advice, you should seek the services of a competent attorney or other professional.

American Casebook Series is a trademark registered in the U.S. Patent and Trademark Office.

© 2009 Thomson Reuters
  610 Opperman Drive
  St. Paul, MN 55123
  1–800–313–9378
Printed in the United States of America

ISBN: 978–0–314–18043–8

 TEXT IS PRINTED ON 10% POST CONSUMER RECYCLED PAPER

To Mark, Rosie and Thea

*

PREFACE

Professional responsibility is a challenging and fascinating course to teach. It is fascinating because lawyers, what they do, and the situations into which legal work plunges them are endlessly interesting; it is challenging because it is, for the most part, a required course to which at least some students come with less than their usual enthusiasm. At the same time, the course is perhaps the only one in law school that addresses how lawyers can attend to and protect their own interests and obligations as well as those of their clients. My hope is that students emerge from the course surprised by and attuned to the ways in which the course will be relevant to their lives in practice; the frequent phone calls I get from former students suggest that they do.

This book is designed with many interests in mind. The first is that desire to surprise students with the engaging and compelling nature of this material—and to keep them awake. The text, accordingly, includes a variety of contemporary materials, many dealing with the practice experiences of relatively junior lawyers. The book is designed to work through the range of duties that lawyers owe to various stakeholders, but also to approximate the arc of representation, starting at the beginning (am I competent to represent this client? how do I become someone's lawyer?), and working through the obligations (confidentiality, loyalty) that inure to the client once that relationship is formed. The later chapters deal with duties that the lawyer owes to others besides the client, including the court, third parties, or the legal system, as well as what I call duties to the guild, involving the preservation of the lawyer's professional monopoly.

Another concern is that students in a class on professional responsibility are destined for a broad variety of practices. Some may be headed for a large corporate law firm, while others may be planning a solo practice or government service. The book addresses issues that arise in a diverse range of practice environments; the goal is to equip all students to recognize the issues that are pertinent to their practices and experiences, and to think about them concretely and practically.

One other issue is the optimal level of coverage in a book like this. The book is appropriate for a 2– or 3–credit course in professional responsibility, but teachers and students come to such courses with a wide range of goals. I want the book to be intellectually rigorous and challenging, but also to arm the user with a firm grounding in the most fundamental issues in the law of professional responsibility. It is tempting to include every esoteric issue that anyone in the field might conceivably want to teach, but that desire has to be tempered by the goal of making the book usable and keeping it under fifty pounds. The compromise is the problems that finish each chapter. These problems are taken, for the most part, from contemporary cases or news stories, and can be used to enrich the basic text and expand the material in many different directions. They are also useful for students as a vehicle for review.

The book is designed for use with a rules supplement that includes the ABA's Model Rules of Professional Conduct, though the book recognizes throughout that model rules are not the rules anywhere and that it is incumbent upon lawyers to inform themselves about the governing rules in the jurisdictions where they practice.

The materials in this casebook have been edited. Significant omissions have been indicated, for the most part, through the use of ellipses, but not all deletions are indicated, and omission of citations or footnotes in case materials is not indicated. The goal is to make the materials comprehensible and easy to use. Footnotes in cases have been renumbered to reflect editing.

ACKNOWLEDGMENTS

I have had a great deal of assistance in preparing this book, and owe thanks to many people: to my assistant, Amanda Bibb, for her extraordinary efforts and good humor; to my student research assistants, Andrew Benjamin, Allen Best, Lindsey Karls, Benton Page, Anna Timmerman, and Nora Tauke, for their research and proofreading assistance; to our Law Library staff and student assistants, for their research support; and to the students in my Professional Responsibility classes in the spring and fall of 2008, who lent themselves with vigor and energy to the task of making the book the best it could be. There is no substitute for the comments and suggestions of students who have actively wrestled with the material. In particular, I want to acknowledge the assistance of Kristin Bjella, Laura Folkerts, Mari Kaluza, Amy Kretkowski, Gina Lavarda, Lacee Oliver, Emily Stegmaier, and Charlie Williams. I also appreciate the assistance of attorney Mike Gross.

The support of my colleagues and the administration at the University of Iowa College of Law is, as always, gratefully appreciated.

*

Summary of Contents

ix

CHAPTER 14.   DUTIES TO THE GUILD: ADMISSION TO THE BAR AND UNAUTHORIZED PRACTICE

CHAPTER 15.   DISCIPLINARY JURISDICTION AND CHOICE OF LAW [p. 609]

*

TABLE OF CONTENTS

CHAPTER 4.   THE DUTY OF COMPETENCE

CHAPTER 5.   WHO IS THE CLIENT? ENTERING INTO AND ENDING THE ATTORNEY–CLIENT RELATIONSHIP

*

TABLE OF CASES

The principal cases are in bold type. Cases cited or discussed in the text are in roman type. References are to pages. Cases cited in principal cases and within other quoted materials are not included.

TABLE OF STATUTES AND RULES

THE LAW AND ETHICS
OF LAW PRACTICE

*

CHAPTER 1

INTRODUCTION: WHY STUDY PROFESSIONAL RESPONSIBILITY?

■ ■ ■

Welcome to Professional Responsibility! This is the one (mostly) required course in law school that involves the study of the law that applies, not to your client, but to you. Its position in the law school curriculum is largely an artifact of history (more on that later), and for decades the subject received relatively little scholarly attention. In recent years, there has been an explosion of interest in the field. It has become a significant practice area of its own, with its own professional organizations, research tools, and specialty journals.

This might be an equally accurate description of many subjects: securities regulation, or environmental law, or tax. While specialists in those subjects might think that courses in those areas should be a required part of the curriculum, at most law schools students have the choice of whether to study them or not. Why is professional responsibility different? Most of you are probably taking this class because it is required. Why do you have to bother with it? Many students may also be thinking, "Why do I need an ethics class? I'm an ethical person. I don't need a semester-long lesson in morality."

It is probably true that your ethical sensibilities with regard to the issues that arise in your ordinary life are already well-ingrained. You go to a store, and the clerk inadvertently gives you $10 too much in change. What do you do? You go through the drive-thru and get the wrong bag of food—$25 worth of snacks, instead of the soda you ordered and paid for. What do you do? Your best friend is planning to marry someone you know is cheating on her—what do you do? You bought cheap tickets in the bleachers, but no one's watching when you walk by the exclusive boxes right behind third base—do you sit in the expensive seats, even though you didn't pay for them? Chances are that, however you answer these questions, you will not find these decisions all that difficult. You are familiar with these kinds of dilemmas, and are probably comfortable with how you would address them. Your views about how to handle these situations may come from a wide range of sources: your religious faith, if you have one; your own moral views; your desire for self-gratification; your sense of your community's standards; your fear of or perhaps the

1

likelihood of getting caught; and your awareness of any applicable rules, as well as the potential sanctions for violating them. To the extent that you find ethical dilemmas challenging in your everyday life, it is probably because they pit two strongly held values against each other: your desire to protect your friend versus your desire not to tattle, perhaps, or your desire to enjoy yourself versus your desire to do the right thing.

Two things are true about the world of legal ethics that are not true of your prior experience. First, you are now entering a new community, and new and different rules apply to your conduct. To some extent, as a lawyer, you are still just a human being, and your moral intuitions will still be extremely relevant to your law practice. But you have some additional obligations and duties imposed by virtue of your role as a lawyer that may affect your choices and decisions. This course will acquaint you with those legal rules. Special rules don't just apply to lawyers, of course. Many professions have specific obligations that apply to their members. It is appropriate for you to learn the rules that apply to yours.

legal rules

The second important factor in developing your sensibility to ethical decisionmaking in the context of law practice is that the situations that will arise in this context, unlike the everyday ones we have already discussed, are neither common to your experience nor intuitive. Can you represent a criminal defendant when one of the witnesses who will testify against him is a former client for whom you wrote a will six years ago? If your client tells you that he has cheated on his taxes, do you have the right to report him to the IRS? Do you have an obligation to do so? Does that depend on whether you helped him cheat on his taxes? If you move from one law firm to another, will your new firm need to withdraw from representing a client in a case if, at your old firm, you worked on the case for the other side? Your ordinary, seat-of-the-pants intuitions about right and wrong are probably of little help to you in addressing these specialized problems. While these kinds of issues may seem novel and somewhat puzzling to you now, this course will help you become familiar with the kinds of issues that are likely to arise in the practice of law and will equip you with the skills you need to address them.

not intuitive

The ethical decisionmaking of lawyers is also problematic because the unique role of the lawyer may create situations in which the lawyer's moral intuition is at odds with what the law requires. Deciding to act in a way which is both moral and legal is not difficult; deciding not to act in a way which is neither moral nor legal is similarly obvious. It is the situations where law and morality conflict that pose the most difficulty.

law and morality sometimes at odds

To analyze problems that pose these kinds of complex concerns, you need to know what your moral intuitions suggest and what the law requires. Learning what the law requires in the context of professional responsibility is, like any other area of the law, harder than it sounds. There are areas where the rules are clear, and areas where they are more nuanced or uncertain. Ethics issues may require the close parsing of statutory or regulatory language, the review and interpretation of caselaw and persuasive authority, and the factual distinction of non-controlling precedent. Lawyers contemplating their ethical obligations need to figure out what the law is. Like any area of law, that means both a base level of fundamental knowledge, and an obligation to advance that knowledge using research tools.

Lawyers also need to contemplate the level of certainty under which they wish to operate. Should lawyers making decisions about their own conduct treat those issues in the same way they treat the defense of past conduct by a client? the same way they treat advising a client about future conduct? in a different and more conservative way than either of those? Should these answers be the same for all lawyers, or should there be a sliding scale that takes into account the risk tolerance of particular individuals or the nature of their practices? There are no clear answers to these questions, though there is a lot of discussion about them. You will want to contemplate them yourself as you go forward.

Professional Responsibility is also a course that is organized different-ly than much of the law school curriculum. Most courses explore an area of the law as it applies to the different players who may be affected by it. In the basic tax course, we learn the law of federal income taxation and think about that area of law from the perspective of both the taxpayer and the government. In criminal procedure, we consider the law as it applies to the police and to criminal defendants. In that respect, most law study is distinctly vertical, requiring the mastery of a field of law in its myriad application to all the actors who are affected by it.

We could, instead, teach horizontally, so that every course considered the application of a range of cross-cutting fields to a particular category of client or situation. But for the most part we don't. We don't ordinarily teach "the law of the police" or "the law of the employer." Instead, we assume that we can learn the law that applies to these various actors through study of the range of legal fields that will affect them. We assume that particular bodies of substantive law have coherence and should be studied together. Attempts to cobble together courses that deal with a range of law that applies to a particular category of activities or people have been criticized; Prof. (and Judge) Frank Easterbrook has argued that this kind of course—which he derisively termed "The Law of the Horse"—"is doomed to be shallow and to miss unifying principles."[1] Yet the importance of guaranteeing that lawyers have been educated about the wide range of law that applies to their conduct overrides that usual hesitancy. This explains why the legal ethics course contains materials that touch on a wide range of law school subjects, including agency law, evidence law, contracts, torts, and regulatory law, as well as the rules of professional responsibility, and why it may have a different "feel" than other areas of law study.

---

1. See Frank H. Easterbrook, *Cyberspace and the Law of the Horse*, 1996 U. Chi. Legal F. 207 (1996).

A. WHOSE INTERESTS ARE REFLECTED IN THE RULES GOVERNING LAWYER CONDUCT?

The rules of lawyer conduct could be viewed as reflecting the interests of several distinct groups of stakeholders. Lawyers themselves, clients or potential clients, courts and judges, and the public may all have distinct interests in the regulation of lawyers. If we consider the range of areas in which lawyer behavior might be regulated, we can see two things.

The first is that at least some of these stakeholders may view the range of areas appropriate for lawyer regulation as very broad. Are lawyers just market actors, subject to market constraints? Or should they be governed by a higher and more demanding set of standards? Should the rules regulate the details of practice, like the fees lawyers may charge or what kinds of cases they can take? How should the law handle more fundamental questions? What should the consequences be if lawyers make mistakes? How closely should they guard their clients' secrets? Should they have a separate duty to protect others besides their clients? Should they have civil liability to all persons who are harmed by their conduct?

The second is that the many stakeholders in these areas will have very different views of the right answers to these questions. They may seek to use their leverage to advance those different views of how lawyers should be regulated. While those views are rarely couched in the language of self-interest, concerns about stakeholder interests are rarely far from the conversation. Issues like the scope of the duty of confidentiality or the attorney-client privilege, the regulation of the unauthorized practice of law, the control of attorney advertising and solicitation, or the control of funds reflect how the battles between stakeholders have been, for the moment, resolved. As you move through the materials in this course, ask yourself whether the balance has been struck properly.

B. LAWYER RULES AND ORDINARY MORALITY: A FIRST LOOK

We have discussed the possibility that the situations that arise in the context of legal practice and the rules that apply to those situations may be different from what you have experienced in everyday life. In the following case, a lawyer was confronted with a unique problem which pitted his obligations as a lawyer against his moral obligations as a human being. This classic of the professional responsibility literature is worth a look as you embark on your study of the subject. Did the lawyer do the right thing? Would you have behaved differently? How?

SPAULDING v. ZIMMERMAN

116 N.W.2d 704 (Minn. 1962)

Thomas Gallagher, Justice.

Appeal from an order of the District Court of Douglas County vacating and setting aside a prior order of such court dated May 8, 1957, approving a settlement made on behalf of David Spaulding on March 5, 1957, at which time he was a minor of the age of 20 years; and in connection therewith, vacating and setting aside releases executed by him and his parents, a stipulation of dismissal, an order for dismissal with prejudice, and a judgment entered pursuant thereto.

Vacated prior order approving settlement

The prior action was brought against defendants by Theodore Spaulding, as father and natural guardian of David Spaulding, for injuries sustained by David in an automobile accident, arising out of a collision which occurred August 24, 1956, between an automobile driven by John Zimmerman, in which David was a passenger, and one owned by John Ledermann and driven by Florian Ledermann.

injuries from car accident

On appeal defendants contend that the court was without jurisdiction to vacate the settlement solely because their counsel then possessed information, unknown to plaintiff herein, that at the time he was suffering from an aorta aneurysm which may have resulted from the accident. . . .

After the accident, David's injuries were diagnosed by his family physician, Dr. James H. Cain, as a severe crushing injury of the chest with multiple rib fractures; a severe cerebral concussion, probably with petechial hemorrhages of the brain; and bilateral fractures of the clavicles. At Dr. Cain's suggestion, on January 3, 1957, David was examined by Dr. John F. Pohl, an orthopedic specialist, who made X-ray studies of his chest. Dr. Pohl's detailed report of this examination included the following:

> " . . . The lung fields are clear. The heart and aorta are normal."

Nothing in such report indicated the aorta aneurysm with which David was then suffering. On March 1, 1957, at the suggestion of Dr. Pohl, David was examined from a neurological viewpoint by Dr. Paul S. Blake, and in the report of this examination there was no finding of the aorta aneurysm.

no initial finding of an aorta aneurysm

In the meantime, on February 22, 1957, at defendants' request, David was examined by Dr. Hewitt Hannah, a neurologist. On February 26, 1957, the latter reported to Messrs. Field, Arveson, & Donoho, attorneys for defendant John Zimmerman, as follows:

> The one feature of the case which bothers me more than any other part of the case is the fact that this boy of 20 years of age has an aneurysm, which means a dilatation of the aorta and the arch of the aorta. Whether this came out of this accident I cannot say with any degree of certainty and I have discussed it with the Roentgenologist and a couple of Internists. . . . Of course an aneurysm or dilatation of

aneurysm identified

the aorta in a boy of this age is a serious matter as far as his life. This aneurysm may dilate further and it might rupture with further dilatation and this would cause his death.

It would be interesting also to know whether the X-ray of his lungs, taken immediately following the accident, shows this dilatation or not. If it was not present immediately following the accident and is now present, then we could be sure that it came out of the accident.

Prior to the negotiations for settlement, the contents of the above report were made known to counsel for defendants Florian and John Ledermann.

The case was called for trial on March 4, 1957, at which time the respective parties and their counsel possessed such information as to David's physical condition as was revealed to them by their respective medical examiners as above described. It is thus apparent that neither David nor his father, the nominal plaintiff in the prior action, was then aware that David was suffering the aorta aneurysm but on the contrary believed that he was recovering from the injuries sustained in the accident.

On the following day an agreement for settlement was reached wherein, in consideration of the payment of $6,500, David and his father agreed to settle in full for all claims arising out of the accident.

Richard S. Roberts, counsel for David, thereafter presented to the court a petition for approval of the settlement, wherein David's injuries were described as:

> ... severe crushing of the chest, with multiple rib fractures, severe cerebral concussion, with petechial hemorrhages of the brain, bilateral fractures of the clavicles.

Attached to the petition were affidavits of David's physicians, Drs. James H. Cain and Paul S. Blake, wherein they set forth the same diagnoses they had made upon completion of their respective examinations of David as above described. At no time was there information disclosed to the court that David was then suffering from an aorta aneurysm which may have been the result of the accident. Based upon the petition for settlement and such affidavits of Drs. Cain and Blake, the court on May 8, 1957, made its order approving the settlement.

Early in 1959, David was required by the army reserve, of which he was a member, to have a physical checkup. For this, he again engaged the services of Dr. Cain. In this checkup, the latter discovered the aorta aneurysm. He then reexamined the X rays which had been taken shortly after the accident and at this time discovered that they disclosed the beginning of the process which produced the aneurysm. He promptly sent David to Dr. Jerome Grismer for an examination and opinion. The latter confirmed the finding of the aorta aneurysm and recommended immediate surgery therefor. This was performed by him at Mount Sinai Hospital in Minneapolis on March 10, 1959.

Shortly thereafter, David, having attained his majority, instituted the present action for additional damages due to the more serious injuries including the aorta aneurysm which he alleges proximately resulted from the accident. As indicated above, the prior order for settlement was vacated. In a memorandum made a part of the order vacating the settlement, the court stated:

> . . . The mistake concerning the existence of the aneurysm was not mutual. For reasons which do not appear, plaintiff's doctor failed to ascertain its existence. By reason of the failure of plaintiff's counsel to use available rules of discovery, plaintiff's doctor and all his representatives did not learn that defendants and their agents knew of its existence and possible serious consequences. Except for the character of the concealment in the light of plaintiff's minority, the Court would, I believe, be justified in denying plaintiff's motion to vacate, leaving him to whatever questionable remedy he may have against his doctor and against his lawyer.

> That defendants' counsel concealed the knowledge they had is not disputed. The essence of the application of the above rule is the character of the concealment. Was it done under circumstances that defendants must be charged with knowledge that plaintiff did not know of the injury? If so, an enriching advantage was gained for defendants at plaintiff's expense. There is no doubt of the good faith of both defendants' counsel. There is no doubt that during the course of the negotiations, when the parties were in an adversary relationship, no rule required or duty rested upon defendants or their representatives to disclose this knowledge. However, once the agreement to settle was reached, it is difficult to characterize the parties' relationship as adverse. At this point all parties were interested in securing Court approval. . . .

> But it is not possible to escape the inference that defendants' representatives knew, or must be here charged with knowing, that plaintiff under all the circumstances would not accept the sum of $6500.00 if he or his representatives knew of the aneurysm and its possible serious consequences. Moreover, there is no showing by defendants that would support an inference that plaintiff and his representatives knew of the existence of the aneurysm but concluded that it was not causally related to the accident.

> When the adversary nature of the negotiations concluded in a settlement, the procedure took on the posture of a joint application to the Court, at least so far as the facts upon which the Court could and must approve settlement is concerned. It is here that the true nature of the concealment appears, and defendants' failure to act affirmatively, after having been given a copy of the application for approval, can only be defendants' decision to take a calculated risk that the settlement would be final. . . .

To hold that the concealment was not of such character as to result in an unconscionable advantage over plaintiff's ignorance or mistake, would be to penalize innocence and incompetence and reward less than full performance of an officer of the Court's duty to make full disclosure to the Court when applying for approval in minor settlement proceedings.

The principles applicable to the court's authority to vacate settlements made on behalf of minors and approved by it appear well-established. With reference thereto, we have held that the court in its discretion may vacate such a settlement, even though it is not induced by fraud or bad faith, where it is shown that in the accident the minor sustained separate and distinct injuries which were not known or considered by the court at the time settlement was approved; and even though the releases furnished therein purported to cover both known and unknown injuries resulting from the accident. The court may vacate such a settlement for mistake even though the mistake was not mutual in the sense that both parties were similarly mistaken as to the nature and extent of the minor's injuries, but where it is shown that one of the parties had additional knowledge with respect thereto and was aware that neither the court nor the adversary party possessed such knowledge when the settlement was approved. . . .

From the foregoing it is clear that in the instant case the court did not abuse its discretion in setting aside the settlement which it had approved on plaintiff's behalf while he was still a minor. It is undisputed that neither he nor his counsel nor his medical attendants were aware that at the time settlement was made he was suffering from an aorta aneurysm which may have resulted from the accident. The seriousness of this disability is indicated by Dr. Hannah's report indicating the imminent danger of death therefrom. This was known by counsel for both defendants but was not disclosed to the court at the time it was petitioned to approve the settlement. While no canon of ethics or legal obligation may have required them to inform plaintiff or his counsel with respect thereto, or to advise the court therein, it did become obvious to them at the time, that the settlement then made did not contemplate or take into consideration the disability described. This fact opened the way for the court to later exercise its discretion in vacating the settlement and under the circumstances described we cannot say that there was any abuse of discretion on the part of the court in so doing. . . .

Affirmed.

NOTES

1.   Imagine that you are not an attorney. You learn that a young man whom you know slightly is suffering from an aneurysm, which, if untreated, could result in his immediate and untimely death. Do you tell him or tell his parents? Why or why not? What caused the lawyer in this case to behave as he did?

2.   If David had not been a juvenile at the time the settlement was entered, would he have obtained relief in this case? Did he have other ways to obtain relief? What were they?

3.   As we will see, the confidentiality provisions of the ethics rules provide an exception for disclosures made with the "informed consent" of the client. If the attorneys for the defense in this case had wanted to disclose David Spaulding's medical condition to David, or perhaps to his parents, at the time of the initial settlement, what would they have had to do? What do you suppose "informed consent" means? See Model Rule 1.0(e) (" 'Informed consent' denotes the agreement by a person to a proposed course of conduct after the lawyer has communicated adequate information and explanation about the material risks of and reasonably available alternatives to the proposed course of conduct.") Imagine the conversation you would have with the client. What disclosures do you think you would need to make? Role-play the conversation with the client.

4.   Suppose that the rules of professional conduct required you to keep David Spaulding's condition a secret. Would you have done so? What would your alternatives have been?

CHAPTER 2

SOURCES OF LAW FOR PROFESSIONAL RESPONSIBILITY

■ ■ ■

What law governs your conduct as a lawyer? You are already familiar with many of the sources of law that apply to lawyers. Lawyer agrees to write an appellate brief for a client for $5000; after reviewing the file, Lawyer realizes that this is a lot more work than she expected, and she calls the client and raises the price to $10,000. What law applies? Lawyer agrees to bring suit against a municipality on behalf of a client who slipped on an icy sidewalk, but then misses the very short deadline for filing a notice of claim against the municipality and causes the client to forfeit her claim. What law applies? Lawyer learns from a friend who works at a corporation of a forthcoming corporate acquisition and buys stock in the company that is being acquired in the hopes that the price of his stock will rise once the acquisition becomes public. What law applies? The law of contracts, torts, and criminal law apply with equal force to lawyers; lawyers must comply with securities laws, money laundering prohibitions, and the tax code. Consistent with the "law of the horse" nature of this course, we will spend some time studying with more specificity how doctrines you may have studied in other areas of law apply specifically to the obligations of lawyers.

In addition, there are several sources of law that apply uniquely to lawyers and law practice.

A. PROFESSIONAL RESPONSIBILITY RULES

Each jurisdiction imposes on lawyers admitted to practice in that jurisdiction (and sometimes beyond that) a set of rules that govern lawyer conduct. In most jurisdictions, these are court rules, adopted by the highest court of the state. Compliance with these rules is a requirement of continued admission to practice. In every jurisdiction, a disciplinary mechanism exists to investigate complaints that lawyers have disobeyed the rules of professional responsibility, to adjudicate claims of violation of the rules, and to impose sanctions when violations are found.

Every jurisdiction writes its own rules of professional responsibility. However, in most jurisdictions, these rules were developed using one of the American Bar Association's models of such rules as a starting point.

The ABA began its role in developing professional responsibility rules by adopting, in 1908, the Canons of Professional Ethics. There were originally thirty-two Canons; they were quite brief, somewhat vague, and highly aspirational in tone. Consider, for example, Canon 14, on suing a client for a fee: "Controversies with clients concerning compensation are to be avoided by the lawyer so far as shall be compatible with his self-respect and with his right to receive reasonable recompense for his services; and lawsuits with clients should be resorted to only to prevent injustice, imposition or fraud." The Canons were added to periodically, but in 1964 the then-President of the ABA, Lewis F. Powell, Jr. (later Justice), appointed a Special Committee on Evaluation of Ethical Standards (the "Wright Committee") to assess whether the Canons needed to be changed. The Committee produced the Model Code of Professional Responsibility, which was adopted by the ABA's House of Delegates in 1969.

The Model Code, like any model statute, was not the law anywhere—the ABA has no power to impose rules of professional responsibility on any jurisdiction. Like other drafters of model statutes, the ABA's goal in drafting model professional responsibility rules was twofold. One goal was to provide an effective template for jurisdictions looking to adopt such codes. Another was to create some uniformity among states with regard to professional responsibility rules. The Model Code was quite successful on both counts. In the years following its adoption by the ABA, many states adopted Model Code-based rules of professional conduct.

The Model Code had a three-tiered structure. The most basic principles were "canons," which were "statements of axiomatic norms." These were extremely brief and were even more broad and nonspecific than the 1908 Canons; for example, the Model Code's Canon 1 provided, "A Lawyer Should Assist in Maintaining the Integrity and Competence of the Legal Profession." Each Canon was followed by Ethical Considerations (or "ECs"), numbered in accordance with their corresponding canons; Canon 1, for example, was followed by ECs 1–1 through 1–6. The Ethical Considerations were "aspirational in character" and were intended to provide "a body of principles upon which the lawyer can rely for guidance in many specific situations." They were not, however, intended to be a basis for discipline. The actual rules whose violation could subject a lawyer to discipline were known as Disciplinary Rules (or "DRs"), and were again numbered in accordance with the corresponding canon; Canon 1, for example, had three disciplinary rules—DR 1–101, 1–102, and 1–103—associated with it. You will often see reported cases referring to previous Model Code-based versions of the disciplinary rules, so it is useful to have a basic understanding of how they were structured.

While widely adopted, Model Code-based ethics rules were subject to some criticism. Some viewed the Code as overly litigation-oriented, paying insufficient attention to the role of transactional and advisory lawyers. More significantly, the Watergate scandal of the early 1970s—which involved lawyers in a wide range of troubling and illegal conduct—convinced some that the ethical structure of the legal profession required a fundamental overhaul. Accordingly, the ABA once again formed a group, this time the Commission on Evaluation of Professional Standards (the "Kutak Commission") to consider whether to revise the Model Code or to start over. Ultimately, the Kutak Commission produced a new and distinct model, the Model Rules of Professional Conduct, which was adopted by the ABA House of Delegates in 1983.

As with the Model Code, the ABA's approval of the Model Rules did not make them the law anywhere. Moreover, the quick and enthusiastic adoption of the Model Code by a number of U.S. jurisdictions was not repeated when the Model Rules were promulgated. While some jurisdictions moved quickly to adopt new versions of their professional responsibility codes based on the Model Rules, others retained their Model Code-based rules of professional conduct. To the extent that consistency was viewed as desirable, this state of affairs was less than ideal. It even affected the bar examination. Reflecting the fact that many jurisdictions had adopted Model Rules-based ethics codes and that some had retained Model Code-based rules, for many years, the Multistate Professional Responsibility Examination (MPRE), the multiple choice professional responsibility examination that in most jurisdictions is a component of the bar examination, asked only questions that could be answered the same way under either the Model Code or the Model Rules. This approach was chosen intentionally so that the exam would be an acceptable testing vehicle for states with either Code-based or Rules-based ethics standards. This policy ended in 1999, and the MPRE now tests only the Model Rules, not the Model Code. Over the years some desire for uniformity (and the problem of testing ethics for jurisdictions which still had a Model Code-based set of professional responsibility rules once the MPRE moved to a Model Rules-only examination) has resulted in most jurisdictions moving to a Model Rules-based set of professional responsibility rules.

The ABA launched another commission, known as "Ethics 2000," in 1997. The Ethics 2000 commission produced significant changes to the Rules in 2002 (and again in 2003), but those changes retained the underlying format of the Model Rules.

Because many jurisdictions have adopted a Rules-based format for their own regulation of professional responsibility, the Model Rules are worthy of considerable time and attention. Remember, though, that in any given jurisdiction significant deviations from the Model Rules are possible; the only way to know what the professional responsibility rule is on a particular issue in a particular state is to look at the state's own rule, as well as the cases and ethics opinions decided under it. Be careful not to make assumptions; there are many areas in which considerable deviation from the Model Rules is commonplace.

The Model Rules have a two-level format: there are Rules and Comments. Rules are organized in chapters, very roughly arranged in terms of the function the rules serve. For example, the first chapter deals with the client-lawyer relationship. The rules in that chapter, numbered from 1.1 to 1.18, deal with various facets of that relationship, from the distribution of responsibility within that relationship (Rule 1.2) to the rules governing the lawyer's relationship with an entity client (Rule 1.13) or a client with diminished capacity (Rule 1.14). Associated with each Rule is a set of Comments, which are numbered individually and referred to by that number and by the rule with which they are associated. For example, the third comment to Rule 1.1 is described as "Comment [3] to Model Rule 1.1." (Yes, you have to use the brackets.) The first Model Rule, 1.0, is a definitions section, which you will find helpful as you interpret the Rules.

Read the Preamble and the Scope Note to the Model Rules. What is the significance of a Rule? A Comment? Do the Rules give rise to civil liability? How else are they used?

B. SPECIALIZED REGULATION OF PARTICULAR PRACTICE AREAS

The ethics rules do not represent the entire universe of lawyer regulation. Additional layers of regulation apply to lawyers engaged in the practice of law in particular specialized practice areas. Typically, these regulations are imposed by agencies before which the lawyers practice, and they reflect concerns that are specific to the area of practice. With some exceptions, lawyers in these practice areas must obey both their jurisdiction's rules of professional responsibility and the additional regulations imposed upon them. Some examples follow. What if the requirements of the federal practice area conflict with the state ethics rule? Which rule governs? *See North Carolina Formal Ethics Op. 2005–9.*

1. SARBANES–OXLEY

The corporate scandals of the early 2000s produced a clamor for closer regulation of, among other persons, attorneys involved in advising corporations. In response, Congress passed the Sarbanes–Oxley Act of 2002. Section 307 of the Act expressly directed the Securities and Exchange Commission (SEC) to promulgate rules regarding the conduct of attorneys "appearing and practicing before the Commission," 15 U.S.C. § 7245. The SEC accordingly promulgated those rules, which appear at 17 C.F.R. §§ 205.1–205.7. While you might think that very few lawyers—perhaps only those involved in hearings or proceedings before the SEC—are "appearing and practicing before the Commission," the definition of that term is much broader than a casual reading would suggest. The standards define "appearing and practicing before the Commission" to include "[p]roviding advice in respect of the United States securities laws or the Commission's rules or regulations thereunder regarding any document that the attorney has notice will be filed with or submitted to, or incorporated into any document that will be filed with or submitted to, the Commission, including the provision of such advice in the context of preparing, or participating in the preparation of, any such document." 17 C.F.R. 205.2 (2007). This means that any lawyer who advises a client about what should or should not be disclosed to the SEC (and that could be an environmental lawyer or an employment law specialist as well as a securities lawyer) is "appearing and practicing before the Commission" even if the lawyer knows nothing about securities law and even if she does not go anywhere near Washington, D.C.

A lawyer who is "appearing and practicing before the Commission" has a series of specific obligations if he or she is representing an issuer of securities and becomes aware of evidence of a "material violation" of law by the issuer. Those obligations involve reporting to legal counsel and, if the response is not satisfactory, ultimately require "up the ladder" reporting to higher authority in the organization. These obligations are discussed in more detail in Chapter 7. For now, though, it is important to recognize that these obligations are imposed by federal regulations, and apply in addition to the applicable state professional responsibility rules. Failure to comply with them can subject the lawyer to sanction for civil violation of the securities laws and may in addition subject the lawyer to discipline by the Commission, which can "result in an attorney being censured, or being temporarily or permanently denied the privilege of appearing or practicing before the Commission." 17 C.F.R. § 205.6.

2. CIRCULAR 230

Much as Sarbanes–Oxley's provisions regulate lawyers who practice before the Securities and Exchange Commission, Circular 230 (another name for 31 C.F.R. §§ 10.0–10.93) regulates attorneys and others who "practice before the Internal Revenue Service." The regulations, again, define this more broadly than you might anticipate; anyone "rendering written advice with respect to any entity, transaction, plan or arrangement . . . having a potential for tax avoidance or evasion" is deemed to be engaged in practice "before the Internal Revenue Service." 31 C.F.R. § 10.2. These regulations govern several categories of behavior by tax lawyers, including specific rules about the giving of tax opinions. Sanctions for violation of these regulations can range from censure to disbarment from practice before the Service. Monetary penalties are also available.

3. PATENT AND TRADEMARK OFFICE REGULATIONS

The Patent and Trademark Office (PTO) regulates attorneys who practice before it. 37 C.F.R. Part 10. Practice before the Office is limited to proceedings "pending before the Office." 37 C.F.R. § 10.1(s). The PTO has, in effect, its own rules of professional responsibility, many of which mirror the traditional professional responsibility rules, others of which are unique to the area of practice. Violation of these rules can subject a lawyer to sanction, including reprimand, suspension, or exclusion from practice before the PTO.

4. BANKRUPTCY CODE

The Bankruptcy Code imposes affirmative obligations on a lawyer filing any pleading in a bankruptcy matter. 11 U.S.C. § 707(b)(4)(C), for example, provides that "[t]he signature of an attorney on a petition, pleading, or written motion shall constitute a certification that the attorney has (i) performed a reasonable investigation into the circumstances that gave rise to the petition, pleading, or written motion; and (ii) determined that the petition, pleading, or written motion (I) is well grounded in fact; and (II) is warranted by existing law or a good faith argument for the extension, modification, or reversal of existing law and does not constitute an abuse under paragraph (1)." Failure to comply with these requirements subjects the attorney to liability for attorney's fees and costs.

5. RULE 11 AND OTHER SANCTIONS PROVISIONS

You may have considered Federal Rule of Civil Procedure 11 in your civil procedure course. Rule 11(b) provides that by signing a submission to a court, a lawyer certifies that, to the best of her "knowledge, information, and belief, formed after an inquiry reasonable under the circumstances," the submission

(1) . . . is not being presented for any improper purpose, such as to harass, cause unnecessary delay, or needlessly increase the cost of litigation;

(2) the claims, defenses, and other legal contentions are warranted by existing law or by a nonfrivolous argument for extending, modifying, or reversing existing law or for establishing new law;

(3) the factual contentions have evidentiary support or, if specifically so identified, will likely have evidentiary support after a reasonable opportunity for further investigation or discovery; and

(4) the denials of factual contentions are warranted on the evidence or, if specifically so identified, are reasonably based on belief or a lack of information.

Failure to comply with this Rule subjects the attorney to sanctions, which can include "nonmonetary directives; an order to pay a penalty into court; or, if imposed on motion and warranted for effective deterrence, an order directing payment to the movant of part or all of the reasonable attorney's fees and other expenses directly resulting from the violation." F.R.C.P. 11(c)(4).

One might consider Rule 11 an additional set of professional responsibility regulations for the litigator. There are other bases for the imposition of federal court sanctions on lawyers, including Federal Rules of Civil Procedure 16, 26, and 37 as well as 28 U.S.C. § 1927, which permits the imposition of sanctions on a lawyer "who so multiplies the proceedings in any case unreasonably and vexatiously." The sanction can include attorneys' fees. The federal courts also have the "inherent authority" to sanction lawyers for bad faith conduct. *Chambers v. NASCO, Inc.*, 501 U.S. 32 (1991).

6. PRECATORY STANDARDS

Some areas of practice have recommended codes of conduct which have been proffered by professional organizations. These are advisory only and there is no sanction for violating them; they are in some sense recommendations of best practices. Consider, for example, the Code of Pretrial Conduct and Code of Trial Conduct promulgated by the American College of Trial Lawyers. The American Bar Association has adopted Standards Relating to the Administration of Criminal Justice, with separate standards for the Prosecution Function and the Defense Function. These rules cannot be the subject of discipline, but they are often cited and referred to as guides to appropriate lawyer behavior.

The message here is that each area of practice may be governed by its own distinct set of ethical rules, and that any lawyer embarking on practice in a particular area needs to learn what rules apply to practice in that discipline and before the requisite agencies. These obligations are in addition to, not in lieu of, a lawyer's obligations under his or her state ethics rules.

C. SOURCES OF GUIDANCE: FINDING THE LAW OF PROFESSIONAL RESPONSIBILITY

We have considered the rules of professional conduct and other regulations governing attorney conduct. As most law students know, however, a rule or statute seldom provides a clear and unambiguous answer to a legal issue. Professional responsibility law is law first and foremost, and like any other area will present issues that are complex and do not have easy or obvious answers. Where does a lawyer look to find the answer to professional responsibility problems?

1. CASELAW

Judicial decisions often address issues of professional responsibility. These might include decisions in disciplinary cases, or in other matters in which the rules of professional responsibility are for some reason relevant. Accordingly, you will spend more time than you might have imagined reading judicial decisions on professional responsibility issues. Many of the materials in this book are reported judicial decisions.

2. ETHICS OPINIONS

The ABA Standing Committee on Ethics and Professional Responsibility publishes opinions dealing with ethics issues. The ABA used to issue two types of ethics opinion: formal and informal. Formal ethics opinions dealt with broader issues, while informal opinions addressed narrower and more specific inquiries. As a theoretical matter, informal opinions are still possible, but the Committee issued its last informal opinion in 1989. Even though these opinions are advisory only, they can be of persuasive force. In addition, many jurisdictions have a mechanism for seeking an "ethics opinion" about a specific issue or problem; those opinions are often published. These "ethics opinions" can also be helpful in interpreting state professional responsibility rules.

3. THE RESTATEMENT OF THE LAW GOVERNING LAWYERS

Completed in 2000, the Restatement (Third) of the Law Governing Lawyers attempts a broader synthesis of the law governing lawyers. It includes not only matters addressed by the ethics rules, but matters addressed by other areas of the law, such as torts, contracts, and evidence law. Like any other Restatement, it is not a definitive statement of the law anywhere, but has persuasive value and is a useful resource.

4. OTHER RESEARCH RESOURCES

There are a wide range of treatises and looseleaf sources available for research in the area of professional responsibility; many state bar websites also provide access to state professional responsibility rules, disciplinary decisions, and ethics opinions.

CHAPTER 3

CONSEQUENCES OF VIOLATING THE DISCIPLINARY RULES

■ ■ ■

A. SANCTIONS AND PROCEDURES

What happens to lawyers who violate the disciplinary rules? In theory, they are subject to discipline. In many cases, however, nothing happens to lawyers who violate the rules. Attorney discipline procedures vary from state to state, but as a general rule they involve assessment of a preliminary complaint, a determination that there is probable cause to proceed with the complaint, and a formal hearing process at which the attorney's misconduct must be proved. In order for an attorney to be disciplined, several steps have to take place: reporting of a complaint, investigation by disciplinary authorities, a determination of probable cause, and (barring a concession of wrongdoing) a formal adjudicative proceeding.

Consider what factors might hamper effective enforcement at each stage of this process. For example, what factors might tend to make the filing of a complaint more or less likely? Who is likely to be the source of disciplinary complaints? As we will see, lawyers have an obligation to report certain categories of disciplinary violations by other lawyers, but lawyers report other lawyers less often than such a rule might suggest. Can you think why? Is there a particular category of lawyer that you might expect to bring disciplinary complaints? Do you think judges are likely to bring disciplinary complaints? Clients, of course, are a significant source of complaints. Are certain clients or categories of clients more likely than others to use the disciplinary process to express dissatisfaction with their attorneys? According to one study, "the largest percentage of formal grievances involve criminal practice, personal injury practice, or domestic relations practice." Patricia W. Hatamyar & Kevin M. Simmons, *Are Women More Ethical Lawyers? An Empirical Study*, 31 Fla. State U. L.Rev. 785, 830 (2004). Why might this be the case? What other vehicles might a client use to retaliate against an attorney with whom the client is unhappy? Might there be categories of lawyers who are likely to be subjected to more disciplinary complaints from their clients than others? Given that the disciplinary system is complaint-based, we might question whether the disciplinary process is likely to succeed in identifying all

18

lawyers who have violated the rules of professional responsibility. There is little empirical evidence nationwide about the identity of disciplined lawyers, but what evidence there is suggests that solo and small-firm practitioners are disproportionately the recipients of attorney sanctions. If this is actually the case, can you speculate about why that might be? Hatamyar & Simmons also conclude that female attorneys are disciplined at lower rates than male attorneys. Why do you suppose that is?

Attorney discipline processes also turn on the availability of staff—often called bar or disciplinary counsel—to investigate and prosecute attorney sanctions. One statistic that might reflect whether the discipline process is hampered by a shortage of staff is the processing time for a disciplinary complaint. In 2006, the average time from receipt of a complaint to the filing of a formal disciplinary charge ranged from 89 days in Connecticut to 616 days in Massachusetts.[1] This was not by any means an anomalous statistic: this time period was 523 days in North Carolina, 426 days in Washington and a brisk 18 months in Iowa. If the primary purpose of attorney discipline is client protection, how effective is that discipline if years pass between the initial complaint and the ultimate punishment of the attorney?

Part of the lengthy processing time for complaints might reflect the high volume of complaints: the percentage of complaints that result in a probable cause determination and a charge against the lawyer varies from jurisdiction to jurisdiction, but on a national level something less than 4% of complaints filed against lawyers resulted in a finding of probable cause and a formal disciplinary complaint against the lawyer. Why do you suppose there are so many complaints, and why are so many of them deemed to be unfounded by disciplinary counsel?

Given that attorney discipline is a slow and sometimes unlikely consequence of misconduct, the legal system must rely on lawyers' internal commitment to the rules and values of the profession to ensure compliance with those standards most of the time. Consider Paragraph [16] of the Scope Note to the Model Rules of Professional Conduct: "Compliance with the Rules, as with all law in an open society, depends primarily upon understanding and voluntary compliance, secondarily upon reinforcement by peer and public opinion and finally, when necessary, upon enforcement through disciplinary proceedings." Are you confident that voluntary compliance and social norms will adequately ensure compliance with the ethics rules? Consider that question again later in the semester, after you have studied in some detail the rules applicable to the practice of law and the temptations against which they attempt to guard.

Violations of ethical rules can give rise to attorney discipline. Different jurisdictions impose different varieties of discipline and call them by different names. In general terms, disbarment—taking away the lawyer's right to practice law—is the most severe sanction. Contrary to most

---

1. These statistics are taken from the American Bar Association's 2006 Survey on Lawyer Discipline Systems (SOLD), available at http://www.abanet.org/cpr/discipline/sold/home.html.

perceptions, however, in many jurisdictions, disbarment is not permanent. Attorneys who have been disbarred can, under some circumstances, seek reinstatement to practice.

The next level of sanction is a suspension—removal from the practice of law for a period of time. What do you suppose happens to a lawyer who is suspended from the practice of law? What do you think such a lawyer must do—and avoid doing—during the period of his suspension? Who, besides the lawyer, is harmed by that sanction? Does that seem a sensible result? Some disciplinary authorities may require additional efforts from suspended lawyers, including in some cases retaking the MPRE or taking a course in professional responsibility, before the lawyer can be reinstated.

The next level of sanction involves some form of reprimand. Such sanctions can be public or private (the ABA considers a "reprimand" a public sanction and an "admonition" a private sanction, but not all jurisdictions follow this terminology). As an unhappy client, would you be satisfied with a censure of your lawyer after a finding of wrongdoing? Why or why not? Would it matter to you whether the sanction was private or public? As a prospective client, would you have an opinion about this matter?

One might think that fines would be a likely category of attorney discipline, but under most discipline systems, this is not an available punishment option. Should it be? What about a restitutionary sanction, as, for example, returning money to a client from whom it has been improperly taken? In some jurisdictions, disciplinary authorities have the power to award these; in others, the authorities can and sometimes do condition the resolution of the disciplinary matter on providing restitution to the aggrieved client. And in many jurisdictions, the cost of the disciplinary proceeding can be charged to the disciplined attorney.

How is the sanction selected? In past years there was substantial criticism that sanctions were unevenly and inequitably applied; the same conduct might result in radically different sanctions for identical misconduct in different jurisdictions or even for two different lawyers in the same jurisdiction. In response, the ABA promulgated "Standards for Imposing Lawyer Sanctions." Some states have adopted the standards, while others have adopted their own or permit the consideration of the standards as relevant. The standards recommend considering the nature of the duty violated, the lawyer's mental state, and the injury caused by the misconduct, and then permit consideration of "aggravating" and "mitigating" factors. What sorts of lawyer misconduct do you think should be worthy of the most severe sanction? Can you think of some misconduct that you might view as relatively minor? What kinds of factors might you view as aggravating or mitigating? The standards have been criticized by some as not providing sufficient guidance to promote uniformity.

NOTES

1.   In some jurisdictions, a court may impose as a condition of reinstatement to practice that the lawyer obtain malpractice insurance. *See In re Sullivan*, 2003 WL 22701634 (Del. 2003). Sullivan was suspended from practice after misconduct, which had resulted in several malpractice suits being brought against him, at least one of which resulted in a civil judgment. As a condition of his reinstatement he was required to obtain malpractice insurance. He claimed that he was unable to obtain coverage and asked that the condition be waived. The court declined. It concluded, " 'it would be a breach of our duty to the public if we were to permit a lawyer with Sullivan's history of malpractice to be reinstated as an active member of the Bar without adequate malpractice insurance coverage.' "

2.   Can a disciplinary authority require a lawyer to pay a malpractice judgment as part of an attorney discipline proceeding? In *Kentucky Bar Ass'n v. Greene*, 63 S.W.3d 182 (Ky. 2002), the attorney was hired to bring a tort claim on a client's behalf, but he did nothing and the suit was ultimately barred by the statute of limitations. The client obtained a malpractice judgment for $3,003.74. The attorney was then charged with unethical conduct. The state Supreme Court, in addition to suspending the lawyer from practice for ninety days, directed him to pay the malpractice judgment. A dissenting justice indicated his disapproval: "I do not believe this Court should use its disciplinary authority to order attorneys to satisfy civil judgments when clients have suffered economic loss as a result of an attorney's negligence. The existing provisions for collecting judgments are adequate and grafting such requirements onto our disciplinary sanctions unnecessarily expands the role of this Court."

B.   THE TANGLED WEB: GETTING INTO TROUBLE IN A DISCIPLINARY PROCEEDING

STATE OF OKLAHOMA EX REL. OKLAHOMA BAR ASS'N v. ALLFORD

152 P.3d 190 (Okla. 2006)

COLBERT, J.

The Oklahoma Bar Association filed this disciplinary proceeding against Patricia Ann Allford. The Bar and Allford stipulated to the facts and jointly requested that Allford receive a private reprimand. At a hearing before a panel of the Professional Responsibility Tribunal (PRT), Allford contradicted many of the facts to which she had stipulated, demonstrated a failure to comprehend the seriousness of her actions, refused to acknowledge her culpability, and expressed little remorse. The PRT unanimously recommended that she receive a public reprimand. We reject that recommendation and suspend Allford from the practice of law for six months. . . .

This disciplinary proceeding arises from Allford's representation of a single client. Richard Mackey paid Allford $750 on March 30, 1992, to probate his mother's and father's estates. The probate was not completed by October 16, 2001, when Mackey terminated Allford's services by a letter in which he stated that she "had failed to keep appointments or return phone calls to review and discuss the completion of the case." Allford would not return the file and persuaded Mackey to let her attempt to finish the matter.

The probate remained incomplete on January 24, 2003, when Mackey sent another letter terminating Allford and asking for the return of the file. Once again, Allford refused to return the file and persuaded Mackey to allow her to complete the case.

Mackey filed a written grievance with the Bar on April 9, 2004. The Bar opened a formal investigation and sent a letter to Allford on April 27, 2004, asking her to respond to Mackey's allegations within twenty days. When she finally responded on June 1, 2004, Allford did not respond to the allegations, but stated only that she had been unable to contact Mackey.

The Bar sent Allford a second letter by certified mail on June 9, 2004, and directed her to respond to Mackey's allegations within five days. Although Allford received the letter on July 1, 2004, she did not respond until Tuesday, July 20, 2004. She still did not respond to the allegations, but stated only:

> I have met with Mr. Richard Watson Mackey and he desires that I continue with the probate case on his parents. I have completed an inventory of the real property, which contains fifteen legal descriptions for mineral and surface interests in four counties. An accounting is being prepared regarding the income produced by these interests.
>
> I anticipate this estate will be completed within the next six months. This is satisfactory with Mr. Mackey. I will keep you posted.

At this point, the Bar issued a subpoena for Allford's deposition, to take place at the Oklahoma Bar Center on July 29, 2004, at 9:00 a.m. Allford did not appear. Instead, she called the Assistant General Counsel, Mike Speegle, at approximately 9:20 a.m. on the day of her scheduled deposition and stated that she did not appear at the appointed time because Mackey did not want her to.

Although Allford eventually did appear by agreement for her deposition, troubling facts surfaced about the events surrounding her receipt of the subpoena. Employees at the Hughes County Sheriff's office called Allford when they received the subpoena. Allford came to the Sheriff's office and accepted personal service on Friday, July 23, 2004, at 8:00 a.m. However, she asked two of the Sheriff's employees to falsify the date of service to show that it was not served until 8:00 a.m. on July 29th (the date of the scheduled deposition). Because she assured them that the "matter would be dropped and that it wasn't a big deal," the employees honored her request. They admitted their role in the deception when the Bar called the

Sheriff's office on the morning of the 28th (the day before the scheduled deposition) to confirm that Allford had been served with the subpoena.

The Bar filed a formal complaint on September 24, 2004. When Allford filed her response on November 15, 2004, she attached Mackey's affidavit stating that he wished to withdraw his grievance and continue the probate with Allford as his attorney. The disciplinary matter was continued several times and Allford finally completed the probate sometime in 2005.

When the hearing before the PRT convened, Allford formally stipulated to the Bar's allegations, admitting that she had repeatedly refused to return Mackey's file and that she had asked the Sheriff's employees to falsify the service date on the subpoena. Allford's testimony, however, differed materially from her stipulations. Although she repeatedly affirmed the truth of the stipulations and stated that "I accept full responsibility," and "I was dilatory," her responses to specific questions by the panel members were less apologetic and full of inconsistencies between her stated desire to accept full responsibility and her efforts to deflect any real culpability by admitting only to "mistakes." . . .

Allford began by attributing the situation to the complexity of the probate case and her lack of skill: "I no longer practice in that area of the law. It's not something that I enjoy doing or felt very skilled at doing." She then attributed her failure to keep appointments with Mackey to simple miscommunication and lack of a full-time secretary. Finally, she implied that she failed to return phone calls because Mackey would "call right back" after she had already explained "things" to him.

Allford's testimony contained so many internal inconsistencies that it was apparent she was not willing to admit to any of the facts underlying the stipulations. Allford's testimony upon being confronted is equally troubling.

> [Allford]: What happened was, I want to take full responsibility for that. They asked me what date do you want us to put on this and I said I don't care, put whatever date you want to, in a fit of anger and I was very upset and just not thinking clearly.
>
> [PRT]: What you have admitted to in these stipulations is different than what you've just testified to.
>
> [Allford]: Yes. Yes, I have.
>
> [PRT]: Stipulations say you admitted asking them to put a false date on there. Now you're saying you didn't really ask that, but instead you said put whatever date you want to on there? There's a big difference there.
>
> [Allford]: There's a big difference, but that's what I said to them and I realize this affidavit was drafted by the assistant district attorney and that was drafted in the worst light towards me, but I want to accept full responsibility. I should not have said that. I should have accepted the papers. I should not have put them in any kind of jeopardy.

[PRT]: Did you ask them to specifically put a false date on there? Not just put any date you want to, but did you ask them to put a false date on there?

[Allford]: I asked them to put whatever they wanted to on it, that I didn't care, in a fit of anger that day.

[PRT]: The *AFFIDAVIT* . . . said you came in and asked that [they] . . . show that it was served on July 29th at 8 o'clock a.m. Is that a true or false statement?

[Allford]: That's a true statement.

[PRT]: That's different than what you just testified to.

[Allford]: It is, but I will agree with that statement, yes.

[PRT]: That concerns me. That means you may have given false testimony to us just now by saying put whatever date in that you want to.

[Allford]: I agree to this because I do not want them to be in jeopardy. I should have accepted the papers. They have families. It could be their jobs and—and yes, I agree with this.

[PRT]: Let's be—let's be clear. Did you ask [her] to put the date of July 29th on the papers?

[Allford]: If that's what the *AFFIDAVIT* says, yes.

Allford was also quite certain that she had admitted her behavior during the deposition, but could not remember specifically what she admitted.

Allford stipulated that she violated Rules 1.1, 1.2, 1.3, 1.4, 4.1(a), & 8.4(a-d) of the Rules of Professional Conduct, addressing competence, diligence, client communication, truthfulness, and conduct involving dishonesty and trustworthiness. The Bar also alleged that Allford violated Rules 1.3 and 5.2 of the Rules Governing Disciplinary Proceedings, by . . . failing to cooperate in the Bar's investigation.

We are inexorably drawn to the conclusion that even a public censure is insufficient in this matter. The primary problem is no longer Allford's dilatory representation of her client; it is her refusal to acknowledge the Bar's and this Court's authority to oversee her practice and investigate a complaint against her. Allford has failed to accept any real responsibility for her actions. Even the dry, written transcript of her testimony before the PRT displays a degree of irritation toward the Bar and the disciplinary process at odds with the respect demanded of those *permitted* to practice law in this state. Allford was clearly saying whatever was necessary to get through the process and go on.

The record provides no basis for concluding that Allford's behavior and attitude will improve if she is allowed to continue her legal practice without interruption. Moreover, the facts of Allford's misconduct bring into question her professional judgment and expose an attitude of mis-placed irritation and a habit of ignoring a growing problem in hopes that it will simply disappear. These characteristics are at odds with the mature, thoughtful, and professional approach to any matter required of attorneys. . . .

> Honesty and integrity are the cornerstones of the legal profession. Nothing reflects more negatively upon the profession than deceit. There can be little doubt that the attorney has brought discredit upon the legal profession.

. . . Allford has never before received any formal discipline. Her behavior, although unacceptable, did not result in a client or a member of the public suffering a legal or financial loss. Indeed, the attempted stipulations, however clumsy, reflected her effort to avoid having others lose their jobs because of her actions. We reject the Bar's suggestion of a private reprimand and the PRT's suggestion of a public censure and conclude that a 6-month suspension is the appropriate discipline.

NOTES

1.   What was the initial problem that brought attorney Allford to the attention of the disciplinary authorities? Clients often complain about the service they have received from their lawyers. Do the complaints here seem justified? Why or why not?

2.   Attorney Allford's initial problem seemed relatively minor—a disagreement with a client about whether she had been dilatory in pursuing a probate matter. Such complaints are often dismissed, particularly if the lawyer promptly seizes the opportunity to complete the matter to the client's satisfaction; even if the complaint is not dismissed, such misconduct rarely results in such a severe sanction. What did the lawyer do in this case that justified her six-month suspension?

3.   Imagine that Allford had consulted you as a professional responsibility attorney upon receiving the initial complaint in this matter. What would you have advised her to do? Based on what you have seen in this case, what do you think are the most important elements of defense in a discipline proceeding?

4.   As the opinion makes clear, honesty is important. Cooperation is also significant; it is possible for the disciplinary authority to find the underlying disciplinary complaint to be unfounded but to discipline the lawyer, nonetheless, for failing to cooperate adequately with the disciplinary process.

5.   Many things can cause lawyers to violate their ethical obligations. One is addictive behaviors. Attorney Michael Burke was disbarred in the state of Michigan for embezzling $1.6 million from clients. He committed the thefts in order to fund his compulsive gambling habit. By the time he turned himself in, Burke was gambling five days a week; in the previous two months, he had spent $600,000 of his clients' money gambling. In addition to losing his license, Burke spent time in prison. *See* Stephanie Francis Ward, *Learning the Hard Way*, ABA Journal, May 2008.

PROBLEMS

1.   Lawyer was an assistant district attorney trying a criminal homicide case. Defense counsel inquired about a police report that contained an exculpatory statement from a witness. The judge asked Lawyer if he knew where the witness was; Lawyer told the judge that his office was looking, but had not yet located the witness. The witness was then located and Lawyer met with her. Four days later the judge renewed his inquiry about the whereabouts of the witness. Lawyer falsely told the judge, on the record, that he did not know where she was. What would be the appropriate discipline for Lawyer? *See In re Stuart*, 803 N.Y.S.2d 577 (N.Y. App. Div. 2005).

2.   Attorney agreed to file a lawsuit on behalf of Client, who had been injured in a motorcycle accident. Over the next two years, the case proceeded slowly, in part because Attorney was not prompt in responding to defense discovery requests, but also because the defendant's insurance company filed for bankruptcy. Attorney and Client agreed that Attorney should voluntarily dismiss the action and refile it after the insurance company's bankruptcy stay was lifted and some of Client's medical problems were resolved. Attorney, however, miscalculated how much time he had to refile the case and permitted the statute of limitations to lapse. Upon realizing his error, he immediately told Client to consult another lawyer about a potential malpractice claim against Attorney. Attorney also had no malpractice insurance. Ultimately, Client sued Attorney for malpractice; that claim was settled and Attorney paid Client in full. Should Attorney be subject to disciplinary sanctions? *See Disciplinary Counsel v. Sabol*, 886 N.E.2d 191 (Ohio 2008).

3.   Client gave Lawyer $76,000 as an anticipated payment to settle a case, but the case did not settle as planned. Client asked for the money back, but Lawyer kept it in his trust account. Within one week after Client gave Lawyer the money, Lawyer drew out $500 from Client's money for his own use. Within a year Lawyer had used all of Client's money for himself. What is the appropriate sanction for Lawyer? *See Florida Bar v. Barley*, 831 So.2d 163 (Fla. 2002).

4.   Lawyer hit another driver while driving an uninsured vehicle. He told his insurer, however, that he was driving a different vehicle, which was insured. He also asked the other driver to tell his insurer that he was driving the other, insured vehicle. The other driver declined to do so. Lawyer was prosecuted for insurance fraud and pled guilty to a misdemeanor. Should he be subject to attorney discipline? Would the following information be relevant to your decision: the fact that Lawyer, "at the time of the accident . . . was under extreme financial and emotional duress because: (1) he had grown up poor and incurred substantial debt in obtaining his law degree; (2) he had not been earning enough to provide for his family from his practice representing low-income clients; (3) his wife's salary had recently been reduced because of employment restructuring; (4) his wife had also required an extended stay in the hospital due to complications during birth; (5) one of his three children had been in and out of the hospital for severe allergies; and (6) his father had recently moved in with the family because he was suffering from Alzheimer's disease," or that Lawyer's "professional life, until this incident, reflect[ed] his integrity, commitment to serving the public, and commitment to the legal profession"? *See In re Grew's Case*, 934 A.2d 537 (N.H. 2007).

CHAPTER 4

THE DUTY OF COMPETENCE

■ ■ ■

You hire someone to mow your lawn, and he does a terrible job. What can you do about it? You might complain to him, or to his boss; you might ask for your money back. But the most likely consequence is that you won't hire him again. In many circumstances, assessments of the competency of service providers are reflected in future consumption choices. The market, accordingly, functions as a constraint on incompetence; those folks who are bad at mowing lawns, and whose customers don't return to them and don't refer others to them, will find the business of mowing lawns unprofitable and will soon leave it.

The market may well impose some informal discipline on lawyers, but we have other additional mechanisms for enforcing the duty of competence. Is that because the market is an inadequate vehicle for policing attorney competence? Why might that be the case?

Whenever we contemplate a competence issue, there are two concerns: the consequences for the lawyer, who has acted incompetently and may do so again; and the consequences for the client, who may have been disserved by an incompetent lawyer. As you study the materials in this chapter, consider which of these concerns, if any, are addressed by the various mechanisms presented here. Should we be doing something more or different to ensure attorney competence?

A. ETHICAL RULES REGARDING COMPETENCE

Model Rule 1.1 provides:

A lawyer shall provide competent representation to a client. Competent representation requires the legal knowledge, skill, thoroughness and preparation reasonably necessary for the representation.

Review the Comments to Rule 1.1. Is it clear to you what competence is? As a new lawyer, what kinds of matters do you feel you will be competent to handle? If you do not believe you are competent, how will you become competent?

defendants allege denial of effective assistance of counsel

IN RE DOCKING

869 P.2d 237 (Kan. 1994)

PER CURIAM:

This is an original uncontested attorney disciplinary proceeding. The parties stipulated to the following facts.

Kent Owen Docking is an attorney at law, Kansas attorney registration No. 12265, admitted to the Bar of the State of Kansas on September 20, 1985. . . .

On June 4, 1986, three Korean nationals were each charged with two counts of aggravated kidnapping. Shortly after being charged, all three defendants retained the respondent to represent them in the criminal proceedings. Docking received a fee from each defendant.

Prior to the preliminary examination, Docking met with his clients on several occasions, sometimes with and sometimes without an interpreter. . . . On September 5, 1986, each defendant pleaded guilty to an amended charge of kidnapping, a Class B felony. On October 10, 1986, Judge Frederick Stewart heard motions filed by Docking on behalf of all three defendants to withdraw their pleas of guilty. The basis for the motions was that the defendants were unable to understand the "terms and conditions of the plea" because of a lack of understanding and communication between the interpreter and the defendants. Docking argued in support of the motions. The defendants did not testify. Judge Stewart denied defendants' motions to withdraw their pleas and sentenced each defendant to the custody of the Secretary of Corrections for a minimum term of 10 years and a maximum term of 20 years. On February 27, 1987, the court heard motions filed by Docking on behalf of each defendant to modify the sentences. The court reduced the sentences to a minimum term of 5 years and a maximum term of 20 years.

On November 18, 1988, defendants filed motions alleging that they had been denied effective assistance of counsel by Docking. . . .

Docking voluntarily appeared as a witness at the hearing. . . . He testified at length, without the benefit of counsel during the hearing.

conflict of interest

Judge Stewart noted that Docking undertook representation of the three defendants even though it was apparent that conflicts of interest existed among the positions of the three clients. The court observed that there was no evidence that the possible conflict of interest was explained to or waived by each of the clients.

lacked experience

Judge Stewart found that Docking did not have the experience or competence to represent clients charged with two counts of aggravated kidnapping, a Class A felony. The judge noted that Docking had no felony trial experience, had not previously handled a Class A or B felony, and had only been out of law school for one year. In addition, Docking did not remedy his lack of experience by associating with a Korean-speaking lawyer

competent to handle the case. Although Docking had provided one interpreter for his clients, he did not ensure simultaneous translation during
the criminal proceedings. He also had failed to properly investigate the
case. A witness was known but was not sought or used.... There was
evidence that the statement given by one client could have been suppressed if a motion to suppress had been filed. Docking had erroneously
advised his clients that if probation was not granted, the clients could
withdraw their pleas. Docking then informed his clients that they had no
right to appeal the denial of the motion to withdraw the pleas. He further
advised his clients that a habeas corpus petition must be filed in federal
court by inmates without assistance of counsel. Finally, the judge found
that although Docking was aware his clients were illegal aliens, he had
failed at the sentencing hearing to request that his clients should not be
deported.

At the conclusion of the hearing, the judge found that Docking had not
provided his clients with reasonable effective assistance of counsel. The
judge determined that the defendants' rights to a fair trial had been
prejudiced by Docking's ineffective assistance. Judge Stewart vacated the
sentences of the defendants and set aside their pleas of guilty. The three
clients had been incarcerated for approximately two and one-half years.
The State subsequently declined to reprosecute the defendants.

On October 21, 1990, a formal complaint was filed by the Disciplinary
Administrator alleging that Docking had violated [several rules of professional responsibility, including "handling a legal matter which he knew or
should have known that he was not competent to handle" under DR 6–
101(A)(1), the competency provision under the then-governing Kansas
code.].

The parties agreed that Docking had violated ... DR 6–101(A)(1)....

Docking offered testimony in mitigation of his conduct. Docking admitted
during the early years of his practice he was too inexperienced to defend a
major felony case. Docking further acknowledged that he had failed to
associate with an experienced criminal attorney to assist with the defense
of three Korean nationals who, in turn, were poorly equipped to grasp the
effect of potential conflicts of interest among themselves. Docking acknowledged that public censure would be an appropriate discipline for his
violation of the disciplinary rules in effect at the time of his misconduct.

The hearing panel recommended that Kent Owen Docking be disciplined
by public censure by the Supreme Court of Kansas and that the costs of
this action be taxed to respondent....

The court, having considered the record herein and the report of the
panel, and, after considering the mitigating factors, accepts and concurs in
the findings, conclusions, and recommendations of the hearing panel.

IT IS THEREFORE ORDERED that Kent Owen Docking be, and he is
hereby, disciplined by censure ... for his violations of the Code of
Professional Responsibility.

ABBOTT, JUSTICE, concurring:

I concur in the result. Respondent stipulated to certain violations and a recommendation of published censure. My concern is that the bench and bar will interpret the opinion as saying a recent law school graduate is not competent to handle a criminal case involving a felony and that a lawyer speaking an accused's primary language must be engaged as cocounsel. Such is not required. There may be felony cases that, due to unique facts or the severity of the crime charged, an inexperienced lawyer should not handle, but that would be the exception and not the rule.

It is not required that a recently admitted lawyer, or any other lawyer, associate with a lawyer speaking an accused's primary language. All that is required is that the lawyer be able to communicate with the client either personally or through an interpreter.

COMMITTEE ON PROFESSIONAL ETHICS AND CONDUCT OF THE IOWA STATE BAR ASS'N v. MILLER

412 N.W.2d 622 (Iowa 1987)

LARSON, JUSTICE.

The grievance commission of this court recommended a suspension of the license of Carl H. Miller as a sanction for his neglect of two estates and his refusal to respond to letters of inquiry from the Committee on Professional Ethics and Conduct. All of the material allegations of the complaint concerning Miller's neglect of the estates and his failure to respond to committee inquiries were admitted by him at the hearing. We agree with the findings and recommendations of the commission and order Miller's license to be suspended for a minimum of three months.

I. *The Probate Matters.*

The estate of Dorcas L. Hoff was opened on September 16, 1981, and Miller was designated as attorney. It was a small estate, consisting only of a parcel of real estate valued at $4000. Title problems arose on the proposed sale of the real estate, but Miller made virtually no effort to cure them. As various filing deadlines passed, Miller received a notice of delinquency from the clerk of district court and inquiries from the ethics committee, which had received a complaint from the executor.

Despite the delinquency notice and the committee inquiries, the estate continued to languish in inaction. At the commission hearing, attorney Miller candidly admitted he "[hadn't] the faintest idea" how to close the estate and, at the time of the commission hearing in January 1987, it was apparently still open.

While Miller testified he was an alcoholic who had been sober for only nine months as of the time of the hearing, he did not blame this problem for his mishandling of the estate. He offered no explanation except he was over his head when he got into probate matters.

We agree with the commission that [Miller violated, inter alia, DR 6–101(A) of the Iowa Code of Professional Responsibility, precluding a lawyer from handling legal matters which the lawyer was not competent to handle].

violation #1

II. *Failure to Cooperate in Investigation.*

A lawyer's failure to cooperate in an investigation by the ethics committee constitutes a separate violation of the code of professional ethics. . . .

violation #2

In the Hoff estate, the committee wrote to Miller on August 26, 1985, notifying him that a complaint had been filed by the executor and enclosing a copy of the complaint. The committee requested Miller's response. When he did not respond, the committee wrote a second letter, on September 26, 1985, again requesting a response and informing Miller that his continued failure to respond could result in a disciplinary complaint. On October 11, 1985, still not having received a response, the committee wrote a third letter advising Miller that, if a response was not received in ten days, the complaint would be forwarded to the grievance commission of the supreme court. Miller did not respond, and the matter was referred to the commission. Miller admitted at the commission hearing that he had received all three letters but had not responded to any of them.

We believe Miller's failure to cooperate in the investigation . . . justified disciplinary action by the court as separate violations of these provisions of the Code of Professional Responsibility: DR 1–102(A)(5) (conduct prejudicial to administration of justice) and (6) (engaging in conduct adversely reflecting fitness to practice law).

III. *Disposition.*

We conclude these ethical violations warrant an indefinite suspension of Miller's license to practice law with no possibility of reinstatement for three months from the date of this opinion. . . . In any application for reinstatement, Miller shall establish that he has established office practices that will assure his completion of future legal matters in a timely manner.

NOTES

1. Lawyers are rarely disciplined purely for violations of the duty of competency. Sanctions for violations of Rule 1.1 typically reflect egregious violations, and are usually accompanied by other findings of wrongdoing. Why? Is that because incompetence alone is not a sufficient basis for discipline, or because incompetent lawyers often violate other obligations as well? In that regard, consider Model Rule 1.3 and 1.4. Do you think violations of Rule 1.1 are often accompanied by violations of these rules? Why? *See also In re Yetman*, 552 A.2d 121 (N.J. 1989).

2. Who pays to make the lawyer competent? In *Attorney Grievance Commission of Maryland v. Manger*, 913 A.2d 1 (Md. 2006), the lawyer, a transaction-

al practitioner, undertook to represent a woman with bipolar disorder in a custody proceeding. He spent considerable time educating himself about mental health issues and learning about this (to him) previously unfamiliar area of law. The court concluded that "Respondent's education at his client's expense went too far. . . . The bulk of Respondent's research was of a general nature and should not have been billed to the client. A client who engages counsel has a right to expect that the attorney will have sufficient general knowledge to competently represent her. While it may be appropriate to charge a client for case-specific research or familiarization with a unique issue involved in a case, general education or background research should not be charged to the client."

3. The concurring justice in the *Docking* case was concerned that the case might send the mistaken impression that recent law graduates are not competent to handle felony cases. Are recent law graduates competent to handle felony cases? If you were to undertake one, how would you assure that you were providing competent representation to your client?

B. MALPRACTICE

Legal malpractice is, for the most part, treated as a <u>tort claim</u>: a negligence claim against an attorney. Proving legal malpractice requires proof of the elements of negligence: a duty, a breach of the duty, proximate causation, and damages.

Who gets sued for malpractice?[1] Well over half of all malpractice claims are filed against firms with five or fewer lawyers. Does that mean that it is more risky to practice alone or in a small firm? Claims against lawyers in large firms are increasing; between the ABA's 1999 study of malpractice claims and its 2003 study, the percentage of claims against lawyers in firms of 100 or more increased by 8.15%. Broken down by practice area, plaintiffs' personal injury lawyers had the highest rate of claims—approximately 20%—followed by real estate practitioners. Is that necessarily because there is more malpractice in these areas? Areas like antitrust, international law, and admiralty law represent a very low percentage of malpractice claims. Is that because practitioners in those areas are more competent? What would you need to know to answer these questions? This data is obtained from insurance companies that handle legal malpractice claims. How do you think inclusion of malpractice claims against uninsured lawyers would change this data?

Not all malpractice claims have merit. The ABA study indicated that during the period 2000–2003, approximately 70% of files were closed without any payment to the plaintiff, either because the claim was abandoned or was dismissed. In about 27% of cases, settlements were paid to the plaintiff. Plaintiffs won judgments in less than 3% of cases.

---

1. The information in this discussion is taken from American Bar Association Standing Committee on Lawyers' Professional Liability, Profile of Legal Malpractice Claims 2000–2003 (2005).

What kinds of activities subject lawyers to malpractice claims? In 28% of claims, the client alleged administrative error. That included things like failing to calendar a matter, failing to file a document, or losing a file or evidence. Substantive errors were asserted in 47% of claims. These included issues like failing to determine a deadline, failing to apply the law properly, or conducting inadequate discovery or investigation.

1. ELEMENTS OF THE CLAIM

LOPEZ v. CLIFFORD LAW OFFICES, P.C.

841 N.E.2d 465 (Ill. App. 2005)

JUSTICE GORDON delivered the opinion of the court:

This is an appeal from a dismissal of a legal malpractice action. After Elizabeth Lopez, the daughter of plaintiff Jose Lopez, drowned in a pool that was allegedly maintained by the Rockford School District, Lopez retained defendant Clifford Law Offices (the Clifford firm) to represent him and Elizabeth's estate in a wrongful death action. Several months later, defendant Thomas K. Prindable, an attorney with the Clifford firm, wrote to Lopez, informing him that the firm was unable to continue representing him and the estate. Prindable's letter incorrectly advised Lopez that the applicable statute of limitations was two years, when, in fact, it was only one year from the date of Elizabeth's death. Ultimately, another attorney—whom Lopez retained after the expiration of the one-year statute of limitations applicable to municipalities, but before the second anniversary of Elizabeth's death—filed the wrongful death action. However, because the wrongful death action was filed after the expiration of the applicable statute of limitations, it was dismissed.

The Clifford firm and Prindable (collectively, the Clifford defendants) . . . moved to dismiss the malpractice action . . . on the grounds that the wrongful death action was still viable when the Clifford firm ceased to represent the estate. The circuit court granted the motions to dismiss. For the reasons that follow, we reverse and remand.

BACKGROUND

In his August 19, 2003, complaint, Lopez alleged the following. Elizabeth died on February 20, 2001. Shortly thereafter, Lopez retained the Clifford firm "for the purpose of advising [him] of his legal rights." At all pertinent times, Prindable was an employee, servant and/or agent of the Clifford firm and acting within the scope of his agency. On August 20, 2001, Prindable wrote to Lopez a letter which stated, in pertinent part:

> I am writing . . . to confirm our telephone conversation in [sic] August 14, 2001, wherein I informed you that Clifford Law Offices is unable to continue to assume professional responsibility on behalf of the Estate of your daughter, Elizabeth, as a result of her tragic death on February 20, 2001. This decision does not represent an opinion as to the merit of any cause of action the Estate may have.

Please be advised that the statute of limitations in Illinois provides that a civil action to recover compensation for your daughter's injuries must be filed within two years after the cause of action occurred. Therefore, should you decide to pursue this matter further, we respectfully suggest that you contact an attorney of your choice immediately so that the Estate's legal rights may be fully protected. Do not delay.

The letter was attached as an exhibit to the malpractice complaint. Lopez alleged that Prindable's advice as to the statute of limitations, upon which he reasonably relied, was incorrect because the Rockford School District was a "local public entity" ... and no civil action may be commenced against a "local public entity" after one year from the date of the injury. Lopez claimed that as a result of the Clifford defendants' negligence, he and the estate irrevocably lost their rights of action, and had the wrongful death action not been aborted because of the statute of limitations defense, it would have succeeded on the merits. Although Lopez subsequently amended his complaint several times, these allegations remained unchanged throughout.

The record shows that in September of 2001, shortly after the Clifford defendants terminated their attorney-client relationship with Lopez but before the one-year statute of limitations would have expired, Lopez consulted with another attorney, Joseph Loran, about representing him and the estate in the wrongful death action. By a letter dated October 5, 2001, Loran declined to take the case. On March 22, 2002, a month after the one-year period of limitations expired, but almost a full year before a two-year period of limitations would have run, Lopez consulted yet another attorney regarding the wrongful death matter. That attorney informed Lopez that his previous attorney may have committed malpractice in letting the statute of limitations expire. The record indicates that Lopez did not consult any attorneys in the period between October 5, 2001, and March 22, 2002.

In their motion to dismiss, the Clifford defendants urged that the malpractice action against them could not stand because they terminated their attorney-client relationship with Lopez within the one-year limitations period when the wrongful death action was still viable and, furthermore, Loran's "intervention" within that one-year period extinguished any duty the Clifford defendants owed to Lopez. In support, among other things, the Clifford defendants attached Loran's October 5, 2001, letter to Lopez, wherein Loran stated, in pertinent part:

I have come to the conclusion that I do not believe I can accept representation of your daughter's claim. Other attorney's [sic] may feel differently and I encourage you to contact other lawyers.

Please be advised that all lawsuits are limited by a period prescribed by statute. You need to have your daughter's case filed within the applicable limitations period. If you do not do so, you may lose whatever rights you have to recovery.

On ... March 10, 2004, Lopez filed a second amended complaint, adding Loran and Loran's firm as respondents....

To assist in formulating his response, Lopez moved to take a discovery deposition of Loran to determine whether an attorney-client relationship was ever undertaken by him. In the deposition, ... Loran testified that he had met with Lopez on one occasion in September of 2001. During that meeting, Loran was trying to obtain an understanding of the facts surrounding Elizabeth's death and did not discuss legal issues. At the end of the meeting, Loran told Lopez that he would contact Prindable in order to determine whether to undertake the representation of the Lopez family. After discussing the matter with Prindable, Loran decided not to take the Lopez case. According to Loran, he never entered into a retainer agreement with Lopez and did not ask for or obtain Elizabeth's medical records or a coroner's report. Nor did Loran open a file or assign a case number to the Lopez matter. After sending the October 5, 2001, letter, Loran had no further contact with Lopez.

Loran's account was corroborated by Lopez's affidavit, which was also attached as an exhibit to the response to the motion to dismiss. In his affidavit, Lopez stated that Loran never said he would accept the matter and did not discuss the statute of limitations. Lopez additionally stated that had he known that the statute of limitations was one year, rather than two, he would have sought another attorney immediately after being turned down by Loran.

Consequently, in his response to the Clifford defendants' motion to dismiss, Lopez argued that the motion should be denied because Loran was never retained as an attorney in the wrongful death matter and, therefore, had no duty to correct the Clifford defendants' incorrect advice. Lopez additionally asserted that Loran did not voluntarily undertake a duty to provide him legal advice and did not offer advice regarding the statute of limitations. Lopez therefore argued that Loran's actions did not break the causal chain between the Clifford defendants' negligence and the ultimate barring of the cause of action by the expiration of the statute of limitations....

The circuit court, however, agreed with the Clifford defendants that the legal malpractice claim against them could not stand because the wrongful death action was still viable when the attorney-client relationship between them and Lopez came to an end. On April 12, 2004, the court granted the Clifford defendants' motion to dismiss....

On June 23, 2004, Lopez timely filed a notice of appeal....

ANALYSIS

On appeal, Lopez admits that his relationship with the Clifford firm was terminated when there were still six months left on the limitations period and that he subsequently consulted with Loran, who declined to take his case on October 5, 2001. Lopez, however, contends that none of these facts are proper grounds for dismissal since he reasonably relied on the advice in Prindable's letter that the applicable statute of limitations was two years, and therefore Prindable's advice was the proximate cause of his and the estate's legal injuries. In response, the Clifford defendants argue that dismissal was proper for the following alternative reasons: (1) they withdrew when the action was still viable; (2) they should be absolved of liability because of Lopez's intervening consultation with Loran; and (3) Lopez did not reasonably rely on Prindable's statute of limitations advice.

It is well established that the elements of a legal malpractice action in Illinois are: (1) the existence of an attorney-client relationship that establishes a duty on the part of the attorney; (2) a negligent act or omission constituting a breach of that duty; (3) proximate cause; and (4) damages. In a legal malpractice action, ordinary negligence principles apply.

In the instant case, the Clifford defendants gave Lopez incorrect legal advice with respect to how much time he had left to file the wrongful death action. It is *prima facie* negligent conduct for an attorney to misadvise a client on such a settled point of law that can be looked up by the means of ordinary research techniques. In this context, we observe that such incorrect advice would undermine the client's sense of urgency to seek replacement counsel and is likely to have much more dire consequences than no advice at all. It seems to be a matter of common sense that a person who was not lulled into a false sense that he had another year and a half to file his action would aggressively seek replacement counsel soon after being discharged as a client.

The Clifford defendants, however, maintain, as they did below, that their alleged negligence would be of no consequence because Lopez's wrongful death action was still viable at the time of the withdrawal. In support of this "viability" theory, they rely on a number of cases, all of which upheld summary disposition of a legal malpractice action....

[Defendants cited a number of cases to the court in which initial counsel was relieved of liability for malpractice when the client hired new counsel while the suit was still viable, and the successor attorney failed to correct the initial lawyer's flawed pursuit of the claim.]

These cases fall into two categories.... The first category involved situations where the original attorney presumably breached his duty to the plaintiff.... However, the original attorney avoided liability because it was held that his negligence did not proximately cause the plaintiff's loss, as a matter of law.... [In those cases,] the involvement of a successor attorney at the point where harm to the client's cause of action could still be averted extinguished a malpractice action against the original negligent attorney.

In the second category ... it was held that the original attorney did not breach his duty of care in failing to file the plaintiff's action because reasonable time remained to allow the plaintiff to find a replacement attorney who would file the case. In other words, the law did not impose a duty on the original attorney to file the plaintiff's action under such circumstances. More importantly, it was never alleged ... that the original attorney gave incorrect advice to the client, especially of the kind that would underplay the urgency of promptly obtaining replacement counsel. Here, on the other hand, although the Clifford defendants were not remiss in failing to file Lopez's wrongful death action, they did impart incorrect legal advice to their client which may very well have contributed to his failure to timely retain successor counsel. Under the established negligence principles discussed earlier in this opinion, it is of no import that the breach of duty occurred in communicating with the client rather than with respect to the case itself. However, the line of reasoning employed in the first category of cases invokes the concept of superceding cause which breaks the chain of causation, so that a negligent actor is excused from liability. Accordingly, we must examine whether a superceding cause operated here, so as to cut off the liability of the Clifford defendants.

Superceding cause and proximate cause are interrelated concepts. With regard to proximate cause, we ordinarily ask: "Was the defendant's negligence a material and substantial element in bringing about the injury, and, if so, was the injury of the type that a reasonable person would see as a likely result of his or her conduct?"

Where there are successive negligent actors, however, the negligence of the second actor, under certain circumstances, may be deemed a superceding cause relieving the original negligent actor of liability, as a matter of law. . . .

Our prior cases . . . appear to have taken the position . . . that when the duty of care shifts from the original attorney to the successor, so does the liability, provided that the successor had the opportunity to undo or avert the harm precipitated by the actions or omissions of the original attorney. . . .

[I]n this case no successor counsel was retained before the statute of limitations actually ran. While the Clifford defendants look to Lopez's interim consultation with another attorney, Loran, that fact is of no avail because Loran did not undertake any representation in the Lopez wrongful death matter. The cases relied upon by the Clifford defendants do not suggest that an attorney who declines to accept a case after a preliminary exploratory meeting with a prospective client assumes responsibility and corresponding liability for the preceding attorney's mistakes. The Clifford defendants assert that "[a]t minimum, Loran, by declining the case after consultation, was responsible for advising Lopez as to the exact amount of time remaining on the limitations period." We disagree with this proposition. We do not find any Illinois authority which would impose that burden upon an attorney on the strength of an exploratory meeting which did not result in an acceptance of the case. Nor can such cursory involvement suffice to be characterized as a superceding cause so as to relieve the original attorney of liability for his mistakes and shift it to the shoulders of the second attorney. Finally, we note that Loran's generic advice to Lopez that "all lawsuits are limited by a period prescribed by statute" was not inconsistent with Prindable's and could not have put

Lopez on notice that a shorter period of limitations governed the wrongful death action—thereby breaking the chain of causation.

In sum ... Lopez did not retain a successor counsel until after the expiration of the statute of limitations, i.e., when the successor counsel could not have cured the problem created by the incorrect advice. This outcome, as discussed below, may well be attributable to Lopez's reliance on Prindable's very advice.

For the foregoing reasons, since no superceding cause operated so as to defeat the Clifford defendants' liability as a matter of law, proximate cause in the instant case should be decided not as a matter of law, but by a trier of fact....

The Clifford defendants argue that, intervening superceding cause aside, the complaint and external submissions fail to allege cause in fact because they "indisputably" establish that Lopez in no way relied on Prindable's advice. Additionally, the Clifford defendants argue that Prindable's contemporaneous advice to Lopez to "contact an attorney of your choice immediately.... Do not delay" was an antidote to the incorrect statute of limitations advice. It would seem that this latter argument goes to the reliance not being reasonable, as a matter of law. We disagree with both arguments. In his complaint, Lopez, as noted, alleged that he reasonably relied on the Clifford defendants' advice. In addition, in his affidavit, Lopez stated:

"If I had known the statute of limitations in my daughter's case was one year, I would have obtained an attorney immediately after seeing Loran."

As discussed, Lopez's reliance on Prindable's parting advice was not unreasonable, as a matter of law. Whether Prindable's advice, in its totality, gave Lopez an impression that he had 18 months, as opposed to 6, to retain another attorney and file the wrongful death action is for the trier of fact. It would certainly not be unreasonable to conclude that although Lopez consulted with Loran within weeks of being dropped as a client by the Clifford firm, Prindable's advice caused Lopez to delay making an appointment with another counsel after being turned down by Loran.... The complaint, together with the affidavit supporting its allegations, is sufficient to create questions of fact as to these issues....

Accordingly, because questions of fact exist as to causation, the dismissal of the Clifford defendants was improper....

NOTES

1. What were the elements of Lopez's malpractice claim? What was the attorney's error here? To what standard of care were the lawyers here held? Was that a fair standard?

2. Was Lopez a client of the Clifford firm? If not, why didn't his malpractice claim fail as a matter of law?

3. Why didn't Lopez sue attorney Loran initially? Why wasn't his consultation with Loran sufficient to create a superceding cause and relieve the Clifford firm of liability?

4. At trial, what damages would Lopez be entitled to receive if he proved that the Clifford defendants committed malpractice? How would Lopez go about proving his damages case? What would the Clifford defendants be trying to prove in response to Lopez's damages case? Is there anything strange about the way this plays out in the context of a malpractice case?

5. Are lost punitive damages part of a client's damages in a successful claim for legal malpractice? The argument that they should be payable is that the damages in a malpractice suit should compensate the client for the attorney's negligence—if the client would have received punitive damages if his lawyer had behaved as a reasonable lawyer would have, the client should receive them in the malpractice suit. The contrary argument contends that since punitive damages are intended to punish and deter the original wrongful actor, there would be no purpose in imposing them on the malpracticing attorney. Nor would they be required to make the malpractice plaintiff "whole," which can be accomplished by an award of compensatory damages. Authorities on this issue are divided, though the weight of authority seems to suggest that punitive damages are not recoverable in a legal malpractice action. *See, e.g., Tri–G, Inc. v. Burke, Bosselman & Weaver*, 856 N.E.2d 389 (Ill. 2006). Is this a fair result?

6. When calculating damages in a malpractice case, what should be done about attorneys' fees? There are two issues here. The first is whether, in a situation in which a malpractice plaintiff would have owed a contingency fee to the lawyer had the lawyer succeeded in obtaining a recovery, the plaintiff's recovery in the malpractice case should be reduced by the fee she would have had to pay the malpracticing lawyer. The law on this issue is inconsistent. Some authorities say yes, on the theory that, if the deduction were taken, "the judgment would accurately reflect the amount the client would have recovered if the attorney had not committed malpractice." *Horn v. Wooser*, 165 P.3d 69, 71 (Wyo. 2007). However, the client who is the victim of malpractice will ordinarily incur a second legal fee, paid to the malpractice attorney, to secure a recovery. Some courts consider that this second attorney's fee in effect "cancels out" the fee the plaintiff would have had to pay to the original attorney, and therefore do not require fees to be deducted from the malpractice judgment. *See Shoemake v. Ferrer*, 182 P.3d 992 (Wash. App. 2008).

The second question is whether the plaintiff may claim as damages the attorneys' fees incurred in bringing the malpractice action. While the "prevailing rule is that a plaintiff cannot recover attorneys' fees incurred in prosecuting the malpractice action," 3 Ronald E. Mallen and Jeffrey M. Smith, *Legal Malpractice* § 20:14 at 47–48 (2007), there are decisions to the contrary. *See DiStefano v. Greenstone*, 815 A.2d 496 (N.J. App. 2003) (plaintiff is entitled to full recovery of damages she would have received in contingent fee case without reduction for the fee she would have had to pay, and in addition, may recover fees paid to her new lawyer for bringing the malpractice case). The *DiStefano* court reasoned that while this approach gave the plaintiff a double recovery, it was preferable "to crediting the attorney with an undeserved fee where he has botched the job," and, in effect, the client deserved the windfall for "having to endure two lawsuits." Is this consistent with the so-called "American rule," which holds that each party is generally responsible, in the absence of statutory authority to the contrary, for his own fees and costs? Does this put the plaintiff in a legal malpractice case in a better position than any other similarly situated plaintiff?

7. The elephant in the room with regard to attorney malpractice is the existence of malpractice insurance. Only one U.S. jurisdiction—Oregon—requires lawyers to obtain professional liability insurance. In the absence of a requirement, what percentage of lawyers do you suppose will carry insurance? A recent study in Washington state revealed that 87% of lawyers carried malpractice insurance. Percentages were higher for lawyers admitted for less than six years and lower for sole practitioners. A growing trend is to require lawyers to disclose whether they have malpractice coverage. Some states require that information to be disclosed directly to current or prospective clients, *see, e.g.*, Pennsylvania Rule of Professional Conduct 1.4(c) (requiring written disclosure to clients if the lawyer does not have professional liability insurance meeting certain coverage limits), while others require that the information be disclosed as part of the periodic attorney registration process. Idaho Bar Commission Rule 302(a)(7). Many of these rules are based on the ABA's Model Court Rule on Insurance Disclosure, though some jurisdictions have made this a provision of the disciplinary rules. The Model Rule does not require any particular level of coverage; it simply requires a lawyer to certify "whether the lawyer is currently covered by professional liability insurance and intends to maintain insurance during the period of time the lawyer is engaged in the private practice of law." What do you think of a mandatory disclosure rule? Is it an effective way to compel lawyers to obtain insurance coverage? If a jurisdiction is going to require disclosure, why not just require coverage? Most malpractice insurance is "claims made" insurance, which means that it covers only claims that are made during the policy period. Since the fact that a lawyer has insurance at the moment the client engages him is irrelevant to whether he will have insurance at some point in the future when a claim arises, is a disclosure requirement inherently misleading?

8. In a case like *Lopez*, where the plaintiff claims that the lawyer's malpractice deprived him of a cause of action, his damages will be the damages he would have obtained had the lawyer preserved his claim adequately. The proof of those damages requires proof that had the client been able to bring his suit, he would have won it and would have been awarded damages. This "case-within-a-case" requires the lawyer to prove in the malpractice suit the elements of the claim he did not have the opportunity to prove in the original lawsuit. Suppose the lawyer persuades the client to settle the case, and the client claims that if he had not settled, he would have obtained a better outcome. What must the client prove? *See Environmental Network Corp. v. Goodman Weiss Miller L.L.P.*, 893 N.E.2d 173 (Ohio 2008).

What if the claim is not litigation-based? Suppose the client alleges malpractice in transactional representation. What are the client's damages if he claims that, because of a lawyer's failure, his deal did not go forward or closed on less favorable terms to him than it might have? How will he go about proving those damages? Such a claim arose in *Viner v. Sweet*, 70 P.3d 1046 (Cal. 2003). The Viners engaged counsel to assist them in selling their interest in Dove, an audio book business which they had founded and in which they still held a substantial ownership interest. With the assistance of attorney

Sweet they entered into an agreement to sell their shares in Dove to MIE and to terminate their employment with Dove. In exchange, the Viners were to receive monthly payments over a period of five years. The Viners subsequently claimed the agreement did not protect them adequately and had not been explained to them clearly. The Viners won a $13 million verdict, but it was overturned on appeal. The court concluded that, notwithstanding the difficulties of proof, plaintiffs in a transactional malpractice case still had to show that "but for the alleged malpractice, it is more likely than not that the plaintiff would have obtained a more favorable result." *Id.* at 1054. Otherwise, in the court's view, it would be "far too easy to make the legal advisor a scapegoat for a variety of business misjudgments." *Id.* at 1051.

Imagine that you represented the Viners. How would you show that, but for their lawyer's errors, they would have gotten a better deal—or perhaps that they would not have made the deal at all and would have been better off as a result? Is this harder than proving litigation malpractice? Why or why not?

2. THE STANDARD OF CARE

Courts differ in the way they define the standard of care to which an attorney should be held. One typical formulation is that the lawyer must exercise the care, skill and diligence commonly possessed and exercised by lawyers in the jurisdiction. What exactly does that mean? Suppose you practice in a small town. Is the relevant standard of care the standard in your small town, or should the standard be more general? In *Chapman v. Bearfield*, 207 S.W.3d 736 (Tenn. 2006), the defendant in a malpractice case claimed that summary judgment should be granted because the plaintiffs' expert was not adequately familiar with "the professional standard of care required of attorneys in that part of east Tennessee" where the defendant practiced. Should that be the standard? What would the drawbacks and benefits be of such a standard? The court in *Chapman* adopted a statewide standard.

How does the plaintiff prove that the attorney violated the standard of care? Ordinarily, through the testimony of an expert. As Mallen and Smith note, "The standard of care is predicated on the skill and care ordinarily exercised by lawyers, a measure rarely within the common knowledge of laypersons." 4 Ronald E. Mallen and Jeffrey M. Smith, *Legal Malpractice* § 33.17, at 1116 (2007). Some violations are so "egregious and extreme," however, that the testimony of an expert may not be necessary. These include failing to communicate settlement offers to the client, or missing a statute of limitations. *Id.* at 1123–25. Was expert testimony required in the *Lopez* case? Why or why not?

Does violation of a rule of professional responsibility constitute a violation of the standard of care? Paragraph [20] of the Scope Note to the Model Rules of Professional Conduct says no. "Violation of a Rule should not itself give rise to a cause of action against a lawyer nor should it create any presumption in such a case that a legal duty has been breached." Why? According to the Note, "[t]he Rules are designed to provide guidance to lawyers and to provide a structure for regulating conduct through disciplinary agencies. They are not designed to be a basis for civil liability." Is that persuasive? In other contexts, the violation of a statutory standard of due care is deemed negligence per se; why not in the context of the ethical rules?

While the Rules are not dispositive, they are often relevant as evidence of the appropriate standard of care, and the Scope Note recognizes this: "[S]ince the Rules do establish standards of conduct by lawyers, a lawyer's violation of a Rule may be evidence of breach of the applicable standard of conduct." Scope Note to the Model Rules, paragraph [20].

3.   WHO MAY CLAIM MALPRACTICE?

Lopez states that a duty to the client is an essential element of a malpractice claim, and that the attorney-client relationship creates such a duty. Do attorneys have duties to anyone other than their clients that might create malpractice liability?

BARCELO v. ELLIOTT
923 S.W.2d 575 (Tex. 1996)

PHILLIPS, CHIEF JUSTICE, delivered the opinion of the Court. . . .

The issue presented is whether an attorney who negligently drafts a will or trust agreement owes a duty of care to persons intended to benefit under the will or trust, even though the attorney never represented the intended beneficiaries. The court of appeals held that the attorney owed no duty to the beneficiaries, affirming the trial court's summary judgment for the defendant-attorney. Because the attorney did not represent the beneficiaries, we likewise conclude that he owed no professional duty to them. We accordingly affirm the judgment of the court of appeals.

I

After Frances Barcelo retained attorney David Elliott to assist her with estate planning, Elliott drafted a will and inter vivos trust agreement for her. The will provided for specific bequests to Barcelo's children, devising the residuary of her estate to the inter vivos trust. Under the trust agreement, trust income was to be distributed to Barcelo during her lifetime. Upon her death, the trust was to terminate, assets were to be distributed in specific amounts to Barcelo's children and siblings, and the remainder was to pass to Barcelo's six grandchildren. The trust agreement contemplated that the trust would be funded by cash and shares of stock during Barcelo's lifetime, although the grandchildren contend that this never occurred. Barcelo signed the will and trust agreement in September 1990.

Barcelo died on January 22, 1991. After two of her children contested the validity of the trust, the probate court, for reasons not disclosed on the record before us, declared the trust to be invalid and unenforceable.

[handwritten margin note: plaintiffs, grandchildren of Barcelo, contend that they would have received much more of the estate if the trust had been valid]

Barcelo's grandchildren—the intended remainder beneficiaries under the trust—subsequently agreed to settle for what they contend was a substantially smaller share of the estate than what they would have received pursuant to a valid trust.

Barcelo's grandchildren then filed the present malpractice action against Elliott and his law firm (collectively "Elliott"). Plaintiffs allege that Elliott's negligence caused the trust to be invalid, resulting in foreseeable injury to the plaintiffs. Elliott moved for summary judgment on the sole ground that he owed no professional duty to the grandchildren because he had never represented them. The trial court granted Elliott's motion for summary judgment.

The court of appeals affirmed, concluding that under Texas law an attorney preparing estate planning documents owes a duty only to his or her client—the testator or trust settlor—not to third parties intended to benefit under the estate plan.

II

The sole issue presented is whether Elliott owes a duty to the grandchildren that could give rise to malpractice liability even though he represented only Frances Barcelo, not the grandchildren, in preparing and implementing the estate plan.

A

At common law, an attorney owes a duty of care only to his or her client, not to third parties who may have been damaged by the attorney's negligent representation of the client. Without this "privity barrier," the rationale goes, clients would lose control over the attorney-client relationship, and attorneys would be subject to almost unlimited liability. Texas courts of appeals have uniformly applied the privity barrier in the estate planning context.

Plaintiffs argue, however, that recognizing a limited exception to the privity barrier as to lawyers who negligently draft a will or trust would not thwart the rule's underlying rationales. They contend that the attorney should owe a duty of care to persons who were specific, intended beneficiaries of the estate plan. We disagree.

B

The majority of other states addressing this issue have relaxed the privity barrier in the estate planning context.

While some of these states have allowed a broad cause of action by those claiming to be intended beneficiaries, others have limited the class of plaintiffs to beneficiaries specifically identified in an invalid will or trust. The Supreme Court of Iowa, for example, held that

> a cause of action ordinarily will arise only when as a direct result of the lawyer's professional negligence the testator's intent as expressed in the testamentary instruments is frustrated in whole or in part and

the beneficiary's interest in the estate is either lost, diminished, or unrealized.

Schreiner v. Scoville, 410 N.W.2d 679, 683 (Iowa 1987).

C

We agree with those courts that have rejected a broad cause of action in favor of beneficiaries. These courts have recognized the inevitable problems with disappointed heirs attempting to prove that the defendant-attorney failed to implement the deceased testator's intentions. Certainly allowing extrinsic evidence would create a host of difficulties. . . . Such a cause of action would subject attorneys to suits by heirs who simply did not receive what they believed to be their due share under the will or trust. This potential tort liability to third parties would create a conflict during the estate planning process, dividing the attorney's loyalty between his or her client and the third-party beneficiaries.

Moreover, we believe that the more limited cause of action recognized by several jurisdictions also undermines the policy rationales supporting the privity rule. These courts have limited the cause of action to beneficiaries specifically identified in an invalid will or trust. Under these circumstances, courts have reasoned, the interests of the client and the beneficiaries are necessarily aligned, negating any conflict, as the attorney owes a duty only to those parties which the testator clearly intended to benefit.

In most cases where a defect renders a will or trust invalid, however, there are concomitant questions as to the true intentions of the testator. Suppose, for example, that a properly drafted will is simply not executed at the time of the testator's death. The document may express the testator's true intentions, lacking signatures solely because of the attorney's negligent delay. On the other hand, the testator may have postponed execution because of second thoughts regarding the distribution scheme. In the latter situation, the attorney's representation of the testator will likely be affected if he or she knows that the existence of an unexecuted will may create malpractice liability if the testator unexpectedly dies.

The present case is indicative of the conflicts that could arise. Plaintiffs contend in part that Elliott was negligent in failing to fund the trust during Barcelo's lifetime, and in failing to obtain a signature from the trustee. These alleged deficiencies, however, could have existed pursuant to Barcelo's instructions, which may have been based on advice from her attorneys attempting to represent her best interests. An attorney's ability to render such advice would be severely compromised if the advice could be second-guessed by persons named as beneficiaries under the unconsummated trust.

In sum, we are unable to craft a bright-line rule that allows a lawsuit to proceed where alleged malpractice causes a will or trust to fail in a manner that casts no real doubt on the testator's intentions, while prohibiting actions in other situations. We believe the greater good is served by preserving a bright-line privity rule which denies a cause of action to all beneficiaries whom the attorney did not represent. This will ensure that attorneys may in all cases zealously represent their clients without the threat of suit from third parties compromising that representation.

We therefore hold that an attorney retained by a testator or settlor to draft a will or trust owes no professional duty of care to persons named as beneficiaries under the will or trust.

D

Plaintiffs also contend that, even if there is no tort duty extending to beneficiaries of an estate plan, they may recover under a third-party-beneficiary contract theory. While the majority of jurisdictions that have recognized a cause of action in favor of will or trust beneficiaries have done so under negligence principles, some have allowed recovery in contract.

In Texas, however, a legal malpractice action sounds in tort and is governed by negligence principles. Even assuming that a client who retains a lawyer to draft an estate plan intends for the lawyer's work to benefit the will or trust beneficiaries, the ultimate question is whether, considering the competing policy implications, the lawyer's professional duty should extend to persons whom the lawyer never represented. For the reasons previously discussed, we conclude that the answer is no.

CORNYN, JUSTICE, joined by ABBOTT, JUSTICE, dissenting.

With an obscure reference to "the greater good," the Court unjustifiably insulates an entire class of negligent lawyers from the consequences of their wrongdoing, and unjustly denies legal recourse to the grandchildren for whose benefit Ms. Barcelo hired a lawyer in the first place. I dissent.

By refusing to recognize a lawyer's duty to beneficiaries of a will, the Court embraces a rule recognized in only four states, while simultaneously rejecting the rule in an overwhelming majority of jurisdictions. Notwithstanding the fact that in recent years the Court has sought to align itself with the mainstream of American jurisprudence, the Court inexplicably balks in this case.

The threshold question in a negligence action, including a legal malpractice suit, is duty. Whether a defendant owes a duty to the plaintiff depends on several factors, including risk, foreseeability, and likelihood of injury weighed against the social utility of the actor's conduct, the magnitude of the burden of guarding against injury, and the consequences of placing the burden on the defendant.

The foreseeability of harm in this case is not open to serious question. Because Ms. Barcelo hired Mr. Elliott to accomplish the transfer of her estate to her grandchildren upon her death, the potential harm to the beneficiaries if the testamentary documents were incorrectly drafted was plainly foreseeable. Foreseeability of harm weighs heavily in favor of recognizing a duty to intended beneficiaries.

Additionally, the Court's decision means that, as a practical matter, no one has the right to sue for the lawyer's negligent frustration of the testator's intent. A flaw in a will or other testamentary document is not likely [to] be discovered until the client's death. And, generally, the estate suffers no harm from a negligently drafted testamentary document. Allowing beneficiaries to sue would provide accountability and thus an incentive for lawyers to use greater care in estate planning. Instead, the Court decides that an innocent party must bear the burden of the lawyer's error. The Court also gives no consideration to the fair adjustment of the loss between the parties, one of the traditional objectives of tort law. These grounds for the imposition of a legal duty in tort law generally, which apply to lawyers in every other context, are no less important in estate planning.

Nor do the reasons the Court gives for refusing to impose a duty under these circumstances withstand scrutiny. Contrary to the Court's view, recognizing an action by the intended beneficiaries would not extend a lawyer's duty to the general public, but only to a limited, foreseeable class. Because estate planning attorneys generally do not face *any* liability in this context, potential liability to the intended beneficiaries would not place them in a worse position than attorneys in any other setting.

The Court also hypothesizes that liability to estate beneficiaries may conflict with the attorney's duty to the client. Before the beneficiaries could prevail in a suit against the attorney, however, they would necessarily have to show that the attorney breached a duty to the decedent. This is because the lawyer's duty to the client is to see that the client's intentions are realized by the very documents the client has hired the lawyer to draft. No conflicting duty to the beneficiaries is imposed.

Searching for other hypothetical problems that might arise if a cause of action for the beneficiaries is recognized, the Court observes that a will not executed at the testator's death could in fact express the testator's true intentions. Granted, such a scenario may be the result of either the testator's indecision or the attorney's negligence. Similarly, a family member might be intentionally omitted from a will at the testator's direction, or negligently omitted because of the drafting lawyer's mistake. In other words, what appears to be attorney negligence may actually reflect the testator's wishes.

But surely these are matters subject to proof, as in all other cases. Nothing distinguishes this class of cases from many others in this respect. The Court fails to consider that the beneficiaries will in each case bear the burden of establishing that the attorney breached a duty to the testator, which resulted in damages to the beneficiaries. Lawyers, wishing to protect themselves from liability, may document the testator's intentions. . . .

In sum, I would hold that the intended beneficiary of a will or testamentary trust may bring a cause of action against an attorney whose negligence caused the beneficiary to lose a legacy in whole or in part. Accordingly, I would reverse the judgment of the court of appeals and remand this case to the trial court.

NOTES

1.   As the court makes clear, this is a minority rule. But *Barcelo* is still the law in Texas. *See* David J. Beck and Geoff A. Gannaway, *The Vitality of* Barcelo *After Ten Years: When Can An Attorney Be Sued for Negligence by Someone Other Than His Client?*, 58 Baylor L. Rev. 371 (2006). Recent cases in other jurisdictions reaffirm the viability of the rule. *See, e.g., Shoemaker v. Gindlesberger*, 887 N.E.2d 1167 (Ohio 2008). While, as *Barcelo* suggests, courts have differed on the specific question whether the beneficiaries of a will may bring a malpractice claim against the attorney who drafted the will, courts jealously guard against expansion of the right to pursue a claim for legal malpractice to a range of third parties, even those, like the plaintiffs in *Barcelo*, foreseeably injured by the lawyer's failure.

2.   Can one person assign to another the right to bring a malpractice claim? Most courts have said no. *See, e.g., Wagener v. McDonald*, 509 N.W.2d 188 (Minn. App. 1993). Why isn't a malpractice claim just a commercial cause of action, assignable to another person by the plaintiff? Consider the facts of *Weiss v. Leatherberry*, 863 So.2d 368 (Fla. App. 2003). Green was injured when the car she was driving was hit by Leatherberry's car. Leatherberry was at fault. Green sued Leatherberry. Green offered to settle the case for $100,000, but Leatherberry's lawyer failed to enter the settlement properly; the case was subsequently tried and Green obtained a judgment for $977,773.51. After the court upheld the judgment, Green and Leatherberry agreed that Leatherberry would sue his lawyer for malpractice, would be represented by and cooperate with a lawyer of Green's choosing, and would assign all the benefits from the lawsuit to Green; in return, Green agreed not to execute her judgment against Leatherberry's assets. Should the agreement be enforceable? Why or why not?

3.   What about an excess insurer? An excess insurer is an insurer that contracts to provide coverage if liability for the insured exceeds a certain amount. In *Querrey & Harrow, Ltd. v. Transcontinental Insurance Co.*, 861 N.E.2d 719 (Ind. App. 2007), *opinion adopted*, 885 N.E.2d 1235 (Ind. 2008), the insured manufactured trampolines. It was sued by a plaintiff who claimed he was injured while jumping on a trampoline manufactured by the insured. The case was settled for a payment of $6.3 million; the insured paid the first $250,000, its primary liability insurer paid its available coverage, and Transcontinental, the "excess insurer," paid the remaining $3.74 million. Subsequently, Transcontinental brought suit against the lawyers who represented the insured, arguing that if they had handled the case properly, Transcontinental would not have had to pay the excess coverage. Should Transcontinental have been able to sue for malpractice on a third-party beneficiary theory? On any other theory?

4.   Does the person who pays the lawyer have standing to bring a malpractice claim? In *Fox v. White*, 215 S.W.3d 257 (Mo. App. 2007), Fox was the stepfather of Burns, a criminal defendant. Fox paid attorney White to repre-

sent Burns. Burns was convicted and sentenced to 144 years in prison. Fox then brought suit against White for malpractice. The court held that the contract under which Fox undertook to engage White to represent Burns did not create an attorney-client relationship between White and Fox. "Certainly, had Burns been acquitted . . . other family members would have benefitted from that result. Merely acknowledging this fact, however, does not confer upon White a duty to those family members." The lawyer's obligations to a client whose representation is being paid for by a third party is discussed further in Chapter 5.

5.   How about an opposing party? Suppose that a lawyer brings a frivolous claim on behalf of a client against a defendant. The case is dismissed. Is the lawyer liable to the defendant, who was obliged to defend a meritless lawsuit? In *Clark v. Druckman*, 624 S.E.2d 864 (W. Va. 2005), Druckman, an attorney, brought a medical malpractice suit on behalf of client against Clark, a physician. The plaintiff's action was voluntarily dismissed with prejudice. Over two years later, Clark sued Druckman, claiming that Druckman had violated a duty of care owed to her as the opposing party. Should she prevail if Druckman was negligent in bringing a frivolous claim against her? Why or why not?

6.   What about cocounsel? Does a lawyer who undertakes representation of a client jointly with another lawyer owe a duty to that lawyer? That is the subject of the following case.

MAZON v. KRAFCHICK

144 P.3d 1168 (Wash. 2006) (en banc)

C. JOHNSON, J.

This case involves a dispute between two attorneys who had corepresented a client in a personal injury action. The client's lawsuit was dismissed after one of the attorneys failed to timely serve the complaint and the statute of limitations expired. The client brought a claim for malpractice against both attorneys, which was settled for $1.3 million. The dispute here arose when Michael Mazon sued his cocounsel Steven Krafchick, seeking to recover for the loss of his expected contingency fee. . . . The issue presented [is] whether, under these facts, cocounsel may sue one another for the loss of prospective fees. . . .

The trial court dismissed the claims on summary judgment. The Court of Appeals affirmed the trial court's ruling that public policy prohibits one cocounsel from recovering against the other for the loss of an expected contingency fee under any circumstances. . . . We affirm. . . .

FACTS

On May 18, 1999, Tahar Layouni was electrocuted and seriously injured when a drilling company drilled into a buried electric line and caused a charge to surge through the area where Layouni was working. In July 1999, Layouni retained attorney Michael Mazon to represent him to recover damages for his resulting fibromyalgia and chronic pain. With

Layouni's consent, Mazon associated Steven Krafchick, an attorney with special expertise in this area. Mazon and Krafchick agreed in what the parties consider a "joint venture agreement" to split fees and costs equally. They divided the responsibilities informally. Mazon would draft the complaint and find the addresses and agents of defendants to serve, and Krafchick would file and serve the complaint.

After Mazon drafted the complaint and found the addresses of the agents, Krafchick filed the complaint on May 15, 2002. Since the filing of the complaint tolled the statute of limitations for 90 days, the deadline for serving the defendants was August 13, 2002. Krafchick directed his paralegal to serve the complaint. Though she told Krafchick she had timely served the complaint, she had failed to do so until August 16, 2002, after the statute of limitations expired on Layouni's personal injury claim. In late September, Krafchick told Mazon he had failed to timely serve the complaint. He then drafted a letter to Mazon confirming that he had been responsible for filing and serving the complaint.

The client's suit was dismissed. Layouni then asserted a claim against both Krafchick and Mazon for professional negligence. The attorneys were covered by the same malpractice insurance carrier. In mediation, that insurance carrier settled Layouni's claim for $1.3 million. Layouni would not agree to settle his claim unless Mazon also contributed to the settlement and thus the insurance carrier paid $1,250,000 on behalf of Krafchick and $50,000 on behalf of Mazon.

Mazon then filed this lawsuit against Krafchick, asserting causes of action for breach of the agreement, breach of fiduciary duties, professional negligence, and indemnification. Mazon sought damages ... for ... the loss of the fee he expected to earn of $325,000. . . .

On cross motions for summary judgment, the trial court dismissed Mazon's causes of action for breach of the agreement and breach of fiduciary duties. The court denied Mazon's request for prospective attorney fees on the grounds that allowing claims for reduced or lost fees would be potentially inconsistent with cocounsel's overriding duties to their client. . . . The court reasoned that absent gross negligence or intentional misconduct, claims between cocounsel should be strictly limited to lost costs or expenses advanced, if any, by the nonnegligent cocounsel. . . .

The Court of Appeals affirmed the denial of Mazon's expected contingency fee and adopted a broad rule prohibiting cocounsel from suing each other for lost or reduced prospective attorney fees. . . . Mazon filed a petition for review of whether he is entitled to recover prospective fees.

ANALYSIS

The extent to which an attorney may sue cocounsel for the loss of prospective fees is an issue of first impression in Washington. The Court of Appeals followed the approach of the California courts and rejected the argument that cocounsel owe fiduciary duties to each other on the theory that the latter's malpractice in handling their mutual client's case reduced or eliminated the fees the former expected to realize from the case. . . . [T]he Court of Appeals noted, "it would violate public policy to allow attorneys to sue each other on the theory that 'cocounsel have a fiduciary duty to protect one another's prospective interests in a contingency fee.'"

The court recognized that Mazon's claim in this case did not create an actual conflict with his and Krafchick's undivided loyalty to Layouni, but decided that public policy dictates against allowing claims between cocounsel for lost prospective fees because of the potential conflict with the undivided loyalty owed to the client. The court reasoned that a bright-line rule is preferable because it prevents conflicts from arising at any point during the representation, assures the client's interest is paramount regardless of the issue, and is easy to administer. Thus, the court rejected Mazon's claim on the basis that recovering damages for a prospective contingency fee lost through a misfeasance of cocounsel assumes a duty to conduct the lawsuit in a manner that does not diminish or eliminate the fee each expects to collect. We agree. Imposing a duty to protect prospective fees would create potential impermissible conflicts with the duty of loyalty the attorneys owe their clients. . . .

We . . . adopt a bright-line rule that no duties exist between cocounsel that would allow recovery for lost or reduced prospective fees. As cocounsel, both attorneys owe an undivided duty of loyalty to the client. The decisions about how to pursue a case must be based on the client's best interests, not the attorneys'. The undivided duty of loyalty means that each attorney owes a duty to pursue the case in the client's best interests, even if that means not completing the case and forgoing a potential contingency fee.

If we were to recognize an attorney's right to recover from cocounsel prospective fees, potential conflicts of interest that harm the client's interests may arise. Cocounsel may develop an impermissible self-interest in preserving the claim for the prospective fee, even when the client's interests demand otherwise. Additionally, the question of whether an attorney's claim conflicts with the client's best interests may be difficult to answer. Discretionary, tactical decisions, such as whether to advise clients to settle or risk proceeding to trial and determining the amount and structure of settlements, could be characterized by cocounsel as a breach of the contractual duties or general duties of care owed to one another and provide a basis for claims seeking recovery of prospective fees. As the California Supreme Court recognized, in comparing the issue to lawsuits for prospective fees between successive attorneys,

> [p]ublic confidence in the legal system may be eroded by the spectacle of lawyers squabbling over the could-have-beens of a concluded lawsuit, even when the client has indicated no dissatisfaction with the outcome. Considerations of public policy support the conclusion that an attorney's duty of undivided loyalty to his client should not be diluted by imposing upon him obligations to the client's former

attorney, or at least obligations greater than the client himself owed to the former attorney.

Mazon contends that prohibiting cocounsel from suing each other for prospective fees would undermine the public's confidence in the legal system because cocounsel could not be held fully liable to each other. He states that "when an attorney can recover only nominal damages from cocounsel, despite the loss of a substantial prospective fee, but is confronted with a significant claim for professional negligence from the client through no fault of his own, the incentive will be to collude with cocounsel to minimize or to conceal the client's malpractice claim. Absent a viable legal remedy to recover his own damages, an attorney is thus more likely to be less diligent about protecting the interests of the client, rather than more." Under these circumstances, he argues, the attorney's interest in protecting himself from liability will trump his duty of undivided loyalty to the client.

However, we find this argument unpersuasive because it presumes that allowing cocounsel to recover prospective fees will eliminate attorneys' incentive to collude and protect themselves from liability. Instead, we believe that allowing cocounsel to recover prospective fees would create the opposite incentives to overemphasize the informal divisions of responsibilities between cocounsel, overlook any failings of cocounsel, and later claim that cocounsel's failures were not their responsibility. Prohibiting cocounsel from suing each other for prospective fees arising from an attorney's malpractice in representing their mutual client provides a clear message to attorneys: each cocounsel is entirely responsible for diligently representing the client.

The Court of Appeals correctly recognized that this approach encourages cocounsel to back each other up and ensure that there are fewer mistakes in pursuing the best outcome for the client. Cocounsel are in the best position to ensure that they are not injured by each other's mistakes. This approach is consistent with the attorneys' duty to maintain undivided loyalty to the client. The public interest is best served by this approach because attorneys must exercise diligence when choosing and working with cocounsel to preserve the undivided duty to the client. We affirm the Court of Appeals on this issue and adopt the bright-line rule rejecting the recognition of a duty upon which cocounsel could recover from each other prospective attorney fees. . . .

SANDERS, J. (dissenting).

The majority holds an attorney can never recover prospective fees from cocounsel. I disagree. Instead of focusing on the facts at hand, the majority seeks to prevent *any possible conflict* at *any possible time* in *any possible case*. It claims any liability between attorneys for prospective fees creates a fiduciary duty between attorneys, which might interfere with an attorney's duty of loyalty to the client. The duty breached here, however, is the standard duty of due care every professional owes to any foreseeable plaintiff as well as the duty we all have not to break our contracts. And there is no conflict of interest if an attorney recovers fees from cocounsel because cocounsel has already damaged the mutual client's case through his own negligence. . . .

I agree an attorney owes every client an undivided duty of loyalty, and this duty is inviolate and must be protected. But the majority's rule is so broad it insulates attorneys from responsibility for their professional negligence even where there is no remaining duty to the client to protect. After Krafchick breached his duty of care, resulting in dismissal of the case, Layouni no longer needs Krafchick's loyalty. But instead of providing the proper remedy to Mazon for Krafchick's negligence, the majority protects Krafchick, providing a broad shield apparently available only to lawyers.

Any other professional must bear the cost of his negligence. A lawyer owes a duty of care to nonclients when:

> (a) [T]he lawyer ... invites the nonclient to rely on the lawyer's opinion or provision of other legal services, and the nonclient so relies; and

> (b) the nonclient is not, under applicable tort law, too remote from the lawyer to be entitled to protection.

Restatement (Second) of Torts § 51(2), at 356–57. Under this rule Krafchick owed Mazon a duty because Krafchick invited Mazon to rely on the provision of his legal services, and Mazon did rely. Discussing the rule's rationale, the American Law Institute balances the same concerns raised by the majority:

> Lawyers regularly act in disputes and transactions involving nonclients who will foreseeably be harmed by inappropriate acts of the lawyers. Holding lawyers liable for such harm is sometimes warranted. Yet it is often difficult to distinguish between harm resulting from inappropriate lawyer conduct on the one hand and, on the other hand, detriment to a nonclient resulting from a lawyer's fulfilling the proper function of helping a client through lawful means. Making lawyers liable to nonclients, moreover, could tend to discourage lawyers from vigorous representation. Hence, a duty of care to nonclients arises only in the limited circumstances described in the Section.

Id. § 51 cmt. b at 358. And these limited circumstances are present here. Mazon was foreseeably harmed by Krafchick's failure to timely serve the defendant. Concerns militating against liability are not present here. There is no difficulty distinguishing the harm resulting from Krafchick's negligence and Krafchick's assisting his client. Krafchick was not helping his client when he failed to timely serve a complaint. Nor does liability discourage vigorous representation, rather liability encourages zealous advocacy.

Krafchick is also liable under section 56 of the Restatement. This section provides "a lawyer is subject to liability to a client or nonclient when a nonlawyer would be in similar circumstances." *Id.* § 56, at 416. Unlike the majority, the *Restatement* makes no special exemption for attorneys:

> Lawyers are subject to the general law. If activities of a nonlawyer in the same circumstances would render the nonlawyer civilly liable or afford the nonlawyer a defense to liability, the same activities by a lawyer in the same circumstances generally render the lawyer liable or afford the lawyer a defense.

Id. § 56 cmt. b at 416. Krafchick would generally be liable for his negligence. His negligence arguably cost Layouni $1.3 million in potential recovery and Mazon $325,000 in potential fees. Layouni recovered his share in the form of a credit to the settlement. However Mazon recovered nothing.

The majority fears attorneys might "develop an impermissible self-interest in preserving the claim for prospective fees, even when the client's interests demand otherwise." This is fiction. Krafchick's negligence would never be in the client's interest. An attorney must always timely serve a complaint and failure to do so may be negligent. When an attorney commits malpractice and that same misconduct damages cocounsel, there is no reason both the client and cocounsel should not be allowed to recover. This result does not jeopardize an attorney's duty of loyalty, it promotes it. . . .

Equity also supports Mazon's recovery. Assuming the damages calculation was correct, Krafchick's negligence and breach of contract lost a potential $1.9 million recovery. Layouni received the two-thirds he was entitled to. According to the contract, Mazon was entitled to one-half the remainder. But Krafchick never had to pay. . . . The majority allows Krafchick to keep the $325,000 owed to Mazon. . . .

The majority also claims letting attorneys sue one another will erode public confidence—what little remains—in the legal system. This is speculation at most, not adequate reason to deny a lawyer the legal right to recover damages sustained as the result of another's negligence or breach of contractual duty. What will the image of lawyers insulating themselves from liability do? By turning a blind eye to an attorney's negligence, the majority hopes to encourage "cocounsel to back each other up and ensure that there are fewer mistakes in pursuing the best outcome for the client." Apparently Mazon should have checked with Krafchick daily, acting as his cocounsel's keeper. An attorney with enough time to constantly investigate his cocounsel's activities likely does not need cocounsel in the first place. Dividing responsibilities provides common clients extra talent and resources and promotes efficiency.

The majority hopes to send a clear message: "each cocounsel is *entirely* responsible for diligently representing the client." The bright-line rule adopted today does the opposite; Krafchick is only partially responsible for his mistake. He breached his duties of care to both client and cocounsel. Based on the settlement amount, this cost Layouni $1.3 million and

Mazon $325,000. Layouni recovered $1.3 million, while Mazon recovered nothing.

Mazon should be allowed to recover his prospective fees from Krafchick. Accordingly the Court of Appeals should be reversed.

NOTES

1. How did Mazon calculate his damages?

2. In this case, the lawyers agreed to divide the responsibility for the case, and to divide the fees that the client would pay. Agreements about division of fees between lawyers are governed by Rule 1.5(e). Was the agreement here permissible?

3. Next time, will Mazon be likely to engage co-counsel? Do we want to encourage him to do so? Why or why not? What effect might this case have on a lawyer's willingness to share responsibility for his cases?

4. MALPRACTICE CLAIMS IN CRIMINAL DEFENSE

Malpractice in a civil case costs the client money. But malpractice in a criminal case might result in the client's loss of freedom and reputation or even, in capital cases, his life. Does the law recognize this greater potential for harm in assessing malpractice claims against criminal defense lawyers?

ANG v. MARTIN

114 P.3d 637 (Wash. 2005)

OWENS, J.

We are asked to determine whether plaintiffs in a malpractice action against their former criminal defense attorneys were properly required to prove by a preponderance of the evidence that they were actually innocent of the underlying criminal charges. The Court of Appeals concluded that, as an element of their negligence claim, plaintiffs were required "to prove innocence *in fact* and not merely to present evidence of the government's inability to prove guilt." We affirm the Court of Appeals.

FACTS

Psychiatrist Jessy Ang and his wife Editha jointly owned Evergreen Medical Panel, Inc., a company that provided the Washington State Department of Labor and Industries with independent medical examinations of injured workers. As a result of Dr. Ang's contact with a target of a governmental task force investigating social security fraud, Dr. Ang himself became a person of interest. In February 1994, the task force executed a search warrant on Dr. Ang's office and seized copies of two sets of signed tax returns that reported conflicting amounts of income. The Angs were arrested in April 1996, following the execution of a search warrant at their residence. A year later, the Angs were indicted on 18 criminal counts, including conspiracy to defraud the United States, bank and tax fraud, and filing false statements.

The Angs retained defendants Richard Hansen and Michael G. Martin for flat fees of $225,000 and $100,000, respectively. Attorneys Hansen and Martin engaged in a round of plea negotiations prior to trial, but the Angs rejected the plea bargain. The case proceeded to a jury trial before Judge Tanner in federal district court in December 1997. On the fifth day of trial, just prior to the conclusion of the government's case, Hansen and Martin recommended that the Angs accept another proffered plea, one that the Angs viewed as the least attractive of any agreement previously presented. After Dr. Ang was allegedly told that Mrs. Ang could face sexual assault in prison, the Angs agreed to plead guilty to two of the 18 counts.

The Angs then engaged attorney Monte Hester to review the plea discussions and provide a second opinion. Hester concluded that the government had not met its burden of proof and that the plea agreement provided the Angs with no material benefit. Retaining Hester and Keith A. MacFie to represent them, the Angs successfully moved to withdraw the pleas, which Judge Tanner had never formally accepted. In September 1999, the matter again proceeded to trial before Judge Tanner, with the Angs waiving their right to a jury. Although the government offered another plea bargain prior to trial, one requiring no plea on Dr. Ang's part, a misdemeanor or felony for Mrs. Ang, and a $500,000 fine, the Angs rejected the plea and were acquitted on all 18 counts.

The Angs filed the present legal malpractice action against Hansen and Martin in May 2000 in Pierce County Superior Court. The complaint stated claims for legal malpractice.... The trial court denied the defendants' motion for summary judgment, and a jury trial began in November 2001. The trial court instructed the jury that the Angs had to prove by a preponderance of the evidence that they were innocent of the underlying criminal charges. On January 11, 2002, responding to the initial two questions on a special verdict form, the jury found that the Angs had not "proven by a preponderance of the evidence [they were] innocent of all the criminal charges against [them]." As to the verdict form's third question, asking whether "any of the defendants [had been] negligent," the jury made a finding of negligence against Martin only.

The plaintiffs appealed, but the Court of Appeals affirmed. This court granted the plaintiffs' petition for review.

ISSUE

Where a legal malpractice suit stems from the representation of clients in a criminal prosecution, must plaintiffs who were acquitted of the criminal charges prove their actual innocence of the crimes, or does their acquittal satisfy the innocence element of their malpractice action?

ANALYSIS

Essential Elements of Legal Malpractice Claims against Criminal Defense Counsel. A plaintiff claiming negligent representation by an attorney in a civil matter bears the burden of proving four elements by a preponderance of the evidence:

> (1) The existence of an attorney-client relationship which gives rise to a duty of care on the part of the attorney to the client; (2) an act or omission by the attorney in breach of the duty of care; (3) damage to the client; and (4) proximate causation between the attorney's breach of the duty and the damage incurred.

... In a legal malpractice trial, the "trier of fact will be asked to decide what a reasonable jury or fact finder [in the underlying trial or 'trial within the trial'] would have done *but for* the attorney's negligence." Legal causation, however, presents a question of law: "It involves a determination of whether liability *should* attach as a matter of law given the existence of cause in fact." To determine whether the cause in fact of a plaintiff's harm should also be deemed the legal cause of that harm, a court may consider, among other things, the public policy implications of holding the defendant liable. In "criminal malpractice" suits, two elements related to proximate causation have been added. In *Falkner v. Foshaug*, 29 P.3d 771 (2001), the Court of Appeals "conclude[d] that *postconviction relief* is a prerequisite to maintaining [a criminal malpractice] suit and *proof of innocence* is an additional element a criminal defendant/malpractice plaintiff must prove to prevail at trial in his legal malpractice action."

The trial court in the present case thus instructed the jury as follows on the elements of the Angs criminal malpractice claims:

> To prove their legal malpractice claims, the plaintiffs bear the burden of proving by a preponderance of the evidence each of the following:
>
> First, that there is an attorney-client relationship giving rise to a duty owed by a defendant to a plaintiff;
>
> Second, *that plaintiffs have obtained a successful challenge to their convictions* based on their attorneys failure to adequately defend them;
>
> Third, that *plaintiff was innocent of the crimes charged;*
>
> Fourth, that there is an act [or] omission by a defendant that breached the duty of care of an attorney;
>
> Fifth, that a plaintiff was damaged; and
>
> Sixth, that a breach of duty by a defendant is a proximate cause of a plaintiffs [sic] damages....

The Angs assigned error to this instruction, contending that their undisputed acquittal of the criminal charges met not only the additional element of postconviction relief but also the innocence requirement.

By successfully withdrawing their guilty pleas and receiving an acquittal on all charges, the Angs unquestionably received the equivalent of post-conviction relief, but contrary to their contention, they did not thereby satisfy the ... innocence requirement. The Angs mistakenly claim that, under *Falkner,* they were simply required to prove legal innocence, not actual innocence. But the *Falkner* court referred explicitly to the "*actual* innocence requirement" and at no point equated the innocence requirement with *legal* innocence. Plainly, a requirement of legal innocence would have been redundant alongside the additional, unchallenged requirement of postconviction relief....

Moreover, proving actual innocence, not simply legal innocence, is essential to proving proximate causation, both cause in fact and legal causation. Unless criminal malpractice plaintiffs can prove by a preponderance of the evidence their actual innocence of the charges, their own bad acts, not the alleged negligence of defense counsel, should be regarded as the cause in fact of their harm. Likewise, if criminal malpractice plaintiffs cannot prove their actual innocence under the civil standard, they will be unable to establish, in light of significant public policy considerations, that the alleged negligence of their defense counsel was the legal cause of their harm. Summarizing the policy concerns, the *Falkner* court observed that, "[r]equiring a defendant to prove by a preponderance of the evidence that he is innocent of the charges against him will prohibit criminals from benefiting from their own bad acts, maintain respect for our criminal justice systems procedural protections, remove the harmful chilling effect on the defense bar, prevent suits from criminals who may be guilty, [but] could have gotten a better deal, and prevent a flood of nuisance litigation."

In sum, we conclude that the Angs were properly required to prove by a preponderance of the evidence that they were actually innocent of the underlying criminal charges. We therefore affirm the Court of Appeals....

CHAMBERS, J. (concurring in dissent).

I ... write separately to express my indignation that this court, based upon the policy of protecting lawyers, would carve out a special protection for criminal defense attorneys whose acts of professional negligence are harmful to their clients. Under this logic, it is not enough for the injured client to prove actual harm from the attorney's failure to meet professional standards; the injured client must also prove that her hands were always clean. Under this logic, why not give immunity to accountants for professional negligence unless the accountant's client can prove he or she never understated income or requested an unavailable deduction, even when the accountants' bad acts caused actual harm to their clients or society? Surely tax dodgers should not profit from their misdeeds. Under this logic, why not give immunity to health care providers who harm their patients unless the patient can prove perfect good health but for the negligence of the provider? Surely the unhealthy should not profit from their illness.

But this logic ignores the fact that professionals owe a duty to the sick as well as the healthy; to the scrupulously honest business woman as well as the one looking for the angle; to the guilty as well as the innocent. Those of us caught in the grip of the law are always entitled to competent legal representation whether or not we are totally innocent. The heart of the criminal defense lawyer's job is often not to prove absolute innocence; the irreducible core of the job is to make the state prove its case and make the best case for the defendant possible. Often the sole issue is the level of culpability and the sanction to be imposed upon the client. The government may seek multiple counts where a single count is appropriate, seek charges of a higher degree than the evidence supports, or seek a sentence disproportionate to the offense. The negligence of her lawyer may cost her client her fortune, her liberty, or her life. The "actual innocence" requirement is impractical and harmful in the area of criminal malpractice law; it creates an almost impossible burden and provides almost absolute immunity to criminal defense lawyers.

The most troubling aspect of the actual innocence requirement announced by the majority lies with its origin. It is based upon a policy to protect *lawyers* from lawsuits. Tort actions are maintained for a variety of reasons, including the deterrence of wrongful conduct. As a matter of basic policy, accountability, compensation, and deterrence of wrongful conduct should trump protecting lawyers from lawsuits.

Second, while it may be true that a majority of courts that have reached the issue require the plaintiff to establish actual innocence, the numbers do not appear to be great. Only Missouri, New York, Massachusetts, Alaska, Pennsylvania, California, New Hampshire, Nebraska, Illinois, Florida, and Wisconsin require either proof of actual innocence or that the conviction was set aside on postconviction relief. This is hardly a national consensus.

This court should protect the public from lawyers' misdeeds, not the other way around. A plaintiff who is not categorically innocent seeking compensation under ordinary principles of tort law faces no light burden. Such a guilty plaintiff must prove a duty, a breach of that duty, injuries proximately caused by the breach, and the amount of his damages. I see no reason to provide additional protections for lawyers.

NOTES

1. Not every jurisdiction requires the "actual innocence" requirement that *Ang* imposes, but most require some demonstration that the conviction was wrongful. Many, for example, require that the plaintiff have obtained postconviction relief. *See, e.g., Adkins v. Dixon,* 482 S.E.2d 797 (Va. 1997). Adkins was charged with sixteen felonies. In the trial court, he moved pro se to dismiss all sixteen charges because the state had violated his right to a speedy trial. The trial court denied his motion, and he was tried on all sixteen charges. Dixon, his appointed counsel, pursued the speedy trial claim on appeal only with regard to ten of the sixteen felony counts. The appellate

court held that the speedy trial claim had merit, and discharged those ten convictions. The state Supreme Court declined to extend that treatment to the remaining six claims because Dixon had not made a timely claim for that relief. Adkins' sentence on the six felonies was two life sentences plus 45 years. Do you think Adkins should be able to sue Dixon for malpractice? Would Adkins have been better off without a lawyer?

2.   What is the justification for the "actual innocence" rule? Do you think it is legitimate?

3.   What if the malpractice claim is based not on the client's guilt, but on the sentence he received? Suppose that client agrees that he is guilty of the crime charged, but claims that due to his lawyer's malpractice, he received a longer sentence than that authorized by law. Can he claim malpractice, or will he be precluded by the "actual innocence" rule? *See Powell v. Associated Counsel for the Accused*, 129 P.3d 831 (Wash. App. 2006). Powell pled guilty to a gross misdemeanor, for which the maximum sentence was one year. He was erroneously sentenced to 38.25 months of confinement; by the time he was able to secure relief, he had been incarcerated for over 20 months. He sought damages based on the fact that he had spent eight months in excess of his legally authorized sentence in prison. His former lawyer, citing *Ang*, claimed that the case should be dismissed because Powell could not prove his innocence. The court rejected the lawyer's argument, holding that where the allegations of malpractice stemmed entirely from his sentencing rather than the guilt or innocence phase, the causation problems identified in *Ang* were not present, and the "particularly egregious allegation of attorney negligence" was uncommon and unlikely to recur. Powell's case was "more akin to that of an innocent person wrongfully convicted than of a guilty person attempting to take advantage of his own wrongdoing."

4.   What if the lawyer's error resulted in conviction for an offense that did not exist? Client was arrested while riding his moped and was charged with driving on a suspended license. He protested to Lawyer, correctly, that the statute in question expressly excluded mopeds from the list of vehicles a person with a suspended license was prohibited from driving. Lawyer ignored his claim and the court found Client guilty. Subsequently Client, without a lawyer, moved successfully to reopen his case on the ground that his conduct had not constituted a crime at all. The prosecutor agreed and the court entered an order dismissing the charges. Can Client sue Lawyer for malpractice? *See Taylor v. Davis*, 576 S.E.2d 445 (Va. 2003).

5.   In the absence of any civil liability for malpractice, what incentive is there for criminal defense lawyers to perform competently? Are those motivations different than those of civil practitioners?

6.   The requirement in many jurisdictions that the client obtain postconviction relief before he can pursue a claim for attorney malpractice can pose a procedural difficulty: the statute of limitations on the malpractice claim may expire before the postconviction matter can be resolved. What do you suppose the client should do in those circumstances? *See Burnett v. South*, 2006 WL 4497729 (Tenn. App. 2007).

7.   Are there particular reasons to be concerned about the competency and diligence of criminal defense lawyers? A recent Washington Post article noted

that Virginia has created a fund to supplement the fees paid to court-appointed criminal defense lawyers. Without the supplementation—which provides for additional funds under certain circumstances—state law provided that the maximum payment to appointed counsel for a juvenile court case was $120 and for a felony punishable by twenty years or less of imprisonment, $445. For a case such as murder or rape the maximum payment to a lawyer was $1,235. Tom Jackman, *Virginia Court–Appointed Lawyers Shun Fund, Jeopardizing Future*, Wash. Post, Mar. 22, 2008, at B01. Does this suggest a reason to be concerned about the quality of criminal defense representation? Does the doctrine of ineffective assistance of counsel, as discussed in the following section, adequately address these concerns?

C. INEFFECTIVE ASSISTANCE OF COUNSEL

As the preceding section suggests, legal doctrine significantly constrains criminal defendants in securing civil judgments for damages from their attorneys for professional malpractice. But what happens to a defendant who has been convicted in part because of the incompetence of his lawyer? Even if he is not entitled to a damages remedy, is there any way he can obtain relief from his conviction? The Supreme Court addressed this issue in the following case.

STRICKLAND v. WASHINGTON
466 U.S. 668 (1984)

JUSTICE O'CONNOR delivered the opinion of the Court.

This case requires us to consider the proper standards for judging a criminal defendant's contention that the Constitution requires a conviction or death sentence to be set aside because counsel's assistance at the trial or sentencing was ineffective.

I

A

During a 10–day period in September 1976, respondent planned and committed three groups of crimes, which included three brutal stabbing murders, torture, kidnaping, severe assaults, attempted murders, attempted extortion, and theft. After his two accomplices were arrested, respondent surrendered to police and voluntarily gave a lengthy statement confessing to the third of the criminal episodes. The State of Florida indicted respondent for kidnaping and murder and appointed an experienced criminal lawyer to represent him.

Counsel actively pursued pretrial motions and discovery. He cut his efforts short, however, and he experienced a sense of hopelessness about the case, when he learned that, against his specific advice, respondent had also confessed to the first two murders. By the date set for trial, respondent was subject to indictment for three counts of first-degree murder and multiple counts of robbery, kidnaping for ransom, breaking and entering and assault, attempted murder, and conspiracy to commit robbery. Respondent waived his right to a jury trial, again acting against counsel's advice, and pleaded guilty to all charges, including the three capital murder charges.

In the plea colloquy, respondent told the trial judge that, although he had committed a string of burglaries, he had no significant prior criminal record and that at the time of his criminal spree he was under extreme stress caused by his inability to support his family. He also stated, however, that he accepted responsibility for the crimes. The trial judge told respondent that he had "a great deal of respect for people who are willing to step forward and admit their responsibility" but that he was making no statement at all about his likely sentencing decision.

Counsel advised respondent to invoke his right under Florida law to an advisory jury at his capital sentencing hearing. Respondent rejected the advice and waived the right. He chose instead to be sentenced by the trial judge without a jury recommendation.

In preparing for the sentencing hearing, counsel spoke with respondent about his background. He also spoke on the telephone with respondent's wife and mother, though he did not follow up on the one unsuccessful effort to meet with them. He did not otherwise seek out character witnesses for respondent. Nor did he request a psychiatric examination, since his conversations with his client gave no indication that respondent had psychological problems.

Counsel decided not to present and hence not to look further for evidence concerning respondent's character and emotional state. That decision reflected trial counsel's sense of hopelessness about overcoming the evidentiary effect of respondent's confessions to the gruesome crimes. It also reflected the judgment that it was advisable to rely on the plea colloquy for evidence about respondent's background and about his claim of emotional stress: the plea colloquy communicated sufficient information about these subjects, and by forgoing the opportunity to present new evidence on these subjects, counsel prevented the State from cross-examining respondent on his claim and from putting on psychiatric evidence of its own.

Counsel also excluded from the sentencing hearing other evidence he thought was potentially damaging. He successfully moved to exclude respondent's "rap sheet." Because he judged that a presentence report might prove more detrimental than helpful, as it would have included respondent's criminal history and thereby would have undermined the claim of no significant history of criminal activity, he did not request that one be prepared.

At the sentencing hearing, counsel's strategy was based primarily on the trial judge's remarks at the plea colloquy as well as on his reputation as a sentencing judge who thought it important for a convicted defendant to own up to his crime. Counsel argued that respondent's remorse and acceptance of responsibility justified sparing him from the death penalty.

Counsel also argued that respondent had no history of criminal activity and that respondent committed the crimes under extreme mental or emotional disturbance, thus coming within the statutory list of mitigating circumstances. He further argued that respondent should be spared death because he had surrendered, confessed, and offered to testify against a codefendant and because respondent was fundamentally a good person who had briefly gone badly wrong in extremely stressful circumstances. The State put on evidence and witnesses largely for the purpose of describing the details of the crimes. Counsel did not cross-examine the medical experts who testified about the manner of death of respondent's victims.

The trial judge found several aggravating circumstances with respect to each of the three murders. He found that all three murders were especially heinous, atrocious, and cruel, all involving repeated stabbings. All three murders were committed in the course of at least one other dangerous and violent felony, and since all involved robbery, the murders were for pecuniary gain. All three murders were committed to avoid arrest for the accompanying crimes and to hinder law enforcement. In the course of one of the murders, respondent knowingly subjected numerous persons to a grave risk of death by deliberately stabbing and shooting the murder victim's sisters-in-law, who sustained severe—in one case, ultimately fatal—injuries.

With respect to mitigating circumstances, the trial judge made the same findings for all three capital murders. First, although there was no admitted evidence of prior convictions, respondent had stated that he had engaged in a course of stealing. In any case, even if respondent had no significant history of criminal activity, the aggravating circumstances "would still clearly far outweigh" that mitigating factor. Second, the judge found that, during all three crimes, respondent was not suffering from extreme mental or emotional disturbance and could appreciate the criminality of his acts. Third, none of the victims was a participant in, or consented to, respondent's conduct. Fourth, respondent's participation in the crimes was neither minor nor the result of duress or domination by an accomplice. Finally, respondent's age (26) could not be considered a factor in mitigation, especially when viewed in light of respondent's planning of the crimes and disposition of the proceeds of the various accompanying thefts.

In short, the trial judge found numerous aggravating circumstances and no (or a single comparatively insignificant) mitigating circumstance. With respect to each of the three convictions for capital murder, the trial judge concluded: "A careful consideration of all matters presented to the court impels the conclusion that there are insufficient mitigating circumstances . . . to outweigh the aggravating circumstances." He therefore sentenced respondent to death on each of the three counts of murder and to prison terms for the other crimes. The Florida Supreme Court upheld the convictions and sentences on direct appeal.

B

Respondent subsequently sought collateral relief in state court on numerous grounds, among them that counsel had rendered ineffective assistance at the sentencing proceeding. Respondent challenged counsel's assistance in six respects. He asserted that counsel was ineffective because he failed to move for a continuance to prepare for sentencing, to request a psychiatric report, to investigate and present character witnesses, to seek a presentence investigation report, to present meaningful arguments to the sentencing judge, and to investigate the medical examiner's reports or cross-examine the medical experts. In support of the claim, respondent submitted 14 affidavits from friends, neighbors, and relatives stating that they would have testified if asked to do so. He also submitted one psychiatric report and one psychological report stating that respondent, though not under the influence of extreme mental or emotional disturbance, was "chronically frustrated and depressed because of his economic dilemma" at the time of his crimes.

The trial court denied relief without an evidentiary hearing, finding that the record evidence conclusively showed that the ineffectiveness claim was meritless. Four of the assertedly prejudicial errors required little discussion. First, there were no grounds to request a continuance, so there was no error in not requesting one when respondent pleaded guilty. Second, failure to request a presentence investigation was not a serious error because the trial judge had discretion not to grant such a request and because any presentence investigation would have resulted in admission of respondent's "rap sheet" and thus would have undermined his assertion of no significant history of criminal activity. Third, the argument and memorandum given to the sentencing judge were "admirable" in light of the overwhelming aggravating circumstances and absence of mitigating circumstances. Fourth, there was no error in failure to examine the medical examiner's reports or to cross-examine the medical witnesses testifying on the manner of death of respondent's victims, since respondent admitted that the victims died in the ways shown by the unchallenged medical evidence.

The trial court dealt at greater length with the two other bases for the ineffectiveness claim. The court pointed out that a psychiatric examination of respondent was conducted by state order soon after respondent's initial arraignment. That report states that there was no indication of major mental illness at the time of the crimes. Moreover, both the reports submitted in the collateral proceeding state that, although respondent was "chronically frustrated and depressed because of his economic dilemma," he was not under the influence of extreme mental or emotional disturbance. All three reports thus directly undermine the contention made at the sentencing hearing that respondent was suffering from extreme mental or emotional disturbance during his crime spree. Accordingly, counsel could reasonably decide not to seek psychiatric reports; indeed, by relying solely on the plea colloquy to support the emotional disturbance contention, counsel denied the State an opportunity to rebut his claim with psychiatric testimony. In any event, the aggravating circumstances were so overwhelming that no substantial prejudice resulted from the absence at sentencing of the psychiatric evidence offered in the collateral attack.

The court rejected the challenge to counsel's failure to develop and to present character evidence for much the same reasons. The affidavits submitted in the collateral proceeding showed nothing more than that certain persons would have testified that respondent was basically a good person who was worried about his family's financial problems. Respondent himself had already testified along those lines at the plea colloquy. Moreover, respondent's admission of a course of stealing rebutted many of the factual allegations in the affidavits. For those reasons, and because the sentencing judge had stated that the death sentence would be appropriate even if respondent had no significant prior criminal history, no substantial prejudice resulted from the absence at sentencing of the character evidence offered in the collateral attack. . . .

[T]he trial court concluded that respondent had not shown that counsel's assistance reflected any substantial and serious deficiency measurably below that of competent counsel that was likely to have affected the outcome of the sentencing proceeding. The court specifically found: "[A]s a matter of law, the record affirmatively demonstrates beyond any doubt that even if [counsel] had done each of the . . . things [that respondent alleged counsel had failed to do] at the time of sentencing, there is not even the remotest chance that the outcome would have been any different. The plain fact is that the aggravating circumstances proved in this case were completely overwhelming. . . ."

The Florida Supreme Court affirmed the denial of relief. . . .

C

Respondent next filed a petition for a writ of habeas corpus in the United States District Court for the Southern District of Florida. He advanced numerous grounds for relief, among them ineffective assistance of counsel based on the same errors, except for the failure to move for a continuance, as those he had identified in state court. The District Court held an evidentiary hearing. . . .

On the legal issue of ineffectiveness, the District Court concluded that, although trial counsel made errors in judgment in failing to investigate nonstatutory mitigating evidence further than he did, no prejudice to respondent's sentence resulted from any such error in judgment. . . . [T]he District Court concluded that "there does not appear to be a likelihood, or even a significant possibility," that any errors of trial counsel had affected the outcome of the sentencing proceeding. The District Court went on to reject all of respondent's other grounds for relief. . . .

[After a complex procedural history, the en banc Court of Appeals remanded the case for consideration in light of its newly announced standards for deciding claims of ineffective assistance of counsel.]

D

... The petition presents a type of Sixth Amendment claim that this Court has not previously considered in any generality.... [T]he Court has never directly and fully addressed a claim of "actual ineffectiveness" of counsel's assistance in a case going to trial.

For these reasons, we granted certiorari to consider the standards by which to judge a contention that the Constitution requires that a criminal judgment be overturned because of the actual ineffective assistance of counsel....

II

In a long line of cases ... this Court has recognized that the Sixth Amendment right to counsel exists, and is needed, in order to protect the fundamental right to a fair trial. The Constitution guarantees a fair trial through the Due Process Clauses, but it defines the basic elements of a fair trial largely through the several provisions of the Sixth Amendment, including the Counsel Clause:

> In all criminal prosecutions, the accused shall enjoy the right to a speedy and public trial, by an impartial jury of the State and district wherein the crime shall have been committed, which district shall have been previously ascertained by law, and to be informed of the nature and cause of the accusation; to be confronted with the witnesses against him; to have compulsory process for obtaining witnesses in his favor, and to have the Assistance of Counsel for his defence.

Thus, a fair trial is one in which evidence subject to adversarial testing is presented to an impartial tribunal for resolution of issues defined in advance of the proceeding. The right to counsel plays a crucial role in the adversarial system embodied in the Sixth Amendment, since access to counsel's skill and knowledge is necessary to accord defendants the "ample opportunity to meet the case of the prosecution" to which they are entitled.

Because of the vital importance of counsel's assistance, this Court has held that, with certain exceptions, a person accused of a federal or state crime has the right to have counsel appointed if retained counsel cannot be obtained. That a person who happens to be a lawyer is present at trial alongside the accused, however, is not enough to satisfy the constitutional command. The Sixth Amendment recognizes the right to the assistance of counsel because it envisions counsel's playing a role that is critical to the ability of the adversarial system to produce just results. An accused is entitled to be assisted by an attorney, whether retained or appointed, who plays the role necessary to ensure that the trial is fair.

For that reason, the Court has recognized that "the right to counsel is the right to the effective assistance of counsel." Government violates the right to effective assistance when it interferes in certain ways with the ability of counsel to make independent decisions about how to conduct the defense.

Counsel, however, can also deprive a defendant of the right to effective assistance, simply by failing to render "adequate legal assistance."

The Court has not elaborated on the meaning of the constitutional requirement of effective assistance in the latter class of cases—that is, those presenting claims of "actual ineffectiveness." In giving meaning to the requirement, however, we must take its purpose—to ensure a fair trial—as the guide. The benchmark for judging any claim of ineffectiveness must be whether counsel's conduct so undermined the proper functioning of the adversarial process that the trial cannot be relied on as having produced a just result.

The same principle applies to a capital sentencing proceeding such as that provided by Florida law. A capital sentencing proceeding like the one involved in this case . . . is sufficiently like a trial in its adversarial format and in the existence of standards for decision that counsel's role in the proceeding is comparable to counsel's role at trial—to ensure that the adversarial testing process works to produce a just result under the standards governing decision. For purposes of describing counsel's duties, therefore, Florida's capital sentencing proceeding need not be distinguished from an ordinary trial.

III

A convicted defendant's claim that counsel's assistance was so defective as to require reversal of a conviction or death sentence has two components. First, the defendant must show that counsel's performance was deficient. This requires showing that counsel made errors so serious that counsel was not functioning as the "counsel" guaranteed the defendant by the Sixth Amendment. Second, the defendant must show that the deficient performance prejudiced the defense. This requires showing that counsel's errors were so serious as to deprive the defendant of a fair trial, a trial whose result is reliable. Unless a defendant makes both showings, it cannot be said that the conviction or death sentence resulted from a breakdown in the adversary process that renders the result unreliable.

A

As all the Federal Courts of Appeals have now held, the proper standard for attorney performance is that of reasonably effective assistance. . . . When a convicted defendant complains of the ineffectiveness of counsel's assistance, the defendant must show that counsel's representation fell below an objective standard of reasonableness.

More specific guidelines are not appropriate. The Sixth Amendment refers simply to "counsel," not specifying particular requirements of effective assistance. It relies instead on the legal profession's maintenance of standards sufficient to justify the law's presumption that counsel will fulfill the role in the adversary process that the Amendment envisions. The proper measure of attorney performance remains simply reasonableness under prevailing professional norms.

Representation of a criminal defendant entails certain basic duties. Counsel's function is to assist the defendant, and hence counsel owes the client a duty of loyalty, a duty to avoid conflicts of interest. From counsel's function as assistant to the defendant derive the overarching duty to advocate the defendant's cause and the more particular duties to consult with the defendant on important decisions and to keep the defendant informed of important developments in the course of the prosecution. Counsel also has a duty to bring to bear such skill and knowledge as will render the trial a reliable adversarial testing process.

These basic duties neither exhaustively define the obligations of counsel nor form a checklist for judicial evaluation of attorney performance. In any case presenting an ineffectiveness claim, the performance inquiry must be whether counsel's assistance was reasonable considering all the circumstances. Prevailing norms of practice as reflected in American Bar Association standards and the like, e.g., ABA Standards for Criminal Justice 4–1.1 to 4–8.6 (2d ed. 1980) ("The Defense Function"), are guides to determining what is reasonable, but they are only guides. No particular set of detailed rules for counsel's conduct can satisfactorily take account of the variety of circumstances faced by defense counsel or the range of legitimate decisions regarding how best to represent a criminal defendant. Any such set of rules would interfere with the constitutionally protected independence of counsel and restrict the wide latitude counsel must have in making tactical decisions.... Moreover, the purpose of the effective assistance guarantee of the Sixth Amendment is not to improve the quality of legal representation, although that is a goal of considerable importance to the legal system. The purpose is simply to ensure that criminal defendants receive a fair trial.

Judicial scrutiny of counsel's performance must be highly deferential. It is all too tempting for a defendant to second-guess counsel's assistance after conviction or adverse sentence, and it is all too easy for a court, examining counsel's defense after it has proved unsuccessful, to conclude that a particular act or omission of counsel was unreasonable. A fair assessment of attorney performance requires that every effort be made to eliminate the distorting effects of hindsight, to reconstruct the circumstances of counsel's challenged conduct, and to evaluate the conduct from counsel's perspective at the time. Because of the difficulties inherent in making the evaluation, a court must indulge a strong presumption that counsel's conduct falls within the wide range of reasonable professional assistance; that is, the defendant must overcome the presumption that, under the circumstances, the challenged action "might be considered sound trial strategy." There are countless ways to provide effective assistance in any given case. Even the best criminal defense attorneys would not defend a particular client in the same way.

The availability of intrusive post-trial inquiry into attorney performance or of detailed guidelines for its evaluation would encourage the proliferation of ineffectiveness challenges. Criminal trials resolved unfavorably to the defendant would increasingly come to be followed by a second trial, this one of counsel's unsuccessful defense. Counsel's performance and even willingness to serve could be adversely affected. Intensive scrutiny of counsel and rigid requirements for acceptable assistance could dampen the ardor and impair the independence of defense counsel, discourage the acceptance of assigned cases, and undermine the trust between attorney and client.

Thus, a court deciding an actual ineffectiveness claim must judge the reasonableness of counsel's challenged conduct on the facts of the particular case, viewed as of the time of counsel's conduct. A convicted defendant making a claim of ineffective assistance must identify the acts or omissions of counsel that are alleged not to have been the result of reasonable professional judgment. The court must then determine whether, in light of all the circumstances, the identified acts or omissions were outside the wide range of professionally competent assistance. In making that determination, the court should keep in mind that counsel's function, as elaborated in prevailing professional norms, is to make the adversarial testing process work in the particular case. At the same time, the court should recognize that counsel is strongly presumed to have rendered adequate assistance and made all significant decisions in the exercise of reasonable professional judgment.

These standards require no special amplification in order to define counsel's duty to investigate, the duty at issue in this case. As the Court of Appeals concluded, strategic choices made after thorough investigation of law and facts relevant to plausible options are virtually unchallengeable; and strategic choices made after less than complete investigation are reasonable precisely to the extent that reasonable professional judgments support the limitations on investigation. In other words, counsel has a duty to make reasonable investigations or to make a reasonable decision that makes particular investigations unnecessary. In any ineffectiveness case, a particular decision not to investigate must be directly assessed for reasonableness in all the circumstances, applying a heavy measure of deference to counsel's judgments.

The reasonableness of counsel's actions may be determined or substantially influenced by the defendant's own statements or actions. Counsel's actions are usually based, quite properly, on informed strategic choices made by the defendant and on information supplied by the defendant. In particular, what investigation decisions are reasonable depends critically on such information. For example, when the facts that support a certain potential line of defense are generally known to counsel because of what the defendant has said, the need for further investigation may be considerably diminished or eliminated altogether. And when a defendant has given counsel reason to believe that pursuing certain investigations would be fruitless or even harmful, counsel's failure to pursue those investigations may not later be challenged as unreasonable. In short, inquiry into counsel's conversations with the defendant may be critical to a proper assessment of counsel's investigation decisions, just as it may be critical to a proper assessment of counsel's other litigation decisions.

B

An error by counsel, even if professionally unreasonable, does not warrant setting aside the judgment of a criminal proceeding if the error had no effect on the judgment. The purpose of the Sixth Amendment guarantee of counsel is to ensure that a defendant has the assistance necessary to justify reliance on the outcome of the proceeding. Accordingly, any deficiencies in counsel's performance must be prejudicial to the defense in order to constitute ineffective assistance under the Constitution.

In certain Sixth Amendment contexts, prejudice is presumed. Actual or constructive denial of the assistance of counsel altogether is legally presumed to result in prejudice. So are various kinds of state interference with counsel's assistance. Prejudice in these circumstances is so likely that case-by-case inquiry into prejudice is not worth the cost. Moreover, such circumstances involve impairments of the Sixth Amendment right that are easy to identify and, for that reason and because the prosecution is directly responsible, easy for the government to prevent.

One type of actual ineffectiveness claim warrants a similar, though more limited, presumption of prejudice. In *Cuyler v. Sullivan*, 446 U.S. 335, 345–350 (1980), the Court held that prejudice is presumed when counsel is burdened by an actual conflict of interest. In those circumstances, counsel breaches the duty of loyalty, perhaps the most basic of counsel's duties. Moreover, it is difficult to measure the precise effect on the defense of representation corrupted by conflicting interests. Given the obligation of counsel to avoid conflicts of interest and the ability of trial courts to make early inquiry in certain situations likely to give rise to conflicts, it is reasonable for the criminal justice system to maintain a fairly rigid rule of presumed prejudice for conflicts of interest. Even so, the rule is not quite the per se rule of prejudice that exists for the Sixth Amendment claims mentioned above. Prejudice is presumed only if the defendant demonstrates that counsel "actively represented conflicting interests" and that "an actual conflict of interest adversely affected his lawyer's performance."

Conflict of interest claims aside, actual ineffectiveness claims alleging a deficiency in attorney performance are subject to a general requirement that the defendant affirmatively prove prejudice. The government is not responsible for, and hence not able to prevent, attorney errors that will result in reversal of a conviction or sentence. Attorney errors come in an infinite variety and are as likely to be utterly harmless in a particular case as they are to be prejudicial. They cannot be classified according to likelihood of causing prejudice. Nor can they be defined with sufficient precision to inform defense attorneys correctly just what conduct to avoid. Representation is an art, and an act or omission that is unprofessional in one case may be sound or even brilliant in another. Even if a defendant shows that particular errors of counsel were unreasonable, therefore, the defendant must show that they actually had an adverse effect on the defense.

It is not enough for the defendant to show that the errors had some conceivable effect on the outcome of the proceeding. Virtually every act or omission of counsel would meet that test, and not every error that conceivably could have influenced the outcome undermines the reliability of the result of the proceeding. Respondent suggests requiring a showing that the errors "impaired the presentation of the defense." That standard, however, provides no workable principle. Since any error, if it is indeed an error, "impairs" the presentation of the defense, the proposed standard is inadequate because it provides no way of deciding what impairments are sufficiently serious to warrant setting aside the outcome of the proceeding.

On the other hand, we believe that a defendant need not show that counsel's deficient conduct more likely than not altered the outcome in the case. This outcome-determinative standard has several strengths. It defines the relevant inquiry in a way familiar to courts, though the inquiry, as is inevitable, is anything but precise. The standard also reflects the profound importance of finality in criminal proceedings. Moreover, it comports with the widely used standard for assessing motions for new trial based on newly discovered evidence. Nevertheless, the standard is not quite appropriate. . . .

[T]he appropriate test for prejudice finds its roots in the test for materiality of exculpatory information not disclosed to the defense by the prosecution, and in the test for materiality of testimony made unavailable to the defense by Government deportation of a witness. The defendant must show that there is a reasonable probability that, but for counsel's unprofessional errors, the result of the proceeding would have been different. A reasonable probability is a probability sufficient to undermine confidence in the outcome.

In making the determination whether the specified errors resulted in the required prejudice, a court should presume, absent challenge to the judgment on grounds of evidentiary insufficiency, that the judge or jury acted according to law. An assessment of the likelihood of a result more favorable to the defendant must exclude the possibility of arbitrariness, whimsy, caprice, "nullification," and the like. A defendant has no entitlement to the luck of a lawless decisionmaker, even if a lawless decision cannot be reviewed. The assessment of prejudice should proceed on the assumption that the decisionmaker is reasonably, conscientiously, and impartially applying the standards that govern the decision. . . .

The governing legal standard plays a critical role in defining the question to be asked in assessing the prejudice from counsel's errors. When a defendant challenges a conviction, the question is whether there is a reasonable probability that, absent the errors, the factfinder would have had a reasonable doubt respecting guilt. When a defendant challenges a death sentence such as the one at issue in this case, the question is whether there is a reasonable probability that, absent the errors, the sentencer—including an appellate court, to the extent it independently reweighs the evidence—would have concluded that the balance of aggravating and mitigating circumstances did not warrant death.

IV

... Although we have discussed the performance component of an ineffectiveness claim prior to the prejudice component, there is no reason for a court deciding an ineffective assistance claim to approach the inquiry in the same order or even to address both components of the inquiry if the defendant makes an insufficient showing on one. In particular, a court need not determine whether counsel's performance was deficient before examining the prejudice suffered by the defendant as a result of the alleged deficiencies. The object of an ineffectiveness claim is not to grade counsel's performance. If it is easier to dispose of an ineffectiveness claim on the ground of lack of sufficient prejudice, which we expect will often be so, that course should be followed. Courts should strive to ensure that ineffectiveness claims not become so burdensome to defense counsel that the entire criminal justice system suffers as a result.

V

Having articulated general standards for judging ineffectiveness claims, we think it useful to apply those standards to the facts of this case in order to illustrate the meaning of the general principles. The record makes it possible to do so. . . .

Application of the governing principles is not difficult in this case. The facts as described above make clear that the conduct of respondent's counsel at and before respondent's sentencing proceeding cannot be found unreasonable. They also make clear that, even assuming the challenged conduct of counsel was unreasonable, respondent suffered insufficient prejudice to warrant setting aside his death sentence.

With respect to the performance component, the record shows that respondent's counsel made a strategic choice to argue for the extreme emotional distress mitigating circumstance and to rely as fully as possible on respondent's acceptance of responsibility for his crimes. Although counsel understandably felt hopeless about respondent's prospects, nothing in the record indicates ... that counsel's sense of hopelessness distorted his professional judgment. Counsel's strategy choice was well within the range of professionally reasonable judgments, and the decision not to seek more character or psychological evidence than was already in hand was likewise reasonable.

The trial judge's views on the importance of owning up to one's crimes were well known to counsel. The aggravating circumstances were utterly overwhelming. Trial counsel could reasonably surmise from his conversations with respondent that character and psychological evidence would be of little help. Respondent had already been able to mention at the plea colloquy the substance of what there was to know about his financial and emotional troubles. Restricting testimony on respondent's character to what had come in at the plea colloquy ensured that contrary character and psychological evidence and respondent's criminal history, which counsel had successfully moved to exclude, would not come in. On these facts, there can be little question, even without application of the presumption of adequate performance, that trial counsel's defense, though unsuccessful, was the result of reasonable professional judgment.

With respect to the prejudice component, the lack of merit of respondent's claim is even more stark. The evidence that respondent says his trial counsel should have offered at the sentencing hearing would barely have altered the sentencing profile presented to the sentencing judge. As the state courts and District Court found, at most this evidence shows that numerous people who knew respondent thought he was generally a good person and that a psychiatrist and a psychologist believed he was under considerable emotional stress that did not rise to the level of extreme disturbance. Given the overwhelming aggravating factors, there is no reasonable probability that the omitted evidence would have changed the conclusion that the aggravating circumstances outweighed the mitigating circumstances and, hence, the sentence imposed. Indeed, admission of the evidence respondent now offers might even have been harmful to his case: his "rap sheet" would probably have been admitted into evidence, and the psychological reports would have directly contradicted respondent's claim that the mitigating circumstance of extreme emotional disturbance applied to his case. . . .

Failure to make the required showing of either deficient performance or sufficient prejudice defeats the ineffectiveness claim. Here there is a double failure. More generally, respondent has made no showing that the justice of his sentence was rendered unreliable by a breakdown in the adversary process caused by deficiencies in counsel's assistance. Respondent's sentencing proceeding was not fundamentally unfair.

We conclude, therefore, that the District Court properly declined to issue a writ of habeas corpus. The judgment of the Court of Appeals is accordingly

Reversed.

JUSTICE MARSHALL, dissenting.

The Sixth and Fourteenth Amendments guarantee a person accused of a crime the right to the aid of a lawyer in preparing and presenting his defense. It has long been settled that "the right to counsel is the right to the effective assistance of counsel." *McMann v. Richardson*, 397 U.S. 759, 771, n. 14 (1970). The state and lower federal courts have developed standards for distinguishing effective from inadequate assistance. Today, for the first time, this Court attempts to synthesize and clarify those standards. For the most part, the majority's efforts are unhelpful. Neither of its two principal holdings seems to me likely to improve the adjudication of Sixth Amendment claims. And, in its zeal to survey comprehensively this field of doctrine, the majority makes many other generalizations and suggestions that I find unacceptable. Most importantly, the majority fails to take adequate account of the fact that the locus of this case is a capital sentencing proceeding. Accordingly, I join neither the Court's opinion nor its judgment.

I

The opinion of the Court revolves around two holdings. First, the majority ties the constitutional minima of attorney performance to a simple "standard of reasonableness." Second, the majority holds that only an error of counsel that has sufficient impact on a trial to "undermine confidence in the outcome" is grounds for overturning a conviction. I disagree with both of these rulings.

A

My objection to the performance standard adopted by the Court is that it is so malleable that, in practice, it will either have no grip at all or will yield excessive variation in the manner in which the Sixth Amendment is interpreted and applied by different courts. To tell lawyers and the lower courts that counsel for a criminal defendant must behave "reasonably" and must act like "a reasonably competent attorney," is to tell them almost nothing. In essence, the majority has instructed judges called upon to assess claims of ineffective assistance of counsel to advert to their own intuitions regarding what constitutes "professional" representation, and has discouraged them from trying to develop more detailed standards governing the performance of defense counsel. In my view, the Court has thereby not only abdicated its own responsibility to interpret the Constitution, but also impaired the ability of the lower courts to exercise theirs.

The majority defends its refusal to adopt more specific standards primarily on the ground that "[n]o particular set of detailed rules for counsel's conduct can satisfactorily take account of the variety of circumstances faced by defense counsel or the range of legitimate decisions regarding how best to represent a criminal defendant." I agree that counsel must be afforded "wide latitude" when making "tactical decisions" regarding trial strategy, but many aspects of the job of a criminal defense attorney are more amenable to judicial oversight. For example, much of the work involved in preparing for a trial, applying for bail, conferring with one's client, making timely objections to significant, arguably erroneous rulings of the trial judge, and filing a notice of appeal if there are colorable grounds therefor could profitably be made the subject of uniform standards. . . .

B

I object to the prejudice standard adopted by the Court for two independent reasons. First, it is often very difficult to tell whether a defendant convicted after a trial in which he was ineffectively represented would have fared better if his lawyer had been competent. Seemingly impregnable cases can sometimes be dismantled by good defense counsel. On the basis of a cold record, it may be impossible for a reviewing court confidently to ascertain how the government's evidence and arguments would have stood up against rebuttal and cross-examination by a shrewd, well-prepared lawyer. The difficulties of estimating prejudice after the fact are exacerbated by the possibility that evidence of injury to the defendant may be missing from the record precisely because of the incompetence of defense counsel. In view of all these impediments to a fair evaluation of the probability that the outcome of a trial was affected by ineffectiveness of counsel, it seems to me senseless to impose on a defendant whose lawyer has been shown to have been incompetent the burden of demonstrating prejudice.

Second and more fundamentally, the assumption on which the Court's holding rests is that the only purpose of the constitutional guarantee of effective assistance of counsel is to reduce the chance that innocent persons will be convicted. In my view, the guarantee also functions to ensure that convictions are obtained only through fundamentally fair procedures. The majority contends that the Sixth Amendment is not violated when a manifestly guilty defendant is convicted after a trial in which he was represented by a manifestly ineffective attorney. I cannot agree. Every defendant is entitled to a trial in which his interests are vigorously and conscientiously advocated by an able lawyer. A proceeding in which the defendant does not receive meaningful assistance in meeting the forces of the State does not, in my opinion, constitute due process....

II

Even if I were inclined to join the majority's two central holdings, I could not abide the manner in which the majority elaborates upon its rulings. Particularly regrettable are the majority's discussion of the "presumption" of reasonableness to be accorded lawyers' decisions and its attempt to prejudge the merits of claims previously rejected by lower courts using different legal standards.

A

In defining the standard of attorney performance required by the Constitution, the majority appropriately notes that many problems confronting criminal defense attorneys admit of "a range of legitimate" responses. And the majority properly cautions courts, when reviewing a lawyer's selection amongst a set of options, to avoid the hubris of hindsight. The majority goes on, however, to suggest that reviewing courts should "indulge a strong presumption that counsel's conduct" was constitutionally acceptable, and should "appl[y] a heavy measure of deference to counsel's judgments."

I am not sure what these phrases mean, and I doubt that they will be self-explanatory to lower courts. If they denote nothing more than that a defendant claiming he was denied effective assistance of counsel has the burden of proof, I would agree. But the adjectives "strong" and "heavy" might be read as imposing upon defendants an unusually weighty burden of persuasion. If that is the majority's intent, I must respectfully dissent. The range of acceptable behavior defined by "prevailing professional norms," seems to me sufficiently broad to allow defense counsel the flexibility they need in responding to novel problems of trial strategy. To afford attorneys more latitude, by "strongly presuming" that their behavior will fall within the zone of reasonableness, is covertly to legitimate convictions and sentences obtained on the basis of incompetent conduct by defense counsel. . . .

IV

The views expressed in the preceding section oblige me to dissent from the majority's disposition of the case before us. It is undisputed that respondent's trial counsel made virtually no investigation of the possibility of obtaining testimony from respondent's relatives, friends, or former employers pertaining to respondent's character or background. Had counsel done so, he would have found several persons willing and able to testify that, in their experience, respondent was a responsible, non-violent man, devoted to his family, and active in the affairs of his church. Respondent contends that his lawyer could have and should have used that testimony to "humanize" respondent, to counteract the impression conveyed by the trial that he was little more than a cold-blooded killer. Had this evidence been admitted, respondent argues, his chances of obtaining a life sentence would have been significantly better.

Measured against the standards outlined above, respondent's contentions are substantial. Experienced members of the death-penalty bar have long recognized the crucial importance of adducing evidence at a sentencing proceeding that establishes the defendant's social and familial connections. The State makes a colorable—though in my view not compelling—argument that defense counsel in this case might have made a reasonable "strategic" decision not to present such evidence at the sentencing hearing on the assumption that an unadorned acknowledgment of respondent's responsibility for his crimes would be more likely to appeal to the trial judge, who was reputed to respect persons who accepted responsibility for their actions. But however justifiable such a choice might have been after counsel had fairly assessed the potential strength of the mitigating evidence available to him, counsel's failure to make any significant effort to find out what evidence might be garnered from respondent's relatives and acquaintances surely cannot be described as "reasonable." Counsel's failure to investigate is particularly suspicious in light of his candid admission that respondent's confessions and conduct in the course of the trial gave him a feeling of "hopelessness" regarding the possibility of saving respondent's life. . . .

[handwritten margin note: Counsel's strategy not reasonable]

If counsel had investigated the availability of mitigating evidence, he might well have decided to present some such material at the hearing. If he had done so, there is a significant chance that respondent would have been given a life sentence. In my view, those possibilities, conjoined with the unreasonableness of counsel's failure to investigate, are more than sufficient to establish a violation of the Sixth Amendment and to entitle respondent to a new sentencing proceeding.

I respectfully dissent.

NOTES

1. What must a convicted defendant show to make out a claim that his counsel was constitutionally ineffective? What is the remedy if he succeeds in proving that he had the ineffective assistance of counsel? In the ordinary course, when will such a claim need to be made? What are the difficulties of making it?

2. The Court set out the required elements of a successful claim of ineffective assistance of counsel: deficient performance and prejudice. The Court noted, however, that in some cases, where there has been an "[a]ctual or constructive denial of the assistance of counsel altogether," prejudice is presumed and need not be specifically proven. What sorts of circumstances might give rise to a claim of "actual or constructive denial" of counsel? Do you think that defense counsel sleeping through portions of the trial would qualify? *See Burdine v. Johnson*, 262 F.3d 336 (5th Cir. 2001). What about "drinking approximately twelve ounces of rum each evening" during a capital murder trial? *See Frye v. Lee*, 235 F.3d 897 (4th Cir. 2000). How about appointing a lawyer with no criminal defense experience to defend a serious criminal case, and allowing him only 25 days to prepare a case that the government had taken over four years to investigate? *See United States v. Cronic*, 466 U.S. 648 (1984).

3. Denial of counsel of *choice* is another situation in which no prejudice need be proved to make out a Sixth Amendment violation. In *United States v. Gonzalez–Lopez*, 548 U.S. 140 (2006), Gonzalez–Lopez was wrongfully denied his privately engaged counsel of choice at his criminal trial. The court required him to go forward with another lawyer, and he was convicted. Gonzalez–Lopez argued that he was deprived of his Sixth Amendment right to counsel because he was not able to have the lawyer he wanted. The government argued that this deprivation violated Gonzalez–Lopez's Sixth Amendment rights only if he was prejudiced as a result. The Court agreed with Gonzalez–Lopez. Assuming that there was no legitimate reason to deny him the counsel of his choice, "[d]eprivation of the right is 'complete' when the defendant is erroneously prevented from being represented by the lawyer he wants, regardless of the quality of the representation he received." *Id*. at 148. This unfettered right to counsel of choice does not extend to lawyers whom the court has a legitimate basis to exclude, or to clients who require appointed counsel. *Id*. at 151.

4. Suppose you represent a client in a criminal case. Subsequently, the client claims in a postconviction proceeding that you provided ineffective assistance of counsel to her at trial. What do you think your obligation is to that client? Should you resist efforts to have your work deemed constitutionally ineffective? Should you assist in those efforts? Is there a third alternative?

Consider the following affidavit, submitted by trial counsel in an ineffective assistance of counsel proceeding in a death penalty case.

Mr. Kindler's case was my first capital trial. I did not have any experience or training in how to handle capital cases, in particular the penalty phase of the proceeding.

I concentrated my efforts on attempting to create a reasonable doubt as to Mr. Kindler's guilt, although I was aware that there was a strong likelihood that Mr. Kindler would be convicted.

I did not conduct a penalty phase or mitigation investigation. In particular, I did not talk to Mr. Kindler or any of his family members about his family background. Mr. Kindler's family was available to me. His parents had retained me, and they attended the trial. I simply did not think about investigating or presenting evidence concerning family background at the penalty phase.

I also did not attempt to obtain any school, medical or other records relating to Mr. Kindler. I did not have a strategic or tactical reason for not seeking such records; it just did not occur to me that such records could be helpful.

I also did not consider obtaining any mental health evaluation of Mr. Kindler. Again, there was no strategic or tactical reason for my failure to do so.

Would you be willing to write such an affidavit? Might you have concerns about doing so? *See Kindler v. Horn*, 542 F.3d 70 (3d Cir. 2008).

5.   Claims of ineffective assistance of counsel are very rarely successful. In that regard, consider the following case. What made this a strong claim?

GOODMAN v. BERTRAND
467 F.3d 1022 (7th Cir. 2006)

WILLIAMS, CIRCUIT JUDGE.

Fourteen years ago, an individual entered a Milwaukee convenience store, robbed the store's manager and cashier at gunpoint, and then fled in a getaway car. After a first trial ended in a hung jury, a second jury convicted Warren Goodman of armed robbery and being a felon in possession of a firearm, and he was sentenced to twenty-two years' imprisonment. Having exhausted his state court remedies, Goodman petitioned for a writ of habeas corpus pursuant to 28 U.S.C. § 2254, challenging the effectiveness of his counsel during the second trial. The United States District Court for the Eastern District of Wisconsin denied relief. Unlike the district court, we find, under the Antiterrorism and Effective Death Penalty Act of 1996 ("AEDPA"), that the state court decision was contrary to the ineffective assistance of counsel standard set forth in *Strickland v. Washington*. Further, we conclude, under AEDPA, that the state court decision was an unreasonable application of *Strickland* because the cumulative effect of counsel's errors constituted ineffective assistance of counsel. Therefore, we reverse the judgment of the district court and remand for the entry of an order granting the writ.

I. BACKGROUND

On July 28, 1992, an individual robbed Kohl's Food Store, a convenience store in Milwaukee, holding the store's cashier, Ilene Retzlaff, and manager, Daniel Kollath, at gunpoint. After the two complied with the gunman's demands, the assailant fled in a getaway car, driven by an accomplice. Blocks later, the men switched to a second getaway car that was driven by a third accomplice. Later that day, police stopped Mark Smith and Larry Ross, who were riding in a car matching the description of the second getaway car. Police retrieved two handguns and $200 from the car.[1] Smith eventually confessed that he acted as a lookout in the robbery, and fingered Ross as an accomplice. Smith also brokered a deal with prosecutors in which, in exchange for more lenient punishment, he implicated Goodman. In a lineup, the store manager Kollath initially identified another person as the robber, but in a subsequent lineup he chose Goodman. The store cashier, Retzlaff, did not pick Goodman from the lineup, instead choosing another individual as the person who most resembled the robber.

A. Goodman's first and second trials

The case against Goodman went to trial twice. In each instance, the facts of the robbery were essentially undisputed; only the identification of Goodman as the perpetrator was at issue. In the first trial, confessed-lookout Smith and store manager Kollath both testified that Goodman robbed the store. The store cashier testified that she could not identify Goodman as the robber and that she chose another person from the police lineup. Goodman also testified on his own behalf. The court declared a mistrial after the jury was unable to reach a verdict.

Smith received six years' imprisonment for his role in the robbery, in exchange for his testimony in the first trial. Ross, who was serving a seventeen-year sentence for being the driver of the second getaway car, contacted the prosecution after the first trial and agreed to testify against Goodman at the retrial and to identify the driver of the first getaway car, in exchange for a recommendation to reduce his sentence. Ross later named Percy Sallis, who confessed that he was the first getaway car driver.

At the second trial, Goodman was represented by a different lawyer. Kollath, as well as confessed accomplices Smith, Ross, and Sallis, all testified that Goodman committed the robbery. Unlike the first trial, the store's cashier, Retzlaff, did not testify because she was on vacation and Goodman's lawyer failed to subpoena her. Goodman's counsel erroneously believed that a subpoena was unnecessary because the government would call Retzlaff as a witness. Because Goodman's counsel failed to demonstrate that Retzlaff was unavailable to testify in person, the trial court excluded portions of her prior testimony from the second trial. So in the

---

1. There is no indication in the record that the police attempted to retrieve fingerprints from the seized guns.

second trial, four witnesses, including the three accomplices, identified Goodman as the robber, and Retzlaff was not present to testify.

Other problems arose for Goodman's counsel during the course of the second trial. On direct examination, Goodman's counsel asked Goodman a question that ultimately led the court to allow cross-examination on two of Goodman's previous armed robbery convictions.[2] As the parties had earlier stipulated to Goodman's status as a convicted felon, in the normal course of proceedings the prosecution would have been precluded from raising the nature of the prior felonies.

In addition, prosecution witnesses Mark Smith and Larry Ross testified regarding threats they received concerning their participation in the Goodman trial. While the witnesses acknowledged that the threats were not made by Goodman, nor was he present when they were made, the witnesses claimed that the threats were intended to prevent them from testifying against Goodman. Goodman's counsel objected, asserting that the witnesses' testimony impermissibly linked Goodman to the threats in the minds of the jurors. The trial court admitted the testimony on limited grounds, stating, outside the presence of the jury, that such testimony would reflect the witnesses' credibility by demonstrating that they had something to lose as well as something to gain by testifying. Goodman's counsel later failed to request a jury instruction explaining to the jury the limited manner in which they could use the testimony.

In addition, Goodman's counsel did not object after the prosecution made misleading statements on direct examination indicating that the state had not given Ross any reason to testify, when in fact Ross had agreed to do so in the hopes of receiving a reduced sentence. During closing argument the prosecutor also made false statements improperly bolstering Sallis's testimony by stating that Sallis could not have been charged or convicted without his voluntary confession while omitting the fact that Ross had named Sallis as an accomplice before Sallis confessed. Goodman's counsel did not object or request a mistrial.

The jury ultimately found Goodman guilty, and he was sentenced to twenty-two years for the robbery and for being a felon in possession of a firearm during its commission. For his testimony and at the government's recommendation, Ross's initial seventeen-year sentence was later reduced

---

2. During direct examination, Goodman's counsel, while showing Goodman exhibits of guns connected to the crime, abruptly asked, "[D]id you do any armed robberies?" to which the defendant answered, "No." The prosecution asked to approach the bench, and there was an unrecorded sidebar. Goodman's counsel then rephrased the question, asking "Did you do the armed robbery at the Marks Big Boy that they accused you of?" to which the defendant again replied, "No." At the conclusion of Goodman's direct examination, the trial judge briefly dismissed the jury, and ruled that counsel's use of the vague term "any" could leave the jury with the mistaken impression that the defendant had never committed any armed robberies, when in fact he had previously been convicted of two robberies. Goodman's counsel argued that he was clearly referring to the Kohl's Food Store robbery and another robbery at the Marks Big Boy store for which Goodman was charged but later cleared. However, the court disagreed and the prosecution was permitted to cross-examine Goodman on the issue of which armed robberies he had committed.

to twelve years. Sallis received probation, conditioned on six months of work release, for his part in the robbery.

B. Post-conviction proceedings

After his conviction, Goodman sought relief in state court. Goodman argued that, in violation of the Sixth Amendment, his second trial counsel was ineffective for (1) opening the door to cross-examination on Goodman's two prior convictions for armed robbery, (2) failing to procure copies of government witnesses' prior inconsistent testimony, (3) failing to subpoena the store's cashier to testify, and (4) being generally unfamiliar with the case. The trial court denied the motion. The Wisconsin Court of Appeals affirmed stating as follows:

> [W]e, like the trial court, conclude that the record conclusively establishes that Goodman was not prejudiced within the meaning of *Strickland*.... In order to show prejudice, the defendant must show that there is a reasonable probability that, but for counsel's unprofessional errors, the result of the proceeding would have been different. A reasonable probability is a probability sufficient to undermine confidence in the outcome. The *Strickland* test is not an outcome-determinative test. In decisions following *Strickland,* the Supreme Court has reaffirmed that the touchstone of the prejudice component is whether counsel's deficient performance renders the result of the trial unreliable or the proceeding fundamentally unfair.

The court concluded that, even if his counsel's performance was deficient, Goodman's Sixth Amendment claim failed because "none of Goodman's counsel's alleged deficient conduct prejudiced him such that the result of the trial was unreliable."

Goodman then presented his Sixth Amendment claim in a state habeas petition and argued that his trial counsel was ineffective for (1) failing to request a limiting instruction regarding the testimony of threats, (2) failing to object regarding the denial of his right to confront witnesses against him, and (3) failing to object to prosecutorial misconduct during closing arguments. The trial court denied relief, and the appellate court affirmed. The Wisconsin Supreme Court denied habeas review.

Following these adverse rulings in state court, Goodman timely filed his federal habeas petition pursuant to 28 U.S.C. § 2254 in the United States District Court for the Eastern District of Wisconsin. Goodman maintained that, during direct appeal, the state court erred when it required him to prove the alleged errors of his counsel rendered his second trial unreliable or fundamentally unfair. The district court denied habeas relief, holding that the state court decision was not an unreasonable application of, or contrary to, clearly established federal law. Goodman timely appealed.

II. ANALYSIS

This appeal presents two questions: Did the state court apply the wrong legal standard to Goodman's ineffective assistance of counsel claim? And, under the correct legal framework, did the court unreasonably reject Goodman's Sixth Amendment claim? Reviewing the district court's denial of habeas relief de novo, we affirmatively answer both questions.

Under the relevant provision of AEDPA, Goodman is entitled to habeas relief if "the relevant state-court decision was either (1) 'contrary to . . . clearly established Federal law, as determined by the Supreme Court of the United States,' or (2) 'involved an unreasonable application of . . . clearly established Federal law, as determined by the Supreme Court of the United States.' " A state court decision is contrary to clearly established federal law "when the state court applies a rule that contradicts the governing law set forth by the Supreme Court or, on facts materially indistinguishable from the facts of an applicable Supreme Court precedent, reaches a different result." We do not use hindsight to assess whether a law is clearly established; instead our inquiry looks to the law of the Supreme Court at the time of the last state court decision on the merits, which, in this case, is the Wisconsin Court of Appeals decision disposing of Goodman's direct appeal.

In *Strickland,* the Supreme Court announced the framework for assessing Sixth Amendment ineffective assistance of counsel claims, and the *Strickland* framework was clearly established by the time of Goodman's direct appeal. . . . Goodman argues that the state court's decision, requiring him to demonstrate that his second trial was fundamentally unfair, was contrary to the prejudice analysis set forth in *Strickland,* which requires him only to show there is a reasonable probability of a different result. The district court found that the state court decision comported with *Strickland* and, therefore, that Goodman was not entitled to relief. We disagree. . . .

"One of the most obvious ways a state court may render a decision 'contrary to' the Supreme Court's precedents is when it sets forth the wrong legal framework." . . . This case is somewhat more complicated because the state court cited *Strickland* in its opinion, set forth the two-prong *Strickland* test, and even concluded that "Goodman was not prejudiced within the meaning of *Strickland.*" In denying relief, the district court reasoned that these references suggest the appellate court correctly applied the *Strickland* standard. We disagree. There is a difference between what the state court said and what it actually did. Although, in a boilerplate fashion, the court cited the *Strickland* rule, it repeatedly reasoned that Goodman failed to show that his second trial was "fundamentally unfair" or "unreliable." . . . [T]he state court decision is "contrary to" clearly established federal law. 28 U.S.C. § 2254(d)(1).

Even if the Wisconsin Court of Appeals decision were not contrary to federal law, it was an unreasonable application of *Strickland.* The "unreasonable application" prong of AEDPA means the state court's decision lies "well outside the boundaries of permissible differences of opinion." In the habeas context, an "unreasonable" application is more than simply an "incorrect" application, so "a federal habeas court may not issue the writ simply because that court concludes in its independent judgment that the relevant state-court decision applied clearly established federal law erroneously or incorrectly." Instead, "the state-court decision must be both incorrect and unreasonable."

As we have stated, *Strickland* instructs that Goodman must show that his lawyer's performance was deficient and that he was prejudiced as a result. Although counsel is strongly presumed to have rendered adequate assistance based upon his or her reasonable professional judgment, "it is not the role of a reviewing court to engage in a post hoc rationalization for an attorney's actions by constructing strategic defenses that counsel does not offer...."

Goodman argues that his trial counsel's performance fell below an objective standard of reasonableness because his lawyer: (1) opened the door for admission of Goodman's two prior convictions for armed robbery, (2) failed to subpoena the store's cashier to testify, (3) failed to request a limiting instruction regarding the threats evidence, (4) failed to properly object and preserve the record regarding the denial of Goodman's right to confront the witnesses against him, and (5) failed to object and request a mistrial based upon prosecutorial misconduct in closing argument.... Goodman maintains that his counsel was ineffective for failing to subpoena a critical defense witness, who testified in the first trial that she was unable to identify Goodman from a lineup after the robbery. Goodman's lawyer failed to subpoena Retzlaff because he (erroneously) believed the government would call her as a witness; much to his lawyer's dismay and Goodman's peril, this did not occur. Further, counsel's attempts to introduce at retrial portions of Retzlaff's testimony during the first trial were unsuccessful because, under Federal Rule of Evidence 804(b)(1), he failed to demonstrate that she was unavailable to testify in person. There is little tactical wisdom in counsel resting on his hands and assuming the government would help make the defense case for him.

To show prejudice, Goodman points out that his first trial, in which Retzlaff testified, ended in a hung jury. The government counters that Goodman was not prejudiced by counsel's alleged deficiencies because, unlike the first trial where only one accomplice and the store manager testified, by the time of the second trial, three confessed accomplices and the manager testified against Goodman. The Wisconsin Court of Appeals agreed that the error was harmless, reasoning that "even if the witness had testified in the second trial, it would have had no effect on the outcome of the trial because the victim and all three accomplices identified Goodman as the robber."

However, the cumulative effect of trial counsel's errors sufficiently undermines our confidence in the outcome of the proceeding. Rather than evaluating each error in isolation, as did the Wisconsin Court of Appeals, the pattern of counsel's deficiencies must be considered in their totality. In weighing each error individually, the Wisconsin Court of Appeals overlooked a pattern of ineffective assistance and unreasonably applied *Strickland*.

The details of the robbery were largely undisputed at trial; thus, the case centered on the identification of Goodman as the assailant and, crucially, witness credibility. Three confessed accomplices testified against Goodman; but their credibility is questionable, given their incentive to curry favor with the government regarding their own fate. "Where the state's case consists chiefly or solely upon the word of an accomplice ... courts have recognized the great importance to the defendant of evidence of direct contradiction or material corroboration from other sources." ... [T]he testimony of a disinterested eyewitness was a crucial aspect of Goodman's defense. Retzlaff, who chose another individual as the robber, was undoubtedly important to creating reasonable doubt in the state's case against Goodman. Yet, the jury did not have the benefit of Retzlaff's testimony because Goodman's lawyer made no efforts to secure her presence at trial.

Counsel's failure to subpoena store cashier Retzlaff was only the first in a catalog of errors.... While each of these errors considered in isolation may not have been prejudicial to Goodman, viewed in their totality, they create a clear pattern of ineffective assistance, the existence of which "l[ies] well outside the boundaries of permissible differences of opinion."

Given the totality of the evidence before the jury, there is a reasonable probability that the outcome would have been different absent counsel's deficient conduct. Therefore, assuming the Wisconsin Court of Appeals applied the correct legal standard (which we believe it did not), its decision is nonetheless an unreasonable application of the Supreme Court's decision in *Strickland v. Washington*. Goodman's counsel's performance fell below the constitutional minimum guaranteed in the Sixth Amendment.

NOTES

1.   Why did the court need to conclude, not only that the state court's decision was erroneous, but that its decision was either "contrary to ... clearly established Federal law" or "involved an unreasonable application of ... clearly established Federal law"? What effect does this provision have on an individual bringing a claim of ineffective assistance of counsel in a federal habeas proceeding?

2.   What errors did Goodman's lawyer make? Did they render his performance deficient? How did Goodman show prejudice under *Strickland v. Washington*?

3.   You have studied the various approaches the law takes to safeguarding attorney competence. What do you think about them? Are they sufficient to protect clients? Another component of enforcing attorney competence comes from bar admission requirements. You will consider those in Chapter 14.

PROBLEMS

1. Fox and Bennett decided to exchange parcels of real property. Bennett told Fox he would ask his lawyer to prepare the documents for the transaction and that Bennett would pay the legal fees. Lawyer, consulting only with Bennett, prepared the documents. At the closing, Lawyer read the agreement to Fox and asked if he understood it. Fox said yes and all parties signed the agreement. Fox later claimed that the transaction did not comply with his prior oral agreement with Bennett. Can he sue Lawyer for malpractice? *See Fox v. Pollack*, 181 Cal.App.3d 954 (1st Dist. 1986).

2. Sangha and his girlfriend Aggarwal got into a fight. Sangha threw Aggarwal's cellphone at her, and broke her bedroom window. Sangha was arrested. He hired LaBarbera to represent him. LaBarbera counseled Sangha to plead guilty to felony vandalism; under the plea agreement and state law, if Sangha successfully completed three years of probation, the felony would become an expungeable misdemeanor. Sangha agreed and admitted under penalty of perjury, as part of entering his plea, that he had maliciously destroyed property worth more than $400. Subsequently he learned that the felony conviction prevented him from renewing his securities dealer's license. He engaged new counsel, who convinced the court to set aside the earlier guilty plea and enter a plea of guilty to a misdemeanor instead. One month later, Sangha had the misdemeanor conviction expunged from his record. Can Sangha sue LaBarbera for malpractice? *See Sangha v. LaBarbera*, 146 Cal. App.4th 79 (2006).

3. Plaintiff was charged with a federal crime relating to a scheme to help people fraudulently obtain commercial drivers' licenses. Lawyer told Plaintiff that he had a good defense to the criminal charges, but that Plaintiff would have to pay Lawyer a $150,000 fee and $20,000 in expenses for Lawyer to defend him. Plaintiff paid the money. Once Plaintiff had paid Lawyer the full fee, Lawyer told Plaintiff that, because of statements Plaintiff had made to police before he hired Lawyer, Plaintiff could not win at trial and had to plead guilty. Lawyer sent another attorney to represent Plaintiff at the plea hearing; Plaintiff was sentenced to 22 months in federal prison. Plaintiff sued Lawyer for breach of contract and legal malpractice. Lawyer responded that, because Plaintiff was not actually innocent, he could not bring the suit. Result? *See Winniczek v. Nagelberg*, 394 F.3d 505 (7th Cir. 2005) (Posner, J.).

4. M&S hired Law Firm to structure a loan that would be made to Company. Company planned to construct and manage a casino for an Indian tribe. M&S planned to sell participation interests in the loan to several institutional investors; it did not intend to keep any interest in the loan itself. Law Firm prepared the loan agreement, which included a "pledge agreement" that promised Company's management fees as security for the loan. The agreement was submitted to the National Indian Gaming Commission (NIGC) and received necessary approvals. Subsequently, the parties sought to amend the pledge agreement. It was not clear whether such an amendment required the approval of the NIGC, Company was in a hurry to close on the loan, and the NIGC indicated it would need time to review and approve the agreement. Law Firm advised M&S that NIGC approval of the pledge agreement was not

required, and the loan closed. Within a week, M&S had sold all the participation interests in the loan to institutional investors; within a year Company defaulted on the loans. Company claimed that the pledge agreement was unenforceable because it had not been approved by the NIGC. Can the institutional investors sue Law Firm for malpractice? *See McIntosh County Bank v. Dorsey & Whitney, LLP*, 745 N.W.2d 538 (Minn. 2008).

5. Lawyer was retained to represent Client in a capital murder case. Client worked as a cashier at an airport restaurant; he was charged with robbing the restaurant and killing his supervisor. His bloody finger and palm prints were found at the scene. At trial, the evidence suggested that there was blood at the scene, not that of the victim, and that there had been a struggle between the killer and the victim, suggesting that the mystery blood belonged to the actual killer. Lawyer did not have Client's blood tested and did not argue at trial that the blood found at the scene did not belong to Client. He also did not seem to understand blood typing evidence, and spent only 35.1 hours preparing for trial. During closing argument, Lawyer argued that the prosecution should have tested Client's blood; the prosecutor responded that Lawyer would have offered such evidence if it had been favorable to Client. The jury convicted Client and found, as a special circumstances necessary to the imposition of the death penalty, that Client had himself intentionally killed the victim. It sentenced Client to death. Subsequent testing revealed that the blood at the scene was not that of Client. Can Client make a successful claim of ineffective assistance of counsel? *See Duncan v. Ornoski*, 528 F.3d 1222 (9th Cir. 2008).

6. Lawyer told his client, Homeowners' Association (HOA), that it could unilaterally alter the covenants in the homeowners' agreements limiting the owners' ability to rent their properties. Owner objected to the unilateral modifications and sued HOA, which settled with Owner for $52,000. HOA's insurer reimbursed HOA for the settlement. Can the insurer recover the $52,000 from Lawyer? *See State Farm Fire & Casualty Co. v. Weiss*, 194 P.3d 1063 (Colo. App. 2008).

7. Technical, a long-term client of Lawyer, consulted Lawyer about suing UCB, a supplier, for providing faulty goods. Lawyer advised Technical that the statute of limitations on the claim was five years, but Lawyer did not want to undertake the litigation. Technical hired another law firm but did not do so until three years later. The other firm brought suit on Technical's behalf; UCB successfully moved for summary judgment on the ground that the statute of limitations was four years and the suit was untimely. Technical did not appeal. Can Technical sue Lawyer for malpractice? *See Technical Packaging, Inc. v. Hanchett*, 992 So.2d 309 (Fla. App. 2008).

8. Black hired Schultz to bring a sexual harassment complaint against her employer. The company closed the department Black worked in and offered her a severance package. Schultz told Black not to accept the package because if she did she would give up her right to sue for harassment. He also urged her not to take another job to maximize her damages. Black did as Schultz recommended. Schultz never filed Black's lawsuit, but told her he had done so. Black sued Schultz for malpractice. At trial, Schultz admitted that he had given incompetent advice, but argued that he was not liable in damages

because Black could not establish that her sexual harassment claim would have been successful. The jury agreed that Black's harassment claim would have failed. Can she recover any damages from Schultz? *See Black v. Shultz*, 530 F.3d 702 (8th Cir. 2008).

9. As part of Wife's divorce from Husband, the parties agreed to sell one parcel of jointly owned property and share the proceeds; Husband would buy a second parcel. Husband retained attorney Hecht to prepare a quitclaim deed conveying the second parcel to him. Wife's attorney, Skevofilax, renewed the deed and, on her recommendation, Wife signed it. The deed, however, conveyed not one but both parcels of land to Husband. Can Wife sue Hecht for malpractice? *See Breen v. Law Office of Bruce A. Barket, P.C.*, 862 N.Y.S.2d 50 (N.Y.A.D. 2008).

10. Paterek hired Evans to sue Richardson, who had injured him in an automobile accident. Evans failed to file the complaint in a timely manner. Evans conceded liability, but argued that Richardson was judgment-proof and that, regardless of the damages Paterek suffered, the most he could recover in malpractice damages was the amount of Richardson's available insurance of $100,000. The jury returned a verdict of $382,000. Can Paterek collect it? *See Paterek v. Petersen & Ibold*, 890 N.E.2d 316 (Ohio 2008).

CHAPTER 5

WHO IS THE CLIENT? ENTERING INTO AND ENDING THE ATTORNEY– CLIENT RELATIONSHIP

■ ■ ■

As we've seen, lawyers have some significant obligations to their clients. At this point, it becomes important to know when those obligations arise. What creates the lawyer-client relationship and triggers those obligations? How does the attorney-client relationship end so that those obligations owed to current clients no longer apply? Paragraph [17] of the Scope Note to the Model Rules suggests that these questions are a matter of substantive law, outside the scope of the ethics rules. So we will need to look to external law to answer them.

A. FORMATION OF THE ATTORNEY– CLIENT RELATIONSHIP

A client comes to your office to meet with you and, after a consultation, expressly agrees to engage you to handle a discrete legal matter for her. You present a fee agreement, which you explain; the client signs it and writes you a check as an advance on the fees she anticipates paying. After she departs, you write her a letter, setting out the terms of what you have undertaken to do for her and the fee arrangement to which she has agreed. You close the letter with some pleasantries about how you are looking forward to working with the client and hope to bring the matter, whatever it is, to a successful conclusion.

At this point, you should be pretty sure that you have entered into an attorney-client relationship with all the obligations that go with it. We might call this person an "intentional client." You purposely entered into an attorney-client relationship with her, with your eyes wide open. Since that relationship includes taking on duties to the client, the breach of which could give rise to malpractice liability or disciplinary sanctions, it's a good thing you are aware of those obligations.

There are, however, a range of situations in which you may find yourself owing the obligations of the attorney-client relationship to someone even when you didn't intend to undertake those responsibilities.

Sometimes these are what one author calls "accidental clients." *See* Susan R. Martyn, *Accidental Clients*, 33 Hofstra L. Rev. 913 (2005). In other circumstances, the complexity of the situation may create duties to additional persons or parties besides the ones you thought were your clients. Since the attorney-client relationship imposes significant obligations on you as a lawyer, it is worth paying some attention to the ways in which you can acquire the obligations associated with that relationship without intending to.

1.   THE ACCIDENTAL CLIENT

TOGSTAD v. VESELY, OTTO, MILLER & KEEFE

291 N.W.2d 686 (Minn. 1980)

PER CURIAM.

This is an appeal by the defendants from a judgment of the Hennepin County District Court involving an action for legal malpractice. The jury found that the defendant attorney Jerre Miller was negligent and that, as a direct result of such negligence, plaintiff John Togstad sustained damages in the amount of $610,500 and his wife, plaintiff Joan Togstad, in the amount of $39,000. Defendants (Miller and his law firm) appeal to this court from the denial of their motion for judgment notwithstanding the verdict or, alternatively, for a new trial. We affirm.

In August 1971, John Togstad began to experience severe headaches and on August 16, 1971, was admitted to Methodist Hospital where tests disclosed that the headaches were caused by a large aneurism[1] on the left internal carotid artery. The attending physician, Dr. Paul Blake, a neurological surgeon, treated the problem by applying a Selverstone clamp to the left common carotid artery. The clamp was surgically implanted on August 27, 1971, in Togstad's neck to allow the gradual closure of the artery over a period of days.

The treatment was designed to eventually cut off the blood supply through the artery and thus relieve the pressure on the aneurism, allowing the aneurism to heal. It was anticipated that other arteries, as well as the brain's collateral or cross-arterial system would supply the required blood to the portion of the brain which would ordinarily have been provided by the left carotid artery. The greatest risk associated with this procedure is that the patient may become paralyzed if the brain does not receive an adequate flow of blood. In the event the supply of blood becomes so low as to endanger the health of the patient, the adjustable clamp can be opened to establish the proper blood circulation.

In the early morning hours of August 29, 1971, a nurse observed that Togstad was unable to speak or move. At the time, the clamp was one-half (50%) closed. Upon discovering Togstad's condition, the nurse called a

---

1. An aneurism is a weakness or softening in an artery wall which expands and bulges out over a period of years.

resident physician, who did not adjust the clamp. Dr. Blake was also immediately informed of Togstad's condition and arrived about an hour later, at which time he opened the clamp. Togstad is now severely paralyzed in his right arm and leg, and is unable to speak.

Plaintiffs' expert, Dr. Ward Woods, testified that Togstad's paralysis and loss of speech was due to a lack of blood supply to his brain. Dr. Woods stated that the inadequate blood flow resulted from the clamp being 50% closed and that the negligence of Dr. Blake and the hospital precluded the clamp's being opened in time to avoid permanent brain damage. . . .

Dr. Blake and defendants' expert witness, Dr. Shelly Chou, testified that Togstad's condition was caused by blood clots going up the carotid artery to the brain. They both alleged that the blood clots were not a result of the Selverstone clamp procedure. In addition, they stated that the clamp must be about 90% closed before there will be a slowing of the blood supply through the carotid artery to the brain. Thus, according to Drs. Blake and Chou, when the clamp is 50% closed there is no effect on the blood flow to the brain.

About 14 months after her husband's hospitalization began, plaintiff Joan Togstad met with attorney Jerre Miller regarding her husband's condition. Neither she nor her husband was personally acquainted with Miller or his law firm prior to that time. John Togstad's former work supervisor, Ted Bucholz, made the appointment and accompanied Mrs. Togstad to Miller's office. Bucholz was present when Mrs. Togstad and Miller discussed the case.[2]

Mrs. Togstad had become suspicious of the circumstances surrounding her husband's tragic condition due to the conduct and statements of the hospital nurses shortly after the paralysis occurred. One nurse told Mrs. Togstad that she had checked Mr. Togstad at 2 a.m. and he was fine; that when she returned at 3 a.m., by mistake, to give him someone else's medication, he was unable to move or speak; and that if she hadn't accidentally entered the room no one would have discovered his condition until morning. Mrs. Togstad also noticed that the other nurses were upset and crying, and that Mr. Togstad's condition was a topic of conversation.

Mrs. Togstad testified that she told Miller "everything that happened at the hospital," including the nurses' statements and conduct which had raised a question in her mind. She stated that she "believed" she had told Miller "about the procedure and what was undertaken, what was done, and what happened." She brought no records with her. Miller took notes and asked questions during the meeting, which lasted 45 minutes to an hour. At its conclusion, according to Mrs. Togstad, Miller said that "he did not think we had a legal case, however, he was going to discuss this with his partner." She understood that if Miller changed his mind after talking to his partner, he would call her. Mrs. Togstad "gave it" a few days and, since she did not hear from Miller, decided "that they had come to the conclusion that there wasn't a case." No fee arrangements were discussed,

---

2. Bucholz . . . died prior to the trial of the instant action.

no medical authorizations were requested, nor was Mrs. Togstad billed for the interview.

Mrs. Togstad denied that Miller had told her his firm did not have expertise in the medical malpractice field, urged her to see another attorney, or related to her that the statute of limitations for medical malpractice actions was two years. She did not consult another attorney until one year after she talked to Miller. Mrs. Togstad indicated that she did not confer with another attorney earlier because of her reliance on Miller's "legal advice" that they "did not have a case."

On cross-examination, Mrs. Togstad was asked whether she went to Miller's office "to see if he would take the case of (her) husband...." She replied, "Well, I guess it was to go for legal advice, what to do, where shall we go from here? That is what we went for." Again in response to defense counsel's questions, Mrs. Togstad testified as follows:

> Q: And it was clear to you, was it not, that what was taking place was a preliminary discussion between a prospective client and lawyer as to whether or not they wanted to enter into an attorney-client relationship?
>
> A: I am not sure how to answer that. It was for legal advice as to what to do.
>
> Q: And Mr. Miller was discussing with you your problem and indicating whether he, as a lawyer, wished to take the case, isn't that true?
>
> A: Yes.

On re-direct examination, Mrs. Togstad acknowledged that when she left Miller's office she understood that she had been given a "qualified, quality legal opinion that (she and her husband) did not have a malpractice case."

Miller's testimony was different in some respects from that of Mrs. Togstad. Like Mrs. Togstad, Miller testified that Mr. Bucholz arranged and was present at the meeting, which lasted about 45 minutes. According to Miller, Mrs. Togstad described the hospital incident, including the conduct of the nurses. He asked her questions, to which she responded. Miller testified that "(t)he only thing I told her (Mrs. Togstad) after we had pretty much finished the conversation was that there was nothing related in her factual circumstances that told me that she had a case that our firm would be interested in undertaking."

Miller also claimed he related to Mrs. Togstad "that because of the grievous nature of the injuries sustained by her husband, that this was only my opinion and she was encouraged to ask another attorney if she wished for another opinion" and "she ought to do so promptly." He testified that he informed Mrs. Togstad that his firm "was not engaged as experts" in the area of medical malpractice, and that they associated with the Charles Hvass firm in cases of that nature. Miller stated that at the end of the conference he told Mrs. Togstad that he would consult with Charles Hvass and if Hvass's opinion differed from his, Miller would so inform her. Miller recollected that he called Hvass a "couple days" later and discussed the case with him. It was Miller's impression that Hvass thought there was no liability for malpractice in the case. Consequently, Miller did not communicate with Mrs. Togstad further.

On cross-examination, Miller testified as follows:

Q: Now, so there is no misunderstanding, and I am reading from your deposition, you understood that she was consulting with you as a lawyer, isn't that correct?

A: That's correct.

Q: That she was seeking legal advice from a professional attorney licensed to practice in this state and in this community?

A: I think you and I did have another interpretation or use of the term "Advice." She was there to see whether or not she had a case and whether the firm would accept it.

Q: We have two aspects; number one, your legal opinion concerning liability of a case for malpractice; number two, whether there was or wasn't liability, whether you would accept it, your firm, two separate elements, right?

A: I would say so.

Q: Were you asked [at your deposition], "And you understood that she was seeking legal advice at the time that she was in your office, that is correct also, isn't it?" And did you give this answer, "I don't want to engage in semantics with you, but my impression was that she and Mr. Bucholz were asking my opinion after having related the incident that I referred to." The next question, "Your legal opinion?" Your answer, "Yes." Were those questions asked and were they given?

A: Yes, I gave those answers. Certainly, she was seeking my opinion as an attorney in the sense of whether or not there was a case that the firm would be interested in undertaking.

Kenneth Green, a Minneapolis attorney, was called as an expert by plaintiffs. He stated that in rendering legal advice regarding a claim of medical malpractice, the "minimum" an attorney should do would be to request medical authorizations from the client, review the hospital records, and consult with an expert in the field. John McNulty, a Minneapolis attorney, and Charles Hvass testified as experts on behalf of the defendants. McNulty stated that when an attorney is consulted as to whether he will take a case, the lawyer's only responsibility in refusing it is to so inform the party. He testified, however, that when a lawyer is asked his legal opinion on the merits of a medical malpractice claim, community standards require that the attorney check hospital records and consult with an expert before rendering his opinion.

Hvass stated that he had no recollection of Miller's calling him in October 1972 relative to the Togstad matter. He testified that "when a person comes in to me about a medical malpractice action, based upon what the individual has told me, I have to make a decision as to whether or not there probably is or probably is not, based upon that information, medical malpractice. And if, in my judgment, based upon what the client has told me, there is not medical malpractice, I will so inform the client."

Hvass stated, however, that he would never render a "categorical" opinion. In addition, Hvass acknowledged that if he were consulted for a "legal opinion" regarding medical malpractice and 14 months had expired since the incident in question, "ordinary care and diligence" would require him to inform the party of the two-year statute of limitations applicable to that type of action.

This case was submitted to the jury by way of a special verdict form. The jury found that Dr. Blake and the hospital were negligent and that Dr. Blake's negligence (but not the hospital's) was a direct cause of the injuries sustained by John Togstad; that there was an attorney-client contractual relationship between Mrs. Togstad and Miller; that Miller was negligent in rendering advice regarding the possible claims of Mr. and Mrs. Togstad; that, but for Miller's negligence, plaintiffs would have been successful in the prosecution of a legal action against Dr. Blake.... The jury awarded damages to Mr. Togstad of $610,500 and to Mrs. Togstad of $39,000....

In a legal malpractice action of the type involved here, four elements must be shown: (1) that an attorney-client relationship existed; (2) that defendant acted negligently or in breach of contract; (3) that such acts were the proximate cause of the plaintiffs' damages; (4) that but for defendant's conduct the plaintiffs would have been successful in the prosecution of their medical malpractice claim.

This court first dealt with the element of lawyer-client relationship in the decision of *Ryan v. Long*, 29 N.W. 51 (1886). The *Ryan* case involved a claim of legal malpractice and on appeal it was argued that no attorney-client relation existed. This court, without stating whether its conclusion was based on contract principles or a tort theory, disagreed:

> (I)t sufficiently appears that plaintiff, for himself, called upon defendant, as an attorney at law, for "legal advice," and that defendant assumed to give him a professional opinion in reference to the matter as to which plaintiff consulted him. Upon this state of facts the defendant must be taken to have acted as plaintiff's legal adviser, at plaintiff's request, and so as to establish between them the relation of attorney and client.

We believe it is unnecessary to decide whether a tort or contract theory is preferable for resolving the attorney-client relationship question raised by this appeal. The tort and contract analyses are very similar in a case such as the instant one, and we conclude that under either theory the evidence shows that a lawyer-client relationship is present here. The thrust of Mrs. Togstad's testimony is that she went to Miller for legal advice, was told there wasn't a case, and relied upon this advice in failing to pursue the claim for medical malpractice. In addition, according to Mrs. Togstad, Miller did not qualify his legal opinion by urging her to seek advice from another attorney, nor did Miller inform her that he lacked expertise in the medical malpractice area. Assuming this testimony is true, as this court must do [given the jury's verdict], we believe a jury could properly find that Mrs. Togstad sought and received legal advice from Miller under circumstances which made it reasonably foreseeable to Miller that Mrs. Togstad would be injured if the advice were negligently given. Thus, under either a tort or contract analysis, there is sufficient evidence in the record to support the existence of an attorney-client relationship. . . .

[T]here is adequate evidence supporting the claim that Miller was also negligent in failing to advise Mrs. Togstad of the two-year medical malpractice limitations period. . . . One of defendants' expert witnesses, Charles Hvass, testified:

> Q: Now, Mr. Hvass, where you are consulted for a legal opinion and advice concerning malpractice and 14 months have elapsed (since the incident in question), . . . and you hold yourself out as competent to give a legal opinion and advice to these people concerning their rights, wouldn't ordinary care and diligence require that you inform them that there is a two-year statute of limitations within which they have to act or lose their rights?
>
> A: Yes. I believe I would have advised someone of the two-year period of limitation, yes.

Consequently, based on the testimony of Mrs. Togstad, *i.e.*, that she requested and received legal advice from Miller concerning the malpractice claim, and the above testimony of Hvass, we must reject the defendants' contention, as it was reasonable for a jury to determine that Miller acted negligently in failing to inform Mrs. Togstad of the applicable limitations period.

There is also sufficient evidence in the record establishing that, but for Miller's negligence, plaintiffs would have been successful in prosecuting their medical malpractice claim. . . . Thus, the jury reasonably found that had plaintiff's medical malpractice action been properly brought, plaintiffs would have recovered.

NOTES

1. What were the elements of the Togstads' cause of action? How did they satisfy the requirement that there be an attorney-client relationship? Do you think Miller thought he had an attorney-client relationship with Mrs. Togstad? Were there aspects of the communication between the parties that he should have handled differently? Why do you suppose Mrs. Togstad did not call attorney Miller to make sure she had understood the situation correctly? What might that suggest to you about handling interactions with your own clients, particularly those who might be unfamiliar with legal matters?

2. Imagine that you are Jerre Miller. You've just visited with Mrs. Togstad, had the phone call with Charles Hvass you promised her, and decided not to

take the case. What might you do to avoid the liability that was imposed here? If you were a malpractice insurer, what would you require of an insured lawyer in such a situation?

3.   While, as this case shows, attorney-client relationships can be implied, one who seeks the benefit of such an implied attorney-client relationship is required to be quite explicit about what she intends. In *Flaherty v. Filardi*, 2007 WL 2734633 (S.D.N.Y. 2007), the court granted summary judgment to lawyer defendants who were sued for legal malpractice by a plaintiff who claimed that she had engaged a lawyer from defendants' firm and was relying on him to "pitch" a screenplay for her. The court rejected the claim, because the plaintiff had never asked the lawyer to provide representation or been led to believe that he would. "The uncontroverted record shows that Plaintiff never explicitly requested the attorney to represent her in this matter, never was told that the attorney would protect her interests, and was never billed for any services. Plaintiff's deposition testimony indicates that Plaintiff merely gave Tobia her screenplay and does not suggest any request for legal services. Thus, there is no basis upon which to imply the existence of an attorney-client relationship."

4.   Can a unilateral contact by an individual create an attorney-client relationship? You receive an unsolicited email from someone who expresses an interest in engaging you as her attorney. She tells you that she has visited your website and has a matter that is relevant to your expertise, that she is willing to pay your standard hourly fee for the representation, and that she looks forward to working with you. She discloses private information about her situation that would be relevant to you if you chose to represent her. Has she created an attorney-client relationship with you based solely on her communication with you? See Comment [2] to Model Rule 1.18.

5.   These cases are specific examples of the more general principle that the putative client's belief that there is an attorney-client relationship must be reasonable. In *Togstad*, a jury evidently concluded that Mrs. Togstad's belief that Miller was her lawyer was reasonable. A lawyer's view of what would be reasonable under the circumstances might be different, but remember that the reasonableness of the client's belief is likely to be judged by lay people rather than lawyers.

It is not just the representations of the lawyer, but also the lawyer's staff, that can create an attorney-client relationship. Consider the following case:

DeVAUX v. AMERICAN HOME ASSURANCE CO. ET AL.

444 N.E.2d 355 (Mass. 1983)

ABRAMS, JUSTICE.

Injured in a fall, the plaintiff Loretta R. DeVaux wrote a letter to the defendant, Attorney Frank J. McGee, requesting legal assistance in regard to a possible tort claim. The defendant did not discover the plaintiff's letter, however, before the statute of limitations had run. Thereafter, the plaintiff sued the defendant attorney for malpractice, and the defendant's insurance company was impleaded as a third-party defendant.

Pursuant to Mass.R.Civ.P. 53(a), a judge of the Superior Court appointed a master to hear this case. The master concluded that there was no privity and no attorney-client relationship between the plaintiff and the defendant attorney until after the statute of limitations had run. Thus, the master recommended that a finding be entered for the defendants.

[T]he defendants moved for summary judgment. The defendants alleged that the attorney did not learn of the plaintiff's request for his legal assistance until after the statute of limitations had run, and that, in these circumstances, there was no attorney-client relationship until that time. The defendants asserted that, in the absence of an attorney-client relationship, the attorney had no duty to commence a timely action on behalf of the plaintiff. Thus, the defendants claimed that they were entitled to judgment as a matter of law.

The judge granted the defendants' motion and entered a judgment of dismissal against the plaintiff. The plaintiff appealed to the Appeals Court. We transferred the case to this court on our own motion. The plaintiff claims that the judge erred in granting the defendants' motion for summary judgment because there are genuine issues of material fact relating to the existence of an attorney-client relationship. We agree and remand this case for trial. . . .

We summarize the facts found by the master. On July 17, 1971, the plaintiff fell as she entered a Curtis Compact Store in Hanover. The plaintiff claims that she suffered a serious back injury as a result of this fall. On May 11, 1973, the plaintiff was admitted to South Shore Hospital for removal of a spinal disc.

A few days after her fall, the plaintiff called the defendant attorney's office seeking legal advice. That day a secretary in the attorney's office returned the plaintiff's call and advised her to write a letter to the store stating that she had fallen in the store and received an injury. The secretary also arranged a medical examination for the plaintiff with the store's insurance company. Finally, the secretary instructed the plaintiff to write a letter to the defendant attorney requesting legal assistance.

Following that instruction, the plaintiff personally delivered a letter to the attorney's secretary. In this letter, the plaintiff described her fall. The letter ended with the question, "Would you kindly advise me legally?" The secretary misfiled this letter. The defendant did not discover the letter until June, 1974, after the statute of limitations on the plaintiff's tort claim had run.

From the date she delivered the letter in 1971 until June, 1974, the plaintiff did not visit the defendant attorney's office or speak with him. In the interim, the plaintiff called the attorney's office a number of times. Each time, the plaintiff was told that her calls would be returned. But the attorney never returned any of her calls.

In February, 1978, the plaintiff filed a complaint in the Superior Court alleging that she retained the attorney to represent her concerning the fall at the store. In his answer, the defendant attorney denied that he was ever retained to represent the plaintiff in regard to the fall.

Pursuant to Mass.R.Civ.P. 56(c), only "if . . . there is no genuine issue as to any material fact [is] . . . the moving party . . . entitled to a judgment as a matter of law." Thus, the issue is whether the material facts found by the master, require, as a matter of law, a determination that there was no attorney-client relationship before the statute of limitations ran. We conclude that it was improper to grant the defendants' motion for summary judgment.

"It is the general rule that an attorney's liability for malpractice is limited to some duty owed to a client.... Where there is no attorney/client relationship there is no breach or dereliction of duty and therefore no liability." An attorney-client relationship need not rest on an express contract. An attorney-client relationship may be implied "when (1) a person seeks advice or assistance from an attorney, (2) the advice or assistance sought pertains to matters within the attorney's professional competence, and (3) the attorney expressly or impliedly agrees to give or actually gives the desired advice or assistance.... In appropriate cases the third element may be established by proof of detrimental reliance, when the person seeking legal services reasonably relies on the attorney to provide them and the attorney, aware of such reliance, does nothing to negate it." Where reasonable persons could differ as to the existence of an attorney-client relationship, this issue must be resolved by the trier of fact.

On appeal, the plaintiff advances two theories in support of her claim that there was an attorney-client relationship between the plaintiff and the attorney. First, the plaintiff argues that the secretary had actual authority to take the actions that she did. Therefore, the secretary's knowledge of the plaintiff's request for legal assistance can be imputed to the attorney. When an agent acquires knowledge in the scope of her employment, the principal, here the attorney, is held to have constructive knowledge of that information. There is a question for the jury whether the secretary's actions concerning the plaintiff's request for the attorney's services were within the scope of her employment. The plaintiff argues that, because the attorney had constructive knowledge of her problem, she reasonably relied on him to provide her with legal assistance. [T]he plaintiff asserts that, therefore, her reliance established an attorney-client relationship.

The plaintiff also contends that the secretary had apparent authority to establish an attorney-client relationship on behalf of the defendant. Apparent authority "results from conduct by the principal which causes a third person reasonably to believe that a particular person . . . has authority to enter into negotiations or to make representations as his agent." Applying the doctrine of apparent authority to this case, the plaintiff claims that the attorney placed his secretary in a position where prospective clients might reasonably believe that she had the authority to establish an attorney-client relationship. There is a question of fact for the jury whether the attorney permitted his secretary to act as she did, thereby creating the appearance of authority.

Under either theory, the question whether there was an attorney-client relationship depends on the reasonableness of the plaintiff's reliance. The application of the reasonable person standard is uniquely within the competence of the jury. . . .

It is a question for the jury whether the attorney allowed his secretary to act as she did, and whether he knew what she was doing. We believe that an attorney who places his lay employees in a position which may deceive prospective clients as to the attorney's willingness or ability to represent them may be liable for malpractice for the negligence of those employees.

Therefore, there are factual issues for the jury whether the attorney in this case put himself in a position in which he should be liable to the plaintiff. We reverse the judgment of dismissal and remand the case to the Superior Court for trial.

NOTES

1.   What did lawyer McGee do wrong here? What would you advise him to do differently in terms of law office management?

2.   The court discusses the possibility that McGee's secretary had either ACTUAL or APPARENT authority to form the attorney-client relationship with DeVaux on behalf of McGee. What is the difference? How could McGee have avoided giving his secretary actual authority to enter into relationships on his behalf? In fact, McGee claimed that his employees were under strict orders not to enter into fee agreements with clients. Did that solve the problem? How could McGee have avoided cloaking his employees with apparent authority to enter into agreements with potential clients? Is this an easy problem to solve?

3.   The initial mistake in this case was that DeVaux's letter was placed in a preexisting file, because McGee had done other work for her in the past. Were there other opportunities to fix the error here? Consider what some of those opportunities were. How did the problem here become as significant as it did? In this regard, consider Model Rule 1.4.

4.   Was it reasonable for DeVaux to assume, without any communication from McGee, that he was her lawyer? In *McGlone v. Lacey*, 288 F.Supp. 662 (D.S.D. 1968), McGlone suffered a personal injury. McGlone's daughter wrote to Lacey asking him to represent McGlone in securing relief and included an authorization to charge McGlone a contingent fee for the representation. Lacey's partner wrote McGlone that Lacey was currently serving in the legislature, but that he would respond to her upon his return two weeks later. Two months later, having heard nothing, McGlone wrote to Lacey, asking about progress in her case. Lacey responded that the statute of limitations had run on her claim nine days before. In the ensuing legal malpractice case, the court held that Lacey's silence alone could not form an attorney-client relationship; McGlone's communication was merely an offer which Lacey

never accepted. The court in *DeVaux* expressly rejected the holding in *McGlone*.

2. THE ENTITY CLIENT

Lawyers are frequently engaged to represent entities, rather than individuals. Some of the issues about how to handle the representation of an entity client are set out in Model Rule 1.13. Review the rule briefly at this point; you will return to it in more detail later. As you can see, if your client is an entity a distinct set of duties and obligations arises.

For now, though, we are interested in the problem of who the client is. This is a particular problem when one or more individuals asks a lawyer to assist in the formation of an entity. Who is the client before the entity is formed? After the entity is formed? Who was the client in the following case? Why?

MANION v. NAGIN
394 F.3d 1062 (8th Cir. 2005)

suit dismissed

HEANEY, CIRCUIT JUDGE.

Patrick T. Manion, Jr., sued attorney Stephen E. Nagin ... for breach of fiduciary duty, negligence, and tortious interference with contract stemming from Nagin's conduct in the creation and representation of the Boat Dealers' Alliance, Inc. (BDA). The district court dismissed Manion's suit, and we affirm.

BACKGROUND

Because this matter reaches us following a motion to dismiss the complaint, we construe the pleadings liberally in favor of Manion and accept the allegations in his complaint as true. Patrick Manion worked for many years in the pleasure boat industry. In 1995, he came up with a plan to organize, own, and operate an entity made up of retail boat dealers, who would use their buying power to purchase marine equipment at significant discounts.

Stephen Nagin held himself out as an attorney who was experienced in representing buying groups. When Manion contacted Nagin about Manion's idea to create his marine buying group, Nagin boasted that he was a "world class lawyer" working at a "world class law firm." He claimed to be one of the few lawyers in the country who had expertise in organizing buying groups. In the spring of 1995, Nagin agreed to represent Manion in creating and running BDA. Nagin told Manion that he would charge $300 per hour for his work on BDA, but eventually the two agreed that Nagin would charge $150 an hour but also receive ten percent of BDA's preferred stock. Owners of the preferred stock received ten percent of BDA's annual distributable income. Until Nagin suggested he take an ownership interest in BDA's preferred stock, Manion intended to be the sole owner of it.

Nagin incorporated BDA in Florida. Manion questioned whether it was wise to incorporate in this venue, but Nagin shrugged off Manion's concern, stating "I am the attorney. I am the one who is well versed in this. Let me do my job and you do yours." When Nagin prepared BDA's By–Laws, Manion noticed that preferred stock shareholders could only vote for certain changes in the By–Laws, while common stock shareholders had unrestricted voting rights. He questioned Nagin about how he, owning only preferred stock, could control BDA if he could not vote on general matters. Nagin advised Manion that he maintained control over BDA because the value of his preferred stock was so much greater than the value of common stock, and because of a Management Agreement that Nagin had drafted to serve as Manion's employment contract with BDA. Nagin assured Manion that the Management Agreement precluded BDA from removing Manion from his position as executive director for any reason for twenty years.

By 1996, Nagin had become unhappy with his fee structure. He wrote to Manion, asserting that he was not receiving the amount of compensation they had anticipated in crafting the fee agreement. The two agreed on a new fee structure, whereby Nagin received a greater percentage of the preferred stock dividends. Manion was the only other shareholder of the preferred stock, meaning that the increased legal fees would be paid from monies originally due to Manion.

On February 13, 1999, BDA held a special meeting at which BDA terminated Manion. In arbitration proceedings related to Manion's claims of wrongful termination, BDA successfully argued that its termination of Manion was proper because he acted in bad faith against the interests of BDA. The district court confirmed the arbitration award, and this court affirmed. Manion, still a majority shareholder of the preferred stock, decided to attend BDA's April 10, 1999 meeting. At the meeting, Manion learned that Nagin had asked BDA's Finance Committee to search for additional grounds to justify BDA's termination of Manion. When Manion learned about this, he asked Nagin who he was representing. Nagin responded that he represented BDA. Up until this point, Nagin had not told Manion that he did not represent Manion, and Manion considered Nagin to be his lawyer.

Manion filed suit against BDA, its individual members, Nagin, and his law firms. The district court directed arbitration with regard to Manion's complaint against BDA and its members pursuant to the terms of his contract, and stayed his claims against Nagin and the law firms pending the outcome of the arbitration. This court affirmed. Following the arbitrator's decision, Nagin and the law firms moved to dismiss Manion's complaint, contending that the claims were either legally deficient, collaterally estopped, or barred for failure to comply with a Minnesota statute concerning legal malpractice claims. The district court dismissed Manion's complaint, and this appeal followed.

ANALYSIS

... The district court dismissed ... Manion's suit, which alleged negligence and the breach of fiduciary duty related to Nagin's legal work, because it found he failed to state a claim. The lynchpin of this holding was the district court's determination that Nagin was never working as Manion's personal lawyer, and thus owed Manion no duty whatsoever.

To maintain a claim for negligence deriving from legal malpractice, the plaintiff must demonstrate the existence of an attorney-client relationship. Similarly, an attorney undertaking an attorney-client relationship assumes fiduciary duties, the breach of which may be actionable.

[The court noted that there was a question as to whether Minnesota or Florida law governed Manion's claims, but concluded that the result was the same under either state's law.]

In Minnesota, an attorney-client relationship can be created through contract or tort theory. Under the former, the plaintiff must show the creation of the relationship through either express or implied contract. The tort theory of representation recognizes the existence of an attorney-client relationship "whenever an individual seeks and receives legal advice from an attorney in circumstances in which a reasonable person would rely on such advice." Likewise, in Florida the test for determining if an attorney-client relationship exists depends on the client's belief that he is consulting with an attorney for the manifest purpose of obtaining legal advice. In both states, though, an individual's subjective expectation that a lawyer will represent the person is insufficient as a matter of law to create the relationship.

The district court held that the complaint did not sufficiently show that Nagin and Manion had established an attorney-client relationship. The court noted that Nagin's work was solely related to the creation and operation of BDA, and that Nagin never worked on anything for Manion individually. Invoking the well-established rule that a corporate employee does not generally enjoy an attorney-client relationship with corporate counsel, the court dismissed the claims which required proof of that relationship as an element.

Florida and Minnesota have both adopted rules of professional conduct which govern the actions of their states' lawyers. Both states have nearly identical rules about the representation of corporations and similar entities, making clear that the attorney's duty attaches to the entity, not its constituents. Minn. R. Prof. Conduct 1.13(a); R. Regulating Fla. Bar 4–1.13. Cases interpreting these rules have adhered to this proposition. The district court also turned for guidance to a Wisconsin Supreme Court case, *Jesse v. Danforth,* 485 N.W.2d 63 (Wis. 1992). *Jesse* involved a medical malpractice suit against a few named health care professionals. Two of the doctors moved to disqualify the plaintiffs' law firm because the firm had helped those doctors to create a corporation for the purpose of purchasing and operating MRI equipment. The corporation was not a party to the *Jesse* suit. The question presented to the Wisconsin Supreme Court was whether the plaintiffs' law firm must be disqualified where one of its members represented the defendant doctors in their formation of the MRI-related corporation. The court noted that at the initial stages of the firm's relationship with the doctors, it was representing them personally because no corporation had yet been formed. Still, since the representation was limited solely to the creation of the MRI corporation, the court retroactively applied the entity rule to hold that the firm never actually represented the doctors individually:

> [W]here (1) a person retains a lawyer for the purpose of organizing an entity and (2) the lawyer's involvement with that person is directly related to that incorporation and (3) such entity is eventually incorporated, the entity rule applies retroactively such that the lawyer's pre-incorporation involvement with the person is deemed to be representation of the entity, not the person.

Id. at 67.

Relying on *Jesse,* the district court invoked the entity rule to find that Nagin exclusively represented BDA. We agree that if Nagin's only interaction with Manion was to create BDA, Nagin could not be considered Manion's lawyer. Liberally construing the complaint in Manion's favor, though, we cannot agree that Nagin only operated as BDA's attorney. While Nagin may well have represented BDA as its corporate counsel, this does not preclude a finding that Nagin also provided Manion with legal advice and thus established an attorney-client relationship. Manion alleged that he sought and received guidance about how he could maintain control of the corporation. Nagin's advice here was not to BDA, but to Manion personally. Similarly, Manion used Nagin to draft an employment agreement between himself and BDA. Manion expressed his concern that the agreement sufficiently protect his interests, and Nagin accordingly drafted the agreement in a manner that he told Manion would ensure a twenty-year term of employment. When Nagin renegotiated his payment agreement, he and Manion agreed that Nagin would receive a portion of Manion's preferred share dividends. In other words, Nagin was paid for his services, at least in part, out of Manion's pocket.

When Manion asked questions about the incorporation documents and his employment agreement, he was seeking an opinion about the legal interpretation of the documents and whether they benefitted him as contemplated. These matters were not directly related to the formation of BDA—they concerned Manion's personal concerns of how he would be employed, and whether he would have control of the corporation. Providing Manion with advice about his personal interest in BDA and the Management Agreement was obviously beyond the scope of Nagin's job as BDA's attorney, and perhaps contrary to it. If Nagin was truly working exclusively as BDA's lawyer, he should have responded to Manion's questions by clarifying that he worked only for BDA and suggested Manion seek outside counsel. *See* Minn. R. Prof. Conduct 1.13(d); R. Regulating Fla. Bar 4–1.13(d). Instead, Nagin advised Manion that he maintained control over

BDA by having a strong financial interest in the preferred stock shares and by holding a twenty-year employment contract. Manion sought and received legal advice on these matters from Nagin, and that is sufficient to establish that an attorney-client relationship existed between the two of them.

Nonetheless, Manion has not stated a cognizable claim related to his attorney-client relationship with Nagin. Manion has sufficiently alleged that he established an attorney-client relationship with Nagin relating to Manion's employment contract and control of the corporation. But the arbitrator in Manion's related action against BDA found that Manion operated in bad faith against the corporation's interests by overpaying himself and other BDA shareholders and by failing to disclose financial data which would have revealed his bad faith. Bound by that finding, the defect in Manion's claims becomes obvious: he asks us to hold that Nagin committed legal malpractice by not warning him that he may lose control of BDA for committing malfeasance toward it, or protecting Manion from termination once Manion operated in that manner. Such a claim is not viable under either Minnesota or Florida law. *Accord* Minn. R. Prof. Conduct 1.2(c) (forbidding an attorney from assisting a client in fraudulent or deceitful conduct); R. Regulating Fla. Bar 4–1.2(d) (same). Accordingly, we affirm the district court's dismissal of Manion's breach of fiduciary duty and negligence claims as they related to Nagin's legal work.

NOTES

1.   At the outset of the relationship between Nagin and Manion, who was the client? Did that change once BDA was created? What does *Jesse v. Danforth*, discussed in *Manion*, suggest about who the lawyer's client is when a person (or persons) seeks a lawyer's assistance in creating an entity? Does the solution posited in *Jesse* make sense? Why do you suppose the court there created the legal fiction that it did? Authorities agree that the lawyer should make clear at the outset of an entity representation who the client is, and what the implications of that decision are. If the lawyer believes that the person with whom he is dealing misunderstands his role, he has an obligation to correct that misunderstanding. See Model Rule 4.3. Did Nagin comply with that obligation here?

2.   The *Jesse* analysis is not the only possible resolution of this problem. The lawyer forming an entity might intend to represent the persons creating the entity, not the entity itself. In *Manion*, there was only one such individual, but it is often the case in the formation of an entity that there are multiple individuals, with distinct interests, involved. Do you think the lawyer can represent more than one of those individuals? What kind of issues can you imagine that might make this a difficult problem? You will learn more about the complexities of representing multiple clients in Chapter 8.

3.   What about this situation caused the court to distinguish this case from *Jesse*? What elements did the court mention that created an attorney-client relationship between Manion and Nagin? Would it have been possible for Nagin to represent both Manion and BDA?

4. Small closely held corporations or partnerships often involve controlling individuals who, like Manion, work closely with the lawyers representing the entity. It may therefore be difficult for the individuals who control the entity (and for the entity's lawyer) to distinguish between the entity's interests and the personal interests of the controlling individuals. Rule 1.13(a) attempts to make this clear, providing that "A lawyer employed or retained by an organization represents the organization acting through its duly authorized constituents." Because those "duly authorized constituents" are the same individuals working on a day-to-day basis with the lawyer, drawing these lines may be more complicated than the rule suggests.

3. INSURER AND INSURED

Plaintiff slips and falls on the icy pavement outside your house. She is injured, and she sues you. Who will represent you? Ordinarily, if you have homeowner's insurance, your insurer will provide counsel for you. That means the insurance company will hire the lawyer and pay her. Whose lawyer is she, though? Does the lawyer represent you, or the insurer, or perhaps both? Once again, we have a "who is the client" problem. This might not seem like much of an issue; both insurer and insured want to contest liability and avoid paying any damages, so who the client is may not seem terribly important. But in some circumstances, it is critical. You already know of one reason why, which is developed in the following case:

ruling: Farmland cannot maintain a legal action

PINE ISLAND FARMERS COOP
v. ERSTAD & RIEMER, P.A.

649 N.W.2d 444 (Minn. 2002)

1) Liability insurer - Farmland
2) Insured - Pine Island
3) Defense Counsel - Erstad

PAGE, JUSTICE.

This case presents issues concerning the tripartite relationship between a ① liability insurer, an ② insured, and ③ defense counsel hired by the insurer to defend a claim against the insured. The insurer in this case, appellant Farmland Mutual Insurance Company (Farmland), brought a legal malpractice action against defense counsel, respondents Erstad & Riemer, P.A., arguing that Erstad & Riemer represented both the insured, appellant Pine Island Farmers Coop (Pine Island), and Farmland in an action brought by Duane Windhorst against Pine Island. The district court concluded that Erstad & Riemer did not represent Farmland, and that Farmland therefore could not maintain a legal malpractice action on its own behalf against Erstad & Riemer. The district court went on to conclude that Farmland, however, could maintain such an action on behalf of Pine Island under the doctrine of equitable subrogation.[1]

On appeal, the court of appeals affirmed the district court's conclusion that Erstad & Riemer did not represent Farmland, holding that "the insured is the sole client of the defense attorneys hired by the insurer."

---

1. Under equitable subrogation, an insurer who pays a loss on behalf of its insured can pursue the insured's rights against third parties whose negligence or wrongful acts caused the loss.

The court of appeals reversed the district court with respect to the issue of whether Farmland could maintain a legal malpractice action under the doctrine of equitable subrogation.... We affirm, although on somewhat different grounds.

This case stems from an action brought by Windhorst against Pine Island as a result of Pine Island's sale and installation of a milk metering system on Windhorst's dairy farm in 1994. In 1996, Windhorst commenced an action against Pine Island for breach of contract, negligence, and breach of express warranties, alleging that, as a result of Pine Island's failure to properly install the milk metering system, a number of his dairy cows became contaminated with bacteria. Pine Island tendered defense of Windhorst's claim to its liability insurer, Farmland, who retained Erstad & Riemer to represent Pine Island.

Windhorst's claim was tried to a jury in 1998. The jury found that both Pine Island and Windhorst were negligent, that their negligence was a direct cause of Windhorst's damages, and that Pine Island was 90% at fault. Based on this verdict, the district court entered judgment against Pine Island for $1,145,925, which represented 90% of Windhorst's damages as found by the jury.... Pine Island appealed.... In 1999, while Pine Island's appeal was pending, Windhorst and Farmland settled Windhorst's claim for $1,050,000. As a result of the settlement, Pine Island's appeal was withdrawn.

Farmland and Pine Island commenced the present action against Erstad & Riemer for legal malpractice and breach of contract in 2000. The complaint alleged that both Farmland and Pine Island had an attorney-client relationship with Erstad & Riemer. In its answer to the complaint, Erstad & Riemer denied having an attorney-client relationship with Farmland. In addition, Erstad & Riemer asserted a counterclaim against Farmland for unpaid legal fees.

... The district court granted summary judgment for Erstad & Riemer with respect to all of Farmland's claims on the ground that Erstad & Riemer and Farmland did not have an attorney-client relationship and, thus, there was no basis for the claims. The district court noted that, under Minnesota law, attorney-client relationships can be created by contract, either express or implied, or through tort theory. Based on its analysis of the communications and interactions between Erstad & Riemer and Farmland, the district court concluded that Pine Island was Erstad & Riemer's sole client....

Farmland and Pine Island appealed the district court's order. The court of appeals affirmed the district court's conclusion that Erstad & Riemer and Farmland did not have an attorney-client relationship....

Farmland and Pine Island petitioned this court for review of the court of appeals' decision, and we granted the petition to consider two issues: first, whether Erstad & Riemer and Farmland had an attorney-client relationship; and second, if Erstad & Riemer and Farmland did not have an attorney-client relationship, whether Farmland can maintain a legal malpractice action against Erstad & Riemer under the doctrine of equitable subrogation.

To prevail in its legal malpractice action, Farmland must establish that it had an attorney-client relationship with Erstad & Riemer.[2] If Erstad & Riemer and Farmland did not have an attorney-client relationship, then Farmland's claims fail as a matter of law unless the doctrine of equitable subrogation applies.

Farmland and Pine Island argue that we should apply the general rules regarding the formation of attorney-client relationships to determine whether Erstad & Riemer represented Farmland. Under those rules, a person seeking to establish the existence of an attorney-client relationship may do so using either contract or tort theory. *See Togstad v. Vesely, Otto, Miller & Keefe*, 291 N.W.2d 686, 693 (Minn.1980).... Farmland and Pine Island assert that the exchanges that took place between Erstad & Riemer and Farmland during the Windhorst litigation establish that they had an attorney-client relationship under either contract or tort theory.

In response, Erstad & Riemer argues that, at the outset of the representation, defense counsel's sole client is the insured. According to Erstad & Riemer, the question of whether defense counsel also represents the insurer is governed by our decision in *Shelby Mutual Insurance Co. v. Kleman*, 255 N.W.2d 231 (Minn.1977). Erstad & Riemer argues further that, under the principles discussed in *Kleman,* its sole client was Pine Island.

It is well-established under our case law that defense counsel hired by an insurer to defend a claim against its insured represents the insured. Because defense counsel has an attorney-client relationship with the insured, defense counsel owes a duty of undivided loyalty to the insured and must faithfully represent the insured's interests.

> [A]n attorney retained by an insurer to defend its insured, as long as he represents the insured, is under the same obligations of fidelity and good faith as if the insured had retained the attorney personally. The relationship of client and attorney exists the same in one case as in the other.

Thus, it is clear that in an insurance defense scenario, defense counsel has an attorney-client relationship with the insured. A number of jurisdictions have gone a step further, holding that the insured is defense counsel's sole client, and prohibiting defense counsel from forming an attorney-client relationship with the insurer. However, we have never gone so far as to hold that defense counsel cannot have an attorney-client relationship with both the insured and the insurer, and we decline to do so now.

In *Kleman,* we considered whether a law firm representing an insurance company could represent an insured in the same matter. One of the

---

2. We have recognized an exception to this rule, extending an attorney's duty to a nonclient in a "narrow range of factual situations in which the client's sole purpose in retaining an attorney is to benefit directly some third party." This exception is not implicated by the facts of this case, where Farmland retained Erstad & Riemer to represent Pine Island.

opposing parties in that litigation moved the district court to enjoin the law firm that was representing the insurance company from also representing the insured, arguing that there was a conflict of interest between the insurance company and the insured. The district court denied the motion and we affirmed. We identified three reasons for allowing the dual representation to go forward. First, we noted there was "no apparent conflict [of interest]" between the insurance company and the insured. Second, the insured had consulted with an independent attorney, and that attorney had advised the insured that obtaining separate counsel was unnecessary. Finally, the insured had given his express consent to the dual representation "with knowledge of the circumstances."

Consultation and consent were important to our holding in *Kleman* because the interests of the insured and the insurer may conflict, making it difficult for defense counsel to remain loyal to and exercise his or her independent professional judgment for the benefit of each client. The problems caused by conflicts of interest are particularly acute in the insurance defense context, where the potential for conflict exists in every case and actual conflicts are frequent. . . .

Liability insurance contracts grant the insurer rights to participate in and, in some areas, control the defense of claims against the insured. As a result, defense counsel and the insurer inevitably share information about claims. With defense counsel and the insurer in frequent contact over the details of the litigation, the insurer has ample opportunity to inform defense counsel how different approaches to the claim might affect its interests. When the interests of the insurer differ from those of the insured, defense counsel who represents both may find itself in what we have called "an exceedingly awkward position."

The danger is that, if a conflict of interest does arise, the nature of the tripartite relationship makes it likely that defense counsel will tend to favor the interests of the insurer at the expense of those of the insured. As one commentator has stated, defense counsel "may be tempted to help the client [the insurer] who pays the bills, who will send further business, and with whom long-standing personal relationships have developed." Ronald E. Mallen & Jeffrey M. Smith, 4 *Legal Malpractice* § 29.16, at 325 (5th ed. 2000). . . .

As these authorities suggest, it may be rather difficult for defense counsel who represents both the insured and the insurer to provide the insured with "the same 'undeviating and single allegiance' that he would owe to the insured if retained and paid by [the insured]." In this way, permitting dual representation can cause damage to the relationship between defense counsel and the insured by eroding the insured's trust and confidence in defense counsel's ability to faithfully represent his or her interests.

Despite the unique characteristics of the tripartite relationship between defense counsel, insurers, and insureds, Farmland and Pine Island argue that we should simply apply the general rules regarding the creation of attorney-client relationships to the facts of this case to determine whether

Erstad & Riemer represented Farmland.... [M]erely applying the general rules would not adequately address our concerns regarding dual representation in insurance defense cases. In light of the insurer's rights to control the defense of claims, exchanges of information between defense counsel and the insurer—including exchanges in which the insurer seeks, receives, and relies on legal advice from defense counsel—are bound to occur. Thus, a holding that these exchanges, standing alone, are sufficient to create an attorney-client relationship between defense counsel and the insurer would result in a rule that defense counsel represents the insurer in virtually every insurance defense case. Furthermore, such a holding would allow defense counsel to represent the insurer without the insured's consent or knowledge of the significant risks posed by dual representation.

For these reasons, it would be inappropriate to look solely to the general rules to determine whether defense counsel had an attorney-client relationship with an insurer. Instead, it is more appropriate to supplement the general rules with the factors that motivated our decision to permit dual representation in *Kleman*: the absence of a conflict of interest between insured and insurer and the fact that the insured expressly consented to the dual representation after consultation with counsel. This approach provides a bright-line rule to determine whether defense counsel represents the insurer as well as the insured. Without consultation and the express consent of the insured, the insured remains defense counsel's sole client. The twin requirements of consultation and consent make it impossible for the insurer to become defense counsel's co-client without the knowledge of the insured. It also comports with a lawyer's ethical obligations to consult with and obtain the consent of both clients when the lawyer seeks to represent multiple clients in the same matter....

Based on these considerations, we hold that, in the absence of a conflict of interest between the insured and the insurer, the insurer can become a co-client of defense counsel based on contract or tort theory if two conditions are satisfied. First, defense counsel or another attorney must consult with the insured, explaining the implications of dual representation and the advantages and risks involved. Second, after consultation, the insured must give its express consent to the dual representation.

We turn now to an application of our holding to the facts of this case. The record before us does not contain any evidence indicating that defense counsel or another attorney consulted with Pine Island regarding the possibility of dual representation. Nor is there any evidence that Pine Island, after being informed of the risks and advantages of dual representation, consented to dual representation. Based on these facts, we conclude that defense counsel did not represent Farmland in the Windhorst matter, and we therefore hold that defense counsel is entitled to summary judgment with respect to the legal malpractice action brought by Farmland on its own behalf.

Having concluded that Farmland cannot maintain a legal malpractice action on its own behalf against defense counsel, we now address whether

Farmland can assert Pine Island's rights against defense counsel by maintaining a legal malpractice action under the doctrine of equitable subrogation.

Farmland and Pine Island urge us to follow the Michigan Supreme Court's decision in *Atlanta Int'l Ins. Co. v. Bell*, 475 N.W.2d 294 (1991), on this issue. In *Bell*, the Michigan Supreme Court applied the doctrine of equitable subrogation to allow a nonclient insurance company to sue defense counsel for legal malpractice. The insured in *Bell* did not bring a legal malpractice claim against defense counsel. The court's holding was motivated, in part, by the concern that defense counsel would escape malpractice liability if the insurance company was not permitted to go forward with its claim. The Michigan Supreme Court explained: "defense counsel's immunity from suit by the insurer would place the loss for the attorney's misconduct on the insurer. The only winner produced by an analysis precluding liability would be the malpracticing attorney. Equity cries out for application under such circumstances."

In this case, Pine Island has brought a malpractice action against Erstad & Riemer. Consequently, a holding that Farmland cannot bring an equitable subrogation claim will not have the effect of rendering Erstad & Riemer immune from malpractice liability. Thus, the reasoning of the Michigan Supreme Court in *Bell* does not apply to the present case. Similarly, because Pine Island has sought to vindicate its own rights by bringing a malpractice action in its own name, there is no need to allow Farmland to step into Pine Island's shoes to assert Pine Island's rights. Therefore, based on the particular facts and circumstances of this case, we decline to apply the doctrine of equitable subrogation, and we affirm the district court's order dismissing with prejudice all of Farmland's claims.

GILBERT, JUSTICE (concurring in part, dissenting in part).

Today, the majority establishes new standards regarding the formation of an attorney-client relationship. These new standards are based on the presumption that even in the absence of a conflict of interest between the insured and the insurer, the insured is defense counsel's sole client. . . . Applying these new standards, the majority concludes that because there was no evidence in the record that defense counsel consulted with the insured regarding dual representation and there was no evidence that the insured consented to dual representation, defense counsel did not represent the insurer in the Windhorst case. The majority also declines to apply the doctrine of equitable subrogation to permit the insurer to assert a malpractice claim against defense counsel.

Although I concur with the majority's opinion regarding equitable subrogation, I respectfully dissent from the majority's opinion as to whether the insurer had an attorney-client relationship with defense counsel. Under our traditional contract and tort principles, when an individual is licensed as a lawyer, looks like a lawyer, sounds like a lawyer, acts like a lawyer, gives advice like a lawyer, bills like a lawyer, and the client believes he is being represented by a lawyer, the client is being represented by a lawyer. . . .

In this case, the insurer retained defense counsel. Matters of legal strategy relating to investigation, experts, and the appropriate affirmative defenses were discussed and decided by defense counsel and the insurer. For example, defense counsel sought specific approval from the insurer for agreeing to toll the statute of limitations to delay the commencement of the lawsuit and decided not to interplead a third party. There is no indication that these issues were even discussed with the insured. In fact, the law firm did not even meet with the insured until two months after a claim was presented. The billing instructions for representing the insurer or the insured states that "the parties shall be represented," indicating that dual representation was contemplated by the insurer and the insured. . . .

It is ironic that the majority uses this case as a vehicle for establishing new standards to protect the insured from a potential conflict of interest when the facts of this case indicate that there was a unity of interest between the insurer and the insured. The source of the insurer's malpractice claim against defense counsel is that defense counsel failed to assert a limitation of remedy defense as an affirmative defense in the Windhorst suit. This limitation of remedy defense was specified on the back of the contract that formed the basis for the entire Windhorst suit. The reason that defense counsel did not assert this defense is that defense counsel did not even read the contract in preparing its answer and defenses, even through trial. In fact, the lawyer testified at a deposition that he first saw the contract when he and respondent law firm were sued for legal malpractice by the insurer. Significantly, this limitation of remedy defense limits the damage exposure of both the insured and the insurer. On this issue and the other affirmative defenses, there was obviously not only a dual representation with no actual or apparent conflict between the insurer and the insured, but there was a unity of interest to mitigate damages for both the insurer and insured. Because both the insured and the insurer are plaintiffs and appellants in this case, this unity of interest between the insurer and the insured has apparently continued throughout this litigation.

The practical effect of the new standards promulgated by the majority is to grant attorneys a shield of immunity from malpractice claims when there is no conflict of interest between the insurer and the insured. In this case, the insurer paid the judgment at issue and the insured had no meaningful monetary damages except a deductible of $10,000. Now, the majority denies the insurer any effective recourse to even have its claim heard. I would hold that there was an attorney-client relationship between defense counsel and the insurer such that the insurer had standing to bring a malpractice action against defense counsel.

NOTES

1. Is the fact that the insurance company pays the lawyer relevant to the question of who the client is? That a third party is paying the lawyer does not make that party the client and does not entitle the third party to direct the representation. *See* Model Rules 1.8(f) and 5.4(c). What is the difference between the two rules? Insurance defense is one circumstance in which the lawyer is routinely engaged, and paid, by a third party to represent the client; it is not the only one. Imagine a parent paying for a lawyer to represent his child in a juvenile proceeding.

2. As *Pine Island* and the preceding note make clear, the lawyer appointed to represent the insured represents the insured. Whether he also represents the insurer is a complex question, and one which different jurisdictions have decided differently. Why did the court here hesitate to conclude that the lawyer in an insurance defense situation represents the insurer as well as the insured? The court was concerned about conflicts between the insured's interest and the insurer's interest. What kind of situations might present such a conflict? We will consider this problem in Chapter 8.

B. TERMINATION OF THE ATTORNEY–CLIENT RELATIONSHIP

1. ETHICAL RULES CONCERNING WITHDRAWAL

Once you are in an attorney-client relationship, how do you get out of it? Model Rule 1.16 sets out the rule governing termination of representation. Review that rule and its comments carefully. What are the circumstances under which a lawyer is REQUIRED to withdraw from representing a client? This is known as "mandatory withdrawal." Are these also situations in which a lawyer would be prohibited from taking on representation in the first place?

Under what circumstances is withdrawal permitted even if it is not required? This is known as "permissive withdrawal." May a lawyer withdraw from representing a client if the withdrawal will have a material adverse effect on the interests of the client? if the client is not paying the fee that has been agreed upon? if the client's constant phone calls are an unbearable annoyance? if the lawyer and client have a fundamental disagreement about how the case should be handled? Also, note the requirements of Rule 1.16(d). Even a lawyer who is withdrawing has some obligation to protect the client's interests.

In the context of litigation, the mere fact that a lawyer satisfies the requirements for withdrawal under the ethics rules does not mean that withdrawal is automatically permitted. As Rule 1.16(c) reflects, ordinarily in a litigated matter an attorney who has entered an appearance before the court will need the court's permission to withdraw. That can require lawyers or their firms to continue representation that they wish to terminate, even where withdrawal would be permitted—or even re-quired—under Model Rule 1.16. What effect might this possibility have on the lawyer's decision to enter into representation in the first place?

KRIEGSMAN v. KRIEGSMAN

375 A.2d 1253 (N.J. Super. Ct. App. Div. 1977)

MICHELS, J.

Appellants Messrs. Rose, Poley, Bromley and Landers (hereinafter "the Rose firm") appeal from an order of the Chancery Division denying their application to be relieved as attorneys for plaintiff Mary–Ann Kriegsman in this matrimonial action.

On December 22, 1975 plaintiff, who had been previously represented by other counsel, retained the Rose firm to represent her in a divorce action against her husband, defendant Bernard Kriegsman. The Rose firm re-quested and received consent to substitution of attorneys from plaintiff's former attorney. Plaintiff then paid an initial retainer of $1,000, plus $60 in court costs, with the understanding that she would be responsible for additional fees and expenses as litigation progressed. In March 1976 plaintiff paid the Rose firm another $1,000, plus $44 which was to be applied against costs.

During the 3–1/2 months that the Rose firm represented plaintiff prior to its motion the firm had made numerous court appearances and had engaged in extensive office work in plaintiff's behalf. The unusual amount of work required was necessitated in part by the fact that defendant appeared pro se, was completely uncooperative and had refused to comply with some of the orders entered by the court. As of April 5, 1976 the Rose firm alleged that it had spent 110 hours on plaintiff's case, billed at $7,354.50, and had incurred disbursements of approximately $242. Since, by then, plaintiff was on welfare and since she apparently did not have sufficient funds to pay the additional fees incurred, the Rose firm contend-ed that they were entitled to be relieved from further representation. Plaintiff opposed the application before the court, pointing out

> First of all, this case, I think, has accumulated a file this thick. I think at this point, for another attorney to step in, it would be very difficult to acquaint himself with every motion that has been brought up before this court. I feel that Mr. Koserowski (an associate in the Rose firm) has been with me, representing me, for four months, and when this case finally does go to trial, hopefully soon, he has all this knowledge at his fingertips. Whereas another attorney would have to, I don't know how they can, wade through all of this, and really become acquainted with it. That's the first thing. Secondly, when I first went to this law firm, I spoke to Mr. Rose, and he knew exactly my circumstances. He knew that there were very few assets in the marriage. He knew that I would have to borrow money from relatives to pay the thousand dollar retainer fee that they asked for. They

knew that my husband was going to represent himself, which would be a difficult situation. They also knew that he had done certain bizarre things, such as sending letters to people, and doing strange things; so, therefore, we might expect a difficult case from him. Yet, they consented to take my case. Of course, I don't think any attorney can guess, when he consents to represent somebody, what might occur. I imagine some cases go to trial immediately things get resolved, and my case is probably the other extreme, where everything possible has happened. I think it's unfortunate, and I think they've done a very fine job of representing me. I feel they should continue.

Judge Cariddi in the Chancery Division agreed with plaintiff and denied the application of the Rose firm, but set the case down for trial within the month. The Rose firm appealed. . . .

When a firm accepts a retainer to conduct a legal proceeding, it impliedly agrees to prosecute the matter to a conclusion. The firm is not at liberty to abandon the case without justifiable or reasonable cause, or the consent of its client. We are firmly convinced that the Rose firm did not have cause to abandon plaintiff's case, and that the trial judge properly exercised his discretion when he denied the firm's application and scheduled an early trial date. It was to plaintiff's and the firm's advantage that the matter be heard and disposed of as expeditiously as possible. With trial imminent, it would be extremely difficult for plaintiff to obtain other representation, and therefore she clearly would be prejudiced by the Rose firm's withdrawal.

Since the Rose firm undertook to represent plaintiff and demanded and was paid a retainer of $2,000, they should continue to represent plaintiff through the completion of trial. The firm should not be relieved at this stage of the litigation merely because plaintiff is unable to pay to them all of the fees they have demanded. . . . We are not unmindful of the fact that the Rose firm has performed substantial legal services for plaintiff and clearly is entitled to reasonable compensation therefor. Nevertheless, an attorney has certain obligations and duties to a client once representation is undertaken. These obligations do not evaporate because the case becomes more complicated or the work more arduous or the retainer not as profitable as first contemplated or imagined. . . . Attorneys must never lose sight of the fact that "the profession is a branch of the administration of justice and not a mere money-getting trade." As Canon 44 of the Canons of Professional Ethics so appropriately states: "The lawyer should not throw up the unfinished task to the detriment of his client except for reasons of honor or self-respect." Adherence to these strictures in no way violates the constitutional rights of the members of the firm.

NOTES

1. You are the managing partner in the Rose firm. How would you avoid the *Kriegsman* situation in the future? Would Model Rule 1.2(c) help you here? *See* Comments [6] and [7] to Model Rule 1.2.

2. The problem presented by the *Kriegsman* case can create a conundrum for lawyers who undertake work pursuant to a fee arrangement in which the client will pay over time. If the client does not meet the fee obligation in a timely fashion, can the lawyer seek to withdraw? What factors are likely to affect the court's decision whether to permit the lawyer to withdraw? How might that affect the fee schedule you offer your client, or your decision about how quickly to seek permission to withdraw if the client is not able to meet the fee commitments?

3. May a lawyer withdraw if the expenses of litigating the matter have become unreasonable? In February 1984, Attorney agreed to represent Plaintiff, the estate of Rossi, in a lawsuit against cigarette manufacturers. Plaintiff claimed that the defendants' products caused Rossi's untimely death from lung cancer. In November 1992, Attorney sought to withdraw from Plaintiff's case, claiming that he had incurred significant expenses in preparing for trial and that, even if Plaintiff prevailed, recovery would be unlikely to exceed the costs Attorney had already advanced. Under Attorney's agreement with Plaintiff, Attorney would advance the expenses of litigation and would be reimbursed by Plaintiff only if Plaintiff obtained a recovery in the case. Should Attorney be permitted to withdraw? *See Haines v. Liggett Group, Inc.*, 814 F.Supp. 414 (D.N.J. 1993).

4. What are the consequences of withdrawing without court permission? Consider the following case:

ALLISON v. STATE

436 So.2d 792 (Miss. 1983)

The world is much with today's lawyer. His overhead is ever soaring. Litigation is becoming increasingly complex. These developments juxtaposed against the need to provide adequately for one's self and one's family have placed his traditional role in a great tension. Uncooperative and unattractive clients are viewed by some as no more than necessary evils. The romance has gone out of the practice of law.

Still, there are obligations a lawyer may not shirk no matter how inconvenient he may find them. As much as ever, today's lawyer shoulders dual and sometimes conflicting responsibilities of fidelity and service to his clients and to the court. Lawyers differ on the ever present controversy which of these has priority over the other. One thing is certain: both outrank the lawyer's personal whim or convenience.

We are confronted here with a lawyer who has without apology defaulted in his obligation to this Court. His explanation, if it may be called such: an uncooperative client, a steadfast determination not to work without fee, and personal inconvenience. Our Rule 40 provides that

> An attorney who perfects an appeal to this Court on behalf of the appellant shall continue to prosecute the appeal by filing an assignment of errors and brief when due, unless the Court permits such attorney to withdraw from the case.

Cullen C. Taylor, attorney at law, of Brandon, Mississippi, perfected an appeal on behalf of Lenzie Allison. Mr. Taylor entered his appearance in this Court for all purposes. He then proceeded to do nothing. Without filing a motion for leave to withdraw, a by your leave or whatever, Mr. Taylor has defaulted in his obligations under Rule 40. He is in contempt of this Court.

In May of 1982 Lenzie Allison was put to trial in the Circuit Court of Rankin County, Mississippi, on a charge of manslaughter. Prior thereto Taylor had been engaged to serve as defense counsel. Taylor did in fact represent Allison at his trial which resulted in a manslaughter conviction on May 20, 1982. Allison was given a 20 year sentence.

Thereafter, Taylor, acting as counsel for Allison, took the necessary steps to perfect an appeal to this Court. By virtue thereof, Taylor assumed the duty under Rule 40 to prosecute the appeal. We emphasize that this was not merely a duty to his client, Allison, but equally and independently a duty Taylor owed to this Court.

From the papers Taylor has filed with this Court we accept as true Taylor's version of what happened thereafter. Taylor advised Allison that he was perfecting the appeal in order to assure that this right was not lost to Allison. Before he would actually prosecute the appeal, however, an acceptable fee arrangement would have to be made.

In due course, Taylor advised Allison that his fee for handling the appeal would be $3,000. Allison did not respond. On November 18, 1982, Taylor wrote Allison and advised him that the transcript had been prepared. He reiterated that his fee would be $3,000. He told Allison that, if he wished to employ another lawyer, he (Taylor) would be happy to turn over his file to the new attorney. Taylor emphasized to Allison that he needed to act immediately.

Again, on December 1, 1982, Taylor wrote to Allison emphasizing that it was imperative that Allison employ someone to prosecute the appeal.

It may be fairly said that Taylor discharged his duties to his client, Lenzie Allison. Without charge and because the time was short, he perfected the appeal. He arranged for the preparation of the transcript and the trial record. He advised Allison what his fee would be for handling the appeal and assured Allison that he was free to select other counsel if he so desired. Taylor has wholly defaulted, however, in his obligations to this Court.

Our Rule 40 was originally adopted on October 21, 1968. It was amended on July 28, 1975 and has been in its present form since that time. Without equivocation, it requires that an attorney who perfects an appeal *shall continue to prosecute the appeal* unless permitted by the Court to withdraw from the case.[1] The rule then provides that:

---

1. Of considerable importance also is Disciplinary Rule 2–110[A] [1] of the Code of Professional Responsibility of the Mississippi State Bar. D.R. 2–110[A][1] provides

> If an attorney desires to withdraw from a case, he may file a motion giving his reasons for desiring to withdraw and requesting approval of this Court.

Taylor was certainly within his prerogatives in advising Allison that an acceptable fee arrangement would have to be reached regarding the appeal. When it became apparent that no such agreement was possible, Rule 40 made clear to Taylor what he ought to do. Had he filed a motion for leave to withdraw setting forth the facts and circumstances Taylor now presents to us, the Court most likely would have allowed withdrawal.

We reiterate that the appeal was perfected on or about May 28, 1982. One year later, Taylor had done nothing further. On June 1, 1983, this Court entered the following order:

> Cullen C. Taylor, Esq. is hereby ordered within thirty days of the date hereof to show cause, if any he can, why he should not be held in contempt of Court for failure to prosecute the appeal of Lenzie Allison, a/k/a Lindsey Allison to its final disposition or seek relief from this Court from his obligation so to do, and to that end, the said Cullen C. Taylor shall, within thirty days of this date, make such written response as may be appropriate under the circumstances.

Taylor filed his response on June 30, 1983. What is remarkable about this response is that it contains no acknowledgment whatsoever of Taylor's obligations under Rule 40. No excuse whatsoever is offered why Taylor failed to file a Motion for Leave to Withdraw. Taylor does explain that Allison would not pay the $3,000 fee quoted. What Taylor fails to acknowledge, however, is that it is for the Court to determine whether this is a valid reason for allowing him to drop the case. This is not a decision Taylor was entitled to make unilaterally.

Taylor has failed to discharge his obligations to this Court under Rule 40. He has specifically and willfully failed to file an Assignment of Errors and Brief within the time required by the rules of this Court. He has failed to offer any excuse, acceptable or otherwise, for such failure. We hold that Cullen C. Taylor, attorney at law, of Brandon, Mississippi, is in contempt of this Court.

> Rule 40 provides that upon such a finding of contempt the attorney involved shall be
>
> subject to punishment by (1) censure, (2) fine (3) suspension from practice in this Court, depending upon the degree of neglect as determined by this Court.

Under the circumstances of this case, the Court assesses a fine of $100.00. Taylor is ordered and directed within ten days of this date to pay such sum of $100.00 to the clerk of this Court.

Several points bear emphasis.

"If permission for withdrawal from employment is required by the rules of a Tribunal, a lawyer shall not withdraw from employment in a proceeding before that Tribunal without its permission."

First, nothing said here should deter attorneys from doing what Taylor did back in May of 1982. Because the time was short, he acted properly in taking the necessary steps to perfect Allison's appeal to this Court. Nothing said here should give any attorney grounds for believing that, if he takes these procedural steps on behalf of his client, he will then be trapped into handling the entire appeal without fee. When good cause exists for allowing an attorney to withdraw from representation of a client before this Court, upon proper motion, such withdrawal will be allowed.[2] To be sure, in many circumstances the failure of the client to pay a reasonable fee may be a good and valid reason for withdrawal.

Second, when an individual accepts a license to practice law and becomes a member of the bar of this state and of this Court, he assumes many obligations. At least two of these have priority over his certainly legitimate prerogative to charge a legitimate fee for his services. Along with his fellow members of the bar, each lawyer assumes a duty to assume that every person in substantial need of legal service receives that service without regard to ability to pay. Beyond that, each lawyer, in conjunction with his fellow members of the bar, assumes an obligation as an officer of the Court to assure that, before this Court makes the life shattering decisions tendered to it, it has the benefit of competent advocacy on behalf of both sides.

What we say here is a simple reiteration of the values and traditions of the legal profession. These premises are articulated in the ethical considerations underlying the canons in the Code of Professional Responsibility by which all lawyers are bound. There is no doubt that parts of that code relegate to third and fourth priority a consideration of the economics of the practice of law. This is merely a part of the *quid pro quo* the lawyer must be prepared to give when he accepts his license to practice law.

Yes, the world is much with today's lawyer. But so are the ideals and traditions of professional responsibility within the Bar, and so are the Ethical Considerations underlying our Code of Professional Responsibility, with all of which we find the lawyer's obligation under Rule 40 of the rules of this Court to be wholly consistent.

CULLEN C. TAYLOR IS FOUND GUILTY OF CONTEMPT OF THIS COURT AND IS FINED THE SUM OF ONE HUNDRED DOLLARS TO BE PAID IN TEN DAYS SUBJECT TO CONDITIONS STATED HEREINABOVE.

NOTES

1. Taylor was cited for contempt of court. Does that matter? The fine here was relatively modest. Do you think the court has created a significant disincentive for lawyers in Taylor's situation to act as he did? Why or why not?

---

2. Withdrawal will not be automatically allowed. Such factors as the timing of the motion to withdraw, possible prejudice to the adverse party, the court's and the public's interest in the prompt disposition of the matter, and the like, will be relevant considerations. On the other hand, a timely motion to withdraw made for bona fide reasons will normally be looked upon with favor.

2. The court suggested that Taylor acted appropriately in seeking to protect his client's interest and perfect his appeal and indicated that, had he sought to withdraw properly, the request would have been granted. Are you confident of that? If Taylor asked you how he should proceed with his next similarly situated client, what would your recommendation be?

2. FEES ON TERMINATION

As we've seen, the attorney-client relationship can end because the lawyer terminates it, or because the client terminates it. The importance of the client's control over his or her participation in the relationship is reflected in Model Rule 1.16(a)(3), requiring the lawyer to withdraw from representation if the client discharges the lawyer. (This is, of course, subject to the constraint of court permission in a litigated matter, as discussed in the previous section.)

The fact that the client has the unvarnished right to discharge the lawyer does not mean that such a discharge is without consequences. One area where this is a concern is the lawyer's fees. When the relationship is terminated, what happens with regard to fees? That can be a complex question, and one that turns in part on who terminated the arrangement and why. It can be particularly significant, however, when lawyers work on a contingent fee basis, under which the fee is premised on the occurrence of a contingency, typically a positive outcome for the client, and the lawyer is discharged before the work is completed. What fee, if any, should the lawyer receive? One could imagine several possible rules: that the lawyer remains entitled to the entire contingent fee upon the occurrence of the contingency; that the lawyer is entitled to no fee at all; or that the lawyer is entitled to recover in quantum meruit if the client ultimately receives a recovery. What incentives does each rule create? The contemporary rule is set out in the following case.

ROSENBERG v. LEVIN

409 So.2d 1016 (Fla. 1982)

Overton, Justice.

The issue to be decided concerns the proper basis for compensating an attorney discharged without cause by his client after he has performed substantial legal services under a valid contract of employment. . . .

We hold that a lawyer discharged without cause is entitled to the reasonable value of his services on the basis of quantum meruit, but recovery is limited to the maximum fee set in the contract entered into for those services. We have concluded that without this limitation, the client would be penalized for the discharge and the lawyer would receive more than he bargained for in his initial contract. In the instant case, we reject the contention of the respondent lawyer that he is entitled to $55,000 as the reasonable value of his services when his contract fee was $10,000. . . .

The facts of this case reflect the following. Levin hired Rosenberg and Pomerantz to perform legal services pursuant to a letter agreement which provided for a $10,000 fixed fee, plus a contingent fee equal to fifty percent of all amounts recovered in excess of $600,000. Levin later discharged Rosenberg and Pomerantz without cause before the legal controversy was resolved and subsequently settled the matter for a net recovery of $500,000. Rosenberg and Pomerantz sued for fees based on a "quantum meruit" evaluation of their services. After lengthy testimony, the trial judge concluded that quantum meruit was indeed the appropriate basis for compensation and awarded Rosenberg and Pomerantz $55,000. The [appellate] court also agreed that quantum meruit was the appropriate basis for recovery but lowered the amount awarded to $10,000, stating that recovery could in no event exceed the amount which the attorneys would have received under their contract if not prematurely discharged.

The issue submitted to us for resolution is whether the terms of an attorney employment contract limit the attorney's quantum meruit recovery to the fee set out in the contract. This issue requires, however, that we answer the broader underlying question of whether in Florida quantum meruit is an appropriate basis for compensation of attorneys discharged by their clients without cause where there is a specific employment contract. The Florida cases which have previously addressed this issue have resulted in confusion and conflicting views.

[The court set out prior Florida caselaw on the subject.]

There are two conflicting interests involved in the determination of the issue presented in this type of attorney-client dispute. The first is the need of the client to have confidence in the integrity and ability of his attorney and, therefore, the need for the client to have the ability to discharge his attorney when he loses that necessary confidence in the attorney. The second is the attorney's right to adequate compensation for work performed. To address these conflicting interests, we must consider three distinct rules.

Contract Rule

The traditional contract rule adopted by a number of jurisdictions holds that an attorney discharged without cause may recover damages for breach of contract under traditional contract principles. The measure of damages is usually the full contract price, although some courts deduct a fair allowance for services and expenses not expended by the discharged attorney in performing the balance of the contract. Some jurisdictions following the contract rule also permit an alternative recovery based on quantum meruit so that an attorney can elect between recovery based on the contract or the reasonable value of the performed services.

Support for the traditional contract theory is based on: (1) the full contract price is arguably the most rational measure of damages since it reflects the value that the parties placed on the services; (2) charging the full fee prevents the client from profiting from his own breach of contract;

and (3) the contract rule is said to avoid the difficult problem of setting a value on an attorney's partially completed legal work.

Quantum Meruit Rule

To avoid restricting a client's freedom to discharge his attorney, a number of jurisdictions in recent years have held that an attorney discharged without cause can recover only the reasonable value [of] services rendered prior to discharge. This rule was first announced in *Martin v. Camp*, 114 N.E. 46 (N.Y. 1916), where the New York Court of Appeals held that a discharged attorney could not sue his client for damages for breach of contract unless the attorney had completed performance of the contract. The New York court established quantum meruit recovery for the attorney on the theory that the client does not breach the contract by discharging the attorney. Rather, the court reasoned, there is an implied condition in every attorney-client contract that the client may discharge the attorney at any time with or without cause. With this right as part of the contract, traditional contract principles are applied to allow quantum meruit recovery on the basis of services performed to date. Under the New York rule, the attorney's cause of action accrues immediately upon his discharge by the client, under the reasoning that it is unfair to make the attorney's right to compensation dependent on the performance of a successor over whom he has no control.

The California Supreme Court, in *Fracasse v. Brent*, 494 P.2d 9 (Cal. 1972), also adopted a quantum meruit rule. That court carefully analyzed those factors which distinguish the attorney-client relationship from other employment situations and concluded that a discharged attorney should be limited to a quantum meruit recovery in order to strike a proper balance between the client's right to discharge his attorney without undue restriction and the attorney's right to fair compensation for work performed. The *Fracasse* court sought both to provide clients greater freedom in substituting counsel and to promote confidence in the legal profession while protecting society's interest in the attorney-client relationship.

Contrary to the New York rule, however, the California court also held that an attorney's cause of action for quantum meruit does not accrue until the happening of the contingency, that is, the client's recovery. If no recovery is forthcoming, the attorney is denied compensation. The California court offered two reasons in support of its position. First, the result obtained and the amount involved, two important factors in determining the reasonableness of a fee, cannot be ascertained until the occurrence of the contingency. Second, the client may be of limited means and it would be unduly burdensome to force him to pay a fee if there was no recovery. The court stated that: "(S)ince the attorney agreed initially to take his chances on recovering any fee whatever, we believe that the fact that the success of the litigation is no longer under his control is insufficient to justify imposing a new and more onerous burden on the client."

Quantum Meruit Rule Limited By The Contract Price

The third rule is an extension of the second that limits quantum meruit recovery to the maximum fee set in the contract. This limitation is believed necessary to provide client freedom to substitute attorneys without economic penalty. Without such a limitation, a client's right to discharge an attorney may be illusory and the client may in effect be penalized for exercising a right.

The Tennessee Court of Appeals, in *Chambliss, Bahner & Crawford v. Luther*, 531 S.W.2d 108 (Tenn.Ct.App.1975), expressed the need for limitation on quantum meruit recovery, stating: "It would seem to us that the better rule is that because a client has the unqualified right to discharge his attorney, fees in such cases should be limited to the value of the services rendered or the contract price, whichever is less." In rejecting the argument that quantum meruit should be the basis for the recovery even though it exceeds the contract fee, that court said:

> To adopt the rule advanced by Plaintiff would, in our view, encourage attorneys less keenly aware of their professional responsibilities than Attorney Chambliss ... to induce clients to lose confidence in them in cases where the reasonable value of their services has exceeded the original fee and thereby, upon being discharged, reap a greater benefit than that for which they had bargained.

531 S.W.2d at 113. Other authorities also support this position.

We have carefully considered all the matters presented, both on the original argument on the merits and on rehearing. It is our opinion that it is in the best interest of clients and the legal profession as a whole that we adopt the modified quantum meruit rule which limits recovery to the maximum amount of the contract fee in all premature discharge cases involving both fixed and contingency employment contracts. The attorney-client relationship is one of special trust and confidence. The client must rely entirely on the good faith efforts of the attorney in representing his interests. This reliance requires that the client have complete confidence in the integrity and ability of the attorney and that absolute fairness and candor characterize all dealings between them. These considerations dictate that clients be given greater freedom to change legal representatives than might be tolerated in other employment relationships. We approve the philosophy that there is an overriding need to allow clients freedom to substitute attorneys without economic penalty as a means of accomplishing the broad objective of fostering public confidence in the legal profession. Failure to limit quantum meruit recovery defeats the policy against penalizing the client for exercising his right to discharge. However, attorneys should not be penalized either and should have the opportunity to recover for services performed.

Accordingly, we hold that an attorney employed under a valid contract who is discharged without cause before the contingency has occurred or before the client's matters have concluded can recover only the reasonable value of his services rendered prior to discharge, limited by the maximum contract fee. We reject both the traditional contract rule and the quantum meruit rule that allow recovery in excess of the maximum contract price because both have a chilling effect on the client's power to discharge an attorney. Under the contract rule in a contingent fee situation, both the discharged attorney and the second attorney may receive a substantial percentage of the client's final recovery. Under the unlimited quantum meruit rule, it is possible, as the instant case illustrates, for the attorney to receive a fee greater than he bargained for under the terms of his contract. Both these results are unacceptable to us.

We further follow the California view that in contingency fee cases, the cause of action for quantum meruit arises only upon the successful occurrence of the contingency. If the client fails in his recovery, the discharged attorney will similarly fail and recover nothing. We recognize that deferring the commencement of a cause of action until the occurrence of the contingency is a view not uniformly accepted. Deferral, however, supports our goal to preserve the client's freedom to discharge, and any resulting harm to the attorney is minimal because the attorney would not have benefited earlier until the contingency's occurrence. There should, of course, be a presumption of regularity and competence in the performance of the services by a successor attorney.

In computing the reasonable value of the discharged attorney's services, the trial court can consider the totality of the circumstances surrounding the professional relationship between the attorney and client. Factors such as time, the recovery sought, the skill demanded, the results obtained, and the attorney-client contract itself will necessarily be relevant considerations.

We conclude that this approach creates the best balance between the desirable right of the client to discharge his attorney and the right of an attorney to reasonable compensation for his services.... We find the district court of appeal was correct in limiting the quantum meruit award to the contract price, and its decision is approved.

NOTES

1. To what fee would the attorneys have been entitled under the original contract? What fee did they claim after their discharge? Does the court's resolution of the issue sensibly accommodate the competing concerns here?

2. In *Rosenberg*, the discharge of the lawyers by the client was without good cause. What if the client discharges the lawyer because he is not doing a good job?

3. What if the lawyer quits because the case has become too expensive to handle? In *Bell & Marra v. Sullivan*, 6 P.3d 965 (Mont. 2000), Sullivan retained Bell & Marra to represent him in an employment matter. The contract provided for a 40% contingent fee, and provided that "The attorneys may withdraw at any time upon giving reasonable notice." The employment case became very complicated and costly, and Bell & Marra sought to change

the fee arrangement to a more favorable 50% contingency fee, and to require Sullivan to advance funds for the costs of the litigation. The firm told Sullivan that if he did not agree it would withdraw from the case. Sullivan accepted the firm's letter as a notice of withdrawal, and hired new counsel. Ultimately, Sullivan secured a mediated settlement of $155,000. Bell & Marra then sued to recover attorney fees from Sullivan. What result? Would it be different if Bell & Marra had a better reason for withdrawal? The court concluded that "an attorney who voluntarily withdraws from a contingency fee case without good cause forfeits recovery of compensation for services performed," but that "if the withdrawal was for good cause or was justified, then the attorney may recover based on quantum meruit." While the increased financial burden of the case made the withdrawal permissive under the Montana Rules of Professional Conduct, that did not make it "good cause" for purposes of the fee determination.

4. The conclusion in *Rosenberg* that the lawyer may only bring suit for fees on the occurrence of the contingency is not always the rule. Consider *Salmon v. Atkinson*, 137 S.W.3d 383 (Ark. 2003). Salmon consulted Atkinson and Howell about the possibility of claiming damages against the estate of Brown; she had taken care of Brown before he died. She also asked whether she might be treated as Brown's wife and heir. Lawyers and client agreed to a 50% contingent fee agreement. The attorneys did substantial investigation and research on Salmon's claim and concluded that, while Salmon was never married to Brown, she had a legitimate claim for the care she had given Brown before his death. The lawyers prepared a petition for Salmon to file in the probate case. They presented the petition to Salmon for her signature. She replied that she wanted to think about it. She took the petition with her and shortly thereafter sent a letter to the attorneys terminating their services. She then filed the petition *pro se* in the probate matter. The lawyers filed suit against Salmon, seeking recovery in quantum meruit for the work they had done on her case. Salmon argued that they could not recover, because their original contract had provided for payment of a fee only if she had a recovery, and there had not yet been any recovery in the probate matter. What result? Which approach makes more sense? Which is fairer to the client? The lawyer? Do the particular facts of this case make a difference?

3. GETTING YOUR JOB BACK: RESISTING TERMINATION

Model Rule 1.16 makes clear that if the client fires you, your representation is over. Is that always the case? Suppose that your client fires you for a reason that is wrongful, or even for a reason that is against public policy. Should you be able to get your job back? Or, more accurately in most situations, should you be able to claim damages because of the discharge? Below are two cases in which courts dealt with these situations very differently. Is there a good reason for these distinct outcomes?

BALLA v. GAMBRO, INC.

584 N.E.2d 104 (Ill. 1991)

JUSTICE CLARK delivered the opinion of the court:

The issue in this case is whether in-house counsel should be allowed the remedy of an action for retaliatory discharge.

Appellee, Roger Balla, formerly in-house counsel for Gambro, Inc. (Gambro), filed a retaliatory discharge action against Gambro.... Appellee alleged that he was fired in contravention of Illinois public policy and sought damages for the discharge. The trial court dismissed the action on appellants' motion for summary judgment. The appellate court reversed. We granted appellant's petition for leave to appeal and allowed *amicus curiae* briefs from the American Corporate Counsel Association and Illinois State Bar Association.

Gambro is a distributor of kidney dialysis equipment manufactured by Gambro Germany. Among the products distributed by Gambro are dialyzers which filter excess fluid and toxic substances from the blood of patients with no or impaired kidney function. The manufacture and sale of dialyzers is regulated by the United States Food and Drug Administration (FDA)....

Appellee, Roger J. Balla, is and was at all times throughout this controversy an attorney licensed to practice law in the State of Illinois. On March 17, 1980, appellee executed an employment agreement with Gambro which contained the terms of appellee's employment. Generally, the employment agreement provided that appellee would "be responsible for all legal matters within the company and for personnel within the company's sales office." Appellee held the title of director of administration at Gambro. As director of administration, appellee's specific responsibilities included, *inter alia*: advising, counseling and representing management on legal matters; establishing and administering personnel policies; coordinating and overseeing corporate activities to assure compliance with applicable laws and regulations, and preventing or minimizing legal or administrative proceedings; and coordinating the activities of the manager of regulatory affairs. Regarding this last responsibility, under Gambro's corporate hierarchy, appellee supervised the manager of regulatory affairs, and the manager reported directly to appellee.

In August 1983, the manager of regulatory affairs for Gambro left the company and appellee assumed the manager's specific duties. Although appellee's original employment agreement was not modified to reflect his new position, his annual compensation was increased and Gambro's corporate organizational chart referred to appellee's positions as "Dir. of Admin./Personnel; General Counsel; Mgr. of Regulatory Affairs." The job description for the position described the manager as an individual "responsible for ensuring awareness of and compliance with federal, state and local laws and regulations affecting the company's operations and products." Requirements for the position were a bachelor of science degree and three to five years in the medical device field plus two years experience in the area of government regulations. The individual in the position prior to appellee was not an attorney.

In July 1985 Gambro Germany informed Gambro in a letter that certain dialyzers it had manufactured, the clearances of which varied from the package insert, were about to be shipped to Gambro. Referring to these dialyzers, Gambro Germany advised Gambro:

> For acute patients risk is that the acute uremic situation will not be improved in spite of the treatment, giving continuous high levels of potassium, phosphate and urea/creatine. The chronic patient may note the effect as a slow progression of the uremic situation and depending on the interval between medical check-ups the medical risk may not be overlooked.

Appellee told the president of Gambro to reject the shipment because the dialyzers did not comply with FDA regulations. The president notified Gambro Germany of its decision to reject the shipment on July 12, 1985.

However, one week later the president informed Gambro Germany that Gambro would accept the dialyzers and "sell [them] to a unit that is not currently our customer but who buys only on price." Appellee contends that he was not informed by the president of the decision to accept the dialyzers but became aware of it through other Gambro employees. Appellee maintains that he spoke with the president in August regarding the company's decision to accept the dialyzers and told the president that he would do whatever necessary to stop the sale of the dialyzers.

On September 4, 1985, appellee was discharged from Gambro's employment by its president. The following day, appellee reported the shipment of the dialyzers to the FDA. The FDA seized the shipment and determined the product to be "adulterated within the meaning of section 501(h) of the [Federal Act]."

On March 19, 1986, appellee filed a four-count complaint in tort for retaliatory discharge seeking $22 million in damages....

On July 28, 1987, Gambro filed a motion for summary judgment. Gambro argued that appellee, as an attorney, was precluded from filing a retaliatory discharge action in light of the appellate court opinion in *Herbster v. North American Co. for Life & Health Insurance*, 501 N.E.2d 343 (Ill. 1986). Appellee argued that while the *Herbster* opinion declined to extend the tort of retaliatory discharge to the plaintiff/attorney before the court, the opinion did not foreclose the possibility of extending the tort in the future. Appellee argued that the plaintiff in *Herbster* was in-house counsel for a corporation whose duties were restricted to legal matters, whereas he served as the director of administration and personnel and manager of regulatory affairs as well as general counsel for Gambro. Appellee argued that a question of fact existed as to whether he was discharged for the performance of a purely legal function.

On November 30, 1988, the trial court granted appellants' motion for summary judgment. In its opinion, the trial court specifically stated that "the very ground [appellee is] claiming as the basis for retaliatory discharge all [*sic*] involves the decisions which he made applying law to fact to determine whether these things complied with the federal regulations, and that is clearly legal work." Thus, the trial court concluded that the duties appellee was performing which led to his discharge were "conduct clearly within the attorney-client relationship" and that Gambro had the "absolute right" to discharge its attorney. On appeal, the court below held that an attorney is not barred as a matter of law from bringing an action for retaliatory discharge.... [The intermediate appellate court had remanded the case for further findings of fact.]

We agree with the trial court that appellee does not have a cause of action against Gambro for retaliatory discharge under the facts of the case at bar. Generally, this court adheres to the proposition that " 'an employer may discharge an employee-at-will for any reason or for no reason [at all].' " However, in *Kelsay v. Motorola, Inc.*, 384 N.E.2d 353 (Ill. 1978), this court first recognized the limited and narrow tort of retaliatory discharge. In *Kelsay,* an at-will employee was fired for filing a worker's compensation claim against her employer. After examining the history and purpose behind the Workers' Compensation Act to determine the public policy behind its enactment, this court held that the employee should have a cause of action for retaliatory discharge. This court stressed that if employers could fire employees for filing workers' compensation claims, the public policy behind the enactment of the Workers' Compensation Act would be frustrated.

Subsequently, in *Palmateer v. International Harvester Co.*, 421 N.E.2d 876 (Ill. 1981), this court again examined the tort of retaliatory discharge. In *Palmateer,* an employee was discharged for informing the police of suspected criminal activities of a co-employee, and because he agreed to provide assistance in any investigation and trial of the matter. Based on the public policy favoring the investigation and prosecution of crime, this court held that the employee had a cause of action for retaliatory discharge. Further, we stated:

> All that is required [to bring a cause of action for retaliatory discharge] is that the employer discharge the employee in retaliation for the employee's activities, and that the discharge be in contravention of a clearly mandated public policy.

In this case it appears that Gambro discharged appellee, an employee of Gambro, in retaliation for his activities, and this discharge was in contravention of a clearly mandated public policy. Appellee allegedly told the president of Gambro that he would do whatever was necessary to stop the sale of the "misbranded and/or adulterated" dialyzers. In appellee's eyes, the use of these dialyzers could cause death or serious bodily harm to patients. As we have stated before, "[t]here is no public policy more important or more fundamental than the one favoring the effective protection of the lives and property of citizens." However, in this case, appellee was not just an employee of Gambro, but also general counsel for Gambro.

As noted earlier, in *Herbster*, our appellate court held that the plaintiff, an employee and chief legal counsel for the defendant company, did not have a claim for retaliatory discharge against the company due to the presence of the attorney-client relationship. Under the facts of that case, the defendant company allegedly requested the plaintiff to destroy or remove discovery information which had been requested in lawsuits pending against the company. The plaintiff refused arguing that such conduct would constitute fraud and violate several provisions of the Illinois Code of Professional Responsibility. Subsequently, the defendant company discharged the plaintiff.

The appellate court refused to extend the tort of retaliatory discharge to the plaintiff in *Herbster* primarily because of the special relationship between an attorney and client. The court stated:

> The mutual trust, exchanges of confidence, reliance on judgment, and personal nature of the attorney-client relationship demonstrate the unique position attorneys occupy in our society.

The appellate court recited a list of factors which make the attorney-client relationship special such as: the attorney-client privilege regarding confidential communications, the fiduciary duty an attorney owes to a client, the right of the client to terminate the relationship with or without cause, and the fact that a client has exclusive control over the subject matter of the litigation and a client may dismiss or settle a cause of action regardless of the attorney's advice. Thus, in *Herbster,* since the plaintiff's duties pertained strictly to legal matters, the appellate court determined that the plaintiff did not have a claim for retaliatory discharge.

We agree with the conclusion reached in *Herbster* that, generally, in-house counsel do not have a claim under the tort of retaliatory discharge.... [W]e caution that our holding is confined by the fact that appellee is and was at all times throughout this controversy an attorney licensed to practice law in the State of Illinois. Appellee is and was subject to the Illinois Code of Professional Responsibility adopted by this court. The tort of retaliatory discharge is a limited and narrow exception to the general rule of at-will employment. The tort seeks to achieve " 'a proper balance . . . among the employer's interest in operating a business efficiently and profitably, the employee's interest in earning a livelihood, and society's interest in seeing its public policies carried out.' " Further, as stated in *Palmateer*, "[t]he foundation of the tort of retaliatory discharge lies in the protection of public policy." (Emphasis added.)

In this case, the public policy to be protected, that of protecting the lives and property of citizens, is adequately safeguarded without extending the tort of retaliatory discharge to in-house counsel. Appellee was required under the Rules of Professional Conduct to report Gambro's intention to sell the "misbranded and/or adulterated" dialyzers. Rule 1.6(b) of the Rules of Professional Conduct reads:

> A lawyer *shall* reveal information about a client to the extent it appears necessary to prevent the client from committing an act that would result in death or serious bodily injury.

Appellee alleges, and the FDA's seizure of the dialyzers indicates, that the use of the dialyzers would cause death or serious bodily injury. Thus, under the above-cited rule, appellee was under the mandate of this court to report the sale of these dialyzers.

In his brief to this court, appellee argues that not extending the tort of retaliatory discharge to in-house counsel would present attorneys with a "Hobson's choice." According to appellee, in-house counsel would face two alternatives: either comply with the client/employer's wishes and risk both the loss of a professional license and exposure to criminal sanctions, or decline to comply with client/employer's wishes and risk the loss of a full-time job and the attendant benefits. We disagree. Unlike the employees in *Kelsay* which this court recognized would be left with the difficult decision of choosing between whether to file a workers' compensation claim and risk being fired, or retaining their jobs and losing their right to a remedy, in-house counsel plainly are not confronted with such a dilemma. In-house counsel do not have a choice of whether to follow their ethical obligations as attorneys licensed to practice law, or follow the illegal and unethical demands of their clients. In-house counsel must abide by the Rules of Professional Conduct. Appellee had no choice but to report to the FDA Gambro's intention to sell or distribute these dialyzers, and consequently protect the aforementioned public policy.

In addition, we believe that extending the tort of retaliatory discharge to in-house counsel would have an undesirable effect on the attorney-client relationship that exists between these employers and their in-house counsel. Generally, a client may discharge his attorney at any time, with or without cause. This rule applies equally to in-house counsel as it does to outside counsel. Further, this rule "recognizes that the relationship between an attorney and client is based on trust and that the client must have confidence in his attorney in order to ensure that the relationship will function properly." As stated in *Herbster,* "the attorney is placed in the unique position of maintaining a close relationship with a client where the attorney receives secrets, disclosures, and information that otherwise would not be divulged to intimate friends." We believe that if in-house counsel are granted the right to sue their employers for retaliatory discharge, employers might be less willing to be forthright and candid with their in-house counsel. Employers might be hesitant to turn to their in-house counsel for advice regarding potentially questionable corporate conduct knowing that their in-house counsel could use this information in a retaliatory discharge suit.

We recognize that under the Illinois Rules of Professional Conduct, attorneys shall reveal client confidences or secrets in certain situations, and thus one might expect employers/clients to be naturally hesitant to rely on in-house counsel for advice regarding this potentially questionable conduct. However, the danger exists that if in-house counsel are granted a right to sue their employers in tort for retaliatory discharge, employers might further limit their communication with their in-house counsel. . . .

If extending the tort of retaliatory discharge might have a chilling effect on the communications between the employer/client and the in-house counsel, we believe that it is more wise to refrain from doing so.

Our decision not to extend the tort of retaliatory discharge to in-house counsel also is based on other ethical considerations. Under the Rules of Professional Conduct, appellee was required to withdraw from representing Gambro if continued representation would result in the violation of the Rules of Professional Conduct by which appellee was bound, or if Gambro discharged the appellee. In this case, Gambro did discharge appellee, and according to appellee's claims herein, his continued representation of Gambro would have resulted in a violation of the Rules of Professional Conduct. Appellee argues that such a choice of withdrawal is "simplistic and uncompassionate, and is completely at odds with contemporary realities facing in-house attorneys." These contemporary realities apparently are the economic ramifications of losing his position as in-house counsel. However difficult economically and perhaps emotionally it is for in-house counsel to discontinue representing an employer/client, we refuse to allow in-house counsel to sue their employer/client for damages because they obeyed their ethical obligations. In this case, appellee, in addition to being an employee at Gambro, is first and foremost an attorney bound by the Rules of Professional Conduct. . . . An attorney's obligation to follow these Rules of Professional Conduct should not be the foundation for a claim of retaliatory discharge.

We also believe that it would be inappropriate for the employer/client to bear the economic costs and burdens of their in-house counsel's adhering to their ethical obligations under the Rules of Professional Conduct. Presumably, in situations where an in-house counsel obeys his or her ethical obligations and reveals certain information regarding the employer/client, the attorney-client relationship will be irreversibly strained and the client will more than likely discharge its in-house counsel. In this scenario, if we were to grant the in-house counsel the right to sue the client for retaliatory discharge, we would be shifting the burden and costs of obeying the Rules of Professional Conduct from the attorney to the employer/client. The employer/client would be forced to pay damages to its former in-house counsel to essentially mitigate the financial harm the attorney suffered for having to abide by Rules of Professional Conduct. This, we believe, is impermissible for all attorneys know or should know that at certain times in their professional career, they will have to forgo economic gains in order to protect the integrity of the legal profession.

Our review of cases from other jurisdictions dealing with this issue does not persuade us to hold otherwise. . . .

[The court then considered and rejected Balla's argument that he should be treated differently because he acted not in his role as general counsel, but in his distinct role as the manager of regulatory affairs.]

JUSTICE FREEMAN, dissenting:

I respectfully dissent from the decision of my colleagues. In concluding that the plaintiff attorney, serving as corporate in-house counsel, should not be allowed a claim for retaliatory discharge, the majority first reasons that the public policy implicated in this case, *i.e.*, protecting the lives and property of Illinois citizens, is adequately safeguarded by the lawyer's ethical obligation to reveal information about a client as necessary to prevent acts that would result in death or serious bodily harm. I find this reasoning fatally flawed.

The majority so reasons because, as a matter of law, an attorney cannot even contemplate ignoring his ethical obligations in favor of continuing in his employment. I agree with this conclusion "as a matter of law." However, to say that the categorical nature of ethical obligations is sufficient to ensure that the ethical obligations will be satisfied simply ignores reality. Specifically, it ignores that, as unfortunate for society as it may be, attorneys are no less human than nonattorneys and, thus, no less given to the temptation to either ignore or rationalize away their ethical obligations when complying therewith may render them unable to feed and support their families.

I would like to believe, as my colleagues apparently conclude, that attorneys will always "do the right thing" because the law says that they must. However, my knowledge of human nature, which is not much greater than the average layman's, and, sadly, the recent scandals involving the bench and bar of Illinois are more than sufficient to dispel such a belief. Just as the ethical obligations of the lawyers and judges involved in those scandals were inadequate to ensure that they would not break the law, I am afraid that the lawyer's ethical obligation to "blow the whistle" is likewise an inadequate safeguard for the public policy of protecting lives and property of Illinois citizens.

As reluctant as I am to concede it, the fact is that this court must take whatever steps it can, within the bounds of the law, to give lawyers incentives to abide by their ethical obligations, beyond the satisfaction inherent in their doing so. We cannot continue to delude ourselves and the people of the State of Illinois that attorneys' ethical duties, alone, are always sufficient to guarantee that lawyers will "do the right thing." In the context of this case, where doing "the right thing" will often result in termination by an employer bent on doing the "wrong thing," I believe that the incentive needed is recognition of a cause of action for retaliatory discharge, in the appropriate case.

The majority also bases its holding upon the reasoning that allowing in-house counsel a cause of action for retaliatory discharge will have a chilling effect on the attorney-client relationship and the free flow of information necessary to that relationship. This reasoning completely ignores what is very often one of the basic purposes of the attorney-client relationship, especially in the corporate client-in-house counsel setting. More importantly, it gives preeminence to the public policy favoring an unfettered right to discharge an attorney, although "[t]here is no public policy more important or more fundamental than the one favoring the effective protection of the lives and property of citizens." *Palmateer*, 421 N.E. 2d at 880.

One of the basic purposes of the attorney-client relationship, especially in the corporate client-in-house counsel setting, is for the attorney to advise the client as to, exactly, what conduct the law requires so that the client can then comply with that advice. Given that purpose, allowing in-house counsel a cause of action for retaliatory discharge would chill the attorney-client relationship and discourage a corporate client from communicating freely with the attorney only where, as here, the employer decides to go forward with particular conduct, regardless of advice that it is contrary to law. I believe that, just as in-house counsel might reasonably so assume, this court is entitled to assume that corporate clients will rarely so decide. As such, to allow a corporate employer to discharge its in-house counsel under such circumstances, without fear of any sanction, is truly to give the assistance and protection of the courts to scoundrels.

Moreover, to recognize and sanction the corporate employer's freedom (as opposed to its "right") to discharge its in-house counsel under such circumstances, by denying the in-house counsel a cause of action for retaliatory discharge, is to exalt the at-will attorney-client contractual relationship above all other considerations, including the most important and fundamental public policy of protecting the lives and property of citizens. . . .

In holding as it does, the majority also reasons that an attorney's obligation to follow the Rules of Professional Conduct should not be the basis for a claim of retaliatory discharge.

Preliminarily, I would note that were an employee's desire to obey and follow the law an insufficient basis for a retaliatory discharge claim, *Palmateer* would have been decided differently. In this regard, I do not believe any useful purpose is served by distinguishing attorneys from ordinary citizens. . . . An attorney should not be punished simply because he has ethical obligations imposed upon him over and above the general obligation to obey the law which all men have. Nor should a corporate employer be protected simply because the employee it has discharged for "blowing the whistle" happens to be an attorney.

I find the majority's reasoning that an attorney's ethical obligations should not be the basis of a retaliatory discharge claim faulty for another reason. In so concluding, the majority ignores the employer's decision to persist in the questionable conduct which its in-house counsel advised was illegal. It is that conduct, not the attorney's ethical obligations, which is the predicate of the retaliatory discharge claim. That conduct is the true predicate of the claim because it is what required the attorney to act in compliance with his ethical obligations and thereby resulted in his discharge by the employer. As such, granting the attorney a claim for retaliatory discharge simply allows recovery against the party bent on breaking the law, rather than rewarding an attorney for complying with his ethical obligations.

Additionally, I cannot share the majority's solicitude for employers who discharge in-house counsel, who comply with their ethical obligations, by agreeing that they should not bear the economic burden which that compliance imposes upon the attorney. Unlike the majority, I do not believe that it is the attorney's compliance with his ethical obligations which imposes economic burdens upon him. Rather, those burdens are imposed upon him by the employer's persistence in conduct the attorney has advised is illegal and by the employer's wrongful termination of the attorney once he advises the employer that he must comply with those obligations. . . .

In this same regard, it should be borne in mind that this case involves an attorney discharged from his employment, not one who has voluntarily resigned due to his ethical obligations. I believe the majority's reasoning, in general, and with respect to the question of who should bear the economic burdens of the attorney's loss of job, specifically, would be valid grounds for denying a cause of action to an attorney who voluntarily resigns, rather than is discharged. By focusing upon the immediate economic consequences of the discharge, the majority overlooks the very real possibility that in-house counsel who is discharged, rather than allowed to resign in accordance with his ethical obligations once the employer's persistence in illegal conduct is evident to him, will be stigmatized within the legal profession. That stigma and its apparent consequences, economic and otherwise, in addition to the immediate economic consequences of a discharge, also militate strongly in favor of allowing the attorney a claim for retaliatory discharge. . . .

Ultimately, the court's decision in the instant case does nothing to encourage respect for the law by corporate employers nor to encourage respect by attorneys for their ethical obligations. Therefore, I must respectfully dissent.

NOTES

1.   What did the Illinois Rules of Professional Conduct require with regard to the information at issue here? Compare the Illinois rule to Model Rule 1.6(b). Would the case have come out differently under the Model Rules?

2.   Consider Model Rule 1.13. What would it have directed Balla to do? Would the rule ultimately have helped his situation? Would Model Rule 1.13(e) avoid the outcome here? Why or why not?

3.   The majority and the dissent view very differently the possibility that lawyers might be tempted to ignore their obligations under the rules of professional responsibility for fear of losing their jobs. What do you think?

4. *Balla* is a minority rule; most jurisdictions permit a retaliatory discharge action by an attorney, subject to adequate protection of the client's confidential information. *See, e.g., General Dynamics Corp. v. Superior Court*, 876 P.2d 487 (Cal. 1994). Illinois, however, has stuck to its guns, reaffirming *Balla* in *Ausman v. Arthur Andersen, LLP*, 810 N.E.2d 566 (Ill. App. 2004).

WIEDER v. SKALA
609 N.E.2d 105 (N.Y. 1992)

Plaintiff, a member of the Bar, has sued his former employer, a law firm. He claims he was wrongfully discharged as an associate because of his insistence that the firm comply with the governing disciplinary rules by reporting professional misconduct allegedly committed by another associate. The question presented is whether plaintiff has stated a claim for relief either for breach of contract or for the tort of wrongful discharge in violation of this State's public policy. The lower courts have dismissed both causes of action on motion as legally insufficient ... on the strength of New York's employment-at-will doctrine. For reasons which follow, we modify the order and reinstate plaintiff's cause of action for breach of contract.

I.

In the complaint, which must be accepted as true on a dismissal motion ... plaintiff alleges that he was a commercial litigation attorney associated with defendant law firm from June 16, 1986 until March 18, 1988. In early 1987, plaintiff requested that the law firm represent him in the purchase of a condominium apartment. The firm agreed and assigned a fellow associate (L.L.) "to do 'everything that needs to be done.'" For several months, L.L. neglected plaintiff's real estate transaction and, to conceal his neglect, made several "false and fraudulent material misrepresentations." In September 1987, when plaintiff learned of L.L.'s neglect and false statements, he advised two of the firm's senior partners. They conceded that the firm was aware "that [L.L.] was a pathological liar and that [L.L.] had previously lied to [members of the firm] regarding the status of other pending legal matters." When plaintiff confronted L.L., he acknowledged that he had lied about the real estate transaction and later admitted in writing that he had committed "several acts of legal malpractice and fraud and deceit upon plaintiff and several other clients of the firm."

The complaint further alleges that, after plaintiff asked the firm partners to report L.L.'s misconduct to the Appellate Division Disciplinary Committee as required under DR 1–103(A) of the Code of Professional Responsibility,[1] they declined to act. Later, in an effort to dissuade plaintiff from making the report himself, the partners told him that they would reim-

---

1. DR 1–103(A) provides: "A lawyer possessing knowledge, not protected as a confidence or secret, of a violation of DR 1–103 that raises a substantial question as to another lawyer's honesty, trustworthiness or fitness in other respects as a lawyer shall report such knowledge to a tribunal or other authority empowered to investigate or act upon such violation."

burse his losses. Plaintiff nonetheless met with the Committee "to discuss the entire matter." He withdrew his complaint, however, "because the [f]irm had indicated that it would fire plaintiff if he reported [L.L.'s] misconduct." Ultimately, in December 1987—as a result of plaintiff's insistence—the firm made a report concerning L.L.'s "numerous misrepresentations and [acts of] malpractice against clients of the [f]irm and acts of forgery of checks drawn on the [f]irm's account." Thereafter, two partners "continuously berated plaintiff for having caused them to report [the] misconduct." The firm nevertheless continued to employ plaintiff "because he was in charge of handling the most important litigation in the [f]irm." Plaintiff was fired in March 1988, a few days after he filed motion papers in that important case.

Plaintiff asserts that defendants wrongfully discharged him as a result of his insistence that L.L.'s misconduct be reported as required by DR 1–103(A). In his fourth cause of action, he alleges that the firm's termination constituted a breach of the employment relationship. In the fifth cause of action, he claims that his discharge was in violation of public policy and constituted a tort for which he seeks compensatory and punitive damages.

Defendants moved to dismiss the fourth and fifth causes of action as legally insufficient.... Supreme Court granted defendants' motion because his employment relationship was at will....

The Appellate Division affirmed. It also concluded that plaintiff failed to state a cause of action because, as an at-will employee, the firm could terminate him without cause. This Court granted leave to appeal.

II.

We discuss first whether, notwithstanding our firmly established employment-at-will doctrine, plaintiff has stated a legal claim for breach of contract in the fourth cause of action. The answer requires a review of the three cases in which that doctrine is fully explained.

The employment-at-will doctrine is a judicially created common-law rule "that where an employment is for an indefinite term it is presumed to be a hiring at will which may be freely terminated by either party at any time for any reason or even for no reason" (*Murphy v. American Home Prods. Corp.*, 58 N.Y.2d 293, 300). In *Murphy*, this Court dismissed the claim of an employee who alleged he had been discharged in bad faith in retaliation for his disclosure of accounting improprieties. In so doing, we expressly declined to follow other jurisdictions in adopting the tort-based abusive discharge cause of action for imposing "liability on employers where employees have been discharged for disclosing illegal activities on the part of their employers," being of the view "that such a significant change in our law is best left to the Legislature."

With respect to the contract cause of action asserted in *Murphy*, the Court held that plaintiff had not shown evidence of any express agreement limiting the employer's unfettered right to fire the employee. For this reason, the Court distinguished *Weiner v. McGraw–Hill, Inc.*, 443 N.E.2d

441, where such an express limitation had been found in language in the employer's personnel handbook. Finally, in *Murphy*, the Court rejected the argument that plaintiff's discharge for disclosing improprieties violated a legally implied obligation in the employment contract requiring the employer to deal fairly and in good faith with the employee, explaining:

> No New York case upholding any such broad proposition is cited to us by plaintiff (or identified by our dissenting colleague), and we know of none. New York does recognize that in appropriate circumstances an obligation of good faith and fair dealing on the part of a party to a contract may be implied and, if implied will be enforced. *In such instances the implied obligation is in aid and furtherance of other terms of the agreement of the parties. No obligation can be implied, however, which would be inconsistent with other terms of the contractual relationship.* Thus, in the case now before us, plaintiff's employment was at will, a relationship in which the law accords the employer an unfettered right to terminate the employment at any time. In the context of such an employment it would be incongruous to say that an inference may be drawn that the employer impliedly agreed to a provision which would be destructive of his right of termination.

Four years after *Murphy*, the Court decided *Sabetay v. Sterling Drug*, 506 N.E.2d 919. There, the Court dismissed the complaint of an employee who claimed he was fired for "blowing the whistle" and refusing to engage in improper and unethical activities. As in *Murphy*, the Court found no basis for an express limitation on the employer's right to discharge an at-will employee and, adhering to *Murphy* as a precedent, declined to base any such limitation on an implied-in-law obligation of dealing fairly and in good faith with its employee.

Not surprisingly, defendants' position here with respect to plaintiff's breach of contract cause of action is simple and direct, *i.e.*, that: (1) as in *Murphy* and *Sabetay*, plaintiff has shown no factual basis for an express limitation on the right to terminate of the type upheld in *Weiner*; and (2) *Murphy* and *Sabetay* rule out any basis for contractual relief under an obligation implied-in-law. We agree that plaintiff's complaint does not contain allegations that could come within the *Weiner* exception for express contractual limitations. As to an implied-in-law duty, however, a different analysis and other considerations pertain.

In arguing that the law imposes no implied duty which would curtail their unlimited right to terminate the employment contract, defendants rely on the holding in *Murphy*.... The decisions in *Murphy* and *Sabetay*, however, are not controlling here.

As plaintiff points out, his employment as a lawyer to render professional services as an associate with a law firm differs in several respects from the employments in *Murphy* and *Sabetay*. The plaintiffs in those cases were in the financial departments of their employers, both large companies. Although they performed accounting services, they did so in furtherance of their primary line responsibilities as part of corporate management. In contrast, plaintiff's performance of professional services for the firm's clients as a duly admitted member of the Bar was at the very core and, indeed, the only purpose of his association with defendants. Associates are, to be sure, employees of the firm but they remain independent officers of the court responsible in a broader public sense for their professional obligations. Practically speaking, plaintiff's duties and responsibilities as a lawyer and as an associate of the firm were so closely linked as to be incapable of separation. It is in this distinctive relationship between a law firm and a lawyer hired as an associate that plaintiff finds the implied-in-law obligation on which he founds his claim.

We agree with plaintiff that in any hiring of an attorney as an associate to practice law with a firm there is implied an understanding so fundamental to the relationship and essential to its purpose as to require no expression: that both the associate and the firm in conducting the practice will do so in accordance with the ethical standards of the profession. Erecting or countenancing disincentives to compliance with the applicable rules of professional conduct, plaintiff contends, would subvert the central professional purpose of his relationship with the firm—the lawful and ethical practice of law.

The particular rule of professional conduct implicated here (DR 1–103[A]), it must be noted, is critical to the unique function of self-regulation belonging to the legal profession. Although the Bar admission requirements provide some safeguards against the enrollment of unethical applicants, the Legislature has delegated the responsibility for maintaining the standards of ethics and competence to the Departments of the Appellate Division. To assure that the legal profession fulfills its responsibility of self-regulation, DR 1–103(A) places upon each lawyer and Judge the duty to report to the Disciplinary Committee of the Appellate Division any potential violations of the Disciplinary Rules that raise a "substantial question as to another lawyer's honesty, trustworthiness or fitness in other respects." Indeed, one commentator has noted that "[t]he reporting requirement is nothing less than essential to the survival of the profession."

Moreover, as plaintiff points out, failure to comply with the reporting requirement may result in suspension or disbarment. Thus, by insisting that plaintiff disregard DR 1–103(A) defendants were not only making it impossible for plaintiff to fulfill his professional obligations but placing him in the position of having to choose between continued employment and his own potential suspension and disbarment. We agree with plaintiff that these unique characteristics of the legal profession in respect to this core Disciplinary Rule make the relationship of an associate to a law firm employer intrinsically different from that of the financial managers to the corporate employers in *Murphy* and *Sabetay*. The critical question is whether this distinction calls for a different rule regarding the implied obligation of good faith and fair dealing from that applied in *Murphy* and *Sabetay*. We believe that it does in this case, but we, by no means, suggest that each provision of the Code of Professional Responsibility should be deemed incorporated as an implied-in-law term in every contractual relationship between or among lawyers.

It is the law that in "every contract there is an implied undertaking on the part of each party that he will not intentionally and purposely do anything to prevent the other party from carrying out the agreement on his part." The idea is simply that when A and B agree that B will do something it is understood that A will not prevent B from doing it. The concept is rooted in notions of common sense and fairness. . . .

Just such fundamental understanding, though unexpressed, was inherent in the relationship between plaintiff and defendant law firm. Defendants, a firm of lawyers, hired plaintiff to practice law and this objective was the only basis for the employment relationship. Intrinsic to this relationship, of course, was the unstated but essential compact that in conducting the firm's legal practice both plaintiff and the firm would do so in compliance with the prevailing rules of conduct and ethical standards of the profession. Insisting that as an associate in their employ plaintiff must act unethically and in violation of one of the primary professional rules amounted to nothing less than a frustration of the only legitimate purpose of the employment relationship.

From the foregoing, it is evident that both *Murphy* and *Sabetay* are markedly different. The defendants in those cases were large manufacturing concerns—not law firms engaged with their employee in a common professional enterprise, as here. In neither *Murphy* nor *Sabetay* was the plaintiff required to act in a way that subverted the core purpose of the employment. The company rules underlying the firing of *Murphy* and *Sabetay* were not, as in this case, general rules of conduct and ethical standards governing both plaintiff and defendants in carrying out the sole aim of their joint enterprise, the practice of their profession. Unlike *Murphy* and *Sabetay*, giving effect to an implied understanding—that in their common endeavor of providing legal services plaintiff and the firm would comply with the governing rules and standards and that the firm would not act in any way to impede or discourage plaintiff's compliance— would be "in aid and furtherance of [the central purpose] of the agreement of the parties." Thus, the case is distinguishable from *Murphy* and *Sabetay* where giving effect to the implied obligation would have been "inconsistent with" and "destructive of" an elemental term in the agreement. We conclude, therefore, that plaintiff has stated a valid claim for breach of contract based on an implied-in-law obligation in his relationship with defendants. . . .

NOTES

1.   Do you believe Mr. Wieder's version of events? Do you have to?

2.   State law in Illinois was fairly generous in its recognition of wrongful discharge claims, but restrictive in applying that law to lawyers. New York was the reverse. Why did the New York Court of Appeals view *Wieder's* case as more worthy of redress than that of a nonlawyer?

PROBLEMS

1.   Client hires Lawyer. Lawyer's retainer agreement expressly provides that Client agrees in advance to permit Lawyer to withdraw if Client fails to pay agreed fees and expenses in a timely manner. Client falls behind in paying fees and Lawyer withdraws. Has Lawyer acted properly? *See N.Y. State Bar Ass'n Comm. on Prof. Ethics Op.* 805 (1/10/07).

CHAPTER 6

DECISIONMAKING IN THE LAWYER–CLIENT RELATIONSHIP

■ ■ ■

A. STRIKING THE BALANCE: AUTHORITY, AUTONOMY AND ACCOUNTABILITY IN THE ATTORNEY–CLIENT RELATIONSHIP

1. MODELS OF THE RELATIONSHIP

Once you are in an attorney-client relationship, how is authority distributed? That is, who makes decisions about how the representation will proceed and about what its goals and outcomes should be?

One might think that this question should be answered unambiguously by agency law. A lawyer is a client's agent. By that, we mean that the lawyer "acts on behalf of the client, representing the client, with consequences that bind the client." Deborah A. DeMott, *The Lawyer as Agent*, 67 Fordham L. Rev. 301 (1998). An agent is ordinarily subject to the control of the "principal"—the party on whose behalf the agent acts—so we might assume that the client, the lawyer's principal, decides everything about the representation. It might seem sensible to say that it is simply the lawyer's job to do the client's bidding, and that clients should make all decisions about how their legal representation should proceed. But lawyers are also experts, and some decisions may be better left to their considered judgment.

Our vision of who should decide what in the attorney-client relationship might vary depending on our notion of what the lawyer-client relationship is really about. If we understood the typical attorney-client relationship as involving an empowered and educated client and a lawyer intent on using her expertise to serve that client's needs, we might expect the client to be in charge and the lawyer to act largely in response to the client's direction and desires. As Prof. Stephen Ellmann put it, "[c]lients who enjoy economic leverage over their attorneys, clients whose own expertise rivals their lawyers' knowledge, and even, perhaps, clients who are simply so unusually aggressive as to command their lawyers' close attention, may well enjoy legal services that are finely tuned to the clients' own definition of their objectives." *Lawyers and Clients*, 34 U.C.L.A. L. Rev. 717, 718 (1987). If, on the other hand, we conceived the relationship as involving an authoritative and educated lawyer and a disempowered and intimidated client, we might expect the lawyer to direct the decision-making because of her superior knowledge, judgment and status. Prof. Ellmann describes this relationship, as well:

> Attorneys, after all, wield technical expertise, enjoy exclusive or privileged access both to other lawyers and to officials of the state, and bring familiarity and detachment to situations in which clients are often frightened, angry, and uninitiated. Often social status and economic class will also give lawyers a standing to which both lawyer and client may feel deference is due. Even lawyers not eager to embrace class privilege may accept traditions and habits of profession-al autonomy which restrict the spheres of client decisionmaking and active involvement. All of these factors encourage lawyers to assume, and clients to cede, a major role not only in the implementation of client choices but in the making of the choices themselves.

Id. Accordingly, our view of how lawyer-client relationships should be governed and controlled depends on our perception of what the dominant category of those relationships is. Concerns about the first category would suggest that it is important to figure out how to constrain clients' dominance of their lawyers; concerns about the second category might cause us to shape rules designed to encourage and develop clients' autono-my and their capacity to make their own decisions about their representa-tion.

But, in fact, both categories of clients and lawyers exist, and, as one might imagine, critical models of the lawyering relationship have arisen that address both categories. Critics concerned about empowering clients argue that the relationship between lawyer and client should be "client-cen-tered," focusing exclusively on the needs and interests of the client. Advocates of client-centered lawyering emphasize the need for the client to be fully informed and collaboratively involved in strategic decisionmak-ing, and consider that the client should be the ultimate decisionmaker about both the means and ends of the representation. The client-centered model developed as a response to the paternalistic view of lawyers as controlling all aspects of the representation and making decisions based on the lawyer's perception of what was good for the client. Some advocates of the model encourage lawyer neutrality, recognizing that if the client is aware of the lawyer's views, the client may feel the need to defer to the lawyer. The client-centered model developed largely in the context of clinical legal education, and provided an approach for educating future lawyers through the representation of indigent and often disempowered individuals.

Critics more concerned about client dominance of lawyers argue that the lawyer's role should not simply be to advance the client's interest, but to advance broader concerns of justice. This "justice-centered approach" posits a different and more active role for the lawyer. Such an approach contends that lawyers should be more than just "hired guns," reflecting their clients' wishes and desires; instead, lawyers should take account of other interests and actors affected by the client's decisions, and should be actively involved in pursuing what is best for the public. This model was developed reflecting for the most part concerns about lawyers representing large, wealthy, and powerful entity clients.

What would a client-centered view of the lawyer-client relationship mean for the apportionment of decisionmaking responsibility between lawyer and client? How might a justice-centered view of lawyering suggest a different distribution of responsibility? How can one set of rules address the diverse contexts in which these issues arise? One author suggests that the correct approach is power-based, with a more client-centered approach applying to relatively powerless clients and a justice-centered approach applying to more powerful clients. Susan D. Carle, *Power as a Factor in Lawyers' Ethical Deliberation*, 35 Hofstra L. Rev. 115 (2006). Do you find this convincing?

2.   ETHICAL CONSTRAINTS

Consider Model Rule 1.2. According to this rule, which decisions in the course of representation are reserved to the client? Which decisions are for the lawyer to make? Which decisions should the lawyer and client consult about, and what should the lawyer do if there is a difference of opinion between lawyer and client about the matter? You might envision a continuum, where relatively few matters are reserved for the lawyer's sole decision at one end, and for the client's at the other. What should lawyers and clients do with the many decisions in the great middle? Does Comment [2] to Model Rule 1.2 help you here?

Imagine, for example, that shortly before trial opposing counsel calls you and asks you to agree to a continuance. His spouse unexpectedly needs emergency surgery, and going forward as scheduled will create significant hardship for him. You know that if you refuse, the other lawyer will ask the court to reschedule the trial. You also know that the judge is likely to grant the request whether you agree to it or not, and that the judge may be annoyed if you say no and require the other side to make an unnecessary motion. You are also reluctant to play hardball with an opponent you are likely to meet again in other matters and with whom you have an amiable relationship, notwithstanding the fact that you are adversaries in this case. Yet you also know that, if required to proceed, the other side will probably be somewhat disadvantaged by the distraction of its lead counsel, and that this might incline the opposing party to settle more advantageously than it otherwise might have. Should you consult the client about the matter? Suppose the client says that it's time to get tough and that under no circumstances should you agree to a continuance or concede anything. Should you obey the client's direction? Consider Model Rule 1.2, Comment [2] and Model Rule 1.3, Comment [1].

3. OTHER CONSTRAINTS: BINDING THE CLIENT THROUGH THE LAW OF AGENCY

One might think, based on Model Rule 1.2, that there are certain decisions that only clients can make. For example, the rule suggests that only a client can agree to a settlement of a case. This is true as a matter of legal ethics, but legal ethics rules do not govern contract law. How is it that, even though the ethics rules reserve the settlement decision for the client, a client can be bound by a settlement the client claims he or she did not want and did not agree to?

CONWAY v. BROOKLYN UNION GAS CO.
236 F. Supp. 2d 241 (E.D.N.Y. 2002)

Before the court is defendant's motion to enforce the terms of an oral settlement agreement with plaintiff, to enjoin plaintiff from filing further lawsuits against it and its employees and agents, and for attorneys' fees and costs. For the reasons stated below, I respectfully recommend that the settlement agreement be enforced. . . .

Plaintiff Katrina Conway commenced this action against defendant Brooklyn Union Gas Company on December 19, 1996, alleging employment discrimination based on her race and gender. Conway retained attorney Marshall Bellovin ("Bellovin") in January 1997. Settlement discussions took place periodically from 1998 to 2001.

At a settlement conference before me on January 18, 2001, attended by Conway, the parties explicitly agreed to three terms: (1) the Company would convert Conway's termination to a resignation; (2) the Company would provide Conway with a neutral reference for prospective employers; and (3) Conway would withdraw all of her lawsuits pending against the Company, its agents and employees. [The court described a wide range of associated litigation instituted by the plaintiff in this matter.] The parties further agreed that the terms of the settlement would be kept confidential. At the conference, I personally confirmed with the parties that the sole remaining disagreement concerned the monetary amount the Company would pay to plaintiff and that any further negotiations would concern only money. Over the course of the following weeks, I held consensual *ex parte* discussions with each party in an attempt to reconcile their differences on that one remaining issue. At the conclusion of these discussions, I made a settlement recommendation and asked the attorneys to consult with their clients and tell me confidentially whether they accepted the recommendation. I instructed counsel to give me a yes or no answer and expressly stated that if the answer was no, I did not want to hear a counter proposal. I further advised counsel that I would not communicate their response to their adversary unless both parties accepted the recommendation, so that an acceptance could not be used as leverage to obtain further concessions. I also told the parties that an acceptance by both parties would constitute a settlement of the lawsuit. Both parties agreed to this procedure. During a consensual *ex parte* telephone conference on February 9, 2001, Mr. Bellovin notified the court that plaintiff had accepted my settlement recommendation of a monetary amount of $40,000 and reiterated that she also expected a resignation instead of termination; a neutral reference; and strict confidentiality. During the February 9 conference, I confirmed with Bellovin that plaintiff's acceptance of the $40,000 amount constituted an agreement to settle this case on the three terms plaintiff had accepted at the January 18, 2001 conference plus a payment of $40,000.

On March 2, 2001, defendant's counsel Alvin Adelman telephoned my chambers and reported that the Company accepted the court's settlement recommendation and agreed to a monetary payment of $40,000. As of that date, the parties had reached agreement on all terms of the settlement.

On March 5, 2001 the court received a letter, dated March 1, 2001, in which Conway herself wrote directly to the court indicating that she would "settle the two cases that [she had] pending in the Eastern District" but would not agree to dismiss [two related] state court actions.... In the March 1 letter, however, plaintiff did not state that she had discharged her attorney or withdrawn or limited his authority to settle this case on her behalf. Nor did she explain why she was writing directly to the court.

On March 8, 2001, I held a consensual *ex parte* telephone conference with Bellovin and advised him that the case had settled, as the Company had agreed to the $40,000 recommendation. I asked him what if any effect plaintiff's March 1 letter had on his representation or the settlement. Bellovin confirmed that he continued to represent plaintiff and said that, to the best of his knowledge, he continued to have full authority to settle this case on the terms plaintiff had accepted on January 18, 2001 and February 9, 2001. I asked him to consult with his client and to notify me immediately if his authority had changed. The following day, Bellovin confirmed with defendant's counsel that the case had settled for $40,000, a neutral reference, a resignation rather than a termination, and the dismissal of all four pending cases against defendant and its agents. Bellovin asked defendant's counsel to draft the settlement papers.... At that point, the sole outstanding issue was resolved, and the court considered the case settled.

From March 9 to June 12, 2001, however, Conway failed to respond to Mr. Bellovin's phone calls or correspondence. On April 18, 2001, Bellovin advised the court that "plaintiff had not responded to his telephone calls and letters [regarding] the status of [the] settlement." Accordingly, the court scheduled a status conference for May 9, 2001 and directed Conway to attend. On May 3, 2001, Conway faxed a request for a postponement of the May 9 conference because of a family emergency, and the conference was adjourned to June 12. Conway did not say in her letter that she was withdrawing her authority to agree to the settlement. On June 11, 2001, plaintiff informed her attorney that she had commenced and was pursuing *pro se* actions against an employee of the Company. At a status conference on June 12, 2001 before me, plaintiff withdrew her counsel's authority to settle under the terms she had previously accepted. However, she also agreed to withdraw all of her outstanding *pro se* actions. . . .

In August 2001, plaintiff requested a copy of the draft settlement from her attorney. After reviewing it, she returned it with the handwritten comments "No Agreement" and "Never" and indicated that she would only settle the case for $500,000. On September 18, 2001, plaintiff sent a letter to the court against her counsel's advice stating that she could never agree to the terms of the settlement. While she did not deny discussing the four terms mentioned *supra*, she specifically objected to being foreclosed from bringing future lawsuits relating to her termination from the Company.

A final settlement conference was held on October 12, 2001. . . . At the conference, Mr. Bellovin stated that Conway had previously given him authority to agree to the four terms discussed during the February 9 *ex parte* telephone conference. He also indicated that he had informed Conway that a settlement meant she would have to dismiss all of her claims deriving from the same set of facts. Conway stated that, although she had agreed to the settlement generally, she had not realized that she would have to withdraw the actions she had commenced *pro se*. She also stated that she had since decided that $40,000 was not enough money. She maintained that the terms and money would be acceptable if she could file other suits relating to this matter. . . . Defendant's counsel informed the court that defendant was seeking enforcement of the settlement, an order prohibiting Conway from suing the Company in the future, and attorney's fees. Plaintiff's attorney moved to be relieved as counsel, and plaintiff confirmed that she would not reconsider the settlement agreement. [The court granted plaintiff's counsel's motion to withdraw and plaintiff elected to proceed *pro se*.]

Although the decision to settle a case rests with the client, courts will presume that an attorney who enters into a settlement agreement has the authority to do so. A party challenging an attorney's authority to settle a case on his or her client's behalf bears the burden of showing that the attorney lacked the requisite authority to settle the case.

Courts in this Circuit have consistently recognized that an attorney may bind his or her client to a settlement agreement so long as the attorney has apparent authority. Apparent authority in this context is " 'the power to affect the legal relations of [the client] by transactions with third persons, professedly as agent for the [client], arising from and in accordance with the [client's] manifestations to such third persons.' " Apparent authority may only arise from the conduct or representation of the client toward the third party, not that of the attorney. However, if an attorney has apparent authority to settle a case, and the opposing counsel has no reason to doubt this authority, then the settlement will be upheld.

It is clear here that Bellovin had apparent authority from Conway, as he stated such in Conway's presence in open court at the settlement conference before me on October 12, 2001. Conway did not deny that she gave her attorney authority to settle, and in fact has never, to this day, contested the fact that her attorney had authority to enter into the settlement on her behalf. Nor has she argued that Bellovin's authority was limited in any way, either on February 9, 2001 when he accepted the final term of the settlement, or in March when he confirmed the settlement with defendant's counsel and agreed to a stipulation.... She knew Bellovin was involved in settlement negotiations and neither discharged him nor instructed him to revoke the agreement until the June 12, 2001 status conference, well after the parties had agreed on the four-point settlement. Similarly, the Company had no reason to believe that Conway would challenge or withdraw her attorney's authority to settle.[1] Plaintiff has therefore failed to meet her burden of proving with affirmative evidence that her attorney lacked apparent authority. Accordingly, plaintiff is bound by her attorney's acceptance of the settlement terms, assuming the requisite intent.

[The court concluded that, on balance, the parties had manifested an intent to be bound by the oral settlement agreement.]

Although it is not ordinarily a factor that courts consider in deciding whether or not to enforce an oral settlement agreement, I am obliged to note that this court is intimately familiar with the settlement, having worked closely with the parties to settle this case, and I believe that the terms to which they agreed are eminently fair and reasonable.... Since the above factors demonstrate that plaintiff gave her attorney authority to enter into the settlement and unequivocally intended to be bound by the oral settlement agreement—an agreement that provides her with an equitable resolution of her claims—I respectfully recommend that the settlement agreement be enforced....

NOTES

1. Did Conway agree to the terms of the settlement agreement? If not, how can she be held to be bound by them? What about Model Rule 1.2?

2. Clients can sometimes be difficult to deal with. If you had been Conway's lawyer, how would you have dealt with her decisions in this case? Ultimately,

---

1. Plaintiff's March 1, 2001 letter to the court does not alter this conclusion. The fact that plaintiff expressed her emotions directly to the court or defendant was not unusual in this case, as plaintiff had often vented her feelings at settlement conferences, even though her attorney was present. In the end, however, consistent with accepted practice, it was always her attorney who expressed her official position on each issue, whether at the conference or at a later date after private consultation. It is significant that, at plaintiff's urging, Bellovin continued to represent plaintiff after March 1, 2001 until his voluntary withdrawal in October 2001, including at a settlement conference with the court on March 8, 2001 and discussions with defendant on March 9, 2001, when plaintiff's counsel confirmed Conway's agreement to the final term of the settlement. Even after Bellovin sent plaintiff copies of the settlement papers to execute, she did not advise the court, defendant, or her own attorney that Bellovin was not authorized to settle on her behalf. Plaintiff has presented no evidence that she ever placed restrictions on his authority. In such case, defendant was entitled to rely on Bellovin's representations as Conway's attorney. To find otherwise would discourage settlements and undermine the orderly conduct of litigation.

her lawyer sought to withdraw from the matter. Were there grounds for him to withdraw under Model Rule 1.16? If you were the judge, would you grant the request? Why or why not?

B. DECISIONMAKING IN THE CRIMINAL CASE

Model Rule 1.2 sets out some particular decisions that are reserved to the defendant in a criminal case. Because the risks in a criminal case are uniquely borne by the defendant, it makes sense that fundamental decisions regarding criminal cases are left to the defendant's sole discretion.

How far does the client's right to make decisions in the criminal context go? In the following case, the defendant argued for an expansive right to make decisions about the conduct of his appeal. Which side do you think had the better argument?

JONES v. BARNES

463 U.S. 745 (1983)

CHIEF JUSTICE BURGER delivered the opinion of the Court.

We granted certiorari to consider whether defense counsel assigned to prosecute an appeal from a criminal conviction has a constitutional duty to raise every nonfrivolous issue requested by the defendant.

I

In 1976, Richard Butts was robbed at knifepoint by four men in the lobby of an apartment building; he was badly beaten and his watch and money were taken. Butts informed a Housing Authority Detective that he recognized one of his assailants as a person known to him as "Froggy," and gave a physical description of the person to the detective. The following day the detective arrested respondent David Barnes, who is known as "Froggy."

Respondent was charged with first and second degree robbery, second degree assault, and third degree larceny. The prosecution rested primarily upon Butts' testimony and his identification of respondent. During cross-examination, defense counsel asked Butts whether he had ever undergone psychiatric treatment; however, no offer of proof was made on the substance or relevance of the question after the trial judge *sua sponte* instructed Butts not to answer. At the close of trial, the trial judge declined to give an instruction on accessorial liability requested by the defense. The jury convicted respondent of first and second degree robbery and second degree assault.

The Appellate Division of the Supreme Court of New York, Second Department, assigned Michael Melinger to represent respondent on appeal. Respondent sent Melinger a letter listing several claims that he felt should be raised. Included were claims that Butts' identification testimony should have been suppressed, that the trial judge improperly excluded psychiatric evidence, and that respondent's trial counsel was ineffective. Respondent also enclosed a copy of a *pro se* brief he had written.

In a return letter, Melinger accepted some but rejected most of the suggested claims, stating that they would not aid respondent in obtaining a new trial and that they could not be raised on appeal because they were not based on evidence in the record. Melinger then listed seven potential claims of error that he was considering including in his brief, and invited respondent's "reflections and suggestions" with regard to those seven issues. The record does not reveal any response to this letter.

Melinger's brief to the Appellate Division concentrated on three of the seven points he had raised in his letter to respondent: improper exclusion of psychiatric evidence, failure to suppress Butts' identification testimony, and improper cross-examination of respondent by the trial judge. In addition, Melinger submitted respondent's own *pro se* brief. Thereafter, respondent filed two more *pro se* briefs, raising three more of the seven issues Melinger had identified.

At oral argument, Melinger argued the three points presented in his own brief, but not the arguments raised in the *pro se* briefs. On May 22, 1978, the Appellate Division affirmed by summary order. The New York Court of Appeals denied leave to appeal. . . .

[O]n March 31, 1980, [respondent] filed a petition in the New York Court of Appeals for reconsideration of that court's denial of leave to appeal. In that petition, respondent for the first time claimed that his *appellate* counsel, Melinger, had provided ineffective assistance. The New York Court of Appeals denied the application on April 16, 1980.

Respondent then returned to United States District Court for the second time, with a petition for habeas corpus based on the claim of ineffective assistance by appellate counsel. The District Court . . . dismissed the petition, holding that the record gave no support to the claim of ineffective assistance of appellate counsel on "any . . . standard which could reasonably be applied." The District Court concluded:

> It is not required that an attorney argue every conceivable issue on appeal, especially when some may be without merit. Indeed, it is his professional duty to choose among potential issues, according to his judgment as to their merit and his tactical approach.

A divided panel of the Court of Appeals reversed. Laying down a new standard, the majority held that when "the appellant requests that [his attorney] raise additional colorable points [on appeal], counsel must argue the additional points to the full extent of his professional ability." . . .

The Court of Appeals went on to hold that, "[h]aving demonstrated that appointed counsel failed to argue colorable claims at his request, an appellant need not also demonstrate a likelihood of success on the merits of those claims."

The court concluded that Melinger had not met the above standard in that he had failed to press at least two nonfrivolous claims: the trial judge's failure to instruct on accessory liability and ineffective assistance of trial counsel. The fact that these issues had been raised in respondent's own *pro se* briefs did not cure the error, since "[a] pro se brief is no substitute for the advocacy of experienced counsel." The court reversed and remanded, with instructions to grant the writ of habeas corpus unless the State assigned new counsel and granted a new appeal.

We granted certiorari, and we reverse.

II

... [I]n *Griffin v. Illinois* and *Douglas v. California*, the Court held that if an appeal is open to those who can pay for it, an appeal must be provided for an indigent. It is also recognized that the accused has the ultimate authority to make certain fundamental decisions regarding the case, as to whether to plead guilty, waive a jury, testify in his or her own behalf, or take an appeal. In addition, we have held that, with some limitations, a defendant may elect to act as his or her own advocate, *Faretta v. California*, 422 U.S. 806 (1975). [No] decision of this Court suggests, however, that the indigent defendant has a constitutional right to compel appointed counsel to press nonfrivolous points requested by the client, if counsel, as a matter of professional judgment, decides not to present those points.

This Court, in holding that a State must provide counsel for an indigent appellant on his first appeal as of right, recognized the superior ability of trained counsel in the "examination into the record, research of the law, and marshalling of arguments on [the appellant's] behalf." Yet by promulgating a *per se* rule that the client, not the professional advocate, must be allowed to decide what issues are to be pressed, the Court of Appeals seriously undermines the ability of counsel to present the client's case in accord with counsel's professional evaluation.

Experienced advocates since time beyond memory have emphasized the importance of winnowing out weaker arguments on appeal and focusing on one central issue if possible, or at most on a few key issues. Justice Jackson, after observing appellate advocates for many years, stated:

> One of the first tests of a discriminating advocate is to select the question, or questions, that he will present orally. Legal contentions, like the currency, depreciate through over-issue. The mind of an appellate judge is habitually receptive to the suggestion that a lower court committed an error. But receptiveness declines as the number of assigned errors increases. Multiplicity hints at lack of confidence in any one.... [E]xperience on the bench convinces me that multiplying assignments of error will dilute and weaken a good case and will not save a bad one.

Jackson, *Advocacy Before the Supreme Court*, 25 Temple L.Q. 115, 119 (1951).

Justice Jackson's observation echoes the advice of countless advocates before him and since. An authoritative work on appellate practice observes:

> Most cases present only one, two, or three significant questions.... Usually, ... if you cannot win on a few major points, the others are not likely to help, and to attempt to deal with a great many in the limited number of pages allowed for briefs will mean that none may receive adequate attention. The effect of adding weak arguments will be to dilute the force of the stronger ones.

R. Stern, Appellate Practice in the United States 266 (1981).

There can hardly be any question about the importance of having the appellate advocate examine the record with a view to selecting the most promising issues for review. This has assumed a greater importance in an era when oral argument is strictly limited in most courts—often to as little as 15 minutes—and when page limits on briefs are widely imposed. Even in a court that imposes no time or page limits, however, the new *per se* rule laid down by the Court of Appeals is contrary to all experience and logic. A brief that raises every colorable issue runs the risk of burying good arguments—those that, in the words of the great advocate John W. Davis, "go for the jugular"—in a verbal mound made up of strong and weak contentions.[1]

... Here the appointed counsel did just that. For judges to second-guess reasonable professional judgments and impose on appointed counsel a duty to raise every "colorable" claim suggested by a client would disserve the very goal of vigorous and effective advocacy.... Nothing in the Constitution or our interpretation of that document requires such a standard. The judgment of the Court of Appeals is accordingly

Reversed.

JUSTICE BRENNAN, with whom JUSTICE MARSHALL joins, dissenting.

The Sixth Amendment provides that "[i]n all criminal prosecutions, the accused shall enjoy the right ... to have the *Assistance* of counsel for his defence" (emphasis added). I find myself in fundamental disagreement with the Court over what a right to "the assistance of counsel" means. The import of words like "assistance" and "counsel" seems inconsistent with a regime under which counsel appointed by the State to represent a criminal defendant can refuse to raise issues with arguable merit on appeal when his client, after hearing his assessment of the case and his advice, has directed him to raise them. I would remand for a determina-

---

1. The ABA Model Rules of Professional Conduct provide:

"A lawyer shall abide by a client's decisions concerning the objectives of representation ... and shall consult with the client as to the means by which they are to be pursued.... In a criminal case, the lawyer shall abide by the client's decision, ... *as to a plea to be entered, whether to waive jury trial and whether the client will testify.*" Model Rules of Professional Conduct, Proposed Rule 1.2(a) (Final Draft 1982) (emphasis added).

With the exception of these specified fundamental decisions, an attorney's duty is to take professional responsibility for the conduct of the case, after consulting with his client.

tion whether respondent did in fact insist that his lawyer brief the issues that the Court of Appeals found were not frivolous. . . .

The Constitution does not on its face define the phrase "assistance of counsel," but surely those words are not empty of content. No one would doubt that counsel must be qualified to practice law in the courts of the State in question, or that the representation afforded must meet minimum standards of effectiveness. To satisfy the Constitution, counsel must function as an advocate for the defendant, as opposed to a friend of the court. Admittedly, the question in this case requires us to look beyond those clear guarantees. What is at issue here is the relationship between lawyer and client—who has ultimate authority to decide which nonfrivolous issues should be presented on appeal? I believe the right to "the assistance of counsel" carries with it a right, personal to the defendant, to make that decision, against the advice of counsel if he chooses. . . .

[T]he right to counsel is more than a right to have one's case presented competently and effectively. It is predicated on the view that the function of counsel under the Sixth Amendment is to protect the dignity and autonomy of a person on trial by *assisting* him in making choices that are his to make, not to make choices for him, although counsel may be better able to decide which tactics will be most effective for the defendant. . . .

The right to counsel ... is not an all-or-nothing right, under which a defendant must choose between forgoing the assistance of counsel altogether or relinquishing control over every aspect of his case beyond its most basic structure (*i.e.*, how to plead, whether to present a defense, whether to appeal). A defendant's interest in his case clearly extends to other matters. Absent exceptional circumstances, he is bound by the tactics used by his counsel at trial and on appeal. He may want to press the argument that he is innocent, even if other stratagems are more likely to result in the dismissal of charges or in a reduction of punishment. He may want to insist on certain arguments for political reasons. He may want to protect third parties. This is just as true on appeal as at trial, and the proper role of counsel is to *assist* him in these efforts, insofar as that is possible consistent with the lawyer's conscience, the law, and his duties to the court. . . .

[T]he ... Court argues that good appellate advocacy demands selectivity among arguments. That is certainly true—the Court's advice is good. It ought to be taken to heart by every lawyer called upon to argue an appeal in this or any other court, and by his client. It should take little or no persuasion to get a wise client to understand that, if staying out of prison is what he values most, he should encourage his lawyer to raise only his two or three best arguments on appeal, and he should defer to his lawyer's advice as to which are the best arguments. The Constitution, however, does not require clients to be wise, and other policies should be weighed in the balance as well.

It is no secret that indigent clients often mistrust the lawyers appointed to represent them. There are many reasons for this, some perhaps unavoidable even under perfect conditions—differences in education, disposition, and socio-economic class—and some that should (but may not always) be zealously avoided. A lawyer and his client do not always have the same interests. Even with paying clients, a lawyer may have a strong interest in having judges and prosecutors think well of him, and, if he is working for a flat fee—a common arrangement for criminal defense attorneys—or if his fees for court appointments are lower than he would receive for other work, he has an obvious financial incentive to conclude cases on his criminal docket swiftly. Good lawyers undoubtedly recognize these temptations and resist them, and they endeavor to convince their clients that they will. It would be naive, however, to suggest that they always succeed in either task. A constitutional rule that encourages lawyers to disregard their clients' wishes without compelling need can only exacerbate the clients' suspicion of their lawyers.... [T]o force a lawyer's *decisions* on a defendant "can only lead him to believe that the law conspires against him." In the end, what the Court hopes to gain in effectiveness of appellate representation by the rule it imposes today may well be lost to decreased effectiveness in other areas of representation.

The Court's opinion also seems to overstate somewhat the lawyer's role in an appeal. While excellent presentation of issues, especially at the briefing stage, certainly serves the client's best interests, I do not share the Court's implicit pessimism about appellate judges' ability to recognize a meritorious argument, even if it is made less elegantly or in fewer pages than the lawyer would have liked, and even if less meritorious arguments accompany it.... Especially at the appellate level, I believe that for the most part good claims will be vindicated and bad claims rejected, with truly skillful advocacy making a difference only in a handful of cases. In most of such cases—in most cases generally—clients ultimately will do the wise thing and take their lawyers' advice. I am not willing to risk deepening the mistrust between clients and lawyers in all cases to ensure optimal presentation for that fraction-of-a-handful in which presentation might really affect the result reached by the Court of Appeals.

Finally, today's ruling denigrates the values of individual autonomy and dignity central to many constitutional rights, especially those Fifth and Sixth Amendment rights that come into play in the criminal process. Certainly a person's life changes when he is charged with a crime and brought to trial. He must, if he harbors any hope of success, defend himself on terms—often technical and hard to understand—that are the State's, not his own. As a practical matter, the assistance of counsel is necessary to that defense. Yet, until his conviction becomes final and he has had an opportunity to appeal, any restrictions on individual autonomy and dignity should be limited to the minimum necessary to vindicate the State's interest in a speedy, effective prosecution. The role of the defense lawyer should be above all to function as the instrument and defender of the client's autonomy and dignity in all phases of the criminal process....

The Court subtly but unmistakably adopts a different conception of the defense lawyer's role—he need do nothing beyond what the State, not his client, considers most important. In many ways, having a lawyer becomes one of the many indignities visited upon someone who has the ill fortune to run afoul of the criminal justice system.

I cannot accept the notion that lawyers are one of the punishments a person receives merely for being accused of a crime. Clients, if they wish, are capable of making informed judgments about which issues to appeal, and when they exercise that prerogative their choices should be respected unless they would require lawyers to violate their consciences, the law, or their duties to the court. . . .

NOTES

1.   If respondent's claims were not meritorious, why didn't the Court simply decide that he could not show the prejudice required to make out a claim of ineffective assistance of counsel?

2.   If the lawyer was respondent's agent, why wasn't the lawyer required to do as his client directed? Why did the Court conclude that the Constitution did not entitle him to require his lawyer to make the claims he wished on appeal?

C.   SPECIAL SITUATIONS: THE CLIENT OPERATING UNDER A DISABILITY

The rules that govern the attorney-client relationship implicitly assume a significant level of competence and autonomy on the part of the client. As Comment [1] to Model Rule 1.14 puts it, "The normal client-lawyer relationship is based on the assumption that the client, when properly advised and assisted, is capable of making decisions about important matters." But clients are differently situated in their capacities to play this role. Model Rule 1.14 addresses the problem of the client whose "capacity to make adequately considered decisions in connection with a representation is diminished, whether because of minority, mental impairment or for some other reason." The direction of the rule is clear: "the lawyer shall, as far as reasonably possible, maintain a normal client-lawyer relationship with the client." But one can imagine that in many circumstances, this is difficult to do.

The rule expressly mentions two categories of clients to whom it applies: clients who are minors and clients who are mentally impaired. It leaves open the possibility of other reasons for impairment. Students sometimes assume that advanced age alone is a disability that impairs a client's cognitive function, but advanced age, in the absence of other evidence of compromised capacity, is not an impairment.

The representation of minors is complicated by the fact that lawyers may be asked to play different roles with regard to a matter involving a child. A lawyer appointed as a *guardian ad litem* is "viewed as an arm of the court who will advocate in the best-interest of the child," while " 'counsel' for the child will generally have a duty of undivided loyalty and confidentiality to the child." Kristin Henning, *Loyalty, Paternalism, and Rights: Client Counseling Theory and the Role of Child's Counsel in Delinquency Cases*, 81 Notre Dame L. Rev. 245, 266 (2005). Lawyers need to be clear about what role they are playing; this can be particularly difficult because courts and statutes are not always clear about the parameters of the lawyer's role.

The next case concerns a situation in which lawyers confronted a Rule 1.14 problem. What was the lawyers' strategy? Do you think it was appropriate?

UNITED STATES v. KACZYNSKI

239 F.3d 1108 (9th Cir. 2001)

Theodore John Kaczynski, a federal prisoner, appeals the district court's denial of his motion under 28 U.S.C. § 2255 to vacate his conviction. In that motion, Kaczynski alleges that his guilty plea to indictments returned against him as the "Unabomber" ..., in exchange for the United States renouncing its intention to seek the death penalty, was involuntary because his counsel insisted on presenting evidence of his mental condition, contrary to his wishes, and the court denied his *Faretta* request to represent himself.[1] Having found that the *Faretta* request was untimely and not in good faith, that counsel could control the presentation of evidence, and that the plea was voluntary, the district court denied the § 2255 motion without calling for a response or holding a hearing.

... [W]e conclude on the merits that the district court did not err. Therefore, we affirm.

I

The facts underlying Kaczynski's arrest and indictment for mailing or placing sixteen bombs that killed three people, and injured nine others, are well known and we do not repeat them here. Rather, we summarize the pre-trial proceedings that bear on the voluntariness of Kaczynski's plea.

The California Indictment charged Kaczynski with four counts of transporting an explosive in interstate commerce with intent to kill or injure in violation of 18 U.S.C. § 844(d); three counts of mailing an explosive device with intent to kill or injure, in violation of 18 U.S.C. § 1716; and three counts of using a destructive device during and in relation to a crime of violence, in violation of 18 U.S.C. § 924(c). The New Jersey Indictment charged one count of transporting an explosive device in interstate commerce with intent to kill or injure, in violation of 18 U.S.C. § 844(d); one

---

1. *Faretta v. California*, 422 U.S. 806 (1975) (recognizing a criminal defendant's Sixth Amendment right to represent himself).

count of mailing an explosive device with intent to kill or injure, in violation of 18 U.S.C. § 1716; and one count of using a destructive device during and in relation to a crime of violence, in violation of 18 U.S.C. § 924(c). The government gave notice of its intent to seek the death penalty under both indictments on May 15, 1997.

The California Indictment was assigned to the calendar of the Hon. Garland E. Burrell, Jr. Quin Denvir, the Federal Public Defender for the Eastern District of California, and Judy Clarke, the Federal Public Defender for Eastern Washington and Idaho, were appointed to represent Kaczynski. They filed motions to suppress evidence in March, 1997, which were denied.

On June 24, 1997, Kaczynski filed a notice under Fed.R.Crim.P. 12.2(b) of his intent to introduce expert testimony of his mental condition at trial. According to his § 2255 motion, Kaczynski consented to the notice reluctantly and only to allow evidence relating to his "mental condition"—not to a "mental disease or defect." He also avers that the purpose of the notice was to allow psychologist Julie Kriegler, who did not think that he suffered from serious mental illness, to testify.

Jury selection began November 12. Six hundred veniremen were summoned, and 450 questionnaires were filled out. Voir dire of 182 prospective jurors took sixteen days over the course of six weeks.

Kaczynski alleges that he learned in the courtroom on November 25 that his attorneys intended to portray him as suffering from major mental illness (schizophrenia), but that he was deterred from bringing his conflict with counsel to the court's attention as counsel were in plea negotiations with the government. Evidently by December 17 it had become clear that Kaczynski would not go for an unconditional plea and the government would not accept a conditional one. In the meantime, Kaczynski was giving thought to whether he wanted Tony Serra, a San Francisco lawyer whom he believed would not employ a mental state defense, to represent him. On December 16, he received a letter indicating that Serra would be available, but on December 17 Serra withdrew from consideration.

On December 18, Kaczynski's counsel gave the district court three letters in which Kaczynski explained that he had a conflict with his attorneys over the presentation of a mental status defense. The next day the court held an *ex parte, in camera* conference with Kaczynski and counsel, as a result of which he and they undertook to confer over the weekend. On December 22, Clarke and Denvir advised the court that a compromise had been worked out: They agreed to withdraw the Rule 12.2(b) notice and not to present any expert mental health testimony at the guilt phase of the trial, while Kaczynski accepted their control over the presentation of evidence and witnesses to be called, including mental health expert witnesses and members of Kaczynski's family, in order to put on a full case of mitigation at the penalty phase. Kaczynski told the court that he was willing to proceed with his attorneys on this basis, and that "the conflict at least is provisionally resolved." In response to the court's query, Kaczynski also said that he did not want to represent himself. Jury selection was then completed and (to allow for the holidays) opening statements were set to begin January 5, 1998.

On January 5, Kaczynski told the court that he wished to revisit the issue of his relations with his attorneys. He said that he had learned from a preview of the opening statement the evening before (January 4) that counsel intended to present non-expert evidence of his mental state in the guilt phase. Clarke and Denvir explained that they intended to introduce evidence of Kaczynski's physical state, living conditions, lifestyle, and writings to show the deterioration of his mental state over the 25 years he lived in Montana. Kaczynski also raised for the first time with the court the possibility that he might want to have Serra replace Denvir and Clarke. The district court continued the trial to January 8, and appointed Keven Clymo as "conflicts" counsel for Kaczynski.

Another hearing was held January 7. Kaczynski withdrew his January 5 request for Serra to represent him because Clymo had convinced him it would not be in his best interests.... Kaczynski told the court that he would like to be represented by Serra, but said: "As to the question of when he would be able to start, he stated that, of course, he will not be able to start trial tomorrow. He would need a considerable time to prepare." The court refused to allow Serra to take over because of the delay it would cause. After discussing Kaczynski's continuing differences with counsel over mental status evidence, the court also ruled that counsel could control the defense and present evidence of his mental condition over Kaczynski's objection. Again in response to a question from the court, Kaczynski said that he did not want to represent himself. He explained that "if this had happened a year and a half ago, I would probably have elected to represent myself. Now, after a year and a half with this, I'm too tired, and I really don't want to take on such a difficult task. So far I don't feel I'm up to taking that challenge at the moment, so I'm not going to elect to represent myself."

However, the next day (January 8), Kaczynski's counsel informed the court that Kaczynski wanted to proceed as his own counsel. Clarke explained that Kaczynski believed he had no choice, given presentation of a mental illness defense which he "cannot endure." Clarke also indicated that Kaczynski had advised her that he was prepared to proceed *pro se* that day, without delay. Both sides thought that a competency examination should be conducted, given defense counsels' view that his mental condition was Kaczynski's only viable defense. The court also noted that it had learned from the U.S. Marshals office that Kaczynski might have attempted suicide the night before. Accordingly, it ordered a competency examination, to be completed before ruling on the *Faretta* request. The trial was continued to January 22. A court-appointed psychiatrist examined Kaczynski and concluded that he was competent. All parties agreed on January 20 that this resolved the issue.

On January 21, Kaczynski again asked to represent himself. The court denied the request on January 22, finding that it was untimely because it came after meaningful trial proceedings had begun and the jury had been empaneled. The court also found that Kaczynski's request to represent himself was a tactic to secure delay and that delay would have attended the granting of the motion given the complexity of the capital prosecution. Although Kaczynski did not request a continuance, the court found "it was impossible to conceive" that he could immediately assume his own defense without considerable delay for preparation of an adequate defense. This, in turn, would risk losing jurors and having again to go through the arduous process of selecting a new jury. The court also found that Kaczynski's conduct was not consistent with a good faith assertion of his right to represent himself, as he had long known of his attorneys' intention to present mental health evidence and had agreed on December 22 that they could do so at the penalty phase. Accordingly, the court concluded, Kaczynski's conflict with counsel turned solely on the moment when mental evidence would be presented. Finally, the court declined to exercise its discretion to permit Kaczynski to represent himself in spite of the untimely request, noting that to do so would result in Kaczynski's foregoing "the only defense that is likely to prevent his conviction and execution."

Immediately after the *Faretta* request was denied from the bench, Denvir informed the court that Kaczynski would unconditionally plead guilty to both the California and New Jersey Indictments if the government would withdraw its notices of intent to seek the death penalty. (Kaczynski alleges that this condition was counsels' idea, not his.) A written plea agreement was entered into shortly thereafter, and the plea was taken by the court the same day.

Kaczynski was sentenced May 4, 1998 to four consecutive life sentences, plus 30 years imprisonment. He was ordered to pay $15,026,000 in restitution to his victims. Pursuant to the terms of the plea agreement, Kaczynski did not appeal.

On April 23, 1999, he filed a motion under 28 U.S.C. § 2255 seeking to vacate his conviction. The district court denied the motion.... This appeal followed.

II

[The court rejected the contention that Kaczynski was procedurally barred from raising his claims.]

III

On the merits, Kaczynski contends that his plea was involuntary because he was improperly denied his *Faretta* right, or because he had a constitutional right to prevent his counsel from presenting mental state evidence. Even if neither deprivation suffices, still the plea was involuntary in his

view because it was induced by the threat of a mental state defense that
Kaczynski would have found unendurable. . . .

A

. . . [W]e held in *United States v. Hernandez*, 203 F.3d 614 (9th Cir. 2000),
that the erroneous denial of a *Faretta* request [to represent oneself at a
criminal trial] renders a guilty plea involuntary. We reasoned that wrongly denying a defendant's request to represent himself forces him "to
choose between pleading guilty and submitting to a trial *the very structure*
of which would be unconstitutional." Because this deprives the defendant
"of the choice between the only two constitutional alternatives—a plea
and a fair trial," we concluded that a district court's improper *Faretta*
ruling "imposed unreasonable constraints" on the defendant's decisionmaking, thus making a guilty plea involuntary. Therefore, we must
consider whether Kaczynski's plea was rendered involuntary on account of
a wrongful refusal to grant his request for self-representation.

B

. . . We conclude that . . . the propriety of denying Kaczynski's request
necessarily follows from the district court's finding that he asserted the
right to represent himself as a tactic to delay trial proceedings and lacked
bona fide reasons for failing to assert it before January 8, 1998.

The court found that Kaczynski "clearly and unambiguously permitted his
lawyers to adduce mental status evidence at trial, and his complaints to
the contrary, asserted on the day trial was set to commence, evidence his
attempt to disrupt the trial process." Further, the court found that
although Kaczynski contended he made his January 8 request to represent
himself only because he could not endure his attorneys' strategy of
presenting mental status evidence in his defense, the record belied this
contention because Kaczynski had authorized its use. The court also found
that Kaczynski was well aware before January 8 that evidence of his
mental status would be adduced at trial. In addition to the December 22
accord, Kaczynski was present during all but one day of the seventeen
days of voir dire, during which the court observed that he conferred
amicably with his attorneys while they openly and obviously selected
jurors appearing receptive to mental health evidence about him. Finally,
the court found that Kaczynski could not have immediately assumed his
own defense without considerable delay, given the large amount of technical evidence and more than 1300 exhibits that the government intended to
offer.

These findings are well grounded in the record. . . . Although he knew
then that evidence of his mental condition would be presented, Kaczynski
expressly said that he did not want to represent himself. As he agreed to
evidence of his mental state, it cannot be for *this* reason that he later
invoked the right; otherwise, he could have done so on December 22.[2]

---

2. Although Kaczynski correctly points out that the district court had once indicated that he
might have reasonably believed that his attorneys' withdrawal of the 12.2(b) notice meant that no

Instead, on January 5, when opening statements were supposed to start, Kaczynski renewed complaints about the mental status evidence his counsel planned to present in the guilt phase....

As the events preceding Kaczynski's *Faretta* request show, he knew about and approved use of mental state evidence without invoking his right to represent himself. Accordingly, the court could well determine that Kaczynski's avowed purpose of invoking the right in order to avoid a defense he could not endure was not "consistent with a good faith assertion of the *Faretta* right." ... Having found that the request for self-representation was for tactical reasons and not for any good faith reason other than delay, the court properly denied Kaczynski's *Faretta* request. His Sixth Amendment rights were not violated....

C

For essentially the same reasons, neither was Kaczynski's plea rendered involuntary on account of the threat of a mental state defense that he did not want presented.... Kaczynski ... argues that he was coerced into pleading guilty by his counsel's insistence on a mental state defense, that his counsel deceived him in order to gain his cooperation with some such defense, and that he was induced to plead guilty by a choice (being unable to represent himself or to proceed without the mental state defense) that was constitutionally offensive.

Even if Kaczynski were misled by his counsel about the degree to which evidence of his mental state would be adduced in the guilt phase, he learned for sure what their plans were on January 4 when they previewed their opening statement for him and he does not allege, nor does the record show, that they in any way threatened or misled him with respect to the plea or its consequences. Kaczynski ... points out that "the accused has the ultimate authority to make certain fundamental decisions regarding the case, as to whether to plead guilty, waive a jury, testify in his or her own behalf, or take an appeal," *Jones v. Barnes*, 463 U.S. 745, 751 (1983), and argues that evidence about mental status is of the same order of magnitude. The government, on the other hand, submits that it is equally "clear that appointed counsel, and not his client, is in charge of the choice of trial tactics and the theory of defense." We need not decide where along this spectrum control of a mental defense short of insanity lies, because Kaczynski agreed that his counsel could control presentation of evidence and witnesses to be called (including expert witnesses and members of his family who would testify that he was mentally ill) in order to put on a full case of mitigation at the penalty phase. Thus, as the district court found, Kaczynski's claim that his plea was involuntary due

---

lay evidence would be presented on his mental status during the guilt phase of the trial, the court subsequently found that, "after reflecting upon Kaczynski's general acuity, the content of the agreement itself, which was known to him, his awareness of the questions his attorneys asked jurors during voir dire, and his expression and demeanor during voir dire that showed his clear approval of his lawyers' effort to use that defense to save his life, I became convinced that Kaczynski knew that his lawyers intended to offer mental status evidence during the guilt phase of trial."

to his aversion to being portrayed as mentally ill is inconsistent with his willingness to be so portrayed for purposes of avoiding the death penalty. This leaves only the pressure that Kaczynski personally felt on account of his wish to avoid the public disclosure of evidence about his mental state sooner rather than later. We agree with the district court that this does not transform his plea into an involuntary act.

Accordingly, as Kaczynski's guilty plea was voluntary and was not rendered involuntary on account of the wrongful denial of his *Faretta* request or because of anticipation of evidence about his mental condition, his habeas petition was properly denied.

REINHARDT, CIRCUIT JUDGE, dissenting:

I disagree strongly with the majority's decision and regretfully must dissent.

This case involves the right of a seriously disturbed individual to insist upon representing himself at trial, even when the end result is likely to be his execution. It presents a direct clash between the right of self-representation and the state's obligation to provide a fair trial to criminal defendants, especially capital defendants. . . .

The case of Ted Kaczynski not only brings together a host of legal issues basic to our system of justice, it also presents a compelling individual problem: what should be the fate of a man, undoubtedly learned and brilliant, who determines, on the basis of a pattern of reasoning that can only be described as perverse, that in order to save society he must commit a series of horrendous crimes? What is the proper response of the legal system when such an individual demands that he be allowed to offer those perverse theories to a jury as his only defense in a capital case—a defense that obviously has no legal merit and certainly has no chance of success? What should the response be when he also insists on serving as his own lawyer, not for the purpose of pursuing a proper legal defense, but in order to ensure that no evidence will be presented that exposes the nature and extent of his mental problems? The district judge faced these questions and, understandably, blinked. He quite clearly did so out of compassionate and humanitarian concerns. Nevertheless, in denying Kaczynski's request to represent himself, the district court unquestionably failed to follow the law. . . .

Whether Theodore Kaczynski suffers from severe mental illness, and which of the various psychiatric diagnoses that have been put forth is the most accurate, are questions that we cannot answer here. However, it is not now, nor has it ever been, disputed that under the governing legal standards, he was competent to waive his right to the assistance of counsel. Therefore, whatever we may think about the wisdom of his choice, or of the doctrine that affords a defendant like Kaczynski the right to make that choice, he was entitled, under the law as enunciated by the Supreme Court, to represent himself at trial. A review of the transcript makes startlingly clear that, under the law that controls our decision, the denial of Kaczynski's request violated his Sixth Amendment rights. There is simply no basis for the district court's assertion that the request was made in bad faith or for purposes of delay. Because, as the majority acknowledges, the erroneous denial of a self-representation request renders a subsequent guilty plea involuntary as a matter of law, I must respectfully dissent from the majority's holding that Kaczynski's plea was voluntary.

I.

By the time of his arrest in a remote Montana cabin on April 3, 1996, Ted Kaczynski had become one of the most notorious and wanted criminals in our nation's history. For nearly two decades, beginning in 1978, the "Unabomber"—so designated by the FBI when his primary targets appeared to be universities and airlines—had carried out a bizarre ideological campaign of mail-bomb terror aimed at the "industrial-technological system" and its principal adherents: computer scientists, geneticists, behavioral psychologists, and public-relations executives. Three men ... were killed by Kaczynski's devices, and many other people were injured, some severely.

In 1995, Kaczynski made what has been aptly described as "the most extraordinary manuscript submission in the history of publishing." Kaczynski proposed to halt all his killings on the condition that major American newspapers agree to publish his manifesto, "Industrial Society and Its Future." The *New York Times* and *Washington Post* accepted the offer, and that most unusual document, with its "dream ... of a green and pleasant land liberated from the curse of technological proliferation," revealed to the world the utopian vision that had inspired Kaczynski's cruel and inhumane acts. Among the readers of the manifesto was David Kaczynski, who came to suspect that its author was his brother Ted, a former mathematics professor at Berkeley who had isolated himself from society some quarter-century before. David very reluctantly resolved to inform the FBI of his suspicions, although he sought assurances that the government would not seek the death penalty and expressed his strong view that his brother was mentally ill. On the basis of information provided by David, the FBI arrested Kaczynski and, despite David's anguished opposition, the government gave notice of its intent to seek the death penalty.

Following Kaczynski's indictment, Federal Defenders Quin Denvir and Judy Clarke were appointed to represent him. Attorney Gary Sowards joined the defense team some time later. All three are superb attorneys, and Kaczynski could not have had more able legal representatives. From the outset, however, Kaczynski made clear that a defense based on mental illness would be unacceptable to him, and his bitter opposition to the only defense that his lawyers believed might save his life created acute tension between counsel and client. That tension persisted, and periodically erupted, throughout the many months leading up to Kaczynski's guilty plea, and the dispute was not definitively resolved until Judge Burrell ruled on January 7, 1998, that Kaczynski's attorneys could present mental-health evidence even over his vehement objection. It was that ruling, Kaczynski maintains—and the record indisputably reflects—that compelled him to request self-representation the very next day as the only means of preventing his portrayal as a "grotesque and repellent lunatic." In doing so, Kaczynski was merely exercising the right that Judge Burrell had recognized he possessed the day before, immediately after he issued his controversial ruling that counsel, not client, would control the presentation of mental-health evidence.

Whether Kaczynski's self-representation request was made in good faith, as Judge Burrell repeatedly stated on January 8, or whether it was a "deliberate attempt to manipulate the trial process for the purpose of causing delay," as Judge Burrell subsequently held when explaining his reason for denying the request, is the issue before us. Although the answer is absolutely clear from the record, it is helpful to set forth a number of colloquies that demonstrate that everyone involved—including counsel for both sides and the district judge—was fully aware that Kaczynski's request was made in good faith and not for purposes of delay. The record reveals that Kaczynski's aversion to a mental-health defense was, indisputably, heartfelt, and that no one—least of all Judge Burrell—ever questioned Kaczynski's sincerity prior to the time the judge commenced formulating his January 22 ruling.

II.

Kaczynski contends that he first learned on November 25, 1997 that his attorneys intended to present evidence that he suffered from major mental illness, specifically schizophrenia. On that day, in open court, Kaczynski discovered that numerous psychiatric reports, the contents of which he had been assured would be privileged, had been released to the public without his consent. Although it is true, as the majority notes, that Kaczynski had previously been aware that his attorneys were planning to introduce some evidence that he might suffer from neurological problems—he had consented to the filing of a notice under Rule 12.2(b) of the Federal Rules of Criminal Procedure to leave open the possibility of introducing expert testimony on that point—he nevertheless believed that he had the right to prevent the mental-health experts who had examined him from testifying at his trial.

Kaczynski cites to dozens of notes that he wrote to his attorneys in the weeks and months prior to November 25, 1997, in which he expressed, in the strongest terms, his unwillingness to present a mental-health defense at trial. . . . Even when Kaczynski began to suspect that his attorneys intended to use some mental-health evidence and testimony at his trial, he "had no idea they intended to portray him as suffering from major mental illness," and he still believed that all such evidence was privileged and could not be released without his approval.

When, on November 25, 1997, Kaczynski learned that defense experts had diagnosed him as suffering from paranoid schizophrenia, and that the results of those examinations had been released to the government and to the public, he felt "shock and dismay." In the courtroom on that day, Kaczynski wrote to Denvir and Clarke:

> Did Gary [Sowards] give that info to the prosecutors with your knowledge and consent? If you all assume responsibility for revealing what is being revealed now, then this is the end between us. I will not work with you guys any more, because I can't trust you. . . .
>
> This case is developing in a direction that I certainly did not expect. I was lead [sic] to believe that this was not really a "mental health" kind of defense, but that you would try to show that my actions were a kind of "self defense." Gary [Sowards] gave me the impression that we would use only Dr. Kriegler, and would use her only to show I would not "do it again."

In the weeks that followed, Kaczynski also wrote three separate letters to Judge Burrell in which he explained his conflict with his attorneys and sought replacement of counsel. . . .

The letters reveal the depth of the rift that had developed between Kaczynski and his attorneys regarding the issue of mental-health evidence. The first letter, dated December 1, 1997 begins: "Last Tuesday, November 25, I unexpectedly learned for the first time in this courtroom that my attorneys had deceived me." Kaczynski explained that he had been assured by his attorneys that the results of psychiatric examinations that he reluctantly agreed to undergo—and even the fact that he had been examined at all—would be protected by attorney-client privilege and would not be disclosed absent his approval. Moreover, he had been "led to believe that [he] would not be portrayed as mentally ill without [his] consent." . . .

In a letter dated December 18, Kaczynski offered his reasons for objecting to a defense based on mental-health evidence:

> I do not believe that science has any business probing the workings of the human mind, and . . . my personal ideology and that of the mental-health professions are mutually antagonistic. . . . [I]t is humiliating to have one's mind probed by a person whose ideology and values are alien to one's own. . . . [Denvir, Clarke, and Sowards] calculatedly deceived me in order to get me to reveal my private thoughts, and then without warning they made accessible to the public the cold and heartless assessments of their experts. . . . To me this was a stunning blow . . . [and] the worst experience I ever underwent in my life. . . . I would rather die, or suffer prolonged physical torture, than have the 12.2b defense imposed on me in this way by my present attorneys.

Previous consent to such a defense was, Kaczynski contended, "meaningless because my attorneys misled me as to what that defense involved."

Kaczynski proposed three possible solutions: that his attorneys be prevented from using a "12.2b" defense; that he be permitted to represent himself, preferably with appointed counsel to assist him; or that new counsel be appointed for him. After receiving Kaczynski's letters, Judge Burrell ordered an ex parte hearing, to be held on December 22, during which Kaczynski's conflict with counsel would be explored. At that hearing, Kaczynski agreed to an accommodation, which he characterizes as "tentative," according to which Denvir and Clarke would withdraw the 12.2(b) notice (thereby precluding introduction of expert testimony about Kaczynski's mental state during the guilt phase of the trial), but would be permitted to introduce mental-state evidence in the penalty phase. Kaczynski insists that his understanding at the time was that the agreement would preclude the presentation of *any* mental-state evidence during the guilt phase of the trial, even though the rule (the text of which Kaczynski contends he never saw) applies only to *expert* testimony. Kaczynski's misunderstanding was reasonable; in fact, Judge Burrell shared it, as he later acknowledged. . . .

Immediately following the December 22 agreement, the parties exercised their peremptory strikes and the jury was selected. Kaczynski maintains that from December 22 through January 4, he believed that (1) his attorneys would not be permitted to introduce any mental-state evidence during the guilt phase of his trial, and (2) attorney J. Tony Serra—who had written to Kaczynski and offered to represent him without employing a mental-health defense but had subsequently withdrawn the offer of representation—was unwilling to serve as his counsel at trial. Kaczynski first learned of his attorneys' intention to present *non-expert* mental-state testimony at the guilt phase of his trial on the evening of January 4, 1998—the day before trial was to begin. Denvir and Clarke visited him at the jail that evening and read him their opening statement. Kaczynski declares that he was "horrified to learn that his attorneys planned to present extensive nonexpert evidence of severe mental illness in the guilt phase."

On . . . January 7 . . . Judge Burrell ruled that Kaczynski's counsel could present mental-state testimony even if Kaczynski objected. Judge Burrell then offered Kaczynski the option of self-representation, warning: "I don't advise it, but if you want to, I've got to give you certain rights." At the time of the court's offer, Kaczynski declined to accept it, explaining that he was "too tired . . . [to] take on such a difficult task," and that he did not feel "up to taking that challenge at the moment." . . . Later that same day, the court was informed that Tony Serra would, after all, be willing to represent Kaczynski. Kaczynski promptly requested a change of counsel, but Judge Burrell denied the request on the ground that substituting counsel would require a significant delay before trial could commence.

On January 8, Kaczynski decided to accept the court's offer of the previous day and informed the court that he wished to represent himself.[1] Kaczynski's counsel conveyed his request to the court with great reluctance:

---

1. The night before, Kaczynski apparently attempted suicide, although the record shows that Judge Burrell was unaware of that fact until after the January 8 hearing was over.

> Your Honor, if I may address the Court, Mr. Kaczynski had a request
> that we alert the Court to, on his behalf—it is his request that he be
> permitted to proceed in this case as his own counsel. This is a very
> difficult position for him. He believes that he has no choice but to go
> forward as his own lawyer. It is a very heartfelt reaction, I believe, to
> the presentation of a mental illness defense, a situation in which he
> simply cannot endure.

Kaczynski's attorneys made clear that he was not seeking any delay in
proceedings and that he was prepared to proceed *pro se* immediately. . . .

No one disputes that Kaczynski had a constitutional right to represent
himself if, as the court plainly recognized, the assertion of his right was
motivated by the dispute over the mental-state defense. It is therefore no
surprise that Judge Burrell, who repeatedly acknowledged that Kaczynski's request was induced by a genuine aversion to the presentation of
mental-health evidence, signaled his inclination to grant the request. . . .

In fact, when the government tried to advise the court that it strongly
believed that Kaczynski had the right to represent himself, the court
reiterated its agreement with that view, subject only to the question of
competency. . . . At that point, all counsel (including the court-appointed
conflicts counsel) and Judge Burrell agreed that Kaczynski should undergo
a psychiatric evaluation to determine his competency to exercise his right
to self-representation, and the next day the judge issued an order for the
necessary medical examinations.

The competency evaluation would, of course, have been altogether unnecessary had Judge Burrell believed on January 8 that Kaczynski's request
to represent himself was made in bad faith. The judge could simply have
denied the request on that ground. Nevertheless, two weeks later, after
Kaczynski had been determined to be competent by a government psychiatrist, Judge Burrell denied the self-representation request, characterizing
it—in a manner that directly contradicted the numerous statements he
had made at the prior proceedings—as a "deliberate attempt to manipulate the trial process for the purpose of causing delay."

It stretches the imagination to believe that at some point during the two
weeks in which Kaczynski was undergoing mental competency tests,
initially suggested by Judge Burrell, the judge suddenly came to believe
that he had been hoodwinked by Kaczynski from the start. Rather, as
some of his later comments on the subject indicate (*e.g.*, the trial would
become a "suicide forum"), Judge Burrell became more and more appalled
at the grotesque and one-sided spectacle over which he would be forced to
preside were Kaczynski to conduct his own defense. He understandably
developed a strong desire to avoid the chaos, legal and otherwise, that
would have ensued had Kaczynski been allowed to present his twisted
theories to a jury as his defense to a capital murder charge. Not only
would such a trial have had a circus atmosphere but, in light of Kaczynski's aversion to mitigating evidence, it would in all likelihood have
resulted in his execution. It is not difficult to appreciate, therefore, how

the denial of Kaczynski's request for self-representation—regardless of the unquestionable legitimacy of the request—must have seemed the lesser evil.

III.

It is impossible to read the transcripts of the proceedings without being struck by Judge Burrell's exceptional patience, sound judgment, and sincere commitment to protecting Kaczynski's right to a fair trial—and his life. . . .

Nevertheless, Judge Burrell did *not* base his decision denying Kaczynski's *Faretta* rights on his views of the role of the criminal justice system in capital cases; he was not free to do so under controlling law. . . . Because Kaczynski's psychiatric evaluation resulted in a declaration that he was competent, the only available basis for denying his request was to find that it was not made in good faith—but rather for the purpose of delay—even though the record squarely refuted that conclusion.

There can be no doubt that Judge Burrell's admirable desire to prevent an uncounseled, and seriously disturbed, defendant from confronting, on his own, the "prosecutorial forces of organized society"—in this case, three experienced federal prosecutors aggressively seeking that defendant's execution—lay at the heart of his denial of Kaczynski's request for self-representation. . . . [I]t is easy to appreciate why, as one commentator has suggested, "[t]he judicial system breathed a collective sigh of relief when the Unabomber pled guilty." Indeed, all the players in this unfortunate drama—all except Kaczynski, that is—had reason to celebrate Kaczynski's unconditional guilty plea. His attorneys had achieved their principal and worthy objective by preventing his execution. The government had been spared the awkwardness of pitting three experienced prosecutors against an untrained, and mentally unsound, defendant, and conducting an execution following a trial that lacked the fundamental elements of due process at best, and was farcical at worst. Judge Burrell, as noted, had narrowly avoided having to preside over such a debacle and to impose a death penalty he would have considered improper in the absence of a fair trial. It is no wonder that today's majority is not eager to disturb so delicate a balance.

The problem with this "happy" solution, of course, is that it violates the core principle of *Faretta v. California*—that a defendant who objects to his counsel's strategic choices has the option of going to trial alone. Personally, I believe that the right of self-representation *should* in some instances yield to the more fundamental constitutional guarantee of a fair trial. Here, the district court understood that giving effect to *Faretta*'s guarantee would likely result in a proceeding that was fundamentally unfair. However, *Faretta* does not permit the courts to take account of such considerations. Under the law as it now stands, there was no legitimate basis for denying Kaczynski the right to be his own lawyer in his capital murder trial. . . .

NOTES

1. What can you tell from this opinion about what transpired between Kaczynski and his lawyers? Imagine yourself in the position of those lawyers. What do you view as being in your client's interest? How would you handle the situation if the client's view of his interests and yours did not coincide? What about the judge here? Judge Reinhardt's dissent views the judicial decisions sympathetically. Do you? If not, why not? What would Model Rule 1.14 require of these lawyers? Does that make sense in this context?

2. Model Rule 1.14(b) indicates that "[w]hen the lawyer reasonably believes that the client has diminished capacity, is at risk of substantial physical, financial or other harm unless action is taken and cannot adequately act in the client's own interest, the lawyer may take reasonably necessary protective action," including consultation with others who can take action to protect the client "and, in appropriate cases, seeking the appointment of a guardian ad litem, conservator or guardian." Would this rule have provided a possible solution for Kaczynski's counsel? One lawyer who frequently represents incapacitated clients commented about this provision: "If we seek the appointment of a guardian, we are saying, 'This client—MY CLIENT—no longer should have the right to make certain decisions and a guardian should be appointed to make them for him.' That usually is devastating to any trust relationship that might have existed." What do you think of this view?

3. One might think that in criminal cases, the requirement that the defendant be competent to stand trial would avoid some of these problems. Ordinarily it does not, because the standard for competency in criminal cases is quite low. A person who "has sufficient present ability to consult with his lawyer with a reasonable degree of rational understanding and has a rational as well as factual understanding of the proceedings against him" is considered "competent" to stand trial, even if he is suffering from mental illness or other significant disability. *Dusky v. United States*, 362 U.S. 402 (1960). Kaczynski himself was deemed competent to stand trial. The requirement of competency, accordingly, was not a bar to what transpired there.

4. The right of self-representation is not absolute. The Supreme Court recently limited the right of self-representation at trial, holding that the Constitution permits a judge to deny self-representation to persons who are competent to stand trial but "who still suffer from severe mental illness to the point where they are not competent to conduct trial proceedings by themselves." *Indiana v. Edwards*, 128 S.Ct. 2379, 2388 (2008). Based on what you have read about Kaczynski, do you think he could have been denied self-representation on this ground?

5. Kaczynski's case may seem extreme, but the Bureau of Justice Statistics reports that 56% of inmates in state prison suffer from mental health problems; in local jails, that number is 64%. Lawyers dealing with these clients, accordingly, may face these issues more often than they expect.

6. Criminal representation is far from the only circumstance in which the lawyer's view of what is best for the client may deviate from the client's view.

What sorts of practice areas are likely to present these issues repeatedly? If you choose to practice in such an area, how will you deal with these issues?

PROBLEMS

1.   M.R. was a young woman of 21 with Down's syndrome. She was developmentally disabled, functioning at the level of a six- to eight-year-old. M.R. resided with her mother until she turned 18, when she expressed the desire to live with her father. M.R.'s mother sought formal guardianship of M.R. The court appointed lawyer Paul to act as M.R.'s attorney. M.R. told Paul that she wanted to live with her father. Paul concluded that M.R. had more fun at her father's house, but that the more structured environment at her mother's home was a better environment for her. Should Paul have argued to the court for M.R.'s preference, or for the result he thought was in her best interest? *See Matter of M.R.*, 638 A.2d 1274 (N.J. 1994).

2.   Client, accused of murder, insisted that he wanted to plead guilty and did not want his lawyer, Counsel, to resist the state's efforts to impose the death penalty. Client believed that his religion demanded that he receive the death penalty to cleanse himself of his crime. Counsel believed that Client was guilty of the crime but thought he could muster a strong case for a life sentence based on Client's family history. Could Counsel pursue a life sentence for Client? *See* Rebekah Denn & David Fisher, *"Execution Leaves a Trail of Unease,"* Seattle Post–Intelligencer, 8/29/01, at A1.

3.   The court appointed Lawyer to represent Teresa J., who was 16 years old, because of concerns that she was a member of a polygamous sect and had been subjected to sexual abuse by an adult male while she was still under the legal age. Lawyer sought a temporary restraining order to keep a spokesperson for Teresa's church away from her client. Teresa asked the court to replace Lawyer, arguing that Lawyer was "trying to restrict me from every person in my life that I want to talk to or have anything to do with." She also told Lawyer, "The most help you will be to me now is to step aside and let me get a different lawyer that I feel like can help me." Lawyer believed that her client was being pressured by the sect and that the restraining order was necessary to allow her client to make her own choices. "There is no question I am absolutely looking out for her," Lawyer said. "What's happening is really a shame because people who purport to care about her are really doing her a disservice." Teresa denied this, and told Lawyer that "you need to realize that I have a mind of my own and I can do things on my own if I choose to." Should Lawyer do as Teresa asks or pursue what Lawyer believes is in Teresa's best interest? *See* Brooke Adams, *Jeffs' Daughter Wants to Drop Attorney*, Salt Lake Tribune, 6/22/08.

4.   Arko was accused of a domestic assault. The victim claimed that he had intended to kill her; Arko denied this. He was charged with attempted second-degree murder. The jury was instructed on attempted murder and the lesser included offense of attempted reckless manslaughter, and convicted Arko of attempted reckless manslaughter. Arko claimed that the court should have submitted to the jury an instruction on a lesser non-included offense, third-degree assault. (Under somewhat unique state criminal procedure law, a defendant in Colorado may ask to have the jury consider his guilt for a crime

that the state did not initially charge and that is not a lesser included offense, if the evidence at trial would permit the jury to convict him of the less serious uncharged crime.) However, at trial, Arko's counsel had sought to instruct the jury on third-degree assault and Arko had objected. Should the trial court have followed defense counsel's decision on the instruction, or done as Arko requested? *See Arko v. People*, 183 P.3d 555 (Colo. 2008).

CHAPTER 7

THE DUTY TO PROTECT INFORMATION

■ ■ ■

Clients consult lawyers about matters that can be intensely personal, profoundly embarrassing, or hugely significant. Whether the client is contemplating a divorce or a corporate merger, the client fully expects that the lawyer will keep the client's secrets. Is the law's protection of the client's secrets just a client-protection rule, or is there a public benefit as well? The theory, at least, is that the public is better served if lawyers protect their clients' private information. Confidentiality contributes to a relationship of trust between lawyer and client, which results in the client making full disclosure to the lawyer. The lawyer, fully informed, is then able to provide accurate and reliable legal advice. "The client is thereby encouraged to seek legal assistance and to communicate fully and frankly with the lawyer even as to embarrassing or legally damaging subject matter and, if necessary, to advise the client to refrain from wrongful conduct. Almost without exception, clients come to lawyers in order to determine their rights and what is, in the complex of laws and regulations, deemed to be legal and correct. Based upon experience, lawyers know that almost all clients follow the advice given, and the law is upheld." Comment [2] to Model Rule 1.6.

This expectation on the part of clients is honored in some distinct ways. The duty of confidentiality, which is imposed by the rules of professional responsibility, provides for expansive protection of information relating to the representation of a client and sets out limited exceptions to the lawyer's duty not to disclose the information. A rule of ethics, however, does not provide legal protection for a person who wishes to resist judicial compulsion to testify or produce documents. For a legal basis to resist such compulsion, we must look to the attorney-client privilege, a much narrower rule of evidence that protects certain information from judicially compelled disclosure.

We begin with the law of attorney-client privilege.

A. ATTORNEY–CLIENT PRIVILEGE

A client comes to you and asks you to represent him in his upcoming murder trial. You agree and ask him what happened; in response, he tells you that he did, in fact, commit the crime with which he has been charged. Subsequently, you are subpoenaed by the prosecutor, placed under oath, and asked, "What did Client tell you about whether or not he committed the murder?" Must you respond?

The answer, as you might imagine, is no. The lawyer under this circumstance should assert the "attorney-client privilege" and refuse to answer.

What is a privilege? A privilege is a rule of evidence which permits a witness to refuse to provide otherwise relevant, probative evidence. The recognition of a privilege reflects a policy decision that it is important, for some reason, to protect the underlying information from disclosure. Why, for example, might we provide a privilege for communications between doctor and patient? between clergyperson and congregant? What is it about these relationships that is sufficiently important to protect the underlying information from disclosure in a judicial proceeding? Should we have more privileges: a "friend-friend" privilege, perhaps, or a "super-visor-subordinate" privilege? What do you think the policy rationale is for privileging the exchange of information between lawyers and clients?

While the creation of a privilege reflects a policy decision that it is important to protect the free exchange of information in certain categories of relationship, privileges impose a cost on the judicial system. A privilege excludes what would otherwise be relevant and probative evidence to protect the privileged relationship. Accordingly, privileges are interpreted strictly; the person asserting the privilege bears the burden of demonstrating that it should apply.

Privileges can be created by rule or by decisional law, but the elements of the attorney-client privilege are quite consistent. The classic statement of the privilege is Wigmore's: "(1) where legal advice of any kind is sought (2) from a professional legal adviser in his capacity as such, (3) the communications relating to that purpose, (4) made in confidence (5) by the client, (6) are at his instance permanently protected (7) from disclosure by himself or by the legal adviser, (8) except the protection be waived." 8 John Henry Wigmore, *Evidence in Trials at Common Law* § 2292 (John T. McNaughton rev. 1961). Section 68 of the the Restatement of the Law Governing Lawyers offers a somewhat simpler formulation; the attorney-client privilege "may be invoked ... with respect to: (1) a communication (2) made between privileged persons (3) in confidence (4) for the purpose of obtaining or providing legal assistance for the client."

If each of these elements is not satisfied, the privilege will not be recognized. That means that testimony about the communications between attorney and client or compliance with an order to produce information (such as a subpoena to produce documents) that contains such communications can be compelled, absent some other privilege that justifies a refusal to comply.

The existence of the privilege does not protect the underlying *facts* from disclosure. Suppose, for example, that in seeking legal advice about her tax situation, Mary tells her lawyer, Frank, that she failed to disclose income on last year's tax returns. Neither Mary nor Frank can be compelled to testify that she made that communication, assuming the requisites of the privilege are met. But nothing about the attorney-client privilege shields the facts about that situation from disclosure if the government can prove them in other ways. Can a corporate client shield negative research reports about the health effects of the corporation's products from discovery by circulating them to the corporation's lawyers?

Once created, the privilege exists in perpetuity. It survives even the death of the client.

1. FORMATION OF THE PRIVILEGE

STATE v. BRANHAM

952 So.2d 618 (Fla. Dist. Ct. App. 2007)

CANADY, JUDGE.

The State seeks certiorari review of the trial court's order determining that certain testimony is subject to the lawyer-client privilege. Because we conclude that the trial court's ruling was erroneous ... we grant the State's petition.

This certiorari proceeding arises from the prosecution of Michael Branham (the defendant) for the murder of his wife, Janette L. Branham (the victim). In the criminal proceeding, the defendant filed a "Notice of Exercise of Attorney–Client Privilege" with respect to certain communications between W. James Kelly, a practicing lawyer, and the defendant.

Prior to the defendant's indictment, Kelly was subpoenaed by the State to give a sworn statement. After raising the issue of lawyer-client privilege, Kelly was instructed by a circuit judge to answer the State's questions. Kelly then gave a sworn statement in which he testified that during the week preceding the victim's death, the defendant told Kelly that he intended to kill the victim. After the defendant's indictment, Kelly was listed by the State as a "person having information" with respect to the case.

In response to the defendant's notice concerning Kelly, the State filed a motion seeking a determination that the communications between the defendant and Kelly were not subject to the protection of the lawyer-client privilege. After considering the circumstances surrounding the communication by the defendant to Kelly, the trial court entered an order determining that "the Defendant's Exercise of Lawyer–Client Privilege is allowed." The State now seeks to have this order of the trial court quashed.

At the hearing on the State's motion, Kelly testified that several months before the death of the victim, the Branhams began having marital problems and discussed filing for divorce. Because Kelly was a friend to both of the Branhams, Kelly made it clear to them that he would not represent either of them in the divorce proceedings. However, Kelly agreed to act as a "go-between" for the Branhams in their efforts to resolve their differences.

Sometime during the week prior to the victim's death, Kelly went to the defendant's house on a social visit. Kelly testified that he and the defendant were discussing the Branhams' marital problems and that "some of [the discussion] was just shooting the breeze, some of it was just talk." During the conversation, the defendant inquired if Kelly was his attorney and Kelly responded "Sure." Immediately thereafter, the defendant stated that he was going to kill his wife. According to Kelly, the defendant's threat occurred "right in the middle of the conversation." The defendant subsequently repeated the threat several more times during their conversation. Kelly's response to the defendant each time he made the threat was "You're crazy. I don't even want to hear it" and "Don't talk like that." When Kelly was asked whether he gave the defendant advice or counsel, Kelly testified:

> I don't think he was asking me. I don't know what his intentions were. I just know what I replied to him was certainly not in the context of a criminal lawyer. As far as I know, the issue of what he was telling me, I didn't think that had anything to do with anything going on. I mean, it just came whistling out of the clear blue.

Kelly also testified that the defendant never requested Kelly's assistance to plan, commit, or get away with a crime.

When asked if he was "talking to [the defendant] as his attorney with regard to the divorce," Kelly said "No." When asked if he was "talking to [the defendant] strictly as a friend," Kelly said "Yes." Kelly further testified that he warned the victim concerning the threats made by the defendant. There was no testimony before the trial court indicating that in the conversation between the defendant and Kelly, the defendant either sought or received any legal advice concerning any matter.

The trial court's ruling that the lawyer-client privilege was applicable was based on the crucial determination that when Kelly "responded to [the defendant] indicating that he was his lawyer, he became such and [the defendant] had a right to rely on that affirmation." In its certiorari petition, the State argues—as it did before the trial court—that the defendant neither sought nor received legal advice and that the lawyer-client privilege was therefore inapplicable. . . .

Section 90.502(2), Florida Statutes (2005), provides that "[a] client has a privilege . . . to prevent any other person from disclosing . . . the contents of confidential communications when such other person learned of the communications because they were made in the *rendition of legal services to the client*." (Emphasis added.) Under section 90.502(1)(b), *client* is defined as "any person . . . who consults a lawyer with the *purpose of obtaining legal services* or who is *rendered legal services* by a lawyer." (Emphasis added.)

The statute makes clear that the lawyer-client privilege only applies to communications if they "were made in the rendition of legal services to the client." A person cannot be considered a client and therefore cannot obtain the protection of the lawyer-client privilege unless the person either "consult[ed] a lawyer with the purpose of obtaining legal services" or was "rendered legal services by a lawyer."

"The purpose of the [lawyer-client] privilege is to encourage clients to make full disclosure to their attorneys." *Fisher v. United States*, 425 U.S. 391, 403 (1976). The privilege "protects only those disclosures necessary to obtain informed legal advice." *Id.* "[I]f a communication with a lawyer is not made with him in his professional capacity as a lawyer, no privilege attaches." Thus, the lawyer-client privilege "does not extend to every statement made to a lawyer." A statement made "to [a] lawyer merely as a personal friend" is not subject to the privilege. *Id.*

Here, the evidence before the trial court unequivocally established that in the conversation with Kelly at the defendant's home, the defendant never asked for any legal advice and Kelly never gave any legal advice. The defendant did not "consult" Kelly "with the purpose of obtaining legal services," and Kelly did not "render[ ] legal services" to the defendant. § 90.502(1)(b). The defendant's statements to Kelly that the defendant intended to kill his wife were not "made in [connection with] the rendition of legal services to" the defendant. § 90.502(2). In ruling that the statements made by the defendant to Kelly were subject to the lawyer-client privilege, the trial court failed to apply the clear—and clearly applicable—provisions of sections 90.502(1)(b) and 90.502(2).

There is no legal basis for the trial court's conclusion that because Kelly told the defendant that Kelly was the defendant's attorney, the defendant was entitled to rely on the lawyer-client privilege. The lawyer-client privilege is not established by incantation. Nor does the privilege come into existence simply because a party believes that it exists.

Kelly was the defendant's attorney in a then-pending negligence case, and Kelly had previously represented the defendant in other civil matters. But the existence of the lawyer-client relationship between Kelly and the defendant with respect to the negligence case and the other matters did not establish a lawyer-client relationship with respect to the matters discussed in the course of the conversation at issue here. That conversation was totally unrelated to any lawyer-client relationship between Kelly and the defendant.

The State's petition is granted, the writ is issued, and the order on review is quashed.

NOTES

1.   The lawyer in this case was asked to testify to a communication between himself and another person. While the privilege is the client's and is intended to protect the client's interest, it is often the lawyer, not the client, who will need to assert the privilege on the client's behalf.

2. What was missing from the communication between Branham and Kelly that caused Branham's privilege claim to fail? At trial, Branham testified that "he believed Kelly was going to give him legal advice and talk to him about other alternatives after he made the comment." Dan Fearson, *"Powerful Testimony Flows at Branham Trial,"* Highlands Today, 9/8/2007. Kelly testified that Branham went into detail about how he planned to kill his wife and named the specific date he intended to do it. "Branham later called to tell him something came up on Friday and he would do it later." Matt Murphy, *"He Told Me He Was Going To Kill His Wife,"* News–Sun, 9/9/2007. Branham's defense to the murder charge was that his wife had attacked him and he had responded in self-defense, making his earlier statement to Kelly highly relevant.

3. Do you think Kelly had an obligation to do something when Branham told Kelly that he intended to kill his wife? What was he permitted to do? These matters are discussed *infra* in Part B.

4. Must there be a formal and ongoing attorney-client relationship to create the privilege? In *In re Investigating Grand Jury*, 887 A.2d 257 (Pa. Super. Ct. 2005), lawyer Stretton represented Y in his trial for murder, kidnaping, rape and robbery. Y was convicted and sentenced to death, and Stretton withdrew from the representation with leave of the court before Y's appeal. Twenty years later, DNA analysis produced exculpatory evidence; based on that evidence, the case was dismissed and Y was released. Prosecutors suspected that Y had made inculpatory statements to Stretton after Stretton had withdrawn from the case. Stretton was subpoenaed to appear before the grand jury and asked to testify as to "what he was told by 'Mr. Y.'" Stretton asserted the privilege, refused to testify, and was found in contempt. The government argued that the formal representation had ended, that communications between Y and his former lawyer were "not made in the course of seeking legal assistance," and that therefore the communications were not privileged. Stretton argued that at the time of the communications in question, it was not yet clear whether Y had another lawyer, that the conversation was about the case, and that Y believed the conversation to be confidential. The court accepted the claim of privilege. "A case does not automatically end simply because there is a change in lawyers. It is the obligation of a lawyer to continue to cooperate with new counsel. It would not advance public policy to provide that absent a formal contract of representation, legal matters discussed between an attorney and someone seeking legal advice are [not] privileged unless it is clear that there is no lawyer-client relationship and it is just a casual conversation." The court continued, "[b]ecause of the strong public policy encouraging clients to talk freely with their attorneys, the fine line between when there is or is not representation is often not known to clients." The court concluded that it was reasonable for Y to believe that because of his prior relation with Stretton, his communications with him were protected by the privilege. Is *Stretton* consistent with *Branham*? Why or why not?

5. What about a prospective client? Mixon was a suspect in a homicide. He worked at a video store. The store employed a lawyer, Heckler. Mixon called Heckler and the two met to discuss Mixon's situation. Heckler initially agreed to represent Mixon in the homicide, but then realized that Mixon might have

used Heckler's gun in the offense. Heckler then declined to represent Mixon. Did the attorney-client privilege apply to the preliminary discussions even though an attorney-client relationship did not result? *See Mixon v. State*, 224 S.W.3d 206 (Tex. Crim. App. 2007).

Whether communications with an individual are protected by the attorney-client privilege is a more complicated question if the lawyer represents an entity client rather than an individual. The following case deals with this complex issue.

UPJOHN CO. v. UNITED STATES
449 U.S. 383 (1981)

JUSTICE REHNQUIST delivered the opinion of the Court.

We granted certiorari in this case to address important questions concerning the scope of the attorney-client privilege in the corporate context and the applicability of the work-product doctrine in proceedings to enforce tax summonses. With respect to the privilege question the parties and various *amici* have described our task as one of choosing between two "tests" which have gained adherents in the courts of appeals. We are acutely aware, however, that we sit to decide concrete cases and not abstract propositions of law. We decline to lay down a broad rule or series of rules to govern all conceivable future questions in this area, even were we able to do so. We can and do, however, conclude that the attorney-client privilege protects the communications involved in this case from compelled disclosure and that the work-product doctrine does apply in tax summons enforcement proceedings.

I

Petitioner Upjohn Co. manufactures and sells pharmaceuticals here and abroad. In January 1976 independent accountants conducting an audit of one of Upjohn's foreign subsidiaries discovered that the subsidiary made payments to or for the benefit of foreign government officials in order to secure government business. The accountants so informed petitioner, Mr. Gerard Thomas, Upjohn's Vice President, Secretary, and General Counsel. Thomas is a member of the Michigan and New York Bars, and has been Upjohn's General Counsel for 20 years. He consulted with outside counsel and R. T. Parfet, Jr., Upjohn's Chairman of the Board. It was decided that the company would conduct an internal investigation of what were termed "questionable payments." As part of this investigation the attorneys prepared a letter containing a questionnaire which was sent to "All Foreign General and Area Managers" over the Chairman's signature. The letter began by noting recent disclosures that several American companies made "possibly illegal" payments to foreign government officials and emphasized that the management needed full information concerning any such payments made by Upjohn. The letter indicated that the Chairman had asked Thomas, identified as "the company's General Counsel," "to conduct an investigation for the purpose of determining the nature and magnitude of any payments made by the Upjohn Company or any of its subsidiaries to any employee or official of a foreign government." The questionnaire sought detailed information concerning such payments. Managers were instructed to treat the investigation as "highly confidential" and not to discuss it with anyone other than Upjohn employees who might be helpful in providing the requested information. Responses were to be sent directly to Thomas. Thomas and outside counsel also interviewed the recipients of the questionnaire and some 33 other Upjohn officers or employees as part of the investigation.

On March 26, 1976, the company voluntarily submitted a preliminary report to the Securities and Exchange Commission on Form 8–K disclosing certain questionable payments. A copy of the report was simultaneously submitted to the Internal Revenue Service, which immediately began an investigation to determine the tax consequences of the payments. Special agents conducting the investigation were given lists by Upjohn of all those interviewed and all who had responded to the questionnaire. On November 23, 1976, the Service issued a summons pursuant to 26 U.S.C. § 7602 demanding production of:

> All files relative to the investigation conducted under the supervision of Gerard Thomas to identify payments to employees of foreign governments and any political contributions made by the Upjohn Company or any of its affiliates since January 1, 1971 and to determine whether any funds of the Upjohn Company had been improperly accounted for on the corporate books during the same period.

> The records should include but not be limited to written questionnaires sent to managers of the Upjohn Company's foreign affiliates, and memorandums or notes of the interviews conducted in the United States and abroad with officers and employees of the Upjohn Company and its subsidiaries.

The company declined to produce the documents specified in the second paragraph on the grounds that they were protected from disclosure by the attorney-client privilege and constituted the work product of attorneys prepared in anticipation of litigation. On August 31, 1977, the United States filed a petition seeking enforcement of the summons.... That court adopted the recommendation of a Magistrate who concluded that the summons should be enforced. Petitioners appealed to the Court of Appeals for the Sixth Circuit which ... agreed that the privilege did not apply "[t]o the extent that the communications were made by officers and agents not responsible for directing Upjohn's actions in response to legal advice ... for the simple reason that the communications were not the 'client's.'" The court reasoned that accepting petitioners' claim for a broader application of the privilege would encourage upper-echelon management to ignore unpleasant facts and create too broad a "zone of silence." Noting that Upjohn's counsel had interviewed officials such as the Chairman and President, the Court of Appeals remanded to the District Court so that a determination of who was within the "control group" could be made. In a concluding footnote the court stated that the work-product doctrine "is not applicable to administrative summonses issued under 26 U.S.C. § 7602."

II

Federal Rule of Evidence 501 provides that "the privilege of a witness . . . shall be governed by the principles of the common law as they may be interpreted by the courts of the United States in light of reason and experience." The attorney-client privilege is the oldest of the privileges for confidential communications known to the common law. Its purpose is to encourage full and frank communication between attorneys and their clients and thereby promote broader public interests in the observance of law and administration of justice. The privilege recognizes that sound legal advice or advocacy serves public ends and that such advice or advocacy depends upon the lawyer's being fully informed by the client. . . . Admittedly complications in the application of the privilege arise when the client is a corporation, which in theory is an artificial creature of the law, and not an individual; but this Court has assumed that the privilege applies when the client is a corporation, and the Government does not contest the general proposition.

The Court of Appeals, however, considered the application of the privilege in the corporate context to present a "different problem," since the client was an inanimate entity and "only the senior management, guiding and integrating the several operations, . . . can be said to possess an identity analogous to the corporation as a whole." The first case to articulate the so-called "control group test" adopted by the court below reflected a similar conceptual approach:

> Keeping in mind that the question is, Is it the corporation which is seeking the lawyer's advice when the asserted privileged communication is made?, the most satisfactory solution, I think, is that if the employee making the communication, of whatever rank he may be, is in a position to control or even to take a substantial part in a decision about any action which the corporation may take upon the advice of the attorney, . . . then, in effect, *he is (or personifies) the corporation* when he makes his disclosure to the lawyer and the privilege would apply. (Emphasis supplied.)

Such a view, we think, overlooks the fact that the privilege exists to protect not only the giving of professional advice to those who can act on it but also the giving of information to the lawyer to enable him to give sound and informed advice. The first step in the resolution of any legal problem is ascertaining the factual background and sifting through the facts with an eye to the legally relevant. . . .

In the case of the individual client the provider of information and the person who acts on the lawyer's advice are one and the same. In the corporate context, however, it will frequently be employees beyond the control group as defined by the court below—"officers and agents . . .

responsible for directing [the company's] actions in response to legal advice"—who will possess the information needed by the corporation's lawyers. Middle-level and indeed lower-level-employees can, by actions within the scope of their employment, embroil the corporation in serious legal difficulties, and it is only natural that these employees would have the relevant information needed by corporate counsel if he is adequately to advise the client with respect to such actual or potential difficulties. . . .

The control group test adopted by the court below thus frustrates the very purpose of the privilege by discouraging the communication of relevant information by employees of the client to attorneys seeking to render legal advice to the client corporation. The attorney's advice will also frequently be more significant to noncontrol group members than to those who officially sanction the advice, and the control group test makes it more difficult to convey full and frank legal advice to the employees who will put into effect the client corporation's policy.

The narrow scope given the attorney-client privilege by the court below not only makes it difficult for corporate attorneys to formulate sound advice when their client is faced with a specific legal problem but also threatens to limit the valuable efforts of corporate counsel to ensure their client's compliance with the law. In light of the vast and complicated array of regulatory legislation confronting the modern corporation, corporations, unlike most individuals, "constantly go to lawyers to find out how to obey the law," particularly since compliance with the law in this area is hardly an instinctive matter. The test adopted by the court below is difficult to apply in practice, though no abstractly formulated and unvarying "test" will necessarily enable courts to decide questions such as this with mathematical precision. But if the purpose of the attorney-client privilege is to be served, the attorney and client must be able to predict with some degree of certainty whether particular discussions will be protected. An uncertain privilege, or one which purports to be certain but results in widely varying applications by the courts, is little better than no privilege at all. The very terms of the test adopted by the court below suggest the unpredictability of its application. The test restricts the availability of the privilege to those officers who play a "substantial role" in deciding and directing a corporation's legal response. Disparate decisions in cases applying this test illustrate its unpredictability. . . .

The communications at issue were made by Upjohn employees to counsel for Upjohn acting as such, at the direction of corporate superiors in order to secure legal advice from counsel. As the Magistrate found, "Mr. Thomas consulted with the Chairman of the Board and outside counsel and thereafter conducted a factual investigation to determine the nature and extent of the questionable payments *and to be in a position to give legal advice to the company with respect to the payments*." (Emphasis supplied.). Information, not available from upper-echelon management, was needed to supply a basis for legal advice concerning compliance with securities and tax laws, foreign laws, currency regulations, duties to shareholders, and potential litigation in each of these areas. The communications concerned matters within the scope of the employees' corporate duties, and the employees themselves were sufficiently aware that they were being questioned in order that the corporation could obtain legal advice. The questionnaire identified Thomas as "the company's General Counsel" and referred in its opening sentence to the possible illegality of payments such as the ones on which information was sought. A statement of policy accompanying the questionnaire clearly indicated the legal implications of the investigation.... This statement was issued to Upjohn employees worldwide, so that even those interviewees not receiving a questionnaire were aware of the legal implications of the interviews. Pursuant to explicit instructions from the Chairman of the Board, the communications were considered "highly confidential" when made, and have been kept confidential by the company. Consistent with the underlying purposes of the attorney-client privilege, these communications must be protected against compelled disclosure.

The Court of Appeals declined to extend the attorney-client privilege beyond the limits of the control group test for fear that doing so would entail severe burdens on discovery and create a broad "zone of silence" over corporate affairs. Application of the attorney-client privilege to communications such as those involved here, however, puts the adversary in no worse position than if the communications had never taken place. The privilege only protects disclosure of communications; it does not protect disclosure of the underlying facts by those who communicated with the attorney:

> [T]he protection of the privilege extends only to *communications* and not to facts. A fact is one thing and a communication concerning that fact is an entirely different thing. The client cannot be compelled to answer the question, 'What did you say or write to the attorney?' but may not refuse to disclose any relevant fact within his knowledge merely because he incorporated a statement of such fact into his communication to his attorney.

Here the Government was free to question the employees who communicated with Thomas and outside counsel. Upjohn has provided the IRS with a list of such employees, and the IRS has already interviewed some 25 of them. While it would probably be more convenient for the Government to secure the results of petitioner's internal investigation by simply subpoenaing the questionnaires and notes taken by petitioner's attorneys, such considerations of convenience do not overcome the policies served by the attorney-client privilege. As Justice Jackson noted in his concurring opinion in *Hickman v. Taylor*, 329 U.S. 495, 516 (1947): "Discovery was hardly intended to enable a learned profession to perform its functions ... on wits borrowed from the adversary."

Needless to say, we decide only the case before us, and do not undertake to draft a set of rules which should govern challenges to investigatory subpoenas. Any such approach would violate the spirit of Federal Rule of Evidence 501. While such a "case-by-case" basis may to some slight extent undermine desirable certainty in the boundaries of the attorney-client privilege, it obeys the spirit of the Rules. At the same time we conclude that the narrow "control group test" sanctioned by the Court of Appeals, in this case cannot, consistent with "the principles of the common law as . . . interpreted . . . in the light of reason and experience," Fed. Rule Evid. 501, govern the development of the law in this area.

III

Our decision that the communications by Upjohn employees to counsel are covered by the attorney-client privilege disposes of the case so far as the responses to the questionnaires and any notes reflecting responses to interview questions are concerned. The summons reaches further, however, and Thomas has testified that his notes and memoranda of interviews go beyond recording responses to his questions. To the extent that the material subject to the summons is not protected by the attorney-client privilege as disclosing communications between an employee and counsel, we must reach the ruling by the Court of Appeals that the work-product doctrine does not apply to summonses issued under 26 U.S.C. § 7602.

The Government concedes, wisely, that the Court of Appeals erred and that the work-product doctrine does apply to IRS summonses. This doctrine was announced by the Court over 30 years ago in *Hickman v. Taylor.* In that case the Court rejected "an attempt, without purported necessity or justification, to secure written statements, private memoranda and personal recollections prepared or formed by an adverse party's counsel in the course of his legal duties." The Court noted that "it is essential that a lawyer work with a certain degree of privacy" and reasoned that if discovery of the material sought were permitted

> much of what is now put down in writing would remain unwritten. An attorney's thoughts, heretofore inviolate, would not be his own. Inefficiency, unfairness and sharp practices would inevitably develop in the giving of legal advice and in the preparation of cases for trial. The effect on the legal profession would be demoralizing. And the interests of the clients and the cause of justice would be poorly served.

While conceding the applicability of the work-product doctrine, the Government asserts that it has made a sufficient showing of necessity to overcome its protections. . . .

The Government stresses that interviewees are scattered across the globe and that Upjohn has forbidden its employees to answer questions it considers irrelevant. The above-quoted language from *Hickman*, however, did not apply to "oral statements made by witnesses . . . whether presently in the form of [the attorney's] mental impressions or memoranda." As to such material the Court did "not believe that any showing of necessity can be made under the circumstances of this case so as to justify production. . . . If there should be a rare situation justifying production of these matters petitioner's case is not of that type." Forcing an attorney to disclose notes and memoranda of witnesses' oral statements is particularly disfavored because it tends to reveal the attorney's mental processes.

Rule 26 accords special protection to work product revealing the attorney's mental processes. The Rule permits disclosure of documents and tangible things constituting attorney work product upon a showing of substantial need and inability to obtain the equivalent without undue hardship. This was the standard applied by the Magistrate. Rule 26 goes on, however, to state that "[i]n ordering discovery of such materials when the required showing has been made, the court shall protect against disclosure of the mental impressions, conclusions, opinions or legal theories of an attorney or other representative of a party concerning the litigation." Although this language does not specifically refer to memoranda based on oral statements of witnesses, the *Hickman* court stressed the danger that compelled disclosure of such memoranda would reveal the attorney's mental processes. It is clear that this is the sort of material the draftsmen of the Rule had in mind as deserving special protection.

Based on the foregoing, some courts have concluded that *no* showing of necessity can overcome protection of work product which is based on oral statements from witnesses. Those courts declining to adopt an absolute rule have nonetheless recognized that such material is entitled to special protection.

We do not decide the issue at this time. It is clear that the Magistrate applied the wrong standard when he concluded that the Government had made a sufficient showing of necessity to overcome the protections of the work-product doctrine. The Magistrate applied the "substantial need" and "without undue hardship" standard articulated in the first part of Rule 26(b)(3). The notes and memoranda sought by the Government here, however, are work product based on oral statements. If they reveal communications, they are, in this case, protected by the attorney-client privilege. To the extent they do not reveal communications, they reveal the attorneys' mental processes in evaluating the communications. As Rule 26 and *Hickman* make clear, such work product cannot be disclosed simply on a showing of substantial need and inability to obtain the equivalent without undue hardship.

While we are not prepared at this juncture to say that such material is always protected by the work-product rule, we think a far stronger showing of necessity and unavailability by other means than was made by the Government or applied by the Magistrate in this case would be necessary to compel disclosure.... [T]he best procedure with respect to this aspect of the case would be to reverse the judgment of the Court of Appeals for the Sixth Circuit and remand the case to it for such further proceedings in connection with the work-product claim as are consistent with this opinion.

NOTES

1. If the court had not upheld the privilege claim in *Upjohn*, what would the likely result have been? How would you, as corporate counsel, have advised a corporate client to proceed in the future in a similar situation if counsel's investigation in that case had not been deemed privileged? Does the privilege serve a useful function in this regard?

2. The Court indicated that the Government was free to interview Upjohn employees. Wouldn't those interviews result in disclosure of privileged information? If so, how can they be proper?

3. According to the government, Upjohn had "forbidden its employees to answer questions it considers irrelevant." If Upjohn's lawyers gave those instructions, did they behave properly? *See* Model Rule 3.4(f).

4. The court also discusses the work product doctrine. Work product immunity is a distinct basis for challenging the admissibility of information prepared by a lawyer for or in anticipation of litigation. It is broader than the attorney-client privilege in some respects; it is not narrowly limited, as the attorney-client privilege is, to information communicated directly by the client. Restatement of the Law Governing Lawyers, § 87, comment (d). The protection for work product can be more limited, however; while "[a]pplication of the attorney-client privilege absolutely bars discovery or testimonial use ... work-product immunity is a qualified protection that, in various circumstances, can be overcome on a proper showing." *Id.* As the opinion reflects, while work product can be compelled on a showing that there is a "substantial need" for the information and that obtaining it by other means would involve "undue hardship" for the searching party, that standard is not sufficient when the work product, like the notes taken by the attorneys in *Upjohn*, would incorporate the mental impressions or opinions of the attorney.

For the privilege to be created, all the necessary elements must be present. What was missing in the following situation?

LYNCH v. HAMRICK

968 So.2d 11 (Ala. 2007)

SEE, JUSTICE.

Juanita Lynch ("Juanita"), individually and through her son Buddy Lynch ("Buddy"), as her attorney-in-fact (collectively "the Lynches"), appeal the trial court's ruling allowing an attorney who had previously represented Juanita to testify in an action seeking to set aside a deed regarding allegedly confidential communications. We affirm.

Factual and Procedural Background

On August 30, 2004, Juanita executed a deed conveying a 40–acre tract of land to her daughter, Rebecca Lynch Hamrick, the defendant below. According to Hamrick's testimony, Juanita asked Hamrick to take her to an attorney in Huntsville so she could execute a new will and convey the land to Hamrick. Hamrick chose Julie Wills from a listing of attorneys in the telephone book because the advertisement said that Wills specialized in elder law.

Wills met with Juanita and Hamrick together in her office. Wills, who testified at trial over the Lynches' assertion of the attorney-client privilege, could not remember whether she had spoken to Juanita alone at any point during their meeting. Hamrick, however, testified that Wills asked her to leave the room during part of the consultation. On the stand, Wills explained that she was cautious in approaching the representation because a potential beneficiary had brought Juanita in to have a will drafted and to convey real property. Wills testified that she believed that Juanita was competent to execute the will and the deed, and she noted that Juanita's testamentary scheme, including the deed, divided her estate evenly between Hamrick and her brother, Buddy. Further, Hamrick gave Wills a document entitled "Chronology of Events," drafted by Hamrick, that showed that the rest of the real property that Juanita had owned had previously been conveyed to Buddy. Wills later telephoned Juanita at her home, "so [she] could talk to her when her daughter was nowhere around, because [Wills] wanted to verify her desires and what she wanted to do . . . and that she wasn't being influenced by her daughter or anyone else." Satisfied that the disposition of the estate and the real property was in accord with Juanita's wishes, Wills prepared the instruments and scheduled a second appointment.

At the second meeting, Wills spoke with Juanita alone, where "[she] confirmed again that she wanted to deed the property to her daughter. [Juanita said that she had] given other property to her son, and this is what she want[ed]." Juanita executed and Wills notarized the warranty deed Wills had prepared, and Hamrick's husband recorded it the next day.

A few days later, Buddy learned that Juanita had conveyed the 40–acre parcel of property to Hamrick. Buddy testified that, when he asked his mother about giving the land to Hamrick, "[s]he told [him] that she didn't know that she had done anything, that she didn't realize [she had done] that." Buddy, as his mother's attorney-in-fact by virtue of a power of attorney previously executed by his mother, sued to set aside the deed, alleging that Hamrick "deceived and tricked" his mother into executing the deed. Juanita intervened in the action in her own right. Through her own attorney, Juanita requested that the trial court set aside the deed, alleging that she was induced to execute the deed based upon Hamrick's representations and promises that she would care for Juanita during her lifetime. Juanita explained that Hamrick could not afford to care for her and that she wanted the deed set aside so that she could use the real property to support herself.

Hamrick gave notice that she intended to depose Wills, and the Lynches and Wills moved to quash the deposition on the basis of the attorney-client privilege. The trial court ruled that the events surrounding the preparation and execution of the deed were not privileged. Although Wills's deposition was never taken, she testified at trial, over the Lynches' objection, to the conversations she had had with Juanita and Hamrick in her office and with Juanita by telephone. On direct examination by Hamrick, Wills's testimony was limited to her perceptions regarding Juanita's capacity to convey the real property and whether the conveyance was voluntary.

The Lynches' attorneys then cross-examined Wills. The Lynches had Wills read from her notes regarding the two meetings and her telephone call to Juanita, and they questioned Wills regarding Juanita's capacity to convey the property and to execute the will. They also asked Wills to testify about the types of questions Wills had asked Juanita and the advice Wills had given her. At the Lynches' request, Wills testified about communications she had had in private with Juanita. When the Lynches asked to see the "Chronology of Events" Hamrick had prepared, Wills's counsel objected, and the Lynches' attorney stated: "We waive her privilege at this point." Later, the Lynches asked Wills about a communication she had had with Juanita after the attorney then representing Juanita contacted her requesting copies of the instruments Juanita had signed. Again, Wills asserted the attorney-client privilege, and the Lynches' attorney said: "We're still waiving."

The trial court declined to set aside the deed.... The Lynches appealed, arguing that the trial court erred in allowing Wills to testify.

Standard of Review

" 'Whether a communication is privileged is a question of fact to be determined by the trial court from the evidence presented....' " The burden is on the party asserting the attorney-client privilege to establish the existence of an attorney-client relationship as well as other facts demonstrating the claim of privileged information. We review a trial court's ruling on whether a privilege exists to determine whether the trial court, in so ruling, exceeded its discretion.

Analysis

Hamrick argues that any communications Juanita had with Wills in Hamrick's presence were not privileged and that Juanita waived the privilege as it pertained to communications between Juanita and Wills when Hamrick was not present. We agree....

The attorney-client privilege belongs to the client, but it may be asserted by the client's attorney on the client's behalf.... Rule 510, Ala. R. Evid., provides that the client may waive the privilege: "A person upon whom these rules confer a privilege against disclosure waives the privilege if the person ... voluntarily discloses or consents to disclosure of any significant part of the privileged matter."

The Lynches first argue that, because "[Hamrick] was interested in the subject matter of Ms. Wills'[s] representation, i.e., the deed," the communications remained privileged even when Hamrick was present. The

Lynches cite the following statement from *International Brotherhood of Teamsters, Chauffeurs, Warehousemen & Helpers of America v. Hatas*, 252 So.2d 7, 28 (1971):

> [W]here two or more persons interested in the same subject matter are present at a conference with an attorney who represents only one of those present, it has been held that matters discussed at such conference are confidential as to strangers to the conference and accordingly they constitute privileged communications as to such strangers.

... [I]n this case, Hamrick did not have "a sufficient common legal interest in the subject matter" of the representation. The Lynches claimed that Juanita gave Hamrick the property in exchange for a promise to support her, a promise Hamrick denies having made. The Lynches also argued to the trial court that one of the reasons they wanted the deed set aside was that transferring the property had consequences on Juanita's eligibility for Medicaid benefits. The Lynches pointed out that the value of the property could be considered in calculating Juanita's assets if she applied for benefits within a certain time after such a transfer. These allegations demonstrate that Juanita's and Hamrick's interests were not sufficiently aligned to preserve the attorney-client privilege because Hamrick's interests in having her mother transfer the property were adverse to her mother's interests in retaining it.

Next, the Lynches argue that Hamrick's "presence was necessary at the meeting because [Hamrick] set the meeting and drove plaintiff Juanita Lynch there." However, there is no evidence indicating that Hamrick's presence in the meeting was necessary for Wills to prepare Juanita's will and the deed. Wills testified that she addressed her questions to Juanita and that "[she] got [Juanita] to explain things to [her] and talk to [her]." Wills stated that "[w]hen [she] deals with older people [she] gets them to give [her] the information." Wills explained that Juanita appeared competent and appeared to know what she wanted to have done in regard to the disposition of her property. Further, after the will and the deed had been drafted, Juanita drove herself to Huntsville to execute those instruments. The burden is on the party asserting the attorney-client privilege to show that the presence of a third party did not destroy the privilege. [T]he trial court was within its discretion in concluding that Hamrick was an unnecessary third party at the meeting between Juanita and Wills.

Further, we may affirm the judgment of the trial court if it is right for any reason, and there is an alternative ground on which the trial court could have allowed Wills to testify. Wills's testimony on direct examination was limited to the facts that Juanita signed the deed voluntarily, that there was no trickery or deceit used to obtain her signature, and that Juanita appeared coherent and able to understand the contents and the effect of the instrument. Hamrick correctly points out that, under Rule 502(d)(4), Ala. R. Evid., there is no privilege "[a]s to a communication relevant to an issue concerning the intention or competence of a client executing an attested document to which the attorney is an attesting witness, or concerning the execution or attestation of such a document." Wills was the attesting witness to the deed, and she could thus "divulge information received in the attorney's capacity as an attesting witness." Wills's testimony on direct examination was largely limited to information regarding Juanita's intentions and information that Wills had gained in her capacity as the attesting witness, and it did not contain privileged information.

It was only in response to the cross-examination by the Lynches that Wills produced information regarding the representation that could be regarded as learned in her capacity as an attorney. Further, although the Lynches now argue that the trial court erred in allowing Wills to testify regarding private conversations between Wills and Juanita, it was the Lynches, not Hamrick, who elicited such testimony regarding these private conversations. The Lynches asked Wills to read the notes she took at each of her meetings with Juanita. The attorney representing Juanita in this action asked Wills: "Since [the first consultation] was a thirty-minute meeting, why don't you just shortly, briefly, go over your notes for us. Why don't you just read from them." The Lynches also asked Wills to read her notes from the private telephone call Wills made to Juanita after the first meeting, as well as her notes made after the second meeting. According to the Lynches, each of these consultations contained privileged communications.

Further, the Lynches asked Wills about her conclusions regarding Juanita's competency and how she came to those conclusions. The Lynches asked Wills: "[W]hat kind of questions did you ask Mrs. Lynch? . . . Did you ever ask her about her memory?" The Lynches then questioned Wills about how she concluded that Juanita was of "sound mind." They also asked Wills: "Ms. Wills, was there anything to suggest that Mrs. Lynch was either under duress or that she was somehow coerced into making this deed or meeting with you?" The Lynches thus elicited the same information regarding Juanita's competency with greater detail than had Hamrick in her direct examination of Wills.

By inquiring into the substance of what were otherwise confidential and privileged communications between Juanita and Wills, Juanita waived the attorney-client privilege.

Finally, the Lynches, in separate instances, expressly waived the protections of the attorney-client privilege. When she was asked to present the "Chronology of Events," Wills's counsel objected, and the Lynches stated: "We waive her privilege at this point." Later, the Lynches asked Wills about a communication Wills had had with Juanita after she was contacted by the attorney then representing Juanita. Again, Wills asserted the attorney-client privilege, and the Lynches said: "We're still waiving."

For these reasons, it does not appear that the trial court exceeded its discretion in allowing Wills to testify regarding her representation of Juanita.

Conclusion

The Lynches have failed to establish that the protections of the attorney-client privilege apply in this case. The trial court acted within its discretion when it allowed Wills to testify regarding Juanita's intentions and her capacity to execute the warranty deed in Hamrick's favor. Further, by their cross-examination of Wills regarding the confidential communications she had had with Juanita, the Lynches waived any error the trial court may have otherwise committed in permitting Wills to testify.

NOTES

1. Why did the court conclude that the communications made to the attorney by Juanita Lynch in the presence of her daughter, Rebecca Hamrick, were not privileged? Are there circumstances under which the presence of more than one party to the conversation would not defeat the privilege? When a lawyer represents multiple clients together, the presence of the multiple clients does not defeat the privilege. Since each is represented by the lawyer, the communications of each of the clients with the lawyer are confidential, as far as the rest of the world is concerned. Ordinarily, there will not be any privilege as between the multiply represented parties; since they are jointly represented in the same matter, it is assumed that as between them the confidentiality necessary to create privilege does not exist. So if Lawyer represents A and B jointly, and subsequently C sues A and B based on a matter relating to the representation, both A and B can assert the privilege if asked by C to testify to communications with Lawyer. If, however, A sues B, neither A nor B can assert the attorney-client privilege against the other. This was not quite the case in *Lynch*. What was the argument about why the communications made by Lynch in Hamrick's presence were nonetheless privileged, and why did it fail?

2. The court concluded that certain information to which the lawyer testified would not have been protected by the privilege in any event. Why not? Suppose that a lawyer is asked to testify to the appearance of a client at the time of a meeting: whether the client appeared disheveled, for example, or whether she had a cut on her face. Would that information be privileged? Why or why not?

3. The court helpfully distinguishes between the situation in which the privilege never attached and the situation in which the Lynches waived the privilege after it had been created. What information was privileged here and how did the Lynches waive the privilege? Waiver is discussed more extensively in the following section.

4. In this case, the presence of a third party in the consultation between lawyer and client defeated the confidentiality of the communication. Can technology similarly render communications not "confidential" for purposes of the attorney-client privilege? Scott, a physician, claimed that Beth Israel Medical Center, his employer, was in possession of confidential emails he had sent to his lawyer regarding a dispute he was having with the hospital. He argued that the emails were privileged and demanded their return. Beth Israel claimed that the emails could not have been confidential because the

hospital's email policy expressly stated that the hospital's email was for business purposes only and that employees had no privacy right in any materials generated or received using the university's computer systems. "The Medical Center," the policy continued, "reserves the right to access and disclose such material at any time without prior notice." Do you think the company's policy defeated Scott's privilege claim? *See Scott v. Beth Israel Medical Center Inc.*, 847 N.Y.S.2d 436 (N.Y. Sup. Ct. 2007).

⁕ 5. The privilege protects only *communications* between attorney and client. Does this include the identity of the client? In most cases, the answer is no. In *Lefcourt v. United States*, 125 F.3d 79 (2d Cir. 1997), the firm of Gerald Lefcourt, a criminal defense lawyer, was assessed a penalty for violating a tax statute that required the firm to report to the IRS the name of any client who paid the firm more than $10,000 in cash. The firm argued that the client's identity was protected by the privilege because the completed form "would provide the government with evidence of the client's unexplained wealth— evidence that could incriminate the client in the same proceedings for which the client had retained the law firm." *Id.* at 85. The court rejected the argument. A different rule might apply if the disclosure of the client's identity, in effect, amounted to a disclosure of confidential communications.

Are there situations in which this should not be the rule? Lawyer submitted to the IRS a cashier's check for $12,706 in taxes on behalf of a taxpayer, but did not designate the taxpayer's name. The amount was paid on Lawyer's advice, and reflected an underpayment of tax of which the IRS was unaware. The IRS sought to compel Lawyer's testimony about the name of the client for whom he made the payment. Should Lawyer be required to disclose? *See Baird v. Koerner*, 279 F.2d 623 (9th Cir. 1960). Is this the same as *Lefcourt*, or different? Why?

2. DEFEATING THE PRIVILEGE

(A) EXCEPTIONS TO THE PRIVILEGE

(I) THE TESTAMENTARY EXCEPTION

Are there times when the privilege should not apply? Suppose that Client consults Lawyer for the purpose of drafting a will. Lawyer assists Client in drafting the will and it is properly executed. Subsequently, Client dies and family members contest the will on the ground of lack of capacity. Must Lawyer remain silent in the face of this challenge to Client's asserted desires? While the privilege is ordinarily held to survive the client's death, most states recognize a testamentary exception to the privilege in this circumstance, on the ground that there is an implicit waiver where the disclosure by the lawyer would further the client's testamentary intent. See Restatement of the Law Governing Lawyers § 81.

What if the client never completed the will, however? In *Gould, Larson, Bennet, Wells & McDonnell PC v. Panico*, 869 A.2d 653 (Conn. 2005), Panico engaged the Gould firm in 1993 and the firm wrote a will for him. In 2002, Panico consulted the firm about changes to his will. He met with a lawyer from the firm but the firm never prepared or executed a new will for him. Instead, Panico went to another lawyer, who prepared a new will, which Panico signed. Panico died shortly thereafter, and there was a dispute between his heirs about whether the 1993 will or the 2002 will should control. The heirs subpoenaed the Gould lawyer and sought testimony about Panico's consultations with the lawyer regarding the possible drafting of a new will. The lawyer resisted the subpoena and claimed the privilege. The court concluded that in light of the fact that the will had never been executed, there was no basis to assume an implicit waiver of the privilege. "In our view, the testator's intent is expressed, *if at all,* in the creation of an executed will. When no will results from the privileged communications, there is no basis upon which to imply a waiver of that privilege."

(II) THE CRIME–FRAUD EXCEPTION

Another exception to the privilege arises when a client consults a lawyer for the purpose of using the lawyer's assistance to commit a crime or fraud. What are the elements of the crime-fraud exception?

UNITED STATES v. DOE

429 F.3d 450 (3d Cir. 2005)

ROSENN, CIRCUIT JUDGE.

This appeal raises several serious questions concerning the time-respected role of privileged communication between client and attorney and the crime-fraud exception. For almost four years now, the Government has had an active grand jury investigating certain activities of a federal law enforcement officer (hereinafter referred to as "Target"). The Government submitted details of the investigation to the District Court under seal through an *ex parte* affidavit of Peter R. Zeidenberg, a trial attorney of the Criminal Division of the Public Integrity Section of the United States Department of Justice. The Government sought the grand jury testimony of an attorney (hereinafter referred to as "Attorney") from whom Target sought legal advice in connection with an allegedly fraudulent, and likely criminal, course of conduct. Specifically, the Government claims to have discovered evidence that Target proposed to engage in future criminal conduct, and that Target's purpose in consulting Attorney was to ascertain how best to conceal the illegal activity in which he planned to engage.

Attorney refused to respond to a grand jury subpoena, invoking the attorney-client privilege and moving to quash the subpoena. The District Court for the District of New Jersey conducted a sealed hearing on the motion to quash. The Government argued that the crime-fraud exception to the privilege applied to Target's conversations with the lawyer because they were in furtherance of Target's planned criminal activity....

The District Court issued an oral ruling granting the motion to quash, concluding that the crime-fraud exception did not apply.... The Government timely appealed. For reasons set forth below, we reverse and direct the denial of the motion to quash.

... The attorney-client privilege is a well-established historic rule which protects confidential communications between client and attorney. The privilege belongs to the client, not the attorney. The Supreme Court has long emphasized that the central concern of the privilege is to "encourage full and frank communication between attorneys and their clients and thereby promote broader public interests in the observance of law and administration of justice." *United States v. Zolin,* 491 U.S. 554, 562 (1989) (quoting *Upjohn Co. v. United States,* 449 U.S. 383, 389 (1981)).... The privilege is not lost if a client proposes a course of conduct which he is advised by counsel is illegal, but is extinguished when a client seeks legal advice to further a continuing or future crime. Because this ancient and valuable privilege is at the expense of the full discovery of the truth, it should be strictly construed....

We now turn to the Government's principal argument, the crime-fraud exception to the attorney client privilege rule. As the Supreme Court noted in *Zolin,* the attorney-client privilege is not without limitations. A principal and reasonable exception is that the privilege may not be used for the purpose of obtaining advice to promote crime or fraud. Although broad, the privilege does not allow a client to shield evidence of an intent to use an attorney's advice to further a criminal purpose.

The crime-fraud exception to the attorney-client privilege applies to any communications between an attorney and client that are intended "to further a continuing or future crime or tort." In this analysis, "the client's intention controls and the privilege may be denied even if the lawyer is altogether innocent." The privilege is not lost if the client innocently proposes an illegal course of conduct to explore with his counsel what he may or may not do. Only when a client knowingly seeks legal counsel to further a continuing or future crime does the crime-fraud exception apply.

Although the District Court made no formal findings of fact as to the defendant's intent in consulting with his lawyer, the record is sufficient to support a finding that the Government met its burden of establishing a prima facie case to have the subpoena honored. A prima facie showing "requires evidence which, if believed by the fact-finder, would be sufficient to support a finding that the elements of the crime-fraud exception were met." Specifically, the Government must show that "the client was committing or intending to commit a fraud or crime" and that the consultation was "in furtherance of that alleged crime or fraud."

... The record is reasonably clear as to the criminal intent of Target. It shows that Target was an experienced federal law enforcement officer, having served in that capacity for seven years. Witness' business was at the center of an investigation in which Target was responsible for coordinating Witness' activities as an informant. Target consulted Attorney in 1999, asking how he could invest in Witness' business. Witness later informed the Government that Target "sought [Attorney's] advice on how such an investment could be made—and, in particular, whether [Target] could do the investment in [his] wife's name rather than in [Target's] name so that he could not be directly tied to the investment."

The investment would have been a criminal violation of 18 U.S.C. § 208 & 209 which bar any officer or employee of an independent agency of the United States, unless exempted or granted a special exception of the Government, from having a financial interest in any business or any arrangement concerning prospective employment, or from receiving salary or compensation from nongovernmental sources. We think it implausible that an experienced government agent like Target would not know that the proposed investment was a crime. In March 2000, Target made the investment in the business of Witness and received $1000–2000 per week for the duration of the investment. We conclude that the Government has made a prima facie case that the crime-fraud exception applies. . . .

NOTES

1. What is the purpose of the crime-fraud exception? A lawyer is prohibited from advising a client to commit a crime or fraud; see Model Rule 1.2(d). But many consultations with lawyers are not quite as straightforward as the one in this case; few clients ask their lawyers, "How can I get away with this felony?" Might the crime-fraud exception interfere with legitimate attempts on the part of clients to secure legal advice about the propriety of their conduct? Suppose Client comes to you, tells you that he is engaged in a cash business, and asks if he must declare all that income on his tax return. You advise him that he is legally obligated to disclose, and describe to him the penalties for failure to comply and the likelihood that his return will be audited. If he subsequently does not disclose his cash income on his tax return, does the crime-fraud exception apply to your conversation? Should it?

2. As the court notes, the crime-fraud exception is based on the client's intent and knowledge, not the lawyer's. In *In re: Sealed Case*, 162 F.3d 670 (D.C. Cir. 1998), Client came to Lawyer and asked him to prepare an affidavit for her for submission in a court proceeding. Lawyer prepared the affidavit and submitted it as Client requested. Subsequently, it became clear that Client had lied about material matters in the affidavit, though Lawyer did not know that at the time he prepared it. Client's consultations with Lawyer were held to fall within the crime-fraud exception to the privilege. (Client was Monica Lewinsky, and the affidavit concerned her false assertions that she had not had an intimate relationship with President Bill Clinton.)

3. As a procedural matter, what must be shown to defeat the privilege under the crime-fraud exception? The party challenging the privilege has the burden of making a prima facie showing that the communications were in further-ance of an intended or present illegality, and that there is some relationship between the communications and the illegality. How close do you think that relationship should be before the exception applies?

4. Does a finding that the crime-fraud exception applies mean that none of the communications between the attorney and the client are privileged? In *In*

re Grand Jury Subpoena, 419 F.3d 329 (5th Cir. 2005), Lawyer represented Client, a felon, on several weapons possession charges over a period of nine months. Client's girlfriend, Witness, initially claimed in two sworn statements that the weapon in question was not hers, but subsequently sought to change her statement, saying that she had lied when she denied ownership. The prosecution claimed that Client and Witness were trying to obstruct justice by falsely claiming that the weapon belonged to Witness, not Client. It sought to require Lawyer to testify to conversations he had with Client. Client protested that, even if the crime-fraud exception applied, it did not apply to every communication between Client and Lawyer during the entire representation, but only to the communications made to further an ongoing or future crime or fraud. The court agreed; "the proper reach of the crime-fraud exception when applicable does not extend to all communications made in the course of the attorney-client relationship but rather is limited to those communications and documents in furtherance of the contemplated or ongoing criminal or fraudulent conduct." *Id.* at 342.

(B) WAIVER OF THE PRIVILEGE

Once the privilege attaches, it can be waived by conduct inconsistent with the preservation of the privilege. Since confidentiality is the hallmark of the privilege, conduct inconsistent with maintaining the confidentiality of privileged information can waive the privilege. In the *Lynch* case, *supra*, the court concluded that the party claiming the privilege had waived it by asking the lawyer to testify to privileged material. What was the conduct in the following case that led to the claim of waiver? Do you think the court's conclusion was fair?

IN RE QWEST COMMUNICATIONS INT'L INC.

450 F.3d 1179 (10th Cir. 2006)

MURPHY, CIRCUIT JUDGE.

In this mandamus action, Qwest Communications International, Inc. (Qwest), presents an issue of first impression in this circuit, namely, whether Qwest waived the attorney-client privilege and work-product doctrine, as to third-party civil litigants, by releasing privileged materials to federal agencies in the course of the agencies' investigation of Qwest. Qwest urges us to adopt a rule of "selective waiver" or "limited waiver" which would allow production of attorney-client privileged and work-product documents to the United States Department of Justice (DOJ) and the Securities and Exchange Commission (SEC) without waiver of further protection for those materials. On the record before us, we hold that the district court did not abuse its discretion in declining to apply selective waiver.

In early 2002, the SEC began investigating Qwest's business practices. In the summer of 2002, Qwest learned that the DOJ ... had also commenced a criminal investigation of Qwest. During these investigations, Qwest produced to the agencies over 220,000 pages of documents protected by the attorney-client privilege ... (the Waiver Documents). Qwest chose not to produce another 390,000 pages of privileged documents to the agencies.

The production of the Waiver Documents was pursuant to subpoena and pursuant to written confidentiality agreements between Qwest and each agency. In relevant part, these agreements stated that Qwest did not intend to waive the attorney-client privilege.... The SEC agreed to "maintain the confidentiality of the [Waiver Documents] pursuant to this Agreement and ... not disclose them to any third party, except to the extent that the Staff determines that disclosure is otherwise required by law or would be in furtherance of the Commission's discharge of its duties and responsibilities." Similarly, the DOJ agreed to maintain the Waiver Documents' confidentiality and not disclose them to third parties. In addition, Qwest agreed that the DOJ could share the Waiver Documents with other state, local, and federal agencies, and that it could "make direct or derivative use of the [Waiver Documents] in any proceeding and its investigation." In other agreements with the DOJ, Qwest agreed that the agency could

> make full use of any information it obtains under this agreement in any lawful manner in furtherance of its investigation, including, without limitation, analyses, interviews, grand jury proceedings, court proceedings, consultation with and support of other federal, state or local agencies, consultations with experts or potential experts, and the selection and/or retention of testifying experts.

Even prior to the initiation of the federal investigations, plaintiffs had filed civil cases against Qwest that involved many of the same issues as the investigations. More such actions were filed after the federal investigations began. Several of the cases ... were consolidated into a federal securities action designated *In re Qwest Communications International, Inc. Securities Litigation* (the Securities Case). The Real Parties in Interest before us (the Plaintiffs) are the lead plaintiffs in the Securities Case.

In the course of the Securities Case, Qwest produced millions of pages of documents to the Plaintiffs, but it did not produce the Waiver Documents. It argued the Waiver Documents remained privileged despite Qwest's production to the agencies. After the Plaintiffs moved to compel production of the Waiver Documents, the magistrate judge concluded Qwest had waived the attorney-client privilege and work-product protection by producing the Waiver Documents to the agencies and ordered Qwest to produce the Waiver Documents to the Plaintiffs. Qwest objected. The district court refused to overrule the magistrate judge's order compelling production and ordered Qwest to produce the Waiver Documents....

Qwest filed a motion to reconsider the order to produce the Waiver Documents and to certify an interlocutory appeal.... The court ... declined to certify an interlocutory appeal of the waiver issue. Consequently, Qwest filed a petition for a writ of mandamus in this court....

Federal Rule of Evidence 501 provides that privileges in federal-question cases generally are "governed by the principles of the common law as they may be interpreted by the courts of the United States in the light of reason and experience." The Advisory Committee Notes state that the rule "reflect[s] the view that the recognition of a privilege based on a confidential relationship and other privileges should be determined on a case-by-case basis."

The Supreme Court has cautioned that "[t]estimonial exclusionary rules and privileges contravene the fundamental principle that the public . . . has a right to every man's evidence." The Court further has cautioned that such rules and privileges "must be strictly construed and accepted 'only to the very limited extent that permitting a refusal to testify or excluding relevant evidence has a public good transcending the normally predominant principle of utilizing all rational means for ascertaining truth.' " . . .

Because confidentiality is key to the privilege, "[t]he attorney-client privilege is lost if the client discloses the substance of an otherwise privileged communication to a third party." This court has stated, "the confidentiality of communications covered by the privilege must be jealously guarded by the holder of the privilege lest it be waived. The courts will grant no greater protection to those who assert the privilege than their own precautions warrant." . . . "Any voluntary disclosure by the client is inconsistent with the attorney-client relationship and waives the privilege."

In light of this precedent, Qwest will have waived the attorney-client privilege and work-product protection for the Waiver Documents by disclosing them to the SEC and the DOJ, unless this court adopts a selective waiver rule. This court has not yet considered the concept of selective waiver. Our review of the opinions of other circuits, however, indicates there is almost unanimous rejection of selective waiver. Only the Eighth Circuit has adopted selective waiver in circumstances applicable to Qwest.

The Eighth Circuit created the concept of selective waiver in *Diversified Industries, Inc. v. Meredith*, 572 F.2d 596, 611 (8th Cir. 1977). There, a company defending a civil proceeding sought to protect a memorandum and a report prepared by its counsel that it had previously produced to the SEC in response to an agency subpoena. The court's discussion of selective waiver is but a single paragraph:

> We finally address the issue of whether Diversified waived its attorney-client privilege with respect to the privileged material by voluntarily surrendering it to the SEC pursuant to an agency subpoena. As Diversified disclosed these documents in a separate and nonpublic SEC investigation, we conclude that only a limited waiver of the privilege occurred. To hold otherwise may have the effect of thwarting the developing procedure of corporations to employ independent outside counsel to investigate and advise them in order to protect stockholders, potential stockholders and customers.

Id. at 611.

Most circuits have rejected selective waiver of the attorney-client privilege. The D.C. Circuit was the first circuit to consider the issue after *Diversified*. In *Permian Corp. v. United States*, the Department of Energy requested documents from the SEC, which had obtained them from the company. 665 F.2d 1214, 1216–17 (D.C. Cir. 1981). After considering the privilege's purpose of protecting the attorney-client relationship by shielding confidential communications, the court held that the company had "destroyed the confidential status of the seven attorney-client communications by permitting their disclosure to the SEC staff." It found the proposal of selective waiver "wholly unpersuasive."

> First, we cannot see how the availability of a "limited waiver" would serve the interests underlying the common law privilege for confidential communications between attorney and client.... Voluntary cooperation with government investigations may be a laudable activity, but it is hard to understand how such conduct improves the attorney-client relationship. If the client feels the need to keep his communications with his attorney confidential, he is free to do so under the traditional rule by consistently asserting the privilege, even when the discovery request comes from a "friendly" agency.

The court continued, "[t]he client cannot be permitted to pick and choose among his opponents, waiving the privilege for some and resurrecting the claim of confidentiality to obstruct others, or to invoke the privilege as to communications whose confidentiality he has already compromised for his own benefit." "We believe that the attorney-client privilege should be available only at the traditional price: a litigant who wishes to assert confidentiality must maintain genuine confidentiality."

Using similar reasoning, the First, Second, Third, and Fourth Circuits all have joined the D.C. Circuit in rejecting selective waiver. The most recent circuit to reject selective waiver of the attorney-client privilege is the Sixth Circuit.... It concluded, "after due consideration, we reject the concept of selective waiver, in any of its various forms." ...

[W]e conclude the record in this case is not sufficient to justify adoption of a selective waiver doctrine as an exception to the general rules of waiver upon disclosure of protected material. Qwest advocates a rule that would preserve the protection of materials disclosed to federal agencies under agreements which purport to maintain the attorney-client privilege and work-product protection but do little to limit further disclosure by the government. The record does not establish a need for a rule of selective waiver to assure cooperation with law enforcement, to further the purposes of the attorney-client privilege or work-product doctrine, or to avoid unfairness to the disclosing party. Rather than a mere exception to the general rules of waiver, one could argue that Qwest seeks the substantial equivalent of an entirely new privilege, i.e., a government-investigation privilege. Regardless of characterization, however, the rule Qwest advocates would be a leap, not a natural, incremental next step in the common law development of privileges and protections. On this record, "[w]e are unwilling to embark the judiciary on a long and difficult journey to such an uncertain destination.''

Qwest argues selective waiver is necessary to ensure cooperation with government investigations. Selective waiver may well be a means to encourage cooperation with law enforcement, an end with unquestioned benefits to the commonwealth....

The record before us, however, does not support the contention that companies will cease cooperating with law enforcement absent protection under the selective waiver doctrine. Most telling is Qwest's disclosure of 220,000 pages of protected materials knowing the Securities Case was pending, in the face of almost unanimous circuit-court rejection of selective waiver in similar circumstances, and despite the absence of Tenth Circuit precedent. These actions undermine its argument that selective waiver is vitally necessary to ensure companies' cooperation in government investigations....

Further, if selective waiver were as essential to government operations as Qwest claims, it would seem the agencies would support Qwest's position. At the court's request, the DOJ responded to Qwest's petition. Rather than urging the adoption of selective waiver, though, it carefully took no position on the parties' dispute. Additionally, the DOJ declined an invitation to participate in oral argument. It would appear, then, that the government's interest is not as Qwest portrays it.

Qwest also contends the key point distinguishing this case from the majority of the cases rejecting selective waiver is the fact that Qwest entered into confidentiality agreements with the agencies prior to disclosing the Waiver Documents. Some courts have held or indicated that the existence of a confidentiality agreement is irrelevant to a waiver of privileges. Others, however, have indicated that the existence of a confidentiality agreement may justify adopting selective waiver.

The record does not support reliance on the Qwest agreements with the SEC and the DOJ to justify selective waiver. The agreements do little to restrict the agencies' use of the materials they received from Qwest. The agencies are permitted to use the Waiver Documents as required by law and in furtherance of the discharge of their obligations. The DOJ is specifically permitted to share the Waiver Documents with other agencies, federal, state, and local, and make use of them in proceedings and investigations. In its brief, the DOJ illustrates just how far some of the documents may have traveled, stating that, at a minimum, Waiver Documents have been introduced into evidence in a criminal trial, produced as discovery in three separate criminal proceedings, and used as exhibits to SEC investigative testimony. The DOJ also informs us it was not required to ''segregate material obtained from Qwest, file it under seal, keep records of its use, or otherwise deal with the information in any special way,'' and it had made no effort to determine what information had been disseminated to third parties.

The record does not indicate whether Qwest negotiated or could have negotiated for more protection for the Waiver Documents, or whether, as it asserted at oral argument, seeking further restrictions would have so diluted its cooperation to render it valueless. Be that as it may, the confidentiality agreements gave the agencies broad discretion to use the Waiver Documents as they saw fit, and any restrictions on their use were loose in practice. As Qwest has conceded, it is unknown how many or which of the Waiver Documents the agencies have used or disclosed, how those uses or disclosures occurred, who might have had access to the Waiver Documents, and the extent of continuing disclosures. It is therefore not inappropriate to conclude that some undetermined number of Waiver Documents have been widely disseminated and have thus become public information. . . .

In short, Qwest's confidentiality agreements do not support adoption of selective waiver. . . .

Qwest argues that adopting selective waiver would avoid unfairness to Qwest while visiting no unfairness on the Plaintiffs. If companies do not have the assurance of protection, Qwest theorizes, they simply will not release privileged documents to federal authorities. Thus, civil plaintiffs will not have access to them anyway. . . . Allowing Qwest to choose who among its opponents would be privy to the Waiver Documents is far from a universally accepted perspective of fairness.

As discussed above, the record is silent on whether selective waiver truly is necessary to achieve cooperation. Qwest's fairness argument nevertheless rests on that very foundation. It is difficult to understand how a rejection of selective waiver will work an unfairness on Qwest when Qwest disclosed the Waiver Documents in the face of the known threat from Plaintiffs, the absence of Tenth Circuit precedent, and a dearth of favorable circuit authority. It hedged its bets by choosing to release 220,000 pages of documents but to retain another 390,000 pages of privileged documents. Qwest perceived an obvious benefit from its disclosures but did so while weighing the risk of waiver. . . .

Amici curiae, Association of Corporate Counsel and the Chamber of Commerce of the United States of America, support Qwest's position by suggesting their employers and members, respectively, now litigate in a "culture of waiver" instituted by federal prosecutors. They argue that companies facing federal investigations do not choose to waive their privileges; under current enforcement standards, companies cannot risk being labeled as uncooperative; and cooperation, as defined by federal officials, requires producing privileged documents. Amici state that "the demand for privilege waivers by the government as a pre-requisite to fair treatment by prosecutors is now routine." They urge the court "to note with disapproval this culture of waiver as a matter of policy that should be reversed."

Amici's position is supported by commentators. It is not, however, supported by the record. Aside from the anecdotal material serving as the foundation for the purported "culture of waiver," the record is silent regarding its existence, significance, and longevity. More specifically, the record is silent about Qwest's particular dealings with the agencies and whether it experienced the tactics deplored by amici. Even though common sense and human nature suggest there is some level of pressure for companies to satisfy the government by disclosing as much as possible, including even privileged and protected material, this court cannot rely on such a sparse record to recognize a new doctrine of selective waiver or to create a new privilege for government investigations.

For the reasons discussed above, the record in this case does not justify adoption of selective waiver. Consequently, the district court did not abuse its discretion in ordering Qwest to produce the Waiver Documents to the Plaintiffs.

NOTES

1.   Who sought the documents as to which Qwest claimed privilege? What was the conduct that the court deemed to have waived the privilege? Why should the plaintiffs in the securities action benefit from Quest's cooperation with regulators?

2.   What impact does the rejection of a selective waiver claim have on a corporate entity's decision to cooperate with government investigators? Do you think the lawyers for Qwest knew at the time they made the disclosures to the DOJ or the SEC that they were unlikely to succeed in asserting a claim of selective waiver? How do you think that affected the decision to cooperate?

3.   In the court's view, a doctrine of selective waiver did not advance the goals of the attorney-client privilege or the work product doctrine. Do you think that is correct? Imagine that you are Qwest's in-house counsel. Does this decision affect the sort of documents you generate? Why or why not?

4.   Why didn't the parties' agreement that the release of the documents to the federal agencies would not constitute a waiver suffice to protect Qwest? New Federal Rule of Evidence 502(d) provides that a federal court may order that disclosures connected with litigation will not constitute waiver. Rule 502(e), however, makes clear that the parties' agreement about the effect of a disclosure, without more, cannot prevent a finding of waiver and "is binding only on the parties to the agreement, unless it is incorporated into a court order."

5.   Concerns about corporate frauds caused federal prosecutors in the post-Enron era to take an aggressive posture towards corporate entities in criminal investigations. One of the aspects that caused considerable criticism of prosecutors was a claim that they exerted pressure on corporate entities to waive the attorney-client privilege in order to be perceived as having cooperated with the investigation. The 2003 "Thompson memorandum" provided that waiver of attorney-client privilege by a corporation was deemed to reflect "cooperation" with the government, which was assessed in deciding whether to charge a corporate entity with a crime. This policy was extensively criticized, notably in a letter signed by several former senior figures in the

Justice Department, including three former Solicitors General and two former Attorneys General, and by an ABA Task Force on Attorney–Client Privilege, and legislation was proposed to countermand it. The Department of Justice modified its policies in the "McNulty Memo," which claimed to constrain the power of prosecutors to seek waivers of the attorney-client privilege from corporate targets of criminal investigations. The McNulty memo was also subjected to extensive criticism, because it continued to allow a prosecutor to consider a corporation's willingness to waive privileges in assessing whether the entity had cooperated with the government. Under legislative pressure, the Department of Justice in the summer of 2008 once again released new guidelines, this time purporting to assure that "Eligibility for cooperation credit is not predicated upon the waiver of attorney-client privilege or work product protection." *Principles of Federal Prosecution of Business Organizations*, 9–28.720. It remains to be seen whether the new guidelines will alleviate concerns about what Qwest termed the "culture of waiver."

6. In the *Qwest* case, the waiver flowed from an intentional disclosure of information to third parties. What if the disclosure is inadvertent? Should the privilege still be waived? Inadvertent disclosure often happens during document discovery in civil litigation. If a document is called for by a discovery request but there is a viable claim that it is protected by privilege, the proper procedure is to particularize any claim of privilege by listing the document on a "privilege log," not to produce it. If the document is inadvertently produced, should that waive the privilege? Electronic discovery seems likely to exacerbate this problem. *See Victor Stanley, Inc. v. Creative Pipe, Inc.*, 250 F.R.D. 251 (D. Md. 2008) (holding that privilege was waived with respect to 165 documents disclosed in discovery). If you are the recipient of an inadvertently disclosed privileged document, what are your obligations? See Model Rule 4.4(b). The rule requires you to disclose to the sender that you have received the document. Does it permit you to keep it, read it, use it, or claim that your receipt of it waived the privilege? Brand-new Federal Rule of Evidence 502(b) limits the impact of inadvertent disclosure in a federal proceeding; if the holder of the privilege took reasonable steps to prevent disclosure and promptly took reasonable steps to rectify the error, the inadvertent disclosure should not operate as a waiver.

7. The dangers of waiver are exacerbated because waiver as to one document or piece of information is sometimes treated as a waiver of all other privileged information regarding the same subject matter. The principle behind the doctrine of subject matter waiver is fairness. If you know of 500 privileged documents relating to an issue, and three of them are favorable to your position, it would not be fair to let you offer those three documents into evidence without allowing your adversary access to the remaining 497 documents. While this seems reasonable when a party is affirmatively offering privileged material into evidence, it is less convincing when the waiver arises from an inadvertent disclosure of a privileged document. In that situation, no fairness argument exists, and the costs of making sure that privileged matter is never inadvertently disclosed can be extremely high.

New Federal Rule of Evidence 502 proposes a solution to this problem. Rule 502(a) provides that the doctrine of subject matter waiver can be applied only to intentional, as opposed to inadvertent, waivers. Only those seeking to use privileged information as a sword acquire the obligation of complete disclosure, and only when the matters ought in fairness to be considered together.

8.   Waiver is also accomplished by putting the protected information at issue. " 'At issue' waiver of privilege occurs where a party affirmatively places the subject matter of its own privileged communication at issue in litigation." *Deutsche Bank Trust Co. v. Tri–Links Inv. Trust*, 837 N.Y.S.2d 15 (Sup. Ct. 2007). Why would placing the subject matter of the privilege at issue in litigation amount to waiver? For the privileged communications to be at issue, the party must have asserted a claim or defense that it intends to prove using the privileged material; it is not enough that the privileged materials might be relevant to a litigated matter.

B.   THE DUTY OF CONFIDENTIALITY

As we have seen, the attorney-client privilege provides some protection to information exchanged in the course of the attorney-client relationship. But it is quite limited. First, it protects only judicially compelled production of information. That includes subpoenaed documents and discovery material as well as testimony. But it does not apply outside the context of judicial or administrative proceedings. Second, it protects a limited range of information: communications between lawyer and client. As you can imagine, a lawyer might learn sensitive information in the course of representing a client from sources other than communications with the client. The attorney-client privilege does not apply to such information. The broader duty of confidentiality described in the ethics rules therefore comes into play.

Issues of confidentiality permeate the ethics rules. But the basic rule on confidentiality is set out in Model Rule 1.6 and the accompanying comments, which you should read carefully at this point. As you will see, the rule defines what information is protected by the duty of confidentiality, and then describes a set of exceptions to the duty.

1.   DEFINING THE DUTY

Model Rule 1.6 defines what is protected by the duty of confidentiality as "information relating to the representation of a client." This is a broad definition. In the prior Model Code, the duty applied to "confidences" and "secrets." A "confidence" referred to information protected by the attorney-client privilege, and a "secret" was information "gained in the professional relationship that the client has requested be held inviolate or the disclosure of which would be embarrassing or would be likely to be detrimental to the client." ABA Model Code of Professional Responsibility DR 4–101(A). The prior rule both incorporated the law of attorney-client privilege into the ethical rule, and required some elaborate analysis (or a Miranda-style warning from the client, probably at the lawyer's suggestion) to determine what was protected by the duty and what was not. The current rule uncouples the ethical rule from the law of privilege and provides an all-encompassing and straightforward definition of what is confidential.

When we say that confidential information is protected, what do we mean? Model Rule 1.6(a) sets out a default rule: that "[a] lawyer shall not reveal information relating to the representation of a client." This is not an absolute rule, of course; there would be no way to bring a lawsuit or negotiate a settlement on behalf of a client if you could never disclose any information relating to your representation of the client. Model Rule 1.6(a) includes three circumstances under which the lawyer may reveal information protected by Rule 1.6: if the client gives informed consent, the disclosure is "impliedly authorized in order to carry out the representation," or the disclosure is permitted by Rule 1.6(b).

Confidential information is protected not just by prohibitions on revealing that information, but on using it. Model Rule 1.8(b) provides that "A lawyer shall not use information relating to representation of a client to the disadvantage of the client unless the client gives informed consent." Under what circumstances could a lawyer use confidential information about a client without revealing it? See Comment [5] to Model Rule 1.8. Can a lawyer use confidential information if doing so does not disadvantage the client?

The prohibitions on revealing or using confidential information continue even after the lawyer's representation of the client has concluded. See Model Rule 1.9(c). Is there any difference between the confidentiality protection offered to a current client and that offered a former client?

When does the duty of confidentiality attach? Suppose a person consults a lawyer about engaging her, but ultimately, for some reason, no attorney-client relationship results. Does the lawyer owe a duty of confidentiality to that person with regard to the information learned in the course of the consultation? The Model Rules deem "[a] person who discusses with a lawyer the possibility of forming a client-lawyer relationship" a "prospective client." Model Rule 1.18(b) provides that "a lawyer who has had discussions with a prospective client shall not use or reveal information learned in the consultation," except in the circumstances permitted with regard to a former client.

Is everyone who communicates with a lawyer about possible representation a "prospective client"? What about someone who calls a lawyer and leaves a voicemail message, sends an e-mail, or visits a webpage and expresses interest in engaging the lawyer? Should any information transmitted to the lawyer this way be treated as confidential? What factors might be relevant to determining whether the duty of confidentiality exists under these circumstances? See Comment [2] to Model Rule 1.18.

2. EXCEPTIONS TO THE DUTY

Model Rule 1.6(b) sets out a series of exceptions to the duty of confidentiality. Several of these are of quite recent vintage. Over the years, although drafting committees and commissions routinely recommended expanding the scope of the exceptions to the duty of confidentiality, the ABA House of Delegates was routinely skeptical about and resistant to any expansion of a narrow list of existing exceptions. The corporate fraud scandals of recent years caused some well-founded concern that further obligations of disclosure would be imposed on the bar externally, through regulation or legislation, if self-regulation did not address the matter sufficiently. Model Rules 1.6(b)(2) and (b)(3) were added in response to these concerns. How extensive is the exception to the duty of confidentiality created by those provisions?

Another issue that has been the subject of substantial disagreement is the nature of the power to disclose. Model Rule 1.6 provides that if an exception is satisfied, a lawyer "may reveal" otherwise confidential information. From that provision alone, it looks as though disclosure is always permissive and is never required under the Model Rules. Consider, however, Rule 4.1(b), which provides that, "In the course of representing a client a lawyer shall not knowingly fail to disclose a material fact to a third person when disclosure is necessary to avoid assisting a criminal or fraudulent act by a client, unless disclosure is prohibited by Rule 1.6." If disclosure of such information is PERMITTED under Rule 1.6, what does that mean Model Rule 4.1 requires? Model Rule 3.3 also creates a mandatory disclosure obligation that supersedes Model Rule 1.6. See Model Rule 3.3(c).

The express disclosure authority with regard to the exceptions articulated in Model Rule 1.6 is permissive rather than mandatory. Should it be? Many jurisdictions have opted for mandatory disclosure under certain circumstances which the Model Rules treat as permissive. This is an area in which consulting local law is crucial; whether disclosure is permitted at all, and whether it is permissive or mandatory, varies widely from jurisdiction to jurisdiction.

If information is confidential and there is no exception to the duty, disclosure is a violation of the rules of professional responsibility. Consider the situation in which the lawyers in the following article found themselves. Would the current rules of professional responsibility permit them to disclose? If not, should they have done so anyway? Why or why not?

MARIA KANTZAVELOS, *FOLLOWING PROFESSIONAL RULES—AND A MORAL COMPASS*

Chicago Lawyer, Vol. 31, No. 3 (March 2008)
Reprinted with permission from the Law Bulletin Publishing Co.

By the very nature of their practice, criminal defense attorneys can come to harbor plenty of secrets. Some of those secrets can be horrifying, like a client's detailed account of a gruesome murder. Others are plainly sad, like the revelation that the young daughter of a client had been sexually abused. Many of them are mundane, simply bits of information about a client, like his drug or alcohol use, or his broken family situation.

"We have billions of secrets," said William P. Murphy, a criminal defense attorney for 40 years. "I've probably heard so many of them, I forget them."

But there can be the sort of secret too difficult to forget, one that could put a lawyer in a vexing position.

It's one of the age-old problems that law professors who teach ethics include in their classes: What happens if you, as an individual, think something should be done, but the rules of the profession would keep you bound to silence?

Take the 26–year-old secret revealed recently in a Cook County courtroom with the testimony of veteran criminal defense attorneys Dale Coventry and Jamie Kunz, whose story was reported in a Jan. 19 Chicago Tribune article.

The retired assistant Cook County public defenders said they were bound by attorney-client privilege to hold onto their client's admission that he was the man who fatally shot a security guard during a Jan. 11, 1982, robbery at a McDonald's restaurant on the South Side, not another man, Alton Logan, who is still serving a life sentence for the crime.

Coventry and Kunz were representing Andrew Wilson on capital charges in the Feb. 9, 1982, murders of two Chicago police officers. The lawyers said Wilson gave permission for them to reveal his admission in the McDonald's case only after his death. Wilson, who was sentenced to life in prison for the police murders, died last November.

That is why, the lawyers said, they could reveal the secret, which they recorded in a notarized affidavit, sealed in an envelope and kept locked in a metal box for a quarter of a century while Logan, now 54, remained in prison for a crime they believed their client committed.

"It's a classic, legal ethics book hypothetical, and here it is in real life," said Steven Lubet, a legal ethics expert and the director of the program on advocacy and professionalism at Northwestern University School of Law. "Lawyers are often called upon to keep secrets they would rather not keep. This, of course, is one of the most wrenching of those circumstances."

The lawyers' recent testimony and the contents of the affidavit surfaced as part of Logan's request for a new trial based on newly discovered evidence in his post-conviction petition.

In a proceeding set for March 10 before Criminal Court Judge James M. Schreier, Assistant Cook County public defender Harold Winston, who is representing Logan, said he will file a memorandum of law giving reasons why the 1982 affidavit and the lawyers' testimony about it should be admissible as evidence.

Moral imperatives

The story involving the retired public defenders raises the general ethics issue of how lawyers can find themselves in a quandary, forced to reconcile competing personal and professional principles.

"You have two moral imperatives here," said John E. Corkery, dean of The John Marshall Law School and a former chairman of the Illinois State Bar Association's Standing Committee on Professional Conduct. "One is to maintain confidentiality, which you and the law told this person you would give them. The other is: Something bad will happen—an innocent person will go to jail. "There's no standard answer for all these conflicts," Corkery said. "The answer is, you're going to have to pick one side or the other. And one side is probably going to nag at you for a long time."

Kunz said he viewed his professional obligation as a moral obligation.

"I can't extricate my legal obligations—my professional obligations—from my morals," Kunz said recently. "Andrew Wilson was my client. How could I possibly do anything with the information without somehow jeopardizing Andrew Wilson's life?" Kunz said. "It wasn't comfortable, but it wasn't ambiguous. There was no question where my moral loyalty had to lie. His life was in my hands."

Keeping such a secret, Kunz said, "certainly hasn't been easy, but it's nothing like what life has been like for Alton Logan in the last 26 years."

"As a human being I'm disturbed by the prospect of an innocent person in jail, the way any other citizen is," Kunz said. "But as an attorney," he said, his loyalty is "clear and exclusive."

"It's to my client," he said. "It's not a question of protecting my license, it's a question of protecting my client."

Still, Coventry and Kunz said they would have come forward if Logan, who was facing capital charges, had been sentenced to death.

"We were going to do something," Coventry said. "We had a way to get to Governor [James R.] Thompson. We were going to do that. Whether it would've made an impact we don't know. We would've done something to try to prevent the death penalty."

And if there wasn't the possibility that their own client would face the death penalty, "I would've been able to talk him into revealing this information himself," Coventry said. "I would've had him come forward himself, but I wasn't going to take the risk when he was facing the death penalty."

The confidentiality obligation under the attorney-client privilege is far-reaching. There are a few exceptions, like the one spelled out in Rule 1.6 (b) of the Illinois Rules of Professional Conduct: "A lawyer shall reveal information about a client to the extent it appears necessary to prevent the client from committing an act that would result in death or serious bodily harm."

"The question we always ask in class is, 'Is silence an act that would result in death or serious bodily harm?' It's a stretch, but at least it raises the issue. It's a question, and it makes people think," Corkery said.

"You might also keep in mind, though, that if the oath of confidentiality can be broken in this case, and the innocent person in prison saved this time, that next time the lawyers may not get this kind of information because the client will not believe he can trust them with this kind of secret," Corkery said. "But maybe that's worth it if it prevents an innocent person from languishing in jail. On the other hand, you're not going to have the privilege in the same way anymore, if there is an opt-out based on the lawyer's conscience."

Toughest dilemma

Many defense attorneys in Chicago said they could not imagine a more difficult situation than the one described by Coventry and Kunz.

"That's the toughest ethical dilemma a lawyer can have," said William J. Martin, a criminal-defense attorney who also practices in the area of professional responsibility. "It's an awful secret to carry with you, but I don't see where the privilege gives you any alternative." . . .

Anthony Pinelli, a former assistant Cook County public defender, put it this way: "As a normal citizen seeing that, it would be like seeing a little kid stepping into the street in front of a car [saying] 'I've got to stop this.' But the privilege stops you from doing that. Unless your client gives you the permission to do something about it, you can't. You have to literally watch the accident happen. If you really believe in the privilege, you can't make an exception in that circumstance." . . .

The centuries-old attorney-client privilege is the cornerstone of what the profession is all about, said Martin.

"If I can't go to a lawyer and know that what I tell him is confidential, then why the hell do we need lawyers? If a lawyer is an agent for the police or law enforcement, that's just a total distortion of what the adversary system is all about," Martin said.

Longtime criminal-defense attorney Terence P. Gillespie said, sometimes "there are ways to get information out, and hopefully in a way that doesn't compromise your client and compromise yourself."

"I don't know whether those two fellows had a way. It's a touchy subject, but I think it's one where creativity comes into play," Gillespie said. "I don't think it's so hard and fast that one can't put his thought processes in ways to circumvent it. If you've got a rule that's a disaster to an innocent human being, if it's inflexible, then the rule is not serving its purpose. I'd put a lot of energy into talking to people to figure out how in the hell I can get around this."

That's what Kunz and Coventry did.

"I talked to friends about it—mentors, people who were wiser than I was—saying, 'Isn't there something we can do?' " Kunz said. "Maybe there should be an exception, but I'm not intelligent enough to figure out what it would be. I can't think of a way where something can be done, to relax the rules so that I could help Logan. I don't see any way to help Logan, without hurting Wilson."

Even if he had disclosed the secret in the . . . case, Kunz said, "There's no reason to believe the authorities would believe me."

"And if they did believe me, and believed Andrew Wilson, then I'd have to find a way to live with myself, because of what I'd done to the guy I had promised confidence. That would be harder to live with than what I've had to live with as it is."

Plus, said Coventry, "it wasn't going to have an impact anyway."

"First of all, it's hearsay. And our client could've blocked it because it was his privilege," Coventry said. "And it wasn't an unknown fact. This [the contention that Andrew Wilson was the shooter] had been the defense for Logan for 26 years."

Kunz stressed that it was because of the attorney-client privilege, and their promise of confidentiality to their client, that they were even able to get the admission, and the permission to disclose the information after his death.

"What's certainly true is that Coventry and I would never have put the question to him in the first place if it weren't for the privilege," Kunz said.

Many criminal defense lawyers praised the former public defenders for finding a way to remain true to their professional obligations, while taking steps they thought they could take to be able to come forward with the information at some point.

"I don't know if I would've thought that far ahead, that's why I applaud them for at least being able to do that," said criminal defense attorney Thomas M. Breen.

Pinelli, the former public defender, said he could only hope he would handle a similar situation in the way Coventry and Kunz did.

"They actually thought it through to one step more in creating a contingency that didn't, in any way, threaten their client," Pinelli said.

"When they teach ethics, this is a perfect example for a case study to show people what you really need to do to honor the privilege." . . .

NOTES

1. The conviction of Alton Logan, the imprisoned man at issue in this case, was vacated after the disclosure of the affidavit, and a new trial was ordered. In September 2008, the government formally dropped the charges against him.

2. The lawyers interviewed in this article considered the maintaining of Wilson's secret a matter of the attorney-client privilege. Was it? How?

3. One lawyer suggested that "creativity" might have solved the problem for the attorneys in this case. What sort of creative solutions could you imagine for the situation in which the lawyers found themselves? Do they solve the problem?

(A) BODILY HARM OR INJURY

Client tells you that he is going to kill his wife. May you disclose that information? Under Model Rule 1.6(b)(1), the answer is yes, if you reasonably believe it is necessary to make that disclosure to prevent reasonably certain death or substantial bodily harm. The prior version of Model Rule 1.6 provided that the lawyer could disclose "to prevent the client from committing a criminal act that the lawyer believes is likely to result in imminent death or substantial bodily harm." Why do you suppose the language was changed? What if your client tells you that he is planning to commit a crime that will damage the property of another person? May you disclose under Model Rule 1.6?

(B) CLIENT'S CRIME OR FRAUD IN WHICH CLIENT IS US-ING OR HAS USED THE LAWYER'S SERVICES

Model Rule 1.6(b)(2) and (3) are the most recently added exceptions to the duty of confidentiality. Review those sections carefully. What sort of conduct are these provisions designed to address? What are we talking about when we talk about client fraud?

Suppose that you represent a large, publicly traded corporation. The corporation wants to maximize its share price, but has been purchasing many expensive assets; this means the corporation has acquired considerable debt, which adversely affects the corporation's balance sheet.

With the help of its accountants, the corporation decides to solve these problems through the creation of partnerships, called "special purpose entities," with which the corporation will transact business. Under some circumstances, accounting rules permit such special purpose entities to be treated as entirely separate from the corporation. This means that the corporation can treat transactions with the special purpose entities as transactions with an outside party, and can treat the assets and liabilities of the special purpose entities as independent of the corporation's. The reason that the special purpose entities receive this treatment is that they are, at least in part, independent of the corporation; the entity must have an independent investor who invests at least 3% of the assets of the special purpose entity, and the independent investor must control the entity. Your client, however, does not observe these rules. The corporation or its employees control the special purpose entities, and they create and manage them for the sole purpose of manipulating the corporation's financial statements, transferring debt away from the corporation so its earnings look higher, and its debt, lower.

Once a special purpose entity has been created, the corporation can do business with it. The corporation can, for example, sell assets to the special purpose entities that it wants removed from its books. The sales look like transactions with an outside entity: the corporation realizes gain from selling the assets, and the asset (with its associated debt) is transferred to the entity and its debt treated as the entity's debt, not the corporation's. But the transaction isn't real; the corporation has agreed to buy back the assets from the special purpose entity at a later date and to protect the entity against any loss. The transfers are really designed to make the corporation's financial results look better than they are.

This is a fairly simplistic explanation of one of the many machinations at Enron that led to its ultimate scandal-ridden bankruptcy. Enron created special purpose entities, and transacted business with them, in order to communicate inaccurate and misleading information about Enron's true financial position to the market and to its shareholders. Such transactions required the assistance of lawyers, who participated in structuring the transactions and prepared ''opinion letters'' in which they expressed the view that the proposed transactions complied with the law.

Was this fraud? In the words of Prof. Susan Koniak, yes:

> Fraud is, in plain English, lying to someone to get them to give you their stuff. Sometimes the lie is expressed out loud. Other times it is told by speaking and leaving out important information that the person with the ''stuff'' would certainly have wanted to consider before parting with that stuff.... [M]any of Enron's related party transactions were fraudulent. Why? The partnerships were buying assets from Enron and making trades with Enron that Enron was financing. This made it seem as if Enron was generating profits that it was not (a lie). This also made it seem as if Enron had protected itself from potential losses from risky assets and trades (another lie)— risks it was not transferring to the related-entities ... because Enron was promising the investors in those entities a profit, no matter what happened. These lies were told to get people to buy Enron's stock at inflated values—values driven by financial statements that included these lies, thus projecting an intentionally false picture of Enron's financial condition. They were, in other words, lies to get people to give up their stuff.

Susan P. Koniak, Corporate Fraud: See, Lawyers, 26 Harv. J. L. & Pub. Pol'y 195, 198 (2003).

Many have argued that the lawyers in Enron were complicit in the transactions and equally responsible for the fraud. Affirmatively assisting in the commission of a client crime or fraud is expressly prohibited by the rules of professional responsibility. Model Rule 1.2(d) provides that "A lawyer shall not counsel a client to engage, or assist a client, in conduct that the lawyer knows is criminal or fraudulent." Active participation in a client's fraud could make the lawyer liable for fraud as well, and if the lawyer herself makes misleading statements, that could constitute a violation of the securities laws. Why would a law firm involve itself in activities that might amount to fraud or a crime? Consider that Enron was the largest client of law firm Vinson & Elkins, and was responsible for 7.8% of the firm's revenue in 2001. Might that create some incentive on the part of the lawyer to go along with the client's demands, however questionable they became?

Our question here is about confidentiality, however. What if the lawyers did not intentionally participate in planning and executing their client's fraud? Instead, having done some work for the client, they realized that the client had used their work to commit fraud. What would the lawyers' confidentiality obligation permit them to do?

Until 2003, the Model Rules provided no exception to the duty of confidentiality that would permit the lawyer to disclose the client's fraud to parties that had been injured by it, even if the lawyer's services had been used to commit the fraud. The most the rules permitted was that the lawyer could withdraw from representing the client, could give notice that the lawyer was withdrawing, and could "withdraw or disaffirm" any opinion letter or document the lawyer had proffered in the course of representing the client. This was known as the "noisy withdrawal" provision, and it satisfied no one. On the one hand, it sent a clear signal—to those who understood such things—that there was something problematic about the representation and the disaffirmed documents. It therefore did amount to a disclosure of confidential information about the client, albeit an opaque and imprecise one. At the same time, it did not send a clear message about what the client had done wrong, or about what the recipients of this notice might do to protect their interests. It was, accordingly, less protective of the interests of third parties than some advocates thought it ought to be. Nor was the oblique disclosure permitted likely to be sufficient to protect lawyers who were concerned about bearing some liability—civil or even criminal—for assisting in their clients' fraud. While the ABA House of Delegates had been entreated repeatedly to permit disclosure of past client fraud in which the lawyer's services had been used, it resisted pressure to amend Model Rule 1.6 to permit such disclosure. As recently as 2002, the House of Delegates rejected the recommendation of the Ethics 2000 Commission that it adopt an exception to the confidentiality rules in the case of client fraud.

Two things caused the ABA to revisit the issue. One was the pervasive impact of the Enron debacle and an assortment of other large-scale, high-profile corporate frauds in which lawyers' services had been used. The other was a clear indication that the SEC intended to regulate lawyer disclosure in the case of client fraud. Once it became apparent that the involvement of lawyers in extensive financial frauds would be regulated by someone else if attorney self-regulation did not play more of a role, the ABA House of Delegates approved Model Rule 1.6(b)(2) and (3). Read these sections carefully. Do these sections require the lawyer to disclose, or is this merely permissive disclosure?

These sections are more limited than they may appear at first glance. A client, an investment adviser, comes to you asking you to represent him in a suit by a customer alleging that the client defrauded the customer. The client confirms to you that he did, in fact, commit fraud. May you disclose that information? Does it matter whether the fraud has significantly injured the customer?

What about future crimes? Client tells you that he is going to embezzle money from his employer. Can you disclose under 1.6(b)(2) or (3)? Under any other exception to the duty of confidentiality? Is this a sensible result?

When the client is an entity, there is an additional disclosure provision contained in Model Rule 1.13. That rule provides a multi-step process if a lawyer representing an entity "knows that an officer, employee or other person associated with the organization is engaged in action, intends to act or refuses to act in a matter related to the representation that is a violation of a legal obligation to the organization, or a violation of law that reasonably might be imputed to the organization, and that is likely to result in substantial injury to the organization." The rule directs the lawyer to proceed "as is reasonably necessary in the best interest of the organization," and provides that, "[u]nless the lawyer reasonably believes that it is not necessary in the best interest of the organization to do so, the lawyer shall refer the matter to higher authority in the organization." This "reporting up" provision requires the lawyer, if the circumstances warrant it, to refer the matter "to the highest authority that can act on behalf of the organization." Model Rule 1.13(b). If this reporting does not address the problem, and the lawyer "reasonably believes that the violation is reasonably certain to result in substantial injury to the organization," the lawyer may reveal confidential information to the extent the lawyer reasonably believes necessary to prevent "substantial injury" to the entity. This is the case even if the disclosure would not otherwise fall within the exceptions in Model Rule 1.6(b). See Model Rule 1.13(c).

Regulations of the Securities and Exchange Commission promulgated pursuant to the Sarbanes–Oxley Act require a similar process of reporting up. Those regulations are reproduced below.

You might think that regulations of the Securities and Exchange Commission would have limited impact; it might seem as though relatively few attorneys are actually "appearing and practicing before the Commission" or are representing "issuers." It is worth noting that the definitions of these terms, which appear in 17 C.F.R. § 205.2, are considerably broader than you might have anticipated. In addition to transacting business with the Commission or representing a client in a Commission proceeding, "[a]ppearing and practicing before the Commission" includes "[p]roviding advice in respect of the United States securities laws ... regarding any document that the attorney has notice will be filed with or submitted to, or incorporated into any document that will be filed with or submitted to, the Commission, including the provision of such advice in the context of preparing, or participating in the preparation of, any such document," 17 C.F.R. § 205.2(a)(iii), and "[a]dvising an issuer as to whether information or a statement, opinion, or other writing is required under the United States securities laws or the Commission's rules or regulations thereunder to be filed with or submitted to, or incorporated into any document that will be filed with or submitted to, the Commission." 17 C.F.R. § 205.2(a)(iv). The term "issuer" means "any person who issues or proposes to issue any security." See 15 U.S.C. § 78c(a)(8). This means that any lawyer advising a publicly traded company about whether any information should be disclosed in its public filings is accordingly "appearing and practicing before the Commission." That can mean an environmental lawyer advising about a potential liability; it is not limited to securities law practitioners and doesn't have to happen anywhere near Washington, D.C.

17 C.F.R. § 205.3 ISSUER AS CLIENT

(a) Representing an issuer. An attorney appearing and practicing before the Commission in the representation of an issuer owes his or her professional and ethical duties to the issuer as an organization. That the attorney may work with and advise the issuer's officers, directors, or employees in the course of representing the issuer does not make such individuals the attorney's clients.

(b) Duty to report evidence of a material violation [of federal or state securities law or law on fiduciary duty].

>   (1) If an attorney, appearing and practicing before the Commission in the representation of an issuer, becomes aware of evidence of a material violation by the issuer or by any officer, director, employee, or agent of the issuer, the attorney shall report such evidence to the issuer's chief legal officer (or the equivalent thereof) or to both the issuer's chief legal officer and its chief executive officer (or the equivalents thereof) forthwith. By communicating such information to the issuer's officers or directors, an attorney does not reveal client confidences or secrets or privileged or otherwise protected information related to the attorney's representation of an issuer.

>   (2) The chief legal officer (or the equivalent thereof) shall cause such inquiry into the evidence of a material violation as he or she reasonably believes is appropriate to determine whether the material violation described in the report has occurred, is ongoing, or is about to

occur. If the chief legal officer (or the equivalent thereof) determines no material violation has occurred, is ongoing, or is about to occur, he or she shall notify the reporting attorney and advise the reporting attorney of the basis for such determination. Unless the chief legal officer (or the equivalent thereof) reasonably believes that no material violation has occurred, is ongoing, or is about to occur, he or she shall take all reasonable steps to cause the issuer to adopt an appropriate response, and shall advise the reporting attorney thereof. In lieu of causing an inquiry under this paragraph (b), a chief legal officer (or the equivalent thereof) may refer a report of evidence of a material violation to a qualified legal compliance committee under paragraph (c)(2) of this section if the issuer has duly established a qualified legal compliance committee prior to the report of evidence of a material violation.

(3) Unless an attorney who has made a report under paragraph (b)(1) of this section reasonably believes that the chief legal officer or the chief executive officer of the issuer (or the equivalent thereof) has provided an appropriate response within a reasonable time, the attorney shall report the evidence of a material violation to:

(i) The audit committee of the issuer's board of directors;

(ii) Another committee of the issuer's board of directors consisting solely of directors who are not employed, directly or indirectly, by the issuer and are not, in the case of a registered investment company, "interested persons" as defined in section 2(a)(19) of the Investment Company Act of 1940 ... (if the issuer's board of directors has no audit committee); or

(iii) The issuer's board of directors (if the issuer's board of directors has no committee consisting solely of directors who are not employed, directly or indirectly, by the issuer. . . .)

(4) If an attorney reasonably believes that it would be futile to report evidence of a material violation to the issuer's chief legal officer and chief executive officer (or the equivalents thereof) under paragraph (b)(1) of this section, the attorney may report such evidence as provided under paragraph (b)(3) of this section.

(5) An attorney retained or directed by an issuer to investigate evidence of a material violation reported under paragraph (b)(1), (b)(3), or (b)(4) of this section shall be deemed to be appearing and practicing before the Commission. Directing or retaining an attorney to investigate reported evidence of a material violation does not relieve an officer or director of the issuer to whom such evidence has been reported under paragraph (b)(1), (b)(3), or (b)(4) of this section from a duty to respond to the reporting attorney.

(6) An attorney shall not have any obligation to report evidence of a material violation under this paragraph (b) if:

(i) The attorney was retained or directed by the issuer's chief legal officer (or the equivalent thereof) to investigate such evidence of a material violation and:

(A) The attorney reports the results of such investigation to the chief legal officer (or the equivalent thereof); and

(B) Except where the attorney and the chief legal officer (or the equivalent thereof) each reasonably believes that no material violation has occurred, is ongoing, or is about to occur, the chief legal officer (or the equivalent thereof) reports the results of the investigation to the issuer's board of directors, a committee thereof to whom a report could be made pursuant to paragraph (b)(3) of this section, or a qualified legal compliance committee; or

(ii) The attorney was retained or directed by the chief legal officer (or the equivalent thereof) to assert, consistent with his or her professional obligations, a colorable defense on behalf of the issuer (or the issuer's officer, director, employee, or agent, as the case may be) in any investigation or judicial or administrative proceeding relating to such evidence of a material violation, and the chief legal officer (or the equivalent thereof) provides reasonable and timely reports on the progress and outcome of such proceeding to the issuer's board of directors, a committee thereof to whom a report could be made pursuant to paragraph (b)(3) of this section, or a qualified legal compliance committee.

(7) An attorney shall not have any obligation to report evidence of a material violation under this paragraph (b) if such attorney was retained or directed by a qualified legal compliance committee:

(i) To investigate such evidence of a material violation; or

(ii) To assert, consistent with his or her professional obligations, a colorable defense on behalf of the issuer (or the issuer's officer, director, employee, or agent, as the case may be) in any investigation or judicial or administrative proceeding relating to such evidence of a material violation.

(8) An attorney who receives what he or she reasonably believes is an appropriate and timely response to a report he or she has made pursuant to paragraph (b)(1), (b)(3), or (b)(4) of this section need do nothing more under this section with respect to his or her report.

(9) An attorney who does not reasonably believe that the issuer has made an appropriate response within a reasonable time to the report or reports made pursuant to paragraph (b)(1), (b)(3), or (b)(4) of this section shall explain his or her reasons therefor to the chief legal officer (or the equivalent thereof), the chief executive officer (or the equivalent thereof), and directors to whom the attorney reported the evidence of a material violation pursuant to paragraph (b)(1), (b)(3), or (b)(4) of this section.

(10) An attorney formerly employed or retained by an issuer who has reported evidence of a material violation under this part and reasonably believes that he or she has been discharged for so doing may notify the issuer's board of directors or any committee thereof that he or she believes that he or she has been discharged for reporting evidence of a material violation under this section.

(c) Alternative reporting procedures for attorneys retained or employed by an issuer that has established a qualified legal compliance committee.

(1) If an attorney, appearing and practicing before the Commission in the representation of an issuer, becomes aware of evidence of a material violation by the issuer or by any officer, director, employee, or agent of the issuer, the attorney may, as an alternative to the reporting requirements of paragraph (b) of this section, report such evidence to a qualified legal compliance committee, if the issuer has previously formed such a committee. An attorney who reports evidence of a material violation to such a qualified legal compliance committee has satisfied his or her obligation to report such evidence and is not required to assess the issuer's response to the reported evidence of a material violation.

(2) A chief legal officer (or the equivalent thereof) may refer a report of evidence of a material violation to a previously established qualified legal compliance committee in lieu of causing an inquiry to be conducted under paragraph (b)(2) of this section. The chief legal officer (or the equivalent thereof) shall inform the reporting attorney that the report has been referred to a qualified legal compliance committee. Thereafter, pursuant to the requirements under § 205.2(k), the qualified legal compliance committee shall be responsible for responding to the evidence of a material violation reported to it under this paragraph (c).

(d) Issuer confidences.

(1) Any report under this section (or the contemporaneous record thereof) or any response thereto (or the contemporaneous record thereof) may be used by an attorney in connection with any investigation, proceeding, or litigation in which the attorney's compliance with this part is in issue.

(2) An attorney appearing and practicing before the Commission in the representation of an issuer may reveal to the Commission, without the issuer's consent, confidential information related to the representation to the extent the attorney reasonably believes necessary:

(i) To prevent the issuer from committing a material violation that is likely to cause substantial injury to the financial interest or property of the issuer or investors;

(ii) To prevent the issuer, in a Commission investigation or administrative proceeding from committing perjury, proscribed in 18 U.S.C. 1621; suborning perjury, proscribed in 18 U.S.C. 1622;

or committing any act proscribed in 18 U.S.C. 1001 that is likely to perpetrate a fraud upon the Commission; or

(iii) To rectify the consequences of a material violation by the issuer that caused, or may cause, substantial injury to the financial interest or property of the issuer or investors in the furtherance of which the attorney's services were used.

NOTES

1. Why does the rule permit the lawyer to report up within the organization? Why isn't the disclosure of the information to the superiors within the company a breach of the duty of confidentiality?

2. Under both the Sarbanes–Oxley rules and the Model Rules, reporting up is required, while disclosure outside the entity is permitted but not mandated. Why the difference? Should the rules require disclosure outside the entity under some circumstances? What do these rules assume? Is it a fair assumption?

(C) LAWYER PROTECTION

Rule 1.6 is protective of lawyers in a number of ways. One is the recent addition of Rule 1.6(b)(4). Suppose that an ethics issue comes up in your practice, and you need to consult a lawyer to figure out what your obligations are under the law of professional responsibility. Can you do so? What if that consultation will result in the disclosure of your client's confidential information to another lawyer—one outside your firm? *See also* Comment [4] to Rule 1.6, permitting a lawyer to discuss a problem hypothetically "so long as there is no reasonable likelihood that the listener will be able to ascertain the identity of the client or the situation involved."

Another protection for the lawyer is provided by Rule 1.6(b)(6), which provides that if other law or a court order requires a disclosure, that disclosure is permitted. This rule avoids the whipsaw that might affect a lawyer ordered to disclose confidential information that does not fall within the other exceptions in the Rules.

Model Rule 1.6(b)(5) creates what is known as the "self-defense" exception. Its significance is demonstrated in the following case:

MEYERHOFER v. EMPIRE FIRE AND MARINE INS. CO.

497 F.2d 1190 (2d Cir. 1974)

MOORE, CIRCUIT JUDGE:

This is an appeal by Dietrich Meyerhofer and Herbert Federman, plaintiffs, and their counsel, Bernson, Hoeniger, Freitag & Abbey, from an order of the United States District Court for the Southern District of New York, (a) dismissing without prejudice plaintiffs' action against defendants, (b) enjoining and disqualifying plaintiffs' counsel, Bernson, Hoeniger, Freitag & Abbey, and Stuart Charles Goldberg from acting as attorneys for plaintiffs in this action or in any future action against defendant Empire Fire and Marine Insurance Company (Empire) involving the same transactions, occurrences, events, allegations, facts or issues, and (c) enjoining Bernson, Hoeniger, Freitag & Abbey and Stuart Charles Goldberg from disclosing confidential information regarding Empire to others. Intervenor Stuart Charles Goldberg also appeals from said order. . . .

The full import of the problems and issues presented on this appeal cannot be appreciated and analyzed without an initial statement of the facts out of which they arise.

Empire Fire and Marine Insurance Company on May 31, 1972, made a public offering of 500,000 shares of its stock, pursuant to a registration statement filed with the Securities and Exchange Commission (SEC) on March 28, 1972. The stock was offered at $16 a share. Empire's attorney on the issue was the firm of Sitomer, Sitomer & Porges. Stuart Charles Goldberg was an attorney in the firm and had done some work on the issue.

Plaintiff Meyerhofer, on or about January 11, 1973, purchased 100 shares of Empire stock at $17 a share. He alleges that as of June 5, 1973, the market price of his stock was only $7 a share—hence, he has sustained an unrealized loss of $1,000. . . .

On May 2, 1973, plaintiffs, represented by the firm of Bernson, Hoeniger, Freitag & Abbey (the Bernson firm), on behalf of themselves and all other purchasers of Empire common stock, brought this action alleging that the registration statement and the prospectus under which the Empire stock had been issued were materially false and misleading. . . . Damages for all members of the class or rescission were alternatively sought.

The lawsuit was apparently inspired by a Form 10–K which Empire filed with the SEC on or about April 12, 1973. This Form revealed that "The Registration Statement under the Securities Act of 1933 with respect to the public offering of the 500,000 shares of Common Stock did not disclose the proposed $200,000 payment to the law firm as well as certain other features of the compensation arrangements between the Company (Empire) and such law firm (defendant Sitomer, Sitomer and Porges)." Later that month Empire disseminated to its shareholders a proxy statement and annual report making similar disclosures.

The defendants named were Empire, officers and directors of Empire, the Sitomer firm and its three partners, A. L. Sitomer, S. J. Sitomer and R. E. Porges, Faulkner, Dawkins & Sullivan Securities Corp., the managing underwriter, Stuart Charles Goldberg, originally alleged to have been a partner of the Sitomer firm, and certain selling stockholders of Empire shares.

On May 2, 1973, the complaint was served on the Sitomer defendants and Faulkner. No service was made on Goldberg who was then no longer associated with the Sitomer firm. However, he was advised by telephone that he had been made a defendant. Goldberg inquired of the Bernson firm as to the nature of the charges against him and was informed generally as to the substance of the complaint and in particular the lack of disclosure of the finder's fee arrangement. Thus informed, Goldberg requested an opportunity to prove his non-involvement in any such arrangement and his lack of knowledge thereof. At this stage there was unfolded the series of events which ultimately resulted in the motion and order thereon now before us on appeal.

Goldberg, after his graduation from Law School in 1966, had rather specialized experience in the securities field and had published various books and treatises on related subjects. He became associated with the Sitomer firm in November 1971. While there Goldberg worked on phases of various registration statements including Empire, although another associate was responsible for the Empire registration statement and prospectus. However, Goldberg expressed concern over what he regarded as excessive fees, the nondisclosure or inadequate disclosure thereof, and the extent to which they might include a 'finder's fee,' both as to Empire and other issues.

The Empire registration became effective on May 31, 1972. The excessive fee question had not been put to rest in Goldberg's mind because in middle January 1973 it arose in connection with another registration (referred to as 'Glacier'). Goldberg had worked on Glacier. Little purpose will be served by detailing the events during the critical period January 18 to 22, 1973, in which Goldberg and the Sitomer partners were debating the fee disclosure problem. In summary Goldberg insisted on a full and complete disclosure of fees in the Empire and Glacier offerings. The Sitomer partners apparently disagreed and Goldberg resigned from the firm on January 22, 1973.

On January 22, 1973, Goldberg appeared before the SEC and placed before it information subsequently embodied in his affidavit dated January 26, 1973, which becomes crucial to the issues now to be considered.

Some three months later, upon being informed that he was to be included as a defendant in the impending action, Goldberg asked the Bernson firm for an opportunity to demonstrate that he had been unaware of the finder's fee arrangement which, he said, Empire and the Sitomer firm had concealed from him all along. Goldberg met with members of the Bernson firm on at least two occasions. After consulting his own attorney, as well as William P. Sullivan, Special Counsel with the Securities and Exchange Commission, Division of Enforcement, Goldberg gave plaintiffs' counsel a copy of the January 26th affidavit which he had authored more than three months earlier. He hoped that it would verify his nonparticipation in the finder's fee omission and convince the Bernson firm that he should not be a defendant. The Bernson firm was satisfied with Goldberg's explanations and, upon their motion, granted by the court, he was dropped as a defendant. After receiving Goldberg's affidavit, the Bernson firm amended plaintiffs' complaint. The amendments added more specific facts but did not change the theory or substance of the original complaint.

By motion dated June 7, 1973, the remaining defendants moved 'pursuant to Canons 4 and 9 of the Code of Professional Responsibility, the Disciplinary Rules and Ethical Considerations applicable thereto, and the supervisory power of this Court' for the order of disqualification now on appeal.

By memorandum decision and order, the District Court ordered that the Bernson firm and Goldberg be barred from acting as counsel or participating with counsel for plaintiffs in this or any future action against Empire involving the transactions placed in issue in this lawsuit and from disclosing confidential information to others.

The complaint was dismissed without prejudice. The basis for the Court's decision is the premise that Goldberg had obtained confidential information from his client Empire which, in breach of relevant ethical canons, he revealed to plaintiffs' attorneys in their suit against Empire. The Court said its decision was compelled by 'the broader obligations of Canons 4 and 9.'

There is no proof—not even a suggestion—that Goldberg had revealed any information, confidential or otherwise, that might have caused the instigation of the suit. To the contrary, it was not until after the suit was commenced that Goldberg learned that he was in jeopardy. The District Court recognized that the complaint had been based on Empire's—not Goldberg's—disclosures, but concluded because of this that Goldberg was under no further obligation 'to reveal the information or to discuss the matter with plaintiffs' counsel.'

. . . DR 4–101(C) recognizes that a lawyer may reveal confidences or secrets necessary to defend himself against 'an accusation of wrongful conduct.' This is exactly what Goldberg had to face when, in their original complaint, plaintiffs named him as a defendant who wilfully violated the securities laws.

The charge, of knowing participation in the filing of a false and misleading registration statement, was a serious one. The complaint alleged violation of criminal statutes and civil liability computable at over four million dollars. The cost in money of simply defending such an action might be very substantial. The damage to his professional reputation which might be occasioned by the mere pendency of such a charge was an even greater cause for concern.

Under these circumstances Goldberg had the right to make an appropriate disclosure with respect to his role in the public offering. Concomitantly, he had the right to support his version of the facts with suitable evidence.

The problem arises from the fact that the method Goldberg used to accomplish this was to deliver to Mr. Abbey, a member of the Bernson firm, the thirty page affidavit, accompanied by sixteen exhibits, which he had submitted to the SEC. This document not only went into extensive detail concerning Goldberg's efforts to cause the Sitomer firm to rectify the nondisclosure with respect to Empire but even more extensive detail concerning how these efforts had been precipitated by counsel for the underwriters having come upon evidence showing that a similar nondisclosure was contemplated with respect to Glacier and their insistence that full corrective measures should be taken. Although Goldberg's description reflected seriously on his employer, the Sitomer firm and, also, in at least some degree, on Glacier, he was clearly in a situation of some urgency. Moreover, before he turned over the affidavit, he consulted both his own attorney and a distinguished practitioner of securities law, and he and Abbey made a joint telephone call to Mr. Sullivan of the SEC. Moreover, it is not clear that, in the context of this case, Canon 4 applies to anything except information gained from Empire. Finally, because of Goldberg's apparent intimacy with the offering, the most effective way for him to substantiate his story was for him to disclose the SEC affidavit. It was the fact that he had written such an affidavit at an earlier date which demonstrated that his story was not simply fabricated in response to plaintiffs' complaint. . . .

In addition to finding that Goldberg had violated Canon 4, the District Court found that the relationship between Goldberg and the Bernson firm violated Canon 9 of the Code of Professional Responsibility which provides that:

> EC 9–6 Every lawyer [must] strive to avoid not only professional impropriety but also the appearance of impropriety.

The District Court reasoned that even though there was no evidence of bad faith on the part of either Goldberg or the Bernson firm, a shallow reading of the facts might lead a casual observer to conclude that there was an aura of complicity about their relationship. However, this provision should not be read so broadly as to eviscerate the right of self-defense conferred by DR 4–101(C)(4).

. . . To the extent that the District Court's order prohibits Goldberg from representing the interests of these or any other plaintiffs in this or similar actions, we affirm that order. . . .

The burden of the District Court's order did not fall most harshly on Goldberg; rather its greatest impact has been felt by Bernson, Hoeniger, Freitag & Abbey, plaintiffs' counsel, which was disqualified from participation in the case. The District Court based its holding, not on the fact that the Bernson firm showed bad faith when it received Goldberg's affidavit, but rather on the fact that it was involved in a tainted association with Goldberg because his disclosures to them inadvertently violated Canons 4 and 9 of the Code of Professional Responsibility. Because there are no violations of either of these Canons in this case, we can find no basis to hold that the relationship between Goldberg and the Bernson firm was tainted. . . . Since its relationship with Goldberg was not tainted by violations of the Code of Professional Responsibility, there appears to be no warrant for its disqualification from participation in either this or similar actions. *A fortiori* there was no sound basis for disqualifying plaintiffs or dismissing the complaint.

NOTES

1.   Was this a case about confidentiality or privilege? Why?

2.   Why did the defendants seek to disqualify the Bernson firm from representing the plaintiffs? Were they really concerned about the information that Goldberg had shared with plaintiffs' counsel? Disqualification motions are often employed for strategic advantage. What are the strategic benefits of a disqualification motion?

3.   Why weren't Goldberg's actions a violation of his duty of confidentiality to Empire? To Glacier? What was the defense theory of disqualification and why was it unsuccessful?

4.   Goldberg had not been served at the time he invoked his self-defense right. Do you think he should have waited until he was served with the complaint to disclose the information he knew? Must a lawyer wait until he is actually charged or sued to make disclosure? See Comment [10] to Model Rule 1.6.

C. DISTINGUISHING CONFIDENTIAL INFORMATION FROM PHYSICAL EVIDENCE

A client comes to you and tells you that he has committed a bank robbery. He tells you where he has hidden the proceeds of the robbery and the weapon he used to commit the robbery. Can you disclose these matters? Under what circumstances?

Now, assume that the client brings to your office and places on your desk the weapon or the proceeds of the robbery. Do you think the answer should be the same or different? Why? What was the court's conclusion in the following case about how the lawyer should respond in this situation?

PEOPLE v. MEREDITH
631 P.2d 46 (Cal. 1981)

TOBRINER, JUSTICE.

Defendants Frank Earl Scott and Michael Meredith appeal from convictions for the first degree murder and first degree robbery of David Wade. Meredith's conviction rests on eyewitness testimony that he shot and killed Wade. Scott's conviction, however, depends on the theory that Scott conspired with Meredith and a third defendant, Jacqueline Otis, to bring about the killing and robbery. To support the theory of conspiracy the prosecution sought to show the place where the victim's wallet was found, and, in the course of the case this piece of evidence became crucial. The admissibility of that evidence comprises the principal issue on this appeal.

At trial the prosecution called Steven Frick, who testified that he observed the victim's partially burnt wallet in a trash can behind Scott's residence. Scott's trial counsel then adduced that Frick served as a defense investigator. Scott himself had told his former counsel that he had taken the victim's wallet, divided the money with Meredith, attempted to burn the wallet, and finally put it in the trash can. At counsel's request, Frick then retrieved the wallet from the trash can. Counsel examined the wallet and then turned it over to the police.

The defense acknowledges that the wallet itself was properly admitted into evidence. The prosecution in turn acknowledges that the attorney-client privilege protected the conversations between Scott, his former counsel, and counsel's investigator. Indeed the prosecution did not attempt to introduce those conversations at trial. The issue before us, consequently, focuses upon a narrow point: whether under the circumstances of this case Frick's observation of the location of the wallet, the product of a privileged communication, finds protection under the attorney-client privilege.

This issue, one of first impression in California, presents the court with competing policy considerations. On the one hand, to deny protection to observations arising from confidential communications might chill free and open communication between attorney and client and might also inhibit counsel's investigation of his client's case. On the other hand, we cannot extend the attorney-client privilege so far that it renders evidence immune from discovery and admission merely because the defense seizes it first.

Balancing these considerations, we conclude that an observation by defense counsel or his investigator, which is the product of a privileged communication, may not be admitted unless the defense by altering or removing physical evidence has precluded the prosecution from making that same observation. In the present case the defense investigator, by removing the wallet, frustrated any possibility that the police might later discover it in the trash can. The conduct of the defense thus precluded the prosecution from ascertaining the crucial fact of the location of the wallet. Under these circumstances, the prosecution was entitled to present evidence to show the location of the wallet in the trash can; the trial court did not err in admitting the investigator's testimony. . . .

We first summarize the evidence other than that relating to the discovery and location of the victim's wallet. . . .

On the night of April 3, 1976, Wade (the victim) and Jacqueline Otis, a friend of the defendants, entered a club known as Rich Jimmy's. Defendant Scott remained outside by a shoeshine stand. A few minutes later codefendant Meredith arrived outside the club. He told Scott he planned to rob Wade, and asked Scott to go into the club, find Jacqueline Otis, and ask her to get Wade to go out to Wade's car parked outside the club.

In the meantime, Wade and Otis had left the club and walked to a liquor store to get some beer. Returning from the store, they left the beer in a bag by Wade's car and reentered the club. Scott then entered the club also and . . . asked Otis to get Wade to go back out to his car so Meredith could "knock him in the head."

When Wade and Otis did go out to the car, Meredith attacked Wade from behind. After a brief struggle, two shots were fired; Wade fell, and Meredith, witnessed by Scott . . . , ran from the scene.

Scott went over to the body and, assuming Wade was dead, picked up the bag containing the beer and hid it behind a fence. Scott later returned, retrieved the bag, and took it home where Otis and Meredith joined him.

We now recount the evidence relating to Wade's wallet, basing our account primarily on the testimony of James Schenk, Scott's first appointed attorney. Schenk visited Scott in jail more than a month after the crime occurred and solicited information about the murder, stressing that he had to be fully acquainted with the facts to avoid being "sandbagged" by the prosecution during the trial. In response, Scott gave Schenk the same information that he had related earlier to the police. In addition, however, Scott told Schenk something Scott had not revealed to the police: that he had seen a wallet, as well as the paper bag, on the ground near Wade. Scott said that he picked up the wallet, put it in the paper bag, and placed both behind a parking lot fence. He also said that he later retrieved the bag, took it home, found $100 in the wallet and divided it with Meredith, and then tried to burn the wallet in his kitchen sink. He took the partially burned wallet, Scott told Schenk, placed it in a plastic bag, and threw it in a burn barrel behind his house.

Schenk, without further consulting Scott, retained Investigator Stephen Frick and sent Frick to find the wallet. Frick found it in the location described by Scott and brought it to Schenk. After examining the wallet and determining that it contained credit cards with Wade's name, Schenk turned the wallet and its contents over to Detective Payne, investigating officer in the case. Schenk told Payne only that, to the best of his knowledge, the wallet had belonged to Wade.

The prosecution subpoenaed Attorney Schenk and Investigator Frick to testify at the preliminary hearing. When questioned at that hearing, Schenk said that he received the wallet from Frick but refused to answer further questions on the ground that he learned about the wallet through a privileged communication. Eventually, however, the magistrate threatened Schenk with contempt if he did not respond "yes" or "no" when asked whether his contact with his client led to disclosure of the wallet's location. Schenk then replied "yes," and revealed on further questioning that this contact was the sole source of his information as to the wallet's location.

At the preliminary hearing Frick, the investigator who found the wallet, was then questioned by the district attorney. Over objections by counsel, Frick testified that he found the wallet in a garbage can behind Scott's residence.

Prior to trial, a third attorney, Hamilton Hintz, was appointed for Scott. Hintz unsuccessfully sought an *in limine* ruling that the wallet of the murder victim was inadmissible and that the attorney-client privilege precluded the admission of testimony concerning the wallet by Schenk or Frick.

At trial Frick, called by the prosecution, identified the wallet and testified that he found it in a garbage can behind Scott's residence. On cross-examination by Hintz, Scott's counsel, Frick further testified that he was an investigator hired by Scott's first attorney, Schenk, and that he had searched the garbage can at Schenk's request. Hintz later called Schenk as a witness: Schenk testified that he told Frick to search for the wallet immediately after Schenk finished talking to Scott. Schenk also stated that Frick brought him the wallet on the following day; after examining its contents Schenk delivered the wallet to the police. Scott then took the stand and testified to the information about the wallet that he had disclosed to Schenk.

The jury found both Scott and Meredith guilty of first degree murder and first degree robbery. It further found that Meredith, but not Scott, was armed with a deadly weapon. Both defendants appeal from their convictions.

Defendant Scott concedes, and we agree, that the wallet itself was admissible in evidence. Scott maintains, however, that Evidence Code section 954 bars the testimony of the investigator concerning the location of the wallet. We consider, first, whether the California attorney-client privilege codified in that section extends to observations which are the product of privileged communications. We then discuss whether that privileged status is lost when defense conduct may have frustrated prosecution discovery. . . .

Scott's statements to Schenk regarding the location of the wallet clearly fulfilled the statutory requirements [of a claim of privilege]. Moreover, the privilege did not dissolve when Schenk disclosed the substance of that communication to his investigator, Frick. . . . If Frick was to perform the investigative services for which Schenk had retained him, it was "reasonably necessary," that Schenk transmit to Frick the information regarding the wallet. Thus, Schenk's disclosure to Frick did not waive the statutory privilege.

The statutes codifying the attorney-client privilege do not, however, indicate whether that privilege protects facts viewed and observed as a direct result of confidential communication. To resolve that issue, we turn first to the policies which underlie the attorney-client privilege, and then to the cases which apply those policies to observations arising from a protected communication.

The fundamental purpose of the attorney-client privilege is, of course, to encourage full and open communication between client and attorney. . . .

In the criminal context, as we have recently observed, these policies assume particular significance: " 'As a practical matter, if the client knows that damaging information could more readily be obtained from the attorney following disclosure than from himself in the absence of disclosure, the client would be reluctant to confide in his lawyer and it would be difficult to obtain fully informed legal advice.' ... Thus, if an accused is to derive the full benefits of his right to counsel, he must have the assurance of confidentiality and privacy of communication with his attorney."

Judicial decisions have recognized that the implementation of these important policies may require that the privilege extend not only to the initial communication between client and attorney but also to any information which the attorney or his investigator may subsequently acquire as a direct result of that communication. In a venerable decision involving facts analogous to those in the instant case, the Supreme Court of West Virginia held that the trial court erred in admitting an attorney's testimony as to the location of a pistol which he had discovered as the result of a privileged communication from his client. That the attorney had observed the pistol, the court pointed out, did not nullify the privilege: "All that the said attorney knew about this pistol, or where it was to be found, he knew only from the communications which had been made to him by his client confidentially and professionally, as counsel in this case. And it ought therefore, to have been entirely excluded from the jury. It may be, that in this particular case this evidence tended to the promotion of right and justice, but as was well said in *Pearce v. Pearce*, 11 Jar. 52, in page 55, and 2 De Gex & Smale 25–27: 'Truth like all other good things may be loved unwisely, may be pursued too keenly, may cost too much.' "

This unbearable cost ... could not be entirely avoided by attempting to admit testimony regarding observations or discoveries made as the result of a privileged communication, while excluding the communication itself. Such a procedure ... "was practically as mischievous in all its tendencies and consequences, as if it has required (the attorney) to state everything, which his client had confidentially told him about this pistol. It would be a slight safeguard indeed, to confidential communications made to counsel, if he was thus compelled substantially, to give them to a jury, although he was required not to state them in the words of his client."

More recent decisions reach similar conclusions. In *State v. Olwell*, 394 P.2d 681 (Wash. 1964), the court reviewed contempt charges against an attorney who refused to produce a knife he obtained from his client. The court first observed that "(t)o be protected as a privileged communication ... the securing of the knife ... must have been the direct result of information given to Mr. Olwell by his client." The court concluded that defense counsel, after examining the physical evidence, should deliver it to the prosecution, but should not reveal the source of the evidence; "(b)y thus allowing the prosecution to recover such evidence, the public interest is served, and by refusing the prosecution an opportunity to disclose the source of the evidence, the client's privilege is preserved and a balance reached between these conflicting interests."

Finally, we note the decisions of the New York courts in *People v. Belge*, 372 N.Y.S.2d 798 (Sup. Ct. 1975), *aff'd, People v. Belge*, 376 N.Y.S.2d 771 (App. Div. 1975). Defendant, charged with one murder, revealed to counsel that he had committed three others. Counsel, following defendant's directions, located one of the bodies. Counsel did not reveal the location of the body until trial, 10 months later, when he exposed the other murders to support an insanity defense.

Counsel was then indicted for violating two sections of the New York Public Health Law for failing to report the existence of the body to proper authorities in order that they could give it a decent burial. The trial court dismissed the indictment; the appellate division affirmed, holding that the attorney-client privilege shielded counsel from prosecution for actions which would otherwise violate the Public Health Law.

The foregoing decisions demonstrate that the attorney-client privilege is not strictly limited to communications, but extends to protect observations made as a consequence of protected communications. We turn therefore to the question whether that privilege encompasses a case in which the defense, by removing or altering evidence, interferes with the prosecution's opportunity to discover that evidence.[1]

In some of the cases extending the privilege to observations arising from protected communications the defense counsel had obtained the evidence from his client or in some other fashion removed it from its original location; in others the attorney did not remove or alter the evidence. None of the decisions, however, confronts directly the question whether such removal or alteration should affect the defendant's right to assert the attorney-client privilege as a bar to testimony concerning the original location or condition of the evidence.

When defense counsel alters or removes physical evidence, he necessarily deprives the prosecution of the opportunity to observe that evidence in its original condition or location. As the amicus Appellate Committee of the California District Attorneys Association points out, to bar admission of testimony concerning the original condition and location of the evidence in such a case permits the defense in effect to "destroy" critical information; it is as if, he explains, the wallet in this case bore a tag bearing the words "located in the trash can by Scott's residence," and the defense, by taking the wallet, destroyed this tag. To extend the attorney-client privilege to a

---

1. We agree with the parties' suggestion that an attorney in Schenk's position often may best fulfill conflicting obligations to preserve the confidentiality of client confidences, investigate his case, and act as an officer of the court if he does not remove evidence located as the result of a privileged communication. We must recognize, however, that in some cases an examination of evidence may reveal information critical to the defense of a client accused of crime. If the usefulness of the evidence cannot be gauged without taking possession of it, as, for example, when a ballistics or fingerprint test is required, the attorney may properly take it for a reasonable time before turning it over to the prosecution. Similarly, in the present case the defense counsel could not be certain the burnt wallet belonged in fact to the victim: in taking the wallet to examine it for identification, he violated no ethical duty to his client or to the prosecution.

case in which the defense removed evidence might encourage defense counsel to race the police to seize critical evidence.

We therefore conclude that courts must craft an exception to the protection extended by the attorney-client privilege in cases in which counsel has removed or altered evidence. . . .

We therefore conclude that whenever defense counsel removes or alters evidence, the statutory privilege does not bar revelation of the original location or condition of the evidence in question.[2] We thus view the defense decision to remove evidence as a tactical choice. If defense counsel leaves the evidence where he discovers it, his observations derived from privileged communications are insulated from revelation. If, however, counsel chooses to remove evidence to examine or test it, the original location and condition of that evidence loses the protection of the privilege. Applying this analysis to the present case, we hold that the trial court did not err in admitting the investigator's testimony concerning the location of the wallet.

NOTES

1. Was the information that the lawyers received from Scott about the wallet privileged? Was it confidential? If the lawyers had simply kept this information to themselves, would they have had any obligation to disclose to the prosecution the location of the burned wallet?

2. What should a lawyer do who learns from a client the location of physical evidence of a crime? What might that depend on?

3. If the lawyer or his agent retrieves the evidence, as the investigator did here, must the lawyer then testify as to how the prosecution learned of the location of the evidence? Wouldn't that be highly incriminating for the client? What solution does the court propose to this problem?

4. What if the lawyer had learned this information from a third party—a witness to the crime, or a relative of the client—rather than from the client himself? Lee was accused of attempted murder. His wife located some shoes belonging to Lee and contacted the public defender assigned to Lee to ask what she should do with them. The lawyer retrieved the shoes and ultimately turned them over to the prosecutor. The shoes were covered with the victim's blood and were strongly incriminating evidence that Lee had committed the crime. At trial, a representative of the public defender's office was required to

---

2. In offering the evidence, the prosecution should present the information in a manner which avoids revealing the content of attorney-client communications or the original source of the information. In the present case, for example, the prosecutor simply asked Frick where he found the wallet; he did not identify Frick as a defense investigator or trace the discovery of the wallet to an attorney-client communication.

In other circumstances, when it is not possible to elicit such testimony without identifying the witness as the defendant's attorney or investigator, the defendant may be willing to enter a stipulation which will simply inform the jury as to the relevant location or condition of the evidence in question. When such a stipulation is proffered, the prosecution should not be permitted to reject the stipulation in the hope that by requiring defense counsel personally to testify to such facts, the jury might infer that counsel learned those facts from defendant.

testify about how the office had come to take possession of the shoes. Was this proper? *See People v. Lee*, 83 Cal.Rptr. 715 (Cal. App. 1970).

5.   Client, suspected of a homicide, tells Lawyer that he has committed two unrelated homicides and discloses the location of the bodies. Lawyer goes to the place directed by Client, observes the bodies and photographs them, but leaves them as he found them. Must Lawyer disclose what he has seen? May Lawyer disclose? *See N.Y. State Bar Ass'n Comm. on Prof'l Ethics Op. 479* (1978); *People v. Belge*, 376 N.Y.S.2d 771 (App. Div. 1975).

D.   NEW TECHNOLOGIES AND NEW PROBLEMS: PROTECTING CLIENT INFORMATION IN THE ELECTRONIC AGE

The use of electronic transmission of documents creates many complex opportunities for the inadvertent transmission of information. One recent and much-discussed issue has been the treatment of metadata.

What is metadata? Metadata is data concealed within data files. A document prepared using standard word-processing software may contain significant information about the document, including who prepared it initially and when and how it has been edited. If you transmit a data file containing metadata without first removing (or "scrubbing") the metadata, you may be transmitting information about that document as well. As *Alabama Ethics Op. 2007–02* noted, "The disclosure of metadata contained in an electronic submission to an opposing party could lead to the disclosure of client confidences and secrets, litigation strategy, editorial comments, legal issues raised by the client, and other confidential information."

What does the duty of confidentiality require a lawyer to do with regard to metadata? That's the easy question. Disclosure of metadata is a breach of the duty of confidentiality. The harder question—what the recipient should do with metadata unintentionally sent—has sent state ethics authorities in radically different directions. *Compare Ethical Propriety of Mining Metadata, Alabama Ethics Op. 2007–02* ("Absent express authorization from a court, it is ethically impermissible for an attorney to mine metadata from an electronic document he or she inadvertently or improperly receives from another party") *with Ethics of Viewing and/or Using Metadata, Maryland State Bar Association Committee on Ethics Opinion 2007–09* ("there is no ethical violation if the recipient attorney (or those working under the attorney's direction) reviews or makes use of the metadata without first ascertaining whether the sender intended to include such metadata"). What possible justification could there be for such different answers to the same question?

This discussion refers to metadata created by lawyers. Metadata included in documents prepared by clients may be called for in discovery; scrubbing or altering client documents could constitute improper tampering with evidence. As the Alabama ethics opinion noted, "The production of metadata during discovery will ordinarily be a legal matter within the sole discretion of the courts. The Commission advises attorneys, however, to be cognizant of the issue of disclosing metadata during discovery. Both parties should seek direction from the court in determining whether a document's metadata is to be produced during discovery."

NOTES

1.   State bar ethics opinions continue to be quite divided about the propriety of reviewing metadata. What do you think about it? What does the controversy tell you about what your office conventions ought to be with regard to creating and scrubbing your own metadata?

2.   As noted above, once documents are relevant to litigation and may be sought in discovery, the client may be required to produce electronic documents with their metadata intact. What pre-litigation conversations might you have with your clients about their standard procedures for preserving metadata in light of this concern?

PROBLEMS

1.   Lawyer was appointed to represent Client, a minor child, in a dependency proceeding. Client told Lawyer that she was currently being sexually assaulted by an adult at the home where the court has placed her. Client explicitly told Lawyer not to disclose this information to anyone. Can Lawyer disclose? What should Lawyer do? *See L.A. County Bar Ass'n Prof'l Responsibility & Ethics Comm. Form. Eth. Op. No. 504* (5/15/2000).

2.   Lawyer secured labor certification for Client, an undocumented immigrant who was seeking permission to work legally in the United States. A dispute arose between Client and Lawyer about Lawyer's fee. Lawyer filed a lawsuit against Client for payment of his fee. Fourteen months later, while the suit was still pending, Lawyer wrote a letter to the federal authorities stating that Client "lacked the good moral character needed to obtain immigration benefits" because he owed Lawyer over $7000, and asked that the letter be placed in Client's file "to prevent him from obtaining any further immigration benefits." Did Lawyer act properly? *See In re Lim*, 210 S.W.3d 199 (Mo. 2007).

3.   Plaintiff sued Defendant, claiming he was the victim of clergy sexual abuse. Lawyer, who represented Defendant, telephoned Plaintiff and left a message for him on his answering machine. Lawyer, thinking she had finished the call, then had a conversation with Defendant about Plaintiff and his claim. Lawyer had not hung up the telephone receiver properly, and the entire conversation between Lawyer and Defendant was recorded on Plaintiff's answering machine. Is the resulting recording protected by the attorney-client privilege? *See Howell v. Joffe*, 483 F. Supp. 2d 659 (N.D. Ill. 2007).

4.   Client loaned Entity $85 million. Entity was engaged in copyright infringement. Plaintiff claimed that the "loan" Client made to Entity was a sham, and that Client really purchased a controlling interest in Entity, but

structured the transaction as a loan to avoid potential liability for Entity's copyright infringement. Were conversations Client had with its lawyers about structuring the loan protected by the attorney-client privilege? *See In re Napster*, 479 F.3d 1078 (9th Cir. 2007).

5.   Client was charged with possession of a stolen vehicle. He gave his lawyer two documents, a bill of sale and a certificate of title, to turn over to the prosecutor. However, the VIN numbers on the two documents did not match. The government wished to use the fact that Client had produced the two documents to prove that he knew or should have known the vehicle was stolen. Can his lawyer be required to testify that he got the documents from Client? *See Hayden v. State*, 972 So.2d 525 (Miss. 2007).

6.   Madera sought to withdraw his guilty plea in a criminal case, claiming that his lawyer had provided ineffective assistance of counsel and that as a result his guilty plea was not made knowingly because he did not understand the mandatory sentence he would receive. The government subpoenaed Madera's attorney's entire file in the case, arguing that Madera's claim of ineffective assistance of counsel waived the attorney-client privilege. Should the subpoena be quashed? *See People v. Madera*, 112 P.3d 688 (Colo. 2005).

7.   Meeks was charged with a crime and claimed he was incompetent to stand trial. The prosecution subpoenaed Scholle, a lawyer who had previously represented Meeks, to testify at Meeks' competency hearing. Scholle was not asked about specific communications between her and Meeks, but was asked about how she ordinarily proceeded when representing a client and what she would do if she perceived an issue regarding the client's competency. Her testimony clearly implied that she had not believed Meeks to be incompetent at the time she represented him. The judge considered this evidence in concluding that Meeks was competent to stand trial. Did Scholle's testimony violate the attorney-client privilege? *See State v. Meeks*, 666 N.W.2d 859 (Wis. 2003).

8.   Client was arrested when his fingerprints were found in blood in the home of a friend, Jones, who was murdered. Two of Jones' children were missing from the home. Client's mother engaged Lawyer to represent Client. After several conversations with Client over the course of a week, Lawyer thought it highly likely that Client had killed both of the children, but he was not sure. Client told Lawyer that "Jesus saved the kids," and Lawyer did not ask if they were dead. He did ask Client to tell him where the children were. Client did so, drawing a map and giving it to Lawyer, and indicating two isolated locations, sixty miles apart, where the two children were located. Lawyer instructed his secretary to call the sheriff's department anonymously and provide directions to the locations on the map. Law enforcement authorities located the bodies and used forensic evidence found at the scene to convict Client. Did Lawyer behave properly? Was Client deprived of the effective assistance of counsel? *See McClure v. Thompson*, 323 F.3d 1233 (9th Cir. 2003).

9.   Lawyer received an unsolicited email from Victim, the driver of a car that was involved in a multi-vehicle accident. The email said, "I got your email address from the State Bar website. I would like to retain you to represent me in a personal injury case in which I was rear-ended by three cars. I have a lot

of back pain. Prior to the accident, I had a few drinks. Do you think they will find out? I look forward to working with you." Before Lawyer opened this email, he met with Driver, another driver hurt in the same accident. Must Lawyer keep Victim's email confidential? *Compare San Diego County Bar Ass'n Ethics Opinion 2006–1 with Cal. Eth. Op 2005–168*, 2005 WL 3068090.

10. Law Firm represented a large number of individual plaintiffs who claimed that a particular medication, Exco, caused them injury. Law Firm's website included a questionnaire, captioned "Exco Litigation Initial Contact." The questionnaire stated that its purpose was to "garner information about potential plaintiffs who have suffered damaging side effects from Exco," and persons who took the medication, as well as family members of such persons, were invited to complete the questionnaire. To submit a completed questionnaire, the responder had to click a box that acknowledged that the questionnaire did not constitute a request for legal advice and that the responder was not forming an attorney-client relationship with Law Firm by submitting the information. Subsequently, four plaintiffs who had responded to the questionnaire engaged Law Firm and brought suit against Exco's manufacturer. The defense sought the clients' questionnaire responses in discovery. May the firm resist producing them on the ground that they are privileged? *See Barton v. United States District Court*, 410 F.3d 1104 (9th Cir. 2005).

11. Newman was involved in an acrimonious divorce proceeding. While meeting with her lawyer, Friedman, she told him about her plan to kill one of her children and arrange to blame her husband, stating, "You know, I don't have to kill both children. I only need to kill Lars because I can save Herbie, and then [Husband] will go to jail and get what he deserves because he is a criminal, and I can at least save Herbie." Friedman disclosed Newman's statements to a judge and was permitted to withdraw as her lawyer. Newman was subsequently charged with conspiracy to commit murder for participating in an attempt to kill her ex-husband. The state called Friedman to testify at Newman's trial about her statements. Should Friedman's testimony be admitted at Newman's trial? *See Newman v. State*, 863 A.2d 321 (Md. 2004).

12. Client, an undocumented immigrant, contacted Lawyer to ask if Lawyer could assist Client in obtaining legal status in the United States. Lawyer agreed to take on the representation of Client, and Client paid Lawyer $1,250. Client was employed by Employer. Client asked Employer if Employer would file a petition for labor certification which would assist Client in securing legal status, and Employer agreed. Lawyer had a meeting with Employer and Client and discussed what each needed to do to secure legal status for Client. Subsequently, Employer was investigated for unlawfully employing undocumented workers. The government sought to elicit testimony from Lawyer about the meeting with Employer and Client. Must Lawyer testify? *See In re De Mayolo*, 2007 WL 1121303 (N.D. Iowa 2007).

CHAPTER 8

THE DUTY OF LOYALTY

■ ■ ■

A. WHAT IS A CONFLICT OF INTEREST? LESSONS FROM ORDINARY LIFE

A client tells you that she is eager to acquire a particular piece of property for use in her business. You own the property, and you figure that you can sell the property to the client at well above the usual market price since the client wants it so badly. May you do that? The answer, as you might imagine, is no.

Why? You already know of one reason: it would involve the use of confidential information to the client's disadvantage. But a significant additional reason is that a lawyer has a duty of loyalty to a client. Loyalty requires an attorney to put her client's interest first: before the interests of other clients, before the interests of third parties, and before the interest of the lawyer herself.

> [A]n attorney is precluded from assuming any relation which would prevent him from devoting his entire energies to his client's interests. Nor does it matter that the intention and motives of the attorney are honest. The rule is designed not alone to prevent the dishonest practitioner from fraudulent conduct, but as well to preclude the honest practitioner from putting himself in a position where he may be required to choose between conflicting duties, or be led to attempt to reconcile conflicting interests, rather than to enforce to their full extent the rights of the interest which he should alone represent.

Anderson v. Eaton, 293 P. 788, 789–90 (Cal. 1930).

The duty of loyalty creates two distinct problems. The first is defining and understanding the wide and complex range of situations in which the lawyer's loyalty to a client might be impaired because the lawyer is also attending to the interests of others—other clients or perhaps herself. The second is learning and applying the rules that govern those situations.

We often say that a situation in which a lawyer's loyalty may be compromised presents a "conflict of interest," because the lawyer may want—or be required—to pursue two distinct sets of interests that are in conflict with each other. The idea of a conflict of interest is by no means unique to the practice of law. It arises in a wide variety of situations, from business to personal life. Should a college financial aid advisor take gifts from a company that offers loans to students? Should a corporate director encourage the corporation to purchase raw materials from a company in which the director holds a substantial stake, when the transaction will produce a profit for the director? If you're the soccer coach, should you give your kid more playing time than her teammates get? Life is rife with conflict of interest situations; whenever your personal or professional interests create obligations that have the potential to conflict with each other or with your own self-interest, the possibility of a conflict of interest exists.

Each of these situations involves a possible problem of conflicting obligations. The financial aid advisor has a duty to help the students he advises get the best deal possible; receiving gifts from a particular loan company may cause him to recommend that loan provider not because it provides the best rates or the best student service, but because it benefits him personally. The corporate director has a fiduciary duty to advance the interests of the corporation; her financial interest in profiting from a sale to the company might interfere with her exercise of independent judgment on behalf of the corporation. You might be giving your child extra playing time because she's the best player, or just because you love her the most.

Law practice creates many possible conflict of interest situations. First, the lawyer's duty of loyalty to her clients can conflict with her desire to do well for herself or otherwise to advance her personal interests. Second, the lawyer's duty to each client can create conflicts of interest between clients. The lawyer owes a duty of loyalty to every client, and may not unilaterally decide that the interests of one client are more important than the interests of another. Moreover, the lawyer's other duties to her present and former clients—such as the duty of confidentiality—may affect the lawyer's work on behalf of other clients. Third, lawyers retain some obligations towards clients even after their representation ends. The law must consider not only how the lawyer will deal with conflicts of interest involving self-interest, the interests of third parties, or current clients, but also how the lawyer will deal with conflicts involving former clients.

Once we identify a conflict of interest, how should it be managed? The accusation of a "conflict of interest" is sometimes understood as casting aspersions on the integrity of the actor; it seems to suggest that we do not trust the actor to do the right thing. If we recognize that a conflict of interest can be a conflict between equal obligations equally owed to others, however, such a conflict will not always be manageable simply by securing a promise that the lawyer will act honestly or with integrity. Does that mean that conflicts of interest must always be avoided? That they need not be avoided if the parties affected consent to them? Or that they need never be avoided as long as lawyers promise to do the right thing? The Rules of Professional Responsibility take a distinct view of these issues. Conflicts, however, are rarely the subject of disciplinary actions. As you read these materials, consider how conflict of interest issues typically arise and where they are usually resolved. Does this affect, in your view, what the rules about conflicts should be?

B. CONCURRENT CONFLICTS OF INTEREST

1. ETHICAL CONSTRAINTS ON CONFLICTS OF INTEREST

The basic rule on conflicts of interest is Model Rule 1.7. Read it carefully at this point. As you will see, the Rule does three things. First, part (a) defines a "concurrent conflict of interest." Second, part (a) creates a default rule: that "a lawyer shall not represent a client if the representation involves a concurrent conflict of interest." Third, part (b) creates exceptions to the default rule: situations in which a lawyer may proceed to represent a client <u>notwithstanding</u> a concurrent conflict of interest.

Any conflicts problem accordingly requires a two-part analysis. First, is there a "concurrent conflict of interest"? That analysis requires consideration of the two possible types of concurrent conflict of interest defined in Model Rule 1.7(a): conflicts that arise because "the representation of one client will be directly adverse to another client," and conflicts that arise because of a "significant risk that the representation of one or more clients will be materially limited by the lawyer's responsibilities to another client, a former client or a third person or by a personal interest of the lawyer." These are sometimes referred to as "directly adverse" or "materially limited" conflicts. They are not mutually exclusive; a particular fact situation can create both a "directly adverse" and a "materially limited" conflict.

The determination that there is a concurrent conflict of interest does not end the analysis. While the default provision in Model Rule 1.7(a) states that a lawyer may not engage in representation that involves a concurrent conflict of interest, there is an exception in Rule 1.7(b). The next question is therefore whether the exception in Model Rule 1.7(b) applies or whether the default rule of Rule 1.7(a) applies.

Model Rule 1.7(b) permits a lawyer to proceed with representation involving a concurrent conflict of interest if <u>all four</u> of the requirements set out in Rule 1.7(b)(1)-(4) are satisfied. The absence of any one of these elements makes the exception inapplicable and invokes the default rule of Rule 1.7(a).

One of the requirements in Model Rule 1.7(b) is the informed consent of each affected client, confirmed in writing. Rule 1.7(b)(4). But consent alone does not permit a lawyer to proceed with representation in the face of a concurrent conflict of interest. The other requirements of Model Rule 1.7(b) must also be satisfied. Model Rule 1.7(b)(1) requires the lawyer to reasonably believe "that the lawyer will be able to provide competent and diligent representation to each affected client." If the lawyer cannot reasonably believe this, the representation is not permitted, even if the affected clients consent to it. Such a situation is termed a "nonconsentable" conflict.

There are two other limitations in Model Rule 1.7(b). One is that the representation may not be "prohibited by law." Some jurisdictions have prohibitions on representation of two clients in particular situations. For example, in Iowa representation of both spouses in a divorce is expressly prohibited by Iowa Rule of Professional Conduct 1.7(c). Such representation would accordingly be prohibited even if the lawyer reasonably believed it possible to satisfy Rule 1.7(b)(1) and secured informed consent from each affected client.

The last requirement of Model Rule 1.7(b) is that representation may not involve "the assertion of a claim by one client against another client represented by the lawyer in the same litigation or other proceeding before a tribunal." This may seem inherently unlikely to arise, but consider the following case:

IOWA SUPREME COURT ATTORNEY DISCIPLINARY BOARD v. HOWE

706 N.W.2d 360 (Iowa 2005)

TERNUS, JUSTICE.

The complainant, Iowa Supreme Court Attorney Disciplinary Board ... filed disciplinary charges against the respondent, Bradley Howe, a part-time city attorney for the city of Spencer, Iowa....

The matter is now before this court for decision.... [W]e think the misconduct that occurred in this case warrants suspension of Howe's license to practice law in this state for four months.

Bradley Howe has been licensed to practice law in the State of Iowa since 1975. He is a general practitioner, and since 1976 has also served as an assistant city attorney for the City of Spencer. As an assistant city attorney Howe is primarily responsible for prosecuting simple misdemeanor charges filed by the Spencer city police alleging violations of the city code....

By all accounts, Howe is respected in his community and is known as a hard-working, honest attorney. Howe has a reputation for being trustworthy, forthright, and fair. He has not previously been disciplined for an ethical violation....

Mouw Conflict of Interest.

The Spencer police department charged Michael Mouw with four offenses: (1) third-degree burglary on December 11, 2002; (2) speeding on December 29, 2002; (3) underage possession of alcohol on December 30, 2002; and (4) violation of a driving instruction permit restriction on February 22, 2003.

Mouw did not appear for his hearing on the latter charge, and a conviction was entered.

The Clay County attorney prosecuted the burglary charge. Howe defended Mouw in this case, entering a written plea of not guilty on Mouw's behalf on January 27, 2003. At the same time, Howe prosecuted the three city charges against Mouw in his capacity as assistant city attorney. On April 21, 2003, ostensibly acting as the assistant city attorney, Howe filed a motion to rescind Mouw's conviction on the instruction permit violation. Howe also asked the court "to order the Department of Transportation to expunge any record of this conviction." Magistrate Whittenburg granted Howe's motion.

At some point, Mouw's mother talked to Howe about the charges pending against her son. Howe told her he could not represent her son on the charges he was prosecuting. Nonetheless, Howe said he would contact the police and the county attorney to see what they wanted to do. He then wrote to the police department secretary asking whether the charging officers would contact the county attorney so all four charges could be resolved at once. The officers and the county attorney, without Howe's involvement, then agreed to a resolution of all four cases. Howe subsequently told Mouw and Mouw's mother of the proposed disposition and obtained their approval.

The respondent then wrote to the magistrate, informing her of the disposition of the charges that he "was able to work out." In that letter Howe referred to Mouw as his client, entered a plea of guilty to the possession charge on Mouw's behalf, and moved to dismiss the instruction permit and speeding charges on behalf of the city. He stated that the city wanted no more than the minimum fine on the possession charge, and then requested that Mouw be given a couple of months to pay the fine. He also asked the court to waive the costs on the speeding and instruction permit charges.

Howe billed both the city and Mouw for his dual representation in these matters. Although Howe disclaimed any direct participation in the settlement of the four pending charges, his statement to Mouw for $275 included charges for multiple telephone conferences with Magistrate Whittenburg, police officers and the county attorney "re: 3 Spencer charges and state burglary charges (to reach settlement)."

Howe admitted at the hearing that his facilitation of the disposition of the three city charges through a plea agreement was wrong. We agree. Howe's representation of Mouw on the three charges Howe prosecuted on behalf of the city violated DR 5–105(B), which requires a lawyer to decline employment if the lawyer's exercise of independent professional judgment on behalf of the client will likely be adversely affected. *Cf. Iowa Rules of Prof'l Conduct* 32:1.7(b)(3) (prohibiting attorney's representation when it involves "the assertion of a claim by one client against another client represented by the lawyer in the same litigation"). Certainly Howe could not exercise independent professional judgment on behalf of the city in prosecuting Mouw on city charges when he was at the same time seeking to have the identical charges dismissed on behalf of the defendant. . . .

Larson and Olin Dual Representation.

Lance Larson was charged by a Spencer police officer with reckless driving. In a pleading signed by Howe as "attorney for defendant," Howe entered an appearance on behalf of Larson and entered a not-guilty plea to the citation. A month later he filed a motion for leave to amend on behalf of the city, signing as "attorney for plaintiff." In this pleading, he asked the court to amend the reckless driving violation to a cowl-lamp violation "as the result of a plea agreement." Magistrate Whittenburg allowed the amendment and subsequently accepted Larson's guilty plea to the cowl-lamp citation. Larson was fined $100. Howe billed the city for his time on the Larson prosecution, but he did not bill Larson.

[handwritten margin note: acted as prosecutor and defense counsel]

Mavis Olin was Howe's elderly neighbor. Olin was in a traffic accident with a city police car and was issued a citation by a Spencer police officer for failure to yield the right of way at a stop sign. Howe testified that upon hearing of the accident, he visited with Olin at her home. Olin was very concerned about losing her license, so the respondent told her not to worry and that he would "make some calls." Howe then wrote to Magistrate Whittenburg on his law office stationery, stating in part: "Would you please consider this letter to be Mavis' appearance and plea of not guilty for now? I am guessing we will simply cave in down the road and enter no defense." After the charging officer determined that Mavis's insurance would pay for the damage to the city police car, he suggested that the original citation be amended to a cowl-lamp violation. Olin eventually pled guilty to a cowl-lamp charge, and was fined $50.

Howe testified at the hearing before the Commission that he did not represent these defendants and did not intend to represent these defendants. He explained that he viewed his role as that of a public servant; so it was not unusual for him, upon being contacted by a defendant, to offer to make a call or drop a line to the magistrate to take care of the appearance date so the defendant would not have to come to court. A defendant's appearance would delay disposition of the charge and give Howe time to talk with the charging officer about a possible plea bargain. Generally, Howe would simply communicate to the magistrate that he was in the process of negotiating a plea agreement with the defendant and that she should indicate a not-guilty plea for the time being. Both Howe and the magistrate testified such communications are not unusual, and as a practical matter, are necessary to keep the matter moving toward a resolution when the defendant is unrepresented and not familiar with the legal process. Howe said he meant to follow the same procedure in the Larson and Olin cases: to simply pass along the defendants' wishes to the magistrate.

We understand that when a defendant is unrepresented the prosecutor is often thrust into the position of having to communicate the *pro se* defendant's wishes to the court. But Howe did more than that here. He filed a formal appearance for Larson and did the equivalent for Olin in his letter to the magistrate. His later contention that he was not really representing these defendants is belied by the court files.

Howe's simultaneous representation of Larson and Olin, on the one hand, and the city on the other created an obvious and direct conflict of interest because at the same time he prosecuted the criminal charges against these defendants, he was defending them against the same charges. Howe could not exercise independent professional judgment under these circumstances, and therefore, he violated DR 5–105(B).

Although we believe Howe was always motivated by the desire to resolve city charges in a fashion that was just to the city as well as to defendants, he often crossed the line into unethical conduct in disposing of criminal charges.... Howe represented criminal defendants and the city in the same case on more than one occasion. The inappropriateness of this dual representation should have been clear to him. Howe's conflicts of interest affected not only his ability to effectively represent his clients, but also compromised his role as an officer of the court, depriving the court of the advocacy that is a fundamental component of our system of justice....

In summary, we are convinced Howe's license should be suspended.... [W]e suspend Bradley Howe's license to practice law in this state indefinitely with no possibility of reinstatement for a period of four months from the date of the filing of this opinion....

NOTES

1. Why did Howe find himself on both sides of several criminal cases? Is this a relatively uncommon situation in criminal cases in most places? Why or why not? Does that suggest anything about the nature of Howe's practice? Do the rules reflect assumptions about the socioeconomic nature of law practice that may not be true everywhere?

2. Were these conflicts consentable? Why or why not?

3. As you might imagine, lawyers rarely undertake representation that affirmatively violates Model Rule 1.7(b)(3). But representation of clients with potentially conflicting interests is considerably more common, as the following case suggests:

IOWA SUPREME COURT ATTORNEY DISCIPLINARY BOARD v. CLAUSS

711 N.W.2d 1 (Iowa 2006)

LARSON, JUSTICE.

Robert Clauss, Jr., was cited by our attorney disciplinary board for violations of our code of professional ethics.... The Grievance Commission of this court concluded that the violations were established by the board and recommended suspension of Clauss's license for not less than ninety days. We affirm the findings of code violations, but increase the suspension to a minimum of six months.

The ... board's complaint involved a tale of two clients—both of them represented by Clauss despite their conflicting interests. The first client was National Management Corporation, which retained Clauss to collect past-due rental payments from Clauss's second client, Kay Clark.

Clauss called Clark to try to arrange payment of her debt to National. In the course of their conversation, Clark told Clauss she had problems of her own: she had breached a covenant not to compete with a previous employer and had been enjoined from running her competing professional recruitment business. As a result of the conversation, it was decided that Clauss could possibly represent Clark in attempting to get the injunction lifted. That way Clark could operate her business and generate income to apply toward National's judgment against her.

Although the plan appeared to be beneficial to all involved, Clauss saw, with good reason, that problems could arise from this dual representation. He contacted a lawyer more experienced in ethics cases to inquire about whether to proceed and, if so, how to avoid ethical problems. That attorney advised Clauss that he could, consistently with our ethics rules, represent both Clark and National, provided he obtained waivers from both of them. Clauss wrote a letter to Clark concerning a possible waiver:

> I am asking you to waive any conflict I may have in representing you in your covenant not to compete case and National Mgt. Corp. at the same time when you are a debtor of National Mgt. Corp. Ethically, I simply wanted to bring this matter to your attention by way of full disclosure. I spoke with Jerry Woods [acting on behalf of National] and he has no problems under these circumstances. I am sending Jerry an identical letter.

[handwritten margin note: waivers— insufficient / full disclosure required]

Clauss wrote a similar, but not identical, letter to National, stating:

> Per our telephone conversation, I am asking that you waive any conflict I may have in representing you and Kay Clark ... at the same time who is a debtor of National Mgt. Corp. Ethically, I simply wanted to bring this matter to your attention by way of full disclosure. I spoke with Kay Clark and she has no problems under these circumstances. I am sending her an identical letter.

Both National and Clark agreed to waive any conflict, pursuant to Clauss's suggestion.

Despite Clauss's efforts to obtain valid waivers, they were insufficient under our rules. Our disciplinary rules are quite clear on a lawyer's responsibilities under these circumstances.

A waiver of a conflict of interest is not valid unless the attorney has made a full disclosure of the possible consequences of dual representation.

An unconflicted lawyer working on behalf of National would have discovered, perhaps through a debtor's examination, where Clark had deposits or accounts receivable that could be subjected to payment on National's judgment. Clauss did not do that. In fact, as of the time of the commission hearing, he had not remitted any funds to National from Clark, despite the fact he had collected substantial sums for Clark by pursuing claims for her against other parties and had received attorney fees for himself on those collections.

This respondent was required to do more than simply warn his clients that there were potential conflicts and ask them to waive those conflicts. His actions involved conflicts between his clients, and he undertook representation of both clients without making "full disclosure of the possible effect of such representation on the exercise of the lawyer's independent professional judgment on behalf of each," as required by DR 5–105(D) [the predecessor to Iowa's rule 1.7]. We have said,

> [i]n a dual representation situation, it is not enough for a lawyer simply to inform the client that the lawyer is representing both sides. Full disclosure under DR 5–105(D) requires the attorney not only to inform the prospective client of the attorney's relationship with the [other client], but also to explain in detail the pitfalls that may arise in the course of the transaction which would make it desirable that the [prospective client] obtain independent counsel.

must describe pitfalls

We conclude the respondent violated DR 5–101(A) (prohibiting acceptance of employment if the lawyer's professional judgment will reasonably be affected by the lawyer's own financial, property, or personal interests); DR 5–105(C) (providing that a lawyer shall not continue multiple employment if his exercise of professional judgment is likely to be adversely affected by the representation of another client); and DR 5–105(D) (requiring full disclosure of possible effects of multiple representation).

We note, as an aggravating factor in determining the discipline to be imposed, that National was harmed financially because apparently it did not ever get any of the money that Clauss ultimately collected for Clark in other cases in which Clauss represented her. Presumably, National did not obtain another attorney to act for it because Clauss had preempted that responsibility. . . .

Based on these violations, exacerbated by the fact that the respondent benefited financially from his representation of a second client at the expense of the first, and together with his extensive history of disciplinary infractions, we conclude that the ninety-day suspension recommended by the commission is insufficient. Accordingly, we suspend Robert Clauss's license to practice law in this state indefinitely with no possibility of reinstatement for a period of six months from the date of the filing of this opinion.

NOTES

1. Why was there a problem with Clauss representing both Clark and National? Wasn't it possible that National would have more success recover-

ing debt payments from Clark if the company's lawyer was also Clark's lawyer? And wasn't it possible that Clark would get a better deal from National because her lawyer was also National's lawyer? In view of these concerns, what is wrong with Clauss's decision here?

2.   Why was the disclosure Clauss made to the clients inadequate? Was this a nonconsentable conflict, or simply one in which the waiver was invalid because of the nature of the disclosure? If you think this was a consentable conflict, consider the disclosure you would have had to make to secure a valid waiver. What kinds of issues would you have raised? How, if at all, would you have memorialized those disclosures? What does Model Rule 1.7(b) require in this regard?

3.   In this case, the lawyer's conflict of interest was based on his loyalty to two clients with conflicting interests. The conflict in their interests was self-evident. It can be considerably more difficult to spot conflicts when clients have some interests in common, or are members of the same family. Consider the facts of *Cincinnati Bar Association v. Lukey*, 851 N.E.2d 493 (Ohio 2006). Lukey represented grandparents who had adopted their grandson. The child had been charged with arson, and the grandparents, in an attempt to control him, had locked him in the basement. A dependency proceeding was brought to determine whether the grandparents should continue to care for the child. Attorney Lukey told the court that he represented the child, even though the child had a public defender appointed to represent him, and entered a plea agreement on the child's behalf. He then represented in the dependency proceeding that the boy was guilty of the crime and that the grandparents were having difficulty controlling the child. He did not tell the court that the child was "polite and cooperative, played orchestral harp, and displayed no antisocial or criminal behaviors"; as a result, the court subjected the child to a two-week detention pending resolution of the dependency matter. Did attorney Lukey act properly?

4.   A conflict can arise because of the lawyer's own interest as well. In that regard, consider the "attorney of the day" program implemented in a Texas county criminal court. The program provided that a private criminal defense attorney would be present in court to assist in expediting the large number of *pro se* criminal defendants appearing before the court each day. The attorney would volunteer his services, and would be available to criminal defendants to advise them as to their rights and options, on that day only. The "attorney of the day" would not be appointed to represent all the *pro se* defendants who consulted with him, and the defendants would need to sign a statement agreeing to the limited terms of this advisory relationship in order to take advantage of his consulting services. If the criminal defendant chose to resolve his case on that day through a plea of guilty, the "attorney of the day" would, only then, be appointed to represent him and would be paid. Accordingly, under the scheme the "attorney of the day" would be paid a fee only for those cases that resulted in the same-day entry of a defendant's guilty plea. Is there a conflicts problem with this arrangement? If so, is it one that is consentable? *See Texas Ethics Op. 535* (2000).

5.   What about a lawyer who realizes that he has committed malpractice? Lawyer mistakenly filed his client's personal injury claim in the wrong state;

by the time the defendant had succeeded in getting the case dismissed for lack of jurisdiction, the statute of limitations had expired. Lawyer continued to represent the client, seeking unsuccessfully to overturn the dismissal, for several years. Did he act properly? *See In re Hoffman*, 700 N.E.2d 1138 (Ind. 1998) (holding the continued representation "after it became apparent that the representation might be materially limited by the respondent's own interests" was improper). What should the lawyer do in this situation? Is Model Rule 1.8(h) relevant here?

6.   Clients with viable legal claims may be fairly certain of recovery in the future, but may have trouble supporting themselves while they await resolution of their cases, and advancing the expenses associated with litigation. One enterprising lawyer suggested that he organize a consumer moneylending company that would lend money to his cash-strapped clients to help them pay his fees and other litigation expenses. The investors in the company would be the lawyer's relatives, and the lawyer would be the sole manager of the company. Is there a conflict of interest under Model Rule 1.7? Is it consentable? *See Utah State Bar Ethics Advisory Opinion Comm. Op. 06–03.*

2.   CONFLICTS OF INTEREST IN THE CRIMINAL CASE

CUYLER v. SULLIVAN

446 U.S. 335 (1980)

MR. JUSTICE POWELL delivered the opinion of the Court.

The question presented is whether a state prisoner may obtain a federal writ of habeas corpus by showing that his retained defense counsel represented potentially conflicting interests.

I

Respondent John Sullivan was indicted with Gregory Carchidi and Anthony DiPasquale for the first-degree murders of John Gorey and Rita Janda. The victims, a labor official and his companion, were shot to death in Gorey's second-story office at the Philadelphia headquarters of Teamsters' Local 107. Francis McGrath, a janitor, saw the three defendants in the building just before the shooting. They appeared to be awaiting someone, and they encouraged McGrath to do his work on another day. McGrath ignored their suggestions. Shortly afterward, Gorey arrived and went to his office. McGrath then heard what sounded like firecrackers exploding in rapid succession. Carchidi, who was in the room where McGrath was working, abruptly directed McGrath to leave the building and to say nothing. McGrath hastily complied. When he returned to the building about 15 minutes later, the defendants were gone. The victims' bodies were discovered the next morning.

Two privately retained lawyers, G. Fred DiBona and A. Charles Peruto, represented all three defendants throughout the state proceedings that followed the indictment. Sullivan had different counsel at the medical examiner's inquest, but he thereafter accepted representation from the two lawyers retained by his codefendants because he could not afford to pay his own lawyer. At no time did Sullivan or his lawyers object to the multiple representation. Sullivan was the first defendant to come to trial. The evidence against him was entirely circumstantial, consisting primarily of McGrath's testimony. At the close of the Commonwealth's case, the defense rested without presenting any evidence. The jury found Sullivan guilty and fixed his penalty at life imprisonment. Sullivan's post-trial motions failed, and the Pennsylvania Supreme Court affirmed his conviction by an equally divided vote. Sullivan's codefendants, Carchidi and DiPasquale, were acquitted at separate trials.

multiple representation for criminal charges

Sullivan then petitioned for collateral relief under the Pennsylvania Post Conviction Hearing Act. He alleged, among other claims, that he had been denied effective assistance of counsel because his defense lawyers represented conflicting interests. In five days of hearings, the Court of Common Pleas heard evidence from Sullivan, Carchidi, Sullivan's lawyers, and the judge who presided at Sullivan's trial.

main allegation

DiBona and Peruto had different recollections of their roles at the trials of the three defendants. DiBona testified that he and Peruto had been "associate counsel" at each trial. Peruto recalled that he had been chief counsel for Carchidi and DePasquale, but that he merely had assisted DiBona in Sullivan's trial. DiBona and Peruto also gave conflicting accounts of the decision to rest Sullivan's defense. DiBona said he had encouraged Sullivan to testify even though the Commonwealth had presented a very weak case. Peruto remembered that he had not "want[ed] the defense to go on because I thought we would only be exposing [defense] witnesses for the other two trials that were coming up." Sullivan testified that he had deferred to his lawyers' decision not to present evidence for the defense. But other testimony suggested that Sullivan preferred not to take the stand because cross-examination might have disclosed an extramarital affair. Finally, Carchidi claimed he would have appeared at Sullivan's trial to rebut McGrath's testimony about Carchidi's statement at the time of the murders. . . .

The Pennsylvania Supreme Court affirmed both Sullivan's original conviction and the denial of collateral relief. The court saw no basis for Sullivan's claim that he had been denied effective assistance of counsel at trial. It found that Peruto merely assisted DiBona in the Sullivan trial and that DiBona merely assisted Peruto in the trials of the other two defendants. Thus, the court concluded, there was "no dual representation in the true sense of the term." The court also found that resting the defense was a reasonable tactic which had not denied Sullivan the effective assistance of counsel.

state court ruling - no merit to claim

Having exhausted his state remedies, Sullivan sought habeas corpus relief in the United States District Court. . . . The petition was referred to a Magistrate, who found that Sullivan's defense counsel had represented conflicting interests. The District Court, however, accepted the Pennsylva-

federal court (conflicting interests existed)

nia Supreme Court's conclusion that there had been no multiple representation. The court also found that, assuming there had been multiple representation, the evidence adduced in the state post conviction proceeding revealed no conflict of interest.

The Court of Appeals for the Third Circuit reversed. It first held that the participation by DiBona and Peruto in the trials of Sullivan and his codefendants established, as a matter of law, that both lawyers had represented all three defendants. The court recognized that multiple representation " 'is not tantamount to the denial of effective assistance of counsel. . . .' " But it held that a criminal defendant is entitled to reversal of his conviction whenever he makes " 'some showing of a possible conflict of interest or prejudice, however remote. . . .' " The court acknowledged that resting at the close of the prosecutor's case "would have been a legitimate tactical decision if made by independent counsel." Nevertheless, the court thought that action alone raised a possibility of conflict sufficient to prove a violation of Sullivan's Sixth Amendment rights. The court found support for its conclusion in Peruto's admission that concern for Sullivan's codefendants had affected his judgment that Sullivan should not present a defense. To give weight to DiBona's contrary testimony, the court held, "would be to . . . require a showing of actual prejudice."

We granted certiorari. . . . We now vacate and remand.

II

. . . The Court of Appeals carefully recited the facts from which it concluded that DiBona and Peruto represented both Sullivan and his codefendants. The court noted that both lawyers prepared the defense in consultation with all three defendants, that both advised Sullivan on whether he should rest his defense, and that both played important roles at all three trials. In fact, the transcript of Sullivan's trial shows that Peruto rather than DiBona rested the defense. We agree with the Court of Appeals that these facts establish the existence of multiple representation.

III

[The court concluded that ineffective assistance of retained counsel posed a constitutional issue.]

IV

We come at last to Sullivan's claim that he was denied the effective assistance of counsel guaranteed by the Sixth Amendment because his lawyers had a conflict of interest. The claim raises two issues expressly reserved in *Holloway v. Arkansas*, 435 U.S. at 483–84. The first is whether a state trial judge must inquire into the propriety of multiple representation even though no party lodges an objection. The second is whether the mere possibility of a conflict of interest warrants the conclusion that the defendant was deprived of his right to counsel.

A

In *Holloway*, a single public defender represented three defendants at the same trial. The trial court refused to consider the appointment of separate counsel despite the defense lawyer's timely and repeated assertions that the interests of his clients conflicted. This Court recognized that a lawyer forced to represent codefendants whose interests conflict cannot provide the adequate legal assistance required by the Sixth Amendment. Given the trial court's failure to respond to timely objections, however, the Court did not consider whether the alleged conflict actually existed. It simply held that the trial court's error unconstitutionally endangered the right to counsel.

Holloway requires state trial courts to investigate timely objections to multiple representation. But nothing in our precedents suggests that the Sixth Amendment requires state courts themselves to initiate inquiries into the propriety of multiple representation in every case. Defense counsel have an ethical obligation to avoid conflicting representations and to advise the court promptly when a conflict of interest arises during the course of trial. Absent special circumstances, therefore, trial courts may assume either that multiple representation entails no conflict or that the lawyer and his clients knowingly accept such risk of conflict as may exist. Indeed, as the Court noted in *Holloway*, trial courts necessarily rely in large measure upon the good faith and good judgment of defense counsel. "An 'attorney representing two defendants in a criminal matter is in the best position professionally and ethically to determine when a conflict of interest exists or will probably develop in the course of a trial.'" 435 U.S., at 485, quoting *State v. Davis*, 514 P.2d 1025, 1027 (1973). Unless the trial court knows or reasonably should know that a particular conflict exists, the court need not initiate an inquiry.

Nothing in the circumstances of this case indicates that the trial court had a duty to inquire whether there was a conflict of interest. The provision of separate trials for Sullivan and his codefendants significantly reduced the potential for a divergence in their interests. No participant in Sullivan's trial ever objected to the multiple representation. DiBona's opening argument for Sullivan outlined a defense compatible with the view that none of the defendants was connected with the murders. The opening argument also suggested that counsel was not afraid to call witnesses whose testimony might be needed at the trials of Sullivan's codefendants. Finally, as the Court of Appeals noted, counsel's critical decision to rest Sullivan's defense was on its face a reasonable tactical response to the weakness of the circumstantial evidence presented by the prosecutor. On these facts, we conclude that the Sixth Amendment imposed upon the trial court no affirmative duty to inquire into the propriety of multiple representation.

B

Holloway reaffirmed that multiple representation does not violate the Sixth Amendment unless it gives rise to a conflict of interest. Since a possible conflict inheres in almost every instance of multiple representation, a defendant who objects to multiple representation must have the opportunity to show that potential conflicts impermissibly imperil his right to a fair trial. But unless the trial court fails to afford such an opportunity, a reviewing court cannot presume that the possibility for conflict has resulted in ineffective assistance of counsel. Such a presumption would preclude multiple representation even in cases where " '[A] common defense . . . gives strength against a common attack.' "

In order to establish a violation of the Sixth Amendment, a defendant who raised no objection at trial must demonstrate that an actual conflict of interest adversely affected his lawyer's performance. In *Glasser v. United States*, for example, the record showed that defense counsel failed to cross-examine a prosecution witness whose testimony linked Glasser with the crime and failed to resist the presentation of arguably inadmissible evidence. The Court found that both omissions resulted from counsel's desire to diminish the jury's perception of a codefendant's guilt. Indeed, the evidence of counsel's "struggle to serve two masters [could not] seriously be doubted." Since this actual conflict of interest impaired Glasser's defense, the Court reversed his conviction.

Glasser established that unconstitutional multiple representation is never harmless error. Once the Court concluded that Glasser's lawyer had an actual conflict of interest, it refused "to indulge in nice calculations as to the amount of prejudice" attributable to the conflict. Thus, a defendant who shows that a conflict of interest actually affected the adequacy of his representation need not demonstrate prejudice in order to obtain relief. But until a defendant shows that his counsel actively represented conflicting interests, he has not established the constitutional predicate for his claim of ineffective assistance.

C

The Court of Appeals granted Sullivan relief because he had shown that the multiple representation in this case involved a possible conflict of interest. We hold that the possibility of conflict is insufficient to impugn a criminal conviction. In order to demonstrate a violation of his Sixth Amendment rights, a defendant must establish that an actual conflict of interest adversely affected his lawyer's performance. Sullivan believes he should prevail even under this standard. He emphasizes Peruto's admission that the decision to rest Sullivan's defense reflected a reluctance to expose witnesses who later might have testified for the other defendants. The petitioner, on the other hand, points to DiBona's contrary testimony and to evidence that Sullivan himself wished to avoid taking the stand. Since the Court of Appeals did not weigh these conflicting contentions under the proper legal standard, its judgment is vacated and the case is remanded for further proceedings consistent with this opinion.

JUSTICE MARSHALL, concurring in part and dissenting in part.

. . . I dissent from the Court's formulation of the proper standard for determining whether multiple representation has violated the defendant's right to the effective assistance of counsel. The Court holds that in the absence of an objection at trial, the defendant must show "that an actual conflict of interest adversely affected his lawyer's performance." If the Court's holding would require a defendant to demonstrate that his attorney's trial performance differed from what it would have been if the defendant had been the attorney's only client, I believe it is inconsistent with our previous cases. Such a test is not only unduly harsh, but incurably speculative as well. The appropriate question under the Sixth Amendment is whether an actual, relevant conflict of interests existed during the proceedings. If it did, the conviction must be reversed. Since such a conflict was present in this case, I would affirm the judgment of the Court of Appeals.

Our cases make clear that every defendant has a constitutional right to "the assistance of an attorney unhindered by a conflict of interests." *Holloway v. Arkansas*, 435 U.S. 475, 483 n.5 (1978).... If "[t]he possibility of the inconsistent interests of [the clients] was brought home to the court" by means of an objection at trial, the court may not require joint representation. But if no objection was made at trial, the appropriate inquiry is whether a conflict actually existed during the course of the representation.

Because it is the simultaneous representation of conflicting interests against which the Sixth Amendment protects a defendant, he need go no further than to show the existence of an actual conflict. An actual conflict of interests negates the unimpaired loyalty a defendant is constitutionally entitled to expect and receive from his attorney.

Moreover, a showing that an actual conflict adversely affected counsel's performance is not only unnecessary, it is often an impossible task. As the Court emphasized in *Holloway*:

> [I]n a case of joint representation of conflicting interests the evil—it bears repeating—is in what the advocate finds himself compelled to *refrain* from doing.... It may be possible in some cases to identify from the record the prejudice resulting from an attorney's failure to undertake certain trial tasks, but even with a record of the sentencing hearing available it would be difficult to judge intelligently the impact of a conflict on the attorney's representation of a client. And to assess the impact of a conflict of interests on the attorney's options, tactics, and decisions in plea negotiations would be virtually impossible. 435 U.S. at 490–491 (emphasis in original).

Accordingly, in *Holloway* we emphatically rejected the suggestion that a defendant must show prejudice in order to be entitled to relief. For the same reasons, it would usually be futile to attempt to determine how counsel's conduct would have been different if he had not been under conflicting duties.

In the present case Peruto's testimony, if credited by the court, would be sufficient to make out a case of ineffective assistance by reason of a conflict of interests under even a restrictive reading of the Court's standard. In the usual case, however, we might expect the attorney to be unwilling to give such supportive testimony, thereby impugning his professional efforts. Moreover, in many cases the effects of the conflict on the attorney's performance will not be discernible from the record. It is plain to me, therefore, that in some instances the defendant will be able to show there was an actual, relevant conflict, but be unable to show that it changed his attorney's conduct.

It is possible that the standard articulated by the Court may not require a defendant to demonstrate that his attorney chose an action adverse to his interests because of a conflicting duty to another client. Arguably, if the attorney had to make decisions concerning his representation of the defendant under the constraint of inconsistent duties imposed by an actual conflict of interests, the adequacy of the representation was adversely affected. If that is the case, the Court's view and mine may not be so far apart after all.

NOTES

1.   If Sullivan had raised an objection to his treatment at the time of his trial, would the analysis of the problem have been different? Why? In this case, was there any reason to believe that an objection to the joint representation would be raised? Who would have raised it? Is that a fair expectation under the circumstances?

2.   Sullivan was represented by a lawyer who was paid by a third party. Is that permissible? What might be the concerns with such an arrangement? *See* Model Rules 1.8(f) and 5.4(c).

3.   What showing did Sullivan need to make to obtain relief? Do you think he could succeed in making it? Is it different from the showing required to demonstrate ineffective assistance of counsel under *Strickland v. Washington*? How?

4.   Justice Marshall suggests that it may be difficult to expect lawyers in ineffective assistance cases to give the kind of testimony that would be required to make the showing the court required here. Why? What do you think the lawyer's obligations are in that situation?

5.   In *Cuyler v. Sullivan*, the problem was the lawyer's joint representation of multiple defendants charged with involvement in the same case. But conflicts of interest are not limited to multiple representation of co-defendants. What created the conflict in the next case?

STATE v. WATSON

620 N.W.2d 233 (Iowa 2000)

TERNUS, JUSTICE.

The defendant, Nathan Watson, was convicted of murdering his father. On appeal, he claims that the trial court should have *sua sponte* held a hearing on whether his trial counsel suffered from a conflict of interest based on counsel's dual representation of the defendant and a key prosecution witness. We agree that such a hearing was required under the Sixth Amendment to the United States Constitution. Therefore, we reverse and remand.

I. *Background Facts and Proceedings.*

At the time of the events giving rise to Watson's conviction, Watson lived with his father, Rocky Chase, in a converted school bus located on property belonging to Watson's aunt and uncle, Janet and Gene Chase. In the early morning hours of January 16, 1998, Watson ran to the next-door residence of his aunt and told her that his father had shot himself. Law enforcement authorities arrived and determined that Rocky had been shot in the forehead at close range with a shotgun. Disbelieving that Rocky's death was a suicide, the county attorney charged Watson with first-degree murder.

The defendant pled not guilty, maintaining that the shooting was accidental or self-inflicted. Tim Ross–Boon and Brian Sissel of the Linn County Public Defender's Office were appointed to represent the defendant.

The case was tried to a jury. The testimony of expert witnesses called by both sides was conflicting as to whether the shooting was intentional or accidental.

Of greater importance to the present appeal, however, was the testimony of a prosecution witness, David Grunewald. Grunewald testified on direct that he and Watson occupied adjoining cells at the county jail and that Grunewald overheard Watson say "demons made him shoot his dad." Grunewald also testified that his criminal record included, among other things, burglary, public intoxication and possession of marijuana. Grunewald said that he received no benefit for his testimony and came forth voluntarily.

Defense attorney Sissel cross-examined Grunewald. He brought out the fact that Grunewald was a friend of Rocky and saw Rocky almost every day, including the day before Rocky's death. . . . Sissel also established on cross-examination that Grunewald was a substance abuser. Of significance to the issue on appeal was Grunewald's testimony that criminal contempt charges were pending against him at the time he came forward with information concerning Watson's incriminating statement. Grunewald testified that he and his attorney, Ross–Boon (the same Ross–Boon who represented the defendant), had discussed his sentencing with the county attorney before Grunewald told authorities of Watson's statement. Grunewald, however, acknowledged that his sentencing occurred after he told the jailer that Watson had admitted killing his father. Grunewald testified that he was sentenced to serve fourteen days in jail, although the maximum sentence possible was thirty days. It appeared from the record that Grunewald had served his sentence prior to testifying in Watson's trial.

As our review of Grunewald's testimony shows, Grunewald's cross-examination revealed that Ross–Boon simultaneously represented Grunewald and the defendant for some portion of the pre-trial period, including the period during which Grunewald overheard Watson's incriminating statement, reported it to the authorities, and was sentenced on his contempt conviction. No objections were made by anyone at trial concerning the propriety of Ross–Boon's representation of the defendant, and the trial court did not initiate an inquiry into the matter.

The jury returned a conviction of first-degree murder. This appeal followed.

On appeal, Watson asserts that his attorney, Ross–Boon, had an actual conflict of interest or a serious potential conflict of interest when he maintained dual representation of the defendant and Grunewald, a key prosecution witness whose interests were adverse to the defendant. Watson claims that this situation should have been apparent to the trial court upon Grunewald's testimony and that the trial court had a duty *sua sponte* to make an inquiry. The trial court's failure to do so, argues the defendant, requires automatic reversal of his conviction.

II. *Applicable Legal Principles.*

[The court concluded that the Sixth Amendment required reversal if the court knew or should have known of the conflict, regardless of whether there was an adverse effect on counsel's performance under *Cuyler v. Sullivan*.][1]

III. *Application of Legal Principles to Facts.*

The testimony of prosecution witness Grunewald revealed to the trial court that Grunewald was represented by defense counsel Ross–Boon during the pre-trial stages of Ross–Boon's representation of Watson. The testimony established that this period of simultaneous representation included the time frame when Grunewald overheard Watson make an incriminating statement, when Grunewald reported this statement to the police, and when Grunewald was sentenced on the contempt charge. Based on this testimony, the trial court knew of Ross–Boon's dual representation of the defendant and a key prosecution witness. We next consider whether this dual representation gave rise to an actual conflict.

Although most conflict of interest cases arise in the context of one attorney representing multiple defendants, a conflict of interest can arise

---

1. Even if we were to apply the *Cuyler* standard, reversal is required. Ross–Boon's simultaneous representation of the defendant and Grunewald during the time Watson allegedly made the incriminating statement and Grunewald came forward with this information "resulted in an unavoidable conflict as to confidential communications and affected counsel's ability to effectively impeach the credibility of [the] witness...." Although defense counsel established in his cross-examination of Grunewald that Grunewald was not sentenced until after he had informed law enforcement of Watson's incriminating statement, counsel did not challenge Grunewald's denial that his cooperation with the authorities had no impact on his sentence in his criminal case. Nor did defense counsel explore whether Grunewald's substance abuse problem affected his cognitive abilities on the date he overheard Watson talking about Rocky's death. Similarly, Grunewald's relationship with the decedent was not probed to reveal any bias or animosity Grunewald might have toward the defendant. Grunewald's cross-examination simply lacked any aggressive questioning to challenge his credibility.

in other factual scenarios. Basically, "a conflict exists when an attorney is placed in a situation conducive to divided loyalties." We think that, under this standard, an actual conflict of interest existed in the present case.

Unlike the joint representation of codefendants, where there may be a benefit to presenting a united defense, in the case of dual representation of the defendant and an adverse witness, there is no benefit to common representation. To the contrary, the potential for less zealous representation of the defendant is obvious. In a case of dual representation of the defendant and a prosecution witness, the Pennsylvania Superior Court analyzed the divergence of interests that is the hallmark of a conflict of interest:

> [The defendant's] interest and [the witness's] interest diverged with respect to [the attorney's] cross-examination of [the witness]. [The attorney] had an obligation to [the defendant] to use all the information at his disposal to impeach [the witness's] credibility. Yet, [the attorney] also had an obligation to [the witness] to maintain the confidentiality of [the witness's] communications with the Defender Association. Given these inconsistent duties, counsel was forced to make a "Hobson's choice."

> One might argue that [the attorney] had a greater responsibility to [the defendant] than to [the witness]. Yet, the importance of maintaining client confidences cannot be lightly disregarded. Any statements made by [the witness] to the Defender Association in connection with his legal representation were covered by the attorney-client privilege. Moreover, a heightened concern for protecting confidences is particularly appropriate where a lawyer is called upon to cross-examine an individual whom his office represents. . . .

> We find that counsel had a duty to protect [the witness's] rights as well as a duty to protect [the defendant's] rights. Thus, an "actual conflict of interest arose."

In re Saladin, 518 A.2d 1258, 1261–62 (1986). Other courts have also concluded that an actual conflict of interest exists when an attorney represents the defendant and a prosecution witness.

The State attempts to distinguish these authorities on two bases: (1) Ross–Boon no longer represented Grunewald at the time of trial; and (2) Ross–Boon did not cross-examine Grunewald; Ross–Boon's co-counsel, also an attorney with the Public Defender's Office, did. We do not think these facts insulated the defendant's counsel from the actual conflict of interest shown by the record.

We begin our analysis with a review of Ross–Boon's ethical obligations to his clients. Ross–Boon had a duty to Watson to represent him "zealously within the bounds of the law." He also had a duty to Grunewald to maintain the confidences of Grunewald. . . . [T]he ethical obligations of defense counsel extended beyond a prohibition of merely revealing Grunewald's confidences and secrets. Counsel was also obligated to refrain from *using* Grunewald's confidences or secrets "to the disadvantage of [Grunewald]" *or* "for the advantage...of a third party."

With this background, we now consider the State's contention that no conflict existed because, by the time of trial, Ross–Boon no longer represented Grunewald. We initially point out that there was simultaneous representation of Watson and Grunewald during some portion of the pre-trial period. Thus, defense counsel's pre-trial investigation was burdened with the conflict between Grunewald's interests and Watson's interests. Ross–Boon's efforts to ferret out impeachment material based on the relationship between Grunewald and the victim, based on Grunewald's substance abuse problem, or based on any other ground would be dampened by the fact that he also represented Grunewald and had to ensure that he used no information gained in his relationship with Grunewald to Grunewald's disadvantage or to Watson's advantage.

In addition, we think defense counsel's divided loyalties survived the termination of the attorney-client relationship between Ross–Boon and Grunewald. The end of this relationship did not lessen Ross–Boon's ethical obligation to Grunewald. He was still bound to maintain Grunewald's confidences and secrets. Simultaneously with his obligation not to use any "information gained in [his] professional relationship" with Grunewald the disclosure of which would be embarrassing or detrimental to Grunewald, Ross–Boon was also obligated to zealously represent Watson by impeaching Grunewald with any information available to Ross–Boon. Clearly the impeachment of Grunewald would be embarrassing to Grunewald and would help Watson. In our opinion, Ross–Boon was burdened by an actual conflict of interest at trial despite the fact that he no longer represented Grunewald.

As for the State's second argument—that Ross–Boon did not cross-examine Grunewald—we point out that attorneys in the same office are permitted to share confidences. *See* Iowa Code of Prof'l Responsibility EC 4–2 ("Unless the client otherwise directs, a lawyer may disclose the affairs of a client to partners or associates of the lawyer's firm."). Therefore, all members of the Public Defenders Office were bound to protect Grunewald's confidences and secrets. Thus, Ross–Boon's co-counsel labored under the same conflict of interest as did Ross–Boon.

Moreover, Ross–Boon's obligation to zealously represent his client, the defendant, was not suspended simply because his co-counsel was the one who asked Grunewald questions on the witness stand. Ross–Boon still had an obligation to Watson to contribute what he could to the defense team's preparation for Grunewald's cross-examination, including pre-trial investigation. We conclude, therefore, that Ross–Boon's decision not to personally examine Grunewald was insufficient to remove the actual conflict of interest that burdened Watson's defense team.

IV. *Conclusion.*

We hold that the defendant's trial counsel had an actual conflict of interest that the trial court knew or should have known existed when the court became aware of counsel's dual representation of the defendant and a key prosecution witness. Under these circumstances, the court was obligated *sua sponte* to hold a hearing on the propriety of the defendant's representation by the Linn County Public Defender's Office. The court's failure to conduct such an inquiry mandates reversal. Accordingly, we reverse the defendant's conviction and remand for a new trial where the defendant shall be represented by counsel unburdened by a conflict of interest.

NOTES

1. Subsequent to the decision in this case, the U.S. Supreme Court, in *Mickens v. Taylor*, 535 U.S. 162 (2002), rejected the conclusion that where the trial judge knows or should know of a conflict, automatic reversal is required without satisfying the requirements of *Cuyler v. Sullivan*.

2. What was the significance of the fact that Ross–Boon's representation of Grunewald had ended by the time of Watson's trial? Did it matter that Sissel, rather than Ross–Boon, conducted the cross-examination of Grunewald? In that regard, consider Model Rule 1.10(a).

3. Is the witness problem one that the witness can waive? Alberni claimed that he was harmed because his defense counsel, Buchanan, had previously represented a government witness, Flamm. Flamm gave testimony that was harmful to Alberni. Initially, Buchanan refused to cross-examine Flamm, saying, "I just don't wish to cross examine one of my clients. I will ask no questions." The trial court then sought a waiver of the conflict from Flamm. Flamm agreed to be cross-examined, and the court directed Buchanan to proceed. Despite Buchanan's protest that "I don't know whether a client can waive an ethical breach of a confidential relationship," the trial court told Buchanan, "I hereby absolve you of any possible conflict of interest and . . . the Court, as a matter of law, rules that you have no ethical issue with cross examining the witness." Buchanan cross-examined Flamm, but did not impeach him with any of the information available to him. Was Flamm's consent sufficient to obviate the problem? *See Alberni v. McDaniel*, 458 F.3d 860 (9th Cir. 2006).

3. SPECIALIZED CONFLICT SITUATIONS: INSURER AND INSURED

Contracts of insurance typically provide that the insurer will defend all claims. This means that the insurer hires counsel to represent the insured. What conflicts might arise under such a scenario?

First, the insurance defense arrangement presents a situation in which a third party pays for the representation of the client. Such an arrangement is governed by Model Rules 1.8(f) and 5.4(c), and Comments [11] and [12] to Model Rule 1.8. Do those rules adequately address the client's potential concerns about the attorney's loyalty? Does the fact that the client is likely to be a one-time client, while the insurer is a repeat player, create a problem? Suppose that the contract of insurance provides (as most do) that negligent conduct is covered, but intentional conduct is not. Does this create a potential conflict of interest between the insurer and the insured?

Several issues have arisen in recent years regarding the relationship between insurer, insured, and attorney. One is whether a lawyer may agree to constraints, imposed by the insurer, on the representation of the insured, which might require prior approval by the company for hiring experts or conducting depositions, or might limit or prohibit altogether the use of certain strategies or activities. Another is whether an insurance company may use its own salaried attorneys to represent its insureds rather than hiring outside counsel. What conflicts issues might such arrangements present?

4. SPECIAL PROBLEMS OF MULTIPLE REPRESENTATION

The duty of loyalty poses a particular difficulty when a lawyer represents multiple clients in the same matter.

Common representation

AN UNNAMED ATTORNEY v. KENTUCKY BAR ASS'N

186 S.W.3d 741 (Ky. 2006)

LAMBERT, C.J.:

Movant, An Unnamed Attorney, moves this Court to impose the sanction of a Private Reprimand in the above referenced disciplinary proceeding.

In early 2003, Movant was employed as an attorney by John and Jane Doe, husband and wife, to perform an investigation of the circumstances surrounding the fatal shooting of Mrs. Doe's former husband. Neither Mr. nor Mrs. Doe had been charged with any crime in connection with that occurrence; however, they were concerned that one or both of them might be charged with a crime as the official investigation proceeded. The Does advised Movant that neither of them had played any role in the shooting and that they had a common alibi. They sought to employ Movant to investigate the shooting on their behalf, in the hope that the investigation would produce evidence supporting their claim that they were innocent of any involvement.

fails to provide informed consent

Movant advised the Does that a conflict of interest could arise in the course of his work on their behalf. He also advised them that if a conflict of interest did arise he might be required to withdraw from the joint employment. However, he did not advise them that any and all information obtained during the joint representation or obtained in any communication to him by them would be available to each client and exchanged freely between the clients in the absence of a conflict of interest. Movant asserts that he did not anticipate the possibility that the interests of the

Does would become so materially divergent that there would be a conflict of interest in providing the results of the investigation to each of them. He acknowledges that he did not explain the potential ramifications of joint representation in that regard.

After discussing the aforementioned aspects of the employment, Movant agreed to undertake the investigation for a flat fee of $7,500. The Does made an initial payment of $2,500, and Movant commenced work on their behalf. They paid him an additional $3,000 after he began work, leaving a balance of $2,000 still unpaid.

The investigation produced information that indicated that one of the Does was directly involved in the shooting, contrary to what Movant had been told. Upon discovery of this information, and following communications with the KBA Ethics Hotline, Movant determined that he should withdraw from the joint employment. Furthermore, Movant concluded that he should not disclose certain results of his investigation to either Mr. or Mrs. Doe without the consent of each of them, which they declined to give. Movant encouraged each of them to obtain new counsel, and they followed this advice.

After receiving a bar complaint from the Does, the Inquiry Commission authorized a Charge against Movant pursuant to SCR 3.190. The Charge contains two counts, both of which are based on the allegation that Movant did not adequately explain the potential for a conflict of interest and the potential consequences of such a conflict. Count I alleges that Movant violated SCR 3.130–1.4(b), which states: "a lawyer should explain a matter to the extent reasonably necessary to permit the client to make informed decisions regarding the representation." Count II alleges that Movant violated SCR 3.130–1.7(2)(b) which states:

> A lawyer shall not represent a client if the representation of that client may be materially limited by the lawyer's responsibilities to another client or to a third person, or by the lawyer's own interests, unless:
>
>> (1) The lawyer reasonably believes the representation will not be adversely affected; and
>>
>> (2) The client consents after consultation. When representation of multiple clients in a single matter is undertaken, the consultation shall include explanation of the implications of the common representation and the advantages and risks involved.

This rule does not absolutely prohibit common representation. As neither of the Does had been charged at the time the representation commenced, the rule only required that Movant reasonably believe the representation of each client would not be adversely affected by the dual representation, and that each of the clients consent after consultation. In the context of common representation, consent must be informed, and this requires that each client be made aware of the full consequences of such representation. This includes the meaning of confidentiality, and the reasonably foreseeable means that conflicts could adversely affect the interests of each client. Such communication must "include explanation of the implications of the common representation."

In this case there was a lack of required communication by Movant. Specifically, Movant failed to explain that there would be no confidentiality as between the two clients and the lawyer, that all information discovered would be furnished to both, and that each client was owed the same duty. When the investigation uncovered information that was favorable to one client but harmful to the other, Movant refused to release the information he had gathered without the acquiescence of both clients, which was not given. This resulted from his failure to initially explain the implications of common representation to both clients. When the investigation revealed that one of the clients was involved in the homicide, Movant had a duty with respect to that client to keep that fact confidential. On the other hand, he had a duty to the other client to provide exculpatory information which necessarily included information he was obligated to keep confidential.

... This case well illustrates the potential peril lawyers face when undertaking joint representation. SCR 3.130–1.7(2)(b) is mandatory and the consent element must be *informed* consent, including a full explanation of all foreseeable ramifications.

The KBA has expressed its agreement with the motion made by Movant, and we feel that the punishment is appropriate, especially in light of the unique factors of this case. We hereby grant the motion and, it is ORDERED that:

Movant, An Unnamed Attorney, is hereby privately reprimanded.

NOTES

1. The Kentucky court seemed to be of the view that in any joint representation, there would be no confidentiality as among the jointly represented parties. Do the Model Rules take this position? See Comment [31] to Model Rule 1.7. Is there a reason why this *should* be the rule, even if the current Model Rules do not require it?

ABA Formal Op. 08–450 suggested a very different view: that "Absent an express agreement among the lawyer and the clients that satisfies the 'informed consent' standard of Rule 1.6(a)... whenever information related to the representation of a client may be harmful to the client in the hands of another client or a third person, the lawyer is prohibited by Rule 1.6 from revealing that information to any person, including the other client and the third person, unless disclosure is permitted under an exception to Rule 1.6." This opinion has been extensively criticized. Why? Does it matter that the hypothetical addressed by the opinion involved a situation in which a lawyer, retained by an insurer to defend both the insured employer and an employee of the insured, learned information from the employee that might permit the insurer to refuse coverage? Should the rules governing that situation be the same as the rules in a case like *Doe*? In any event, as the lawyer undertaking joint representation, what can you do to assure that if such a situation arises you will know what to do about it? *Compare D.C. Bar Op. 327.*

2. Issues regarding confidentiality in joint representation situations arise frequently in the context of estate planning. A married couple typically consults an attorney together. What if one member of the couple discloses to the lawyer the existence of an out-of-wedlock child, unknown to the spouse, for whom the parent wishes to provide? These problems present both loyalty issues and confidentiality issues. How do the Model Rules suggest the lawyer should address these issues? See Comments [29]–[33] to Model Rule 1.7.

IOWA SUPREME COURT BOARD OF PROFESSIONAL ETHICS AND CONDUCT v. WAGNER

599 N.W.2d 721 (Iowa 1999)

LAVORATO, JUSTICE.

This disciplinary proceeding is a textbook example of the pitfalls that await an attorney who decides to represent both the buyer and the seller in a large commercial transaction. The Iowa Supreme Court Board of Professional Ethics and Conduct alleged that, in representing both the buyer and the seller, attorney John C. Wagner failed to make full disclosures to the buyer as required by our disciplinary rules. The Grievance Commission found that the board had established the violations alleged, and it recommended a three-month suspension. After carefully reviewing the record, we concur in the commission's findings and recommendation. We therefore suspend Wagner's license to practice law in this state indefinitely with no possibility of reinstatement for three months from the date of this opinion. . . .

I. Facts.

. . . Wagner has practiced law in this state since 1979. . . . For a period of time, he served as a part-time judicial magistrate. Wagner devotes at least twenty-five percent of his practice to business and real estate matters and does some domestic and personal injury work.

Before April 1995, Carl Oehl and his family operated a restaurant known as Colony Market Place in South Amana. Titles to the business and the real estate upon which the restaurant was located were in the name of Colony Market Place, Inc., a corporation whose shareholders included Oehl and his family. The restaurant had been in existence for twenty-eight years and included a gift shop and a specialty food line.

In December 1993, Oehl closed all but the gift shop and specialty food line and decided to sell the business. He listed the property for six months with a Cedar Rapids Realtor, and his asking price was $475,000. Oehl received no offers during the listing.

Oehl then listed the property with Great Western, a national organization dealing primarily with the sale of restaurants. Great Western had an appraisal firm, The Fisher Business Group, appraise the property. The Fisher Business Group appraised the property at $750,000. Oehl listed the property at this figure for eight months without success. He then dropped the price to $600,000, but he still had no success.

In February 1995, Oehl and Wagner agreed that, if Wagner found a buyer and would represent Oehl in the sale, Oehl would pay him a commission of ten percent of the gross sale price as compensation for all of Wagner's services. If the property were sold on contract, Wagner was to receive ten percent of the down payment and ten percent of each payment on principal until the purchase price was paid in full.

Shortly thereafter, Wagner and his intern, Jeff Ritchie, visited the restaurant, viewed the appraisal, and reviewed the books and records of the business. Ritchie then prepared a sales brochure listing the asking price at $600,000. At one place in the brochure under the heading, Financial Information, appear the words "assurance of a profitable operation" and "a low risk factor for new ownership." Apparently, Oehl prepared this part of the brochure. Between March 16 and April 18, Ritchie contacted a number of people about buying the business but was unsuccessful in receiving any offers.

On April 18 David Childers met with Wagner at Wagner's Amana office to gather information about Oehl's restaurant. Childers knew that the restaurant had been closed for about fifteen months, but he did not know whether the restaurant was for sale. (At the time, Childers was a kitchen manager at another local restaurant.) Childers went to Wagner because Wagner had represented him in the past and Wagner was the only attorney he knew.

In that first meeting, Childers discussed buying the restaurant and starting his own business. He offered that he had never owned a business and had limited financial resources. Wagner told Childers that he represented Oehl in regard to the sale of Oehl's restaurant, but he could not be involved in negotiating a purchase price. Wagner also told Childers that it may be in his best interest to have independent counsel, but he did not explain why. And Wagner never mentioned he would receive a ten percent commission if he found a buyer for the restaurant. Additionally, Wagner mentioned that Childers could have his own appraisal but this would cost $1000 to $2000. Wagner, however, did not advise Childers that he ought to pay the money and obtain the appraisal. Wagner charged Childers for this meeting and for all subsequent work he did for Childers.

The following day Childers signed a confidentiality agreement regarding any financial information he learned about Oehl's restaurant and received a copy of the sales brochure. Wagner and Ritchie then accompanied Childers to Oehl's restaurant to meet Oehl and view the restaurant.

On the same day, Wagner began making inquiries to a local bank about financing for Childers. Those efforts continued for several more days and resulted in the bank agreeing to finance a portion of the purchase price. Wagner prepared several documents the bank required as a condition for the loan. One of the documents was a subordination agreement for which he charged Childers one-half of the preparation time because the services benefited both Childers and Oehl....

Childers and Oehl agreed to a purchase price of $400,000 with a down payment of $150,000. Wagner prepared the offer to buy, which included these amounts. After Childers signed the offer on April 24, Wagner presented it to Oehl that evening. Oehl wanted some additional terms that Wagner included in a counteroffer. Childers accepted the counteroffer the next day. On the same day, Wagner and Oehl amended their fee agreement, reducing the total amount of compensation from $40,000 to $37,500 and providing that Wagner receive $30,000 immediately instead of $15,000 and the balance a year later.

Two days after the counteroffer was signed, Wagner sent a congratulatory letter to Oehl and Childers in which he stated:

> I know I have repeatedly explained my legal ethics to all of you as this matter progressed, but I want to reiterate that I have represented all of you in the past. In regard to this transaction, it is my opinion that I can continue to provide representation to the Oehl family and to the Childers family as long as you are fully informed of such representation, and as long as there are no controversies. This will also confirm that I took no part with either of you in the development of the purchase price amount or any negotiations relating thereto.

Wagner invited responses only if either party disagreed with these representations.

Wagner prepared the documents for closing, which included required real estate filings, a title opinion to Childers, the real estate contract between the parties, and closing statements for both parties. The closing took place on May 26. Oehl's closing statement disclosed Wagner's commission, but Childers' statement did not. Childers never received a copy of Oehl's closing statement.

In his title opinion to Childers, Wagner wrote:

> Prospective purchasers are also advised that the title examiner also represents the seller on this transaction. Buyers are advised that such representation is a conflict of interest as the interest of the parties are different and likely adverse. Buyers are advised that it would be prudent for them to consult with other counsel concerning this opinion.

To complete the purchase, Childers borrowed the $150,000 down payment from the bank; $50,000 of this amount was secured by a mortgage on his home and $100,000 was secured by the business. Additionally, Childers borrowed $54,000 as working capital from his brother.

Childers took possession of the restaurant on May 26. The first contract payment of $9375 was due December 31. Childers only paid $6000 of that payment. Childers asked Wagner for help regarding his financial problems. In response, Wagner tried to convince the bank to renegotiate the loan but was unsuccessful.

On December 27 Wagner told Childers to retain other counsel. Wagner wrote Oehl a letter telling him the same thing. Childers and Oehl thereafter retained other counsel.

Eventually, Oehl forfeited Childers' contract. Childers, however, still owed the bank nearly $150,000. He also owed his brother the $54,000 he had borrowed from him. Additionally, Childers owed some outstanding restaurant bills.

Wagner found another buyer, a former client, Todd Markillie. Markillie bought the restaurant on contract, agreeing to pay $348,000 with $25,000 down on August 1, 1996. Wagner loaned Markillie $50,000 toward the purchase price. Markillie suffered the same fate as Childers had: Oehl forfeited the contract in January 1997. Wagner was only able to recover $9000 of the $50,000 Wagner had loaned Markillie.

Thereafter, Wagner and his wife purchased the restaurant on contract for $322,000 and a down payment of $2500 on February 21, 1997. Oehl gave Wagner a $6500 credit on the purchase price because of the partially unpaid commission owing on the sale to Childers. The Wagners are presently leasing the property to a couple who apparently are running the business successfully.

Meanwhile, Childers' new attorney learned of Wagner's fee arrangement with Oehl in May 1996. Childers sued Wagner, and the parties later settled. There is no record evidence of the grounds for the suit or the terms of the settlement.

II. Ethical Violations.

The board charged and the commission found that Wagner violated Iowa Code of Professional Responsibility for Lawyers DR 5–101(A), DR 5–105(B), and DR 5–105(C). DR 5–101(A) provides:

> Except with the consent of the client after full disclosure, a lawyer shall not accept employment if the exercise of the lawyer's professional judgment on behalf of the client will be or reasonably may be affected by the lawyer's own financial, business, property, or personal interests.

DR 5–105(B) requires a lawyer to

> decline proffered employment if the exercise of independent professional judgment in behalf of a client will be or is likely to be adversely affected by the acceptance of the proffered employment, except to the extent permitted under DR 5–105(D).

DR 5–105(C) prohibits a lawyer from

> continu[ing] multiple employment if the exercise of independent professional judgment in behalf of a client will be or is likely to be

adversely affected by the representation of another, except to the extent permitted under DR 5–105(D).

In those situations covered by DR 5–105(B) and (C), the Iowa Code of Professional Responsibility allows a lawyer to

> represent multiple clients if it is obvious that the lawyer can adequately represent the interest of each and if each consents to the representation after full disclosure of the possible effect of such representation on the exercise of the lawyer's independent professional judgment on behalf of each.

DR 5–105(D).

A. Differing interests.

The principle underlying Ethical Canon 5 is that a lawyer should not represent parties with differing interests. . . .

Like the commission, we find that from Childers' initial meeting with Wagner, Wagner was representing both Oehl as a seller and Childers as a buyer. Wagner concedes this fact. Although we stop short of finding that Wagner had any role in negotiating the purchase price, we agree with the commission that this fact did not eliminate the conflict. In fact, Wagner recognized this conflict in his title opinion to Childers. As one commentator notes, the differing interests between buyer and seller are obvious, and price is only one of many areas in which those interests differ:

> The process by which a buyer and seller of property transact their business is fraught with conflicts of interests. Indeed, a lawyer's simultaneous representation of a buyer and a seller in the same transaction is a paradigm of a conflict of interest. Beginning with such basic elements as determining the price and describing the property to be sold, what one party gets the other must concede. Terms of payment, security for unpaid balances, warranties of quality and of title, date of closing and risk of loss in the interim, tax consequences, and a host of other details should be addressed by each party or the party's adviser in a well-thought-out transaction. When the transaction is a large one—such as the purchase and sale of a residence, commercial property, or a business—the transaction typically becomes further complicated because the additional interests of banks, brokers, tenants, and title insurance companies may intrude.

Charles Wolfram, *Modern Legal Ethics* § 8.5, at 434 (West 1986) (footnotes omitted).

We also find, as the commission did, that Wagner's own financial stake in the transaction—the ten percent commission—brought his interests into conflict with Childers' interest, a fact that Wagner concedes. Given the uncertainty of the value of the restaurant and the lack of offers from other interested parties, the purchase of the restaurant was a risky proposition. In these circumstances, Childers had a right to expect competent, disinterested advice that would allow him to make an informed decision on whether to proceed with the purchase at all. Wagner's own interest, on the other hand, was to make sure that the sale went through so he could earn his commission.

Wagner's interests conflicted with Childers' interests in two other respects. Childers' interest naturally called for achieving a rock bottom purchase price. In contrast, Wagner's interest called for achieving the highest price possible to maximize his commission. In addition, it was in Wagner's and Oehl's interest that Childers make a sizable down payment. Wagner's up-front commission payment depended upon the size of the down payment. Oehl's interest was what any contract seller would want: the higher the down payment the greater the security. Obviously, Childers' interest was to obtain as small a down payment as possible.

B. Duty of full disclosure.

1. Duty of full disclosure where attorney has financial interest in the transaction. As mentioned, because of Wagner's ten percent commission, his interests conflicted with Childers' interests. In these circumstances, Wagner had the heavy burden of showing that Childers consented to Wagner representing him after Wagner made a full disclosure. Under DR 5–104(A), a lawyer's duty to make full disclosure

> means more than making the client aware of the nature and the terms of the transaction. It also requires the attorney to give the client the kind of advice the client would have received if the transaction were with a stranger.

Committee on Prof'l Ethics & Conduct v. Carty, 515 N.W.2d 32, 35 (Iowa 1994) (citations omitted)....

There is no record evidence that Wagner ever disclosed to Childers his commission arrangement with Oehl. In fact, Wagner readily concedes he made no such disclosure.

As mentioned, Wagner suggested to Childers that it might be in his best interest to have independent counsel, but never explained why. Despite this oral admonition, we think Wagner actually encouraged both parties to proceed without independent counsel. In his letter to Childers and Oehl following Childers' acceptance of the counteroffer, Wagner wrote:

> In regard to this transaction, it is my opinion that I can continue to provide representation to the Oehl family and to the Childers family as long as you are fully informed of such representation, and as long as there are no controversies.

Like the commission, we conclude that Wagner failed to make a full disclosure of his financial interest in the transaction. Thus, any consent on the part of Childers to Wagner's representation was not an informed consent. Without such informed consent, Wagner's representation of Childers was in violation of DR 5–104(A).

2. Duty of full disclosure in dual representation situations. As mentioned, Wagner represented clients with differing interests. Thus, his duty

to make full disclosure was again called into play. Absent such disclosures, Wagner could neither undertake representation of Childers, nor continue such representation once undertaken.

In a dual representation situation, it is not enough for a lawyer simply to inform the client that the lawyer is representing both sides. Full disclosure ... requires the

> attorney not only to inform the prospective client of the attorney's relationship with the seller, but also to explain in detail the pitfalls that may arise in the course of the transaction which would make it desirable that the buyer obtain independent counsel.

In re Dolan, 384 A.2d 1076, 1080 (N.J. 1978).

Such a disclosure is crucial in a large commercial transaction as the one here because as one court put it:

> A client cannot foresee and cannot be expected to foresee the great variety of potential areas of disagreement that may arise in a real estate transaction of this sort. The attorney is or should be familiar with at least the more common of these and they should be stated and laid before the client at some length and with considerable specificity.

In re Lanza, 322 A.2d 445, 448 (N.J. 1974)....

It is true that Wagner informed Childers and Oehl that he was representing both of them in the transaction and that if any controversies arose he would withdraw. In addition, Wagner told Childers about a possibility of a conflict. Wagner, however, did not advise Childers what possible conflicts might arise and why independent counsel was advisable. These disclosures to Childers were not adequate. Wagner did not shed his duty to point out the advantages of obtaining independent counsel even though he shied away from negotiating the purchase price.

III.   Discipline.

... Several aggravating factors militate in favor of the recommended sanction. One is harm to the client. Had Childers known the true facts and received the independent legal advice he was entitled to, he might never have purchased the restaurant and suffered the financial loss that he did. Although this may be speculative, the fact remains that Wagner's dual representation and cover-up denied Childers the opportunity to make an informed choice. Although Childers may have recovered some of his economic loss in his civil suit against Wagner, this fact does not remove the need for a sanction.

Another aggravating factor is Wagner's experience in the practice of law. Sixteen years in the practice with a heavy emphasis in real estate transactions tell us that Wagner should have known better. His own title opinion to Childers showed that he was well aware that his dual representation was "a conflict of interest as the interest of the parties are different and likely adverse."...

In this case, the commission made exhaustive findings, gave a thorough review of appropriate authorities and their application to the facts, and came to a well-reasoned decision on a recommendation for appropriate discipline. We can find no fault with that recommendation. We therefore suspend Wagner's license to practice law in this state with no possibility of reinstatement for three months from the filing date of this opinion.

NOTES

1. The court identifies two distinct conflicts of interest on the part of attorney Wagner. What were they? Why did each of them pose a problem?

2. Does this case mean that a lawyer can never represent both a buyer and a seller in a transactional matter? Consider Comments [26]-[28] to Model Rule 1.7. Why might clients prefer this type of representation? Were there aspects of this transaction that made such an arrangement particularly problematic here?

3. Was this a consentable conflict for which Wagner did not secure appropriate informed consent, or was it a nonconsentable conflict? What would Wagner have had to tell Childers in order to obtain his consent to the joint representation? Could he have made those disclosures? Consider Comments [18] and [19] to Model Rule 1.7.

4. Suppose that a lawyer embarks on what looks like a permitted joint representation, but the situation changes, meaning that there is now a nonconsentable conflict between the parties. The lawyer must withdraw from the multiple representation of both clients. At that point, can she represent either one? *See* Comment [4] to Model Rule 1.7 and Model Rule 1.9. In light of the answer to this question, do you think the lawyer should warn the clients of this possibility when securing informed consent to the joint representation in the first instance? *See* Comment [29] to Model Rule 1.7.

5.   OTHER CONSEQUENCES OF CONFLICTS OF INTEREST

A conflict of interest can subject a lawyer to discipline, and require the disqualification of the lawyer. It can also have significant consequences for the client. What were the consequences of the conflict of interest for the client in the following case?

ANDREW CORP. v. BEVERLY MANUFACTURING CO.

415 F. Supp. 2d 919 (N.D. Ill. 2006)

HOLDERMAN, DISTRICT JUDGE.

On August 31, 2005, plaintiff Andrew Corporation ("Andrew"), filed its first amended complaint alleging that defendant Beverly Manufacturing Company ("Beverly"), infringed three of Andrew's patents.... Beverly wishes to use three opinion letters written by its counsel from the law firm of Barnes & Thornburg in Beverly's defense to Andrew's allegations of willful infringement.

On November 8, 2005, Andrew filed the pending "Motion to Disqualify Counsel and Exclude all Opinion Letters Issued by Counsel," seeking to prevent Beverly from presenting evidence regarding the three Barnes & Thornburg opinion letters and to bar Barnes & Thornburg attorneys from testifying or otherwise participating in this case. Both Andrew and Beverly are current clients of Barnes & Thornburg. Barnes & Thornburg has not filed an appearance in this case on behalf of either party. . . . For the reasons set forth below, this court grants Andrew's motion.

FACTUAL BACKGROUND

Barnes & Thornburg's three opinion letters were issued to Beverly on July 8, 2003, July 15, 2003 and August 28, 2003. Each of these opinion letters state positions that are adverse to Andrew. The July 8, 2003 letter, signed by Barnes & Thornburg attorneys Timothy J. Engling ("Engling"), and Dennis M. McWilliams ("McWilliams"), opined that Beverly's newly "modified stackable hanger does not fall within the claims of [Andrew's] '543 patent." The July 15, 2003 letter, signed by Barnes and Thornburg attorneys Engling and Mark J. Nahnsen ("Nahnsen"), provided a similar opinion that Beverly's newly designed "grounding kit does not fall within the claims of [Andrew's] '056 patent." The July 15, 2003 letter was supplemented by the third opinion letter dated August 28, 2003 which was also signed by Engling and Nahnsen. The August 28, 2003 letter opines that Beverly's "new embodiment of the grounding kit does not literally infringe the '056 patent. . . ."

Beverly was previously represented by McWilliams and Engling when they were members of the law firm of Lee Mann, Smith, McWilliams, Sweeney & Ohlson ("Lee Mann"). In 2000, attorneys from Lee Mann, including Engling, were counsel for Beverly in a dispute that Beverly had with Andrew. In that dispute, Andrew threatened to sue Beverly for unfair competition and misappropriation of trade secrets over Beverly's "snap-in hangers," but before a lawsuit was filed, the parties reached a settlement in which Beverly agreed to adjust the design of the "snap-in hanger." According to the July 8, 2003 opinion letter, Beverly's post–2000 settlement "modified snap-in hanger" is a "variation on a hanger described in Andrew's expired '132 patent." Beverly renamed the modified "snap-in hanger" to be called "the modified stackable hanger." The modified stackable hanger is analyzed in the July 8, 2003 opinion letter and Andrew now asserts in this litigation that Beverly's modified stackable hanger infringes Andrew's '543 patent.

While still at the Lee Mann firm in 2002, McWilliams and Engling began working for Beverly on their opinions with regard to Andrew's patents at issue in this case and opened two legal files in the Lee Mann's filing system regarding that work. According to Barnes & Thornburg's General Counsel, these Lee Mann files, however, did not list Andrew as the adverse party. The Lee Mann law firm merged into Barnes & Thornburg in January 2003 and McWilliams and Engling joined Barnes & Thornburg as partners.

At the time of that merger in January 2003, Andrew was a client of Barnes & Thornburg. Barnes & Thornburg lawyers Daniel P. Albers ("Albers"), and Thomas J. Donovan ("Donovan"), among others, were representing Andrew in the patent infringement case *Andrew Corp. v. Kathrein, Inc.* Barnes & Thornburg's conflicts department analyzed Lee Mann's client information in conjunction with the merger to determine whether Beverly could be a Barnes & Thornburg client. Barnes & Thornburg recognized no conflict between Andrew and Beverly despite the fact that the work McWilliams and Engling performed for Beverly had analyzed Andrew's patents adversely to Andrew. Failing to identify the conflict during the merger, Barnes & Thornburg approved Beverly as one of its new clients without informing Andrew or Beverly of any conflict or requesting consent from either. Barnes & Thornburg in July and August 2003 provided Beverly the three opinion letters that were adverse to Andrew.

Barnes & Thornburg continued not to recognize the conflict during 2003 and the first half of 2004 despite the fact that, as of June 30, 2003, McWilliams, Engling, Nahnsen, Albers and Donovan were all physically located in [the] same Barnes & Thornburg office in Chicago performing patent related services. (Albers and Donovan were representing Andrew and McWilliams, Engling and Nahnsen were representing Beverly.) In August 2004, both Andrew and Beverly contacted Barnes & Thornburg with each seeking representation in the dispute that has led to this litigation between Andrew and Beverly. Barnes & Thornburg finally recognized that it concurrently represented both Andrew and Beverly and declined both companies' request for representation against one another. Consequently, Andrew and Beverly are represented by other law firms in this case. Despite Barnes & Thornburg's August 2004 recognition that it could not represent either Beverly and Andrew against one another, and that Barnes & Thornburg's 2003 opinion letters were adverse to Andrew, lawyers at Barnes & Thornburg still represent both Andrew and Beverly in other matters through the present. . . .

Andrew contends that Barnes & Thornburg breached its fiduciary duties to Andrew by taking positions adverse to Andrew in the July and August 2003 opinion letters provided to Beverly. Therefore, Andrew asserts that Barnes & Thornburg must be disqualified from any participation in this case, that the three July and August 2003 opinion letters must be withdrawn, and that Beverly must be barred from using the opinions or presenting any testimony regarding those opinion letters in this case.

Beverly counters that Barnes & Thornburg cannot be disqualified because it never filed an appearance in this case. Beverly also argues that it is blameless in this situation, and therefore it should not be penalized for any mistakes made by Barnes & Thornburg. Additionally, Beverly argues that Andrew has been aware of the concurrent representation for over a year and that this motion is merely a litigation tactic. . . .

ANALYSIS

This district's Rules of Professional Conduct are patterned after the ABA's Model Rules. Local Rule 83.51.7(a) states that "a lawyer shall not represent a client if the representation of that client will be directly adverse to another client, unless: (1) the lawyer reasonably believes the representation will not adversely affect the relationship with the other client; and (2) each client consents after disclosure." Local Rule 83.51.10(a) states that "no lawyer associated with a firm shall represent a client when the lawyer knows or reasonably should know that another lawyer associated with that firm would be prohibited from doing so by L.R. 83.51.7." . . .

"[L]oyalty to a client prohibits undertaking representation directly adverse to that client without the client's consent. [Local Rule 83.51.7(a)] expresses that general rule. Thus, a lawyer ordinarily may not act as advocate against a person the lawyer represents in some other matter, even if it is wholly unrelated." N.D. Ill. L.R. 83.51.7 Comm. Cmts.

A.   The Conflict

Barnes & Thornburg's attorneys took positions directly adverse to its client Andrew in the July and August 2003 opinion letters on behalf of its other client Beverly, without obtaining informed consent from both Andrew and Beverly, in violation of Local Rules 83.51.7 and 83.51.10. These opinion letters advised Beverly that its products did not infringe Andrew's patents, attacked Andrew's patents, provided potential litigation arguments and provided a factual basis for a potential defense against future claims by Andrew of willful infringement. Barnes & Thornburg possessed sufficient information to have determined that its work for Beverly was adverse to its existing client Andrew, that it would affect its relationship with Andrew and that the Barnes & Thornburg firm as a whole was disqualified under the imputed conflict rule. The initial failure to record in the Lee Mann files that Andrew was an adverse party, and that the project's purpose was evaluating Andrew's patents, does not excuse Barnes & Thornburg's conduct. Nor does Barnes & Thornburg's arguments that no Barnes & Thornburg lawyer worked on both Andrew and Beverly cases, that there was no use of confidential information, and that the Barnes & Thornburg lawyers did not discuss their concurrent representation of Andrew and Beverly relieve Barnes & Thornburg of its ethical responsibilities to comply with Local Rules 83.51.7 and 83.51.10.

B.   The Remedy

Having determined that Barnes & Thornburg issued the July and August 2003 opinion letters while laboring under an actual conflict, this court must now undertake the unpleasant task of determining what remedy, if any, should be provided. To begin, this court must reject Beverly's argument that it is an innocent party and cannot be held liable for Barnes

& Thornburg's errors. It has long been the law that "[l]awyers' errors in civil proceedings are imputed to their clients."

This court agrees with the Seventh Circuit's view that "it is ordinarily preferable to sanction the lawyer for the lawyer's mistake than... to precipitate a second suit—a suit against the lawyer for malpractice." Additionally, this court also recognizes that attorney disqualification is a "drastic remedy which courts should hesitate to impose except when absolutely necessary [because] it may create... delay and deprive parties of their chosen legal advisor." Unfortunately, the circumstances of Barnes & Thornburg's unwaived conflict created by its concurrent representation of two clients with adverse interests eliminates any opportunity to fashion a less restrictive remedy. If Beverly is allowed to use the opinion letters at issue in this case, Andrew will suffer because of Barnes & Thornburg's breach of its ethical duty to Andrew. The public will also suffer if the opinion letters are used in these proceedings because the opinion letters are the product of attorneys laboring under an unwaived conflict of interest. However, if Beverly is not allowed to use the opinion letters in this case, Beverly will suffer because of Barnes & Thornburg's breach of its ethical duty to Beverly resulting from the conflict created by Barnes & Thornburg's representation of Andrew to which Beverly never consented. . . .

The Barnes & Thornburg's attorneys who are members of the bar of this court were engaged in the practice of law when they issued the July and August 2003 opinion letters. Beverly now seeks to bring these attorneys before this court and use their legal analysis, along with their positions as attorneys, to argue against Andrew's contentions of Beverly's willful infringement. Attorneys who are licensed to practice in this district are bound by the ethical obligations of the Rules of Professional Conduct in all aspects of their practice of law, not just when they have filed an appearance in a particular case before the court.

Patent opinion letters are intended by both the attorney and the client to be relied upon and followed by the client in making decisions as to the client's future conduct relative to a patent. . . .

The primary purpose of a client obtaining a patent opinion letter from independent, objective and competent patent counsel is to "ensure that it acts with due diligence in avoiding activities which infringe the patent rights of others," not the mere creation of a prophylactic defense against a potential claim of willful infringement. . . .

The mere act of obtaining an opinion letter, however, is not sufficient to avoid a later finding of willful infringement. The relevant question is the "infringer's investigation and good-faith belief of invalidity or non-infringement." The infringer can still be held liable for willful infringement despite receiving an opinion letter when: (1) the infringer ignores the warnings of a competent counsel, (2) fails to provide sufficient information to allow the lawyer to provide an independent, objective and competent opinion letter, (3) obtains the opinion letter after infringing activity has occurred or merely as a defense to future litigation with no intention of curbing his infringing activities.

"The legal opinion must be 'competent' or it is of little value in showing the good faith belief of the infringer." The competency of an attorney to produce an opinion letter is more than just his or her ability [to] analyze the law and the facts. Attorneys must perform their work within the confines of the ethical obligations that regulate their professional conduct.

Barnes & Thornburg's conflict, which arose from the concurrent representation of both Andrew and Beverly, who were adverse to one another, prevents Barnes & Thornburg from being able to provide the type of competent, independent advice and opinion letters that the law requires. Barnes & Thornburg's fiduciary duties to Andrew prohibited it from taking any position adverse to Andrew.... [I]n the absence of valid consents by both Andrew and Beverly waiving the conflict after full disclosure to each, Barnes & Thornburg's only competent legal opinion in July and August 2003 to Beverly consistent with the Code of Professional Conduct was to refrain from expressing any opinion. Therefore, as a matter of law, this court holds that the July and August 2003 opinion letters were not issued by competent opinion counsel. The only remedy available to enforce adherence to the Rules of Professional Conduct is, to the extent possible, place the parties in the position they would have been in had counsel acted competently in accordance with the Rules of Professional Conduct. Consequently, it appears that to be fair and to uphold the integrity of the profession, no opinion letter by Barnes & Thornburg while laboring under the unwaived conflict of interest, should be used in any manner in this case.

This court appreciates, but disagrees, with Beverly's argument that it is an "innocent" party in this situation. In 2003, Beverly had the affirmative duty to exercise due care to determine whether or not it infringed on Andrew's patents. Included in Beverly's affirmative duty was the duty to seek and obtain competent legal advice from counsel before the initiation of any possible infringing activity. Beverly's affirmative obligation to seek and obtain competent legal advice from counsel included the obligation to obtain legal advice from a counsel who was free from ethical conflicts. That aspect of Beverly's affirmative duty is just as important as Beverly's obligation to seek and obtain counsel with sufficient ability, experience and expertise in patent matters to render a legally competent opinion. It was Beverly who chose Barnes & Thornburg to provide the July and August 2003 opinion letters and, unfortunately, it is Beverly who must now live with the consequences of that choice. There is a clear showing that Barnes & Thornburg was laboring under a clear and unwaived conflict when the July and August 2003 opinion letters adverse to Andrew were provided to Beverly. Barnes & Thornburg was precluded by the conflict from providing those letters. Beverly's apparent lack of knowledge of the existence of the conflict does not change the fact that the conflict, under which Barnes & Thornburg labored, existed. Beverly may seek recourse from Barnes & Thornburg elsewhere if it desires.

In this case, this court must uphold the requirements of the Code of Professional Responsibility and protect the public's confidence in the integrity of the legal profession. Therefore, this court must preclude any use and any mention of the July and August 2003 Barnes & Thornburg opinion letters at trial.

NOTES

1. A finding of willful infringement can expose an infringer to treble damages. The court's suppression of the opinion letters meant that Beverly could not claim that it had obtained competent counsel's advice as to whether it was engaging in infringement. This could have profound consequences for the subsequent litigation, since reliance on the advice of counsel would at the very least be relevant to the issue of whether Beverly's infringement had been willful. Is it fair to hold Beverly responsible for its lawyers' failure to behave ethically? The court says that Beverly had an obligation to "obtain legal advice from a counsel who was free from ethical conflicts." What more could Beverly have done to assure that this was the case? If Beverly lost on the willful infringement claim because it did not have admissible evidence that it had relied on advice of competent counsel, and that resulted in a treble damages award to Andrew, what could Beverly do to recover those losses?

2. What did Barnes & Thornburg do wrong? Was the problem with the conflicts checking procedures of the predecessor firm, or with the process of reviewing the Lee Mann files after the merger? Was this unavoidable? Was the problem here unique to patent litigation, or does it suggest a broader problem with conflicts checking? If you were consulted by a firm seeking to avoid problems with conflicts following a law firm merger, what would you suggest?

3. Why did Barnes & Thornburg have a conflict, given that different lawyers in the firm represented the two different clients? See Model Rule 1.10(a).

C. PERSONAL INTEREST CONFLICTS

A conflict of interest can arise because of the lawyer's conflicting obligations to different clients. A lawyer's own self-interest can also create conflicts with the interests of the client. Those conflicts are governed by different aspects of the Model Rules. The lawyer's own interest ("a personal interest of the lawyer") can create a "materially limited" conflict under Rule 1.7(a)(2). In addition, Rule 1.8 contains an array of specific provisions governing the lawyer's conduct in situations that involve his own self-interest. Review Model Rules 1.8(a), (c), (d), (h), (i), and (j). Do we need these more specific rules, or does the more generalized provision in Rule 1.7(a) adequately address these various issues?

1. BUSINESS TRANSACTIONS WITH A CLIENT

IN RE DATO

614 A.2d 1344 (N.J. 1992)

ORDER

The Disciplinary Review Board having filed a report with the Court, recommending that ROBERT F. DATO ... be suspended for a period of one year for acting with a conflict of interest in his purchase of property from a client, and the Court having heard the arguments of the parties, and good cause appearing;

It is ORDERED that the report and recommendation of the Disciplinary Review Board are adopted and ROBERT F. DATO is hereby suspended for one year....

APPENDIX

Decision and Recommendation of the Disciplinary Review Board

... Respondent was admitted to the New Jersey bar in 1965. He maintains a practice of law in Woodbridge, Middlesex County. In 1984, he was retained by Mary Cinque, a long-standing friend of respondent's wife and her family, to represent her in a divorce action against her husband, the grievant herein.... After a matrimonial action permeated with acrimony, a final judgment of divorce was entered late in 1984.

Mr. Cinque agreed to transfer to Mrs. Cinque his title in the former marital residence, a three-family house located in Port Reading. Although no formal appraisals had been conducted during the divorce proceedings, the parties stipulated, for the purposes of equitable distribution, that the property had a net equity of $90,000....

After the divorce, Mrs. Cinque moved to Arizona, where her daughters resided. She then asked respondent, who continued to represent her in the ongoing matrimonial post-judgment proceedings in New Jersey, to assist her in procuring a buyer for the Port Reading property. According to her testimony, although she left the sales price up to respondent, she hoped to sell it for $95,000.

In the spring of 1985, respondent offered to sell the property to another client, Ralph Mocci, a real estate developer he had known both socially and professionally since the early 1970s. Respondent had also been in partnership with Mocci in some business ventures. Mocci testified that, after he saw the property, he became very interested in purchasing it. His intention was to refurbish and then resell it. In Mocci's words, "... I told [respondent] when I passed by the house, we could possibly make money on the property and that I should go into contract."

Consistent with this understanding, respondent prepared a contract of sale between Mrs. Cinque and Mocci, listing a purchase price of $95,000.

The contract contained no provision for a mortgage contingency or for a brokers' commission. On April 15, 1985, respondent forwarded the contract to Arizona for Mrs. Cinque's review and signature. He did not first obtain Mocci's signature thereon.

Asked, at the hearing, whether it was contemplated that he and respondent would become partners in the deal, Mocci replied that they had an understanding that respondent could choose to participate in any ventures in which he represented Mocci. . . . Respondent vehemently denied that he had any interest in the property at that time.

In any event, after Mrs. Cinque signed the contract and returned it to respondent, neither she nor Mocci heard anything further from respondent about the transaction. When queried at the hearing, respondent offered no explanation for this puzzling turn of events. He replied that ". . . as best as I can remember, when I went to finalize the transaction, Mr. Mocci reconsidered." According to Mocci, however, respondent never presented the contract for his signature, although he had remained interested in the property at all times. Throughout the contract phase of the transaction, respondent acted as the attorney for both Mrs. Cinque and Mocci.

Some months later, in September 1985, respondent decided that he would buy the property from Mrs. Cinque as an investment. He prepared a contract of sale listing a purchase price of $85,000, $10,000 less than the price that Mocci was willing to pay. As in the Mocci transaction, the contract did not contain a mortgage contingency clause or a provision for a real estate commission. The contract also stipulated that Mrs. Cinque would take back a second mortgage of $10,000 for one year, at twelve percent interest.

In an attempt to justify his purchase of the property, respondent testified that Mrs. Cinque was having difficulty in selling it; that she was pressing him for help in selling the property . . .; that it was then, for the first time, that he began to develop an interest in buying the property as an investment; and that, "knowing the area and having some roots there, I indicated to her that I would consider buying [it] and I told her that I thought the house in my opinion . . . might have had a value of upwards of $100,000. That is, anywhere between $80,000 and $100,000. . . . I said to her that if I bought it in order to make it profitable to me and also to make it feasible for her that I would buy it with no conditions whatsoever, no mortgage contingency. . . ." Respondent went on to say that, because of the absence of a broker's commission, Mrs. Cinque would net $85,000, a sum equivalent to a sale for a $100,000 gross purchase price; that the property was "run down"; that the rental income of $800 to $900 monthly was too low and needed to be increased; and that, while this transaction was "in my good interest . . . I was sure that this was good for her."

Asked by the hearing panel whether he had advised Mrs. Cinque to consult with an attorney, respondent replied:

If you permit me, the answer to that question is yes but it's a qualified yes and I have to put it on the record.

As I explained, Mary and my relationship was somewhat beyond attorney/client and for that reason we had formal and informal discussions. She was in Arizona. She was fighting vigorously for her rights relative to her divorce. Her husband had moved in with another woman with a longstanding marriage. Mary's in her 60's. So this was a marriage of 35, 40 years. Her children were siding with her husband and it was a very, very unpleasant situation from her point of view and from mine, knowing the family and knowing her as I did.

When we got into this transaction, not only by virtue of her needing some advice concerning the sale but often I would say to her, Mary, you need an attorney in Arizona to enforce your rights. . . .

Mary did hire an Arizona attorney, I believe, . . . and when this was happening, this transaction, I cannot say to you under oath that I so very specifically told Mary you better get a lawyer on this sale, but there is no question in my mind that while this was happening I was advising Mary to be represented by Counsel in the context of this divorce and I do remember suggesting to her that at least have someone look at what's going on with this house to be sure you want to sell it. Be sure you want to sell it for whatever it is that I'm offering you and be certain you're doing the right thing.

I can't say I added the last ingredient as that and be absolutely certain that the paperwork that I'm preparing is reviewed by a lawyer so that you know that it protects your interest, and the reason I say that [at] all, it was going to be as a deed, it was a cash deal. There was no—I wasn't concerned about her knowing the technical aspects being represented for the technical aspects of this transaction because it was just passing of money. I wanted to be sure she knew what she was doing in selling the house.

Respondent added that his partner represented him at the closing, while Mrs. Cinque "was unrepresented."

Mrs. Cinque denied that respondent had made any suggestions that she have the contract reviewed by an attorney. She explained that she did not show the contract to another lawyer because respondent did not advise her to show it to another lawyer.

It was respondent's estimation that $85,000 was a fair price for the property, in light of the numerous repairs that were needed and of the low rental income generated. Respondent testified that, even before the closing of title, he arranged for extensive repairs to be undertaken, necessitating a cash outlay of $1,000 to $1,500. In addition, respondent contended, he and his wife spent several weekends conducting repairs themselves. Respondent also asserted that, prior to the closing, he began efforts to increase the rents from $800–$900 a month to "$2,000 plus."

Respondent knew that the rental income could be readily increased. In his own words, "I knew the income potential of the property from the moment I looked at it. In fact, I didn't even have to look at it. When Mary Cinque told me what the rents were, I said, Mary, you're not getting enough money there." And then, "[my wife and I] thought it was a good investment because it was going to generate more income than it was going to cost us to carry it."

At the hearing, Mrs. Cinque was asked about the condition of the property at the time of the divorce. She denied that it was in a state of disrepair. She stated that the inside and outside were "nice" and that the portion of the property in which she had lived had been redone. In fact, she had visited the property on the day of the closing and had not observed any repairs, repainting or refurbishing. In her words, "everything looked the same."

Following the signing of the contract, respondent forwarded $1,000 to Mrs. Cinque as a deposit, notwithstanding the fact that the contract provided for a $5,000 deposit. On October 18, 1985, the closing of title took place. . . .

A review of the settlement statement shows that respondent obtained a $96,000 mortgage loan secured by a property that was being sold for $85,000. Respondent testified that he was able to secure a mortgage greater than the purchase price "by virtue of the cleaning up and repairs that were completed at that house, as well as the continuation of the rentals."[1] . . .

As mentioned above, the closing of title in the Cinque to Dato transaction occurred on October 18, 1985. Ten days later, respondent contracted to sell the property to three investors for $150,000, or $65,000 more than what he had paid Mrs. Cinque. This transaction, too, was exclusive of a broker's commission.

Respondent vigorously denied that he had contracted to sell the property to the investors before he bought it from Mrs. Cinque. He testified that, shortly after he bought the property from her, the investors retained him to review a contract of sale for the purchase of a three-family property in South Amboy for $150,000. Respondent recounted the sequence of events that developed as follows:

> A. I advised them that I had this piece and suggested they take a look at it for the purpose of comparing the two and I told them that I could sell this place in Port Reading to them for less than the $150,000 they were going to pay in South Amboy. . . .

---

1. If the bank—with which respondent admittedly had a very close relationship—gave him a mortgage loan equal to 113% of the purchase price, then obviously the bank's appraisal must have shown a much higher value for the property. Because banks typically lend eighty percent of the purchase price, the bank's appraisal must have reflected, at a minimum, a $120,000 value for the house.

So I had renovated that house and I was convinced that—I keep using that word. I was comfortable in my telling them that this is a house they should look at and they did.

Q. Can you give us an idea of approximately how long after your purchase of the Cinque residence this took place?

A. We tried to locate in my diaries. It turns out that the 1985 diary was one that was the subject of an IRS partnership audit and it was used and no one in the office can now find it, but to my recollection— now, I don't recall. It would be foolish for me to tell you when I thought and this is four years later.

Q. So they went at some point in time and looked at the Danielle Street property?

. . .

A. Went back to the house and walked the house inside and out, and then within a day or two, they went back again without me and made their last inspection and then they came back to me and indicated an interest in buying, and as I remember, the figure was higher than I was asking for, more than $137,500. We ultimately got to $137,500.

The contract of sale between respondent, as seller, and Stephen Moore, Sr. and his wife, Stephen Moore, Jr., and Robert Moore, as buyers, listed a $150,000 purchase price. For reasons that neither respondent nor the Moores can recall, on November 15, 1985, fifteen days before the closing of title, the parties executed an amendment to the contract, reducing the purchase price from $150,000 to $137,500.[2] Respondent's profit from the resale of the property, thus, totalled $52,500.

As in the transaction between respondent and Mrs. Cinque, the buyers were not represented by separate counsel. Respondent and the only investor who testified, Stephen Moore, Jr., agreed that the Moores had elected not to be represented by an attorney, notwithstanding respondent's advice, in writing, that they retain separate counsel. The record leaves no doubt, however, that the Moores expected respondent to render some legal services on their behalf. In fact, respondent's performance of certain legal services was more than a mere expectation on the Moores' part; it was a matter of express agreement between the parties. Specifically, it was agreed that respondent would assist the Moores in obtaining a mortgage, obtaining title insurance, and preparing the leases after the closing of title. . . . And, as confirmed by Stephen Moore, Jr., it was the Moores' expectation that respondent would "deal with the bank and prepar[e] papers, obtain[ ] title insurance, [and] various other services," at no charge. . . .

---

2. It has not escaped the Board's attention that the mortgage loan obtained by the Moores, $120,000, coincidentally amounts to eighty percent of $150,000, the purchase price initially quoted on the contract. The Board also noted that the contract providing for a $150,000 purchase price listed a $13,750 deposit, or ten percent of the price ultimately paid by the Moores, $137,500.

Respondent testified that, immediately following his $52,500 windfall, he informed Mrs. Cinque of his good fortune. [He claimed that he chose to "do certain things for her," instead of sharing his extraordinary profit with her.] . . .

Mrs. Cinque denied that respondent had informed her of the resale of the property to the Moores and of the huge profit he had realized therefrom. She testified that she found out about both approximately one year later through one of her daughters, who had been apprised of the events by Mr. Cinque. . . .

Upon a *de novo* review of the record, the Board is satisfied that the conclusion that respondent's conduct was unethical is fully supported by clear and convincing evidence. The Board cannot agree, however, with the recommendation that respondent receive only a private reprimand. In the Board's view, anything short of a suspension would be disproportionate to the ethics offenses and would not adequately vindicate the goals of the disciplinary system to maintain the integrity of the bar and the public's confidence in the profession.

This case is one more sorry example of an attorney's failure to heed the Court's repeated warnings about the dangers of entangling his or her business dealings with a professional relationship.

Respondent's conduct in this entire matter reflected a pattern of conflict of interest that started with his simultaneous representation of opposite sides in a transaction and ended with the overreaching of a client and friend of long standing. Indeed, respondent embarked on one scheming course of conduct after another in order to promote his own interest, to the detriment of his clients.

It all began when respondent asked Mocci, a client, if he was interested in buying the former marital residence of another client, Mrs. Cinque, for a price fixed by respondent and known to him to be below the fair market value. Respondent did not counsel either client to consult with or retain an attorney of their own choosing. Thereafter, respondent prepared a contract of sale between Mocci and Mrs. Cinque and forwarded it to the latter for her signature. She signed it. For some reason that respondent could not explain and Mocci did not know, respondent never gave Mocci the contract for his signature, notwithstanding Mocci's continued interest in the property. Incredibly, some five months later, respondent drafted a contract of sale between Mrs. Cinque and himself, as buyer, this time listing the purchase price as $85,000, $10,000 less than what Mocci had agreed to pay for the property. Once again, respondent failed to advise Mrs. Cinque to retain independent counsel. In fact, even if respondent had given Mrs. Cinque such advice, this precaution would not have been sufficient because of the special circumstances attendant to this case. In light of the parties' close, long-term personal and professional relationship, it is unlikely that Mrs. Cinque would have sought legal counsel. Instead, she would have continued to operate under the belief that respondent was protecting her interests because of the trust and faith that she placed on him. Under these circumstances, respondent's proper course of action should have been either to insist that Mrs. Cinque be represented by counsel or to refuse to proceed with the transaction. Egregiously, however, he was represented by his partner at closing, while she went without legal representation.

Respondent disavowed any improper motives on his part in purchasing the property from Mrs. Cinque. He insisted that $85,000 was a fair price because of the "run down" condition of the property and of the low rental income then collected; he contended that he had "renovated" the property and more than doubled the rents. He also pointed to the absence of a real estate broker's commission and of a mortgage contingency clause, in an attempt to justify the low purchase price. But respondent was unable to produce any proof of the repairs allegedly undertaken and Mrs. Cinque's credible testimony was that, on the closing date, the house looked the same as before. Also, if respondent knew that the rents were too low, then it is difficult to comprehend why he did not factor the real rental value into his computation of the property's fair market value. Moreover, the Cinque to Mocci transaction, too, did not contemplate a broker's commission or a mortgage contingency clause. In fact, the terms of the deal with respondent were less favorable to Mrs. Cinque than the terms of the deal with Mocci: Mrs. Cinque took back a $10,000 mortgage.... A more egregious case of overreaching a helpless client may not be easily envisioned.

Equally incredible was respondent's next course of conduct. A mere ten days after closing title on the property, respondent contracted to sell it to a group of investors for $150,000, or $65,000 more than what he had paid Mrs. Cinque. This transaction, as well, was exclusive of a broker's commission. For reasons not revealed by the record, the parties eventually agreed to reduce the purchase price to $137,500, thus causing respondent to pocket a handsome profit of $52,500....

In sum, respondent's overall conduct in this matter reflected an extreme indifference to his clients' interests and a pattern of self-dealing that is shocking to the minds of reasonable individuals. His behavior toward Mrs. Cinque was abominable. His testimony that he shared his ill-gotten gains with Mrs. Cinque by forbearing the payment of legal fees and expenses and by bestowing upon her certain material benefits is unworthy of belief. Although respondent professed that he acted with nothing but good intentions in his dealings with Mrs. Cinque, the record leaves no doubt that his motivation was greed. Clear and convincing evidence of overreaching abounds.

There remains the question of appropriate discipline for respondent's serious offenses.

Where an attorney involved in a conflict of interest situation has failed to recognize his or her obligation to a client, the discipline imposed has ranged from a public reprimand to disbarment....

Here, respondent overreached one client by a single act; there was no repetitive course of overreaching. Nevertheless, his behavior in this single episode with Mrs. Cinque was egregious. Coupled with his demonstrated indifference to basic conflict of interest considerations and to the well-being of his clients, his conduct is deserving of a lengthy term of suspension.... Accordingly, the Board unanimously recommends that respondent be suspended for a period of one year.

NOTES

1.   What did attorney Dato do wrong? Can't a lawyer, like any other person, take advantage of an opportunity to secure a bargain when the lawyer values the property more highly than the seller does? Why shouldn't we assume that Mrs. Cinque agreed to accept $85,000 for the house because that was her subjective view of its value, and that it was reasonable for her lawyer to pay her what she thought the house was worth?

2.   Was the problem here a procedural one: that the lawyer failed to make proper disclosures or to recommend to his client that she secure independent counsel? Or was it a substantive problem: that the deal was unfair to the client? Consider Model Rule 1.8(a). What does it require of a lawyer who enters a business transaction with a client?

3.   In this case, the lawyer realized profit at the expense of his client. But a lawyer can violate the rules on business transactions with clients even without realizing any profit. Consider *Committee on Professional Ethics and Conduct of the Iowa State Bar Ass'n v. Mershon*, 316 N.W.2d 895 (Iowa 1982). Mershon entered into an agreement with Miller, his client, and Schenk, an engineer, to form a corporation that would develop property owned by Miller. The agreement was that Mershon would provide legal services, Schenk would provide engineering services, and Miller would provide the land. The client conveyed the property to the corporation and got 400 shares of stock; Schenk also got 400 shares, and Mershon got 200 shares in anticipation of his future legal services. The corporation could not find financing and the deal did not proceed; after eight years Miller died. Although the court concluded that Mershon was "forthright and honest and gained no profit from this transaction"—in fact, he had spent some money on the deal that he did not get back—he was nonetheless disciplined. He had done business with his client, Miller, without giving him "the kind of advice Miller should have had if the transaction were with a stranger." In particular, Mershon did not investigate whether the apportionment of the stock was appropriate; he did not explore alternative ways that Miller could have paid for legal or engineering services (other than providing an equity interest in the corporation); and he did not assure that the property would revert to Miller if the project failed. According to the court, Mershon had three alternatives: to refuse to participate in the transaction, to recommend that Miller obtain independent legal advice, or to try to meet the "high standard of disclosure" required. Mershon's attempt at this third, "least desirable choice" was unsuccessful.

4.   In addition to disciplinary consequences, a lawyer's contract for a business transaction with a client may be voidable on the ground of undue influence.

See BGJ Associates, LLC v. Wilson, 113 Cal. App. 4th 1217 (Cal. Dist. Ct. App. 2003).

5.   Are lawyers' transactions with clients that are in the clients' ordinary course of business subject to the strictures of Model Rule 1.8(a)? As a lawyer can you buy a car from a client, engage a client to do accounting work for you, or hire a client to put a new roof on your house, without worrying about the procedural or substantive constraints of Rule 1.8(a)? See Comment [1] to Rule 1.8. Why might the rule be different in this context?

2.   SEX WITH CLIENTS

IN RE RINELLA

677 N.E.2d 909 (Ill. 1997)

CHIEF JUSTICE HEIPLE delivered the opinion of the court:

The Administrator of the Attorney Registration and Disciplinary Commission filed a complaint with the Hearing Board charging respondent, Richard Anthony Rinella, with four counts of professional misconduct for engaging in sexual relations with clients and testifying falsely before the Commission. The Hearing Board found that respondent had committed the misconduct charged in each of the counts and recommended that respondent be suspended from the practice of law for a period of three years and until further order of this court. . . . Respondent is suspended from the practice of law for three years. . . .

[Rinella represented Jane Doe in her divorce.] Jane Doe testified that during her second visit to respondent's office in July 1983, respondent came over to the sofa she was sitting on and began fondling her. She testified that she began crying and that respondent told her to stop crying. She testified that she then performed fellatio on respondent. She also testified that during the sexual activity, respondent said "it would make it easier." She testified that she did not want to engage in sexual activity with respondent but felt she had to because she had just changed lawyers and paid respondent a large retainer.

Doe further testified that one day in the spring of 1984, she and respondent were undressed and engaging in fellatio in her bedroom at her house when her ex-husband, John Doe, walked into the room. Jane Doe testified that she put on a robe and followed John Doe downstairs while respondent hid in a closet. She testified that John Doe then asked where the couple's five-year-old son was, and she responded that he was at a friend's house. She testified that John Doe periodically refers to this incident when she requests timely maintenance or child support payments from him.

John Doe testified before the Hearing Board that the incident in the bedroom at his wife's house occurred a few weeks before the entry of a supplemental judgment resolved issues of property distribution, maintenance, and child support in the Does' dissolution of marriage proceeding.

Also before the Hearing Board, Jane Doe identified two exhibits as photographs of respondent in the nude taken at her house in the spring of

1984. She said the photographs showed wallpaper in her house which she had removed in the fall of 1984.

Jane Doe admitted that she attended a holiday luncheon sponsored by respondent's law firm in 1987 or 1988, and that she sent respondent a humorous postcard in January 1986 which she signed "Lustfully Yours."

Respondent testified before the Hearing Board that while he had engaged in sexual activity with Jane Doe, this activity took place in late 1986, or in 1987 or 1988, after he had stopped representing her. He denied having sex with Jane Doe in his office in July 1983, and denied having sex with her in her house at any time. He testified that he went to Jane Doe's house on a few occasions during his representation of her, and that John Doe came to the house on one of those occasions, but said that he and Jane Doe were standing in an upstairs hallway fully clothed when John Doe encountered them. Respondent also testified that the photographs of him in the nude were taken on an occasion when he and Jane Doe engaged in sexual activity in late 1986, or in 1987 or 1988. Respondent admitted that in prior testimony before the Commission he falsely denied ever having had sex with Jane Doe and having had nude pictures taken, but he stated that he believed these answers were justified because his sexual relationship with Doe occurred after he stopped representing her.

Jeanne Metzger testified that she retained respondent in November 1983, and that on a Saturday in December 1983, she had an appointment at respondent's office to discuss her case. She testified that when she entered respondent's office, respondent closed the door behind her and propped a chair up against the doorknob. She testified that respondent then came towards her, unzipped his pants, and sat down on the couch beside her. She testified that respondent then put his hand on her head, had her lean towards him, and pushed her head down while stating "You don't have to do this if you don't want to." Metzger testified that she then performed fellatio on respondent. She testified that while she did not want to do so, she felt she had to for the welfare of her children, whose custody was contested.

Metzger further testified that respondent scheduled another appointment with her for December 14, 1983, at his office, and that when she arrived, respondent told her to go downstairs and wait on the sidewalk outside the building. She testified that respondent then joined her outside and took her by taxi to an apartment in a high-rise building. She testified that after entering the apartment, respondent undressed and sniffed a bottle of liquid, and then asked her to do the same. She testified that she sniffed the bottle and got an "extreme high," and that the two then had sex. Metzger further testified that on January 11, 1984, after a deposition in her case, respondent again took her to the apartment and asked her to sniff the bottle of liquid, and that the two then had sex again. She testified that on this occasion, respondent told her to make an appointment to get a "tummy tuck," and that he gave her the name of the doctor with whom she should make the appointment. She also testified that on this occasion, respondent said that he wanted to take pictures of her "from the neck down" and offered to let her take similar pictures of him, but that there was no camera in the apartment.

Metzger further testified that respondent told her to bring an instant camera to a court appearance in her case one day in February 1984. She testified that just before the court appearance, respondent instructed her to answer "yes" to all of his questions. She also testified that respondent asked her before the hearing if she had brought the camera, and that she said "yes" because she was afraid telling him the truth would affect his representation that day. She testified that immediately after the court appearance, when she told respondent that she did not really have the camera, he became angry and left abruptly, refusing to discuss with her a number of questions she had regarding the testimony she had given that day. Metzger testified that shortly thereafter, she hired another attorney to replace respondent.

Respondent testified that he never had sexual relations with Metzger. He denied propping a chair up against the door during an appointment with Metzger. He denied ever going with her to an apartment and having sex. He also denied asking her to bring a camera to a court appearance.

Sandra Demos testified before the Hearing Board that she retained respondent's law firm in 1980 to represent her in a dissolution of marriage proceeding, and that respondent's father was the primary attorney on her case. Demos testified that she met respondent for the first time in the lobby of the law firm, and that after this meeting, he began calling her frequently to ask her out for a drink. She stated that although she continually refused to meet him, the phone calls went on for months, and that during the conversations, respondent discussed information he could only have learned by viewing her confidential files, such as her sexual history with her husband.

Demos testified that she finally agreed to meet respondent one day in March 1992. She testified that they met and had several drinks, and that respondent afterwards offered to drive her home. She testified that respondent then drove her to a harbor, parked the car, and began kissing and fondling her. She testified that she did not want to have sexual relations with him, but submitted to his advances because she feared her case would be mishandled if she did not. She further testified that after approximately 15 minutes, respondent, without saying anything to her, drove the car to a motel and took her into a room. She testified that respondent attempted to have sexual intercourse with her, but had trouble maintaining an erection, and that he then began sniffing some liquid in a bottle. She testified that respondent then attempted to force her to perform fellatio on him, but that she refused. She testified that after they had spent approximately one hour in the motel, respondent drove her home.

Respondent testified that he did not recall ever meeting Demos, although he might have met her once briefly in the lobby of his law firm. He denied ever discussing Demos' case with other attorneys at his firm or viewing the firm's files on her case. He also denied that he ever had sexual relations with her or took her to a motel.

The Hearing Board found that respondent engaged in sexual relations with each of the three women while he or his firm represented them. The Board found that this conduct by respondent constituted overreaching because he used his position of influence over the clients to pressure them to engage in sexual relations. The Board noted that all of the women testified that they did not want to engage in sexual relations with respondent but felt that they had to in order to ensure that they were effectively represented and because they could not afford to hire another lawyer.

The Hearing Board also found that respondent violated the following rules of the Code of Professional Responsibility: Rule 1–102(a)(5), by engaging in conduct prejudicial to the administration of justice; Rule 4–101(b)(3), by using client confidences for his own advantage in his dealings with Sandra Demos; Rule 5–101(a), by failing to withdraw from the women's cases when his professional judgment may have been affected by his own personal interest; and Rule 5–107(a), by failing to represent his clients with undivided fidelity. As to count II, the Board found that respondent violated Rules 8.1(a)(1), 8.4(a)(3), 8.4(a)(4), and 8.4(a)(5) of the Rules of Professional Conduct by giving false testimony before the Commission.

Respondent takes exception to the Hearing Board's finding that he committed sanctionable misconduct. He contends that he cannot be sanctioned for engaging in sexual relations with his clients because no disciplinary rule specifically proscribes such conduct, and that imposing a sanction under these circumstances would violate due process because he did not have adequate notice that his conduct was prohibited. . . .

Initially, we reject respondent's contention that attorney misconduct is sanctionable only when it is specifically proscribed by a disciplinary rule. On the contrary, the standards of professional conduct enunciated by this court are not a manual designed to instruct attorneys what to do in every conceivable situation. . . .

The Hearing Board found that respondent failed to withdraw from representation when the exercise of his professional judgment on behalf of his clients reasonably could have been affected by his own personal interests. The Hearing Board also found that respondent failed to represent his clients with undivided fidelity. We believe the record amply supports these findings. The Hearing Board was justified in concluding that respondent took advantage of his superior position as the women's legal representative to gain sexual favors from them during times when they were most dependent upon him. . . . By placing his clients in such situations of duress, respondent compromised the exercise of his professional judgment on their behalf and failed to represent them with undivided fidelity. Furthermore, with regard to Sandra Demos, the record supports the

Hearing Board's finding that respondent used a confidence or secret of a client for his own advantage in violation of Rule 4–101(b)(3).

We also believe the record supports the Hearing Board's finding that respondent engaged in conduct prejudicial to the administration of justice, thereby violating Rule 1–102(a)(5). Two of the women described incidents in which respondent, during appointments he had scheduled with them in his office to discuss their cases, made completely unsolicited sexual advances which included undressing himself. Respondent's sexual relations with all three clients originated solely from the provision of legal services, since he did not know the women prior to their retaining him or his firm. These abuses of respondent's professional relationship with clients were clearly prejudicial to the administration of justice....

Respondent contends that his admittedly false testimony before the Commission is not sanctionable because the questions posed to him were ambiguous, because information concerning his private sexual relations was protected by the right of privacy, and because he later recanted his false testimony. We find no merit in any of these contentions. Respondent was clearly asked if he had ever had sexual relations with Jane Doe, to which he falsely responded "no." ... Finally, we observe that respondent did not voluntarily recant his false testimony, but rather recanted only when confronted with undeniable pictorial evidence that he had lied to the Commission. Under these circumstances, his false testimony is entirely inexcusable.

Respondent contends that the three-year suspension recommended by the Hearing and Review Boards is an excessive sanction for the instant misconduct. In deciding on an appropriate sentence, the Hearing Board considered the following factors in aggravation: respondent's pattern of misconduct, his selfish motive, the nonconsensual nature of his sexual relations with the women, his inability to appreciate the wrongfulness of his conduct, and his false testimony before the Commission. In mitigation, the Board considered that this is respondent's first charged instance of misconduct, as well as the testimony of numerous witnesses regarding respondent's good character and reputation in the legal community.

We do not believe that the recommended three-year suspension is an excessive sanction. Respondent violated numerous ethical standards in his dealings with three separate clients. He then compounded this misconduct by concealing and denying it while it was under investigation....

Accordingly ... Respondent is suspended from the practice of law for three years and until further order of this court.

NOTES

1. Model Rule 1.8(j) imposes an express prohibition on sex with clients. In the *Rinella* case, there was no such explicit rule. Does the case suggest why some might consider a rule appropriate? Does it suggest that such a rule is unnecessary? After all, the Illinois authorities succeeded in sanctioning Rinella without one.

2. Might the existence of a rule make enforcement of improper behavior *more* difficult? Consider *In re Inglimo*, 740 N.W.2d 125 (Wis. 2007), in which the court concluded that participation in a three-way sexual encounter with a client and the client's girlfriend did not violate the prohibition on sex with a client, since, while both Inglimo and the client had sexual relations with the client's girlfriend at the same time and place, Inglimo and the client did not have sexual relations with each other. In the same disciplinary decision, the court concluded that Inglimo's sexual relations with another client's wife in the presence of the client, and allegedly as payment for legal services, violated Rule 1.7 because the attorney's personal interests materially limited the representation of the client. Does this suggest that a specific rule is inadvisable or unnecessary?

3. Are some clients more susceptible to overreaching in this manner than others? Does it make sense to have a blanket prohibition like Rule 1.8(j), or would it be better to target the rule to situations in which an unscrupulous lawyer might seek to take advantage of a vulnerable client?

D. MORE LOYALTY: CONSECUTIVE CONFLICTS AND IMPUTED DISQUALIFICATION

1. FORMER CLIENTS

In Part B, we considered the problem of concurrent conflicts of interest. Those conflicts included conflicts arising from duties owed to another current client. Representations end, however. What loyalty obligations does a lawyer owe to a former client? Model Rule 1.9(a) deals with this problem. The rule provides: "A lawyer who has formerly represented a client in a matter shall not thereafter represent another person in the same or a substantially related matter in which that person's interests are materially adverse to the interests of the former client unless the former client gives informed consent, confirmed in writing." How is this different from the rules about representation directly adverse to a current client which we considered previously?

First, the rule applies only to representation that is "materially adverse" to the former client "in the same or a substantially related matter." What determines whether matters are "substantially related"? Comment [3] to Model Rule 1.9 provides, "Matters are 'substantially related' for purposes of this Rule if they involve the same transaction or legal dispute or if there otherwise is a substantial risk that confidential factual information as would normally have been obtained in the prior representation would materially advance the client's position in the subsequent matter." Why do you suppose that representation adverse to former clients is prohibited only if the representation is in the same or a substantially related matter? What interest is being protected by such a rule? Are there circumstances in which that interest does not need protection? This is the subject of the next case.

Second, there appear to be no "nonconsentable" conflicts under Model Rule 1.9. Remember that under Model Rule 1.7, there are some circumstances in which the lawyer cannot ask for consent or in which consent will not cure a conflict. That does not appear to be the case under Rule 1.9. Remember, however, that Rule 1.9 requires informed consent. A lawyer who is constrained, for example, by a duty of confidentiality to a former client, may not be able to make the disclosure required to obtain informed consent. Is that a Rule 1.9 issue or a Rule 1.7 issue? Remember that duties owed to former clients can create 1.7 conflicts as well as 1.9 conflicts.

BRENNAN'S, INC. v. BRENNAN'S RESTAURANTS, INC.

590 F.2d 168 (5th Cir. 1979)

TJOFLAT, CIRCUIT JUDGE:

This is an action for trademark infringement and unfair competition. This appeal, however, concerns the disqualification of attorneys. The district court barred the appellants' attorneys from further representing them on grounds of conflict of interest. The correctness of this order is the only issue before us.

I

The underlying dispute in this case arises out of the business affairs of the Brennan family of New Orleans, Louisiana, who have been in the restaurant business for many years. All of the corporate parties are owned and closely held by various members of the Brennan family. Appellee Brennan's, Inc., the plaintiff below, owns and operates Brennan's restaurant at 417 Royal Street in New Orleans. The corporate appellants own and operate other restaurants in Louisiana, Texas, and Georgia. There has been no trial as yet, but a review of the facts leading to the present suit, as disclosed by the pleadings and affidavits, is necessary to a decision of this appeal. For convenience, the parties will be referred to in the capacities in which they appear in the court below.

Prior to 1974, all the members of the Brennan family were stockholders and directors of plaintiff, and some of them were stockholders and directors of the corporate defendants. All the corporations were independent legal entities in the sense that none held any of the stock of another, but they were all owned by members of the Brennan family and had interlocking boards of directors. In 1971, Edward F. Wegmann became general counsel for the family businesses, and his retainer was paid pro rata by all the corporations. He continued this joint representation until November 1973.

As part of his services, Mr. Wegmann, in close cooperation with trademark counsel in Washington, D.C., prosecuted applications for the federal registration of three service marks: "Brennan's," "Breakfast at Brennan's," and a distinctive rooster design. A registration for the rooster design was issued in February 1972, but the applications for the other two marks were initially denied on the ground that they were primarily a surname. On the advice of Washington trademark counsel, Mr. Wegmann collected data supporting a demonstration that the marks had acquired a secondary meaning, and the applications were amended to include this material. Registrations were subsequently issued in plaintiff's name in March 1973. These registered service marks are the subject of this lawsuit.

Later in 1973 a dispute developed within the Brennan family over the operation and management of the family businesses. This dispute was resolved in November 1974 by dividing the corporations' stock between the two opposing family groups. Plaintiff became 100% owned by one group and the corporate defendants became 100% owned by the second group, composed of the individual defendants. Mr. Wegmann elected to continue to represent defendants and severed his connections with plaintiff and its shareholders.

At no time during the negotiations which culminated in the November 1974 settlement was there any discussion of who would have the right to use the registered service marks. Both sides claimed ownership of the marks and continued to use them after the settlement. Attempts to negotiate a license or concurrent registration were unsuccessful. Plaintiff filed this suit for trademark infringement and unfair competition on May 21, 1976. In their answer and counterclaim defendants alleged that the marks were registered in plaintiff's name for convenience only, and, "in truth and actuality, the applications were filed and the registrations issued for the benefit and ownership of all of the Brennan family restaurants, including the corporate defendants." Defendants also alleged that the marks and registrations are invalid.

Upon the filing of this suit, Mr. Wegmann, on behalf of the defendants, retained the services of Arnold Sprung, a New York patent and trademark attorney, to assist him in the defense of the case. On October 22, 1976, plaintiff moved for the disqualification of both attorneys: Mr. Wegmann on the ground that his present representation was at odds with the interests of plaintiff, his former client, and Mr. Sprung by imputation of Mr. Wegmann's conflict. After a hearing, the district court granted the motion. It found that the subject matter of the present suit is substantially related to matters in which Mr. Wegmann formerly represented plaintiff, and to allow him now to represent an interest adverse to his former client creates the appearance of impropriety. It also found that "the close working relationship which has been shown to exist between Mr. Wegmann and Mr. Sprung creates a significant likelihood that Mr. Sprung would have had access to or been informed of confidential disclosures made to Mr. Wegmann by his former client."

II

We first consider the disqualification of Mr. Wegmann.

Defendants argue that the district court failed to consider that in his prior representation of plaintiff, Mr. Wegmann also represented defendants. This fact of joint representation is crucial, they assert, since no confidences can arise as between joint clients. Hence, the argument goes, Mr. Wegmann violates no ethical duty in his present representation.

We have not addressed this precise question before. In *Wilson P. Abraham Construction Corp. v. Armco Steel Corp.*, we reaffirmed the standard that "a former client seeking to disqualify an attorney who appears on behalf of his adversary, need only to show that the matters embraced within the pending suit are substantially related to the matters or cause of action wherein the attorney previously represented him," but we acknowledged that "(t)his rule rests upon the presumption that confidences potentially damaging to the client have been disclosed to the attorney during the former period of representation." Defendants contend that this presumption cannot apply in this case. This argument, in our view, interprets too narrowly an attorney's duty to "preserve the confidences and secrets of a client." The fundamental flaw in defendants' position is a confusion of the attorney-client evidentiary privilege with the ethical duty to preserve a client's confidences. Assuming the prior representation was joint, defendants are quite correct that neither of the parties to this suit can assert the attorney-client privilege against the other as to matters comprehended by that joint representation. But the ethical duty is broader than the evidentiary privilege. Information so acquired is sheltered from use by the attorney against his client by virtue of the existence of the attorney-client relationship. This is true without regard to whether someone else may be privy to it. The obligation of an attorney not to misuse information acquired in the course of representation serves to vindicate the trust and reliance that clients place in their attorneys. A client would feel wronged if an opponent prevailed against him with the aid of an attorney who formerly represented the client in the same matter.... The need to safeguard the attorney-client relationship is not diminished by the fact that the prior representation was joint with the attorney's present client.... Since the district court's findings of prior representation and substantial relationship are not disputed, we affirm the disqualification of Mr. Wegmann.

Ruling

III

Whether Mr. Sprung should be disqualified presents a more difficult case. He has never had an attorney-client relationship with plaintiff; the district court disqualified him by imputation of Mr. Wegmann's conflict. Up to this point we have accepted, for the sake of argument, defendants' assertion that they were formerly joint clients with plaintiff of Mr. Wegmann. There is no dispute that plaintiff and defendants were previously represented by Mr. Wegmann simultaneously, but plaintiff maintains that, at least with respect to the registration of the service marks, Mr. Wegmann was representing plaintiff alone. The district court made no findings on the issue. Because we think that the disqualification of Mr.

Sprung may turn on this fact and others not found by the court below, we vacate that part of the court's order relating to Mr. Sprung and remand the cause for further proceedings. For the guidance of the court on remand, we set forth our view of the applicable ethical standards.

If the court finds that Mr. Wegmann previously represented plaintiff and defendants jointly, we can see no reason why Mr. Sprung should be disqualified. As between joint clients there can be no "confidences" or "secrets" unless one client manifests a contrary intent. Thus, Mr. Sprung could not have learned anything from Mr. Wegmann that defendants did not already know or have a right to know. Plaintiff argues that this permits the defendants indirectly to gain the benefit of Mr. Wegmann's services when they could not do so directly. If the representation was joint, however, defendants possess no information as to which plaintiff could have had any expectation of privacy in relation to the defendants. The only remaining ground for disqualification then would be an appearance of impropriety.... [T]here is such an appearance when an attorney represents an interest adverse to that of a former client in a matter substantially related to the subject of the prior representation. Mr. Sprung has never been plaintiff's counsel, however; he is only the cocounsel of one who was. In the case of Mr. Sprung, we think the balance weighs against disqualification. Assuming that Mr. Wegmann's prior retainer was joint, plaintiff has suffered no actual prejudice from communications between Mr. Wegmann and Mr. Sprung....[1]

Under the peculiar facts of this case, we do not think there would be such an appearance of impropriety in Mr. Sprung's continued representation of defendants as to warrant his disqualification.

If the district court finds that Mr. Wegmann did not previously represent these parties jointly, it does not necessarily follow that Mr. Sprung should be disqualified. Mr. Sprung should not be disqualified unless he has learned from Mr. Wegmann information the plaintiff had intended not be disclosed to the defendants.

NOTES

1. The court concluded that Wegmann was disqualified from representing his client in the current matter. Why? Why did it conclude that Sprung was not disqualified? Did the court's analysis make any sense? Is there a better way to understand it?

2. The court also noted that Wegmann might well be a witness to the proceeding. If that was true, could he also represent a client in the matter? For guidance on whether a lawyer can be a witness in a proceeding when he is also an advocate, *see* Model Rule 3.7.

---

1. It is very likely that Mr. Wegmann will be a witness in this case. He handled the registrations for the service marks which are the subject of this suit. Moreover, he prepared and notarized two affidavits that were executed at the time the registrations were issued. Defendants rely on these affidavits in support of their claim of ownership of the marks. The circumstances of their execution and the facts to which these affidavits purport to attest will undoubtedly be a subject of dispute at trial and Mr. Wegmann's knowledge may be relevant....

2.   PRESENT CLIENT OR FORMER CLIENT?

As we have seen, the rules for representation adverse to former clients are considerably more permissive than the rules relating to representation adverse to current clients. Representation adverse to a current client is a concurrent conflict of interest and is impermissible without satisfying the requirements of Rule 1.7(b); in some situations, such representation is nonconsentable. By contrast, representation adverse to a former client is prohibited only if the party represented is materially adverse to the former client in the same or a substantially related matter. Is it possible to convert current clients to former clients by firing them once an advantageous adverse representation opportunity presents itself? This is what the lawyers tried to do in the following case. Why? Did they succeed?

SANTACROCE v. NEFF

134 F. Supp. 2d 366 (D.N.J. 2001)

LIFLAND, DISTRICT JUDGE.

The "Hot Potato Doctrine" has evolved to prevent attorneys from dropping one client like a "hot potato" to avoid a conflict with another, more remunerative client. Upon review of the undisputed facts and the inferences drawn therefrom, the Court concludes that this is exactly what happened to plaintiff Stefania Santacroce ("Santacroce"). Accordingly, RPC 1.7(a) and 1.9(a)(1) of the New Jersey Rules of Professional Conduct preclude the firm of Jaffe & Asher from representing Arthur Goldberg's Estate in this case.

Hot Potato Doctrine [handwritten margin note]

Ruling [handwritten margin note]

BACKGROUND

Arthur Goldberg ("Goldberg") was a longstanding client of Jaffe & Asher. The firm represented Goldberg in personal matters and represented many of Goldberg's corporations, including DiGiorgio Corporation, Bally Total Fitness Corporation, and Dice Investments.

In 1998, Goldberg and Santacroce became romantically involved. According to Santacroce, Goldberg requested that she leave her apartment in New York City, abandon her business, EuroJewels, Inc. ("EuroJewels"), and live with Goldberg in New Jersey to medically care for him and provide companionship.

At Goldberg's request, Jaffe & Asher was retained in November, 1999 to represent Santacroce and EuroJewels in connection with a contractual dispute with Damiani International ("Damiani"), a manufacturer of jewelry products. Santacroce's legal fees in the Damiani matter were paid by Goldberg until his death. On Santacroce's behalf, Jaffe & Asher filed a complaint in the New York Supreme Court, New York County, against Damiani, regarding the termination of an exclusive agency agreement

("Damiani matter"). Santacroce filed an affidavit with the New York Supreme Court in the Damiani matter on November 5, 1999. As Santacroce's counsel, Jaffe & Asher prepared her affidavit which states that Damiani terminated the agency agreement with EuroJewels without good cause or reasonable notice and Damiani misappropriated confidential customer information from EuroJewels. Santacroce's affidavit generally claims that EuroJewels did nothing to provoke Damiani's "commercially unreasonable termination" of the agency agreement.

Although the New York action was dismissed due to improper venue, Jaffe & Asher continued to provide Santacroce with legal services and helped her obtain local counsel in the proper venue. Moreover, Jaffe & Asher "also assisted EuroJewels in connection with minor business disputes with its landlord and freight forwarder."

On October 19, 2000, Goldberg died. Richard Neff, one of the Goldberg Estate's Executors, approached Asher and stated that the Estate wanted Jaffe & Asher to represent its interests in any forthcoming litigation.

Goldberg's Last Will and Testament did not leave anything to Santacroce. In December, 2000, Santacroce retained Michael Rosenbaum ("Rosenbaum") as counsel with the intent to file a palimony suit against the Goldberg Estate ("Estate"). Frank Stifelman ("Stifelman") was then counsel to the Estate. In December, 2000, Rosenbaum gave a "courtesy copy" draft of Santacroce's complaint to Stifelman. Rosenbaum agreed not to file the complaint while settlement negotiations were pending.

On December 22, 2000, Jaffe & Asher sent Santacroce a letter withdrawing as counsel in the Damiani matter. The letter stated that "[i]n light of the fact that you have commenced an action against the estate of Arthur Goldberg, a conflict of interest has arisen in our representation of you. Regrettably, we must therefore withdraw as your attorneys effective immediately.... At this time, we ask that you pay in full your current outstanding legal bills for legal fees and disbursements in the amount of $8,828.20."

On January 4, 2001, Santacroce filed the complaint in this Court, alleging breach of promise for support and breach of promise to make a will.... Santacroce alleges that Goldberg persuaded her to move to New Jersey and abandon EuroJewels in exchange for Goldberg's promise of financial security for the rest of her life.

Jaffe & Asher seek to represent the Estate in this matter.[1] On February 7, 2001, Santacroce sought, and the Court signed, an Order to Show Cause why Jaffe & Asher should not be disqualified. The Court conducted a hearing.... [T]he undisputed facts and inferences therefrom compel the disqualification of Jaffe & Asher in this case.

---

1. On January 3, 2001, Stifelman called Rosenbaum to inform him that Stifelman was being replaced by Jaffe & Asher as counsel to the Estate. On the same day, Asher called Rosenbaum to request that Santacroce waive any conflict. Santacroce did not provide a waiver.

DISCUSSION

I.   RPC 1.7

RPC 1.7(a) governs a potential conflict of interest when an attorney concurrently represents clients with adverse interests. RPC 1.7(a) provides:

> A lawyer shall not represent a client if the representation of that client will be directly adverse to another client unless:
>
> > (1) the lawyer reasonably believes that representation will not adversely affect the relationship with the other client; and
> >
> > (2) each client consents after a full disclosure of the circumstances and consultation with the client.

Under RPC 1.7(a), an attorney may not concurrently represent two clients when 1) the clients' interests are materially adverse, 2) the relationship of one of the clients with the attorney will be adversely affected and 3) either client does not consent to the dual representation. In this case, there is no question that the interests of the Estate and Santacroce are directly adverse because they are opposing parties in the present suit. Accordingly, if Jaffe & Asher represented the Estate in this case, the firm's relationship with Santacroce would be adversely affected. Furthermore, RPC 1.7(a)(2) is not satisfied because Santacroce never consented to Jaffe & Asher's representation of the Estate.

Jaffe & Asher argue that RPC 1.7(a) does not apply in this situation because Santacroce was a former client when the present complaint was filed. It points to the December 22, 2000 firing of Santacroce as a client and the January 4, 2001 filing of the complaint. The Court looks to RPC 1.7 when the movant is an actual, not a former, client during the events pertinent to this motion. Although a party may have become a former client soon after the complaint against him was filed, "[t]he relevant date for determining status as a present or former client is the date on which the complaint was filed." Here, Jaffe & Asher argue that Santacroce became a former client before the complaint was filed, and that therefore, RPC 1.7 does not apply. The Court disagrees. The complaint's actual filing date is not particularly significant when notice of the proposed complaint is what precipitated the events pertinent to this motion.

Here, Santacroce was fired as a client by Jaffe & Asher because it got wind of her proposed complaint against the Estate. This conclusion is compelled by the timing of the December 21 or 22 sharing of the complaint by Rosenbaum with Stifelman, the then-attorney for the Estate, coupled with the December 22 letter, which referred to her commencing an action against the Estate, asserted a conflict and fired her as a client. Thus, the appropriate date for evaluating the applicability of RPC 1.7(a) is not the filing date of the complaint, by which time Santacroce was a former client of Jaffe & Asher. Under the circumstances here, the appropriate date is after Jaffe & Asher found out about the proposed complaint but before the firm fired Santacroce. During that interval, Jaffe & Asher represented both Santacroce and the Estate. At that time, there was a clear conflict (as Jaffe & Asher asserted in the December 22 letter) and RPC 1.7(a) applies and precludes Jaffe & Asher's representation of defendants herein.

In any event, the "hot potato doctrine" serves as an exception to the general rule that the status of a client must be determined by the date of the filed complaint. An attorney may not drop one client like a "hot potato" in order to avoid a conflict with another, more remunerative client. "Such behavior is unethical as it violates attorneys' duty of loyalty...."

... [A] firm may not circumvent Model Rule 1.7 by dropping a present client or characterizing him as a former client in order to take on a conflicting and, quite possibly, more lucrative client. Were it otherwise, both the duty of undivided loyalty to the client and public confidence in attorneys and the legal system would be undermined.

When Jaffe & Asher found out that the firm's two clients, Santacroce and the Estate, were at odds, it dropped Santacroce like a "hot potato." The firm dropped Santacroce even before suit was filed in a transparent attempt to represent the extraordinarily more remunerative client, the Estate of multimillionaire Goldberg. Although Jaffe & Asher claim that they terminated representation of Santacroce only due to her inability to pay legal fees, this is belied by their own words. The firm itself refers to the "conflict of interest" in their December 22, 2000 letter to Santacroce.

The Court concludes that RPC 1.7(a) precludes Jaffe & Asher from representing the Estate in this matter....

II. RPC 1.9

Even if the Estate is a successor client to Santacroce, Jaffe & Asher must be disqualified under RPC 1.9 as well. RPC 1.9(a)(1), governing successive representation, provides:

> (a) A lawyer who has represented a client in a matter shall not thereafter:
>
> > (1) represent another client in the same or a substantially related matter in which that client's interests are materially adverse to the interests of the former client unless the former client consents after a full disclosure of the circumstances and consultation with the former client....

Under RPC 1.9(a)(1), Jaffe & Asher cannot represent the Estate in this matter unless 1) the matters are not substantially related, or 2) Santacroce consents, or 3) the interests of Santacroce and the Estate are not materially adverse. As noted previously, the second and third prongs of RPC 1.9(a)(1) analysis have not been met in this case. The Court must decide whether the matters in which Jaffe & Asher represented Santacroce are substantially related to her suit against the Estate.

Jaffe & Asher argue that their firm's representation of Santacroce in the case against Damiani is not substantially related to the present matter because Santacroce did not reveal any information or confidences which would give the defendants an advantage. The Court disagrees.

In the Damiani matter, Asher prepared Santacroce's affidavit, which claims that Damiani terminated the agency agreement with EuroJewels without cause. Under Jaffe & Asher's guidance, Santacroce argued that EuroJewels never gave Damiani any reason to discontinue their business relationship.

This causes a problem in the instant case because the Estate is now faced with Santacroce's claim that Goldberg asked her to abandon EuroJewels to live with him in New Jersey and become his caretaker and social companion. Santacroce alleges that Goldberg knew his request would cause EuroJewels to falter so he promised to provide Santacroce with financial security for the rest of her life. The Estate, through the work of Jaffe & Asher when it represented Santacroce and prepared her affidavit in the Damiani matter, is provided with a defense to Santacroce's claim herein. That affidavit, which implies that EuroJewels was operating efficiently, directly contradicts Santacroce's allegations that she abandoned EuroJewels in consideration for Goldberg's promises. Accordingly, Jaffe & Asher's representation of Santacroce and EuroJewels in the Damiani matter is substantially related to Santacroce's present complaint against the Estate. . . .

In conclusion, under both RPC 1.7(a) and RPC 1.9(a)(1), Jaffe & Asher cannot represent the Estate . . . in this matter.

NOTES

1.   What was the subject matter of Jaffe & Asher's representation of Santacroce? If Santacroce were a former client, what would the issue be with regard to whether Jaffe & Asher could represent the estate in the palimony matter? If Santacroce were a current client, what would the issue be? Does this explain why the firm tried to do what it did? If the court had accepted Jaffe & Asher's argument that Santacroce was a former client, would the firm have been able to represent the estate?

2.   Once Santacroce had sued the estate, could Jaffe & Asher have continued to represent her in the Damiani matter? If not, then what did the firm do wrong?

3.   The firm tried to secure Santacroce's consent to the representation, but that consent was not forthcoming. What sort of disclosure do you think the firm would have needed to make to get a valid consent from Santacroce?

4.   In this case, the Court concluded that the firm was engaged in current representation of Santacroce at the time the conflict arose. Whether a client is a current or former client can be a more complex issue if the firm does occasional work for the client. In between representations, is the client a current client or a former client? That was the issue in the following case.

OXFORD SYSTEMS, INC. v. CELLPRO, INC.

45 F. Supp. 2d 1055 (W.D. Wash. 1999)

ZILLY, DISTRICT JUDGE.

This matter comes before the Court on intervenor Becton Dickinson's motion to disqualify Perkins Coie from representing Lyon & Lyon, L.L.P., in this litigation. The Court hereby GRANTS Becton Dickinson's motion to disqualify Perkins Coie.

Background

Johns Hopkins University (JHU) owns certain patents which it has licensed to Becton Dickinson (Becton). Becton has in turn sublicensed these patents to Baxter Healthcare Corporation (Baxter).

In April 1992 CellPro filed a complaint in this district against Baxter and Becton seeking a declaratory judgment of non-infringement, invalidity, and unenforceability of the JHU patents. The complaint also alleged violations of the Sherman and Clayton Acts. CellPro was represented in the action by Lyon & Lyon, with Seed & Berry acting as local counsel. Becton Dickinson hired a Boston law firm to handle the antitrust claims, a New York firm to handle the patent issues, and Perkins Coie to serve as local counsel.

JHU was not named in the Washington lawsuit even though it was the owner of the patents. Baxter and Becton filed a motion to dismiss the complaint, arguing that JHU was a necessary party and that JHU was not subject to personal jurisdiction in this district. In September 1993, District Judge Carolyn Dimmick found that JHU was a necessary party with respect to the patent claims and that the Court did not have jurisdiction over JHU. Accordingly, the Court dismissed the portion of the Complaint related to the patent claims, and stayed the antitrust claims.

In early 1994, Becton, Baxter, and JHU filed a complaint against CellPro in Federal District Court for the District of Delaware alleging that CellPro infringed one of the JHU patents. In response to the filing of the Delaware complaint, CellPro filed a second complaint in this district against JHU, Becton, and Baxter alleging further antitrust violations. CellPro then moved to consolidate the two Washington actions, and JHU, Becton, and Baxter moved to transfer the Washington cases to Delaware. In April 1994, Judge Dimmick granted CellPro's motion to consolidate the two Washington cases, and also granted the defendants' motion to transfer the consolidated cases to the Delaware court.

Perkins Coie was not counsel of record in the Delaware litigation. Perkins partner David Burman states in his declaration that the Office of the Clerk of the District Court of Delaware notified Perkins that it could not continue as counsel in the Delaware litigation unless it retained local counsel and applied for admission pro hac vice. It is undisputed that Becton never asked Perkins to make application to the Delaware court, and Perkins never sought to be admitted pro hac vice in Delaware. Nevertheless, Perkins did continue to assist Becton with aspects of the Delaware litigation, particularly "organiz[ing] and prepar[ing] documents for exhibits," preparing and serving subpoenas, and arranging depositions in Seattle. Notably, Perkins assisted Becton with preparing a subpoena for Coe Bloomberg, a partner with Lyon & Lyon, which Perkins now represents.

The Delaware patent infringement case was tried to a jury beginning on July 24, 1995. Although the jury found that the claims of all of the JHU patents were invalid as obvious in light of prior art, the district court granted the plaintiffs' post-trial motion for judgment as a matter of law as to some issues and for a new trial on other issues. A second jury trial commenced on March 4, 1997. On March 11, 1997, the jury returned with verdicts finding that plaintiffs had proven damage in the amount of $2.3 million and that CellPro's infringement of the patents had been wilful. Plaintiff then moved for enhancement of damages pursuant to 35 U.S.C. § 284, arguing that CellPro had no reasonable, good faith basis to believe the JHU patents were invalid. CellPro's defense to the bad faith allegation was that it relied on the advice of its counsel, Lyon & Lyon, that the JHU patents were invalid. The district court rejected this defense, stating:

> ... CellPro almost proved plaintiff's case for them, with its weak and disingenuous defense of alleged good-faith reliance on the advice of counsel.... The Lyon & Lyon opinions were so obviously deficient, one might expect a juror to conclude the only value they had to CellPro in the world outside the courtroom would have been to file them in a drawer until they could be used in a cynical effort to try to confuse or mislead what CellPro, its Board, and counsel must have expected would be an unsophisticated jury.

The Delaware court, having concluded that CellPro acted in bad faith, trebled the jury's damage award.

Following the district court's decision, JHU, Becton, and Baxter requested that the Court award attorneys' fees and costs of approximately $7.0 million against CellPro and Lyon & Lyon based on Rule 11 and 28 U.S.C. § 1927. The district court stated that it would address that motion in a separate decision after the Court of Appeals had had an opportunity to review the case on appeal. On August 11, 1998, the Federal Circuit affirmed. On September 30, 1998, the district court entered judgment against CellPro for attorneys' fees and costs in the amount of $8.7 million. The district court's order expressly reserved decision "on whether to award additional fees and costs against CellPro's trial counsel, Lyon & Lyon, and whether Lyon & Lyon should be declared jointly and severally liable for some or all of the fees and costs hereby awarded against CellPro." Becton asserts that it intends to pursue a claim against Lyon & Lyon for fees.

On March 10, 1998, while Becton's and JHU's patent litigation remained pending in Delaware, this securities fraud action was filed. Both CellPro and Lyon & Lyon are named as defendants. In the Complaint, the plaintiff shareholders allege, among other things, that

> Lyon & Lyon had access to the adverse non-public information about CellPro's wilful patent infringement. In furtherance of defendants' common scheme, Lyon & Lyon issued false and misleading opinions and defended CellPro in litigation based on those opinions.

The Complaint goes on to allege that Lyon & Lyon knew or recklessly disregarded that CellPro continued to utilize the patent opinions, and that CellPro purported to base the legitimacy of its infringing activities on those opinions. Thus, Lyon & Lyon's opinions on the validity of the JHU patents and Lyon & Lyon's conduct in the Delaware litigation are central to the securities fraud allegations in this lawsuit.

Lyon & Lyon is represented in this lawsuit by Perkins Coie. Becton Dickinson, who is not a party to this lawsuit, has intervened in this action for the sole purpose of moving to disqualify Perkins Coie as counsel for Lyon & Lyon. Becton argues that Perkins' representation of Lyon & Lyon is a conflict of interest that requires Perkins' disqualification. Perkins argues there is no conflict of interest because Becton is a former client, not a current client; the Perkins partner who handled the patent suit as local counsel left Perkins in 1996; and no current Perkins attorneys who previously worked on the patent matter have any material confidential information about Becton that could be used in this securities litigation.

Discussion

... The Washington Rules of Professional Conduct (RPC) have different conflict-of-interest rules for current clients than for former clients. With respect to current clients, the rules provide that a lawyer cannot represent any client with interests directly adverse to the interests of another client unless each client consents in writing after full disclosure. With respect to former clients, the rules provide that a lawyer may not represent a client if he or she is utilizing confidences to the disadvantage of the former client, or the former client's interests are adverse and the matter is substantially related. *See* RPC 1.9. A firm is not prohibited from representing a client under these circumstances, however, where the lawyer who previously represented the former client has terminated his or her association with the firm, and no lawyers remaining at the firm possess secrets or confidences of the former client. *See* RPC 1.10.

Becton asserts that in April 1998, when Perkins began representing Lyon & Lyon, Becton was a current client of Perkins, and therefore Perkins was prohibited from representing Lyon & Lyon in a substantially related matter absent Becton's written consent. Perkins concedes that this securities litigation and the former patent action are substantially related matters, but it argues that Becton was a former client, not a current client, in April 1998. Perkins further argues that the partner who represented Becton in the patent matter left the firm in 1996, and no lawyers remaining at Perkins had acquired any secrets or confidences. If Becton was a current client of Perkins Coie at the time Perkins agreed to represent Lyon & Lyon, and its representation of Lyon & Lyon is adverse to the interests of Becton, then Perkins *must* be disqualified because Becton has not consented in writing to Perkins' representation of Lyon & Lyon.

I. *Was Becton a Former or Current Client of Perkins Coie in April 1998?*

Whether an attorney-client relationship exists is a question of fact, the essence of which may be inferred from the parties' conduct. "The existence of the relationship 'turns largely on the client's subjective belief that it exists.'" The client's subjective belief, however, does not control the issue unless it is reasonably formed based on the attending circumstances, including the attorney's words or actions.

Perkins Coie has represented Becton on various matters for thirteen years, and since 1990, Becton has used Perkins Coie exclusively for its legal work in Washington State. Robert M. Hallenbeck, Associate General Counsel of Becton, describes in his declaration the nature of the work performed by Perkins since 1985:

> Perkins Coie has represented Becton as counsel of record or in an advisory capacity in matters ranging from employment/breach of contract and defamation, products liability, corporate acquisitions and patent litigation. The nature of the legal work performed by Perkins Coie on behalf of Becton has included, generally, rendering advice on state appellate practice, preparation of briefs and oral argument before lower and appellate courts in Washington, review of documents for production, preparation of answers to interrogatories, taking and defending depositions of Becton's witnesses and other witnesses, negotiations and discussions with attorneys for other parties, review of corporate records as part of "due diligence," review of and comment on a merger agreement and tax issues related thereto, and rendering advice on the State Bulk Transfer Act.

Becton last engaged Perkins in 1996 in the matter of *Nyland v. Becton Dickinson*, a product liability action. Becton retained Perkins as local counsel in that matter and Perkins performed services for Becton through May 1997, when the case was settled.

Becton contends that based on its thirteen year relationship with Perkins and its past practice of using Perkins exclusively for legal work in Washington, it reasonably believed in April 1998, when Lyon & Lyon sought to engage Perkins, that Perkins and Becton had an existing attorney-client relationship. Perkins argues that there is no retainer agreement or other agreement with Becton that establishes an ongoing attorney-client relationship, and in the absence of such an agreement an existing attorney-client relationship should not be presumed. Perkins argues that such presumptions create indefinite attorney-client relationships based on past legal work, rather than present responsibilities, and unduly hamper the law firm's ability to take on new clients. These are valid concerns, but not in the context of this case.

Washington law is clear that the existence of an attorney-client relationship turns largely on the client's subjective understanding of whether such a relationship exists, provided that subjective belief is reasonable under all the circumstances. Thus each case turns on its facts, and in this case, the facts demonstrate that Becton reasonably believed in April 1998 that it had an ongoing relationship with Perkins. That belief was based on the duration of the attorney-client relationship, Becton's practice of using Perkins exclusively as its local counsel in Washington matters whenever such matters arose, and the fact that Perkins had been actively participating in the *Nyland* matter within the last year. The relationship between Becton and Perkins was of sufficient scope and duration that Becton reasonably assumed that Perkins would continue to represent Becton in further matters that arose in Washington State. Moreover, while Perkins was not counsel of record in the Delaware patent action, the firm had been retained to handle the patent matter, had performed substantial work on that matter, and had continued to perform legal work on the case after it had been transferred to Delaware. At the time Lyon & Lyon approached Perkins in April 1998, the patent action was still ongoing in Delaware and the question of whether fees should be awarded against CellPro and Lyon & Lyon had not been resolved. Thus, while Perkins was not actively working on the Delaware case in April 1998, it was reasonable for Becton to believe that based on Perkins' previous engagement and involvement in the patent matter, Perkins would not agree to represent another client with interests directly adverse to those of Becton in a substantially related matter. . . .

The Court concludes that Becton and Perkins had an ongoing attorney-client relationship in April 1998, and therefore pursuant to RPC 1.7 Perkins was prohibited from representing Lyon & Lyon absent Becton's written consent. Because Becton timely objected to Perkins' representation of Lyon & Lyon, the Court concludes that Perkins must be disqualified as counsel for Lyon & Lyon in this matter.

The Court further concludes that even if Becton was a former client of Perkins in April 1998, Perkins would still have to be disqualified under RPC 1.9.

II. *Even if Becton Was a Former Client, Perkins Should Be Disqualified*

RPC 1.9 provides:

> A lawyer who has formerly represented a client in a matter shall not thereafter:
>
> > (a) Represent another person in the same or a substantially related matter in which that person's interests are materially adverse to the interests of the former client unless the former client consents in writing after consultation and a full disclosure of the material facts; or

(b) Use confidences or secrets relating to the representation to the disadvantage of the former client. . . .

RPC 1.9 is stated in the alternative: "an attorney may not proceed if (1) he or she is utilizing confidences to the disadvantage of the former client, **or** (2) the former client's interests are adverse **and** the matter is substantially related." Thus, proof of disclosure of confidential information is not necessary if the matters are substantially related. . . .

The Court finds, and Perkins concedes, that the two matters are substantially related despite the difference in claims. Although the first case involved patent infringement and this case alleges securities fraud, Cell-Pro's reliance on Lyon & Lyon's patent opinions is a central issue in both cases. It is also clear that the interests of Becton and Lyon & Lyon are adverse. The Delaware court has ruled that it will consider either awarding attorneys' fees against Lyon & Lyon or holding Lyon & Lyon jointly and severally liable for fees and costs awarded against CellPro. Thus, Becton has a claim against Lyon & Lyon for fees and costs in the patent litigation based on Lyon & Lyon's misconduct surrounding the issuance of the patent opinion to CellPro. Perkins, as the lawyer for Becton in the patent action, necessarily would have had to take the position that Lyon & Lyon's patent opinion was a sham and that CellPro could not have in good faith relied on that opinion. In the current securities action, Perkins, as counsel for Lyon & Lyon, must necessarily take the position that Lyon & Lyon's opinion was valid and based on a good faith review of the JHU patent. The two matters are substantially related, and Lyon & Lyon's interests in this suit are materially adverse to Becton's interests in the patent litigation.

Perkins acknowledges that the two matters are substantially related and in the usual circumstance RPC 1.9 would prohibit Perkins from representing Lyon & Lyon. Perkins argues, however, that because the partner who handled the Becton patent matter, David Wagoner, left the firm in 1996, disqualification is not required. In so arguing, Perkins relies on RPC 1.10, which provides:

(c) When a lawyer has terminated an association with a firm, the firm is not prohibited from thereafter representing a person with interests materially adverse to those of a client represented by the formerly associated lawyer unless:

(1) The matter is the same or substantially related to that in which the formerly associated lawyer represented the client; **and**

(2) Any lawyer remaining in the firm has acquired confidences and secrets . . . that are material to the matter.

Unlike RPC 1.9, RPC 1.10 does not require disqualification merely because the matters are substantially related. Under RPC 1.10, the firm's disqualification will not be required unless the matters are substantially related **and** remaining lawyers have acquired confidences and secrets.

Perkins argues that no lawyers remaining at the firm have acquired any material confidences or secrets of Becton.

There is a presumption that attorneys who work together share secrets and confidences. This presumption is the basis for RPC 1.10's imputed disqualification provision, which provides that "while lawyers are associated with a firm, none of them shall knowingly represent a client when any one of them practicing alone would be prohibited from doing so." The presumption that lawyers within a firm share confidences is rebuttable, however.

Perkins submits declarations from two attorneys who assisted David Wagoner in the patent litigation, Joseph Bringman and Elizabeth (Betsy) Alaniz. Each states: "I do not now possess, and never have acquired, any secrets or confidences of Becton Dickinson of any type, much less any that would be material to the securities litigation." Perkins argues these declarations are sufficient to rebut the presumption that Mr. Wagoner shared Becton's secrets and confidences with other lawyers at the firm.

Perkins attorney Joseph Bringman billed one half hour of work on the Becton patent matter in June 1992. Betsy Alaniz billed 10.25 hours in April 1994, and 2.4 hours in February and March 1995, on the Becton matter. Perkins argues that Bringman and Alaniz's time on the Becton matter was too minimal to require disqualification under RPC 1.9. Perkins further argues that the limited amount of work performed by these two lawyers demonstrates that they were not exposed to any secrets or confidences of Becton while the patent matter was pending. Finally, Perkins argues that Alaniz performed only ministerial tasks and, therefore, she did not in fact represent Becton on any matters related to the current litigation. Becton counters that the fact that Alaniz and Bringman billed only for a short period of time does not preclude disqualification.

Becton is correct that the amount of time billed on the matter is not dispositive of the disqualification issue. Nevertheless, the extent of a lawyer's involvement in the previous case is a factor to consider in determining both whether that lawyer should be disqualified under RPC 1.9, and whether that lawyer, or any other lawyers remaining at the firm, have acquired secrets or confidences of the former client for purposes of RPC 1.10(c)(2).

According to Bringman's time sheet, his work on the Becton patent matter was limited to reviewing the proposed protective order and having a conference with David Wagoner regarding that protective order. Although Bringman's work was arguably peripheral in light of the limited task he performed and the minimal amount of time billed on the matter, Alaniz's work was more substantial. In her declaration, Alaniz describes her work in the Becton matter as follows:

> [T]he tasks involved coordinating filings related to a motion to transfer the case to Delaware in April 1994, and assisting in 1995 with the issuance of deposition subpoenas for depositions in the Delaware action to be taken locally. To the best of my knowledge, I believe that

my involvement did not extend beyond the rather ministerial involvement described in the time entries, and that I did not thereby, or otherwise, acquire any secrets or confidences of Becton Dickinson.

Although the tasks performed in 1995 appear to be ministerial in nature (i.e., assisting with deposition arrangements and subpoenas), billing records show that Alaniz played a more substantive role in 1994. Alaniz had numerous telephone conferences with Thomas Burt, counsel for co-defendant Baxter International, and Donald Ware, Becton's antitrust counsel in Boston, and she participated in telephone conferences with opposing counsel. She also billed time for a conference with partner David Wagoner on April 15, 1994.

Becton also submits a letter dated April 1, 1994 from David Wagoner to Donald Ware, Becton's Boston counsel, which states:

> As I indicated I am leaving on Sunday to handle an ICC arbitration in Geneva, returning to Seattle probably Friday the 15th of April. In my absence, please refer any matters in the CellPro case to Betsy Alaniz. I have brought her up to date on the status of pending matters.

... Alaniz's time sheets for this period indicate that she had telephone conferences with counsel for Baxter "regarding motion to dismiss, opposition briefing and reply briefing." She also "coordinate[d] the response to CellPro's opposition" and "coordinate[d] filing of opposition briefing." Alaniz billed 3.25 hours on April 14, 1994 for a telephone conference with co-counsel for Becton, and a telephone conference with counsel for Baxter. On the next day she "review[ed] the pleadings" and had a telephone conference with co-counsel for Becton, as well as a conference with David Wagoner.

Perkins argues that the motions to consolidate Washington cases, transfer Washington cases to Delaware, and stay discovery pending transfer involved only procedural matters and, therefore, Alaniz did no substantive work that would have exposed her to Becton confidences and secrets. Under these circumstances, Perkins argues, disqualification would be inappropriate. The Court rejects as without merit Perkins' distinction between "procedural" work and "substantive" work for purposes of determining whether Ms. Alaniz represented Becton in the patent matter. Although the nature of the work done by the lawyer is a factor to consider in determining whether confidences were likely disclosed, there is no basis for concluding that work on "procedural" matters constitutes some lower level of representation than work on "substantive" matters.

The work done by Alaniz on the Becton patent matter was not minimal or peripheral, and the patent matter she worked on was substantially related to this litigation.... Although Alaniz did not spend a large amount of time on the case, it is evident that she was Wagoner's lead associate on the matter and he prepared her to take charge in his absence. This is not peripheral or minimal representation, despite Perkins' characterizations to the contrary.

Alaniz's involvement in the Becton matter was substantial enough that confidential information would normally have been imparted to her. Whether such disclosures were in fact made is not the proper inquiry. . . . Because Alaniz previously represented Becton in the patent matter, she is prohibited under RPC 1.9 from representing Lyon & Lyon in a substantially related matter. Alaniz's disqualification is in turn imputed to the entire firm under RPC 1.10(a).

Even if the Court was to conclude that Alaniz's role in the patent litigation was "minimal," as alleged by Perkins, the Court would still find that Perkins must be disqualified because it has not met its burden under RPC 1.10(c)(2) of proving that no lawyers remaining at Perkins have acquired confidences and secrets of Becton. Although Perkins focuses on the work of only two of its lawyers, the invoices sent to Becton show that Perkins billed Becton for a substantial amount of work on the patent matter. Becton was billed approximately $27,000 for professional legal services in connection with the patent case, and, according to Becton, more than 45 hours of legal services were attributable to Perkins personnel other than Wagoner, Bringman, or Alaniz. . . . There is no evidence in the record indicating who these individuals are and whether any of them were exposed to confidences or secrets of Becton. . . . That there were several other unidentified Perkins employees, whether attorneys or paralegals, who knew of Becton's concerns about Lyon & Lyon's patent opinions demonstrates how difficult it is to determine whether confidential information was in fact disclosed to persons at the firm. Because so many Perkins employees worked on the Becton matter, the declarations of two Perkins lawyers who billed only a fraction of the total time billed on the Becton matter are inadequate to rebut the presumption that confidences were shared. . . .

In determining whether to exercise discretion to disqualify counsel, the court has several obligations. First, it must balance the right of the former client to preserve confidences against a party's right to employ counsel of its own choosing. Second, the court must be mindful that "the interests of the clients are primary, and the interests of the lawyers are secondary." Finally, the Court should resolve any doubts in favor of disqualification. Here, the parties present a bona fide dispute on the conflicts issue, but the Court concludes that the evidence clearly weighs in favor of disqualification. Although disqualification has the immediate adverse effect of depriving Lyon & Lyon of the attorney of its choice, removal is necessary to protect Becton's confidences and to preserve the integrity of the adversary process.

Perkins argues that its client Lyon & Lyon will be severely prejudiced if it is disqualified. However, by letter dated May 20, 1998, Becton promptly gave notice to Perkins of the conflict issue and advised Perkins of its "strong objection" to representation of Lyon & Lyon. Perkins cannot be heard to complain about the time it has spent on this case since it has known almost from the very beginning that Becton objected to Perkins' representation of Lyon & Lyon. . . .

NOTES

1. The first problem in this case is whether, at the time Perkins Coie initiated its representation of Lyon & Lyon, Becton was a current client or a former client. What created the ambiguity about whether the client was a current or a former client? Why do you suppose the firm was not clearer about the nature of the relationship?

2. What is the central concern when considering disqualification based on the prior representation of a materially adverse party in a substantially related matter? Is it preservation of confidential information? Why did the court not require a showing that confidential information was improperly shared?

3. Why did Perkins Coie argue that the lawyer who had handled the matter for Becton had left the firm? Model Rule 1.10(a) imputes disqualification to all lawyers currently associated in a firm. What happens after a lawyer leaves the firm is addressed by Rule 1.10(b), which provides that the disqualification of Rule 1.10(a) continues if any lawyer in the firm still possesses confidential information. Accordingly, Perkins argued that there was none. Why was that argument unsuccessful?

4. Why did Perkins argue that "Alaniz performed only ministerial tasks and, therefore, she did not in fact represent Becton on any matters related to the current litigation"? Perkins was confronted with two distinct problems in the case. First, if any lawyer who had "formerly represented a client" in the matter remained at the firm, that lawyer would be disqualified from representing a materially adverse party in a substantially related matter under Rule 1.9(a), and her disqualification would be imputed to the rest of the firm under Rule 1.10(a). Second, even if no lawyer remained who had actually "represented" Becton in the substantially related matter, the firm would still be precluded from materially adverse representation in a substantially related matter under Rule 1.10(b) if "any lawyer remaining in the firm has information protected by Rules 1.6 and 1.9(c) that is material to the matter." To be permitted to continue its representation of Lyon & Lyon, Perkins had to address both problems. What was the court's conclusion on each issue?

5. In this case, the court concluded that the firm was disqualified based largely on information drawn from the time sheets of junior associate Betsy Alaniz. Do you think it was fair to conclude that Alaniz "represented" Becton, or that she probably was in possession of confidential information about the client? What evidence did the court rely on in reaching its conclusions? Why do you suppose the evidence the court considered looked the way it did? Does that suggest anything to you about how you should record the activities for which you bill time once you are in practice? Might that conflict with other concerns you might have?

3. PROSPECTIVE CLIENTS

Someone who is thinking about hiring a lawyer (we call her a "prospective client") consults an attorney about the possibility of employing the attorney to represent her in a matter. For some reason, the client does not hire the attorney. How should we treat that attorney for purposes of conflict of interest issues?

If we treated the lawyer as though she had represented the prospective client, that would make the prospective client a "former client" for conflict of interest purposes. If the client were a "former client," the consulted lawyer could not represent the opposing party (who would be "materially adverse" to the prospective client) in the same matter. This would impose a significant limit on the other party's ability to hire the counsel of its choice. Moreover, if this were the rule, prospective clients who wanted to game the system might systematically consult the most desirable attorneys with the relevant specialty in a particular geographic area, intentionally manufacturing a conflict that would disqualify the best lawyers from representing the other side. This strategy is not the exclusive province of the high-powered entity client; in *Virginia State Bar Legal Ethics Opinion 1794*, a husband facing a divorce in a small community tried this approach to prevent his wife from obtaining adequate counsel in their divorce proceeding.

In addition, if we treated the client as a former client, the usual rules of imputed disqualification would apply the consulted lawyer's disqualification to the lawyer's entire firm. That would mean that a brief consultation with a prospective client could potentially generate a broad range of disqualifications.

At the same time, if we treated the potential client as imposing no potential future disqualifications on the lawyer—as a sort of "non-client"—that would not adequately protect the confidential information that the lawyer might have learned in the course of her interaction with the prospective client. Communications between a lawyer and a prospective client are protected as both privileged and confidential; any rule that applied to prospective clients would need to respect that person's confidential information.

Model Rule 1.18 offers a solution to this problem. Read the rule carefully. Like many of the rules we have studied, it imposes a default rule, and then creates exceptions to the default rule. The default rule, in Rule 1.18(c), is that the individual lawyer who consulted with the prospective client is disqualified from representing a client materially adverse to the prospective client in the same or a substantially related matter, and that disqualification is imputed to the lawyer's law firm. Does this rule look familiar? Rule 1.18(d) creates an exception to the default rule. What is the exception? May the lawyer who consulted with the prospective client ever represent the materially adverse party in the same or a substantially related matter? May the lawyer's firm? What must the lawyer do to invoke the exception? If you were a lawyer in a firm about to have a meeting with a prospective client, what would you want to do to make sure that the exception in Rule 1.18(d) applied to your situation?

E. IMPUTED DISQUALIFICATION AND MOBILE LAWYERS

Conflicts issues become more complex when we consider that lawyers often practice in firms rather than individually. The default assumption about the treatment of conflicts in the context of lawyers practicing in law firms is embodied in Model Rule 1.10(a). Read Rule 1.10 carefully. What assumptions does it make about how lawyers who work for the same firm interact with each other? Are those assumptions accurate? Is there an alternative to those assumptions?

Conflicts issues would be complex even if lawyers did not change jobs. But they do, all the time. The conflicts rules not only affect the representation of clients, but the mobility and job security of lawyers. What created the conflict in the following case, and how was it resolved? Does that consequence have a significant effect on the mobility of lawyers?

ROBERTS & SCHAEFER CO. v. SAN–CON, INC.

898 F. Supp. 356 (S.D. W. Va. 1995)

GOODWIN, DISTRICT JUDGE.

Pending before the Court is the motion of the defendant San Con, Inc. (San Con) to disqualify Daniel A. Ruley, Jr. and the law firm of Steptoe & Johnson as counsel for the plaintiffs Roberts & Schaefer Company (Roberts & Schaefer) and Mingo Logan Coal Company (Mingo Logan). The Court finds that Mr. Ruley's continued representation of the plaintiffs presents a conflict of interest. The Court therefore concludes that absent a waiver of the conflict of interest by San Con, Mr. Ruley and Steptoe & Johnson are disqualified from continuing to represent the plaintiffs.

I. Background

Roberts & Schaefer hired San Con as a sub-contractor to build a coal storage silo for Mingo Logan. Within a year after San Con completed work on the silo, the silo collapsed. This case addresses liability for that collapse.

After the silo's collapse but before this lawsuit, Mt. Hawley Insurance Company (Mt. Hawley), San Con's insurer, hired the law firm of Steptoe & Johnson to evaluate the dispute. Mt. Hawley forwarded materials relating to San Con's role in the matter to James R. Watson, a partner in Steptoe & Johnson. Mr. Watson's office is in Charleston, West Virginia. Not realizing that Steptoe & Johnson had a conflict of interest because of its ongoing representation of Roberts & Schaefer (not the precise subject of this motion to disqualify),[1] Mr. Watson agreed to review the matter for

---

1. Apparently, Steptoe & Johnson conducted a conflict-of-interest determination, pursuant to the requirements of Rule 1.7 of the West Virginia Rules of Professional Conduct, but failed to

San Con. Mr. Watson performed the requested review and then prepared and forwarded an evaluation letter to San Con and its insurer Mt. Hawley.

Thereafter, Roberts & Schaefer contacted Steptoe & Johnson about representing Roberts & Schaefer in its dispute with San Con over liability for collapse of the silo. Only at this point did Steptoe & Johnson discover the original conflict of interest that should have precluded Steptoe & Johnson from representing San Con in the first place. Mr. Watson and Steptoe & Johnson then withdrew from their representation of San Con. Steptoe & Johnson likewise declined to represent Roberts & Schaefer and Mingo Logan because of Mr. Watson's former representation of San Con in this precise matter.

Shortly after Steptoe & Johnson's withdrawal, San Con retained its current counsel Pietragallo, Bosick & Gordon. Roberts & Schaefer hired Daniel A. Ruley, Jr., then a partner in the Parkersburg, West Virginia law firm of Ruley & Everett. Mr. Ruley filed this lawsuit on the plaintiffs' behalf. In May 1995, the law firms of Steptoe & Johnson and Ruley & Everett merged. The merger announcement stated in pertinent part:

> The law firms of Steptoe & Johnson of Clarksburg, Charleston, Morgantown, Martinsburg, Charles Town, Wheeling, West Virginia and Hagerstown, Maryland and Ruley & Everett of Parkersburg, West Virginia are pleased to announce the merger of their practices under the name of Steptoe & Johnson.

A list of all the attorneys in the newly merged firm, including the name of Daniel A. Ruley, Jr., accompanied the announcement.

Before the formal merger announcement, Steptoe & Johnson, apparently believing that it otherwise would have to withdraw, wrote to San Con and its insurer Mt. Hawley requesting "a waiver of any conflict of interest in Ruley's continued employment" as counsel for the plaintiffs in this lawsuit. Before receiving a response, Steptoe & Johnson and Ruley & Everett merged. Shortly afterward, San Con declined to waive the conflict and requested that the plaintiffs obtain other counsel. Mr. Ruley and Steptoe & Johnson did not step aside. Instead, in an effort to turn two "wrongs" into a "right," they filed a motion to determine that Mr. Ruley was not disqualified from continuing to represent the plaintiffs.

... San Con has filed a motion to disqualify Mr. Ruley and Steptoe & Johnson from representing the plaintiffs. Thus the issue of disqualification is properly before the Court.

San Con bases its motion to disqualify Mr. Ruley and Steptoe & Johnson on the plain language of W.Va.R.Prof.Conduct 1.9 and 1.10. Mr. Ruley and Steptoe & Johnson argue, however, that their "of counsel" relationship makes W.Va.R.Prof.Conduct 1.10 inapplicable. Alternatively, Mr. Ruley and Steptoe & Johnson argue that the Court should not strictly apply those rules in this case, but instead should permit them to continue to

---

discover the conflict because Steptoe & Johnson previously had listed Roberts & Schaefer under the name of its parent company, Jupiter Industries, Inc.

represent the plaintiffs because they have set up a "Chinese wall" around Mr. Watson and the information gained from San Con and its insurer Mt. Hawley. In an affidavit, Robert M. Steptoe, managing partner of Steptoe & Johnson, states that he advised Mr. Watson and Mr. Ruley not to discuss this litigation and instructed Mr. Watson to place his entire file in a safety deposit box and to delete all related documents from Steptoe & Johnson's computers and word processing equipment. Mr. Ruley and Steptoe & Johnson believe that these safeguards should be sufficient to protect any confidential information from San Con, while permitting Mr. Ruley to continue to represent the plaintiffs.

II. Discussion

... In reviewing San Con's motion to disqualify Mr. Ruley and Steptoe & Johnson, the Court is guided by the principle that motions to disqualify counsel should be viewed with extreme caution because of their potential as a method of harassment. On the other hand, disqualification is appropriate when representation of a client will result in the violation of the Rules of Professional Conduct or other law.

A.

The plaintiffs concede that Mr. Watson, the Steptoe & Johnson attorney who originally reviewed the case for San Con, now is disqualified from representing the plaintiffs in this litigation by W.Va.R.Prof.Conduct 1.9. Rule 1.9 provides in relevant part:

> A lawyer who has formerly represented a client in a matter shall not thereafter:
>
> > (a) represent another person in the same or substantially related matter in which that person's interests are materially adverse to the interests of the former client unless the former client consents after consultation....

Mr. Watson has represented San Con in the precise matter that is the subject of this litigation, and the plaintiffs' interests are materially adverse to the interests of San Con. Watson therefore cannot represent the plaintiffs in this litigation regardless of "whether confidences were in fact imparted to [Mr. Watson] by [San Con or Mt. Hawley]" in the prior representation.

B.

Despite conceding that Mr. Watson cannot represent them in this litigation, the plaintiffs argue that there is no conflict of interest because Mr. Ruley will be of counsel, not a partner, associate, or employee of Steptoe & Johnson. According to Mr. Ruley, "of counsel" status makes him an independent contractor to Steptoe & Johnson and the imputed disqualification rule inapplicable. On the record before the Court, this argument appears to be little more than a post hoc effort to deal with the conflict of interest caused by the merger of Steptoe & Johnson and Ruley & Everett.

The merger announcement clearly lists Mr. Ruley as an attorney at Steptoe & Johnson. The comment to Rule 1.10 states: "[I]f [two practitioners] present themselves to the public in a way suggesting that they are a firm or conduct themselves as a firm, they should be regarded as a firm for purposes of the Rules." Once the merger occurred and Steptoe & Johnson and Ruley & Everett held themselves out as one firm with Mr. Ruley as an attorney in that firm, it was too late for the parties to recharacterize their relationship.

Furthermore, even if Mr. Ruley characterizes himself as "of counsel" to Steptoe & Johnson, such an arrangement would be insufficient to avoid having Steptoe & Johnson's conflicts imputed to Mr. Ruley. Rule 1.10 applies to lawyers who are "associated" in a firm. *Black's Law Dictionary* defines "association" as "the act of a number of persons in uniting together for some special purpose or business." Assuming that Mr. Ruley and Steptoe & Johnson intended to create an "of counsel" relationship, such was a combining for a special purpose and thus qualifies as an association within the meaning of Rule 1.10.

C.

The plaintiffs also argue that the Court should not impute Mr. Watson's disqualification to Mr. Ruley and Steptoe & Johnson. W.Va.R.Prof.Conduct 1.10, which addresses imputed disqualification of law firms, provides in relevant part:

> (a) While lawyers are associated in a firm, none of them shall knowingly represent a client when any one of them practicing alone would be prohibited from doing so by Rules 1.7, 1.8(c), 1.9 or 2.2.

> (b) When a lawyer becomes associated with a firm, the firm may not knowingly represent a person in the same or a substantially related matter in which that lawyer, or a firm with which the lawyer was associated, had previously represented a client whose interests are materially adverse to that person and about whom the lawyer had acquired information protected by Rules 1.6 and 1.9(b) that is material to the matter.

The plain language of both Rule 1.10(a) and 1.10(b) clearly preclude Mr. Ruley and Steptoe & Johnson from continuing to represent the plaintiffs. The plaintiffs do not dispute that San Con is a former client within the meaning of Rule 1.9. The plaintiffs similarly do not dispute that during his representation of San Con, Mr.Watson acquired confidential information protected by Rules 1.6 and 1.9(b), that the representation was in the same or a substantially related matter, or that San Con's interests are materially adverse to the plaintiffs' interests.

Rather, the plaintiffs argue that the provisions of Rule 1.10 are not as absolute as they first would appear. The plaintiffs cite the comments to Rule 1.10, the language of other provisions in the Rules, and case law, as well as a trend to liberalize the rules of imputed disqualification as support for their proposition. The Court finds none of these arguments persuasive.

1.

The comment to W.Va.R.Prof.Conduct 1.10 states in pertinent part:

> When lawyers have been associated in a firm but then end their association ... the problem is more complicated. The fiction that the law firm is the same as a single lawyer is no longer wholly realistic. There are several competing considerations. First, the client previously represented must be reasonably assured that the principle of loyalty to the client is not compromised. Second, the rule of disqualification should not be so broadly cast as to preclude other persons from having reasonable choice of legal counsel. Third, the rule of disqualification should not unreasonably hamper lawyers from forming new associations and taking on new clients after having left a previous association....
>
> A rule based on a functional analysis is more appropriate [than per se rules of disqualification or the "appearance of impropriety" standard] for determining the questions of vicarious disqualification.

The plaintiffs read this language as requiring the Court to conduct a functional analysis of the competing interests involved separate and apart from Rule 1.10 to determine whether screening procedures would be appropriate. The plaintiffs miss the point. Rule 1.10 is "[a] rule based on a functional analysis" and incorporates the competing interests within its language. As far as Rule 1.10(b) is concerned, for example, the balance of competing interests tips in favor of disqualification when a member of the firm has acquired confidential information from the former client, the representation is in the same or a substantially related matter, and the interests of the former client are materially adverse to those of the new client; otherwise, the balance tips against disqualification.

2.

The plaintiffs also point to W.Va.R.Prof.Conduct 1.11(b), which permits law firms to set up screening procedures around former government attorneys with confidential government information, as support for their assertion that screening procedures would be appropriate in this case. But Rule 1.11(b) merely illustrates that a functional approach to conflicts of interest may lead to different rules in different contexts. As the Second Circuit [has] explained:

> [Disapproval of screening procedures] may hamper the government's efforts to hire qualified attorneys; the latter may fear that government service will transform them into legal "Typhoid Marys," shunned by prospective private employers because hiring them may result in the disqualification of an entire firm in a possibly wide range of cases.

Because of the differences between government-to-private-firm moves and private-firm-to-private-firm moves, the West Virginia Supreme Court of Appeals and the drafters of the Model Rules adopted different rules for these different types of moves. The fact that they chose to do so weakens, rather than strengthens, the plaintiffs' argument.

3.

The plaintiffs rely on *INA Underwriters Ins. Co. v. Rubin*, 635 F.Supp. 1 (E.D.Penn.1983), and *Nemours Foundation v. Gilbane*, 632 F.Supp. 418 (D.Del.1986), as support for their argument that screening is permissible in the private-firm-to-private-firm context. The Court agrees that *Rubin* and *Nemours*, although distinguishable, can be read as support for the plaintiffs' argument. The Court, however, notes that the majority of courts considering this issue have rejected the approach taken by the *Rubin* and *Nemours* courts.

In *Rubin*, the conflict of interest arose because an attorney for the firm that represented the plaintiff previously had met with the defendant in a prospective client interview. In that interview, the defendant provided the attorney with confidential information substantially related to the litigation. The *Rubin* court, in concluding that screening was appropriate, relied primarily on the fact that the attorney had never represented or attempted to represent the plaintiff as a client. The *Rubin* court's approach, although decided under the Code of Professional Responsibility, is consistent with the letter, although possibly not the spirit, of W.Va.R.Prof.Conduct 1.9 and 1.10 because these rules apply to "clients" and "former clients." The defendant in *Rubin* was neither.

In *Nemours*, an attorney who worked in a minor role as counsel for the plaintiff, went to work for the firm representing the defendants. The district court in *Nemours* conducted a functional analysis separate and apart from Delaware's Rules of Professional Conduct. The facts in *Nemours* are distinguishable from this case because the attorney's role in *Nemours* had been minor (i.e., "the duties which typically characterize the life of a young associate"), he only worked on the case over a four month period, and he had no recollection of any confidential information. In this case, by contrast, Mr. Watson's role as primary evaluator of San Con's case appears far more significant. Additionally, the *Nemours* court implied that the plaintiff's motive in raising this issue five months after the attorney's move was harassment. The Court does not question San Con's motives in this case. Despite being able to distinguish *Nemours* and *Rubin*, the Court, as explained below, must note its discomfort with those courts' decisions to sacrifice ethical standards for the sake of expediency.

4.

The Court recognizes that there is a trend to liberalize the rules governing imputed disqualification of law firms when a lawyer associated with that firm would be prohibited from representing the client. W.Va.R.Prof.Conduct 1.11 (former government attorneys) and 1.12 (former judges, arbitrators, and law clerks) illustrate well this trend, as does Tentative Draft No. 4 of the proposed *Restatement of the Law Governing Lawyers*. Section 204 of the proposed *Restatement* provides in relevant part:

> The restrictions upon an affiliated lawyer ... do not restrict that lawyer when: ...
>
> > (2) The restriction is of representation adverse to a former client ... and there is no reasonable prospect that confidential information of the former client will be used with material adverse effect on the former client because:
> >
> > > (a) The confidential client information communicated to the personally-prohibited lawyer is not likely to be significant in the later case;
> > >
> > > (b) Adequate screening measures are in effect to eliminate involvement by the personally-prohibited lawyer in the representation; and
> > >
> > > (c) Timely and adequate notice of the screening has been provided to all affected clients....

In this case, however, even the proposed *Restatement* rule would not permit Mr. Ruley to continue to represent the plaintiffs because Mr. Watson and Steptoe & Johnson, in attempting to create a Chinese wall around Mr. Watson, apparently believe that Mr. Watson has confidential information bearing on the central issues in this case.

Even so, the Court is troubled by the trend to dispose of centuries-old confidentiality rules solely for the convenience of modern lawyers who "move from one association to another several times in their careers." Lawyers and law firms are more than mere business entities.... In an age of sagging public confidence in our legal system, maintaining confidence in that system and in the legal profession is of the utmost importance. In this regard, courts should be reluctant to sacrifice the interests of clients and former clients for the perceived business interest of lawyers, especially when the state supreme court, in promulgating the Rules of Professional Conduct, has failed to adopt contrary rules. While these considerations may dampen law firm mergers, such is the price that lawyers must pay for their special status in our society....

The firms clearly recognized the obvious conflict of interest involved in this case—Steptoe and Johnson when it originally declined to represent the plaintiffs and Mr. Ruley when he wrote to San Con and Mt. Hawley asking for their consent to his continued representation of the plaintiffs. The problem in this case is that the firms apparently did not discover the conflict of interest involved until shortly before their official merger date. As a result, they were left in an awkward position when San Con refused the consent to Mr. Ruley's continued representation of the plaintiffs. Lawyers and law firms must consider and address the effects of mergers and new associations on their clients well in advance of when such events occur.

D.

The Court notes the concerns of Mr. Ruley and Steptoe & Johnson that their professional integrity and ability to guard client confidences are being called into question by the disqualification motion. . . .

This Court certainly does not question the integrity of Mr. Ruley and the other Steptoe & Johnson attorneys involved in this case nor their assurances that San Con's confidences will remain confidential. This Court also understands the sensitivity of lawyers who perceive that opposing counsel is questioning their personal integrity and ability to guard client confidences.

Nevertheless, lawyers must avoid responding to such motions with personal attacks. In their response to San Con's motion to disqualify Mr. Ruley and Steptoe & Johnson, the plaintiffs wrote:

> It appears that what San Con really intends to communicate darkly . . . is insinuation and innuendo to the effect that Steptoe & Johnson in general and Bob Steptoe, Jim Watson and Dan Ruley in particular lack sufficient integrity to not breach the confidences communicated between San Con and Watson and to suggest otherwise is naive. *It is fair to add that the experience of the undersigned has been that people who throw such insinuation or innuendo at others sometimes have personal familiarity with it.* (Emphasis added.)

West Virginia's Code of Professional Courtesy states: "While my duty is to zealously represent my client, I will treat opposing counsel with courtesy and respect. I will refrain from unnecessary or unjustified criticism of the Court, my adversary or my adversary's client." The comment to W.Va.R.Prof.Conduct 3.5 provides that "[r]efraining from abusive or obstreperous conduct is a corollary of the advocate's right to speak on behalf of litigants." The Court believes that the above statement crossed the line between zealous representation and unnecessary ad hominem personal attack and thus has no place in a litigant's brief. . . .

III. Conclusion

For the foregoing reasons, the Court GRANTS San Con's motion to disqualify Daniel A. Ruley, Jr. and Steptoe & Johnson from continued representation of the plaintiffs in this action.

NOTES

1. Who had the conflict that precluded the firm's representation of Roberts & Schaefer? When considering whether a conflict will be imputed to the rest of the firm, your analysis should always start with the lawyer who is most likely to have a conflict. Under Model Rule 1.10(a), what happens if any lawyer in the firm has a Rule 1.7 or Rule 1.9 conflict? There is an exception for prohibitions "based on a personal interest of the prohibited lawyer." What do you suppose that means? See Comment [3] to Rule 1.10, and Comments [10] and [11] to Rule 1.7. Rule 1.10 does not include an imputation rule for

conflicts that arise under Rule 1.8. Why not? See Rule 1.8(k) and Comment [20] to Rule 1.8. Which prohibition under Rule 1.8 is not imputed to the lawyer's law firm? Why not?

2.   Sometimes, conflicts are created when lawyers move; in this case, the conflict was created by a law firm merger. Conflicts can also be created through changes in the structure of an entity client; these are sometimes called "thrust-upon conflicts."

3.   As the case suggests, the representation that Steptoe & Johnson originally undertook also involved a conflict of interest. How was it that Steptoe & Johnson failed to recognize this? This is not the first case you have read which involved a messy disqualification issue that arose because of a large firm's failure to conduct adequate conflicts checking as part of a law firm merger; this was also the problem in *Andrew Corp. v. Beverly Manufacturing Co.*, *supra*. What do you suppose a large law firm needs to do in order to ensure that it is not making this kind of mistake?

4.   The firm in this case proposed to erect a "Chinese wall" between the two representations. That's an old-fashioned phrase; these days what the law firm proposed is usually described as "screening." Model Rule 1.10 does not permit screening as a solution to the problem of imputed disqualification. There are, however, other places in the rules where screening is recognized as a solution to the imputed disqualification problem. Consider Rule 1.18 and Rule 1.11. Under what circumstances do these rules recognize screening as a legitimate alternative to disqualification of an entire firm? What are the policy justifications behind the decision to permit screening in those circumstances but not in Rule 1.10? Do you think those justifications are adequate to support the rejection of screening in ordinary cases of imputed disqualification?

There have been several proposals to amend the Model Rules to permit screening in an increased range of circumstances, but those proposals have up until now been unsuccessful. In some jurisdictions, however, limited screening has replaced imputed disqualification. Consider, for example, Utah Rules of Professional Conduct 1.10, revised in 2005:

UTAH RULE OF PROF. CONDUCT 1.10.   IMPUTATION OF CONFLICTS OF INTEREST: GENERAL RULE

(a) While lawyers are associated in a firm, none of them shall knowingly represent a client when any one of them practicing alone would be prohibited from doing so by Rules 1.7 or 1.9, unless the prohibition is based on a personal interest of the prohibited lawyer and does not present a significant risk of materially limiting the representation of the client by the remaining lawyers in the firm.

(b) When a lawyer has terminated an association with a firm, the firm is not prohibited from thereafter representing a person with interests materially adverse to those of a client represented by the formerly associated lawyer and not currently represented by the firm, unless:

(1) the matter is the same or substantially related to that in which the formerly associated lawyer represented the client; and

(2) any lawyer remaining in the firm has information protected by Rules 1.6 and 1.9(c) that is material to the matter.

(c) When a lawyer becomes associated with a firm, no lawyer associated in the firm shall knowingly represent a person in a matter in which that lawyer is disqualified under Rule 1.9 unless:

(1) the personally disqualified lawyer is timely screened from any participation in the matter and is apportioned no part of the fee therefrom, and

(2) written notice is promptly given to any affected former client.

(d) A disqualification prescribed by this Rule may be waived by the affected client under the conditions stated in Rule 1.7.

(e) The disqualification of lawyers associated in a firm with former or current government lawyers is governed by Rule 1.11.

NOTES

1. What is the difference between the Utah rule and the Model Rule? What do you suppose is the justification for this difference? Is this a sensible outcome?

2. The ethics rules consider the problem of lawyer mobility and address it in a range of rules that are not intuitively obvious. There are two sets of concerns. The first is what happens to a firm's conflicts of interest if the lawyer whose work created the conflict departs. This issue is addressed by Rule 1.10(b), which addresses whether the departure of the lawyer removes the conflict on the part of the firm. This was the issue in the *Oxford Systems* case, *supra*. The second concern is whether a lawyer who has a conflict of interest when working at firm A carries that conflict with her when she moves to firm B. This issue is governed by Rule 1.9(b).

The nature of these rules has a significant impact on lawyer mobility. This may not be intuitively obvious, but consider the following rule, which was DR 5–108 of Nebraska's Code of Professional Responsibility until 2005:

FORMER NEBRASKA DR 5–108. LAWYERS— CONFLICT OF INTEREST

(A) A lawyer who has personally represented a former client in a matter shall not thereafter represent a current client in the same or a substantially related matter in which the current client's interests are materially adverse to the interests of the former client unless the former client consents after consultation.

(B) When a former client is represented by a lawyer's firm but not personally by the lawyer and the lawyer leaves the firm, the lawyer shall not represent a client whose interests are materially adverse to the former client in the same or a substantially related matter in which the firm with which the lawyer formerly was associated had previously represented the former client, unless the former client consents after consultation.

(C) When a lawyer has terminated an association with a firm, that firm is prohibited from thereafter representing a client with interests adverse to those of a former client personally represented by the formerly associated lawyer, unless the matter is not the same or substantially related to that in which the formerly associated lawyer represented the former client, or unless the former client consents to such representation.

NOTE

What do you suppose this rule meant for lawyer mobility in Nebraska? Might it have had an impact on attorney salaries in the state? As a junior lawyer contemplating your first job, what concerns would you have about making your choice of employer in a state with this disqualification rule?

PROBLEMS

1. Zonen, a prosecutor, prosecuted several individuals responsible for the kidnapping and murder of a 15-year-old boy. Hollywood, the alleged ringleader, fled and became a fugitive. A film director and screenwriter approached Zonen and asked him to help write a screenplay about the murder. Zonen did so, but was not compensated. Two years later Hollywood was apprehended. Did Zonen have a conflict of interest that prevented him from serving as the prosecutor in Hollywood's case? *See Hollywood v. Superior Court*, 182 P.3d 590 (Cal. 2008); Model Rule 1.8(d); *see also Haraguchi v. Superior Court*, 182 P.3d 579 (Cal. 2008).

2. Lawyer agreed to bring a personal injury claim on behalf of Client. Lawyer was not diligent and failed to bring the claim within the statute of limitations period. What was Lawyer's obligation at this point? Would it make a difference if Lawyer's malpractice insurer insisted that Lawyer keep silent about the error? *See N.Y. State Bar Ass'n Comm. on Prof'l Ethics Op. 734* (2000).

3. Lawyer worked for Law Firm. In addition, he was a member of the City Council. Client, a local business owner, asked Law Firm to represent him in a lawsuit against City. Client claimed that he was injured by a city police officer and that when he complained City retaliated against him by restricting his business permit. May Lawyer represent Client in suing City? May another lawyer at Law Firm do so? *See Shannon v. City of Sioux City*, No. C07–4028–MWB (N.D. Iowa May 16, 2007).

4. Lawyer was appointed by Insurer to represent Insured, whose son injured a neighbor. While the company's claims adjuster believed the act to be unintentional (and therefore covered by Insured's policy), Lawyer obtained confidential medical records from Insured from which he concluded that the son acted intentionally. Lawyer informed Insurer of this information. Has

Lawyer behaved appropriately? *See Parsons v. Continental Nat'l American Group*, 550 P.2d 94 (Ariz. 1976).

5. A law firm may hesitate to undertake representation of a client if the firm fears that, in the future, the representation will create a conflict that will require the firm to decline other lucrative work. May the firm condition its agreement to the representation on the client's signing an "advance waiver" of conflicts—in effect, agreeing in advance that if a future conflict arises, the client will consent to the representation notwithstanding the conflict? What factors might be relevant in answering this question? *See Association of the Bar of the City of New York Comm. on Prof'l and Judicial Ethics Formal Op. 2006–1 (2/17/06)*; *ABA Formal Op. 05–436*; *D.C. Bar Legal Ethics Comm. Op. 309*.

6. Lawyer agreed to represent 154 individual plaintiffs, franchisees, in a lawsuit against their franchisor. The retainer agreements signed by each plaintiff provided that the matter would be settled if a majority of the individual plaintiffs voted to accept a settlement offer. A settlement was negotiated; a majority of the plaintiffs approved it, but 18 of the plaintiffs did not. The defendants sought to enforce the settlement against all the plaintiffs, including the 18 objectors. Is the settlement enforceable? Did Lawyer act properly? *See Tax Authority, Inc. v. Jackson Hewitt, Inc.*, 898 A.2d 512 (N.J. 2006); Model Rule 1.8(g); *ABA Formal Op. 06–438* (2006).

7. Lawyer was employed as an assistant county prosecutor responsible for juvenile prosecutions. After three years of this work, she was hired as the director of the Youth Law Center, a nonprofit organization that employed attorneys as *guardians ad litem* in juvenile cases in the same county. Lawyer acted as guardian ad litem—advocating for the best interest of the child—in two cases in which she had previously been involved as a prosecutor. Has Lawyer acted properly? *See Iowa Supreme Court Attorney Disciplinary Board v. Johnson*, 728 N.W.2d 199 (Iowa 2007); Model Rule 1.11(a)(2).

8. Daniel consulted Flatt, an attorney, about a ruling in his divorce case concerning the ownership of his business. Prior to the divorce, Daniel had hired Hinkle, an attorney, to structure the acquisition of his business. After reviewing documents Daniel provided, Flatt told Daniel that Hinkle had not structured the acquisition competently and that Daniel could sue Hinkle for malpractice. A week later Flatt told Daniel she could not represent him in the malpractice case because of a conflict of interest—her firm represented Hinkle's firm in an unrelated matter. Flatt did not advise Daniel of the statute of limitations or the need to act promptly. Daniel did not consult another attorney for a year and a half. Subsequently, Daniel, represented by new counsel, sued both Hinkle and Flatt, arguing that if his claim against Hinkle was time-barred, Flatt was responsible. Is Flatt liable to Daniel? *See Flatt v. Superior Court*, 885 P.2d 950 (Cal. 1994).

9. Martinez contacted attorney Buchanan about representing Morante, who was charged with selling methamphetamine that Martinez had provided. Buchanan met with Morante, his parents, and Martinez and Martinez's wife, all together. Mrs. Martinez paid Buchanan $25,000 in cash for the representation of Morante, by far the most Buchanan had ever received in a case. Buchanan told Morante his options were "either plead guilty or go to trial."

Morante had previously had another lawyer, to whom Morante had expressed an interest in cooperating with the government, but Buchanan never asked Morante if he wanted to cooperate. Has Buchanan behaved properly? *See In re Buchanan*, 2007 WL 3287353 (N.D. Tex. 2007).

10. Firm was hired by Insurer to represent Cab Co. in a tort action brought by Plaintiff. Firm represented Cab Co. but was replaced by different counsel before trial. The case settled during trial for more than the policy limit; Cab Co. had to contribute a substantial amount to the settlement. Subsequently, Cab Co. sued Insurer, claiming bad faith refusal to settle Plaintiff's case for policy limits. Can Firm represent Cab Co. in its bad faith suit against Insurer? *See Nevada Yellow Cab Corp. v. Eighth Judicial District Court*, 152 P.3d 737 (Nev. 2007).

11. Law Firm represented Client, a music distribution company, in negotiations with the Department of Justice about whether, in prior copyright litigation, Client had improperly withheld documents and engaged in deceptive conduct. Subsequently, Client sued Startup, a social networking site, claiming that Startup enabled others to infringe Client's copyrights. Startup retained Law Firm to defend it in the suit. Can Client seek to disqualify Law Firm? Would it make a difference if, at the time Law Firm undertook the representation of Client, Client had agreed to waive any future conflicts of interest arising out of the representation? *See UMG Recordings, Inc. v. MySpace, Inc.*, 526 F. Supp. 2d 1046 (C.D. Cal. 2007).

12. Herzog prepared documents for Damron to sell his business to Wheatley. The deal included a Stock Purchase Agreement under which Wheatley would make periodic payments to Damron. The transaction was completed. Nine years later, Wheatley consulted Herzog about his obligations under the Stock Purchase Agreement. Herzog advised Wheatley to stop making the required payments because Damron had not complied with his obligations under the Agreement. Did Herzog act properly? If not, what remedy can Damron seek? *See Damron v. Herzog*, 67 F.3d 211 (9th Cir. 1995).

13. Lawyer represented Taylor in a bankruptcy matter; as part of the representation, Taylor provided Lawyer with information about his finances on an intake form. Lawyer never filed the bankruptcy petition. One year later, Lawyer represented Brookins, Taylor's girlfriend, in a paternity action against Taylor. The petition sought custody and child support. Did Lawyer behave properly? *See In re Balocca*, 151 P.3d 154 (Or. 2007).

14. Law Firm employed Associate two days per week. The rest of the time Associate had her own solo practice. Buyer asked Associate, in her role as a sole practitioner, to represent him in acquiring some real estate from Seller. Seller asked Law Firm to represent it in the same transaction. May Associate represent Buyer? *See N.Y. State Bar Ass'n Comm. on Prof. Ethics Op. 807 (1/29/07)*.

15. Hospital terminated Doctor's privileges and Doctor brought suit. One of the reasons Hospital claimed it terminated Doctor's privileges was that Doctor did not report to Hospital that he had been sued by Patient. Doctor claimed that he did not report the suit on the advice of his lawyer, Borum. Hospital's lawyer is Stewart, who was Borum's partner during the pendency of Patient's suit against Doctor. Stewart left Borum's firm three months after Patient's

case settled. Should Stewart be disqualified from representing Hospital? *See In re Basco*, 221 S.W.3d 637 (Tex. 2007).

16. Client hired Lawyer to represent her in a discrimination suit against her former employer, Fox. Client claimed that she had been fired for taking too much pregnancy leave, while Fox claimed that a project on which she had provided legal advice did not go well. Fox moved to disqualify Lawyer on the ground that Lawyer had previously been associated with a firm that represented Fox on intellectual property issues. Should Lawyer be disqualified from representing Client? *See Fox Searchlight Pictures, Inc. v. Paladino*, 89 Cal. App. 4th 294 (Cal. Dist. Ct. App. 2001).

17. Wife was browsing the Internet for a potential divorce lawyer and came upon Law Firm's web site. The site provided a form which enabled an inquirer to send a question to Law Firm. Wife typed in her contact information, and then explained that she was interested in a divorce. She indicated that she was contemplating being re-certified as a teacher in order to return to full-time work, stated that she wanted sole custody of her child, and mentioned that she was concerned that Husband would find out about an extra-marital affair she had had which he appeared not to know about. She concluded, "I like your web site and would like you to represent me." Immediately below the box was a list of "Terms," which included the statement, "I agree that I am not forming an attorney-client relationship by submitting this question. I also understand that I am not forming a confidential relationship." Wife had to click a box agreeing to the "Terms" in order to submit her question. She did so. It turned out that Law Firm was already representing Husband in the divorce proceeding. Should Law Firm be disqualified? *See State Bar of California Standing Committee on Professional Responsibility and Conduct Formal Op. No. 2005–168.*

18. Client asked Lawyer to represent Client in Client's suit against Company. Lawyer had previously defended Company in a different case involving some of the same facts as Client's suit. Lawyer declined to represent Client at trial. Some time later, Client once again asked Lawyer to represent Client in the matter involving Company. Can Lawyer represent Client if Lawyer restricts her representation to preparing a certiorari petition for Client on a narrow and purely legal issue of federal appellate jurisdiction in the case, and refuses to be involved in any dispute involving factual issues between Client and Company? *See D.C. Ethics Op. 343*; Model Rule 1.2(c).

19. Lawyer Flyght worked at the DeWitt firm. He was retained by a group of physicians, including Danforth, to assist them in creating a corporate entity that would purchase and operate an MRI machine. Flyght did so, incorporating MRI Associates, Inc. Danforth became president of MRI Associates, Inc. and Flyght continued to represent the entity. Lawyer Farnsworth also worked at the DeWitt firm. Jesse hired Farnsworth to bring suit against Danforth for medical malpractice. Danforth sought to disqualify Farnsworth and the DeWitt firm from representing Jesse in his suit against Danforth. What result? *See Jesse v. Danforth*, 485 N.W.2d 63 (Wis. 1992).

20. Cole was a school principal. She claimed she was discharged from her administrative position because of her gender and brought suit against the school district. The district hired the law firm of Simons Cuddy & Friedman

to represent it. Cole moved to disqualify the firm, arguing that because she had consulted with the firm about the dismissal of several employees while she was principal, she had an attorney-client relationship with the firm. Should she prevail? *See Cole v. Ruidoso Municipal Schools*, 43 F.3d 1373 (10th Cir. 1994).

21.   Passante represented Upper Deck, a start-up business that sought to place holograms on baseball cards to prevent counterfeiting. The business was in desperate need of cash, and Passante offered to arrange a loan of $100,000 from the brother of his law partner. In gratitude, the directors of the company accepted the loan and agreed that Passante should be given three percent of the company's stock. Upper Deck later became a highly profitable company and sought to renege on its promise of stock to Passante. Can Passante enforce the arrangement? *See Passante v. McWilliam*, 53 Cal.App.4th 1240 (Cal. Dist. Ct. App. 1997).

CHAPTER 9

FEES AND FIDUCIARY OBLIGATIONS

■ ■ ■

A. FEES

Many lawyers bill fees for paying clients. Are there any legal or ethical constraints on fee arrangements? At one extreme, we could treat fee arrangements as simple contracts, and permit lawyers to charge whatever fees they could get willing clients to pay. At the other extreme, we could treat all fee arrangements as business transactions with clients and subject them to the stringent constraints of Model Rule 1.8(a), which requires not just procedural but substantive fairness to the client. As you will see, the rules apply neither of these extremes. Comment [1] to Model Rule 1.8 makes clear that Model Rule 1.8(a) does not apply to "ordinary fee arrangements between client and lawyer," though there are some situations—where the lawyer "accepts an interest in the client's business or other nonmonetary property as payment of all or part of a fee," or, in some jurisdictions, where the lawyer seeks to renegotiate the fee arrangement partway through the representation—in which Model Rule 1.8 will apply. But Model Rule 1.5 imposes some substantive constraints on the fee that even a willing client can be required to pay.

How do lawyers ordinarily charge fees? There are a range of possibilities and some new and novel approaches developing in the current market for legal services.

1. HOURLY FEES

Many lawyers bill fees on an hourly basis. The lawyer charges a fee per hour of work; the fee for the work is determined by multiplying the number of hours worked by the lawyer times the hourly fee. This is how many major law firms bill their clients.

Are there problems with hourly billing? What do you suppose clients like about hourly fees? What about this method of being charged for legal services might cause them concern? Are there inherent incentives for lawyers in an hourly billing environment to act in ways that are contrary to the interest of the client? One empirical study suggests that class action cases tend to settle more quickly in courts that usually award attorneys' fees as a percentage of settlements, while the cases settle more slowly if they are pending before judges who use the time spent by the lawyer as the basis for assessing fees.[1] What, if anything, does this suggest about the impact hourly billing might have on attorney behavior? Are there ways to police the concerns clients might have about hourly billing? One prominent commentator says that hourly billing in six-minute increments "has placed virtually every lawyer in America in a position in which he or she is guilty of multiple mini-frauds every day," Lawrence J. Fox, 17 *The Professional Lawyer* No. 3, and that the emphasis on hourly billing and on hourly expectations and minimums has a "distortive effect" on the way in which lawyers account for their time. Do you agree?

As you might imagine, hourly fees require a method for keeping track of attorney time so that it can ultimately be billed to the client. The maintenance of time records is an essential element of practice in such environments, though most lawyers, regardless of fee structure, keep track of what they are doing with their time. Do you think lawyers are honest about their billing? Why or why not?

One factor that might be relevant to this question is what employers expect of lawyers with regard to billable hours. The billable hour expectations for lawyers at most major law firms have increased significantly in recent decades. According to one author, "Thirty years ago, most partners billed between 1200 and 1400 hours per year and most associates between 1400 and 1600 hours. . . . Today, many firms would consider these ranges acceptable only for partners or associates who had died midway through the year." Patrick J. Schiltz, *On Being a Happy, Healthy, and Ethical Member of an Unhappy, Unhealthy and Unethical Profession*, 52 Vanderbilt L. Rev. 871, 891 (1999). In 2004, associates in the American Lawyer's annual survey billed an average of 2072 hours, and "reports of 2,300 or 2,400 hours were plentiful." Amy Kolz, *Don't Call Them Slackers*, American Lawyer, Oct. 2005, at 114. This may not sound like very many hours, but consider how many hours a lawyer must spend in the office in order to bill eight or ten legitimate hours a day, and you may begin to understand why billable hour requirements are a major concern of junior lawyers. Might high billable hour expectations heighten your concern about billing behaviors?

Several perennial issues arise with hourly billing. One is the problem of working for two clients at once. Suppose you are flying to Los Angeles for a meeting for Client X, and while you're on the plane you are working on a memo to Client Y. Can you bill the time on the plane to both Client X and Client Y? (Most authorities say no; *see, e.g., ABA Formal Opinion 93–379.*)

Another is the billing increment. What unit of time is used for billing time to a client? Different firms with different software might have

---

1. *See* Eric Helland & Jonathan Klick, *The Impact of Attorney Compensation on the Timing of Settlements*, 1st Annual Conference on Empirical Legal Studies Paper, *available at http://ssrn.com/abstract=906154.*

different approaches; some typical approaches are billing in six-minute, ten-minute, or quarter-hour increments. Suppose you make a phone call to a client. The client is out and you leave a message on her voice mail. Dialing the call and leaving a message might take thirty seconds. Do you bill the minimum increment for this work? If not, you are leaving work unbilled and uncharged to the client (and you are not making any progress towards your billable hour expectation). If so, the client will be charged for ten or fifteen minutes' work for a thirty-second phone call. If your billing rate is $250 per hour, how much did the client pay for you to dial the phone? Was it worth it? If the firm rewards high billable hours, what incentive does that create for lawyers?

Hourly billing also creates some concerns for law firm management. Imagine that you, the lead partner on a case, receive the time records for lawyers who have been working on a client matter so you can prepare the bill. The number of hours and the cost of the work seems high to you, and the client is already concerned about the high cost of your firm's representation. What can you do? One choice is not to bill out all the time worked on a matter; at one time law firms "ate" a considerable amount of time worked by junior lawyers, chalking it up to training and not charging the client for it. That becomes more difficult as the starting salaries for junior lawyers increase; in order to make hiring junior lawyers cost-effective, the firm needs them to pay their own way and then some. What does that mean for the hiring and training of junior lawyers? Firms are in a competitive environment and must compete for the business of clients; clients are increasingly scrutinizing bills and may refuse to pay to have junior lawyers work on their matters at high billing rates. Is there a solution to this problem? Is it good for junior lawyers?

2. FLAT FEES

In some areas of practice, lawyers may charge a "flat fee"—a set amount for performance of an agreed-upon task. This is quite common in criminal defense practice, and for some kinds of family law practice, such as the preparation of a will or a straightforward marital dissolution. What are the advantages and disadvantages of a flat fee arrangement? As a lawyer, does the flat fee create incentives for you that may be inconsistent with the client's interests? As the client, might you tend to overuse a resource that you have already paid for in full? What could be done to alleviate these concerns?

3. PROPORTIONATE FEES

A lawyer can charge a fee that is a proportion of some stated amount. Statutory fees are sometimes set this way; for example, the fee for probating an estate might be a percentage of the value of the estate.

4. CONTINGENT FEES

A contingent fee is a fee that is "contingent" on some occurrence; that is, it does not need to be paid until the contingency happens. Often, the contingency is a recovery of damages in a dispute, and the fee may be a percentage of the successful recovery. A fee that is based on a percentage of the recovery is both proportionate and contingent. Not all contingent fees need be proportionate; a retainer agreement providing that "if Lawyer secures the desired zoning variance on Client's behalf, Client will pay Lawyer $10,000" is a contingent fee.

The contingent fee is widely viewed as problematic. Why? The theory of the contingent fee is that it properly aligns the interests of the lawyer and the client: the lawyer's interest in recovering a significant fee is congruent with the client's interest in obtaining a significant recovery. Is that accurate, or are there distinct behavioral incentives for the lawyer and the client in the contingent fee context? Is there a way to address those concerns?

A contingent fee arrangement may result in a fee that seems high relative to other fee types. Imagine, for example, that Attorney agrees to represent Client in a personal injury matter; the retainer agreement provides for a contingent fee of one-third of Client's recovery. After gathering information and making a demand on the tortfeasor, Lawyer receives a settlement offer of $300,000, and Client accepts the offer. If Lawyer has spent ten hours securing this settlement for Client, Lawyer will receive $10,000 per hour for his work for Client. While some lawyers will reduce this fee in light of the small commitment of time and resources required to earn it, others will not. What justifies such an exorbitant fee?

The theory is that a contingent fee representation entails a certain amount of risk, and the upside potential of a high fee compensates the lawyer for the risk that she will recover nothing. Because of this, the courts have held that contingent fees are not permitted in cases where there is, in effect, no contingency and therefore no risk. A lawyer seeking payment on a life insurance policy where there is no question about the obligation of the company to pay, *see Committee on Legal Ethics v. Tatterson*, 352 S.E.2d 107 (1986), or seeking an automatic payment under a no-fault insurance scheme, see *Attorney Grievance Commission v. Kemp*, 496 A.2d 672 (Md. App. 1985), is therefore precluded from charging a contingent fee. But many cases which in theory bear a risk of nonpayment for the lawyer may in fact involve very little. Experienced, specialized lawyers may be very effective at screening cases and have enough business to turn away cases that involve any substantial risk of nonrecovery, meaning that they accept only cases in which their recovery of a fee is virtually certain.[2] Is it proper for those lawyers to charge a contingent fee? Why or why not?

---

2. *See* Lester Brickman, *ABA Regulation of Contingency Fees: Money Talks, Ethics Walks*, 65 Fordham L. Rev. 247, 283 (1996) ("there is overwhelming evidence that contingency fee lawyers only accept cases in which there is at least a good prospect for recovery.").

The principal benefit of the contingent fee is access: the promise of fees at the conclusion of a successful dispute might enable clients who would otherwise not have the money to pay lawyers to secure representation. Some believe there is also a benefit to the "screening" function, on the theory that lawyers will sift out nonmeritorious cases and will pursue only those cases in which a recovery for the client, and a fee payment to them, is likely. Others counter that the possibility of a nuisance payment to settle a nonmeritorious claim reduces the value of the screening function.

Ordinarily, when the contingency does not occur, the lawyer cannot recover the contingent fee. This can be frustrating for the lawyer if the failure to recover is, in the lawyer's view, the result of the client's bad decision. But the existence of a contingent fee agreement does not change the essential division of authority in decisionmaking between lawyer and client. In *Keck & Associates v. Vasey*, 834 N.E.2d 486 (Ill. App. 2005), Lawyer represented Client in a libel suit. Client agreed to pay hourly rates till the fee reached $10,000, and after that, 33% of any recovery over the $10,000. The engagement letter did not say anything about an appeal. Client lost the case at trial, and decided not to appeal. In the letter urging him to appeal, Lawyer wrote, "By . . . preventing us from filing the Notice of Appeal, you would be denying us the right to recover our contingent fee for our services. In such case, you would be assuming responsibility to pay us the reasonable value of the legal services that we have rendered to you." Lawyer sued Client for the reasonable value of its services. The court denied the claim. "The client, and not his attorney, must decide whether to appeal from the trial court's judgment. Nowhere in the contract did Vasey surrender his right to decide whether to appeal from the trial court's judgment. Requiring Vasey to pay Keck hourly fees, far in excess of the contractual contingent fee, would make the right to decide whether to appeal largely meaningless." *See also Culpepper & Carroll, PLLC v. Cole*, 929 So.2d 1224 (La. 2006). There, the lawyer recommended to the client that he accept a settlement. The client refused and fired the lawyer; ultimately the client brought suit on his own, but recovered nothing. The lawyer sued for the contingent fee he would have received had the client followed his advice and accepted the settlement. The court held that the client was not liable to pay a contingent fee, because that would interfere with the client's authority to decide whether to settle. "[I]t is clear that the decision to accept a settlement belongs to the client alone. Therefore, regardless of the wisdom of Mr. Cole's decision, his refusal to accept the settlement was binding on Mr. Culpepper. To allow Mr. Culpepper to recover a contingent fee under these circumstances would penalize Mr. Cole for exercising his right to reject the settlement."

One last issue is the basis on which the contingent fee is calculated. Often, a lawyer will advance the expenses involved with conducting contingent fee litigation. See Model Rule 1.8(e). When the contingent fee is paid, should it be calculated based on the gross recovery to the client—the amount of money paid by the opposing party—or on the net recovery to the client after the costs of the litigation have been subtracted? What does Model Rule 1.5(c) say about this issue? Is one approach fairer than the other? For a distinct perspective on this issue, *see* W. William Hodes, *Cheating Clients with the Percentage-of-the-Gross Contingent Fee Scam*, 30 Hofstra L. Rev. 767 (2002).

5. NO FEES

It is perfectly permissible for a lawyer to do work for no fee. This is typically called "pro bono" work, short for "pro bono publico"—for the public good. The lawyer's duties to the client are the same whether or not the lawyer is paid for her services.

6. STATUTORY FEES

A statute may provide that the prevailing party may recover attorneys' fees from the losing party. This type of statute alters the traditional "American rule" that parties are responsible for paying their own attorneys' fees regardless of the outcome of the case.

7. LESS TRADITIONAL FEE STRUCTURES

The above-listed fee arrangements are some of the traditional ways in which lawyers are compensated for their work. Lawyers have not always been satisfied with the results they achieve with these more traditional fee vehicles, and neither have clients. Several suggestions have been made about fee structures that might address these concerns, and some lawyers use them. Many combine the types of fees listed above—for example, an hourly or flat fee with a contingent fee component. Some are task-based: each phase of a representation might have a flat fee associated with it. Some firms are adopting what is called "success-fee" or "outcome-dependent" billing, in which the firm negotiates a fee arrangement based on the accomplishment of a specific objective for the client.

One possibility is taking some kind of equity share in the client's business. This may be attractive to a client who is starting up a venture and may not have a lot of ready cash. Such arrangements are not treated as traditional fee agreements and are subject to the constraints on business transactions with clients. This was the way many "dotcom" startups got legal services. How would the parties assess whether a share of a startup of uncertain future was "fair and reasonable" to the client?

What about bonuses? Some lawyers have begun including a term in their agreements that suggests that the client should consider a bonus for the lawyer in the event of a positive outcome. Can a client be required to pay a bonus? In *Hedlund & Hanley, LLC v. Board of Trustees of Community College District No. 508*, 876 N.E.2d 1 (Ill. App. 2007), a law firm entered into a fee agreement that included the following provision: "While there would be no commitment to do so, we would hope that, at the conclusion of the litigation, City Colleges would give favorable consideration to a bonus request from my firm based upon results achieved, efficiency of our work at the hourly rates approved, and overall reasonableness." The law firm secured a good outcome for the client and submitted a written request for an "efficiency bonus." The client denied the request. The lawyers brought suit, claiming that the client "flatly refused to undertake any good-faith, fair, or reasonable consideration of their bonus request," and that this wrongly deprived them of the benefit intended. The court rejected the claim; the agreement provided that the decision to grant a bonus (or not) was in the sole discretion of the client.

B. CONSTRAINTS ON FEES

1. THE ETHICAL RULES

Model Rule 1.5 deals with attorney fees. Read the rule with some care at this point. What does it require? The requirement that fees not be "unreasonable" is pretty vague. How does the rule help define what an "unreasonable" fee might be?

In addition to the prohibition on unreasonable fees, there are some procedural obligations with regard to the fee agreement. Must fee agreements be in writing? Why or why not? Under what circumstances do the rules require a written agreement, and what do they require be specified in the agreement? Why do you suppose that is?

There are also some fee arrangements that are expressly prohibited by the ethical rules. Model Rule 1.5(d) specifically prohibits contingent fees in domestic relations matters and in criminal cases. Why do we prohibit contingent fees in these contexts and not in others? Is this rational, or does it reflect a bias against certain categories of clients or lawyers? The domestic relations prohibition has had to be modified in some jurisdictions to make clear that it does not apply to subsequent enforcement of judgments for child support. Why?

In addition to the ethics rules, other law can also be the source of prohibitions on contingent fees; for example, Circular 230, which governs lawyers practicing before the Internal Revenue Service, imposes limits on contingent fees in tax matters. *See* 31 C.F.R. § 10.27.

One other constraint is the rule governing the division of fees between lawyers. Model Rule 1.5(e) provides, "A division of a fee between lawyers who are not in the same firm may be made only if: (1) the division is in proportion to the services performed by each lawyer or each lawyer assumes joint responsibility for the representation; (2) the client agrees to the arrangement, including the share each lawyer will receive, and the agreement is confirmed in writing; and (3) the total fee is reasonable." Why might lawyers in different firms decide to divide fees? How might this rule affect the decision to enter into an agreement to divide fees?

2. ENFORCEABILITY OF CONTRACTS

A violation on the prohibition against charging an unreasonable fee can subject a lawyer to discipline. It can also, as the case below reflects, affect the enforceability of a contract to pay attorney fees. Is the reasonableness of the fee, as determined by the factors set out in Model Rule 1.5, the only issue? Or is there a hidden additional factor the courts may consider in determining whether an attorney's fee is "reasonable"?

HAUPTMAN, O'BRIEN, WOLF & LATHROP, P.C. v. TURCO

735 N.W.2d 368 (Neb. 2007)

STEPHAN, J.

Louis J. Turco, Jr., engaged the law firm of Hauptman, O'Brien, Wolf & Lathrop, P.C., to represent his minor daughter, Lucia Turco, with respect to her personal injuries and the death of her unborn child resulting from a motor vehicle accident. Louis executed a contingent fee agreement with the firm. After receiving a settlement offer, but before accepting it, Louis advised the firm that he was terminating its services. The firm then brought this action to enforce an attorney lien against Louis and Lucia (collectively the Turcos) in an amount computed in accordance with the contingent fee agreement. The Turcos asserted various defenses, including a claim that the amount of the fee was unreasonable. The district court granted the firm's motion for summary judgment, and the Turcos appealed. Because the record does not afford a sufficient basis for determining the reasonableness of the claimed fee, we conclude that there are genuine issues of material fact which preclude summary judgment and therefore reverse, and remand for further proceedings.

BACKGROUND

On June 20, 2004, Lucia was a passenger in an automobile involved in an accident with another vehicle. Lucia was a minor at the time of the accident and was 31 weeks pregnant. She suffered a broken femur and the loss of her unborn child. She was hospitalized for 6 days.

Several days after the accident, Louis contacted the law firm on Lucia's behalf and met with an attorney from the firm. During the meeting, he explained that Lucia had been a passenger in an automobile which was struck by a drunk driver and that her unborn child had died as a result. Louis did not employ the law firm at this initial meeting, but he did leave the office with a brochure and a copy of the firm's contingent fee agreement.

On July 8, 2004, Louis, his wife, and Lucia again met with attorneys from the law firm. During this meeting, the parties discussed Lucia's injuries, responsibility for medical bills, issues relating to the possible wrongful death claim, and the length of time it would take to resolve the matters.

The details and particulars of the accident and Lucia's injuries were related to the law firm. From the attorneys' comments, Louis understood that "it would be a lot of work to get the insurance companies to pay the claim" and that the firm would not consider settling for 6 to 8 months because of uncertainty as to the extent of Lucia's injuries and the resulting medical bills. The contingent fee agreement was explained during this meeting, and Louis signed it.

The agreement provided that the firm's fee would be "thirty-three and one-third percent (33–1/3%) of the gross amount recovered either by judgment or by settlement . . . calculated independently of any costs or bills owed by client." It included an acknowledgment that the fee was "dependent upon the outcome of client's claim" and that the firm had explained that the case "could be handled at an attorney's regular hourly rate, plus expenses, payable monthly as billed, but client prefers that this matter be handled on a contingent fee basis." The agreement also included the following provision:

> In the event of termination of attorney's representation, attorney shall have a lien for fees and expenses, which lien will be imposed upon any sums recovered by, for, or on behalf of client. For purposes of computing the contingency fee to which attorney is entitled, the 33 1/3 percentage shall be computed based upon the last settlement offer received by attorney from defendant's representatives. If no such settlement offer has been tendered, attorney shall be allowed fees in an amount equal to his/her standard hourly rate for the hours expended, as well as the hourly rate of paralegal and other support staff utilized on client's behalf.

Members of the firm explained to the Turcos that this provision was necessary to protect it from clients who would terminate its services in order to avoid payment of a fee.

On August 9, 2004, an attorney from the firm telephoned Louis' wife and informed her that the liability insurance carrier for the driver of the other vehicle involved in the accident had offered to settle for its policy limits. The attorney told her that the next step would be to pursue underinsured coverage. Neither Louis nor his wife told the attorney that they would accept the settlement offer, which was in the amount of $194,000.

Following a court hearing in September 2004, Louis became dissatisfied with the firm. On September 14, he delivered a letter to the law firm terminating its services. Although he was aware of the provision of the contingent fee agreement specifying the fee payable upon termination, he felt that the law firm had expended little time and effort and that the fee of 33 1/3 percent of the settlement offer was excessive for the amount of work done.

After the firm tried unsuccessfully to resolve the dispute regarding the fee, it served notice of an attorney lien on the attorney representing the party which had made the settlement offer. The notice stated that the lien was in the amount of $64,600 and represented fees owed pursuant to the contingent fee agreement signed by Louis. New counsel retained by Louis subsequently advised the firm that while Louis agreed that it was entitled to be compensated for the "reasonable value of services provided up to the time of [the firm's] termination" and reimbursed for expenses incurred, the amount of the claimed lien was excessive.

The law firm subsequently brought this action against the Turcos, generally alleging breach of contract. In their answer, the Turcos alleged that terms of the contingent fee agreement were unconscionable, that the execution of the agreement was fraudulently induced, and that the amount of the fee claimed by the firm was "unreasonable and excessive." The firm filed a motion for summary judgment, as did the Turcos. The district court granted the law firm's motion and denied that filed by the Turcos. The Turcos perfected this appeal. . . .

ASSIGNMENTS OF ERROR

The Turcos assign that the district court erred in granting the law firm's motion for summary judgment because (1) there are genuine issues of material fact as to whether the fee is excessive for the amount of work actually performed, (2) the law firm failed to present evidence that the terms of the fee agreement were reasonable, and (3) there are genuine issues of material fact as to whether the law firm made fraudulent representations that the Turcos relied upon to their detriment. . . .

ANALYSIS

The party moving for summary judgment has the burden to show that no genuine issue of material fact exists and must produce sufficient evidence to demonstrate that it is entitled to judgment as a matter of law. The evidence offered by the law firm in support of its motion for summary judgment included the contingent fee agreement and notice of attorney lien, the deposition of Louis, and the termination letter Louis delivered to the firm. These latter documents reflect Louis' dissatisfaction with the firm's services and his reasons for claiming that the amount of the fee was unreasonable. The law firm also offered the affidavit of an attorney who opined that the contingent fee agreement utilized in this case "is a reasonable fee agreement and is not excessive" and that the firm was experienced and enjoyed an "outstanding reputation" in the legal, insurance, and medical communities. However, this affidavit does not address the reasonableness of the fee itself.

The firm contends that the reasonableness of its claimed fee is not at issue. In its brief, the firm argues that it has not claimed that the fee is owed "only because [it] is reasonable." Instead, it argues that the fee computed in accordance with the contingent fee agreement "is owed because [the Turcos] agreed to pay that specific amount." It further argues that whether that amount "has been shown to be 'reasonable' is not relevant" to its claim for breach of contract. In support of this argument, the firm relies in part upon *Mecham v. Colby*, which it cites for the proposition that written, unambiguous fee agreements between attorney and client are enforceable where the agreement contains a set or identifiable amount of the fee owed to the attorney.

In *Mecham*, we affirmed a summary judgment in favor of an attorney who had negotiated a settlement on behalf of a client involved in a complex dispute relating to an estate's inherited shares of corporate stock. After the settlement was consummated, the attorney billed the client in the amount of $2,000 and the client approved the statement in writing. The client later refused to pay the fee. We held that the client's written approval of the billing statement constituted a contract enforceable by the attorney, notwithstanding the client's subsequent claim that the settlement was not in her best interests. The record in *Mecham* included affidavits establishing that the attorney had achieved "the best possible settlement that was obtainable" for the client and that the "reasonable value" of his services was "between $7,500 and $10,000," far in excess of the $2,000 fee established in the contract. The opinion does not recite any evidence placing the value of the attorney's services at less than the amount claimed. Thus, *Mecham* does not support an argument that an attorney fee contract is enforceable in the absence of some showing that the amount of the claimed fee is reasonable.

Our jurisprudence recognizes that an attorney fee agreement is different from conventional commercial contracts. The difference arises from the fact that an attorney may not recover for services rendered if those services are rendered in contradiction to the requirements of professional responsibility and are inconsistent with the character of the profession.

The Code of Professional Responsibility, which was in effect when the legal services at issue in this case were performed, provided: "A lawyer shall not enter into an agreement for, charge, or collect an illegal or clearly excessive fee." Under the code, a fee was deemed "clearly excessive when, after a review of the facts, a lawyer of ordinary prudence would be left with a definite and firm conviction that the fee is in excess of a reasonable fee." The code enumerated eight factors to be considered as guides in determining the reasonableness of the fee, one of which was "[w]hether the fee is fixed or contingent." The Nebraska Rules of Professional Conduct, which are currently in effect, similarly provide that a lawyer "shall not make an agreement for, charge, or collect an unreasonable fee," and list the same eight factors to be considered in determining the reasonableness of a fee. The official comment 3 to rule 1.5 specifically states: "Contingent fees, like any other fees, are subject to the reasonableness standard of paragraph (a) of this Rule."

Citing authority from other jurisdictions, we have held that "[a] contingent fee which is not fair and reasonable can not be recovered in an action for attorney fees." . . .

We conclude that an attorney fee computed pursuant to a contingent fee agreement is subject to the same standard of reasonableness as any other attorney fee. To hold otherwise would require us to ignore the ethical principle which prohibits a lawyer from making an agreement for, charging, or collecting an unreasonable fee.... Under the Code of Professional Responsibility applicable to this case and the Nebraska Rules of Professional Conduct currently in effect, whether a fee is fixed or contingent is only one factor to be considered in determining whether the fee is reasonable.

In a suit to recover an unpaid fee, "the lawyer has the burden of persuading the trier of fact, when relevant, of the existence and terms of any fee contract, the making of any disclosures to the client required to render a contract enforceable, and the extent and value of the lawyer's services." The value of an attorney's services is ordinarily a question of fact. Here, the evidence offered by the law firm in support of its motion for summary judgment established that Louis signed a contingent fee agreement which was reasonable on its face and included an acknowledgment that the law firm had offered Louis the alternative of an hourly fee billed monthly, which he declined. There is also evidence that the law firm is experienced and respected in handling personal injury suits. However, the law firm presented no evidence of the extent and value of the professional services which it performed during the period from July 8, 2004, when the contingent fee agreement was executed until September 14, 2004, when Louis terminated the representation. Without such evidence, there is no factual basis upon which to determine whether or not the claimed fee computed pursuant to the contingent fee agreement is reasonable. The district court erred in sustaining the law firm's motion for summary judgment because the firm did not meet its initial burden, as the moving party, of showing that there is no genuine issue of material fact and that it is entitled to judgment as a matter of law.

GERRARD, J., concurring.

I agree with the majority opinion, which clearly explains the basic principles involved in this kind of fee dispute. It is well established that a contingent fee which is not fair and reasonable cannot be recovered in an action for attorney fees. I write separately, in light of further proceedings in this case, because the parties have a fundamental disagreement on the evidence necessary for a lawyer to establish a prima facie case that the fees sought are reasonable....

As our opinion explains, in a suit to recover an unpaid fee, the lawyer has the burden of proving the existence and terms of any fee contract, the making of any disclosures to the client required to render a contract enforceable, and the extent and value of the lawyer's services. A lawyer can establish the extent and value of his or her services in a contingency fee case by producing evidence showing, for example, the results obtained, the quality of the work, and whether the lawyer's efforts substantially contributed to the result. We have also identified other factors relevant to the reasonableness of a contingency fee, such as the time and labor required, the novelty and difficulty of the legal issues involved, the skill required to do the work properly, and the experience, reputation, and ability of the lawyer performing the services. While the pertinent factors will differ from case to case, generally, the inquiry should focus on the circumstances of the agreement and the work performed.

At that point, the burden of going forward with evidence shifts to the client, and the client must object with specificity to demonstrate why the documented fees are not reasonable. The client must, for instance, produce competent evidence disputing specific facts respecting the reasonableness of the fees or set forth the basis for a qualified opinion that the fees are unreasonable. In particular, it will generally be insufficient to simply conclude that the size of a contingent fee, compared to the length of the litigation, makes the fee unreasonable. There are a number of reasons why, in any particular case, a contingency fee agreement may be more advantageous to a client than an hourly fee paid on a monthly basis. A contingency fee will generally be reasonable if the lawyer offered the client a free and informed choice between an hourly fee and a contingency fee, the contract provides for a fee within the range commonly charged by other lawyers in similar representations, and there was no subsequent change in circumstances that made the fee contract unreasonable.

And while events may occur after a fee agreement was made so that a contingent fee arrangement that was fair in the first instance becomes unfair in its enforcement, courts should be reluctant to disturb contingent fee arrangements freely entered into by knowledgeable and competent parties. A prompt and efficient attorney who achieves a fair settlement without litigation serves both the client and the interests of justice. It should therefore be the unusual circumstance that a court refuses to enforce a fully informed contingent fee arrangement because of events arising after the contract's negotiation.

A contingent-fee contract . . . allocates to the lawyer the risk that the case will require much time and produce no recovery and to the client the risk that the case will require little time and produce a substantial fee. Events within that range of risks, such as a high recovery, do not make unreasonable a contract that was reasonable when made.

NOTES

1. The Hauptman firm represented itself in this case. Do you think that was wise?

2. Who bears the burden of proving that a fee agreement was reasonable? By what standards do we judge the agreement—by the circumstances that the parties knew about at the time the agreement was made, or by the circumstances that prevailed at the time the lawyer sought to collect the fee? Does that make sense in this case?

3. Why would it be the case that a contract for legal fees is not governed by traditional principles of contract law? If the parties knowingly agreed to the payment of a fee, why should that agreement be unenforceable based on an external normative assessment that the fee was unreasonable?

4. Limits on the fee contract may extend beyond the amount of the fee to other terms of the agreement. In *Ween v. Dow*, 822 N.Y.S.2d 257 (App. Div.

1st Dep't 2006), Dow retained attorney Ween to represent her in a real estate matter. The retainer agreement provided that if the client failed to pay fees in a timely manner and the lawyer had to bring a legal action to recover fees, the client would be liable for the attorneys' fees incurred in bringing the collection action. Ween wound up suing Dow, claiming that Dow did not pay her fees, and demanded attorneys' fees for the collection action, arguing that the clause was valid "pursuant to general contract law." Dow contended that the provision was void as against public policy. The court held the provision "fundamentally unfair and unreasonable" and therefore unenforceable. "Aside from its lack of mutuality," the court wrote, "the clause ... has the distinct potential for silencing a client's complaint about fees for fear of retaliation for the nonpayment of even unreasonable fees."

5.   This case demonstrates the wisdom of maintaining attorney time records even in contingent fee matters.

     Was the fee in the following case reasonable? Why or why not?

BROBECK, PHLEGER & HARRISON v. TELEX CORP.

602 F.2d 866 (9th Cir. 1979)

PER CURIAM:

This is a diversity action in which the plaintiff, the San Francisco law firm of Brobeck, Phleger & Harrison ("Brobeck"), sued the Telex Corporation and Telex Computer Products, Inc. ("Telex") to recover $1,000,000 in attorney's fees. Telex had engaged Brobeck on a contingency fee basis to prepare a petition for certiorari after the Tenth Circuit reversed a $259.5 million judgment in Telex's favor against International Business Machines Corporation ("IBM") and affirmed an $18.5 million counterclaim judgment for IBM against Telex. Brobeck prepared and filed the petition, and after Telex entered a "wash settlement" with IBM in which both parties released their claims against the other, Brobeck sent Telex a bill for $1,000,000, that it claimed Telex owed it under their written contingency fee agreement. When Telex refused to pay, Brobeck brought this action. Both parties filed motions for summary judgment. The district court granted Brobeck's motion, awarding Brobeck $1,000,000 plus interest. Telex now appeals.

Telex was the plaintiff in antitrust litigation against IBM in the United States District Court for the Northern District of Oklahoma. On November 9, 1973 the District Court found that IBM had violated section 2 of the Sherman Act, and entered judgment for Telex in the amount of $259.5 million, plus costs and attorney's fees of $1.2 million. The court also entered judgment in the sum of $21.9 million for IBM on its counterclaims against Telex for misappropriation of trade secrets and copyright infringement.

On appeal, the Tenth Circuit reversed the entire judgment that Telex had won in the district court. It also reduced the judgment against Telex on

IBM's counterclaim to $18.5 million and affirmed the district court's judgment as modified.

Having had reversed one of the largest antitrust judgments in history, Telex officials decided to press the Tenth Circuit's decision to the United States Supreme Court. To maximize Telex's chances for having its petition for certiorari granted, they decided to search for the best available lawyer. They compiled a list of the preeminent antitrust and Supreme Court lawyers in the country, and Roger Wheeler, Telex's Chairman of the Board, settled on Moses Lasky of the Brobeck firm as the best possibility.

Wheeler and his assistant made preliminary phone calls to Lasky to determine whether Lasky was willing to prepare the petition for certiorari. Lasky stated he would be interested if he was able to rearrange his workload. When asked about a fee, Lasky stated that, although he would want a retainer, it was the policy of the Brobeck firm to determine fees after the services were performed. Wheeler, however, wanted an agreement fixing fees in advance and arranged for Lasky to meet in San Francisco on February 10th to discuss the matter further with Telex's president, Stephen Jatras, and Floyd Walker, its attorney in the IBM litigation.

The San Francisco meeting was the only in-person meeting between Lasky and the Telex officials on the subject of Brobeck's compensation. Jatras told Lasky that Wheeler preferred a contingency fee arrangement. Lasky replied that he had little experience with such arrangements but proposed a contingency fee of 5% of either the judgment or settlement. Jatras thought there should be a ceiling and someone proposed that the ceiling be set at 5% of the first $100 million. Jatras also proposed that anything due IBM on its counterclaim judgment be deducted before calculating the 5% fee. Lasky rejected this, but suggested as a compromise that the amount of the counterclaim judgment be deducted if Telex received $40 million or less in judgment or settlement.

Lasky added that if there was to be [a] ceiling on the contingent fee, there ought to be a minimum fee as well, and suggested that the minimum fee be $1 million. In his deposition, Jatras acknowledged that Lasky proposed a minimum fee, but disputed the other participants' account of the remainder of the discussion. According to Jatras, he told Lasky that Telex would not pay a minimum fee "unless we got something to pay it from." Lasky denied hearing such a proposal. The parties reached no final agreement at the San Francisco meeting. . . .

The next day Walker drafted a memorandum to Jatras recounting the San Francisco meeting and including a proposed fee agreement. . . . The pertinent portion of this proposal, paragraph three, is set forth below:

> Once a Petition for Writ of Certiorari has been filed with the Clerk of the United States Supreme Court then Brobeck will be entitled to the payment of an additional fee in the event of a recovery by Telex from IBM by way of settlement or judgment in excess of the counterclaim judgment; and, such additional fee will be 5% of the first

$100,000,000.00 of such recovery, the maximum contingent fee to be paid is $5,000,000.00 and the minimum is $1,000,000.00.

On the day he received the letter and proposed fee agreement, Lasky telephoned Jatras to tell him the proposal was not acceptable and that he would draft changes. Later that same day, Lasky sent to Jatras a letter in which he agreed to represent Telex and enclosed a memorandum agreement. This agreement, which Lasky had already signed, is set forth in full:

MEMORANDUM

1.   Retainer of $25,000.00 to be paid. If Writ of Certiorari is denied and no settlement has been effected in excess of the Counterclaim, then the $25,000.00 retainer shall be the total fee paid; provided however, that

2.   If the case should be settled before a Petition for Writ of Certiorari is actually filed with the Clerk of the Supreme Court, then the Brobeck firm would bill for its services to the date of settlement at an hourly rate of $125.00 per hour for the lawyers who have worked on the case; the total amount of such billing will be limited to not more than $100,000.00, against which the $25,000.00 retainer will be applied, but no portion of the retainer will be returned in any event.

3.   Once a Petition for Writ of Certiorari has been filed with the Clerk of the United States Supreme Court then Brobeck will be entitled to the payment of an additional fee in the event of a recovery by Telex from IBM by way of settlement or judgment of its claims against IBM; and, such additional fee will be five percent (5%) of the first $100,000,000.00 gross of such recovery, undiminished by any recovery by IBM on its counterclaims or cross-claims. The maximum contingent fee to be paid is $5,000,000.00, provided that if recovery by Telex from IBM in less than $40,000,000.00 gross, the five percent (5%) shall be based on the net recovery, i.e., the recovery after deducting the credit to IBM by virtue of IBM's recovery on counterclaims or cross-claims, but the contingent fee shall not then be less than $1,000,000.00.

4.   Once a Writ of Certiorari has been granted, then Brobeck will receive an additional $15,000.00 retainer to cover briefing and arguing in the Supreme Court.

5.   Telex will pay, in addition to the fees stated, all of the costs incurred with respect to the prosecution of the case in the United States Supreme Court.

Jatras signed Lasky's proposed agreement, and on February 28 returned it to Lasky with a letter and a check for $25,000 as the agreed retainer. To "clarify" his thinking on the operation of the fee agreement, Jatras attached a set of hypothetical examples to the letter. This "attachment" stated the amount of the fee that would be paid to Brobeck assuming judgment or settlements in eight different amounts. In the first hypothetical, which assumed a settlement of $18.5 million and a counterclaim judgment of $18.5 million, Jatras listed a "net recovery" by Telex of "$0" and a Brobeck contingency fee of "$0."

Lasky received the letter and attachment on March 3. Later that same day he replied:

> Your attachment of examples of our compensation in various contingencies is correct, it being understood that the first example is applicable only to a situation where the petition for certiorari has been denied, as stated in paragraph 1 of the memorandum.

No Telex official responded to Lasky's letter.

Lasky, as agreed, prepared the petition for certiorari and filed it in July 1975. In the meantime Telex began to consider seriously the possibility of settlement with IBM by having Telex withdraw its petition in exchange for a discharge of the counterclaim judgment. Telex officials planned a meeting to discuss whether to settle on this basis, and Walker asked Lasky to attend in order to secure Lasky's advice on the chances that the petition for certiorari would be granted.

The meeting was held on September 5. Lasky told the assembled Telex's officials that the chances that the petition for certiorari would be granted were very good. Wheeler, however, was concerned that if the petition for certiorari was denied, the outstanding counterclaim judgment would threaten Telex with bankruptcy. Wheeler informed Lasky that Telex was seriously considering the possibility of a "wash settlement" in which neither side would recover anything and each would release their claims against the other. Lasky responded that in the event of such a settlement he would be entitled to a fee of $1,000,000. Wheeler, upon hearing this, became emotional and demanded to know from the others present whether this was what the agreement provided. Walker agreed that it had. Jatras said he didn't know and would have to read the correspondence.

Two days later Jatras wrote a memorandum for the Telex Board of Directors in which he stated:

> Lasky claims that his deal guarantees him $1 million fee in the event that Telex settles after the Petition for Writ is filed if the settlement is at least a 'wash' with the counterclaim judgment.

> Wheeler doesn't agree that the Lasky interpretation is correct and has asked Jatras to review his notes and recollections of this matter. Jatras has done so and has no independent knowledge beyond the documents.

Having returned to San Francisco, Lasky, at Telex's request, prepared a reply brief to IBM's opposition to the petition for certiorari, and sent it to the Supreme Court on September 17th for filing. In the meantime, Wheeler opened settlement discussions with IBM. He telephoned Lasky periodically for advice.

On October 2 IBM officials became aware that the Supreme Court's decision on the petition was imminent. They contacted Telex and the parties agreed that IBM would release its counterclaim judgment against Telex in exchange for Telex's dismissal of its petition for certiorari. On October 3, Lasky had the petition for certiorari withdrawn. Thereafter, he sent a bill to Telex for $1,000,000. When Telex refused to pay, Brobeck filed its complaint. . . . [T]he district court granted Brobeck's motion for summary judgment. . . .

Paragraph three of the memorandum agreement provided that Brobeck was entitled to an additional fee "in the event of a recovery by Telex from IBM by way of settlement or judgment of its claims against IBM." Telex contends that the wash settlement reached by IBM and Telex was not such a recovery because the contract contemplated that Brobeck would be entitled to its contingent fee only if Telex actually received money in settlement of its suit with IBM. Telex contends that as a result of this "ambiguity," what the parties actually intended the contract to mean, as evidenced by their words and conduct, is a factual matter that cannot be resolved on a motion for summary judgment.

Under California law, the determination of whether a written contract is ambiguous is a question of law that must be decided by the court. . . .

Paragraph one of the agreement provided that:

> 1. Retainer of $25,000.00 to be paid. If Writ of Certiorari is denied and no settlement has been effected in excess of the Counterclaim, then the $25,000.00 retainer shall be the total fee paid; provided, however, that. . . .

Thus, paragraph one narrowly limits Brobeck's fee to its $25,000 retainer to one situation: where there has been no settlement in excess of the counterclaim and where the writ of certiorari has been denied. Telex would have us construe the agreement as if the conditions stated in this paragraph were fulfilled, which they were not. Rather, the language in paragraph one ("provided, however") clearly contemplated a different computation of the fee where the conditions in either of the succeeding two paragraphs were fulfilled.

Paragraph three began with the language "(o)nce a Petition for Writ of Certiorari has been filed with the Clerk of the United States Supreme Court. . . ." Thus, the filing of the petition for certiorari triggered the operation of paragraph three. The paragraph proceeds to outline the manner in which Brobeck's fee would be computed in the event of settlement. The fee was to be contingent on two ranges of settlement. For settlements of less than $100 million but greater than or equal to $40 million, Brobeck's fee would be 5% of the "gross" recovery, i.e., the amount "undiminished by any recovery by IBM on its counterclaims or cross-claims." For any settlement of less than $40 million gross, the 5% would be computed on the "net" recovery, i.e., the recovery after deducting the credit to IBM by virtue of IBM's recovery against Telex "but the contingent fee shall not then be less than $1,000,000." Because the settlement reached with IBM was for less than $40 million gross, Brobeck was entitled to the $1 million contingent fee.

Telex argues that, because it received no money by virtue of the wash settlement with IBM, there was "no recovery by Telex from IBM by way of settlement or judgment of its claims against IBM," and therefore, the condition on which Brobeck would be paid was never fulfilled. Such a construction would create anomalies in the agreement that we cannot reasonably believe that the parties could have intended. First, Telex's requirement that it receive some cash by way of settlement of its claims against IBM could be satisfied by receipt of $1.00 from IBM. We agree with Brobeck that a construction of the contract that would condition the $1 million fee upon Telex's receipt of any amount of cash, no matter how slight, is untenable. Second, had Telex received $18.5 million from IBM in settlement of its antitrust claim, instead of receiving a discharge from its counterclaim judgment, it would have been in the same position as the wash settlement left it. Yet, Telex does not appear to dispute that in such a situation that Brobeck would be entitled to its $1 million fee. Telex's version of the agreement clearly exalts form over substance. Finally, Telex's construction of paragraph three is incompatible with paragraph two. Paragraph two provides that if the case is settled before the petition for a writ of certiorari is actually filed, then Brobeck could bill its services on an hourly basis not to exceed $100,000. It makes no sense to interpret paragraph three such that Telex pays less in attorney's fees where the petition is filed than when it is not. Not only would Brobeck have expended more time and effort where it actually completes and files the petition, but it also would have conferred on Telex the ability to use the completed petition as bargaining leverage in its negotiations with IBM. The substantial leverage that Telex gained by having filed a petition for certiorari is an explanation why Telex was willing to pay substantially more for a filed petition, and in fact, Telex appears to have benefited significantly by having filed the petition.

We conclude, therefore, that the contract was unambiguous on its face. [H]owever, California law allows a party to challenge a contract that is unambiguous on its face, and accordingly, Telex presented extrinsic evidence to the district court to show that the contract was susceptible of its interpretation.... Having carefully reviewed this evidence, taking the facts presented by Telex as true and resolving all doubts in its favor, we ... find that this evidence, if anything, compels our interpretation of the contract.

Three persons were involved in the formation of the Telex–Brobeck agreement: Lasky, Jatras, Telex's president, and Walker, Telex's counsel. In their depositions, Lasky and Walker consistently agreed that the contract should be interpreted in the manner advanced by Brobeck: once the petition for certiorari was filed, Brobeck was entitled to collect at least $1 million unless Telex lost.[1]

---

1. For instance, Walker wrote to Wheeler after the September 5th meeting: "In view of your statement that Telex may decide to 'throw in the sponge' I feel I should call to your attention the obligations for attorney fees which Telex will have in the event it pursues that course and a settlement is made by which the antitrust issues are given up in return for cancellation of the

The extrinsic evidence advanced by Telex to support its interpretation of the contract consists almost exclusively of Jatras' belief that an additional fee would be paid only if there was a net recovery (i.e., a settlement in excess of the counterclaim judgment). Jatras claims that he expressed his belief to Lasky on several occasions.

To the extent that Telex is relying on Jatras' subjective belief to establish the meaning of the contract, we must disagree. Under the modern theory of contracts we look to objective, not subjective, criteria in ascertaining the intent of the parties. . . .

[I]t appears that the construction of the contract that Telex is presently advancing on appeal is the one contained in the version that was rejected by Brobeck. Telex explicitly proposed that Brobeck would be entitled to an additional fee in the event of a recovery in "excess of the counterclaim judgment." In other words, Telex proposed a contract whereby it would pay Brobeck only if Telex recovered an amount in excess of the amount owed on the counterclaim judgment. Brobeck, however, by excluding this limitation in its version . . . to which the parties finally agreed, specifically rejected such a contract. We think that the only correct inference to be drawn from the omission of Telex's proposal in the final contract is that the parties agreed that Brobeck would be entitled to its additional fee in the event of a settlement between IBM and Telex, without regard to whether the amount of settlement was greater than the counterclaim judgment.

The events surrounding the cryptic "attachment" that Jatras sent to Brobeck after the contract was signed also belie Telex's interpretation of the contract. The first example in the series of eight hypotheticals supports Jatras's interpretation that the contingent fee would be paid only if there was a net recovery to Telex. Lasky, by a return letter, promptly disagreed with this interpretation, stating that it applied only in the situation when the petition for certiorari was denied. As Telex admitted in a request for admission:

> neither Mr. Jatras nor anyone else connected with defendants at any time wrote or spoke to Mr. Lasky concerning any statement in the letter of March 3, 1975, and particularly concerning the last paragraph. . . .

We regard Telex's inaction as acquiescing to Brobeck's interpretation of the contract. . . .

Finally, Telex contends that the $1 million fee was so excessive as to render the contract unenforceable. Alternatively it argues that unconscionability depends on the contract's reasonableness, a question of fact that should be submitted to the jury.

Counterclaim judgment. My understanding of the arrangement between Telex and the Brobeck firm is that they are to receive a minimum fee of $1 million if settlement is entered into subsequent to the filing of the Petition for Writ."

Preliminarily, we note that whether a contract is fair or works an unconscionable hardship is determined with reference to the time when the contract was made and cannot be resolved by hindsight.

There is no dispute about the facts leading to Telex's engagement of the Brobeck firm. Telex was an enterprise threatened with bankruptcy. It had won one of the largest money judgments in history, but that judgment had been reversed in its entirety by the Tenth Circuit. In order to maximize its chances of gaining review by the United States Supreme Court, it sought to hire the most experienced and capable lawyer it could possibly find. After compiling a list of highly qualified lawyers, it settled on Lasky as the most able. Lasky was interested but wanted to bill Telex on [an] hourly basis. After Telex insisted on a contingent fee arrangement, Lasky made it clear that he would consent to such an arrangement only if he would receive a sizable contingent fee in the event of success.

In these circumstances, the contract between Telex and Brobeck was not so unconscionable that "no man in his senses and not under a delusion would make on the one hand, and as no honest and fair man would accept on the other." This is not a case where one party took advantage of another's ignorance, exerted superior bargaining power, or disguised unfair terms in small print. Rather, Telex, a multi-million corporation, represented by able counsel, sought to secure the best attorney it could find to prepare its petition for certiorari, insisting on a contingent fee contract. Brobeck fulfilled its obligation to gain a stay of judgment and to prepare and file the petition for certiorari. Although the minimum fee was clearly high, Telex received substantial value from Brobeck's services. For, as Telex acknowledged, Brobeck's petition provided Telex with the leverage to secure a discharge of its counterclaim judgment, thereby saving it from possible bankruptcy in the event the Supreme Court denied its petition for certiorari. We conclude that such a contract was not unconscionable.

NOTES

1. In the *Hauptman* case, the court rejected the notion that the client was bound by the terms of a contract to which it fairly consented, and insisted that the lawyer seeking to enforce a fee contract bore the burden of demonstrating the reasonableness of the fee. Is the approach the same in *Brobeck*? Why or why not?

2. Originally, when consulted by Telex, attorney Lasky said that "it was the policy of the Brobeck firm to determine fees after the services were performed." What do you suppose he meant by that? Would that have been a better choice for the client here? Why was that arrangement unacceptable to the client? The analogy in ordinary life might be deciding whether to pay a flat fee for an open bar for your wedding, or to pay by the drink. What factors would enter into your decision about such a matter?

3. In this case, Telex's counsel, as a fact witness, took a position with regard to the fee that was contrary to the client's interest. Was that proper? Do you

suppose it was difficult? The lawyer's obligation of candor to the court is considered in Chapter 10.

3. IMPERMISSIBLE FEES

CLUCK v. COMMISSION FOR LAWYER DISCIPLINE

214 S.W.3d 736 (Tex. App. 2007)

DAVID PURYEAR, JUSTICE.

The State Bar of Texas Commission for Lawyer Discipline brought a disciplinary action against attorney Tracy Dee Cluck, alleging that he committed professional misconduct by violating multiple provisions of the Texas Disciplinary Rules of Professional Conduct in connection with his representation of Patricia A. Smith. Both parties filed motions for summary judgment. The trial court denied Cluck's motion and granted the Commission's motion, holding that Cluck committed professional misconduct by violating each of the rules cited by the Commission. Cluck appeals, arguing that his conduct did not violate any disciplinary rules. We will affirm the judgment of the district court.

BACKGROUND

Smith approached Cluck in June 2001, looking for an attorney to represent her in a divorce case. Cluck agreed to represent Smith and had her sign a contract for legal services, which states, "In consideration of the legal services rendered on my behalf in the above matter I agree to pay TRACY D. CLUCK a non-refundable retainer in the amount of $15,000...." Following that sentence, a handwritten provision explains, "Lawyer fees are to be billed at $150 per hour, first against non-refundable fee and then monthly thereafter. Additional non-refundable retainers as requested." The contract states that "no part of the legal fee is to be refunded ... should the case be discontinued, or settled in any other matter."

Smith paid Cluck $15,000 on June 28, 2001. Cluck began work on Smith's divorce, including filing the petition and obtaining service on Smith's husband. On July 7, Smith asked Cluck to cease action on her divorce because she wished to reconcile with her husband. Because her husband had already been served, Cluck advised Smith to leave the action pending in case she changed her mind; Smith agreed. On July 12, 2002, Smith contacted Cluck about resuming work on her divorce. Cluck requested that Smith sign an amendment to their contract, in which she agreed to pay an additional $5,000 "non-refundable fee" and to increase Cluck's hourly rate to $200 per hour. Smith signed the amendment and paid Cluck the $5,000, and Cluck resumed work on her case.

On August 22, 2002, Smith terminated Cluck as her attorney because she was dissatisfied with the lack of progress made by Cluck on her case and his lack of responsiveness to her phone calls. She requested the return of her file, which she picked up two weeks later. On October 10, 2002, Smith wrote a letter to Cluck asking for a detailed accounting and a refund of the $20,000, less reasonable attorney's fees and expenses. Cluck replied on December 4, 2002, explaining that he did not respond sooner because he was on vacation when Smith's letter arrived and because an electrical storm destroyed his computer and phone systems. He stated that an itemization of his expenses and time billed was included in her file and in bills he had previously mailed to her. Cluck advised Smith that he did not believe she was entitled to a refund.

The parties dispute the number of hours that Cluck spent working on Smith's case. The Commission asserts that Cluck's billing indicates that he worked 11 hours, while Cluck contends he worked 28.5 hours. It is undisputed that Cluck ultimately collected $20,000 from Smith, which he deposited in his operating account, and that Cluck failed to refund any portion of the collected fees to Smith.

Smith filed a complaint with the State Bar of Texas, and the Commission initiated this suit, alleging that Cluck committed professional misconduct by violating several Texas Disciplinary Rules of Professional Conduct. The Commission claimed that Cluck failed to promptly comply with a reasonable request for information; contracted for, charged, and collected an unconscionable fee; failed to adequately communicate the basis of his fee; failed to hold funds belonging in whole or in part to a client in a trust account; and failed to promptly deliver funds his client was entitled to receive and render a full accounting regarding those funds upon the client's request.

Cluck and the Commission both filed motions for summary judgment. The trial court denied Cluck's motion and granted the Commission's motion, finding that Cluck violated all the disciplinary rules cited by the Commission and thus committed professional misconduct. The court imposed a twenty-four-month fully probated suspension from the practice of law on Cluck and ordered him to pay court costs and restitution to Smith in the amount of $15,000. Cluck appeals, contending that he did not violate the disciplinary rules.

DISCUSSION

... We first address the trial court's finding that Cluck violated rule 1.14(a) by failing to hold the $20,000 paid by Smith in a trust account. Cluck argues that the fee paid by Smith was a nonrefundable retainer that was earned at the time it was received and that he was not obligated to hold the funds in a trust account because they did not belong in whole or in part to Smith. The Commission argues that, despite the contractual language, the fee was neither nonrefundable nor a retainer but was instead an advance fee that should have been held in a trust account.

An opinion by the Texas Committee on Professional Ethics discusses the difference between a retainer and an advance fee. The opinion explains that a true retainer "is not a payment for services. It is an advance fee to secure a lawyer's services, and remunerate him for loss of the opportunity to accept other employment.'' The opinion goes on to state that ''[i]f the lawyer can substantiate that other employment will probably be lost by obligating himself to represent the client, then the retainer fee should be deemed earned at the moment it is received.'' If a fee is not paid to secure the lawyer's availability and to compensate him for lost opportunities, then it is a prepayment for services and not a true retainer. ''A fee is not earned simply because it is designated as non-refundable. If the (true) retainer is not excessive, it will be deemed earned at the time it is received, and may be deposited in the attorney's account.'' However, money that constitutes the prepayment of a fee belongs to the client until the services are rendered and must be held in a trust account.

We are convinced that no genuine issue of material fact exists regarding whether the fees charged by Cluck were true retainers and, thus, whether Cluck was obligated to hold the funds in a trust account. First, the contract for legal services does not state that the $15,000 payment compensated Cluck for his availability or lost opportunities; instead, it states that Cluck's hourly fee will be billed against it. Second, the $5,000 additional payment requested by Cluck in 2002 makes clear that the $15,000 paid in 2001 did not constitute a true retainer; as the trial court noted in its judgment, ''if the first $15,000 secured [Cluck]'s availability, it follows that he should not charge another 'retainer' to resume work on the divorce. He was already 'retained' for the purposes of representing Smith in the matter.''

Finally, Cluck concedes in his brief that the fees did not represent a true retainer. However, he argues that he did not violate any disciplinary rules by depositing the money in his operating account because the contract states that the fees are nonrefundable. We disagree. ''A fee is not earned simply because it is designated as non-refundable.'' Tex. Comm. on Prof'l Ethics, Op. 431, 49 Tex. B.J. 1084 (1986). Advance fee payments must be held in a trust account until they are earned. . . .

retainers must be held in a trust account

Cluck violated rule 1.14(a) because he deposited an advance fee payment, which belonged, at least in part, to Smith, directly into his operating account. Accordingly, we must affirm the trial court's summary judgment holding that Cluck committed professional misconduct because he violated a disciplinary rule.

NOTES

1. You will often hear the term ''retainer.'' As this opinion makes clear, there are different types of ''retainer'' agreement. What the court refers to here as a ''true'' retainer is sometimes called a ''general retainer.'' The Restatement of the Law Governing Lawyers calls it an ''engagement retainer fee'' and defines it as ''a fee paid, apart from any other compensation, to ensure that a lawyer will be available for the client if required.'' Restatement of the Law Governing Lawyers, § 34, comment e. This payment to assure the availability of a lawyer is earned when paid and, according to the Restatement, is separate from the fee actually charged for the services. The most

typical use of the term "retainer" actually refers to a "special retainer," which is an advance payment of fees that the client anticipates owing the lawyer in the future. When a client gives a lawyer a special retainer, to whom does that money belong? This becomes important when we consider the lawyer's duties with regard to the handling of other people's money in the following section.

2. This is another instance in which the lawyer relied on the contract between the parties to establish the legitimacy of his fee claim. Once again, the court rejected the lawyer's argument that, in a fee context, it is the court's duty simply to enforce the agreement that the parties have made. As should be apparent by now, lawyer-client fee agreements are not always pure creatures of contract.

3. The Model Rules do not expressly prohibit non-refundable retainers that are not "true" retainers, but most jurisdictions do. Why? Consider the situation if the client, dissatisfied with his lawyer's representation, decided to discharge the lawyer. What would happen to the nonrefundable retainer if that arrangement were permitted? What would that mean for the client's power to discharge the attorney?

4. Lawyer undertook to represent Client in a divorce. The fee agreement provided, "My hourly rate is $250 an hour. The initial retainer for the matter is $3500. Upon retention, $1500 is assessed to the client for the lost opportunity cost to the attorney for her immediate and permanent inability to represent any other party in the case. The remaining funds will be deposited in the attorney's trust account and will be billed against at the hourly rate described for services rendered." Permissible "true" retainer, or an impermissible nonrefundable retainer? *See Columbus Bar Ass'n v. Halliburton–Cohen*, 832 N.E.2d 42 (Ohio 2005).

5. A lawyer may not be able to compel a client to pay an unreasonable or unethical fee; can a lawyer compel another lawyer to do so? Saggese agreed to refer clients to Kelley's law firm in exchange for one-third of the fees received for services provided to the referred client. Kelley paid the referral fee for a while but when his firm received a large fee in a referred case, he declined to pay. Saggese brought suit. Kelley claimed that the referral fee agreement did not comply with the relevant Rule of Professional Conduct, because the client had not consented to the referral fee, and that the agreement was therefore unenforceable. Should the lawyer nonetheless be required to pay? *Compare Saggese v. Kelley*, 837 N.E.2d 699, 703 (Mass. 2005) (upholding the referral fee agreement) *with Judge v. McCay*, 500 F. Supp. 2d 521 (E.D. Pa. 2007) (holding agreement unenforceable under New Jersey law).

6. Model Rule 5.4(a) contains an express prohibition on sharing legal fees with nonlawyers. Why? The theory is that fee-sharing has the potential to interfere with the lawyer's exercise of independent judgment on behalf of a client. Is such a sharing agreement nonetheless enforceable? In *Patterson v. Goldstein*, 980 So.2d 1234 (Fla. App. 2008), Goldstein, a lawyer, hired Patterson as a paralegal and agreed to pay her a salary plus a bonus of 10% of the fees that Goldstein earned in the cases on which Patterson worked. Goldstein refused to pay the bonus and Patterson brought suit to recover it. Goldstein argued that the contract to pay the bonus was unenforceable as against public

policy because it was prohibited by the ethics rules. Should Goldstein win? Why or why not?

7.   In addition to violating the professional responsibility rules, fee-sharing agreements can in some circumstances constitute a crime. Lawyers at Milberg Weiss LLP, a prominent New York class action firm, were charged with engaging in a racketeering conspiracy for secretly agreeing to pay individuals who agreed to act as lead plaintiffs in class action lawsuits brought by the firm a portion of the attorneys' fees the firm would receive from the representation of the class. The lawyers intentionally concealed this information from the courts in the cases and made false and misleading statements to avoid getting caught. In March 2008, partner Melvyn I. Weiss pleaded guilty to racketeering and agreed to pay $250,000 in fines and forfeit $9.75 million in fees. He was sentenced to 30 months in federal prison. Other partners also pleaded guilty. *See* Tiffany Hsu, *Melvyn Weiss Sentenced for Class-Action Kickback Scheme*, L.A. Times, 6/03/08.

C. FIDUCIARY OBLIGATIONS: TAKING CARE OF OTHER PEOPLE'S MONEY

As we saw in the previous section, a "retainer" paid by a client to a lawyer is often an advance payment of fees to be earned. At the time a fee advance is paid to the lawyer, the retainer is still the client's money, and it remains the client's money until the lawyer has earned it. This is a very common instance in which lawyers are in possession and control of other people's money, but it is far from the only one. Another is the payment of a settlement or judgment. Ordinarily, the payment will go directly to the lawyer, not the client. It is the lawyer's obligation to account for the proceeds of the case promptly and to remit to the client what belongs to her. The possibilities for lawyer conversion or fraud are significant.

Because law practice often places a lawyer in the position of being responsible for money or property that belongs to others, the ethical rules—and, in many jurisdictions, a more specific statute or court rule—impose strict requirements on the way in which the lawyer must take care of and account for other people's money or property. Review Model Rule 1.15 at this point. The rule requires the property of others be held separate from the lawyer's own property.

That is easy to do with personal property, but what about money? The lawyer must hold funds that do not belong to him in a "trust account," and keep those funds strictly separate from the lawyer's own office accounts. Mistakes about this—even negligent or careless ones—can be the subject of severe discipline. This is true, understandably, when the lawyer treats as his own money that really belongs to the client. Interestingly enough, it is equally true when the lawyer treats his own money as though it belonged in the trust account. In *North Carolina State Bar v. Speckman*, 360 S.E.2d 129 (N.C. App. 1987), for example, Speckman received a settlement payment on behalf of a client. He properly deposited it into his trust account, but after he paid the client what was owed to her, he left the remainder—the fee to which he was entitled—in the trust account. Notwithstanding the claim that he did so in order to assure that the check to the client would clear quickly, Speckman was disciplined. (He did leave the money in the trust account for several months and wrote checks against the trust account for office expenses.) It is the loss of the separateness of the trust account—the so-called "commingling of funds"— that is problematic, regardless of whether the client is harmed. Harm to the client, however, may be relevant to the severity of the discipline imposed.

Rules about the nature and handling of the trust account can be quite specific. Following are Iowa's rules for handling the client trust account. Under these rules, how would you

(i) handle a $5000 special retainer that was an advance payment from a client for future services?

(ii) compensate yourself for several hours of work at an agreed-upon hourly rate from the special retainer?

(iii) handle the funds if the client discharged you while some of the retainer was still in your trust account?

(iv) deal with a situation in which you and the client disagreed about whether she was entitled to all the money that was left in the trust account when she discharged you?

IOWA CLIENT TRUST ACCOUNT RULES

Rule 45.1   Requirement for client trust account.

Funds a lawyer receives from clients or third persons for matters arising out of the practice of law in Iowa shall be deposited in one or more identifiable interest-bearing trust accounts located in Iowa. The trust account shall be clearly designated as "Trust Account." No funds belonging to the lawyer or law firm may be deposited in this account except:

1.   Funds reasonably sufficient to pay or avoid imposition of fees and charges that are a lawyer's or law firm's responsibility ... may be deposited in this account; or

2.   Funds belonging in part to a client and in part presently or potentially to the lawyer or law firm must be deposited in this account, but the portion belonging to the lawyer or law firm may be withdrawn when due unless the right of the lawyer or law firm to receive it is disputed by the client, in which event the disputed portion shall not be withdrawn until the dispute is finally resolved....

Rule 45.2   Action required upon receiving funds.

45.2(1) *Authority to endorse or sign client's name.* Upon receipt of funds or other property in which a client or third person has an interest, a lawyer shall not endorse or sign the client's name on any check, draft, security, or evidence of encumbrance or transfer of ownership of realty or personalty, or any other document without the client's prior express authority. A lawyer signing an instrument in a representative capacity shall so indicate by initials or signature.

45.2(2) *Maintaining records, providing accounting, and returning funds or property.* A lawyer shall maintain complete records of all funds, securities, and other properties of a client coming into the lawyer's possession and regularly account to the client for them. Except as stated in this chapter or otherwise permitted by law or by agreement with the client, a lawyer shall promptly deliver to the client or third person any funds or other property that the client or third person is entitled to receive and shall promptly render a full accounting regarding such property....

Rule 45.3   Type of accounts and institutions where trust accounts must be established.

Each trust account referred to in rule 45.1 shall be an interest-bearing account in a bank, savings bank, trust company, savings and loan association, savings association, credit union, or federally regulated investment company selected by the law firm or lawyer in the exercise of ordinary prudence. The financial institution must be authorized by federal or state law to do business in Iowa and insured by the Federal Deposit Insurance Corporation, the National Credit Union Share Insurance Fund, or the Federal Savings and Loan Insurance Corporation. Interest-bearing trust funds shall be placed in accounts from which withdrawals or transfers can be made without delay when such funds are required, subject only to any notice period which the depository institution is required to observe by law or regulation.

Rule 45.4   Pooled interest-bearing trust account.

45.4(1) *Deposits of nominal or short-term funds.* A lawyer who receives a client's or third person's funds shall maintain a pooled interest-bearing trust account for deposits of funds that are nominal in amount or reasonably expected to be held for a short period of time. A lawyer shall inform the client or third person that the interest accruing on this account, net of any allowable monthly service charges, will be paid to the Lawyer Trust Account Commission established by the supreme court.

45.4(2) *Exceptions to using pooled interest-bearing trust accounts.* All client or third person funds shall be deposited in an account specified in rule 45.4(1) unless they are deposited in:

   a. A separate interest-bearing trust account for the particular third person, client, or client's matter on which the interest, net of any transaction costs, will be paid to the client or third person; or

   b. A pooled interest-bearing trust account with sub-accountings that will provide for computation of interest earned by each client's or third person's funds and the payment thereof, net of any transaction costs, to the client or third person.

45.4(3) *Accounts generating positive net earnings.* If the client's or the third person's funds could generate positive net earnings for the client or third person, the lawyer shall deposit the funds in an account described in rule 45.4(2). In determining whether the funds would generate positive net earnings, the lawyer shall consider the following factors:

a. The amount of the funds to be deposited;

b. The expected duration of the deposit, including the likelihood of delay in the matter for which the funds are held;

c. The rates of interest or yield at the financial institution in which the funds are to be deposited;

d. The cost of establishing and administering the account, including service charges, the cost of the lawyer's services, and the cost of preparing any tax reports required for interest accruing to a client's benefit;

e. The capability of financial institutions described in rule 45.3 to calculate and pay interest to individual clients; and

f. Any other circumstances that affect the ability of the client's funds to earn a net return for the client.

45.4(4) *Directions to depository institutions.* As to accounts created under rule 45.4(1), a lawyer or law firm shall direct the depository institution:

a. To remit interest or dividends, net of any allowable monthly service charges, as computed in accordance with the depository institution's standard accounting practice, at least quarterly, to the Lawyer Trust Account Commission;

b. To transmit with each remittance to the Lawyer Trust Account Commission a copy of the depositor's statement showing the name of the lawyer or law firm for whom the remittance is sent, the rate of interest applied, the amount of allowable monthly service charges deducted, if any, and the account balance(s) for the period covered by the report; and

c. To report to the Client Security Commission in the event any properly payable instrument is presented against a lawyer trust account containing insufficient funds....

Rule 45.7 Advance fee and expense payments.

45.7(1) *Definition of advance fee payments.* Advance fee payments are payments for contemplated services that are made to the lawyer prior to the lawyer's having earned the fee.

45.7(2) *Definition of advance expense payments.* Advance expense payments are payments for contemplated expenses in connection with the lawyer's services that are made to the lawyer prior to the incurrence of the expense.

45.7(3) *Deposit and withdrawal.* A lawyer must deposit advance fee and expense payments from a client into the trust account and may withdraw such payments only as the fee is earned or the expense is incurred.

45.7(4) *Notification upon withdrawal of fee or expense.* A lawyer accepting advance fee or expense payments must notify the client in writing of the time, amount, and purpose of any withdrawal of the fee or expense, together with a complete accounting. The attorney must transmit such notice no later than the date of the withdrawal.

45.7(5) *When refundable.* Notwithstanding any contrary agreement between the lawyer and client, advance fee and expense payments are refundable to the client if the fee is not earned or the expense is not incurred.

NOTES

1.   Under these rules, what determines the nature of the account into which you place the client's money? If you put the client's funds into a pooled account, what happens to the interest that it earns? In Iowa these funds go to the Lawyers Trust Account Commission, from which the Commission makes grants for the provision of legal services to indigent clients. In most states these are called IOLTA funds, an acronym for Interest On Lawyer Trust Accounts.

2.   Rule 45.3 requires that the financial institution in which the trust account is established be insured by the Federal Deposit Insurance Corporation (FDIC) or other comparable insurer. The FDIC insures the deposits of each individual depositor in an insured institution up to a set limit. The prospect of bank failures following the subprime credit crisis has raised some concern about assuring that trust account deposits are fully insured by the FDIC. Could depositing client funds that exceed the FDIC limit in a trust account create malpractice liability if the bank fails? In *Bazinet v. Kluge*, 788 N.Y.S.2d 77 (N.Y. App. Div. 2005), attorney Reiser was acting as escrow agent for his client, who was selling two cooperative apartments in New York. Reiser deposited the two down payments—a total of $2.73 million—in a trust account at the Connecticut Bank of Commerce. Before the transaction could be completed, the bank was closed. At the time, the FDIC-insured amount was $100,000 per depositor per bank. The client did not receive all of his money, and he sued Reiser. What do you think his claim was? Should he have succeeded?

3.   Originally, lawyer trust accounts were not permitted to be interest-bearing. This created something of a windfall for banks, for whom lawyers became highly favored clients. After banking law changed to permit the payment of interest on these accounts, the problem of who owned the interest earned on the trust fund deposits became acute. The lawyer could not keep the money, because it did not belong to her. Nor could it be distributed among the clients whose funds were in the account without burdensome and costly accounting procedures. The solution was the IOLTA account.

IOLTA accounts were subjected to lengthy constitutional challenge. The opinion below reflects the Supreme Court's ultimate resolution of these claims. Can you imagine them arising again? Under what circumstances?

BROWN v. LEGAL FOUNDATION OF WASHINGTON

538 U.S. 216 (2003)

JUSTICE STEVENS delivered the opinion of the Court.

The State of Washington, like every other State in the Union, uses interest on lawyers' trust accounts (IOLTA) to pay for legal services provided to the needy.... In *Phillips v. Washington Legal Foundation*, 524 U.S. 156 (1998), a case involving the Texas IOLTA program, we held "that the interest income generated by funds held in IOLTA accounts is the 'private property' of the owner of the principal." We did not, however, express any opinion on the question whether the income had been "taken" by the State or "as to the amount of 'just compensation,' if any, due respondents." We now confront those questions.

I

[I]n the course of their legal practice, attorneys are frequently required to hold clients' funds for various lengths of time. It has long been recognized that they have a professional and fiduciary obligation to avoid commingling their clients' money with their own, but it is not unethical to pool several clients' funds in a single trust account. Before 1980 client funds were typically held in non-interest-bearing federally insured checking accounts. Because federal banking regulations in effect since the Great Depression prohibited banks from paying interest on checking accounts, the value of the use of the clients' money in such accounts inured to the banking institutions.

In 1980, Congress authorized federally insured banks to pay interest on a limited category of demand deposits referred to as "NOW accounts." In response to the change in federal law, Florida adopted the first IOLTA program in 1981 authorizing the use of NOW accounts for the deposit of client funds, and providing that all of the interest on such accounts be used for charitable purposes. Every State in the Nation and the District of Columbia have followed Florida's lead and adopted an IOLTA program, either through their legislatures or their highest courts. The result is that, whereas before 1980 the banks retained the value of the use of the money deposited in non-interest-bearing client trust accounts, today, because of the adoption of IOLTA programs, that value is transferred to charitable entities providing legal services for the poor. The aggregate value of those contributions in 2001 apparently exceeded $200 million....

In 1984, the Washington Supreme Court established its IOLTA program....

[The Court ... described the four essential features of its IOLTA Program]: (a) the requirement that all client funds be deposited in interest-

bearing trust accounts, (b) the requirement that funds that cannot earn net interest for the client be deposited in an IOLTA account, (c) the requirement that the lawyers direct the banks to pay the net interest on the IOLTA accounts to the Legal Foundation of Washington (Foundation), and (d) the requirement that the Foundation must use all funds received from IOLTA accounts for tax-exempt law-related charitable and educational purposes. It explained:

1.   All client funds paid to any Washington lawyer or law firm must be deposited in identifiable interest-bearing trust accounts separate from any accounts containing non-trust money of the lawyer or law firm. The program is mandatory for all Washington lawyers.

2.   The new rule provides for two kinds of interest-bearing trust accounts. The first type of account bears interest to be paid, net of any transaction costs, to the client. This type of account may be in the form of either separate accounts for each client or a single pooled account with subaccounting to determine how much interest is earned for each client. The second type of account is a pooled interest-bearing account with the interest to be paid directly by the financial institution to the Legal Foundation of Washington (hereinafter the Foundation), a nonprofit entity to be established....

3.   Determining whether client funds should be deposited in accounts bearing interest for the benefit of the client or the Foundation is left to the discretion of each lawyer, but the new rule specifies that the lawyer shall base his decision solely on whether the funds could be invested to provide a positive net return to the client. This determination is made by considering several enumerated factors: the amount of interest the funds would earn during the period they are expected to be deposited, the cost of establishing and administering the account, and the capability of financial institutions to calculate and pay interest to individual clients....

. . .

5.   Lawyers and law firms must direct the depository institution to pay interest or dividends, net of any service charges or fees, to the Foundation, and to send certain regular reports to the Foundation and the lawyer or law firm depositing the funds.

The Foundation must use all funds received from lawyers' trust accounts for tax-exempt law-related charitable and educational purposes....

In 1995, the Washington Supreme Court amended its IOLTA rules to make them applicable to Limited Practice Officers (LPOs) as well as lawyers. LPOs are non-lawyers who are licensed to act as escrowees in the closing of real estate transactions. Like lawyers, LPOs often temporarily control the funds of the clients.

II

This action was commenced by a public interest law firm and four citizens to enjoin state officials from continuing to require LPOs to deposit trust funds into IOLTA accounts.... The defendants, respondents in this Court, are the justices of the Washington Supreme Court, the Foundation, which receives and redistributes the interest on IOLTA accounts, and the president of the Foundation....

Brown and Hayes ... both allege that they regularly purchase and sell real estate and in the course of such transactions they deliver funds to LPOs who are required to deposit them in IOLTA accounts. They object to having the interest on those funds "used to finance the Recipient Organizations" and "to anyone other than themselves receiving the interest derived from those funds." [They allege] that the "taking" of the interest earned on their funds in the IOLTA accounts violates the Just Compensation Clause of the Fifth Amendment; and ... that the requirement that client funds be placed in IOLTA accounts is "an illegal taking of the beneficial use of those funds." The prayer for relief sought a refund of interest earned on the plaintiffs' money that had been placed in IOLTA accounts, a declaration that the IOLTA Rules are unconstitutional, and an injunction against their enforcement against LPOs....

After discovery, the District Court granted the defendants' motion for summary judgment. As a factual matter the court concluded "that in no event can the client-depositors make any net returns on the interest accrued in these accounts. Indeed, if the funds were able to make any net return, they would not be subject to the IOLTA program." As a legal matter, the court concluded that the constitutional issue focused on what an owner has lost, not what the " 'taker' " has gained, and that petitioners Hayes and Brown had "lost nothing."

While the case was on appeal, we decided *Phillips v. Washington Legal Foundation*, 524 U.S. 156 (1998). Relying on our opinion in that case, a three-judge panel of the Ninth Circuit decided that the IOLTA program caused a taking of petitioners' property and that further proceedings were necessary to determine whether they are entitled to just compensation.

The Court of Appeals then reconsidered the [*Brown*] case en banc. The en banc majority affirmed the judgment of the District Court, reasoning that, under the ad hoc approach applied in *Penn Central Transp. Co. v. New York City*, 438 U.S. 104 (1978), there was no taking because petitioners had suffered neither an actual loss nor an interference with any investment-backed expectations, and that the regulation of the use of their property was permissible. Moreover, in the majority's view, even if there were a taking, the just compensation due was zero.

The three judges on the original panel, joined by Judge Kozinski, dissented....

We granted certiorari.

III

While it confirms the state's authority to confiscate private property, the text of the Fifth Amendment imposes two conditions on the exercise of such authority: the taking must be for a "public use" and "just compensation" must be paid to the owner. In this case, the first condition is unquestionably satisfied.... Even if there may be occasional misuses of IOLTA funds, the overall, dramatic success of these programs in serving the compelling interest in providing legal services to literally millions of needy Americans certainly qualifies the Foundation's distribution of these funds as a "public use" within the meaning of the Fifth Amendment.

Before moving on to the second condition, the "just compensation" requirement, we must address the type of taking, if any, that this case involves. As we made clear just last term:

> The text of the Fifth Amendment itself provides a basis for drawing a distinction between physical takings and regulatory takings. Its plain language requires the payment of compensation whenever the government acquires private property for a public purpose, whether the acquisition is the result of a condemnation proceeding or a physical appropriation. But the Constitution contains no comparable reference to regulations that prohibit a property owner from making certain uses of her private property. Our jurisprudence involving condemnations and physical takings is as old as the Republic and, for the most part, involves the straightforward application of per se rules. Our regulatory takings jurisprudence, in contrast, is of more recent vintage and is characterized by "essentially ad hoc, factual inquiries," designed to allow "careful examination and weighing of all the relevant circumstances."

We agree that a per se approach is more consistent with the reasoning in our *Phillips* opinion than *Penn Central's* ad hoc analysis. As was made clear in *Phillips*, the interest earned in the IOLTA accounts "is the 'private property' of the owner of the principal."

We therefore assume that Brown and Hayes retained the beneficial ownership of at least a portion of their escrow deposits until the funds were disbursed at the closings, that those funds generated some interest in the IOLTA accounts, and that their interest was taken for a public use when it was ultimately turned over to the Foundation. As the dissenters in the Ninth Circuit explained, though, this does not end our inquiry. Instead, we must determine whether any "just compensation" is due.

IV

"The Fifth Amendment does not proscribe the taking of property; it proscribes taking without just compensation." All of the Circuit Judges and District Judges who have confronted the compensation question, both in this case and in *Phillips*, have agreed that the "just compensation" required by the Fifth Amendment is measured by the property owner's loss rather than the government's gain. This conclusion is supported by consistent and unambiguous holdings in our cases. . . .

Applying the teaching of these cases to the question before us, it is clear that neither Brown nor Hayes is entitled to any compensation for the nonpecuniary consequences of the taking of the interest on his deposited funds, and that any pecuniary compensation must be measured by his net losses rather than the value of the public's gain. For that reason, both the majority and the dissenters on the Court of Appeals agreed that if petitioners' net loss was zero, the compensation that is due is also zero.

V

. . . [L]awyers and LPOs may occasionally deposit client funds in an IOLTA account when those funds could have produced net interest for their clients. It does not follow, however, that there is a need for further hearings to determine whether Brown or Hayes is entitled to any compensation from the respondents.

The Rules adopted and administered by the Washington Supreme Court unambiguously require lawyers and LPOs to deposit client funds in non-IOLTA accounts whenever those funds could generate net earnings for the client. Thus, if the LPOs who deposited petitioners' money in IOLTA accounts could have generated net income, the LPOs violated the court's Rules. Any conceivable net loss to petitioners was the consequence of the LPOs' incorrect private decisions rather than any state action. Such mistakes may well give petitioners a valid claim against the LPOs, but they would provide no support for a claim for compensation from the State, or from any of the respondents. . . .

The categorical requirement in Washington's IOLTA program that mandates the choice of a non-IOLTA account when net interest can be generated for the client provided an independent ground for the en banc court's judgment. It held that the program did not work a constitutional violation with regard to Brown's and Hayes's property: Even if their property was taken, the Fifth Amendment only protects against a taking without just compensation. Because of the way the IOLTA program operates, the compensation due Brown and Hayes for any taking of their property would be nil. There was therefore no constitutional violation when they were not compensated.

We agree with that holding.

VI

To recapitulate: It is neither unethical nor illegal for lawyers to deposit their clients' funds in a single bank account. A state law that requires client funds that could not otherwise generate net earnings for the client to be deposited in an IOLTA account is not a "regulatory taking." A law that requires that the interest on those funds be transferred to a different owner for a legitimate public use, however, could be a per se taking requiring the payment of "just compensation" to the client. Because that compensation is measured by the owner's pecuniary loss—which is zero whenever the Washington law is obeyed—there has been no violation of the Just Compensation Clause of the Fifth Amendment in this case. Accordingly, the judgment of the Court of Appeals is affirmed.

JUSTICE SCALIA, with whom THE CHIEF JUSTICE, JUSTICE KENNEDY, and JUSTICE THOMAS join, dissenting.

The Court today concludes that the State of Washington may seize private property, without paying compensation, on the ground that the former owners suffered no "net loss" because their confiscated property was created by the beneficence of a state regulatory program. In so holding the Court creates a novel exception to our oft-repeated rule that the just compensation owed to former owners of confiscated property is the fair market value of the property taken.

As the Court correctly notes, Washington's IOLTA program comprises two steps: First, the State mandates that certain client trust funds be placed in an IOLTA account, where those funds generate interest. Second, the State seizes the interest earned on those accounts.... With regard to step one, we held in *Phillips, supra,* that any interest earned on client funds held in IOLTA accounts belongs to the owner of the principal, not the State or the State's designated recipient of the interest. As to step two, the Court assumes, arguendo, that the appropriation of petitioners' interest constitutes a "taking," but holds that just compensation is zero because without the mandatory pooling arrangements (step one) of IOLTA, petitioners' funds could not have generated any interest in the first place. This holding contravenes our decision in *Phillips*—effectively refusing to treat the interest as the property of petitioners we held it to be—and brushes aside 80 years of precedent on determining just compensation....

II

When a State has taken private property for a public use, the Fifth Amendment requires compensation in the amount of the market value of the property on the date it is appropriated.

In holding that any just compensation that might be owed is zero, the Court neither pretends to ascertain the market value of the confiscated property nor asserts that the case falls within one of the two exceptions where market value need not be determined. Instead, the Court proclaims that just compensation is to be determined by the former property owner's "net loss," and endorses simultaneously two competing and irreconcilable theories of how that loss should be measured....

A

Under the Court's first theory, just compensation is zero because, under the State Supreme Court's Rules, the only funds placed in IOLTA accounts are those which could not have earned net interest for the client in a non-IOLTA savings account. This approach defines petitioners' "net loss" as the amount of interest they would have received had their funds been deposited in separate, non-IOLTA accounts....

This definition of just compensation has no foundation in reason. Once interest is earned on petitioners' funds held in IOLTA accounts, that money is petitioners' property. It is at that point that the State appropriates the interest—after the interest has been generated in the pooled accounts—and it is at that point that just compensation for the taking must be assessed.

It may very well be, as the Court asserts, that petitioners could not have earned money on their funds absent IOLTA's mandatory pooling arrangements, but just compensation is not to be measured by what would have happened in a hypothetical world in which the State's IOLTA program did not exist. When the State takes possession of petitioners' property— petitioners' money—and transfers it to [the Foundation], the property obviously has value. The conclusion that it is devoid of value because of the circumstances giving rise to its creation is indefensible....

B

The Court's rival theory for explaining why just compensation is zero fares no better. Contrary to its aforementioned description of petitioners' "net loss" as the amount their funds would have earned in non-IOLTA accounts, the Court declares that just compensation is "the net value of the interest that was actually earned by petitioners,"—net value consisting of the value of the funds, less "transaction and administrative costs and bank fees" that would be expended in extracting the funds from the IOLTA accounts. To support this concept of "net value," the Court cites nothing but the cases discussed earlier in its opinion, which establish that just compensation consists of the value the owner has lost rather than the value the government has gained. In this case, however, there is no difference between the two. Petitioners have lost the interest that *Phillips* says rightfully belongs to them—which is precisely what the government has gained. The Court's apparent fear that following the Constitution in this case will provide petitioners a "windfall" in the amount of transaction costs saved is based on the unfounded assumption that the State must return the interest directly to petitioners. The State could satisfy its obligation to pay just compensation by simply returning petitioners' money to the IOLTA account from which it was seized, leaving others to incur the accounting costs in the event petitioners seek to extract their interest from the account....

Perhaps we are witnessing today the emergence of a whole new concept in Compensation Clause jurisprudence: the Robin Hood Taking, in which the government's extraction of wealth from those who own it is so cleverly achieved, and the object of the government's larcenous beneficence is so highly favored by the courts (taking from the rich to give to indigent defendants) that the normal rules of the Constitution protecting private property are suspended. One must hope that that is the case. For to extend to the entire run of Compensation Clause cases the rationale supporting today's judgment—what the government hath given, the government may freely take away—would be disastrous.

The Court's judgment that petitioners are not entitled to the market value of their confiscated property has no basis in law. I respectfully dissent.

PROBLEMS

1. In 1970, Law Firm agreed to provide legal services to Loveless, who wanted to form a joint venture to build a shopping mall. The lawyers agreed to provide legal fees to Loveless at a discounted rate for two and a half years, after which they would charge full fees. In exchange for the reduced fees, Law Firm would receive 5% of the cash distributions produced by the joint venture. The reduced fee cost the firm $8000. In the early 1980s, the venture began making distributions, and by 2001 had distributed $380,000 to Law Firm. The joint venture informed Law Firm that it was terminating payments under the agreement, and Law Firm sued to enforce it. What result? *See Holmes v. Loveless*, 94 P.3d 338 (Wash. App. 2004).

2. Lawyer entered into a fee agreement with Kelly, who had suffered personal injuries in an automobile accident. The fee agreement provided that Lawyer would receive one-third of any recovery if the case settled before suit, and 40% of any recovery after suit or a request for arbitration had been filed. In addition, the agreement provided that Lawyer "may, at his sole discretion, compromise any medical bill and retain as an additional fee the difference between the compromised amount and the bill for medical services, if anything." The agreement further provided that the fee was to be taken from the total amount recovered, before deduction of any costs or expenses. Was the agreement proper? *See In re Silverton*, 2004 WL 60709 (Cal. Bar. Ct. 2004).

3. Lawyer agreed to represent Client in locating assets belonging to her deceased sister. Initially, Lawyer refused to represent Client on a percentage basis, insisting instead on an hourly fee. Client agreed to pay Lawyer $110 per hour and provided a $2000 retainer. After Client located substantial assets belonging to the estate of the sister, however, Lawyer met with Client and presented her with a written contingent fee agreement providing for a 33–1/3 percent fee. Client refused. Lawyer agreed to modify the agreement to 21% of all assets he recovered, plus 4% of the value of the estate as a fee for administering it. Lawyer told Client that "he was unwilling to perform any further work in the case without a signed contingent fee agreement," and suggested that "he expected the case would go to trial and that it would be a long and difficult battle." Client decided to think it over. In the meantime, Lawyer found out that the estate included at least $356,000 in assets, and that the person holding them was prepared to turn them over to the estate voluntarily, but he did not tell Client that information. Client signed the contingent fee agreement, and Lawyer submitted it for judicial approval without informing Client. Ultimately, Lawyer claimed he was entitled to a payment of $101,544.14, which was 21% of the assets that were returned to

the Estate. Lawyer worked on the case for 48 hours. Were the fees proper? *See In re Hefron*, 771 N.E.2d 1157 (Ind. 2002).

4. Walton hired Law Firm to recover unpaid royalties from several oil and gas companies operating on his 32,500 acre ranch. The fee agreement provided that Law Firm would receive a 30% contingent fee on all claims collected in one trial. It also provided, "You may terminate the Firm's legal representation at any time. Upon termination by you, you agree to immediately pay the Firm the then present value of the Contingent Fee, plus all costs then owed to the Firm." Law Firm began the representation, making a $58.5 million settlement demand. The opposing party rejected this, but a month later offered $6 million to settle the claims and purchase part of Walton's ranch. Walton said he would take the $6 million to settle the royalties claim, but had no intention of selling any land. Law Firm urged him to sell. Walton became dissatisfied and fired Law Firm. Ultimately, Walton, with new counsel, settled his case for $900,000. Law Firm sent him a bill for $1.7 million (30% of $6 million). Was Walton required to pay Law Firm? *See Hoover Slovacek LLP v. Walton*, 206 S.W.3d 557 (Tex. 2006).

5. Client was divorced in 1973. The divorce agreement provided that Client's husband would retain the community property, valued at $1.3 million, and would purchase Client's interest in the property for a payment of $50,000 and a $600,000 promissory note. The note provided that Client could demand annual payments of up to $50,000 of principal, and that Husband was to make interest payments on the unpaid portion of the note until it was paid in full; the interest payments would constitute alimony payments to Client. Client made two demands for principal payments, then ceased doing so. By 1998, Husband was still making interest payments on the note and the annual interest payments were more than $100,000. Husband sued Client, claiming that Client had a duty in good faith to make demands for principal payments and allow him to pay off the note. Client hired Lawyer to represent her. While Lawyer offered her an hourly fee arrangement, Client insisted that Lawyer take the case on a contingency fee basis, and the parties agreed on a one-third contingency fee. Lawyer negotiated a payment of $600,000 from Husband, and claimed an entitlement to a $200,000 fee. Can Lawyer enforce the contingency fee agreement? *See Marquis & Aurbach v. Eighth Judicial District Court*, 146 P.3d 1130 (Nev. 2006); *see also Sheresky Aronson & Mayefsky, LLP v. Whitmore*, 2007 WL 2894237 (N.Y. Sup. 2007).

6. Attorney wants to include the following provision in a retainer agreement for representation of clients in contingency fee cases: "In the event Client terminates this agreement, the reasonable value of Attorney's services shall be valued at $200 per hour for attorney time and $65 per hour for legal assistant time for all services rendered. In the alternative, the Attorney may, where permitted by law, elect compensation based on the agreed contingency fee for any settlement offer made to Client prior to termination." Is this provision enforceable? *See Virginia Legal Ethics Op. 1812* (2008).

7. Hepler worked in a bank. A customer, Hughes, named Hepler the personal representative of his estate and sole beneficiary under his will; he had no spouse or surviving children or grandchildren. At the time Hughes executed the will, he was blind and infirm and living in a nursing home. While the

attorney who drafted Hughes's will was convinced that Hughes was competent at the time he executed his will, Hepler was concerned that Hughes' relatives might contest the will. Hepler consulted attorney Flaniken about representing her in connection with the probate of Hughes's will. Flaniken proposed an hourly fee and a retainer; Hepler declined. The two agreed that upon finalization of the probate, Hepler would pay Flaniken a contingency fee of one-third of the gross amount due Hepler; if the will was contested, Flaniken would receive forty percent of the amount received by Hepler. The will was not contested. Flaniken filed the probate, wrapped up the estate, and claimed that under the contingency fee agreement he was entitled to one-third of Hepler's total inheritance of $451,413.54. Did Flaniken violate the ethical rules regarding reasonable fees? *See Oklahoma Bar Association v. Flaniken*, 85 P.3d 824 (Okla. 2004).

CHAPTER 10

THE DUTY TO THE COURT

■ ■ ■

Up until now we have been considering the duties that a lawyer owes to a client. Those duties include the duties of competency, confidentiality, and loyalty, and the questions we have asked about those obligations are predictable: to whom are these duties owed, to what do they extend, and under what circumstances can breach of those duties give rise to discipline, civil liability, or other sanction.

But a lawyer owes duties to others besides the client. In this chapter, we consider the duties that a lawyer owes to the court. Lawyers have duties "as officers of the court to avoid conduct that undermines the integrity of the adjudicative process." Comment [2] to Model Rule 3.3. What happens when the lawyer's duty to the client conflicts with the lawyer's duty to the court? The duty to the client is limited to some extent by the duty to the court; the zeal with which the lawyer pursues the client's objective must be tempered by this duty to the tribunal.

A. THE DUTY OF CANDOR TO THE COURT: CLIENT PERJURY

A lawyer owes a duty of "candor toward the tribunal." Read Model Rule 3.3 at this point. As you can see, several of the requirements of the rule are directed toward the lawyer's own behavior: a lawyer is prohibited, for example, from knowingly making a false statement of material fact or law to a tribunal, and from failing to correct such a false statement after it is made. A lawyer has an obligation of candor with regard to law as well as fact: she must disclose to the tribunal controlling adverse legal authority if the other side does not. (More on that later.)

A lawyer's obligation to be truthful to the court extends beyond her own conduct, however, to the evidence that she presents. A lawyer is also precluded from offering evidence "that the lawyer knows to be false." Model Rule 3.3(a)(3). This, of course, can include the testimony of the lawyer's own client, which brings us to the rules on client perjury.

Before we talk about the ethics rules on client perjury, it's useful to understand what perjury is. 18 U.S.C. § 1623, the federal perjury statute, provides: "Whoever under oath . . . in any proceeding before or ancillary to any court or grand jury of the United States knowingly makes any false material declaration," is guilty of perjury. Perjury is a crime. False testimony under oath is perjury, whether given in open court, in a deposition, or even in a written declaration (like an affidavit) that is attested to by oath or affirmation.

Under Model Rule 3.3, the lawyer is prohibited from offering evidence that the lawyer knows to be false, regardless of the source. This duty to the court extends to all evidence offered by the lawyer, not just the testimony of the lawyer's client. But the most dramatic juxtaposition of the lawyer's duties to the client and to the tribunal are presented when the lawyer is compelled to deal with the false testimony of her own client. The difficulties this presents have caused this issue to be the subject of vigorous debate and intense criticism. We will consider the current rule and its critics. Why has this historically been viewed as such a challenging area to regulate?

In contemplating the ethical rules that govern this area, there are two distinct sets of parameters to keep in mind. One is the stage at which the situation presents itself. We can imagine three. In the first, the lawyer has not yet offered the client's testimony, but has reason to believe that the client intends to testify falsely. In the second, the lawyer is deciding, based on her knowledge and her conversations with her client, whether to offer the client's testimony. In the third, the lawyer has already offered the false testimony. Each of these stages demands distinct conduct on the part of the lawyer.

The second question is whether we are dealing with a civil or criminal case. As we will see, this distinction somewhat constrains the choices that are available to the lawyer.

1. BEFORE THE CLIENT TESTIFIES: THE DUTY TO REMONSTRATE

Imagine that a lawyer is preparing for a criminal trial. The client comes to the office to be prepared to give his testimony. At the close of the session, the client says to the lawyer, "I'll say what I need [to] say to help myself out and if I have to say something untruthful I'll say that. I need to help myself out." (These are the real facts of *State v. McDowell*, 681 N.W.2d 500, 505 (Wis. 2004).)

The client has not yet testified, but based on the client's comments, the lawyer has a concern that the client is planning to testify falsely at trial. What should the lawyer do?

The Model Rules are clear that the lawyer's obligation at this preliminary stage is to urge the client to tell the truth: "If a lawyer knows that the client intends to testify falsely or wants the lawyer to introduce false evidence, the lawyer should seek to persuade the client that the evidence should not be offered." Comment [6] to Model Rule 3.3. How would a lawyer persuade her client to testify truthfully? What kind of arguments would the lawyer bring to bear? One reason that the rules on false testimony developed as they have is to provide some leverage for the lawyer in this situation.

2. DECIDING TO OFFER TESTIMONY

What is the lawyer's obligation when deciding whether to offer the client's testimony? Remember that under Model Rule 1.2(a), the decision whether to testify in a criminal case is exclusively the client's to make. The rules also require, however, that a lawyer "shall not knowingly . . . offer evidence that the lawyer knows to be false." Model Rule 3.3(a)(3). That means that the lawyer is precluded from offering even his own client's testimony if the lawyer affirmatively knows that it will be false.

Model Rule 3.3(a)(3) further provides that "A lawyer may refuse to offer evidence . . . that the lawyer reasonably believes is false." But this is true only in a civil case; if the lawyer represents a defendant in a criminal matter, the lawyer cannot refuse to offer the client's testimony based only on her reasonable belief that the client will testify falsely. In a criminal case, "[u]nless the lawyer knows the testimony will be false, the lawyer must honor the client's decision to testify." Comment [9] to Model Rule 3.3.

How high is the "knowledge" standard? Consider that question in the context of the following case:

NIX v. WHITESIDE

475 U.S. 157 (1986)

CHIEF JUSTICE BURGER delivered the opinion of the Court.

We granted certiorari to decide whether the Sixth Amendment right of a criminal defendant to assistance of counsel is violated when an attorney refuses to cooperate with the defendant in presenting perjured testimony at his trial.

I

A

Whiteside was convicted of second-degree murder by a jury verdict which was affirmed by the Iowa courts. The killing took place on February 8, 1977, in Cedar Rapids, Iowa. Whiteside and two others went to one Calvin Love's apartment late that night, seeking marihuana. Love was in bed when Whiteside and his companions arrived; an argument between Whiteside and Love over the marihuana ensued. At one point, Love directed his girlfriend to get his "piece," and at another point got up, then returned to his bed. According to Whiteside's testimony, Love then started to reach under his pillow and moved toward Whiteside. Whiteside stabbed Love in the chest, inflicting a fatal wound.

Whiteside was charged with murder. . . . Gary L. Robinson was . . . appointed and immediately began an investigation. Whiteside gave him a statement that he had stabbed Love as the latter "was pulling a pistol from underneath the pillow on the bed." Upon questioning by Robinson, however, Whiteside indicated that he had not actually seen a gun, but that he was convinced that Love had a gun. No pistol was found on the premises; shortly after the police search following the stabbing, which had revealed no weapon, the victim's family had removed all of the victim's possessions from the apartment. Robinson interviewed Whiteside's companions who were present during the stabbing, and none had seen a gun during the incident. Robinson advised Whiteside that the existence of a gun was not necessary to establish the claim of self-defense, and that only a reasonable belief that the victim had a gun nearby was necessary even though no gun was actually present.

Until shortly before trial, Whiteside consistently stated to Robinson that he had not actually seen a gun, but that he was convinced that Love had a gun in his hand. About a week before trial, during preparation for direct examination, Whiteside for the first time told Robinson and his associate Donna Paulsen that he had seen something "metallic" in Love's hand. When asked about this, Whiteside responded: "[I]n Howard Cook's case there was a gun. If I don't say I saw a gun, I'm dead."

Robinson told Whiteside that such testimony would be perjury and repeated that it was not necessary to prove that a gun was available but only that Whiteside reasonably believed that he was in danger. On Whiteside's insisting that he would testify that he saw "something metallic" Robinson told him, according to Robinson's testimony:

> [W]e could not allow him to [testify falsely] because that would be perjury, and as officers of the court we would be suborning perjury if we allowed him to do it; ... I advised him that if he did do that it would be my duty to advise the Court of what he was doing and that I felt he was committing perjury; also, that I probably would be allowed to attempt to impeach that particular testimony.

Robinson also indicated he would seek to withdraw from the representation if Whiteside insisted on committing perjury.

Whiteside testified in his own defense at trial and stated that he "knew" that Love had a gun and that he believed Love was reaching for a gun and he had acted swiftly in self-defense. On cross-examination, he admitted that he had not actually seen a gun in Love's hand. Robinson presented evidence that Love had been seen with a sawed-off shotgun on other occasions, that the police search of the apartment may have been careless, and that the victim's family had removed everything from the apartment shortly after the crime. Robinson presented this evidence to show a basis for Whiteside's asserted fear that Love had a gun.

The jury returned a verdict of second-degree murder, and Whiteside moved for a new trial, claiming that he had been deprived of a fair trial by Robinson's admonitions not to state that he saw a gun or "something metallic." The trial court held a hearing, heard testimony by Whiteside and Robinson, and denied the motion. The trial court made specific findings that the facts were as related by Robinson.

The Supreme Court of Iowa affirmed respondent's conviction. That court held that the right to have counsel present all appropriate defenses does not extend to using perjury, and that an attorney's duty to a client does not extend to assisting a client in committing perjury. Relying on DR 7–102(A)(4) of the Iowa Code of Professional Responsibility for Lawyers, which expressly prohibits an attorney from using perjured testimony, and Iowa Code § 721.2 (now Iowa Code § 720.3 (1985)), which criminalizes subornation of perjury, the Iowa court concluded that not only were Robinson's actions permissible, but were required. The court commended "both Mr. Robinson and Ms. Paulsen for the high ethical manner in which this matter was handled."

B

Whiteside then petitioned for a writ of habeas corpus in the United States District Court for the Southern District of Iowa. In that petition Whiteside alleged that he had been denied effective assistance of counsel and of his right to present a defense by Robinson's refusal to allow him to testify as he had proposed. The District Court denied the writ. Accepting the state trial court's factual finding that Whiteside's intended testimony would have been perjurious, it concluded that there could be no grounds for habeas relief since there is no constitutional right to present a perjured defense.

The United States Court of Appeals for the Eighth Circuit reversed and directed that the writ of habeas corpus be granted. The Court of Appeals accepted the findings of the trial judge, affirmed by the Iowa Supreme Court, that trial counsel believed with good cause that Whiteside would testify falsely and acknowledged that ... a criminal defendant's privilege to testify in his own behalf does not include a right to commit perjury. Nevertheless, the court reasoned that an intent to commit perjury, communicated to counsel, does not alter a defendant's right to effective assistance of counsel and that Robinson's admonition to Whiteside that he would inform the court of Whiteside's perjury constituted a threat to violate the attorney's duty to preserve client confidences. According to the Court of Appeals, this threatened violation of client confidences breached the standards of effective representation set down in *Strickland v. Washington*, 466 U.S. 668 (1984). The court also concluded that *Strickland*'s prejudice requirement was satisfied by an implication of prejudice from the conflict between Robinson's duty of loyalty to his client and his ethical duties. ... We granted certiorari, and we reverse.

II

A

The right of an accused to testify in his defense is of relatively recent origin. Until the latter part of the preceding century, criminal defendants in this country, as at common law, were considered to be disqualified from giving sworn testimony at their own trial by reason of their interest as a party to the case. . . .

By the end of the 19th century, however, the disqualification was finally abolished by statute in most states and in the federal courts.

B

In *Strickland v. Washington*, we held that to obtain relief by way of federal habeas corpus on a claim of a deprivation of effective assistance of counsel under the Sixth Amendment, the movant must establish both serious attorney error and prejudice. To show such error, it must be established that the assistance rendered by counsel was constitutionally deficient in that "counsel made errors so serious that counsel was not functioning as 'counsel' guaranteed the defendant by the Sixth Amendment." To show prejudice, it must be established that the claimed lapses in counsel's performance rendered the trial unfair so as to "undermine confidence in the outcome" of the trial.

In *Strickland*, we acknowledged that the Sixth Amendment does not require any particular response by counsel to a problem that may arise. Rather, the Sixth Amendment inquiry is into whether the attorney's conduct was "reasonably effective." To counteract the natural tendency to fault an unsuccessful defense, a court reviewing a claim of ineffective assistance must "indulge a strong presumption that counsel's conduct falls within the wide range of reasonable professional assistance." In giving shape to the perimeters of this range of reasonable professional assistance, *Strickland* mandates that "[p]revailing norms of practice as reflected in American Bar Association Standards and the like, . . . are guides to determining what is reasonable, but they are only guides."

Under the *Strickland* standard, breach of an ethical standard does not necessarily make out a denial of the Sixth Amendment guarantee of assistance of counsel. When examining attorney conduct, a court must be careful not to narrow the wide range of conduct acceptable under the Sixth Amendment so restrictively as to constitutionalize particular standards of professional conduct and thereby intrude into the state's proper authority to define and apply the standards of professional conduct applicable to those it admits to practice in its courts. In some future case challenging attorney conduct in the course of a state-court trial, we may need to define with greater precision the weight to be given to recognized canons of ethics, the standards established by the state in statutes or professional codes, and the Sixth Amendment, in defining the proper scope and limits on that conduct. Here we need not face that question, since virtually all of the sources speak with one voice.

C

We turn next to the question presented: the definition of the range of "reasonable professional" responses to a criminal defendant client who informs counsel that he will perjure himself on the stand. We must determine whether, in this setting, Robinson's conduct fell within the wide range of professional responses to threatened client perjury acceptable under the Sixth Amendment.

In *Strickland*, we recognized counsel's duty of loyalty and his "overarching duty to advocate the defendant's cause." Plainly, that duty is limited to legitimate, lawful conduct compatible with the very nature of a trial as a search for truth. Although counsel must take all reasonable lawful means to attain the objectives of the client, counsel is precluded from taking steps or in any way assisting the client in presenting false evidence or otherwise violating the law. This principle has consistently been recognized in most unequivocal terms by expositors of the norms of professional conduct since the first Canons of Professional Ethics were adopted by the American Bar Association in 1908. . . .

These principles have been carried through to contemporary codifications of an attorney's professional responsibility. Disciplinary Rule 7–102 of the Model Code of Professional Responsibility (1980), entitled "Representing a Client Within the Bounds of the Law," provides:

> (A) In his representation of a client, a lawyer shall not . . .
>
>> (4) Knowingly use perjured testimony or false evidence . . .
>>
>> (7) Counsel or assist his client in conduct that the lawyer knows to be illegal or fraudulent.

This provision has been adopted by Iowa, and is binding on all lawyers who appear in its courts.

Both the Model Code of Professional Responsibility and the Model Rules of Professional Conduct also adopt the specific exception from the attorney-client privilege for disclosure of perjury that his client intends to commit or has committed. Indeed, both the Model Code and the Model Rules do not merely *authorize* disclosure by counsel of client perjury; they *require* such disclosure. *See* Rule 3.3(a)(4); DR 7–102(B)(1); *Committee on Professional Ethics and Conduct of Iowa State Bar Assn. v. Crary*, 245 N.W.2d 298 (Iowa 1976).

These standards confirm that the legal profession has accepted that an attorney's ethical duty to advance the interests of his client is limited by an equally solemn duty to comply with the law and standards of professional conduct; it specifically ensures that the client may not use false evidence. This special duty of an attorney to prevent and disclose frauds upon the court derives from the recognition that perjury is as much a crime as tampering with witnesses or jurors by way of promises and threats, and undermines the administration of justice. . . .

It is universally agreed that at a minimum the attorney's first duty when confronted with a proposal for perjurious testimony is to attempt to dissuade the client from the unlawful course of conduct. A statement directly in point is found in the commentary to the Model Rules of Professional Conduct under the heading "False Evidence":

> When false evidence is offered by the client, however, a conflict may arise between the lawyer's duty to keep the client's revelations confidential and the duty of candor to the court. Upon ascertaining that material evidence is false, the lawyer *should seek to persuade the client that the evidence should not be offered* or, if it has been offered, that its false character should immediately be disclosed.

Model Rules of Professional Conduct, Rule 3.3, Comment (1983) (emphasis added).

The commentary thus also suggests that an attorney's revelation of his client's perjury to the court is a professionally responsible and acceptable response to the conduct of a client who has actually given perjured testimony. Similarly, the Model Rules and the commentary, as well as the Code of Professional Responsibility adopted in Iowa, expressly permit withdrawal from representation as an appropriate response of an attorney when the client threatens to commit perjury. Withdrawal of counsel when this situation arises at trial gives rise to many difficult questions including possible mistrial and claims of double jeopardy.

The essence of the brief *amicus* of the American Bar Association reviewing practices long accepted by ethical lawyers is that under no circumstance may a lawyer either advocate or passively tolerate a client's giving false testimony. This, of course, is consistent with the governance of trial conduct in what we have long called "a search for truth." The suggestion sometimes made that "a lawyer must believe his client, not judge him" in no sense means a lawyer can honorably be a party to or in any way give aid to presenting known perjury.

D

Considering Robinson's representation of respondent in light of these accepted norms of professional conduct, we discern no failure to adhere to reasonable professional standards that would in any sense make out a deprivation of the Sixth Amendment right to counsel. Whether Robinson's conduct is seen as a successful attempt to dissuade his client from committing the crime of perjury, or whether seen as a "threat" to withdraw from representation and disclose the illegal scheme, Robinson's representation of Whiteside falls well within accepted standards of professional conduct and the range of reasonable professional conduct acceptable under *Strickland.*

The Court of Appeals' holding that Robinson's "action deprived [Whiteside] of due process and effective assistance of counsel" is not supported by the record since Robinson's action, at most, deprived Whiteside of his contemplated perjury. Nothing counsel did in any way undermined Whiteside's claim that he believed the victim was reaching for a gun. Similarly, the record gives no support for holding that Robinson's action "also impermissibly compromised [Whiteside's] right to testify in his own defense by conditioning continued representation ... and confidentiality upon [Whiteside's] *restricted* testimony." The record in fact shows the contrary: (a) that Whiteside did testify, and (b) he was "restricted" or restrained only from testifying falsely and was aided by Robinson in developing the basis for the fear that Love was reaching for a gun. Robinson divulged no client communications until he was compelled to do so in response to Whiteside's post-trial challenge to the quality of his performance. We see this as a case in which the attorney successfully dissuaded the client from committing the crime of perjury....

Whatever the scope of a constitutional right to testify, it is elementary that such a right does not extend to testifying *falsely*....

The paucity of authority on the subject of any such "right" may be explained by the fact that such a notion has never been responsibly advanced; the right to counsel includes no right to have a lawyer who will cooperate with planned perjury. A lawyer who would so cooperate would be at risk of prosecution for suborning perjury, and disciplinary proceedings, including suspension or disbarment.

Robinson's admonitions to his client can in no sense be said to have forced respondent into an *impermissible* choice between his right to counsel and his right to testify as he proposed for there was no *permissible* choice to testify falsely. For defense counsel to take steps to persuade a criminal defendant to testify truthfully, or to withdraw, deprives the defendant of neither his right to counsel nor the right to testify truthfully....

On this record, the accused enjoyed continued representation within the bounds of reasonable professional conduct and did in fact exercise his right to testify; at most he was denied the right to have the assistance of counsel in the presentation of false testimony. Similarly, we can discern no breach of professional duty in Robinson's admonition to respondent that he would disclose respondent's perjury to the court. The crime of perjury in this setting is indistinguishable in substance from the crime of threatening or tampering with a witness or a juror. A defendant who informed his counsel that he was arranging to bribe or threaten witnesses or members of the jury would have no "right" to insist on counsel's assistance or silence. Counsel would not be limited to advising against that conduct. An attorney's duty of confidentiality, which totally covers the client's admission of guilt, does not extend to a client's announced plans to engage in future criminal conduct. In short, the responsibility of an ethical lawyer, as an officer of the court and a key component of a system of justice, dedicated to a search for truth, is essentially the same whether the client announces an intention to bribe or threaten witnesses or jurors or to commit or procure perjury. No system of justice worthy of the name can tolerate a lesser standard.

The rule adopted by the Court of Appeals, which seemingly would require an attorney to remain silent while his client committed perjury, is wholly incompatible with the established standards of ethical conduct and the laws of Iowa and contrary to professional standards promulgated by that State. The position advocated by petitioner, on the contrary, is wholly consistent with the Iowa standards of professional conduct and law, with the overwhelming majority of courts, and with codes of professional ethics. Since there has been no breach of any recognized professional duty, it follows that there can be no deprivation of the right to assistance of counsel under the *Strickland* standard.

E

We hold that, as a matter of law, counsel's conduct complained of here cannot establish the prejudice required for relief under the second strand of the *Strickland* inquiry. . . .

JUSTICE BRENNAN, concurring in the judgment.

This Court has no constitutional authority to establish rules of ethical conduct for lawyers practicing in the state courts. Nor does the Court enjoy any statutory grant of jurisdiction over legal ethics.

Accordingly, it is not surprising that the Court emphasizes that it "must be careful not to narrow the wide range of conduct acceptable under the Sixth Amendment so restrictively as to constitutionalize particular standards of professional conduct and thereby intrude into the state's proper authority to define and apply the standards of professional conduct applicable to those it admits to practice in its courts." I read this as saying in another way that the Court *cannot* tell the States or the lawyers in the States how to behave in their courts, unless and until federal rights are violated.

Unfortunately, the Court seems unable to resist the temptation of sharing with the legal community its vision of ethical conduct. But let there be no mistake: the Court's essay regarding what constitutes the correct response to a criminal client's suggestion that he will perjure himself is pure discourse without force of law. As Justice BLACKMUN observes, *that* issue is a thorny one, but it is not an issue presented by this case. Lawyers, judges, bar associations, students, and others should understand that the problem has not now been "decided." . . .

JUSTICE BLACKMUN, with whom JUSTICE BRENNAN, JUSTICE MARSHALL, and JUSTICE STEVENS join, concurring in the judgment.

How a defense attorney ought to act when faced with a client who intends to commit perjury at trial has long been a controversial issue. But I do not believe that a federal habeas corpus case challenging a state criminal conviction is an appropriate vehicle for attempting to resolve this thorny problem. When a defendant argues that he was denied effective assistance of counsel because his lawyer dissuaded him from committing perjury, the only question properly presented to this Court is whether the lawyer's actions deprived the defendant of the fair trial which the Sixth Amendment is meant to guarantee. Since I believe that the respondent in this case suffered no injury justifying federal habeas relief, I concur in the Court's judgment.

On February 7, 1977, Emmanual Charles Whiteside stabbed Calvin Love to death. At trial, Whiteside claimed self-defense. On direct examination, he testified that Love's bedroom, where the stabbing had occurred, was "[v]ery much dark," and that he had stabbed Love during an argument because he believed that Love was about to attack him with a weapon:

Q. Did you think that Calvin had a gun?

A. Most definitely I thought that.

Q. Why did you think that?

A. Because of Calvin's reputation, his brother's reputation, because of the prior conversation that Calvin and I had, I didn't have no other choice but to think he had a gun. And when he told his girl friend to give him his piece, I couldn't retreat.

Whiteside's testimony was consistent with that of other witnesses who testified that the room was dark, and that Love had asked his girlfriend to get his "piece" (which they all believed referred to a weapon). No gun, however, was ever found.

Whiteside, who had been charged with first-degree murder, was convicted of second-degree murder, and sentenced to 40 years' imprisonment. He moved for a new trial, contending that his court-appointed attorneys, Gary Robinson and Donna Paulsen, had improperly coerced his testimony. Whiteside now claimed that he had seen a gun, but had been prevented from testifying to this fact.

At an evidentiary hearing on this motion, Whiteside testified that he had told Robinson at their first meeting that he had seen a weapon in Love's hand. Some weeks later, Robinson informed Whiteside that the weapon could not be found and, according to Whiteside, told him to say only that he thought he had seen a gun, rather than that he in fact had seen one. Whiteside "got the impression at one time that maybe if I didn't go along with—with what was happening, that it was no gun being involved, maybe that he will pull out of my trial."

Robinson's testimony contradicted Whiteside's. According to Robinson, Whiteside did not initially claim to have seen a gun, but rather claimed only that he was convinced Love had had one. Roughly a week before the trial, however, in the course of reviewing Whiteside's testimony, Whiteside "made reference to seeing something 'metallic'.... I don't think he ever did say a gun."

> And at the end Donna asked him about that, because that was the first time it had ever been mentioned either to her or to myself. His response to that was, 'in Howard Cook's case there was a gun. If I don't say I saw a gun, I'm dead.' I explained to him at that time that it was not necessary that the gun be physically present for self-defense, one; two, that to say that would be perjury on his part because he had never at any time indicated that there was a gun ...; three, that we could not allow him to do that ...; four, I advised him that if he did do that it would be my duty to advise the Court of what he was doing ...; also, that I probably would be allowed to attempt to impeach that particular testimony. I told him that there was no need

for him to lie about what had happened, that he had a good and valid defense on the facts as he had related them to us, and we felt we could present a good self-defense case on the facts he had stated to us.

Robinson acknowledged that Whiteside's claim of self-defense would have been stronger had the gun been found, but explained that at trial "we tried to create a gun", through testimony from people who had seen Love carrying a gun on other occasions, through a stipulation that Love had been convicted of possession of a weapon, and through suggestions made during cross-examination of the State's witnesses that the initial police search had been too cursory to discover the weapon and that Love's girlfriend had removed it from the apartment prior to a second, more thorough, search. . . .

The Court approaches this case as if the performance-and-prejudice standard requires us in every case to determine "the perimeters of [the] range of reasonable professional assistance," but *Strickland v. Washington* explicitly contemplates a different course:

> Although we have discussed the performance component of an ineffectiveness claim prior to the prejudice component, there is no reason for a court deciding an ineffective assistance claim to approach the inquiry in the same order or even to address both components of the inquiry if the defendant makes an insufficient showing on one. In particular, a court need not determine whether counsel's performance was deficient before examining the prejudice suffered by the defendant as a result of the alleged deficiencies. . . . If it is easier to dispose of an ineffectiveness claim on the ground of lack of sufficient prejudice, which we expect will often be so, that course should be followed.

In this case, respondent has failed to show any legally cognizable prejudice. . . .

The touchstone of a claim of prejudice is an allegation that counsel's behavior did something "to deprive the defendant of a fair trial, a trial whose result is reliable." *Strickland v. Washington*, 466 U.S. at 687. The only effect Robinson's threat had on Whiteside's trial is that Whiteside did not testify, falsely, that he saw a gun in Love's hand. Thus, this Court must ask whether its confidence in the outcome of Whiteside's trial is in any way undermined by the knowledge that he refrained from presenting false testimony. . . .

In addition, the lawyer's interest in not presenting perjured testimony was entirely consistent with Whiteside's best interest. If Whiteside had lied on the stand, he would have risked a future perjury prosecution. Moreover, his testimony would have been contradicted by the testimony of other eyewitnesses and by the fact that no gun was ever found. In light of that impeachment, the jury might have concluded that Whiteside lied as well about his lack of premeditation and thus might have convicted him of first-degree murder. And if the judge believed that Whiteside had lied, he could have taken Whiteside's perjury into account in setting the sentence. In the face of these dangers, an attorney could reasonably conclude that dissuading his client from committing perjury was in the client's best interest and comported with standards of professional responsibility. In short, Whiteside failed to show the kind of conflict that poses a danger to the values of zealous and loyal representation embodied in the Sixth Amendment. A presumption of prejudice is therefore unwarranted.

In light of respondent's failure to show any cognizable prejudice, I see no need to "grade counsel's performance." The only federal issue in this case is whether Robinson's behavior deprived Whiteside of the effective assistance of counsel; it is not whether Robinson's behavior conformed to any particular code of legal ethics.

Whether an attorney's response to what he sees as a client's plan to commit perjury violates a defendant's Sixth Amendment rights may depend on many factors: how certain the attorney is that the proposed testimony is false, the stage of the proceedings at which the attorney discovers the plan, or the ways in which the attorney may be able to dissuade his client, to name just three. The complex interaction of factors, which is likely to vary from case to case, makes inappropriate a blanket rule that defense attorneys must reveal, or threaten to reveal, a client's anticipated perjury to the court. Except in the rarest of cases, attorneys who adopt "the role of the judge or jury to determine the facts," pose a danger of depriving their clients of the zealous and loyal advocacy required by the Sixth Amendment.

I therefore am troubled by the Court's implicit adoption of a set of standards of professional responsibility for attorneys in state criminal proceedings. The States, of course, do have a compelling interest in the integrity of their criminal trials that can justify regulating the length to which an attorney may go in seeking his client's acquittal. But the American Bar Association's implicit suggestion in its brief *amicus curiae* that the Court find that the Association's Model Rules of Professional Conduct should govern an attorney's responsibilities is addressed to the wrong audience. It is for the States to decide how attorneys should conduct themselves in state criminal proceedings, and this Court's responsibility extends only to ensuring that the restrictions a State enacts do not infringe a defendant's federal constitutional rights. Thus, I would follow the suggestion made in the joint brief *amici curiae* filed by 37 States at the certiorari stage that we allow the States to maintain their "differing approaches" to a complex ethical question. The signal merit of asking first whether a defendant has shown any adverse prejudicial effect before inquiring into his attorney's performance is that it avoids unnecessary federal interference in a State's regulation of its bar. Because I conclude that the respondent in this case failed to show such an effect, I join the Court's judgment that he is not entitled to federal habeas relief.

JUSTICE STEVENS, concurring in the judgment.

Justice Holmes taught us that a word is but the skin of a living thought. A "fact" may also have a life of its own. From the perspective of an appellate judge, after a case has been tried and the evidence has been sifted by another judge, a particular fact may be as clear and certain as a piece of crystal or a small diamond. A trial lawyer, however, must often deal with mixtures of sand and clay. Even a pebble that seems clear enough at first glance may take on a different hue in a handful of gravel.

As we view this case, it appears perfectly clear that respondent intended to commit perjury, that his lawyer knew it, and that the lawyer had a duty—both to the court and to his client, for perjured testimony can ruin an otherwise meritorious case—to take extreme measures to prevent the perjury from occurring. The lawyer was successful and, from our unanimous and remote perspective, it is now pellucidly clear that the client suffered no "legally cognizable prejudice."

Nevertheless, beneath the surface of this case there are areas of uncertainty that cannot be resolved today. A lawyer's certainty that a change in his client's recollection is a harbinger of intended perjury—as well as judicial review of such apparent certainty—should be tempered by the realization that, after reflection, the most honest witness may recall (or sincerely believe he recalls) details that he previously overlooked. Similarly, the post-trial review of a lawyer's pretrial threat to expose perjury that had not yet been committed—and, indeed, may have been prevented by the threat—is by no means the same as review of the way in which such a threat may actually have been carried out. Thus, one can be convinced—as I am—that this lawyer's actions were a proper way to provide his client with effective representation without confronting the much more difficult questions of what a lawyer must, should, or may do after his client has given testimony that the lawyer does not believe. The answer to such questions may well be colored by the particular circumstances attending the actual event and its aftermath.

Because Justice BLACKMUN has preserved such questions for another day, and because I do not understand him to imply any adverse criticism of this lawyer's representation of his client, I join his opinion concurring in the judgment.

NOTES

1.   Did the lawyers in *Whiteside* know that their client did not see a gun in the victim's hand? If so, how did they know it? The Supreme Court, of course, was not deciding this issue because of the state court's findings of fact. If you were the lawyers here, would you have "known" that Whiteside's intended statement that he saw a gun was false? Could a more sophisticated client have created more doubt in your mind?

2.   Do you have some concerns about how accurately you will be able to reach conclusions about the truthfulness of your client's intended testimony? Might these concerns be exacerbated if the client comes from a different age, ethnic and cultural group than you do and, in addition, profoundly mistrusts you as her state-appointed advocate? Might those factors affect your certainty about whether the client intends to give false testimony at trial?

3. The question of knowledge is complex. In the *Crary* case, cited by the Court, the lawyer knew his divorce client was lying at her deposition when asked about her whereabouts at particular times because he had been with her at those times; the lawyer had been having illicit trysts with the client. *Committee on Professional Ethics & Conduct of the Iowa State Bar Ass'n v. Crary*, 245 N.W.2d 298 (Iowa 1976). But the lawyer's knowledge about the truthfulness of a client's intended testimony will rarely come from firsthand information. Where will it ordinarily come from?

4. What does Justice Blackmun mean when he expresses concern that "attorneys who adopt 'the role of the judge or jury to determine the facts,' pose a danger of depriving their clients of the zealous and loyal advocacy required by the Sixth Amendment"? In that regard, consider the following case.

UNITED STATES v. MIDGETT

342 F.3d 321 (4th Cir. 2003)

TRAXLER, CIRCUIT JUDGE:

In November 2000, Paul Dameron Midgett was convicted of ... bank robbery, and threatening a bank teller with gasoline in the course of a bank robbery.... He received life sentences on all three convictions.... Because the court erred in forcing Midgett to choose between his right to a lawyer and his right to testify on his own behalf, we vacate and remand for a new trial.

I.

In October 1999, J.W. Shaw, Jr., was eating lunch in his van at a worksite in Mecklenburg County, North Carolina, when a man approached him with a cup of gasoline, threw it in his face, and demanded his money. After Shaw gave the man his billfold, the assailant ignited the gasoline with a lighter, inflicting burns to Shaw's face, neck, ears, and hands. In November 1999, Paul Midgett and Theresa Russell were charged with this crime (Count One), as well as with using a similar technique later the same day to rob a bank in Union County, North Carolina (Counts Two and Three). Russell eventually agreed to cooperate with the government; Midgett decided to go to trial.

From the outset, Midgett and his lawyer appear to have been at odds. Before trial began, Midgett's lawyer moved to withdraw because of disagreements with his client as to how to proceed. Among other matters, Midgett complained about his lawyer's degree of preparation and his unwillingness to pursue certain issues to Midgett's satisfaction—including a "third person" defense Midgett sought to offer in relation to the Count One crime. Midgett steadfastly maintained to his lawyer that a friend of Russell was driving around with the two of them at the time they encountered Shaw. According to Midgett, it was Russell's friend, and not Midgett, who had committed the assault on Shaw, while Midgett lay in a drug-induced sleep in the back of the vehicle. Midgett was prepared to offer this testimony himself, but his lawyer did not want Midgett to take the stand because he did not believe Midgett's version of events.

Notified of problems emerging between client and attorney prior to trial, the court conducted a hearing and determined that there was no reason justifying withdrawal, Midgett's counsel having demonstrated due diligence in planning and preparing for trial. For the first of several times, the court offered Midgett the choice of proceeding on his own or continuing with his lawyer. Midgett remarked that "there's no way I could do it myself," and so his lawyer remained. The next day, before the jury was impaneled, the court asked Midgett whether he intended to testify, to which Midgett replied, "We haven't made a decision yet and I really—to be honest, my lawyer really doesn't want me, but I kind of wanted to, but we haven't made a decision yet." Trial began and several government witnesses testified, from whom defense counsel was able on cross-examination to bring out certain facts helpful to Midgett. For example, Midgett's lawyer elicited that Shaw had not been able to identify Midgett in a photographic lineup and that another witness to the attack on Shaw had described the culprit to investigators as a tall individual (Midgett being relatively short).

Later that day, after a private conference with Midgett, his lawyer announced to the court that he "must pursuant to the rules of professional conduct move to withdraw." The judge and Midgett's counsel then left the courtroom for what appears to have been an off-the-record discussion which neither Midgett nor the government attorney attended. When they returned, the court addressed Midgett:

> [Y]our attorney explains to me that you are requesting him to offer evidence and present a defense which he does not intend to offer and considers improper to make ... and has so advised you, but you nevertheless insist that you are going to offer the defense, whatever it is, if he doesn't.... I have told him that I will give you the option of proceeding without an attorney from this point or continuing in his representation.... So you better talk with [him] and let me know if you want him to continue to represent you or if you want him to step aside and we'll continue the trial.

Midgett ultimately responded that "I'll continue with [him] being my attorney, but I don't want it, I do it under protest. I do not agree with it at all." ... The government then continued its case, during which defense counsel subjected Midgett's co-defendant Theresa Russell to cross-examination as to the favorable plea agreement she expected in exchange for her testimony against Midgett.

The following day, after the government rested its case and Midgett's motion for acquittal was denied, the court asked whether the defense had evidence to present. Again, Midgett's lawyer raised the issue of his conflict with his client. Defense counsel stated that he had repeatedly recommended to Midgett that testifying was not in his best interests. At the court's prompting, Midgett's lawyer further asserted that

I indicated to you in chambers that I felt I needed to withdraw because I was duty bound to make that motion, and you directed me to tell you why, and at that point I indicated that it is my belief that Mr. Midgett is going to offer information when he testifies that is not in any way truthful or in existence that I can determine from any source.... [A]nd based on what has been represented to me and I understand is about to happen if and when he takes the stand, I am duty bound to move to withdraw at this point. I can say that the issue relates to whether or not a third person was at the scene at the time of the destruction incident when Mr. Shaw was burned, a third person actually did the act. And I have investigated that, I have asked for an identity from this supposed person. I have asked the co-defendant directly whether this person exists.... There's nothing whatsoever that I can find to corroborate any such representation.

Rather than permitting his lawyer to withdraw, the court offered Midgett the choice of either acceding to defense counsel's refusal to put him on the stand or representing himself without further assistance of counsel. Midgett repeated that he did not "feel ... qualified to [represent himself]... I'm saying I want to [take the stand], but I can't." In response, Midgett's lawyer told the court: "I don't think he's being denied his right to testify. He's got a choice here today what he wants to do. He knows the parameters. I have asked him a number of times to give me the name or a way to find this person, and he can't do it and no one else corroborates it." The court agreed, stating that "if the defendant chooses to take the witness stand, I will permit [him] to withdraw." Midgett responded: "I say again, Your Honor, I want to take the witness stand, but I can't because I can't do it without counsel." The court finally told Midgett that

if there is any problem with your taking the stand and not being able to take the stand because of your wanting to bring before the jury an issue that doesn't exist and for which you have absolutely no evidence to offer other than your own testimony ... the court is of the opinion that any resulting problem is a problem of your own making, and the trial will not be further delayed.... The time has come that we're going to finish the case, and you and the appellate courts may take it from there.

Midgett declined to testify and his lawyer offered no other evidence. In his closing statement, defense counsel referred to various weaknesses and inconsistencies in the statements of certain witnesses, including Theresa Russell's motive to give testimony favorable to the government and Shaw's inability to identify Midgett in the photographic lineup. The jury took little time to convict Midgett on all three counts.

After trial the court granted defense counsel's motion to withdraw, stating that:

It was clear throughout the course of the trial that [Midgett] repeatedly conferred with counsel and was satisfied with counsel's performance except as it related to ... [the] defense that a third party was responsible for the crime charged in Count One, when counsel's thorough investigation and the overwhelming evidence indicated the guilt of the Defendant and no one else.

New counsel was appointed and immediately filed a motion for new trial, which was denied; several further motions for new trial were subsequently filed and denied in turn. This appeal followed.

Midgett . . . claims that the district court erred in conditioning his right to counsel on his waiver of his right to testify.

II.

The question of what a lawyer should do when confronted by potentially perjurious testimony has long caused consternation in the legal profession, producing heated debate and little consensus. On the one hand are the series of constitutional rights to which a defendant is entitled and for which the defendant's lawyer is called to provide zealous advocacy; on the other hand are the lawyer's obligations to the court to seek the furtherance of justice. Similarly, the court itself is obliged to ensure that the constitutional rights of the defendant are protected, while also seeing that proceedings are conducted fairly and truthfully. Midgett argues that these obligations were not adequately met when his lawyer, disbelieving Midgett's proffered testimony, sought to withdraw from representing him and approached the court to discuss the lack of corroborative evidence in support of Midgett's case. Likewise, Midgett argues that the court should not have confronted him with a choice between exercising his right to take the stand and his right to be represented by counsel. Under these circumstances, we agree.

The Sixth Amendment guarantees a criminal defendant the right to the assistance of counsel at trial. It is also clear that a criminal defendant has a constitutional right to testify on his own behalf at trial. . . . Notwithstanding its constitutional stature, however, the defendant's right to testify is "not unlimited." In particular, "the right to testify clearly does not include the right to commit perjury." This limitation was explicitly recognized in *Nix v. Whiteside*, 475 U.S. 157 (1986), the case upon which the government relies in answer to Midgett's argument on appeal.

. . . Under *Nix* . . . the defendant's right to counsel and his right to testify on his own behalf are circumscribed in instances where the defendant has made manifest his intention to commit perjury. Unlike *Nix*, however, where the defendant actually admitted to his lawyer that he planned to perjure himself, Midgett never told his lawyer or otherwise indicated to him that his intended testimony was perjurious. Rather, Midgett consistently maintained that his third-person defense was true and that he believed his co-defendant could corroborate his story.

The question, then, is whether the information known to defense counsel was sufficient to show that Midgett's testimony would be perjurious so as to bring this case within the rule set forth in *Nix*. We conclude that it was not. We recognize that Midgett's "mystery man did it" defense lacked other corroboration. Among other things, Midgett's co-defendant actually testified that no one else was in the van during the arson/robbery, and, although he had been unable to do so in an earlier photographic lineup, Shaw did identify Midgett in court as his assailant. Midgett also sent a letter to Shaw that might have been interpreted by the jury as a feeble apology for what had happened to the victim—though the letter is altogether too vague and indirect to be described as an acknowledgment of guilt.

Notwithstanding these obstacles to his case, Midgett had apparently been consistent in his interviews with his lawyer that a third person committed the Count One crime and that he did not. Defense counsel's responsibility to his client was not dependent on whether he personally believed Midgett, nor did it depend on the amount of proof supporting or contradicting Midgett's anticipated testimony regarding how the incident happened. In this situation, Midgett never indicated to his attorney that his testimony would be perjurious. Thus, his lawyer had a duty to assist Midgett in putting his testimony before the jury, which would necessarily include his help in Midgett's direct examination.

Defense counsel's mere belief, albeit a strong one supported by other evidence, was not a sufficient basis to refuse Midgett's need for assistance in presenting his own testimony. This assessment is consistent with Rule 3.3(a)(3) of the Model Rules of Professional Conduct, which requires that a lawyer "not knowingly offer evidence that the lawyer *knows* to be false," but also states that "[a] lawyer may refuse to offer evidence, *other than the testimony of a defendant in a criminal matter*, that the lawyer *reasonably believes* is false." (emphasis added). Far-fetched as Midgett's story might have sounded to a jury, it was not his lawyer's place in these circumstances to decide that Midgett was lying and to declare this opinion to the court.

As this discussion makes clear, we believe Midgett's trial lawyer failed to carry out his duty to zealously defend his client. The issue on appeal, however, is not whether counsel was ineffective so as to warrant a new trial, but whether the district court erred by forcing Midgett to choose between testifying or retaining counsel. We believe that, in the circumstances of this case, the court did err in this regard, given that the court effectively mirrored defense counsel's error by deciding that Midgett's testimony would be perjurious. To be sure, the court had an obligation not to permit *known* perjury from being placed before the jury. In this case, however, the court merely believed the defendant's potential testimony would be dramatically outweighed by other evidence, a situation that did not warrant the extreme sanction imposed by the court.

The record reveals that, during the colloquy after the close of the government's case, the court defended the choice it imposed on Midgett by declaring that "your wanting to bring before the jury an issue that doesn't exist and *for which you have absolutely no evidence to offer other than your own testimony* ... [amounts to] a problem of your own making." (emphasis added). Thus, the court based its ultimatum on an inappropriate weighing of the evidence. Specifically, the court treated as irrefutable proof of an intent to commit perjury the fact that Midgett did not produce corroborating witnesses and sought merely to offer his own testimony. The defendant was told to waive either his right to counsel or his right to testify because neither his counsel nor the court was satisfied that his testimony would be truthful. In so doing, the court leveled an ultimatum upon Midgett which, of necessity, deprived him of his constitutional right to testify on his own behalf. Forcing this "Hobson's choice" upon the defendant constituted error that calls for a new trial. . . .

Notes

1.   Why was the result different in *Midgett* than in *Nix v. Whiteside*? Do you agree with the court's conclusion about what happened in *Whiteside*? The court seems convinced by the fact that in *Whiteside*, the client told the lawyer two different stories, while in *Midgett*, the client stuck to his guns throughout. Does this mean that a lawyer only knows that a client is lying if the client tells him so? According to one court, the knowledge that a client intends to testify untruthfully, "[a]bsent the most extraordinary circumstances . . . must be based on the client's expressed admission of intent to testify untruthfully. While we recognize that the defendant's admission need not be phrased in 'magic words,' it must be unambiguous and directly made to the attorney." *State v. McDowell*, 681 N.W.2d 500, 513 (Wis. 2004). Does this seem like a reasonable rule? In *McDowell*, the client was charged with sexual assault; DNA evidence of his semen was found at the scene of the crime. The client wanted to testify that the reason his DNA was found at the scene was that he had had consensual sexual activity with his girlfriend at the very same location the day before. Does this rule mean the lawyer had to offer the testimony, however preposterous, unless the client admitted that it was untrue? Does the rule unfairly benefit sophisticated clients?

2.   Could Whiteside have fired his lawyer, hired another, and told the new lawyer that he saw a gun in Love's hand? Would that have put him in the same position as Midgett? Would the former lawyer still have a duty to disclose to the court that he knew Whiteside had testified falsely?

Issues of suspected client perjury often come to the court's attention, as they did in *Midgett*, when counsel seeks to withdraw. The lawyer believes that the rules preclude him from knowingly offering false testimony; the court may be reluctant to excuse counsel, delaying the trial and perhaps simply inviting a renewal of the same issue later on with new counsel, or concealing the problem altogether because the client will be more savvy with her new lawyer. What should a court do under the circumstances? Denying the client the right to testify in her own defense might deprive her of her constitutional rights; permitting her to testify falsely would corrupt the trial process.

A few jurisdictions affirmatively approve a third solution to the client perjury problem: the so-called "narrative approach." The lawyer, instead of guiding the client through a traditional direct examination, permits the client to testify in "narrative" form, simply telling his story. As one judge described this procedure to a defendant: " 'What this means . . . is with regard to your testimony . . . while [your attorney] will be here, he will not be conducting that examination. It will not be a question and answer situation as we see with other witnesses. Rather, you . . . will be allowed to testify in a free-flow narrative way.' " *People v. Gadson*, 19 Cal. App. 4th 1700 (2d Dist. 1993).

The good news about the narrative approach? The lawyer does not participate in the offering of false evidence, and the defendant is not fully deprived of his right to testify in his own defense. The bad news? This unusual procedure telegraphs to all knowledgeable players that there is something terribly wrong with the testimony. And if, in fact, the testimony is truthful, the client has been deprived of the assistance of counsel in offering it. The Model Rules unambiguously reject the narrative approach, but some jurisdictions affirmatively approve it, either through their ethics rules, *see D.C. Rule of Professional Conduct 3.3(b)*; *Comment [7] to South Carolina Rule of Professional Conduct 3.3*; or through caselaw. *See, e.g., People v. Andrades*, 828 N.E.2d 599, 603 (N.Y. 2005), describing the appropriate procedure: "Should the client insist on perjuring himself, counsel may seek to withdraw from the case. If counsel's request is denied, defense counsel, bound to honor defendant's right to testify on his own behalf, should refrain from eliciting the testimony in traditional question-and-answer form and permit defendant to present his testimony in narrative form." *See also Brown v. Commonwealth*, 226 S.W.3d 74 (Ky. 2007), *Commonwealth v. Mitchell*, 781 N.E.2d 1237 (Mass. 2003), *People v. Johnson*, 62 Cal. App. 4th 608 (Cal. App. 1998). Even in jurisdictions that do not expressly approve of the narrative method, courts may sometimes resort to it as the best of a bad set of options. What do you think of it?

Those jurisdictions permitting the use of the narrative approach do so only when the lawyer knows that the client intends to offer false testimony. Mere suspicion will not suffice.

3. AFTER THE CLIENT TESTIFIES: THE DUTY TO TAKE "REASONABLE REMEDIAL MEASURES"

What if you have offered material evidence and subsequently learn that it is false? Model Rule 3.3(a)(3) provides that "If a lawyer, the lawyer's client, or a witness called by the lawyer, has offered material evidence and the lawyer comes to know of its falsity, the lawyer shall take reasonable remedial measures, including, if necessary, disclosure to the tribunal."

If the testimony comes from the client, Comment [10] to Model Rule 3.3 makes clear that the lawyer's "proper course" is to "remonstrate with the client confidentially, advise the client of the lawyer's duty of candor to the tribunal and seek the client's cooperation with respect to the withdrawal or correction of the false statements or evidence."

How could a lawyer get a client to reveal to a court that the client has testified falsely? Again, the stick that the lawyer has at her disposal is the threat that the lawyer will disclose to the tribunal that the client has testified untruthfully if the client does not. "[U]nless it is clearly understood that the lawyer will act upon the duty to disclose the existence of false evidence, the client can simply reject the lawyer's advice to reveal the false evidence and insist that the lawyer keep silent." Comment [11] to Model Rule 3.3.

If the client does not remedy the situation, the lawyer must. "If withdrawal from the representation is not permitted or will not undo the effect of the false evidence, the advocate must make such disclosure to the tribunal as is reasonably necessary to remedy the situation, even if doing so requires the lawyer to reveal information that otherwise would be protected by Rule 1.6." Comment [10] to Model Rule 3.3. If Rule 3.3 requires disclosure of confidential information, but Rule 1.6 requires that it be kept confidential, which rule governs? See Model Rule 3.3(c). Model Rule 3.3 thus adds an exception—not mentioned in the text of Model Rule 1.6—to the duty of confidentiality. Even if the lawyer must disclose, the Restatement admonishes that the lawyer should be careful to minimize the adverse effect on the client. Restatement of the Law Governing Lawyers, § 120, comment (h).

How long does the disclosure obligation continue? Model Rule 3.3(c) states that the duties in Model Rule 3.3(a) and (b) "continue to the conclusion of the proceeding." Comment [13] further clarifies that "[a] proceeding has concluded within the meaning of this Rule when a final judgment in the proceeding has been affirmed on appeal or the time for review has passed." The Restatement suggests that this obligation is not terminated simply because the lawyer withdraws or is discharged by the client. Restatement of the Law Governing Lawyers, § 120, comment (h).

Under the Model Rules, the duty to disclose false testimony and the conclusion that the disclosure obligation trumps the confidentiality obligation are unambiguous. The Model Rules approach has, however, been broadly criticized. In a classic law review article, Prof. Monroe Freedman argued that the situation created three distinct and conflicting obligations on the part of the lawyer, what Prof. Freedman memorably termed the "perjury trilemma." In a recent publication, Professor Freedman summarized the problem. "The first ethical obligation is that the lawyer learn everything possible about a client's case. The second obligation is that the lawyer keep knowledge about the client's case confidential except to advance the client's interests. The third obligation is that the lawyer reveal the client's confidential information to the court if doing so should become necessary to expose what the lawyer knows to be perjurious testimony by the client." Monroe Freedman, *Getting Honest About Client Perjury*, 21 Geo. J. Legal Ethics 133, 134 (2008). Prof. Freedman's concern was that these three obligations are in irreconcilable conflict. Can a lawyer in good faith assure the client of confidentiality in order to obtain as much information as possible about a case, knowing that she may need to disclose to the court later on if the client seeks to testify falsely? If the lawyer, cognizant of this concern, describes to the client the limits on the confidentiality obligation at the outset, does she run the risk of learning less than the full information required to represent her client zealously? Prof. Freedman's controversial answer to this challenging problem was to permit lawyers, after attempting to dissuade their clients from committing perjury, to offer their testimony in the ordinary way without disclosing to the court that the testimony was false. As Prof. Freedman notes in his article, the proposal resulted in the bringing of an ethics complaint against him, which was dismissed. 21 Geo. J. Legal Ethics at 133.

Some suggest that the way to avoid this problem is to avoid learning the full truth from the client, thereby avoiding the "knowledge" that would invoke the disclosure obligation and that might prevent the client from giving the most advantageous testimony at trial. Is this an appropriate response to the problem? The ABA's Standards Relating to the Administration of Criminal Justice firmly reject this approach; Standard 4–3.2 for the Defense Function explicitly states that "Defense counsel should not instruct the client or intimate to the client in any way that the client should not be candid in revealing facts so as to afford defense counsel free rein to take action which would be precluded by counsel's knowing of such facts." These standards are advisory only; as a criminal defense lawyer, would you follow them? Why or why not?

B. THE DUTY OF CANDOR TO THE COURT: FALSIFYING EVIDENCE

From the client perjury materials, it might seem as though the problem is that clients want to give false testimony and lawyers want to prevent them from doing so. Lawyers, however, are sometimes themselves involved in the creation of false testimony or evidence. Model Rule 3.4(b) expressly prohibits such conduct; it provides, "A lawyer shall not ... falsify evidence, counsel or assist a witness to testify falsely, or offer an inducement to a witness that is prohibited by law."

In some circumstances, it is easy to tell when a lawyer is counseling a witness to testify falsely. In *In re Attorney Discipline Matter*, 98 F.3d 1082 (8th Cir. 1996), Lawyer represented D.G. in a divorce case in which the custody of her daughter was at issue. During a court hearing, a witness testified that he and D.G. had had sexual intercourse in the presence of the child. Lawyer requested a recess to discuss this damaging testimony, and the following conversation ensued:

Lawyer: What about the business about the [motel]? Did that happen?

D.G.:		Yeah, it happened.
Lawyer:		God-damn. What were you thinking about?
D.G.:		She was only three months—I mean 18 months. I couldn't leave him. I don't know. I don't know.
Lawyer:		You better deny this. Eighteen months old, Jesus.... You better deny this, buddy. You better deny it.... I think the thing that hurts you is taking the kid in the room and screwing with the kid in the room. He said that you two had sex in the bed next to your kid, your little kid that was in the other bed. *You're going to have to do something with it.*
D.G.:		*What can I do with it that won't make it seem like I'm lying?*
Lawyer:		I don't know. That's up to you. *It could be your word against his. It's up to you.*
D.G.:		*Are you saying if I deny it then—*
Lawyer:		*If you said it didn't happen, it didn't happen....*

After the recess, Lawyer elicited the following testimony from D.G. on direct examination:

Lawyer:		Do you ever—*under oath now, do you ever remember going to a motel with your daughter with [J.M.]?*
D.G.:		*No.*
Lawyer:		That's a lie, isn't it?
D.G.:		Yes.
Lawyer:		What would possess him to tell that?
D.G.:		I don't know....

98 F.3d at 1084–85. During the recess, the court reporter's recording equipment was inadvertently left running, providing for a verbatim transcript of Lawyer's colloquy with his client. Lawyer was disbarred for this conduct. Why do you suppose he engaged in it? Given the range of bad options with which he and his client were presented, how might he have proceeded without running afoul of the ethical rules?

It is clear that a lawyer may not affirmatively direct a witness to testify falsely. But what sorts of conduct, short of that direction, overstep the appropriate bounds of lawyer conduct? This is worth thinking about, because lawyers routinely prepare clients and witnesses for courtroom or deposition testimony. Witness preparation creates a unique opportunity to generate false testimony. Certain preparation strategies—urging the witness to be truthful, directing him not to volunteer information and to answer only the question asked, and to dress and behave appropriately—are clearly part of the job. But can witness preparation move from preparing a witness to comply with the somewhat unfamiliar norms of the legal process to generating or encouraging false testimony?

This issue came to the forefront when, in 1997, a memo came out that a law firm, Baron & Budd, was using to prepare clients—plaintiffs who claimed they had been injured by workplace exposure to asbestos—for their depositions. The memo did several things. First, it provided detailed descriptions of the various asbestos products that the clients might have seen or used in the workplace. It further advised clients that, once they determined what they had been exposed to, they should study and memorize the products they had worked with:

> Your responses to questions about asbestos products and how you were exposed to them is the most important part of your deposition. You must PROVE you worked with or around the products listed on your Work History Sheets. You must be CONFIDENT about the NAMES of each product, what TYPE of product it was, how it was PACKAGED, who used it and HOW it was used. You must be able to show that you were close to it often enough while it was being applied to have inhaled the fibers given off while it was being mixed, sanded, sawed, compressed, drilled or cut, etc. You will be required to do all this from MEMORY, which is why you MUST start studying your Work History Sheets NOW! ... [I]t is best to MEMORIZE all your products and where you saw them BEFORE your deposition.

The memo went on to advise as to what would be the best answers to particular questions that might be asked:

> You may be asked how you are able to recall so many product names. The best answer is to say that you recall seeing the names on the containers or on the product itself. The more you thought about it, the more you remembered! If the defense attorney asks you if you were shown pictures of products, wait for your attorney to advise you to answer, then say that a girl from Baron & Budd showed you pictures of MANY products, and you picked out the ones you remembered. If there is a MISTAKE on your Work History Sheets, explain that the "girl from Baron & Budd" must have misunderstood what you told her when she wrote it down.

Finally, the memo gave particular advice about some specific issues:

> You will be asked if you ever saw any WARNING labels on containers of asbestos. It is important to maintain that you NEVER saw any labels on asbestos products that said WARNING or DANGER.... You will be asked if you ever used respiratory equipment to protect you from asbestos. Listen carefully to the question! If you did wear a mask for welding or other fumes, that does NOT mean you wore it for protection from asbestos! The answer is still "NO"! ... Do NOT say you saw more of one brand than another, or that one brand was more commonly used than another. At some jobs there may have been more of one brand. At other jobs there may have been more of another brand, so throughout your career you were probably exposed equally to ALL the brands. You NEVER want to give specific quantities or percentages of any product names. The reason for this is that the other manufacturers can say you were exposed more to another brand than to theirs, and so they are NOT as responsible for your illness. Be CONFIDENT that you saw just as much of one brand as all the others. All the manufacturers sued in your case should share the blame equally!

The memo is reproduced in S.Rep. 108–118, The Fairness in Asbestos Injury Resolution Act of 2003 (July 30, 2003) (Additional View of Sen. Kyl).

The clients in these cases were workers, perhaps with serious illnesses, who were being asked to remember specifics about workplace exposure that had taken place many decades before. In light of that, was the memo an appropriate refreshment of witness recollection, or did it go beyond that to the improper creation of testimony? Did its use constitute zealous representation or subornation of perjury? The Model Rules say nothing about witness preparation. Should they?

C. THE DUTY OF CANDOR TO THE COURT: LAWYER HONESTY

IN RE WILKA

638 N.W.2d 245 (S.D. 2001)

GILBERTSON, CHIEF JUSTICE.

Attorney Timothy J. Wilka (Wilka) was reported to the Disciplinary Board of the State Bar of South Dakota by Second Circuit Judge Glen Severson for violations of the Model Rules of Professional Conduct, stemming from Wilka's use of an incomplete drug report during a visitation hearing and his misleading responses to Judge Severson's questions regarding the report. The Board recommended discipline in the form of a public censure. We agree.

FACTS AND PROCEDURE

Wilka, a graduate of the University of South Dakota School of Law, was admitted to practice in South Dakota in 1983. He is currently engaged in private practice with one associate in Sioux Falls, South Dakota.

In July 2000, Wilka was representing Travis Van Overbeke (Client) in a divorce action against Carla Van Overbeke (Mother). Mother was seeking to restrict Client's visitation rights with his three-year-old daughter to supervised visitation on the basis that Client was using methamphetamines. Second Circuit guidelines regarding child visitation provide that if either parent is using drugs, visitation may be suspended. Additionally, Mother had deprived Client of visitation. Therefore, Client responded with a cross motion to hold Mother in contempt. A hearing was scheduled before Judge Severson for July 31, 2000.

In preparation for the hearing, Wilka counseled Client to undergo a urinalysis test for methamphetamines at Avera McKennan Hospital in Sioux Falls. Client was tested on July 18, 2000. However, the test conducted by McKennan screened for a battery of drugs. While Client tested negative for methamphetamines, he did test positive for cannabinoids, which signaled recent use of marijuana.

The lab technician who performed the analysis telephoned the results to Wilka, who later received a printed report of the substance abuse screen. The screen showed the positive result for cannabinoids and a "not detected" result for seven other substances, including methamphetamines. Wilka then contacted the technician and informed her that, because there were no allegations of marijuana use in his case, he needed a report only indicating the methamphetamine results. He requested a new test be completed, one that screens only for methamphetamine use. The technician informed Wilka that they were unable to separate the screen but that she could provide him with a second report, one without the cannabinoids result. The technician accomplished this by simply tearing or cutting off the bottom portion of the drug screen results, omitting the positive result for cannabinoids.

Following the receipt of the partial report, Wilka made a copy of the report and sent it to opposing counsel, Doug Thesenvitz (Thesenvitz), to refute the charge of methamphetamine use by Client. Thesenvitz had indicated that he would withdraw his motion for supervised visitation if Client tested negative for methamphetamine use. As a former prosecutor, however, Thesenvitz was apparently familiar with the drug screen report and noticed that the cannabinoids result was conspicuously missing. Therefore, he decided to proceed with the hearing.

During the July 31 hearing, Wilka had the partial report marked as Exhibit A and presented it to Client's wife initially for impeachment purposes on cross-examination. Wilka then asked that the partial report be admitted into evidence and it was received by the court. Immediately upon admission, the court asked "Is this cut off or is this the entire—" Wilka responded, "That's what I was provided by the hospital, Your Honor." Again, the court inquired "Is this the entire thing?" Wilka replied "That's what I have Judge. That's what I asked them to screen for."

Before closing statements, the court again addressed the partial report by stating "Mr. Wilka, this wasn't offered for the truth of what the results are. It was—" Wilka responded with "—to show that on July 18th there was no methamphetamine or any of the other drugs detected in his system." The court informed Wilka that the irregularities of the partial report, its torn uneven appearance, made the report "suspect" and it was not competent evidence. Wilka responded "I understand. This is exactly what was provided to me by the people at McKennan Hospital, and if you don't want to receive it, Your Honor, then I understand." Finally, the court ordered Client to undergo an additional drug screen, which came back negative for all drugs, and directed Wilka to provide a certified result of Exhibit A. Wilka did disclose the entire report to the court and opposing counsel while the case was still pending, with no apparent harm being done to either party.

Judge Severson reported Wilka's conduct to the Minnehaha County State's Attorney, the Disciplinary Board and to this Court. Criminal charges were initiated by the State's attorney but were ultimately pled down to a civil contempt charge. On November 7, 2000, Wilka appeared before Judge Severson and entered the following statement

> Your Honor, I sincerely apologize to the Court for failing to fully disclose to the Court that the report I offered as evidence on July 31, 2000, is incomplete. My answers to the Court's questions were misleading and I am sorry.

Wilka was found in contempt and fined $100.

After the disciplinary hearing was conducted on June 15, 2001, the Board concluded that Wilka had violated the following Rules of Professional Conduct: 3.3(a)(1), (2) and (4) and 3.3(b) concerning candor toward the tribunal; 3.4(a) concerning fairness; 4.1(a) concerning truthfulness; and 8.4(a), (c) and (d) concerning professional misconduct. The Board also found that Wilka "showed little genuine remorse for his conduct" and recommended public censure.

The Referee disagreed. The Referee concluded as a matter of law that Wilka did *not* violate the following rules: 3.3(a)(1) because his statements to the court were not false; 3.4(a) because he did not obstruct another party's access to evidence or unlawfully alter, destroy or conceal a document or other material having potential evidentiary value; or 4.1(a) because the report sent to Thesenvitz was not a false statement of a material fact and he had no obligation to disclose the second report revealing marijuana use. The Referee did, however, find that Wilka violated the following rules: 3.3(a)(2) because he failed to answer the court's questions and therefore failed to reveal a material fact; 3.3(a)(4) not because the report itself was false, but because Wilka's evasive answers purported it to be something other than incomplete; 8.4(a) because a violation of the Rules of Professional Conduct is professional misconduct; 8.4(c) because he was deceitful in that his answers to the court were misleading; and 8.4(d) because Wilka failed to answer the plain and understandable questions of the court. Finally, the Referee made a finding of fact that "without hesitancy and without a doubt, [Wilka] is very remorseful and genuinely sorry for what has occurred." Additionally, he noted that Wilka apologized to Judge Severson "on three separate occasions, once in person, once during the contempt proceeding, and again during the disciplinary proceeding," and that not only did he receive his contempt citation in open forum in Sioux Falls with considerable press coverage, he was also charged criminally. As a result, the Referee concluded that Wilka "has been held sufficiently accountable" and recommended discipline by way of private censure. Thus, the only question before this Court is:

> Whether submitting an incomplete report into evidence and refusing to fully answer the questions of the court regarding that evidence, thereby misleading the court, warrants a public censure.

ANALYSIS AND DECISION

In determining the appropriate discipline, this Court reviews the totality of the circumstances leading to the attorney's misconduct.... Wilka's conduct in this case, as well as his prior record,[1] lead us to conclude that public censure is appropriate.

"This Court has previously imposed public censure for misrepresentations to the court." While Wilka may not have directly lied to the court, he intentionally evaded the plain and understandable questions of Judge Severson. In doing so, he misled the court and misrepresented the evidence as being more than it was.

Clearly, the requirement of candor towards the tribunal goes beyond simply telling a portion of the truth. It requires every attorney to be fully honest and forthright.

We cannot overemphasize the importance of attorneys in this state being absolutely fair with the court. Every court ... has the right to rely upon an attorney to assist it in ascertaining the truth of the case before it. Therefore, candor and fairness should characterize the conduct of an attorney at the beginning, during, and at the close of litigation.

There is no allowance for interpretation.

Wilka's intent to mislead the court is not mitigated by his concerns over Client's right to confidentiality. The dilemma in which Wilka found himself was one of his own making. Options other than evading the questions of the court remained open to him....

We respect Wilka's desire to represent Client without betraying confidentiality. Nevertheless, there is a line that even the zealous advocate cannot cross. Herein, the referee found Wilka's conduct to be "deceitful and he misled Judge Severson and this was intentional in nature." Such conduct clearly crosses the line into improper and unprofessional conduct.

Wilka argues that what he has had to endure because of this incident already amounts, in reality, to a public censure. He points to having been the subject of criminal investigations, the recipient of a $100 fine for civil contempt and to the corresponding press coverage that apparently was substantial. We have consistently refused to recognize such claims for leniency to avoid professional discipline. The purpose of a criminal prosecution is to punish a crime against the State. The purpose of civil contempt is to punish the wrongdoer. The purpose of attorney disciplinary proceedings is not to punish the attorney anew, but rather to take sufficient measures for the protection of the public and its legal system from a repetition of these types of incidents....

The Referee also found that Wilka was "remorseful and contrite." When he appeared before this Court, he personally expressed this remorse. At

---

1. Wilka has had 10 complaints filed against him and investigated by the Disciplinary Board since 1990. Four of those complaints were dismissed. For the remaining six, he has received discipline in the form of two cautions, two admonitions and two private reprimands.

this point in these proceedings, we have no reason to doubt the sincerity of his statement.

Therefore, based on a totality of the circumstances, Timothy J. Wilka is hereby publicly censured. . . .

NOTES

1.   What exactly did Wilka do wrong here? Did he make a false statement? What was it? The information that his client had tested positive for cannabinoids was doubtless damaging to the client's right to visitation. Was Wilka obliged to disclose that information? If not, how should he have handled the matter? Consider Model Rule 3.4(a).

2.   The court says that Wilka had alternatives. What were they?

3.   Fraud on the court is an ethical violation. It can also be a crime. John Gellene, a partner at a prominent New York law firm, undertook to represent a client, Bucyrus–Erie Corp., in a bankruptcy proceeding. The bankruptcy rules required Gellene to provide a sworn declaration disclosing "any connection" that his firm had with "the Debtors, their creditors, or any other party in interest." Gellene disclosed that his firm had represented one creditor, but failed to disclose that it represented another creditor, as well as its manager and the manager's financial adviser. Gellene did some of the work for those other clients himself. Gellene filed a supplemental affidavit affirming the false statements and testified to them again at a court hearing. When his false statements came to light, he was charged with and ultimately convicted of two counts of bankruptcy fraud and one count of perjury. He was sentenced to 15 months in prison and a $15,000 fine; his firm was required to disgorge its $1.8 million fee in the bankruptcy case, and his convictions led to his disbarment. *See United States v. Gellene*, 182 F.3d 578 (7th Cir. 1999); *Matter of Gellene*, 676 N.Y.S.2d 161 (N.Y.A.D. 1998).

4.   Lawyers often lie to get themselves out of trouble. In *In re Aguilar and Kent*, 97 P.3d 815 (Cal. 2004), a lawyer failed to appear for oral argument before the state Supreme Court in a matter. He represented to the court that he was unaware of the time and date of the argument. In subsequent proceedings the court concluded that Aguilar lied. The court imposed a $1000 fine and referred him to the state bar for discipline. As *Aguilar* suggests, lying to get out of trouble sometimes gets a lawyer into bigger trouble. But lawyers do not always lie or mislead only to save themselves. What was the lawyer's intention in the following case? Do you think he was treated fairly?

PEOPLE v. SIMAC (IN RE SOTOMAYOR)

defense attorney knowingly misled court about identity of client

641 N.E.2d 416 (Ill. 1994)

CHIEF JUSTICE BILANDIC delivered the opinion of the court:

The sole issue in this appeal is whether appellant, David Sotomayor, an attorney licensed to practice law in this State, was properly found in direct criminal contempt of court. During a traffic proceeding in DuPage County, appellant substituted an individual other than defendant at counsel's table, without the court's permission or knowledge. The trial judge found that such conduct constituted direct criminal contempt, and fined appellant $500. The appellate court, with one justice dissenting, affirmed the finding of direct criminal contempt, but reduced the fine to $100. We granted appellant's petition for leave to appeal. We allowed the National Association of Criminal Defense Lawyers to submit a brief as *amicus curiae* on appellant's behalf.

The incident that gave rise to the contempt citation occurred during appellant's representation of defendant, Christopher Simac, for charges that arose from a car accident on March 20, 1990. Defendant was charged with driving with a revoked license and failure to yield while making a left-hand turn. After several delays, the case was called for trial on December 11, 1990. The State's only witness was Officer Ronald H. LaMorte. The complaining witness, Beth Nelson, never appeared at the trial.

Before trial, appellant seated David P. Armanentos, a clerical worker employed at his law firm, next to him at counsel's table. Defendant was seated at another location in the courtroom. Armanentos and defendant shared similar physical characteristics, in that they were both tall, thin, dark blond-haired men who wore eyeglasses. On the date of trial, Armanentos wore a white shirt with blue stripes, while defendant was dressed in a white shirt with red stripes.

Appellant did not ask the court's permission, or notify the court that he had substituted Armanentos in the customary place for a defendant at counsel's table. The State's Attorney also was not notified of the substitution. The court ordered all witnesses who were going to testify to come forth and be sworn. The clerk asked appellant, "Is your defendant [going to be sworn]?" Appellant replied, "No."

In the State's case in chief, Officer LaMorte testified regarding the automobile accident that he investigated on March 20, 1990, which resulted in injuries to a woman and her young child. He described the intersection where the accident occurred and the position of the cars. LaMorte testified that he asked defendant for identification; however, he believed that defendant was unable to produce his driver's license.

LaMorte identified Armanentos, who was seated next to appellant at counsel's table, as the person who was involved in the accident. The court noted LaMorte's identification of Armanentos as the defendant for the record. Appellant did not inform the court of the misidentification at this time or reveal that defendant was seated elsewhere in the courtroom.

After the State rested its case in chief, appellant made a motion to exclude witnesses. The motion was granted, and LaMorte left the courtroom. Appellant then called Armanentos, the person whom LaMorte previously identified, as a witness. Armanentos was sworn at this time, as he did not come forward to be sworn when the court called for witnesses at the beginning of the trial. When Armanentos stated his name for the record, the court received the first indication that a misidentification had occurred.

On direct examination, Armanentos testified that he was not driving a motor vehicle at the intersection in question on March 20, 1990. The defense then rested. Under cross-examination, Armanentos testified that he had never met defendant. He stated that he temporarily worked as a clerical employee in the appellant's law firm. It was his understanding that he was brought to court by appellant and instructed to sit at counsel's table to see whether the testifying officer would identify him as the defendant. Armanentos testified that he was told that he resembled defendant. He further admitted that he looked similar to defendant, as they were both tall, thin, and Caucasian. In response to the court's inquiry, Armanentos admitted that he did not approach the clerk to be sworn in as a witness before the commencement of the trial.

Appellant stated for the record that Armanentos never approached the bench. He was not sworn in, and was seated in the corner of the courtroom until appellant directed him to sit in the chair next to him. Appellant argued that no fraud was perpetrated on the court, for defendant was in open court as required. He asked that a directed finding of not guilty be entered in the traffic case based on the misidentification.

After appellant said that he did not intend to call any further witnesses, the State called defendant to testify. After taking the stand and stating his name for the record, defendant invoked his fifth amendment privilege and was excused. The court refused the State's request to call appellant as a witness. The State then asked that defendant take his position next to his attorney. The court replied: "[H]e can sit any place he wants to in the courtroom. He is here." Over appellant's objection, the court allowed the State to recall LaMorte. LaMorte again misidentified Armanentos as the defendant. The court granted appellant's request for a directed finding of not guilty based upon the misidentification. In addition, the court entered an order for contempt of court against the appellant for placing the witness in such a manner as to mislead the State's Attorney and the arresting officer. The court stated that the person seated next to appellant did not look like co-counsel or anyone employed in an attorney's office. The court stated that appellant had seated Armanentos next to him to purposely mislead the court. The order prepared by the court stated that "defense attorney is held in direct contempt of court for having a person bearing the likeness of [defendant] sit at the counsel table with him in the location usually occupied by defendant." The court imposed a $500 fine on appellant for direct criminal contempt.

[handwritten margin note: attorney charged w/ contempt of court]

The next day, the court made the following supplemental findings concerning this episode:

> The court finds that it was the totality of the conduct of [defense] attorney in court in connection with this case that is the basis for the court['s] finding of criminal contempt for misrepresentation by inference including the following findings:

1. That a person with the likeness of the defendant, a young, white male, was the only person with defense attorney at the counsel table when defense attorney came to the bench and said, "Here is my jury waiver."

2. That person was dressed in jeans and a shirt with no tie that is not the courtroom attire of an attorney or co-counsel, yet that person sat in the customary location of a defendant throughout the State's case.

3. That person was asked by the clerk to be sworn with other witnesses at the start of the trial, to which defense attorney said that said person was not going to testify. The obvious inference of this comment to the court and clerk was that the person was the defendant because witnesses were excluded except for defendant.

4. That person was identified as the defendant by the State witness police officer, and all of the foregoing resulted in the court's comment that the record could show that the defendant was identified for the record; there was no defense attorney response to this court's comment that advised of the court's impression and finding based on all that had occurred and that the court was misled as to the identity of the defendant.

5. That person's only apparent purpose in the courtroom, in a defendant's customary location with defense attorney, was to create an inference to the court that he was the defendant, and this was done with the knowledge of defense attorney.

6. That while there was no express misrepresentation by words, there was a misrepresentation by inference by the totality of the conduct of the defense attorney, and that was the basis of the criminal contempt of court finding.

On the same day that these supplemental findings were filed, appellant presented a motion to reconsider the order holding him in direct criminal contempt. In support of the motion, appellant stated that defendant was seated in the courtroom at the commencement of the trial. Appellant also stated that he made no representation to the court or State's Attorney concerning the identity of the person sitting next to him. Armanentos never approached the bench, nor did he take any affirmative action to falsely represent his identity. The motion to reconsider also described the six persons seated in the courtroom at the time of the misidentification. Appellant argued that his conduct did not embarrass, hinder or obstruct the court. He noted that the State was afforded every opportunity for the police officer to make an identification. The motion for reconsideration was denied. Appellant appealed the conviction of direct criminal contempt.

On appeal, a divided appellate court affirmed the judgment of direct criminal contempt, but reduced the fine from $500 to $100 . . . .

Before this court, appellant argues that his conduct of placing a substitute at counsel's table is not contemptuous. Appellant contends that the appellate court's holding violates both principles of direct criminal contempt as well as principles of professional responsibility. First, appellant argues that the appellate court improperly eliminated from the offense of direct criminal contempt the element of intent to embarrass, hinder, derogate or obstruct the court. Second, appellant contends that requiring him to disclose to the court or opposing counsel his strategy of substitution to test the State's identification testimony would be in conflict with his responsibilities under the Code of Professional Responsibility. We will address each of appellant's arguments separately.

ANALYSIS

It is well established law that all courts have the inherent power to punish contempt; such power is essential to the maintenance of their authority and the administration of judicial powers.... This court has defined criminal contempt of court "as conduct which is calculated to embarrass, hinder or obstruct a court in its administration of justice or derogate from its authority or dignity, thereby bringing the administration of law into disrepute." A finding of criminal contempt is punitive in nature and is intended to vindicate the dignity and authority of the court. However, the exercise of such power is "a delicate one, and care is needed to avoid arbitrary or oppressive conclusions." ...

def. of contempt of court

Direct criminal contempt is contemptuous conduct occurring "in the very presence of the judge, making all of the elements of the offense matters within his own personal knowledge." ... Direct contempt is "strictly restricted to acts and facts seen and known by the court, and no matter resting upon opinions, conclusions, presumptions or inferences should be considered." Direct criminal contempt may be found and punished summarily because all elements are before the court and, therefore, come within its own immediate knowledge. On appeal, the standard of review for direct criminal contempt is whether there is sufficient evidence to support the finding of contempt and whether the judge considered facts outside of the judge's personal knowledge.

I. Intent

In contending that the appellate court's holding violates principles of direct criminal contempt, appellant argues that the intent necessary to support a conviction of direct criminal contempt was not within the circuit court's personal knowledge and, therefore, his conviction must be overturned. In this regard, appellant argues that he has an ethical obligation to vigorously represent his client. Appellant asserts that, by placing a substitute at counsel's table, he merely intended in good faith to fulfill his ethical duties of zealous advocacy by testing the veracity of the State's identification testimony. Appellant argues that he was operating in unchartered waters, and that his intent was to facilitate rather than impede the administration of justice by preventing the conviction of a potentially innocent defendant based on a tainted in-court identification. He asserts that there was no evidence known to the court to establish an intent to obstruct the administration of justice or to derogate from the court's dignity or authority. Therefore, appellant asserts that, by its holding, the appellate court has improperly eliminated from the offense of direct criminal contempt the intent to embarrass, hinder, derogate, or obstruct the court.

Before citing one with contempt, a court must find that the alleged contemnor's conduct was willful. . . .

In light of the aforementioned principles, we reject appellant's argument. We find that appellant's conduct clearly reveals that his intent was not merely to test the State's identification testimony. Rather, we find that appellant intended to cause a misidentification, thereby misleading not only the State and its witness but also the court itself. Appellant commissioned a clerical employee from his office to sit with him at the defendant's customary place at counsel's table. Appellant's employee resembled the defendant in important identification characteristics. Moreover, both the substitute and the defendant wore glasses and were similarly dressed. Under these circumstances, we find that appellant calculated to cause a misidentification.

Additionally, appellant's conduct before the court indicates appellant's intent to create a misapprehension and thereby cause a misidentification. It is evident to us that appellant's conduct was intended to deceive. For instance, appellant responded in the negative to the clerk's direct inquiry as to whether his defendant would be sworn. Appellant responded negatively even though, at the same time, he obviously anticipated that the substitute would eventually testify as a witness concerning the misidentification. Clearly, appellant was aware that the only inference the court could draw from the totality of these circumstances was that the person sitting next to appellant at counsel's table was the defendant and that the defendant was not going to testify at trial.

Most revealing of appellant's intent to deceive, however, was appellant's failure to correct the court and the record upon the court's erroneous statement for the record that the witness had identified the defendant. At this point, as an officer of the court, appellant had a responsibility to the court and the integrity of the proceedings to correct the court and the record. When the court made the erroneous statement for the record, appellant clearly knew that the court was laboring under a misconception as to the identity of the defendant, yet he took no action to correct the court's mistaken impression. If appellant had not calculated to cause such a misconception, he would have taken some action to clarify the defendant's identity.

As this court has stated, "An attorney's zeal to serve his client should never be carried to the extent of . . . seeking to secure from a court an order or judgment without a full and frank disclosure of all matters and facts which the court ought to know." . . . The true identity of the defendant is clearly a fact "which the court ought to know" because it is the responsibility of the court to ensure the defendant's right to be present at all stages of the proceedings against him. Therefore, an attorney must not deceive the court as to the defendant's identity despite the attorney's obligation to vigorously represent his client. Such a deception prevents the court from fulfilling its obligation and derogates from the court's dignity and authority.

Furthermore, we reject appellant's claim that he merely intended in good faith to test the veracity of the State's identification testimony. Appellant could have easily achieved this purpose without resorting to deceptive and misleading practices. Many alternative methods are available to an attorney to test identification testimony. These available alternatives include conducting an in-court lineup, having defendant sit in the gallery without placing a substitute at counsel's table, or placing more than one person at counsel's table. It is readily apparent, therefore, that appellant could have achieved his goal as an advocate without misleading or deceiving the court, the State, and the witness and thereby remained within the bounds of his responsibilities as an officer of the court.

For the foregoing reasons, we conclude that there is sufficient evidence in the record to support appellant's conviction for direct criminal contempt. Appellant's actions derogated from the court's dignity and authority by causing the court to erroneously find for the record that the witness had identified the defendant, and his conduct delayed the proceedings. In view of appellant's actions and the surrounding circumstances, we find that appellant's conduct was calculated to and actually did embarrass, hinder, and obstruct the court and the proceedings.

II. Professional Responsibility

Appellant argues that requiring a defense attorney to give the court prior notice and obtain its permission before placing a substitute at counsel's table would violate principles of professional responsibility. Appellant contends that, in a bench trial such as this where the court also functions as the trier of fact, prior disclosure to the court of his concern regarding an identification issue would somehow influence the court's ability to render a just verdict based solely on evidence presented during the proceedings. Additionally, appellant argues that, since he cannot engage in ex parte communications with the court, he would also have to reveal his concern and strategy to the prosecution in violation of ethical obligations. Further, appellant contends that the prosecutor would then be placed in the ethical dilemma of deciding whether to inform the State's identification witness what to expect, or to seek a just result by refraining from influencing the identification witness' testimony.

We reject appellant's arguments.... [T]he court and prosecution are frequently made aware of defense concerns and potential strategies in situations involving motions *in limine*. Such pretrial motions occur on a daily basis. Defense attorneys who utilize this pretrial procedure do not violate their ethical obligations to their clients. Nor has the State ever indicated that such motion practice places it in an ethical dilemma. Many times in cases where the defense attorney's motion *in limine* has been granted, the prosecution is aware of evidence which it cannot use or allude to at trial. Nevertheless, the prosecution has been able to proceed with its function without violating its professional responsibilities. We find the practice of giving the court prior notice and obtaining its permission to place a substitute at counsel's table to be analogous to the filing and arguing of motions *in limine*. Therefore, we dismiss appellant's argument. . . .

For the reasons stated, the judgment of the appellate court, which affirmed the judgment of the circuit court in finding appellant guilty of direct criminal contempt but reduced the fine imposed to $100, is affirmed.

JUSTICE NICKELS, dissenting:

I do not agree that placing an individual in the defendant's customary place at counsel's table, without more, is a sufficient basis from which to infer an intent to hinder or obstruct the administration of justice or impugn the integrity of the court. After a thorough review of the record, I believe that defense counsel was acting in good faith to protect his client from a suggestive in-court identification. . . .

At trial, the judge made two findings regarding the basis for the contempt charge. The first finding occurred after defense counsel asked the judge to state for the record the reason for the contempt. The judge responded, "You have brought a person in here to sit next to you as defendant, *to mislead the State's Attorney and to mislead the police officer. That's my finding.*" (Emphasis added.) I am not aware of a duty imposed upon a defense attorney to assist an eyewitness or the State by providing a suggestive identification setting. In refusing to assist the State's eyewitness, defense counsel's conduct is not calculated to embarrass, hinder or obstruct the court. Instead, counsel is merely requiring the State to prove its case. Thus, this finding is not sufficient to support the contempt charge.

On the trial record, the judge made a second statement to support his finding of direct criminal contempt. The judge stated, "You have not had a person sitting beside you that looked like your co-counsel or anyone that is an attorney from your office. And you have, I think, purposely done this to mislead the court." Similarly, the majority also finds that defense counsel intended to deceive the court by placing Armanentos in the defendant's customary place at counsel's table.

A contemptuous state of mind can be inferred from an act calculated to embarrass or obstruct the court. However, not every questionable act can give rise to such an inference, particularly where the conduct involves a defense counsel's representation of a client. . . .

In determining whether the necessary contumacious intent can be inferred from a particular act, I agree with the majority that a reviewing court must look to the surrounding circumstances and the character of the action of the defendant. My examination of the record reveals that defense counsel's conduct was a good-faith attempt to protect his client from a suggestive in-court identification, and not an attempt to deceive or obstruct the court.

First, the surrounding circumstances show a good-faith reason to test the State's ability to identify the defendant. The trial had been delayed by the State, the State had no complaining witness, and the entire case rested on the testimony of Officer LaMorte. In addition, Officer LaMorte testified that he had not taken defendant's driver's license at the scene of the accident. Second, the character of defense counsel's conduct does not show disrespect for the court's authority or an attempt to disrupt the proceedings. Defense counsel showed respect to the court during the entire trial. At no point did defense counsel address the court in an inappropriate manner, disobey an order, or disrupt the proceedings. Immediately after the misidentification, defense counsel placed Armanentos on the stand in order to disclose his identity. Given the unreliability of an identification based only upon the placement of defendant at counsel's table, defense counsel acted in good faith and on behalf of his client. This is not conduct that evidences a contumacious design.

The majority finds that defense counsel intended to deceive the court and such conduct is sufficient to support a charge of contempt. In support of this conclusion, the majority relies on defense counsel's actions in telling the clerk that his defendant would not testify and the brief delay in alerting the court to the misidentification. However, my examination of the judge's order and the record do not support drawing this conclusion.

The judge's supplemental findings charge that defense counsel misrepresented to the court clerk that the person seated next to him was the defendant in the case. However, the record does not support a finding that any misrepresentation took place. The record discloses only that when witnesses were called to be sworn, the court clerk asked, "Is your defendant [going to be sworn]?" In reply, defense counsel answered, "No." The judge's findings state that "the obvious inference of this comment to the court and the clerk was that person was the defendant because witnesses were excluded."

However, because of the dangers inherent in summary contempt, this court has repeatedly stated that "it should be exercised with utmost caution and strictly restricted to acts and facts seen and known by the court, and no matter resting upon opinions, conclusions, presumptions or *inferences* should be considered." . . .

The supplemental findings also state that defense counsel's conduct caused the trial court to make a false finding and that counsel's silence in this circumstance misled the court. The majority also finds that defense counsel's silence directly after the misidentification evinces a contumacious intent to deceive the court.

I disagree. The finding entered into the record was based upon the testimony of Officer LaMorte and the court's own assumptions, not any misrepresentation by counsel. A defense attorney has no obligation to assist the State by alerting an identification witness as to defendant's location. Although defense counsel did not alert Officer LaMorte to his misidentification by immediately disclosing defendant's location, counsel did promptly place Armanentos on the stand after Officer LaMorte was excused to disclose his identity to the court. Defense counsel's silence was brief and lasted only as long as necessary to protect his client. In light of the seriousness of allowing an identification based only upon defendant's placement in the courtroom, defense counsel acted in good faith and on behalf of his client. Such conduct is insufficient to support a charge of contempt. . . .

I recognize that several jurisdictions which have considered the issue require counsel to inform the court before testing an in-court identification by placing someone other than defendant at counsel's table. . . . I agree with the majority that there are a variety of better ways to protect a defendant from such suggestive in-court identifications, including in-court lineups or other experiments done with the court's permission. The issue presented for review is not whether counsel made the best choice, but whether his specific conduct showed disregard for the court's authority and the administration of justice. . . . Under these facts, I believe counsel successfully charted a narrow pathway through a questionable course of conduct.

For the reasons stated, I would vacate the order finding defense counsel in direct criminal contempt of court.

NOTES

1.   What are the elements of direct criminal contempt? How were they shown here? Why is a finding of contempt a problem for a lawyer? Note that in the *Wilka* case, there was substantial press coverage of the contempt proceeding. Would that be important to you?

2.   Did Sotomayor at any point mislead the court, in your opinion? Was there a reason to do so? A courtroom is a suggestive environment in which to make an identification; ordinarily, the witness would expect—as did the witness in this case—that the person sitting at the defense table is, in fact, the defendant. Given that, what should attorney Sotomayor have done to protect his client's right to an unbiased identification procedure? The court suggested that the lawyer should have gone to the court to ask for an in-court identification procedure. Consider the prohibition on ex parte contacts in Rule 3.5(b). What does that mean about the lawyer's request for such a procedure? If you were a prosecutor and had been advised that the defense lawyer in the case was planning to use an unorthodox procedure to challenge an eyewitness's ability to identify the defendant, what might you do? Consider Rule 3.4.

3.   The lawyer's duty of candor becomes even more expansive in an ex parte proceeding. An ex parte proceeding is a proceeding in which, for some reason, one side is legally authorized to appear before the court without the other side being present. (Without legal authorization, the ex parte contact is prohibited under Model Rule 3.5(b); this was the concern Sotomayor expressed.) Model

Rule 3.3(d) requires a lawyer in an ex parte proceeding to "inform the tribunal of all material facts known to the lawyer that will enable the tribunal to make an informed decision, whether or not the facts are adverse." Why do we require full and fair disclosure of facts—even adverse ones—in an ex parte proceeding while we do not in an ordinary adversary proceeding?

D. OTHER DUTIES

1. THE DUTY TO DISCLOSE CONTRARY AUTHORITY

MASSEY v. PRINCE GEORGE'S COUNTY

907 F.Supp. 138 (D. Md. 1995)

MESSITTE, DISTRICT JUDGE.

I.

The Court takes this occasion to address the matter of counsel's responsibility for bringing legal authority to its attention in appropriate fashion.

What the Court *sua sponte* decides is to reverse its earlier decision dismissing certain causes of action in this case and to keep the matter in federal court; the manner in which this reversal has come about, however, merits discussion in its own right.

II.

Plaintiff Willie Massey alleges that in the early morning hours of November 4, 1992 he was sleeping in a vacant or abandoned building in Cheverly, Maryland. He contends that all of a sudden he was awakened by Prince George's County police officers who, without warning, set their police dog upon him. Massey says that although he offered no resistance, the animal proceeded to bite him and inflict painful and permanent injury all over his body. In his Third Amended Complaint before the Court, Massey has sued the individual officers for assault and battery under Maryland law and for deprivation of his Fourth Amendment rights, *i.e.* for use of excessive force, under 42 U.S.C. § 1983. The officers have denied liability, claiming that Massey was warned about the dog in a loud voice and that he resisted their efforts to arrest him.

Earlier in these proceedings, Defendants filed a fifteen page Motion for Summary Judgment. With regard to the Section 1983 claims, Defendants argued that their seizure of Plaintiff and the force used by them were reasonable as a matter of law. After citing general Supreme Court law regarding such claims, defense counsel invited the Court's attention to the case of *Robinette v. Barnes*, 854 F.2d 909 (6th Cir.1988), in which the U.S. Court of Appeals for the Sixth Circuit concluded that the use of a trained police dog in circumstances comparable to those in the case at bar was reasonable as a matter of law. Among other things, the Sixth Circuit Court observed:

... that the circumstances warranted the use of deadly force. The facts indicate that Barnes had probable cause to believe that Briggs, a suspected felon hidden inside a darkened building in the middle of the night, threatened his safety and the safety of the other officers present. As the district court succinctly put it: a reasonably competent officer would believe that a nighttime burglary suspect, who, the officers had good reason to believe, knew the building was surrounded, who had been warned ... that a dog would be used, and who gave every indication of unwillingness to surrender, posed a threat to the safety of the officers.... [T]his is a case where an officer was forced to explore an enclosed unfamiliar area in which he knew a man was hiding. Under the totality of the circumstances, Barnes was justified in using whatever force was necessary, even deadly force, to protect himself and the other officers to apprehend the suspect.

854 F.2d at 913–14.

In the present case, Plaintiff's Response to Defendants' Motion for Summary Judgment consisted of a single page, his Statement of Material Facts in Dispute barely more than two. In these, Plaintiff's counsel cited one case and one alone, namely the *Robinette* case already cited by defense counsel, which Plaintiff's counsel did no more than attempt to distinguish on its facts.

When the matter came on for oral argument, defense counsel again argued the applicability of *Robinette* to the present case, while Plaintiff's counsel again tried to distinguish *Robinette* on its facts, offering no further citation to authority.

At the conclusion of oral argument, largely on the strength of *Robinette*, the Court announced its decision to dismiss the two counts of excessive force, finding the officers' actions reasonable as a matter of law. What remained open, however, was the issue of whether Plaintiff's state law cause of action for assault and battery could survive in the face of the Court's ruling with regard to the two federal constitutional torts. The parties were invited to submit supplemental statements with regard to that limited issue.

III.

Defense counsel has now submitted a one-page letter brief in conformity with the Court's request. Plaintiff's counsel has submitted a six-page letter which, while it comports with the Court's directive in part, in effect invites the Court to reconsider its dismissal of the two federal constitutional counts. Plaintiff seems to understand that his request for reconsideration is out of order at this time, but there is a feature of counsel's letter that cannot go unremarked even now. The critical feature is that for the first time Plaintiff's counsel cites legal authority directly on point to the case at bar. The case, *Kopf v. Wing*, 942 F.2d 265 (4th Cir. 1991), is not only an excessive force case involving a police dog, but is the controlling law in this Circuit. As the Court will discuss presently, that case clearly mandates denial of Defendants' Motion for Summary Judgment, which is to say reinstatement of the excessive force claims the Court recently dismissed. But the fact that *Kopf* has been cited for the first time by Plaintiff's counsel in a supplemental letter—well after the filing of his threadbare initial response to Defendants' Motion for Summary Judgment and his equally scant oral argument on the motion—is a cause for considerable concern. At the same time, the fact that this case has never been cited by defense counsel in his initial pleadings, in oral argument or indeed to this day, gives cause for even greater concern.

IV.

In *Kopf*, a member of the bench in this district granted summary judgment on the following facts:

City police received a report of an armed robbery of a carry-out pizza shop in Hyattsville, Maryland, in which an individual with a handgun stole $100.00. Witnesses had recorded the license plate of the perpetrator's van and within minutes county police officers spotted the van and gave chase. Two of the occupants jumped from the vehicle and attempted to hide behind a shed in the backyard of a house in a residential neighborhood. One of the officers was accompanied by a canine unit dog which, the officer testified he warned in an extremely loud voice, would be released if the suspects did not come out. On deposition the suspects testified that they never heard any warning, although other police officers indicated that it was given. When the dog was released, it began to bite one of the suspects who responded by kicking at it. Although the police contended that the suspect was resisting arrest, other evidence suggested he may only have been trying to make the dog stop biting. As the Fourth Circuit later phrased it, the suspect was soon after taken to a local hospital, "frightfully mauled."

On appeal, the Fourth Circuit reversed. It found genuine issues of material fact with regard to such matters as the alleged loud police announcement that a police dog was on the scene and that the suspects were called on to surrender. It also found a dispute of fact, based on experts' affidavits, with regard to whether releasing a dog without allowing time for a suspect to give up, especially where the suspect is cornered and escape impossible, is reasonable and appropriate to any legitimate purpose for the use of a dog. The court determined that a jury could have found it objectively unreasonable to require someone to put his hands up and calmly surrender while a police dog bit his private parts. Finally, the court held that "even if it found that force was necessary to arrest (the victim), a reasonable jury could nonetheless find the degree of force excessive."

The parallels between *Kopf* and the case at bar are striking and need little elaboration. The Court accepts without question that, on the authority of *Kopf,* Plaintiff ought to have prevailed as against Defendants' Motion for Summary Judgment. Notwithstanding this, neither Plaintiff's nor Defendants' counsel brought the case to the Court's attention even through oral argument. Thereafter, only Plaintiff's counsel, never defense counsel, cited the case, and then only because the Court had directed briefing on another point of law.

V.

One must assume that had Plaintiff's counsel, in preparing his initial Opposition to the Motion for Summary Judgment, exhibited the same degree of diligence that ultimately permitted him to locate the case in untimely fashion, he could have located the case in timely fashion. Instead, counsel offered only the sketchiest statement of grounds, reflecting a bare minimum of legal research, showing every sign of having been dictated on the run. The net effect of this truncated effort was to consume valuable court time in oral argument and the preparation of supplemental briefs (not to mention preparation of the present Opinion), all of which could have been avoided by earlier diligence on counsel's part. Counsel appears to have forgotten two of the most fundamental rules of professional conduct. First, Rule of Professional Conduct 1.1 provides that:

> [a] lawyer shall provide competent representation to a client. Competent representation requires the legal knowledge, skill, thoroughness and preparation reasonably necessary for the representation....

The other Rule of Professional Conduct counsel has apparently misplaced is Rule 1.3 which holds that "[a] lawyer shall act with reasonable diligence and promptness in representing a client." Failure to pursue applicable legal authority in timely fashion may well constitute a violation of this rule.

The action of defense counsel in this case raises a far more serious concern. It is possible that defense counsel also overlooked the *Kopf* precedent, but if he did, the oversight was glaring and extremely troublesome. *Kopf* not only deals with a claim of excessive force against police where a police dog was involved; individual Prince George's County police officers and the County itself were defendants in that case. Indeed, at least one attorney for Prince George's County in *Kopf*, as shown in the reported case, was an individual, whom the Court judicially notices, was still in the County Attorney's office at the time of the filing of the present Motion for Summary Judgment.[1]

The regrettable inference is that defense counsel in the instant case may in fact have deliberately failed to disclose to the Court directly controlling authority from this Circuit. If so, the action would constitute a clear violation of the Rules of Professional Conduct.

---

1. *Kopf*, moreover, could hardly have been a run-of-the-mill case in Prince George's County's experience. Following the Fourth Circuit decision, the County filed a petition for *certiorari* to the Supreme Court, which was denied *sub. nom. Prince George's County v. Kopf*, 502 U.S. 1098 (1992). Further, upon remand and retrial, the trial court again entered judgment in favor of the County and the police officers, and the case went to the Fourth Circuit a second time, where it was again reversed. *See Kopf v. Skyrm*, 993 F.2d 374 (4th Cir.1993). On the County's second brief to the Fourth Circuit, in addition to the Assistant who continues in the office to this day, was the County Attorney for Prince George's County who, at least as of the time the Motion for Summary Judgment was filed in the present case, was also still in office.

Rule 3.3(a)(3) provides that "a lawyer shall not knowingly ... fail to disclose to the tribunal legal authority in the controlling jurisdiction known to the lawyer to be directly adverse to the position of the client and not disclosed by opposing counsel." In federal court, the "controlling jurisdiction" is the circuit in which the district court sits. Particularly disturbing is the type of case encountered here—a litigant who was an unsuccessful party to a directly relevant adverse precedent who has failed to cite that precedent to the court.[2] The Court cannot help but ponder the County's actions.

Under the circumstances, the Court will direct defense counsel to show cause to the Court in writing within thirty (30) days why citation to the *Kopf* case was omitted from his Motion for Summary Judgment, oral argument, and indeed from any pleading or communication to date.

The Court also recollects that in the last several months counsel for Prince George's County was before the Court in at least one other police dog excessive force case in which a Motion for Summary Judgment in favor of the County was granted. It may be that *Kopf* was omitted from the pleading in that proceeding as well. Accordingly, the Court directs defense counsel and the Office of the Prince George's County attorney, within sixty (60) days to disclose to the Court the status of that case and any and all police dog excessive force cases involving Prince George's County that were pending as of August 9, 1991, the date *Kopf* was decided by the Fourth Circuit, or that have been filed from that date to the present.... [The court required the county, *inter alia*, to disclose in each of those cases whether a dispositive motion had been made by the county and whether it had cited *Kopf* in any pleadings in those cases.] Any further sanctions that may be imposed by the Court will depend on the County's showing of cause pursuant to this directive.

Enough has been said for now. No formal Motion for Reconsideration need be filed by Plaintiff's counsel since, as indicated, *Kopf* clearly dictates reinstatement of the excessive force claims.

NOTES

1. The court seems annoyed with both advocates here. Why?

2. Why should it be the obligation of a lawyer to disclose adverse precedent? Isn't it inconsistent with your duty of loyalty to your client? Why isn't it the other side's job to find the law that supports the client's case? How is requiring a lawyer to disclose contrary precedent consistent with the adversary system?

3. As the *Massey* court makes clear, it is not permissible to withhold adverse precedent simply because you think it is wrongly decided. "While it is

---

2. To the extent that defense counsel or Prince George's County may believe *Kopf* was wrongfully decided, that of course would be beside the point. While it may be true that other circuits, including the Sixth Circuit in *Robinette*, have granted summary judgment in comparable police dog cases, nonetheless Fourth Circuit precedent controls in the Maryland federal district until the Circuit or the U.S. Supreme Court say otherwise. Counsel or the County's obligation to disclose *Kopf* would in no way be diminished by their disagreement with the *Kopf* rationale.

acceptable to make a rejected argument for purposes of preserving it for en banc or Supreme Court consideration while acknowledging that it has been rejected by the court," wrote the Ninth Circuit, "it is not acceptable to repeat an argument already rejected without acknowledging the case that rejected it." *Singh v. Gonzales,* 502 F.3d 1128 (9th Cir. 2007). In *Singh,* as in *Massey,* it was a party to the case establishing the prior adverse precedent who failed to cite it. The court imposed costs and fees as a sanction for the behavior.

4. This opinion required the county to explain why its brief in the case did not cite *Kopf.* The response indicated that there were two reasons; first, the particular Assistant County Attorney representing the county in the case did not know about *Kopf* and was not working in the office when it was decided; and second, the *Kopf* decision was distinguishable and was therefore not "directly adverse" to their position. Do you think either of these arguments was persuasive to the court? Why or why not? In response to the court's direction to disclose the status of other excessive force cases involving police dogs, the court learned that 18 such cases had been filed; in five of those, the county had made dispositive motions in which it had not cited the *Kopf* case. Does this suggest mere carelessness, or something else? The court concluded that it would contact the judge in each such case and bring the *Kopf* issue to the attention of each judge. *Massey v. Prince George's County,* 918 F.Supp. 905 (D. Md. 1996).

2. DUTY TO AVOID FRIVOLOUS CLAIMS

Model Rule 3.1 provides that "A lawyer shall not bring or defend a proceeding, or assert or controvert an issue therein, unless there is a basis in law and fact for doing so that is not frivolous." A claim is not frivolous if it "includes a good faith argument for an extension, modification or reversal of existing law." Why? Rule 3.1 includes an express exception for lawyers representing criminal defendants, who are permitted "to defend the proceeding as to require that every element of the case be established." Why?

3. TRIAL BEHAVIOR

Your client is engaged in acrimonious litigation against a neighbor. He wants you to ask the neighbor, on the witness stand, whether she is an alcoholic. You have no reason to believe that she is. Can you do so, in the hopes that even the asking of the question will cause the jury to have a negative opinion of her? See Model Rule 3.4(e).

Rule 3.4(e) imposes some significant and sometimes subtle constraints on a lawyer's trial behavior. "My client is innocent." Permissible? How about "The evidence should make clear to you that my client is innocent"? Is the statement, "I know that at the factory, every possible precaution is taken to protect the safety of Allied's workers," really any different from the statement, "The foreman, Frank Scott, told you that at the factory, every possible precaution is taken to protect the safety of Allied's workers"? Do the Rules treat these differently? Why?

PROBLEMS

1.   Domingo–Gomez was on trial, charged with arson. The identity of the perpetrator was disputed, and Domingo–Gomez and some of his friends testified that he was elsewhere at the time of the crime. In closing argument, the prosecutor stated that Domingo–Gomez and other defense witnesses "lied, testified untruthfully, and/or made up their stories." He further remarked that the state had a "screening process" that cases had to go through before the state filed charges and that the evidence in the case had successfully passed the process. The jury indicated that it was having difficulty with the case and that some members were not sure that the state had proved the identification of Domingo–Gomez beyond a reasonable doubt, but after they were instructed to continue deliberating, they returned a guilty verdict. Did the prosecutor act properly? What relief, if any, should Domingo–Gomez receive? *See Domingo–Gomez v. People*, 125 P.3d 1043 (Colo. 2005).

2.   Collins represented Levine in a palimony suit in Essex County. The trial court, in an unpublished decision, dismissed Levine's claim, holding that cohabitation was a necessary element of a palimony claim. Collins appealed that ruling. While the appeal was pending, Brundage retained Collins to bring a palimony claim on her behalf in Union County against the estate of her deceased paramour. Brundage had not cohabited with the paramour prior to his death. The estate moved to dismiss Brundage's complaint, on the ground that cohabitation was an essential element of a palimony claim. In Collins's brief in response to the motion to dismiss, he stated that "no New Jersey case has held cohabitation to be a requirement for the enforceability of a palimony agreement," that "nowhere has there been articulated in any reported decision in New Jersey a rule of law to the effect that in order for a palimony agreement to be enforceable, it is necessary that the parties live in the same residence," that "no reported decision in New Jersey has held that the absence of the sharing of a single residence by the parties to a palimony agreement renders it unenforceable," and that if the judge held for the defense, he would "do so in the absence of any New Jersey precedent." The court denied the motion to dismiss, and the intermediate appellate court denied a request for interlocutory appeal. Collins did not disclose the existence of the Levine case in his opposition to the interlocutory appeal. The case settled, but before the settlement was completed, the Levine case was decided adverse to Levine and Brundage's position. Has Collins behaved properly? Should there be any consequences for Collins's client? Would it matter if the other side's lawyer in the Brundage matter could have learned about the pendency of the Levine appeal but did not? *See Brundage v. Estate of Carambio*, 951 A.2d 947 (N.J. 2008).

3.   May a lawyer assist a pro se litigant in preparing pleadings or other legal documents? *Compare American Bar Ass'n Formal Ethics Op. 07–446 with Connecticut Ethics Op. 98–5* (1/30/1998).

4.   Client asked Lawyer to bring a personal injury claim on his behalf. Lawyer investigated the claim and learned that the claim would have been viable, but that the claim was time-barred. In the relevant jurisdiction, the contention that the claim is time-barred is an affirmative defense; if the

defendant does not raise the statute of limitations in its responsive pleading the defense is deemed waived. May Lawyer bring the claim? *See Oregon Ethics Op. 1991–21*; *ABA Formal Ethics Op. 94–387.*

5.   Poje collided with another vehicle while driving; a woman was killed in the accident. Poje hired Seelig to represent him. Poje was cited for several motor vehicle offenses by the municipal prosecutor and was also charged with manslaughter by the county prosecutor. On Seelig's advice, Poje appeared in municipal court and pled guilty to the motor vehicle violations; under state law, as Seelig knew, this would preclude on double jeopardy grounds Poje's prosecution on the manslaughter charge. Seelig responded briefly but truthfully to any question he was asked by the municipal court judge during the taking of the plea; however, Seelig did not disclose to the municipal court judge that Poje was facing a manslaughter charge arising out of the incident. The court did not inquire into the extent of the injuries or the factual basis for Poje's guilty plea before taking the plea. Did Seelig behave properly? *See In re Seelig*, 850 A.2d 477 (N.J. 2004).

6.   During the 1970s and 1980s, about 1800 taxpayers participated in a tax shelter. While it was marketed as a legitimate investment which entitled the participants to claim deductions on their individual tax returns, the IRS pursued participants for tax deficiencies, claiming that the shelter transactions were shams. Because there were so many taxpayers involved, the taxpayers and the IRS agreed that a relatively small number of "test cases" would be tried. 1300 taxpayers agreed to be bound by the outcome of the test cases. The IRS's lawyers then made secret deals with some of the test case petitioners which provided them with advantageous individual resolutions of their individual tax cases; they, however, had to keep secret that their cases had been settled and participate in the test case trials. The Tax Court conducted proceedings in the test cases and concluded that the taxpayers were liable for the assessed deficiencies. The test case petitioners then sought to set aside the adverse judgments and obtain their more favorable secret deals. The secret arrangements came to light at that time. The IRS lawyers in the test cases at no time disclosed to the court that the parties had settled and that there was no real controversy remaining in their cases. One test case petitioner testified in the test case trial that there had been no discussion of a reduction of his tax deficiency in exchange for his testimony; the lawyers did nothing although that testimony was false. Did the lawyers act properly? What should the consequences be? *See Dixon v. Commissioner of Internal Revenue*, 316 F.3d 1041 (9th Cir. 2003).

7.   Mullins was a lawyer admitted to practice in Indiana. Lawrance, a patient in a chronic vegetative state, resided in Hamilton County, Indiana, and Lawrance's parents petitioned the court in Hamilton County to withdraw her nutrition and hydration. The court issued an order holding that Lawrance's parents had the authority to consent to the withdrawal of nutrition and hydration. Lawrance was then moved from a nursing home in Hamilton County to a hospice in Marion County. After the hearing, Mullins created an Indiana corporation, the "Christian Fellowship with the Disabled, Inc." Once Lawrance was moved to Marion County, Mullins, on behalf of the Fellowship, petitioned in an ex parte proceeding for an emergency guardianship of Lawrance in the Marion County court. Mullins represented to the court that

"Lawrance is the victim of intentional, willful, and purposeful neglect and/or abuse by her parents, her medical doctors, and/or her health care providers, in that she is being denied essential nutrition and hydration." Mullins did not disclose to the Marion County court all relevant information about the prior Hamilton County proceeding. Has Mullins behaved properly? *See In re Mullins*, 649 N.E.2d 1024 (Ind. 1995).

8.   Client, a habitual traffic violator, had his driver's license suspended for ten years beginning on March 6, 1991. On March 10, 1999, he was stopped for making an illegal U-turn and was charged with driving while suspended as a result. Page represented Client on the driving while suspended case in Shelby Superior Court. Page did not ask Client if he had, in fact, been driving on March 10, and Client never told Page that he had not been. On October 28, 1999, in a separate proceeding, Page prepared a petition for a probationary license for Client, which would relieve Client from the ten-year suspension order. The petition was submitted to the Marion Circuit Court. It stated that Client "has not violated the terms of his suspension by operating a vehicle." At a hearing on the petition, the presiding commissioner asked Client, "Have you driven an automobile in the last nine years, sir?" Client, under oath, responded "No." Page was present in the courtroom at the time and said nothing. Has Page violated the ethics rules? *See In re Page*, 774 N.E.2d 49 (Ind. 2002).

CHAPTER 11

DUTIES TO THIRD PARTIES

■ ■ ■

We have talked about the lawyer's obligations to the client and the lawyer's obligations to the court. What obligations does a lawyer have to others?

Not many, as it turns out. In the words of Prof. Geoffrey C. Hazard, "a third party is entitled to very little from the lawyer." Geoffrey C. Hazard, Jr., *Triangular Lawyer Relationships: An Exploratory Analysis*, 1 Geo. J. Legal Ethics 15, 26 (1987). If the law envisions clients as fully entitled to the loyalty, zeal, and best efforts of the lawyer, it envisions strangers to that relationship as entitled to none of those things. At the same time, the lawyer is not free to act criminally or to defraud third parties, or to mislead them as to the nature of his engagement or his relationship with his client.

We have already considered, in some situations, the duties that a lawyer owes to someone who is not a client, but who might fairly be described as an "almost" client. For example, Model Rule 1.18 addresses the status of the prospective client, who consults the lawyer about possible representation. As we've seen, the lawyer owes that prospective client many of the duties the lawyer owes an actual client, though there are some significant differences. We also considered the third-party beneficiary, who in some limited circumstances may be entitled to enforce a duty of competency through malpractice liability. And we considered the party who, while not nominally a client, is owed some fiduciary obligation or duty of confidentiality by virtue of the lawyer's representations and the non-client's reasonable expectations.

In this chapter, we consider the lawyer's obligation to strangers. By that we don't mean people the lawyer has never met, but people with whom the lawyer has no professional relationship. The lawyer's obligations to those strangers differ significantly depending on whether they are represented by lawyers. Do those differences protect the third party, or protect the perquisites of another lawyer? After you have studied the different rules that apply to lawyer contacts with represented and unrepresented strangers, you will be in a position to consider that question.

A. STRANGERS WITH LAWYERS: MODEL RULE 4.2

Model Rule 4.2 imposes a default rule: an outright prohibition on communicating with a person who is represented by a lawyer. What are the limitations on that prohibition? Consider the language of the rule: "In representing a client, a lawyer shall not communicate about the subject of the representation with a person the lawyer knows to be represented by another lawyer in the matter, unless the lawyer has the consent of the other lawyer or is authorized to do so by law or a court order."

What is the justification for the strict rules on contact with represented parties? Consider the following disciplinary case.

IN RE DALE

2005 WL 1389226 (Review Dep't, State Bar Ct. of California, 2005)

Epstein, J.

Respondent, Joshua M. Dale, compromised the integrity of the criminal justice system when he systematically befriended and then cajoled Darryl Geyer, an incarcerated 22–year-old with a 10th grade education, into giving a confession about an arson fire at an apartment building. Geyer had previously confessed to the police about the fire, and the voluntariness of that confession was the key issue upon which he was appealing his second degree murder conviction. Respondent, who was representing the tenants in a negligence lawsuit against the apartment owner arising from the same fire and was facing the owner's summary judgement motion, needed Geyer's statement about the condition of the premises when he set the fire.

Respondent knew that the declaration he obtained from Geyer could be used as evidence at Geyer's re-trial if his conviction were reversed on appeal. Geyer's trial and appellate attorneys refused respondent's requests to contact Geyer, and they advised Geyer not to speak with respondent. Nevertheless, respondent intentionally used his status as an attorney to gain access to Geyer while he was in jail and to meet with him in private. He skillfully took advantage of Geyer's vulnerability and exacerbated Geyer's dissatisfaction with his attorneys. Respondent offered his services to represent Geyer at his parole hearing if he would sign the incriminating declaration, and Geyer acquiesced. Even after obtaining the declaration, respondent continued to curry favor with Geyer so that he would make himself available as a percipient witness at the civil trial. Respondent ultimately obtained a $400,000 settlement in his civil case.

The hearing judge found respondent culpable of violating the Rules of Professional Conduct by improperly communicating with a represented party. . . .

. . . Darryl Geyer confessed to the police that he set several fires, including a fire to an apartment building at 1011 Bush Street, San Francisco on

June 11, 1996. One of the occupants died in the fire, several were injured and many suffered property damage. Attorney Kenneth Quigley was appointed to represent Geyer in the criminal matter on June 28, 1996. In July 1996, William Burke and several of the tenants at 1011 Bush Street asked respondent to represent them in a suit for personal injuries against the owner of the apartment building, Grace Chen, based on allegations that the premises were maintained negligently, which contributed to the fire. Geyer was not named in the suit, but he was a percipient witness to the condition of the building at the time he set fire to it.

Geyer was indicted on 13 counts of arson, one count of auto theft, and one count of murder with arson special circumstances. His criminal trial commenced on July 23, 1999, and lasted until July 27, 1999, when Geyer withdrew his not guilty plea and submitted a guilty plea to six counts of arson. The homicide charge was submitted to the judge who found Geyer guilty of second-degree murder. However, in a carefully crafted plea agreement, Geyer retained his right to appeal the homicide conviction on the grounds of an illegal confession.

Meanwhile, respondent, who was admitted in 1994 and was inexperienced as a civil lawyer, was facing a motion for summary judgement by the owner's attorneys. Respondent believed that Geyer's declaration about his involvement in setting the fire at 1011 Bush Street, and his observations about the condition of the premises at the time he set the fire, were vital to his ability to defeat the summary judgement motion. Sometime during the pendency of the case, and while Geyer was incarcerated, respondent contacted Quigley and asked him if he could interview Geyer in connection with his civil suit. Quigley refused to give his permission. Nevertheless, on at least three occasions respondent waited in the hallway at the Hall of Justice where inmates were kept while they were awaiting court proceedings, specifically to observe Geyer and make contact with him. The only persons with access to this area were court personnel and attorneys. Respondent succeeded in exchanging nods with Geyer, and on one occasion spoke to him, saying in effect "we are going to have to talk someday."

On July 30, 1999, after the conclusion of the trial, but prior to Geyer's sentencing, respondent visited Geyer in the San Francisco County Jail. During this visit respondent gained direct access to Geyer by using the entrance and the procedures reserved for attorneys rather than regular visitors, thus enabling respondent to speak to Geyer face-to-face and in private, rather than through a glass partition in the public reception area. He told Geyer he would need his statement about the 1011 Bush Street fire for his civil trial. Geyer said he wanted to speak with his attorney before he would agree to give a statement, and he followed up with a letter to respondent on August 5, 1999, stating: "I have been unable to contact my attorney Kenneth M. Quigley about giving you a deposition on the events that took place at 1011 Bush Street. . . . I will be unable to respond to questions in regards to 1011 Bush Street. I'm sure that you understand." Respondent persisted with five more visits to the county jail, all of which were prior to Geyer's sentencing and while Quigley was Geyer's counsel of record. Each time respondent had face-to-face conversations with Geyer in private by utilizing the special procedures reserved for attorneys. The purpose of these visits was to befriend Geyer in order to cultivate him as a favorable witness in respondent's personal injury case. During these visits, they discussed current events, the challenges of life in jail and Geyer's hopes and dreams, in addition to his involvement as a witness in the *Chen* case.

On August 25, 1999, Geyer told Quigley that he was dissatisfied with him and that he wanted to fire him and employ new counsel. However, Geyer did not succeed in replacing Quigley, who remained his court appointed attorney.... On September 28, 1999, Geyer was sentenced to 20 years to life, with the possibility of parole, at the earliest, in 2013. On September 30, 1999, Quigley signed and filed a notice of appeal, which was lodged in the Court of Appeal on October 29, 1999. Geyer was listed on the Notice of Appeal as representing himself in pro per.

Meanwhile, on October 21, 1999, respondent again visited Geyer, who by this time had been transferred to San Quentin prison. Respondent brought with him a letter agreement, typed on his letterhead, which stated:

> Pursuant to our many conversations, I offer you the below contract between the two of us. If you date and sign the enclosed declaration, under penalty of perjury, I will do what I can to assist you when you come up for parole, including but not limited to, being your attorney if you choose, or your witness. As your witness at any hearing, I would tell how you took responsibility early on.... I will also encourage the tenants of 1011 Bush Street to do the same, and some are willing only if you take the first step by telling the truth about the fire, how you entered the building, and what else occurred in the basement of that building on June 11, 1996. The declaration is made up of the facts your [sic] told in your video taped confession to the police.

Geyer testified that he was grateful for respondent's offer of legal assistance with his parole hearing since he had no confidence in Quigley and could not afford to hire other counsel. With this contract as an inducement, Geyer acquiesced to signing the declaration, which respondent had prepared and brought with him to San Quentin. The declaration stated, in part:

> In the early morning hours of June 11, 1996, I was walking in the vicinity of Bush Street and Jones with a friend, Gabriel Cano. As I walked along Jones Street, I noticed an empty door. I entered through that door and found it lead [sic] to a basement area. I later found out that this was the basement of 1011 Bush Street.... While in the basement of 1011 Bush Street I noticed a large amount of paper and cardboard. I also noticed that the walls of the basement were made of exposed wood. Mr. Cano and I stayed in the basement for approximately ten minutes before deciding to leave. Just before I left the

basement, I lit a single match and threw it in some of the paper and cardboard I had seen in the basement area.

However, before Geyer would sign this statement, he insisted that respondent add the following, which was inserted in respondent's handwriting: "Addendum: I have been assured by Joshua M. Dale, Esq., that this document cannot and will not be used or effect [*sic*] my appeal of my conviction in the San Francisco Superior court matter."

After respondent signed the addendum, Geyer signed the declaration under penalty of perjury.

The one area where there is conflicting evidence relates to the nature of respondent's verbal assurances to Geyer at the time he signed the above statement. Respondent asserts that he assured Geyer that his declaration would not harm his appeal, but that he also discussed how Geyer's statement could be used against him at re-trial if he won his appeal. Geyer testified that he was not advised of the full import of his declaration, and that respondent told him repeatedly that the statement could not hurt him in any respect, but would only help him with his eventual parole hearing. Geyer explained: "My primary intention was to make right what I had done to the tenants but I wouldn't have done it if I thought it would hurt me."

Respondent filed the declaration in the superior court in the *Burke v. Chen* case on October 23, 1999. When Quigley found out about the declaration he was furious and demanded that respondent withdraw it. In a letter dated October 25, 1999, to respondent, Quigley stated that respondent had "used [his] status as an attorney to get in the San Francisco County Jail and interview Mr. Geyer, who is still my client.... [T]he result of that interview is that you have obtained a declaration that contains admissions by Mr. Geyer that are devastating to his criminal case ... [and] so destructive of Mr. Geyer's interest that it could result in him spending his life in a small cage." The following day, respondent attempted to head off any fallout from Quigley's anger by writing to Geyer: "Kenneth Quigley is trying to get my law license for talking to you even though you'd fired him, and he wasn't even your attorney after sentencing. I'd say you should expect a visit or letter from him, or his representative, soon.... I'll write to you soon regarding all the commotion that your declaration has created. I again think that your telling the truth is the best thing you could have done." In that same letter, he informed Geyer that he had talked with the district attorney (D.A.) about his appeal and parole, and that the D.A. had told him if Geyer won his appeal, he would only serve eight years. Respondent also advised that the D.A. "agrees that you should do your best to make your first parole hearing count."[1]

Respondent communicated with Geyer by mail on at least three other occasions for the purpose of currying his favor as a witness at the upcoming civil trial. For example, one letter, dated November 3, 1999, said, *"Your declaration saved the tenants' case.* Thank you. Your letter of

---

1. The D.A. disputed that he had such a conversation with respondent.

apology is spectacular, and the tenant [sic] will, and some have already, forgive [*sic*] you for the disruption to their lives. You have much to be proud of and I look forward to visiting soon ... you are a special person on earth...." [Emphasis in the original.]

John Jordan was appointed as Geyer's appellate counsel of record on January 18, 2000. Nevertheless, respondent continued to communicate with Geyer. Thus, on January 28, 2000, respondent wrote to Geyer, warning him: "I'd really be careful with any promises if they've seen you. They are the ones that got you convicted, remember?" In the same letter, respondent persisted with his cultivation of Geyer's friendship, stating: "I'm enclosing some things for you like before. I've talked with several of the people at your new location. There are many things that you may do there.... I'll be able to do more down the road if you begin to send me promising things about you." Three days later, respondent filed a motion in the civil case to obtain a court order to produce Geyer at the trial. Respondent did not serve the notice on Jordan or otherwise notify him and no attorney appeared for Geyer. The motion was granted on February 10, 2000. Respondent settled the *Chen* case in mid-February 2000 for $400,000. He never again communicated with Geyer, and he provided no further legal assistance to him. Geyer lost his appeal, although his declaration did not affect the outcome.

Geyer filed a complaint with the State Bar on May 3, 2000. After an investigation by the State Bar, a three-count Notice of Disciplinary Charges (NDC) was filed on April 3, 2002, alleging respondent violated rule 2–100 by improperly communicating with a represented party....

The rule provides: "While representing a client, a member shall not communicate directly or indirectly about the subject of the representation with a party the member knows to be represented by another lawyer in the matter, unless the member has the consent of the other lawyer."

Respondent argues that he did not violate rule 2–100 because: 1) Geyer was not represented by an attorney at the time respondent obtained his declaration; and 2) Geyer was not a party to the civil case, *Burke v. Chen.*

We can readily dispose of respondent's first contention. Respondent stipulated that his meeting with Geyer on October 21, 1999, when he obtained Geyer's declaration, was the culmination of at least five previous meetings, all of which took place while Geyer was awaiting sentencing and was represented by Quigley. Additionally, respondent communicated with Geyer at least two more times while Geyer was represented by appellate counsel, John Jordan. From the outset, respondent's communications were directed at securing Geyer's declaration and, ultimately, his testimony at trial about his involvement with the arson fire—the very facts that were the crux of Geyer's defense at his murder trial and were the basis of his appeal.

Respondent's second contention that rule 2–100 is inapplicable because Geyer was not a represented "party" in the *Burke v. Chen* personal injury suit is not so readily disposed of. Geyer's involvement with the civil suit was only as a witness. Thus, in order to find a violation of rule 2–100, we must construe the proscription against communicating with a represented "party" to mean represented "person." This was the approach taken by the hearing judge below, but we find very limited support for this broad interpretation of rule 2–100....

We find scant authority in the drafting history of rule 2–100, the rules of statutory construction, and the decisional law for construing rule 2–100 so as to prohibit contacts with a non-party. Indeed, the drafting history of rule 2–100 provides us with precious little guidance. When the rule was adopted by the Supreme Court in 1988, changes were made to the predecessor rule 7–103, which were directed at contacts with corporate parties. No consideration was given to the usage of the term "party" or whether non-parties were to be included within the definition.

Turning to rules of statutory construction, we note that the language of rule 2–100 specifically uses the term "person" within its own definition of "party." We therefore must presume that the drafters were aware of the distinction between "party" and "person" when they simultaneously used both terms in the very same statutory definition. "If possible, significance should be given to every word, phrase, sentence and part of an act in pursuance of the legislative purpose."

The few cases that have interpreted rule 2–100 have given it a narrow construction, albeit while focusing on different provisions of the rule than those of concern here....

Discipline has been imposed under rule 2–100 and its predecessors only in those instances when a member made an ex parte communication with an opposing party....

Finding no rule of construction or persuasive legal precedent to support a broad interpretation, we conclude we are not at liberty to re-write rule 2–100, which by its plain language is limited to a represented "party." We recognize that a strict construction of the rule, limiting its applicability only to represented parties to litigation or to a transaction could, as in this case, defeat the important public policy underlying the rule: "The rule against communicating with a represented party without the consent of that party's counsel shields a party's substantive interests against encroachment by opposing counsel.... [T]he trust necessary for a successful attorney-client relationship is eviscerated when the client is lured into clandestine meetings with the lawyer for the opposition." Our Supreme Court echoed this same assessment: "[The no contact rule] shields the opposing party not only from an attorney's approaches which are intentionally improper, but, in addition, from approaches which are well intended but misguided. The rule was designed to permit an attorney to function adequately in his proper role and to prevent the opposing attorney from impeding his performance in such role."

The instant case illustrates how the concern about interference with the attorney-client relationship is equally relevant when the represented individual is not a party to the proceedings. But we defer to the Board of

Governors and the Supreme Court for any curative efforts should they determine that the purpose of rule 2–100 is ill-served by its present language. We therefore are compelled to conclude that respondent is not culpable for his communications with Geyer under rule 2–100 because Geyer was not a represented party in the *Burke v. Chen* lawsuit, and we dismiss Count One with prejudice.

[In the rest of the opinion, the court concluded that Dale's conduct was nonetheless sanctionable based on other misconduct, including misrepresenting to Geyer the possible consequences of making his declaration if his pending appeal were successful, and acquiring—and breaching—a fiduciary obligation to Geyer by giving him legal advice. The court imposed a two-year period of probation and a four-month suspension, and, *inter alia*, required Dale to retake the MPRE.]

NOTES

1. Why did the court conclude here that Dale did not violate the prohibition on communication with a party represented by counsel? Would the outcome have been the same under Model Rule 4.2? The prior version of the Model Rule used the word "party," as the California rule does; it was modified in 1995. Does this case explain why the rule was changed? Is the change appropriate? Does it solve the problem?

2. Although attorney Dale was not disciplined for violation of the communication rule, what does this case suggest about why such a rule might be appropriate?

3. In this case, Dale sought—and was denied—permission from Geyer's counsel to communicate with him. The rule permits these communications if made with the consent of the represented person's lawyer. Why does the rule place the control of this decision in the hands of the lawyer rather than the client? Is this appropriate? Suppose, for example, that you represent the defendant in a personal injury matter. Your client has made a settlement offer, but you learn—perhaps through an uninvited email or phone message from the plaintiff—that your offer has not been communicated to the plaintiff by her lawyer. Can you simply tell the plaintiff yourself that your client has made an offer? Can you ask your paralegal or assistant to communicate with the plaintiff directly and tell her this information? *See* Comment [4] to Model Rule 4.2; see also Model Rule 8.4(a). Can you advise your client to communicate with the plaintiff directly since you cannot? If so, are there any limits on the permitted scope of such communications? *See In re Pyle*, 91 P.3d 1222 (Kan. 2004). Pyle represented Moline, who was injured at Gutzman's home. On behalf of Moline, Pyle filed suit against Gutzman. Counsel for the defendant, hired by the defendant's insurer, answered the complaint. Subsequently, Pyle prepared an affidavit for Gutzman's signature and sent it to Moline, with a letter stating, "Enclosed please find a proposed affidavit to be signed by Mr. Gutzman. As a party to the case, you have the right to communicate with Mr. Gutzman. Therefore, please talk with him and see if he will sign the enclosed affidavit. The affidavit will help us with your claim

and will help him tremendously to defeat any claim by the insurance company . . . ." Proper contact between clients, or a violation of Rule 4.2?

4. Does it matter who initiates the communications? What if the represented person insists that she wants to communicate with the opposing party's lawyer? Should the client's wishes control? In *Iowa Supreme Court Attorney Disciplinary Bd. v. Box*, 715 N.W.2d 758 (Iowa 2006), Hillard, a widow, was involved in a complex family property dispute. She consulted a lawyer, who prepared an estate plan for her. Her lawyer wrote to attorney Box, counsel for two of the other relatives, and advised that Hillard had counsel and that Box should not contact her directly. Hillard nonetheless attended a meeting at Box's office. When Box stated that perhaps he should not be talking to her because she had another lawyer, Hillard "responded testily that she could speak with whatever lawyer she chose." Box proceeded to prepare and document a sale of her property; he was disciplined for violating the no-contact rule.

5. Suppose a prospective client consults you. He tells you he has another lawyer, but he is dissatisfied with the lawyer's services in the matter and asks you for a second opinion. Can you speak with him, or are such contacts barred by Rule 4.2? *See Louisiana State Bar Association Public Opinion* 07–RPCC–014. Should you call the other lawyer and tell him you have been consulted? Would that be a proper courtesy, or a violation of Rule 1.6? *See Philadelphia Bar Ethics Opinion 2004–1.*

6. What should the consequences be of violating the rule? Myerchin sued Family Benefits on a contract claim. One month later, he agreed to settle the case and dismiss his suit in exchange for a cash payment. Myerchin was paid the money and spent it, but refused to dismiss the case, claiming that Family Benefits' attorney had negotiated the settlement with him directly notwithstanding the fact that the attorney knew that Myerchin was represented in the matter. Should Myerchin be able to claim that the settlement agreement is unenforceable because the other side's lawyer violated the no-contact rule? Does it matter that Myerchin had been negotiating with opposing counsel for two months before hiring his lawyer and bringing suit? *See Myerchin v. Family Benefits, Inc.*, 162 Cal. App. 4th 1526 (4th Dist. 2008).

Does the no-contact rule apply in criminal cases? This is important, because at times it may be in the government's interest to communicate with a criminal defendant—already represented by counsel—to gather information or secure cooperation. Must such contacts go through defendant's counsel? If so, at what point does that obligation arise? Does it apply only when the defendant has been formally charged, or does it attach as soon as the prosecution knows that the person is represented?

This problem arose in *United States v. Hammad*, 846 F.2d 854 (2d Cir. 1988). Hammad was under investigation for arson. The government suspected that Hammad had been committing Medicaid fraud and had burned the building to conceal evidence of the fraud. Investigation revealed a witness, Goldstein, who said that he had provided Hammad with false invoices necessary for the insurance fraud. The Assistant United States Attorney (AUSA) directed Goldstein to meet with Hammad, pretend that he had been subpoenaed to testify before the grand jury about the fraud, and record the resulting conversations. The recordings were used to secure indictments of Hammad for fraud and obstruction of justice. Hammad claimed that he was represented at the time of Goldstein's contacts with him, that the AUSA knew it, and that Goldstein's contacts with him, at the AUSA's direction, violated the no-contact rule.

Why would contacts with a non-lawyer violate the rule? Under Model Rule 8.4(a), a lawyer may not violate the Rules of Professional Conduct "through the acts of another." If the Rules prohibit a lawyer from taking a particular action, Rule 8.4(a) prohibits the lawyer from avoiding that obligation by directing someone else to do what the lawyer herself is prohibited from doing. If the AUSA in *Hammad* was prohibited from contacting Hammad directly, he was precluded from directing Goldstein to do so as well.

The government argued that the no-contact rule only applied once a prosecution had been initiated. The Second Circuit disagreed. Because the timing of formal charge is largely within the prosecutor's control, if the rule were interpreted to apply only after formal charge, "a government attorney could manipulate grand jury proceedings to avoid its encumbrances." *Id.* at 859. This is not the universal rule, however. *See, e.g., United States v. Balter*, 91 F.3d 427 (3d Cir. 1996) (Rule 4.2 did not apply to preindictment investigations because they were "authorized by law"). The government's attempt to argue that this rule did not apply at all to federal prosecutors is catalogued in Chapter 12.

The rule regarding communications with a represented party gets more complicated when we consider entity clients. Which of the entity's employees or officers are considered to be "represented" by counsel for purposes of the no-contact rule?

MURIEL SIEBERT & CO., INC. v. INTUIT INC.

868 N.E.2d 208 (N.Y. 2007)

PIGOTT, J.

Plaintiff Muriel Siebert & Co., Inc., a discount brokerage firm, entered into a "strategic alliance" agreement with defendant Intuit Inc., a manufacturer of financial software, to jointly create and operate an Internet brokerage service. Although the parties were initially successful in that endeavor, their relationship became strained when Siebert asserted that Intuit had failed to promote the Internet brokerage service to its customers. In September 2003, Siebert commenced an action against Intuit for, among other things, breach of contract and breach of fiduciary duty in failing to promote Siebert's business interests.

Nicholas Dermigny, Executive Vice President and Chief Operating Officer for Siebert, was both an important participant in the events at issue in the Intuit lawsuit and a member of Siebert's "litigation team" after the lawsuit began. He participated in the negotiations of the Siebert–Intuit agreement and discussions with Intuit relating to its implementation. He also assisted in drafting the complaint and responses to interrogatories, was privy to discussions concerning Siebert's litigation strategy, and engaged in privileged and confidential communications with Siebert's counsel. In May 2005, Dermigny took a leave of absence to negotiate the terms of his impending separation and eventual termination from Siebert. Counsel for Siebert sought to continue representation of Dermigny at his scheduled deposition, but Dermigny refused. Siebert's counsel informed an attorney for Intuit that Siebert could not produce Dermigny for the deposition because it no longer had control over him. Therefore, Intuit subpoenaed Dermigny for a deposition rescheduled for September 26, 2005.

Dermigny was terminated by Siebert on September 6, 2005. Upon learning of Dermigny's termination, Intuit's attorneys contacted him without Siebert's knowledge and arranged for an interview. Before commencing the interview, Intuit's attorneys advised Dermigny that he should not disclose any privileged or confidential information, including any conversations with Siebert's counsel, or offer any information concerning Siebert's legal strategy. Dermigny was further cautioned that if, during the interview, he was asked a question that could potentially lead to the disclosure of such information, he should so advise Intuit's attorneys and decline to answer the question. Intuit's attorneys then questioned Dermigny about the underlying facts of the case, but did not elicit any privileged information nor inquire about Siebert's litigation strategy.

Days later, Siebert's counsel, upon learning of the interview, moved to disqualify Intuit's attorneys from the case, enjoin them from using any information provided by Dermigny, and stay Dermigny's deposition. Supreme Court granted Siebert's motion, disqualified Intuit's attorneys from the case, ordered the destruction of all notes from their interview with Dermigny, enjoined them from communicating the information they learned during the interview to others, and struck the notice of deposition for Dermigny until such time as Intuit obtained new representation. Supreme Court specifically noted that it was not basing its disqualification determination on DR 7–104(a)(1)[1] of the Code of Professional Responsibility, acknowledging that the rule did not apply because Dermigny was not a Siebert employee at the time of the interview. Rather, Supreme Court held that the disqualification of Intuit's attorneys was warranted, regardless of whether they actually received privileged information, because there was an "appearance of impropriety" based upon the possibility that privileged information had been disclosed during the interview.

The Appellate Division reversed, holding that disqualification was not justified because Intuit's attorneys had advised Dermigny not to disclose privileged information and, based on the record, no such information had been disclosed. In so holding, the Appellate Division noted that this Court's opinion in *Niesig v. Team I*, 558 N.E.2d 1030 (1990) "makes it

---

1. DR 7–104(a)(1) provides that:

(a) During the course of the representation of a client a lawyer shall not:

   (1) Communicate or cause another to communicate on the subject of the representation with a party the lawyer knows to be represented by a lawyer in that matter unless the lawyer has the prior consent of the lawyer representing such other party or is authorized by law to do so.

clear that ex parte interviews of an adversary's former employee are neither unethical nor legally prohibited.'' We now affirm. . . .

In *Niesig*, we held that DR 7–104(a)(1) applies only to certain current employees of a party. We made clear that ex parte communications with nonmanagerial employees are permitted, but adversary counsel are prohibited from directly communicating with employees who have the power to bind the corporation in litigation, are charged with carrying out the advice of the corporation's attorney, or are considered organizational members possessing a stake in the representation. By so holding, we struck a balance between protecting represented parties from making imprudent disclosures, and allowing opposing counsel the opportunity to unearth relevant facts through informal discovery devices, like ex parte interviews, that have the potential to streamline discovery and foster the prompt resolution of claims.

The policy reasons articulated in *Niesig* concerning the importance of informal discovery underlie our holding here that, so long as measures are taken to steer clear of privileged or confidential information, adversary counsel may conduct ex parte interviews of an opposing party's former employee. Indeed, there is no disciplinary rule prohibiting such conduct. At the time of the interview, Dermigny no longer had the authority to bind Siebert in the litigation, was no longer charged with carrying out the advice of Siebert's counsel, and did not have a stake in the representation.

We conclude that disqualification of Intuit's attorneys is not warranted merely because Dermigny was at one time privy to Siebert's privileged and confidential information. That does not mean, however, that the right to conduct ex parte interviews is a license for adversary counsel to elicit privileged or confidential information from an opponent's former employee. Counsel must still conform to all applicable ethical standards when conducting such interviews (*see, e.g., Merrill v. City of New York*, 2005 WL 2923520, *1 (S.D.N.Y. 2005) (adversary counsel prohibited from asking former employee about privileged communications); *Wright v. Stern*, 2003 WL 23095571, *1 (S.D.N.Y. 2003) (adversary counsel must refrain from seeking to elicit attorney-client communications from an opponent's former employee); *ABA Comm. on Ethics and Prof. Responsibility Formal Op. 91–359* (1991) (adversary counsel may interview former employees of an opponent but must disclose their role in the matter and whom they represent, and must not induce former employees to disclose privileged communications)).

In this case, Intuit's attorneys properly advised Dermigny of their representation and interest in the litigation, and directed Dermigny to avoid disclosing privileged or confidential information. They also directed Dermigny not to answer any questions that would lead to the disclosure of such information. Dermigny stated that he understood the admonitions and, on this record, no such information was disclosed. Thus, there is no basis for disqualification.

NOTES

1. The court discusses its holding in *Niesig v. Team I*, which is widely recognized as setting an appropriate standard for which employees and officers of an entity should be deemed to be "represented" by the entity's counsel for purposes of the no-contact rule. Why not simply decide that all employees of an entity are represented by entity counsel? What would that mean for the conduct of litigation against an entity? Why does the court seem to believe that some kind of balance must be established, and that it would be inappropriate to simply preclude all communications with an entity's employees?

2. Given Dermigny's role in the company and the litigation, he would plainly have been a person to whom the no-contact rule would have applied had he been a current employee at the time of the interview at issue. Was it a strategic error for the company to discharge him?

3. As the opinion makes clear, in New York a former employee does not receive the protections of the no-contact rule. *See also* Comment [7] to Model Rule 4.2 ("Consent of the organization's lawyer is not required for communication with a former constituent.") There is, however, some danger if the communication with the former constituent encroaches on privileged information, or on information protected by the constituent's contractual obligations to the former employer. *See* Comment [7] to Model Rule 4.2 ("In communicating with a current or former constituent of an organization, a lawyer must not use methods of obtaining evidence that violate the legal rights of the organization. See Rule 4.4."). If you are talking to a former employee, do you think you should warn him that communicating fully with you might violate a nondisclosure agreement that he has entered into with his employer? Why or why not? Consider Model Rule 4.4(a).

B.   UNREPRESENTED STRANGERS: RULE 4.3

Contacts with persons that the lawyer knows are represented by counsel are governed by Rule 4.2. What about persons who do not have lawyers? Rule 4.3 imposes a very limited set of obligations on the lawyer in this circumstance. First, the lawyer "shall not state or imply that the lawyer is disinterested." Second, "When the lawyer knows or reasonably should know that the unrepresented person misunderstands the lawyer's role in the matter, the lawyer shall make reasonable efforts to correct the misunderstanding." Last of all, "The lawyer shall not give legal advice to an unrepresented person, other than the advice to secure counsel, if the lawyer knows or reasonably should know that the interests of such a person are or have a reasonable possibility of being in conflict with the interests of the client." In the context of represented persons, we seem quite concerned about the potential for overreaching in the lawyer's interactions with other lawyers' clients. Why is the lawyer granted more freedom, not less, when dealing with unrepresented persons?

BARRETT v. VIRGINIA STATE BAR

611 S.E.2d 375 (Va. 2005)

AGEE, JUSTICE.

Timothy M. Barrett and Valerie Jill Rhudy were married in 1990. Barrett was admitted to practice law in the Commonwealth of Virginia in 1996 and operates as a sole practitioner in the City of Virginia Beach. Rhudy served as his secretary during their marriage.

In the summer of 2001, Barrett and Rhudy separated. She took the couple's six children and moved from the marital home in Virginia Beach to her parents' home in Grayson County.

Rule 4.3(b) provides as follows:

> A lawyer shall not give advice to a person who is not represented by a lawyer, other than the advice to secure counsel, if the interests of such person are or have a reasonable possibility of being in conflict with the interest of the client.

The Board found that Barrett violated this rule because it concluded certain statements in two electronic mail ("e-mail") communications he wrote to Rhudy after the separation, but before she retained counsel, constituted legal advice. On July 25, 2001, Barrett sent an e-mail to Rhudy containing the following:

> Venue will not be had in Grayson County. Virginia law is clear that venue is in Virginia Beach.... Under the doctrine of imputed income, the Court will have to look at your skills and experience and determine their value in the marketplace.... You can easily get a job ... [making] $2,165.00 per month ...
>
> In light of the fact that you are living with your parents and have no expenses ... this income will be more than sufficient to meet your needs. I ... just make enough to pay my own bills ... Thus, it is unlikely that you will ... obtain spousal support from me.
>
> I ... will file for ... spousal support to have you help me pay [sic] fair share of our $200,000+ indebtedness. Since I am barely making it on my income and you have income to spare, you might end up paying me spousal support....
>
> In light of the fact that ... I ... am staying in the maritial [sic] home ... I believe that I will obtain the children.... The Court will prefer the children staying with a [parent] ... [T]here is no question that I can set up a home away from home and even continue to home school our kids. Therefore, it is likely that you will lose this fight. And of course, if I have the kids you will be paying me child support....

("July e-mail").

Barrett sent Rhudy another e-mail on September 12, 2001, in which he included the following:

I will avail myself of every substantive law and procedural and evidentiary rule in the books for which a good faith claim exists. This means that you, the kids and your attorney will be in Court in Virginia Beach weekly.... [Y]ou are looking at attorney's expenses that will greatly exceed $10,000.... I will also appeal ... every negative ruling ... causing your costs to likely exceed $30,000.00....

You have no case against me for adultery.... [The facts] show[ ] that you deserted me.... [Y]our e-mails ... show ... that you were cruel to me. This means that I will obtain a divorce from you on fault grounds, which means you can say goodbye to spousal support....

[T]he family debt ... is subject to equitable distribution, which means you could be socked with half my lawschool [sic] debt, half the credit care [sic] debt, have [sic] my firm debt, etc.

("September e-mail").

The foregoing e-mail passages were interwoven with many requests from Barrett to Rhudy to return home, professing his love for her and the children and exhorting Rhudy for reasons of faith to reunite the family because it was God's will....

In finding that Barrett gave unauthorized legal advice to an unrepresented person in violation of Rule 4.3(b), the Board opined that "Barrett cannot send those two e-mails stating what he did." Barrett contends that Rule 4.3(b) was not meant to bar communications between a husband and wife, and that construing it as such interferes with the sanctity of marriage. He further contends the e-mails only stated his opinions and were not advice to Rhudy.

Prior decisions of the Board reveal that conduct usually found to be in violation of Rule 4.3(b) is much more egregious than Barrett's conduct in this case....

Comment [1] to Rule 4.3 of the Virginia Rules of Professional Conduct cautions that "[a]n unrepresented person, particularly one not experienced in dealing with legal matters, might assume that a lawyer is disinterested in loyalties or is a disinterested authority on the law."

... In the case at bar ... Barrett expressed only his opinion that he held a superior legal position on certain issues in controversy between himself and Rhudy. His statements may have been intimidating, but he did not purport to give legal advice. Rhudy knew that Barrett was a lawyer and that he had interests opposed to hers. We find that the concern articulated by the Comment to Rule 4.3 is not borne out in this case.

While the Bar argues that there is no "marital" exception to Rule 4.3(b), neither does it ask us to set out a per se rule that all communication by a lawyer, to his or her unrepresented spouse in a divorce proceeding discussing legal issues pertinent to the divorce, is prohibited under Rule 4.3(b). We do not find there is such a per se rule, but ... upon our independent review of the entire record, we find that there was not sufficient evidence to support the Board's finding that Barrett's e-mail statements to Rhudy were legal advice rather than statements of his opinion of their legal situation. Therefore, we will set aside the Board's finding that Barrett violated Rule 4.3(b). . . .

JUSTICE KEENAN, with whom CHIEF JUSTICE HASSELL and SENIOR JUSTICE COMPTON join, concurring in part and dissenting in part.

I respectfully dissent from the majority's holding that Barrett did not violate Rule 4.3(b). In my opinion, the majority's holding effectively creates a "spousal exception" to the Rule and permits a lawyer to engage in otherwise prohibited conduct dispensing legal advice as long as the lawyer's spouse, rather than an unrelated person, is the affected pro se party. . . .

In reaching its conclusion that Barrett did not violate Rule 4.3(b), the majority states that Barrett "did not purport to give [his wife] legal advice." A brief review, however, of the statements considered by the majority leads me to the opposite conclusion.

In his statements to his estranged wife, Barrett advised her that under Virginia law, all court proceedings would be held in Virginia Beach. With regard to the issue of spousal support, Barrett explained that the court would employ the legal doctrine of imputed income to determine the value of her skills and experience "in the marketplace."

Barrett further stated that "spousal support is based on the maxim [of] . . . the needs of the one versus the other's ability to pay." Citing facts relating to the parties' situation, Barrett then offered his judgment that it was "unlikely" that his wife would be able to obtain court-ordered support. With regard to the issue of child custody, Barrett told his wife that the "court will prefer the children staying with a [parent]," rather than with a substitute caregiver during working hours.

I would hold that these explanations constituted legal advice intended to influence the conduct of a party who had conflicting legal interests and who was not represented by counsel. Without question, Barrett's conduct would have been a violation of Rule 4.3(b) had he communicated this advice to a pro se litigant whose spouse Barrett was representing. Thus, the majority's conclusion necessarily implies that there is a "spousal exception" to Rule 4.3(b), under which an attorney may attempt to influence his or her spouse's conduct by imparting legal advice in a harassing manner regarding the parties' conflicting legal interests.

Such a conclusion, however, is contrary to the plain language of Rule 4.3(b), which provides no "spousal exception." Moreover, Barrett's use of legal advice as a "sword" in his marital conflict is clearly a type of conduct that Rule 4.3(b) is designed to discourage. It is hard to imagine a situation in which an attorney would be in a stronger position to improperly influence another's conduct by giving legal advice.

NOTES

1. Do you think attorney Barrett violated Rule 4.3? The dissent seems to think that the court's decision implies a "spousal exception" to Rule 4.3. Could you articulate the exception differently? Consider the court's statement that "Rhudy knew that Barrett was a lawyer and that he had interests opposed to hers." Does that suggest a basis for an exception to Rule 4.3? Do you think it is legitimate?

2. On some level, the court seems troubled about how to treat the lawyer proceeding pro se. Do we treat him like a lawyer, or like a client? Is the dissent correct that "Barrett's conduct would have been a violation of Rule 4.3(b) had he communicated this advice to a pro se litigant whose spouse Barrett was representing"? If so, why would that situation be different from this one?

KENSINGTON INTERNATIONAL LTD. v. REPUBLIC OF CONGO

2007 WL 2456993 (S.D.N.Y. 2007)

PRESKA, U.S.D.J.

Civil litigation is not always civil. In the instant motion, plaintiff Kensington International Limited, represented by Dechert LLP and Quinn Emanuel Urquhart Oliver & Hedges LLP, claims that the attorneys for defendant Republic of Congo, Cleary Gottlieb Steen & Hamilton LLP, here represented by Simpson Thatcher & Bartlett LLP, in bad faith attempted to dissuade a non-party witness from attending a post-judgment deposition. Kensington asks the Court to sanction Cleary through formal reprimand and reimbursement of costs spent on bringing this motion. For the reasons that follow, the Court finds that Cleary did act in bad faith, and thus the motion for sanctions is GRANTED.

BACKGROUND

... Kensington is a financial institution in the business of, among other things, investing in debt and equity instruments issued by domestic and foreign entities....

In the underlying case, Kensington sought recognition and enforcement of a final money judgment rendered against Congo by the High Court of Justice, Queen's Bench Division, Commercial Court in London. Further to that end, on September 30, 2004, the Court granted Kensington's motion against Congo for partial summary judgment, entered a money judgment of $56,911,991.47, and certified the judgment as final pursuant to Rule 54(b). Thereafter, Kensington began taking discovery in aid of execution of the judgment. Among those subpoenaed in this process was non-party witness Medard Mbemba, a citizen of France and Congo with residences in France and the Ivory Coast and an office in Washington, D.C. Mbemba, through his company, African Partners, was involved in various business dealings with the Congolese government and its officials and agencies, including aspects of the shipping and oil and gas industries. Kensington hoped Mbemba possessed knowledge of the whereabouts of Congo's assets and served on him a subpoena which noticed a deposition for December 23, 2004 in Washington, D.C.

Mbemba's native language is French. Though he does not speak English, his son, Frank Mbemba, does. Frank Mbemba accepted service of the subpoena on December 6, 2004. At some point thereafter, Mbemba consulted with a friend who was an attorney about his obligations under the subpoena; the friend informed him that he was required to testify and suggested an attorney in the United States who could accompany him. After considering the cost of counsel, Mbemba decided he would attend alone. His son communicated with Arnon Siegel, an attorney at Dechert, to coordinate a date and place for the deposition.

Some early scheduling conflicts due to Mbemba's health notwithstanding, on January 28, 2005, Frank Mbemba called Siegel and told him his father was with him in Washington and would appear for deposition on Friday, February 4, 2005. Mbemba was scheduled to be in Washington until Saturday, February 5 and would not return for several months. Siegel informed an attorney at Cleary, Boaz Morag, of the scheduled deposition (and of the fact that Mbemba was not represented by counsel). Morag replied by email and by phone that neither he nor any other Cleary attorney familiar with the case could attend the deposition on February 4, complained of the short notice, and asked that it be rescheduled; Siegel refused, claiming there was no other suitable time during Mbemba's limited stay in Washington. Though Morag proposed that the deposition be held at a later date in France, no agreement was reached on that score, and Siegel informed Morag the deposition would occur as scheduled. As early as Monday, January 31, 2005, Morag informed Siegel of his intention to have the Court intervene to postpone the deposition, but no application was ever made.

On Monday, January 31, and again on Wednesday, February 2, 2005, Morag contacted Jean–Pierre Vignaud, a partner in Cleary's Paris office, to update him on the status of the Mbemba deposition. Vignaud is a member of Cleary's ten-member worldwide executive committee and, though he had no prior substantive role in the instant case, he is the relationship partner for Congo and has, and is known for having, extensive connections with Congo's political leadership. At Morag's request, Vignaud contacted Mbemba on February 3. First, he emailed Mbemba at the address listed on the African Partner's website. The message, in translation, stated:

> Dear Sir:
>
> Our firm represents the interests of the Republic of Congo in a number of legal proceedings involving certain creditors, particularly in the United States.

My colleagues in our New York office have just learned that you agreed to . . . give a deposition concerning your knowledge of commercial or financial transactions of the Republic of Congo and assets belonging to the Republic in the United States and outside the United States.

I wish to call your attention to the very particular nature of depositions in U.S. procedural law. These depositions are given under oath, and it is extremely rare to agree to submit to this procedure without preparation or the assistance of an attorney who is completely familiar with the case. My colleague, Boaz Morag of our New York office will be at a hearing the whole day on Friday and therefore will not be able to assist you on that occasion. Under these circumstances, giving a deposition without the assistance of an attorney who is familiar with the case seems to us to present very serious risks and inconveniences that I will leave to you to assess. In any event, I suggest you urgently contact Boaz Morag . . . or myself at the number below.

He also placed two calls to the Washington D.C. contact number on the African Partner's website, leaving one voice mail message.

On Thursday, February 4, 2005, Mbemba called Vignaud at his office in France. The call was forwarded to Vignaud's home or cell phone. Mbemba recalled at his deposition the following about the conversation:

A: [Vignaud] said we have learned that you are going to go and meet with a lawyer for Kensington in order to give a deposition, and I'm talking now to you in your capacity as Congolese patriot and I want you to understand that these steps are going to affect the stability of Congo. . . .

A: I told him I did not know the matter. I said that if my deposition is going against the interests of my country, then I am against giving the deposition, I'm saying no out of patriotism. And [Vignaud] said yes it is dangerous for your country. So, I said I do not know the United States and I do not know customs there and lawyers. I do not have a lawyer so he said well, this is one more reason you should not go. So, he asked that my son take the initiative to cancel this appointment. . . .

Q: Did you understand Mr. Vignaud to be telling you not to go to this deposition?

A: Yes, that's what he said, not to come.

Mbemba recalled at his deposition that Vignaud said "I want to inform you that your deposition can hurt the Congo," specifically that

these are people who buy loans at percent of their value and who are very dangerous. Then they hire lawyers and they can destabilize the economies of countries, and I'm warning you so that you'll know and not participate in this kind of a game because it is a bad thing for your country. I [Mbemba] said bad for the government or for the population or for certain persons? He [Vignaud] said bad for the population. I said, sir, Mr. Vignaud, I don't have the honor of knowing you and I'm telling you that I will not go to this lawsuit. Not because this is what you are telling me to do, but out of patriotism.

When asked whether he felt Vignaud was trying to persuade him not to attend, Mbemba replied, "It is not an impression, he told me as such not to go."

Mbemba testified that he knew Vignaud to be someone with "privileged connections to ... the authorities in Congo." When asked if he felt threatened by Vignaud's statements, Mbemba replied, "So, when somebody tells you that something is bad for your country and that I feel obliged to warn you, yes, it sounds like a threat." It was Mbemba's state of mind, even before he spoke with Vignaud, that testifying against Congo in a matter over Congo's debt was "dangerous."

Following the call to Mbemba, Vignaud called Morag to tell him to notify Dechert that Mbemba was not testifying. Morag informed Vignaud that he thought it would be better if Mbemba called Dechert directly and asked Vignaud to convey as much to Mbemba. Vignaud called Mbemba, this time at the Watergate Hotel where Mbemba was staying.

In this, the second conversation, Vignaud asked Mbemba if he would communicate his intention directly to Dechert through his son. Mbemba said he did not want to get his son further involved and asked that Cleary contact Dechert; Vignaud agreed to have an email sent to Dechert....

In neither of the conversations did Vignaud mention the need or the possibility of rescheduling the deposition.

At 4 p.m. on Thursday, Morag sent the following email to Siegel:

> M. Mbemba contacted our firm this afternoon and asked us to relay to you his intention not to appear tomorrow. He stated that he had been unaware of the precise nature of the proceeding tomorrow and now that he understands that he will be asked questions under oath on a number of subjects, he stated that he feels uncomfortable appearing without having consulted with a lawyer, which he has not apparently done. He said that he travels to the United States often and there should be another occasion to schedule the deposition.

Upon receiving the email, Siegel contacted Frank Mbemba who confirmed that his father would not appear for his deposition. Siegel informed Frank that the subpoena required his father by law to appear at the deposition. Frank then spoke with Mbemba and convinced him to testify at the deposition.... Frank Mbemba called Siegel back and told him that his father had changed his mind and would attend the deposition and Siegel informed Morag by email that the deposition would go forward as planned.

The following morning, Friday, February 3, Vignaud—having received the Siegel email from Morag—attempted to call Mbemba several times and spoke with him once, just before Mbemba was to leave for his deposition. Mbemba recounts the conversation:

["W]e have just learned that you are going for the deposition in spite of what we discussed. It's incredible that somebody would go make a deposition without a lawyer.["] At that moment I remembered—I remembered at that moment that Congo has been using Vignaud as a lawyer for the last 20 or 30 years. We lost lots of lawsuits. We could have paid all this public debt instead of paying Mr. Vignaud. I said to Mr. Vignaud thank you very much but do you know how old I am?— and I tell him how old I was—therefore, I am old enough to be able to make my own decisions. And then I hung up on him. . . .

Mbemba went to the deposition. Vignaud attempted to reach Mbemba at the Watergate two more times after Mbemba had already left.

Needless to say, Vignaud's account of the substance of the phone calls differs considerably. . . .

Vignaud denies that it was he who "spoke of . . . 'patriotism' to the Congo" and denies that he told Mbemba that it was "dangerous" for the Congo or would "hurt" the Congo if Mbemba testified. He denies threatening Mbemba in any way. He denies ever telling Mbemba not to sit for deposition. . . . He admits, however, that he described the litigation as "the Congo . . . fighting to conserve its assets from foreign vulture creditors," and that he intended to include Kensington in this description. Indeed, while he claims "I did not dissuade [Mbemba] from attending the deposition," he admits "[I] expressed my view that testifying under oath at a deposition in the United States for a non-native English speaker without proper representation was unwise and that, if representatives of the Congo were unable to attend such a deposition, it would put the Congo at a disadvantage in its litigation to protect its sovereign assets from creditors." Vignaud never fully explained how the presence of "representatives of the Congo" at the deposition could in any way serve to protect Mbemba or advance Congo's litigation interests. In fact he admitted he never offered to have Cleary (or another firm) represent or otherwise counsel Mbemba, and further that he only offered his "free advice" to protect the interests of his client, the Congo. Indeed, at several times during his testimony in Court, Vignaud candidly admitted that the interests of the Congo animated his conversations with Mbemba. ("Q: So just to be clear, you were not looking to protect Mr. Mbemba's interest in your conversations with him, right? A: Right. Q: You were looking to protect the interests of the Congo? A: Yes.")

ANALYSIS

A. Applicable Law

The parties do not dispute the law applicable to this case. The Supreme Court has held that federal courts have the "inherent power" to impose sanctions when a party or its counsel acts "in bad faith, vexatiously, wantonly, or for oppressive reasons." . . .

B. *The Court's Factual Findings Demonstrate Cleary's Attorneys Acted in Bad Faith*

The Court finds that sanctions are appropriate here. It so holds because it finds that the evidence clearly demonstrates Cleary's attorneys acted without legal justification and in fact acted to delay or obstruct the post-judgment discovery process in this case. . . .

(1) *Cleary declines to seek a protective order and elects to act on its own*

The sequence of events relevant to this motion begins with Cleary in a jam: it wanted Morag to attend Mbemba's deposition but, because of the late notice from Mbemba as to his availability and Dechert's refusal to reschedule, he could not. Morag's initial impulse to seek a protective order to prevent the deposition was the proper one and evidences Cleary's intention to postpone the deposition. Perhaps Cleary decided that there were no legitimate grounds to seek a protective order; perhaps it feared a court would inquire as to whether Cleary had a sufficient interest in attending the deposition of a non-party witness to warrant delay of the deposition; or perhaps it never had any intention of going to court. But in any event, the record is clear that, in forgoing the legal means at its disposal for postponing or defining the terms of the deposition, Cleary made a choice to achieve its goals through illegitimate means: contacting Mbemba directly and persuading him to avoid the deposition.

(2) *Cleary selects Vignaud to contact, and influence, Mbemba*

Had Cleary done as it claimed and only informed Mbemba of the nature of depositions and the prudence of obtaining counsel—even if its motives were not entirely altruistic—the Court would not find Cleary acted solely in bad faith. But a review of the findings of fact shows Cleary did much more than disinterestedly inform Mbemba of American legal custom.

Cleary's story begins to falter with the selection of Vignaud as the attorney to contact Mbemba. The Court does not believe that Vignaud— Cleary's relationship partner for Congo and a member of Cleary's 10– lawyer worldwide executive committee—was the only attorney at Cleary's disposal who could speak French and relay the nature of a deposition.[1] . . . Nor was Vignaud particularly involved in this case.

The evidence adduced at the hearing, however, compels the conclusion that Vignaud was selected in the hope that he could assert influence over Mbemba. As a well known figure in Congo, he could make a convincing argument that the deposition was "us vs. them" and force Mbemba to pick a side. A Cleary associate in New York who speaks conversational French could not, with adequate gusto, inspire Mbemba to join the fight against the "vulture creditors" threatening Congo's stability. Nor could anyone but Vignaud even create the impression that acquiescence in his demands might yield a benefit; disobedience, a penalty. In a case where

---

1. Vignaud confirmed that Cleary's New York office has at least 15 attorneys who speak French; presumably, they understand the nature of depositions as well.

innuendo was needed in place of explicit commands, Vignaud appears to have been the only man for the job.

(3) *Vignaud's communications with Mbemba demonstrate bad faith*

Vignaud delivered on the promise of his influence. His first act, the February 3 email to Mbemba, standing alone, would probably not suffice to show bad faith. It does, however, begin a theme for the remainder of the communications with Mbemba: the blurring of the line between Congo's interest and Mbemba's. For instance, given that Vignaud later testified Cleary had no intention of representing Mbemba at the deposition, it is unclear what he meant by "assist" when he wrote "[m]y colleague, Boaz Morag of our New York office will be at a hearing the whole day on Friday and therefore will not be able to assist you." Cleary never availed itself of the opportunity to explain what assistance it was going to offer Mbemba.

. . . Mbemba, through his testimony firmly establishes that Cleary acted in bad faith in trying to persuade him not to attend the deposition. His testimony shows that Vignaud appealed to him in his "capacity as Congolese patriot" and told him that the litigation and his deposition testimony was going to "affect the stability of Congo," would "hurt the Congo," could "destabilize" Congo's economy, and was "bad for [Congo's] population." Vignaud told Mbemba that Kensington was "very dangerous" and Vignaud would later add that he told Mbemba that creditors like Kensington were "foreign vulture creditors." . . . Vignaud never mentioned rescheduling the deposition—a topic that would have made sense if Vignaud's true motive was only to assure that Mbemba was represented. Instead, Vignaud urged Mbemba to decline to testify out of patriotism—a reason Mbemba acquiesced in and that Vignaud would not expect to change before his next visit to the United States.

This testimony, which the Court finds to be true and accurate, by itself establishes that Cleary acted in bad faith to persuade Mbemba to avoid the deposition. . . .

(4) *Morag's follow-up email was designed to mislead Dechert and conceal the actual contents of Vignaud's communications with Mbemba*

Having successfully persuaded Mbemba not to attend the deposition, Cleary then attempted to have Mbemba call Dechert himself to cancel. Doing so might possibly insulate Cleary from Mbemba's ultimate decision not to attend, but Mbemba refused. The resulting communique demonstrates Cleary's attempt to obscure what actually transpired between Vignaud and Mbemba and suggests the law firm had something to hide. Morag wrote the email to make Cleary seem the passive recipient of Mbemba's decision ("Mbemba contacted our firm this afternoon . . ."), omitted those aspects of the conversation damaging to Cleary (*e.g.*, no mention of Mbemba's references to his own patriotism or Vignaud's reference to "foreign vulture creditors"), and misrepresented that rescheduling was discussed in the conversations between Mbemba and

Vignaud (it was not). Indeed, neither Vignaud, nor his efforts to contact Mbemba, nor the contents of those communications, nor Mbemba's stated reason for refusing to testify was mentioned in the email. . . .

C. *Sanctions are Warranted*

Sanctions serve three purposes: (1) to prevent a party from benefitting from its own improper conduct, (2) to provide specific deterrents, and (3) to provide general deterrence. Here, Cleary did not benefit from its own improper conduct. But Cleary is an ideal candidate for specific deterrence. It has shown a willingness to operate in the murky area between zealous advocacy and improper conduct, and here it crossed the line. . . . This conduct is inconsistent with counsel's obligations under the Federal Rules of Civil Procedure and recognized ethical strictures. *See, e.g.*, ABA Model Rules of Prof'l Conduct R. 3.4(f) (prohibiting a lawyer from "requesting a person other than a client to refrain from voluntarily giving relevant information to another party"); *id.* at R. 3.4 Cmt. 1 ("Fair competition in the adversary system is secured by prohibitions against destruction or concealment of evidence, improperly influencing witnesses, obstructive tactics in discovery procedure, and the like."); Restatement (Third) of the Law Governing Lawyers § 116(3) (2000) (stating a "lawyer may not unlawfully induce or assist a prospective witness to evade or ignore process obliging the witness to appear to testify"). This case is far from over, and sanctions are necessary to remind Cleary that it has obligations beyond representing its client. Accordingly, Cleary is hereby sanctioned pursuant to the Court's inherent authority. Cleary is directed to pay to Kensington the reasonable costs and attorney's fees incurred by Kensington in connection with this motion. . . .

NOTES

1. The court never addresses the rules about dealing with unrepresented persons. Do you think they applied to Cleary's conduct here? Does the case suggest something about the dangers of permitting lawyers to engage in unconstrained interaction with unrepresented persons? What else did the Cleary lawyers do that skirted the ethics rules?

2. What was the sanction that the court imposed on Cleary? Do you think it was sufficient? Partner Vignaud was not admitted to practice in the United States. Is there any lawyer at the firm who could have been subjected to discipline?

3. Is there a necessity exception to this rule? Consider the facts of *In re Pautler*, 47 P.3d 1175 (Colo. 2002). Deputy District Attorney Mark Pautler learned that William Neal, a suspect in a gruesome multiple homicide and sexual assault, had contacted a sheriff's deputy offering to surrender. Neal insisted, however, on speaking to a lawyer first. After attempting unsuccessfully to contact the lawyer of Neal's choosing, Pautler decided to speak to Neal, pretending to be public defender "Mark Palmer." After his phone conversation with "Palmer," Neal surrendered. Pautler told no one of his deception; it finally unraveled when Neal insisted on speaking to his lawyer,

"Palmer." Pautler was charged with disciplinary violations, including a violation of Rule 4.3. Pautler argued that his violation of the rules was justified because he acted as he did in order to assure the apprehension of Neal. Is that argument convincing? Why or why not? What other rule, besides 4.3, do you think Pautler was alleged to have violated?

C. DUTIES OF CANDOR

1. IN THE COURSE OF REPRESENTING A CLIENT

The ethics rules contain several express prohibitions on false and misleading behavior. One is contained in Model Rule 4.1(a), which provides that, "In the course of representing a client a lawyer shall not knowingly make a false statement of material fact or law to a third person."

Are there times when a lawyer has to lie or mislead? Consider the following case. In this disciplinary proceeding, amicus curiae briefs were submitted by, among others, the United States Department of Justice, the Oregon Consumer League, and the Fair Housing Counsel of Oregon. Why did this small case attract so much attention and concern?

IN RE GATTI
8 P.3d 966 (Ore. 2000)

PER CURIAM.

In this lawyer discipline proceeding, the Oregon State Bar (Bar) seeks review of a decision by a trial panel of the Disciplinary Board. The Bar charged the accused with violating Code of Professional Responsibility Disciplinary Rule (DR) 1–102(A)(3) (conduct involving dishonesty, fraud, deceit or misrepresentation), DR 7–102(A)(5) (knowingly making false statement of law or fact), and ORS 9.527(4) (willful deceit or misconduct in the legal profession). The accused defended, in part, on the theory that there are or should be exceptions to those rules and the statute in some situations. The trial panel concluded that the accused had committed the violations, but it dismissed the Bar's amended complaint, holding that the Bar was estopped from prosecuting the accused. We review the decision of the trial panel de novo. For the reasons that follow, we hold that the Bar was not estopped from prosecuting the accused, that the accused violated both the rules and statute identified above, and that the accused's defense based on the state and federal constitutions is not well taken. We also conclude that, under the circumstances of this case, the appropriate sanction is a public reprimand.

I. FACTS

We find the following facts by clear and convincing evidence. Before the accused engaged in the conduct at issue in this proceeding, he represented several chiropractors who had been charged with racketeering and fraud. Those charges arose out of an undercover investigation, called Operation Clean Sweep, that SAIF Corporation (SAIF) and the Oregon Department of Justice (DOJ) had conducted. In 1992, the accused filed a complaint with the Bar, alleging that the lawyers involved in Operation Clean Sweep had advised SAIF investigators to have individuals pose as janitors and injured workers for the purpose of infiltrating chiropractors' and lawyers' offices to obtain information about suspected fraudulent workers' compensation claims. The accused's complaint asserted that the lawyers who provided that advice had violated several rules of the Code of Professional Responsibility, including the rules that are at issue in this proceeding.

The Bar investigated the accused's complaint. On June 16, 1993, disciplinary counsel to the Bar wrote to the accused:

> Our preliminary research focused on whether a governmental agency, and lawyers working for that agency, have more latitude in carrying out the agency's regulatory powers in a surreptitious fashion than members of the Bar in the private sector. The answer to that question is not clear; however, our research does suggest that a prosecutor is required only to avoid the use of illegal means to obtain evidence directly or indirectly through others. The cases we have reviewed seem to indicate that a prosecutor oversteps his bounds when he causes another to give false testimony under oath or to appear before a court or other agency who has not first been apprised of the deception and the reasons therefore.

> Our preliminary conclusion is that if SAIF is considered to have public authority to root out possible fraud, then attorneys assisting SAIF in this endeavor are not acting unethically in providing advice on how to conduct a legal undercover operation. It is our understanding that no court has found Operation Clean Sweep to have been illegal or to constitute prosecutorial misconduct.

Disciplinary counsel thereafter submitted the accused's complaint to the State Professional Responsibility Board (SPRB). On March 25, 1994, an assistant disciplinary counsel to the Bar wrote to the accused that the SPRB had closed its file on the complaint because ''there was no evidence that any [SAIF or DOJ] attorney violated any provision of the Code of Professional Responsibility in connection with Operation Clean Sweep or any other operation involving [SAIF or DOJ].''

In April 1994, Dr. Saboe, a chiropractor with whom the accused was acquainted, told the accused that a California company, Comprehensive Medical Review (CMR), had contacted Saboe to inquire whether he would serve as a medical reviewer for CMR. At that time, one of CMR's clients was State Farm Insurance Company (State Farm), and CMR provided it with medical review reports recommending whether to accept or deny medical claims. Saboe had a sense of ''unease'' about the methods that CMR used to recommend that State Farm deny benefits. The accused subsequently came to believe that individuals other than medically trained personnel were preparing reports for CMR, that they were using a "formula" that was designed to help State Farm contain costs, and that medical reviewers were signing the reports.

On May 17, 1994, the accused received a copy of a CMR report that had been signed by Dr. Becker, a California chiropractor, concerning a claim that a client of the accused had filed with State Farm. The accused believed that State Farm had denied the claim based on Becker's report. The denial made the accused angry, and he made three telephone calls to CMR personnel. Before placing the calls, he did not perform any legal research regarding this court's case law on the subject of whether a lawyer who misrepresents his or her identity or purpose violates lawyer disciplinary rules. According to the accused, he made the calls intentionally, but they were "an absolute fluke" and he made them "out of stupidity more than anything."

The accused first called Becker. He identified himself to Becker as a chiropractor and asked Becker about Becker's qualifications. Becker became uncomfortable with the accused's questioning and quickly discontinued the conversation, which the accused had tape recorded.

The accused then called Adams, a vice-president and director of operations for CMR. The accused introduced himself to Adams as a doctor with experience performing independent medical examinations and reviewing insurance claims. The accused contends that he did not tell Adams that he was a chiropractor, but he admits that he "wanted [Adams] to believe that [he] was a chiropractic physician." The accused told Adams that he saw patients, that he performed independent medical examinations, that he performed file and case reviews, and that he was interested in participating in CMR's educational programs for insurance claims adjusters. The accused also told Adams that both Becker and State Farm had referred him to CMR, and that he was interested in working for CMR as a claim reviewer. The accused tape recorded most of his conversation with Adams, which he then had one of his secretaries transcribe. For his part, Adams took notes of the conversation.

Adams believed that the accused was a chiropractor and a likely prospect to work for CMR in Oregon. Adams referred the accused to Householder in CMR's Vancouver, Washington, office to discuss employment opportunities with CMR. The accused called Householder, who knew that the accused was a lawyer and that he was not interested in working for CMR. After he had made the calls to Becker, Adams, and Householder, the accused developed a plan for a fraud investigation involving CMR.

In June 1994, based on information that he had acquired from sources other than his telephone calls to Becker, Adams, and Householder, the accused filed an action in the United States District Court for the District of Oregon against CMR, State Farm, and Householder, alleging fraud and intentional interference with contractual relations.

In July 1994, Adams filed with the Bar the present complaint. Among other things, Adams stated that the accused represented himself as an Oregon chiropractor who was interested in working with our company. He specifically stated that he was a Diplomate of the American Board of Chiropractic Orthopaedics.

. . . He continuously attempted to elicit specific information regarding the CMR protocols and guidelines which are used in preparing our reports. We consider much of this information to be confidential and proprietary. . . .

The telephone call was made for the sole purpose of gathering unauthorized discovery for [his] lawsuit.

On August 2, 1994, in response to a request from assistant disciplinary counsel, Hicks, about Adams' complaint, the accused wrote that he had called Adams "as a result of an investigation that we have been conducting against Mr. Adams, Dr. Becker, Comprehensive Medical Review, and several others for racketeering and fraud." The accused's letter stated, in part:

In answer to Mr. Adams' specific charge that I represented myself as a chiropractor, that is absolutely false. I specifically told him that I was inquiring about their educational programs for claims adjusters and that I would like to participate in those programs. Mr. Adams asked if I was a doctor. He did not ask if I was a chiropractor. I told him I was a doctor and that I did file reviews by the hundreds. This, of course, is true.

Hicks then asked the accused to provide her with a copy of his medical license. The accused responded:

I am quite shocked at your request that I provide you with a copy of my medical license. . . . Your records reflect that I am a Doctor of Juris Prudence [sic] and that is not a misrepresentation.

There was no representation that I was a medical doctor and even if there was, under the circumstances of this fraudulent activity, that would not be unethical.

[Subsequently, a transcript of the conversation with Adams, prepared by the accused, was turned over to the bar disciplinary authorities; it made clear that the accused had told Adams that he was interested in working for CMR, that he was a doctor, that he saw patients, that he performed independent medical examinations, and that he was interested in becoming involved with CMR's educational seminars.]

II. ESTOPPEL DEFENSE TO ALLEGED VIOLATIONS

. . . The Bar charged the accused with violating DR 1–102(A)(3), DR 7–102(A)(5), and ORS 9.527(4), all arising from his telephone calls to Becker and Adams. We first address whether the trial panel erred in dismissing the Bar's complaint on the ground that the Bar was estopped from prosecuting the accused.

According to the trial panel, Bar counsel's responses to the accused's 1992 complaint against SAIF and DOJ lawyers "essentially represented to the

Accused that SAIF's lawyers [sic] conduct does not violate the Code of Professional Responsibility, rather than representing to Accused that SAIF's lawyers were accorded a prosecutorial exception to the disciplinary rules." In the trial panel's view, the accused reasonably inferred from those letters that, in the Bar's view, it is ethical for a lawyer in private practice to use deceptive methods to investigate other private parties. Accordingly, the trial panel concluded that, when the accused made the telephone calls to Becker and Adams, he believed that he was acting ethically. . . .

This court has held that a lawyer violates DR 7–102(A)(5) by misrepresenting the lawyer's identity while engaged in the practice of law. Even assuming that the accused relied on the Bar's letters in making the calls, his reliance was not reasonable. The Bar's letters neither stated nor implied that lawyers in the private practice of law may misrepresent their identity or purpose in investigating a matter. Moreover, advice from disciplinary counsel is not a defense to a disciplinary violation. The trial panel erred in holding that the Bar was estopped from prosecuting the accused for the alleged misconduct at issue in this case. We turn to the merits.

III. ALLEGED VIOLATIONS

The Bar's complaint alleged that the accused represented himself to Becker as a chiropractor and that he made several misrepresentations to Adams, including that he did independent medical examinations, that he was interested in working for CMR, that he did file and case reviews, that he saw patients, and that he was interested in participating in CMR's educational programs for insurance claims adjusters. The complaint also alleged that the accused failed to disclose that he was a lawyer, that he was preparing to sue CMR, and that he hoped that he would obtain information from the telephone calls that he could use in claims against CMR and Adams.

In his answer to the Bar's complaint, the accused admitted that he had engaged in the conduct alleged. The evidence demonstrates, as the trial panel found, that the accused was engaged in the practice of law when he made the telephone calls to Becker and Adams and that he had committed each of the charges. . . .

DR 1–102(A)(3) provides that "it is professional misconduct for a lawyer to . . . engage in conduct involving dishonesty, fraud, deceit or misrepresentation." The term "dishonesty" in the rule connotes lack of trustworthiness and integrity. Misrepresentation is a broad term that encompasses the nondisclosure of a material fact. A misrepresentation may be a lie, a half-truth, or even silence. A material fact consists of information that, if disclosed, would have influenced the recipient's conduct. Even a misrepresentation that is made with the best of intentions can be a misrepresentation under DR 1–102(A)(3).

A misrepresentation becomes fraud or deceit "when it is intended to be acted upon without being discovered." However, a finding of fraud or deceit under the rule does not require evidence that the recipient of the misrepresentation relied on it.

The prohibitions against dishonesty, fraud, deceit, and misrepresentation in DR 1–102(A)(3) are not limited to litigation or even to the representation of clients.

As noted, the accused's answer to the Bar's complaint admitted the conduct alleged. It is undisputed that the accused made affirmative misrepresentations to both Becker and Adams, and that he omitted material facts in his conversations with them. The accused also testified that his conduct was deceitful: He wanted Becker and Adams to believe that he was a chiropractor who wanted to work for CMR, and he intended to have both Becker and Adams make damaging statements about CMR's file-review practices.

We turn to the Bar's allegation that the accused violated DR 7–102(A)(5). That rule provides that, in the course of representing a client or the lawyer's own interests, "a lawyer shall not ... knowingly make a false statement of law or fact." To violate the rule, the false statement must be made with at least a knowing or reckless mental state. The focus of the rule is on the falsehood; it is of no significance that the recipient of the false statement was not misled by it.

In this case, the accused admits that he made a false statement to Becker when he told Becker that he was a chiropractor and that he made several false statements to Adams. For example, he told Adams that he saw patients and performed independent medical examinations, which he does not do, and that he was interested in working for CMR, when in fact he was not. . . .

IV.   PROPOSED EXCEPTIONS TO RULES AND STATUTE

The accused contends that this court should adopt an investigatory exception to the disciplinary rules. . . . He asks this court to adopt the following exception:

> As long as misrepresentations are limited only to identity or purpose and [are] made solely for purposes of discovering information, there is no violation of the Code of Professional Responsibility.

According to the accused, such an exception is necessary if lawyers in private practice, like their counterparts in the government, are to be successful in their efforts to "root out evil."

The trial panel refused to recognize an exception to the rules or statute either for government lawyers or lawyers in private practice. It held that "the standards of conduct provided by the disciplinary rules apply to all members of the Bar, without exception." The trial panel also stated that, in failing to prosecute the SAIF and DOJ lawyers about whom the accused had complained in 1992, the Bar erroneously had relied on a "prosecutorial exception" to the rules. It warned that the Bar's "continued reliance on such an exception" will lead to more situations, such as occurred in this case, "where [the] Accused was seeking evidence of fraudulent conduct by CMR, and properly alleges that his attempt to uncover fraud is no less important than SAIF's attorneys' attempts."

Before this court, the United States Attorney for the District of Oregon, appearing as amicus curiae, objects to the trial panel's holding that there is no "prosecutorial exception" to the Code of Professional Responsibility in Oregon. She argues that the trial panel reached that conclusion "without examining the important purposes that are served by legitimate law enforcement undercover operations." The United States Attorney explains that the United States Department of Justice "regularly supervises and conducts undercover operations in Oregon that necessarily involve a degree of deception." Such covert operations involve both civil and criminal cases, ranging from enforcement of civil rights statutes to international narcotics conspiracies. She contends that federal courts long "have upheld the use of deceptive law enforcement tactics" and that she has "not found a single case in which deception and subterfuge are prohibited as a tool of law enforcement." The United States Attorney asks this court to adopt the following rule:

> Government attorneys who advise, conduct or supervise legitimate law enforcement activities that involve some form of deception or covert operations do not violate DR 1–102(A)(3).

The Attorney General for the State of Oregon agrees with the United States Attorney. He contends that this court should

> not interpret DR 1–102(A)(3) in a manner that would determine that government attorneys who advise, conduct or supervise legitimate law enforcement activities that involve covert operations violate that disciplinary rule.

The accused and, to a lesser extent, the United States Attorney, point to legal commentary and authority from other jurisdictions for the argument that this court should recognize an exception to the disciplinary rules that prohibit conduct involving dishonesty, fraud, deceit, misrepresentation, or false statements of law or fact. Those authorities assert that public policy favors an exception that, at the least, allows investigators and discrimination testers to misrepresent their identity and purpose when they are investigating persons who are suspected of engaging in unlawful conduct. The rationale for such an exception is that there may be no other way for investigators or discrimination testers to determine if a person who is suspected of unlawful conduct actually is engaged in unlawful conduct. Therefore, the argument goes, the public benefits more from allowing lawyers to use deception than allowing unlawful conduct to go unchecked.

The Oregon Consumer League, Fair Housing Counsel of Oregon, Oregon Law Center, and numerous individual lawyers, also appearing as amici curiae, object to suggestions that only government lawyers should be exempt from certain rules of professional conduct. They contend that there is no principled reason to permit government lawyers to engage in covert operations, but to label the same practices by the private bar as "unacceptable vigilantism" even if it, too, is for the purpose of rooting out fraud and illegality. Accordingly, those amici propose the following rule:

> Provided that the conduct does not violate any other provision of law or Disciplinary Rule, and notwithstanding DR 1–102, DR 7–102 and ORS [9.527(4)], a lawyer, personally or through an employee or agent, may misstate or fail to state his or her identity and/or purpose in contacting someone who is the subject of an investigation for the purpose of gathering facts before filing suit.

The Bar contends that whether there is or ought to be a prosecutorial or some other exception to the disciplinary rules is not an issue in this case. Technically, the Bar is correct. However, the issue lies at the heart of this case, and to ignore it here would be to leave unresolved a matter that is vexing to the Bar, government lawyers, and lawyers in the private practice of law. A clear answer from this court regarding exceptions to the disciplinary rules is in order.

As members of the Bar ourselves—some of whom have prior experience as government lawyers and some of whom have prior experience in private practice—this court is aware that there are circumstances in which misrepresentations, often in the form of false statements of fact by those who investigate violations of the law, are useful means for uncovering unlawful and unfair practices, and that lawyers in both the public and private sectors have relied on such tactics. However, ORS 9.490(1) provides that the rules of professional conduct "shall be binding upon all members of the bar."

Faithful adherence to the wording of DR 1–102(A)(3), DR 7–102(A)(5), ORS 9.527(4), and this court's case law does not permit recognition of an exception for any lawyer to engage in dishonesty, fraud, deceit, misrepresentation, or false statements. In our view, this court should not create an exception to the rules by judicial decree. Instead, any exception must await the full debate that is contemplated by the process for adopting and amending the Code of Professional Responsibility.

Under the circumstances of this case ... we conclude that a public reprimand is the appropriate sanction. The accused is reprimanded.

NOTES

1. The Oregon Rules of Professional Conduct were subsequently modified; Rule 8.4(b) now provides:

> [I]t shall not be professional misconduct for a lawyer to advise clients or others about or to supervise lawful covert activity in the investigation of violations of civil or criminal law or constitutional rights, provided the lawyer's conduct is otherwise in compliance with these disciplinary rules. "Covert activity," as used in this rule, means an effort to obtain information on unlawful activity through the use of misrepresentations or other

subterfuge. "Covert activity" may be commenced by a lawyer or involve a lawyer as an advisor or supervisor only when the lawyer in good faith believes there is a reasonable possibility that unlawful activity has taken place, is taking place or will take place in the foreseeable future.

Very few jurisdictions have modified their rules of professional conduct in this manner, but the Oregon Supreme Court's express statement in *Gatti* that the rule applies to all lawyers without exception was also quite unusual.

2. Gatti himself made the misrepresentations that gave rise to the disciplinary charges here. When the SAIF investigation was going on, the lawyers themselves did not make the misrepresentations in question; instead, they directed others to do so. This was also the situation the U.S. Attorney envisioned when she expressed concern about the use of "deceptive law enforcement tactics"; the lawyers would not be engaging in the covert tactics themselves, but would be advising and directing the law enforcement officers who were engaging in them. Would the fact that the lawyers were not themselves making the misrepresentations shield them from disciplinary liability? *See* Model Rule 8.4(a), *see also* Model Rule 5.3.

3. How do the prohibitions on making false statements of fact apply to negotiations? Suppose the other side's lawyer asks you, "Do you have authority to settle the case for $50,000?" You do. Can you answer, "No"? Is there a solution to this problem? Comment [2] to Rule 4.1 suggests that certain statements are by definition not statements of "material fact." "Estimates of price or value placed on the subject of a transaction and a party's intentions as to an acceptable settlement of a claim are ordinarily in this category." Do you find this convincing? *ABA Standing Committee on Ethics and Professional Responsibility Formal Op. 06–439* (2006) suggests that "posturing" or "puffing" statements can and should be distinguished from statements of material fact on which another party would be expected to rely. "An example of a false statement of material fact would be a lawyer representing an employer in labor negotiations stating to union lawyers that adding a particular employee benefit will cost the company an additional $100 per employee, when the lawyer knows that it actually will cost only $20 per employee. Similarly, it cannot be considered 'posturing' for a lawyer representing a defendant to declare that documentary evidence will be submitted at trial in support of a defense when the lawyer knows that such documents do not exist or will be inadmissible." In light of this explanation, is the distinction between "posturing" and "material facts" clear to you?

4. Are there misstatements that go beyond the "puffery" of negotiation to affirmative wrongdoing? How about failing to disclose that the client has died? Geisler filed a suit on behalf of McNealy for injuries sustained in a car accident. McNealy died in January 1995. Shortly thereafter, Geisler contacted opposing counsel and stated that "her client wanted to settle the case" and asked him to forward an offer of settlement. After a series of offers and counter-offers, the matter was settled and a check in settlement was forwarded. Only after the deceased's son, as administrator of the estate, executed the settlement documents did opposing counsel learn that Geisler's client had

died. Was the failure to disclose a violation of Rule 4.1? *See Kentucky Bar Ass'n v. Geisler*, 938 S.W.2d 578 (Ky. 1997); *see also* Model Rule 4.1(b).

2. WHEN NOT REPRESENTING A CLIENT: MODEL RULE 8.4(c)

Model Rule 8.4(c) provides that "It is professional misconduct for a lawyer to ... engage in conduct involving dishonesty, fraud, deceit or misrepresentation." Unlike Model Rule 4.1(a), this prohibition is not limited to actions taken in the course of representing a client. This means that lawyers, in the course of their everyday lives, are subject to discipline if they engage in "dishonesty, fraud, deceit or misrepresentation," even if that conduct would not be criminal or civilly actionable. Is this fair? Why can't lawyers engage in the kind of casual dishonesty that is endemic in society? Do lawyers observe this prohibition, do you think? Why or why not?

BOSSE'S CASE

920 A.2d 1203 (N.H. 2007)

DALIANIS, J.

On November 13, 2006, the attorney discipline office (ADO) appealed the decision of the Supreme Court Professional Conduct Committee (PCC) to suspend the respondent, Leigh D. Bosse, from the practice of law in New Hampshire for six months. We order the respondent suspended from the practice of law in New Hampshire for two years.

I.

The parties stipulated to the following: The respondent has been an attorney admitted to the practice of law in New Hampshire since 1975. At all material times, he was self-employed as both a real estate agent and an attorney. In February 2003, he wrote to landowners on a small lake in Hillsboro, informing them that he could "almost guarantee a quick sale" of their lots "for at least $10,000.00" to one of three builders with whom he was working. In response to this letter, the respondent received a telephone call from Raymond Grimard who expressed interest in selling his lot for $10,000.00. The respondent told Grimard that he would send him a listing packet and, if he could contact one of the builders identified in the letter, he would also send a purchase and sale agreement.

The next day, at the request of one of the builders, the respondent prepared a $10,000.00 offer to purchase Grimard's property. Also, at the builder's request, the respondent prepared a listing for the house to be constructed on Grimard's property and entered the listing into his office computer. The respondent then uploaded this information to the Northern New England Real Estate Network (NNEREN), which is the computerized multiple listing service for New Hampshire.

Two days after the respondent uploaded the listing to the NNEREN, James Boike, the administrator of the NNEREN, asked him for documents to verify the listing. The respondent attempted, unsuccessfully, to reach Grimard. Rather than tell Boike that he had uploaded the Grimard listing too soon, he signed Grimard's name to the exclusive listing agreement and the purchase and sale agreement. Although the respondent expected Grimard to forward executed documents to him shortly thereafter, he signed Grimard's name without his consent or authorization. The respondent then forwarded the documents to Boike and falsely informed him that the purchase and sale agreement was "in effect."

Unbeknownst to the respondent, Grimard had decided not to list his property with the respondent and had listed his property with a different realtor. When the respondent discovered this, he wrote to Boike: "I don't know what's going on. Grimard now says he listed with [another realtor] for twice as much and I have withdrawn my agreement & listing."

The ADO originally charged the respondent with violating New Hampshire Rules of Professional Conduct (Rules) 8.4(a), (b) and (c). The parties eventually stipulated that the respondent's conduct violated Rules 8.4(a) and (c)....

Rule 8.4(a) makes it professional misconduct to violate the Rules. Rule 8.4(c) makes it professional misconduct for an attorney to engage in conduct involving dishonesty, fraud, deceit or misrepresentation. The respondent violated this rule when he signed Grimard's name to the exclusive listing agreement and purchase and sale agreement without Grimard's knowledge or consent, and forwarded these documents to the NNEREN so that Boike would believe that the respondent had secured Grimard's agreement to list his property with the respondent and to sell it to the builder. He also violated this rule when he falsely informed Boike that the purchase and sale agreement between Grimard and the builder was "in effect." When the respondent signed the documents and forwarded them to the NNEREN, he knew that he lacked Grimard's consent to sign them.

For the above misconduct, the ADO recommended disbarment and the respondent requested public censure. The PCC ordered the respondent suspended from the practice of law in New Hampshire for six months. The ADO moved for reconsideration, which the PCC denied, and this appeal followed.

II

... In determining a sanction, we are mindful that the purpose of attorney discipline is to protect the public, maintain public confidence in the bar, preserve the integrity of the legal profession, and prevent similar conduct in the future; the purpose is not to inflict punishment. We judge each attorney discipline case upon its own facts and circumstances, taking into account the severity of the misconduct and any mitigating circumstances appearing in the record....

The respondent's conduct involved "intentional ... dishonesty, fraud, deceit [and/or] misrepresentation that seriously adversely reflects on [his] fitness to practice." Even though he engaged in this conduct in his capacity as a real estate agent, his conduct adversely reflects upon his fitness to practice....

We next consider the actual or potential injury from the respondent's conduct. The *Standards* define "[i]njury" as "harm to a client, the public, the legal system, or the profession which results from a lawyer's misconduct." The PCC determined that the injury was "subjective in nature and not quantifiable," but that "[w]henever an attorney engages in ... deceit, ... the injury to the integrity of the New Hampshire Bar is substantial." We agree with the PCC that the injury to the integrity of the legal profession is substantial whenever an attorney engages in deceit.

There is no evidence, however, of any injury to Grimard.... Nor is there any evidence of injury to the NNEREN....

The respondent's conduct was significantly less egregious than that of the attorneys in cases in which we have ordered disbarment. The respondent's Rule violations, unlike those of the attorneys in disbarment cases, involved an isolated instance of misconduct. His conduct did not span "several years," or even "several months," nor did it involve a continuing course of dishonest conduct, including lying to the PCC. Moreover ... the respondent has no prior disciplinary offenses. Additionally ... he cooperated fully with the PCC's investigation and "displayed genuine remorse by admitting his misconduct in the stipulation."

Based upon our consideration of all of the above, we agree with the PCC's recommendation that the respondent be suspended from the practice of law. We decline the ADO's invitation to disbar the respondent for the single episode of deceit at issue. While there may be instances where a single episode of deceit is sufficiently egregious to warrant disbarment, this is not such an instance.

We disagree with the PCC, however, that a six-month suspension is sufficient "to protect the public, maintain public confidence in the bar, preserve the integrity of the legal profession, and prevent similar conduct in the future." Weighing the severity of the respondent's misconduct, his dishonest or selfish motive and his years of experience against his lack of a prior disciplinary record, his cooperation and remorse, and the loss of his real estate license, we conclude that the respondent should be suspended from the practice of law for two years.

NOTES

1. Was Bosse acting as a lawyer at the time of his misconduct? Does that matter? Lawyers might believe that if they are in business (as title insurers, realtors, escrow agents, etc.) and are not practicing law, the rules of professional conduct do not apply to those activities. As this case shows, Rule 8.4(c) applies to lawyers in all aspects of their lives.

2.   What about a situation which involves purely personal conduct? A month after he was admitted to practice, Lawyer hit a parked car with his vehicle. The car Lawyer was driving at the time of the accident was an Econoline van which was not insured. Lawyer called his insurer and falsely reported that he had been driving a different, insured vehicle, his green Ford Windstar van, at the time of the accident. He then called the victim of the accident and told him, falsely, that he had been driving the Windstar at the time of the accident and urged the victim to tell the insurance company that; he left the victim a voice mail suggesting that the victim give Lawyer a call "so we can [get] the facts straight." Ultimately, Lawyer admitted his wrongdoing and paid the claim out of his own pocket. Lawyer pled guilty to a misdemeanor charge of insurance fraud. Did he, in addition, violate the rules of professional conduct? *See In re Grew's Case*, 934 A.2d 537 (N.H. 2007).

PROBLEMS

1.   Ferrer worked for Construction Company, which was wholly owned by Talao. Talao employed Brose, a lawyer, to represent both him and Construction Company. The United States Attorney's Office began a criminal investigation of Construction Company for wage and hour violations. Ferrer was subpoenaed to testify before the grand jury. Ferrer came to the United States Attorney's Office the day before she was scheduled to testify and asked to see Harris, the Assistant United States Attorney in charge of the case. Harris was not there so Ferrer spoke to Harris's supervisor. Ferrer told the supervisor that Talao was pressuring her to give false testimony and that she did not want Brose present when she was testifying. The supervisor said that he would not be present as lawyers were not permitted inside the grand jury room. The next day, Ferrer met Harris. She told Harris that she did not want to be represented by Brose, that Talao had been pressuring her to give false testimony, and that she thought Brose was there to intimidate her. Did Harris act properly in talking with Ferrer? *See United States v. Talao*, 222 F.3d 1133 (9th Cir. 2000).

2.   Lavery, unhappy with his law school performance, prepared a false law school transcript and "bogus and extremely favorable letters of recommendation over the photocopied signatures of several of his law school professors." He sent these documents out along with letters of application for jobs. He claimed that he was carrying out a research project "to find out if it is not What you know, but Who you know, that counts when a young law graduate looks for a job." He was charged with violating the prohibitions on attorney dishonesty. What result? *See In re Lavery*, 587 P.2d 157 (Wash. 1978).

3.   Lawyer obtained over $19,000 of cash advances on his credit cards in order to pursue his gambling habit. He obtained five of the seven total cash advances during a three-day period in early June 1994. The rest were obtained in late May and early July. On July 20, 1994 he filed for bankruptcy. In the bankruptcy proceeding it was determined by a preponderance of the evidence that Lawyer fraudulently obtained the advances without intending to repay them. Was his conduct in securing the cash advances a violation of the rules of professional responsibility? *See In re Petilla*, 2001 WL 664247 (Review Dep't, State Bar Ct. of Ca., 2001).

4. Goodman, an assistant public defender, was precluded from engaging in the private practice of law. He also ran a business, InterMall. A customer of InterMall failed to pay its bill and Goodman filed suit against the customer. He falsely represented, however, that he was Herman, a former law partner of Goodman's who had left the state. He prepared letterhead with Herman's name on it for the suit and pretended to opposing counsel that he was Herman. He then told opposing counsel that "Herman" could not attend the trial, but that Goodman would attend instead. Suspicious that "Herman" and "Goodman" had the same voice, opposing counsel told the judge that Goodman had pretended to be Herman. Goodman denied this to the judge. Did Goodman violate Rule 8.4(c)? Did he violate any other rules? If so, what sanction was appropriate? *See Attorney Grievance Comm'n of Maryland v. Goodman*, 850 A.2d 1157 (Md. App. 2004).

5. Smith, General Counsel of Company, was concerned that confidential communications among the Board of Directors of Company seemed to be winding up in the business press. Smith hired an investigator, who contacted the telephone service providers for members of the Board and, by pretending to be someone he was not, convinced the providers to turn over the board members' telephone records. This behavior was known as "pretexting." Did Smith violate any rules of professional responsibility? On what facts might that issue depend? *See* Yuki Noguchi and Ellen Nakashima, *House Panel Digs Deep in Spy Case*, Washington Post, 09/29/2006, at D01. Such behavior might violate state privacy laws; in that regard, *see also* Model Rule 4.4(a).

6. Prosecutor was conducting a deposition in a criminal case. Defendant was present and was writing notes on a pad and sharing the notes with his counsel. Prosecutor wanted to use the notes as a handwriting exemplar. When Defendant and his lawyer left the room to confer, Prosecutor tore the notes from the legal pad Defendant was using and concealed them under a stack of files. When Defendant returned to the room and began looking for the notes, Prosecutor did not say where they were or that she had taken them; instead, she rummaged through her own papers, pretending to look for the notes. When Defendant saw the edge of a yellow piece of paper protruding from Prosecutor's files, Prosecutor admitted having the notes and returned them. Has Prosecutor violated the rules of professional conduct? *See In re Winkler*, 834 N.E.2d 85 (Ind. 2005).

7. Lawyer represented Defendant in a criminal matter. Lawyer asked Prosecutor to agree to drop a more serious charge in exchange for a guilty plea to a lesser charge. Prosecutor asked Lawyer if he had obtained the arresting officer's agreement to the plea agreement, and Lawyer said that he had. In fact, Lawyer had not discussed the matter with the arresting officer, and Prosecutor testified that he did not ordinarily agree to plea bargains unless the arresting officer concurred in them. Is Lawyer subject to discipline? Does it matter if, under the facts, Defendant was not guilty of the more serious offense? *See Office of Disciplinary Counsel v. Diangelus*, 907 A.2d 452 (Pa. 2006).

8. Miller was suspected of involvement in a corporate fraud. The corporation's lawyer learned that a search warrant of the premises was being executed, called the police, and specifically asked that employees not be

interviewed if counsel was not present. At the time, Miller was being interviewed by police. The police consulted the prosecutor and, following his advice, declined to stop the interview or to notify Miller that the lawyer wanted to speak with him. Violation of the no-contact rule? *See State v. Miller*, 600 N.W.2d 457 (Minn. 1999).

9.   Lawyer represented Client, who was charged with sexually assaulting a minor. Lawyer directed a private investigator to contact the minor, pretend to be from a computer company doing market research, and offer to swap the minor's old computer for a new one. The minor agreed and the investigator took the minor's computer, giving him a new Hewlett–Packard computer in exchange. Lawyer then had Analyst review the minor's computer in search of exculpatory evidence for Client. Proper strategy or unacceptable deceit? *See* Ryan J. Foley, *"Lawyer's Hoax Spurs Legal Tactics Debate,"* Findlaw, March 21, 2007; *Referee's Report & Recommendation, Office of Lawyer Regulation v. Hurley*, Case No. 07 AP 478–D (Wis. 2008). As of 2008, the case was pending before the Wisconsin Supreme Court.

10.   In May 2005, McMillan, a lawyer, sued the Association that managed her condominium. McMillan was represented when the complaint was filed. After a year of litigation, in July 2006, McMillan substituted a new lawyer in the case. In September 2006, McMillan filed a substitution of attorney, removing her attorney from the case and substituting herself as attorney of record. In October 2006, lawyer Schlaff sent a letter to opposing counsel, Paulos, indicating that he would be assisting McMillan on the case "in a limited fashion" but would not be substituting in as attorney of record. On December 7, 2006, Paulos called McMillan and spoke with her. They discussed court dates and the possibility of settlement; Paulos told McMillan not to disclose to him anything she had discussed with her attorneys. Schlaff then moved to disqualify Paulos because of his conversation with McMillan. Should the motion succeed? *See McMillan v. Shadow Ridge At Oak Park Homeowner's Association*, 165 Cal. App. 4th 960 (2d Dist. 2008).

CHAPTER 12

DUTIES TO THE SYSTEM

■ ■ ■

As we've seen, lawyers have duties to their clients and to the courts. They also have some limited duties to third parties. There is another category of duties that is somewhat more amorphous. We could characterize them, perhaps, as duties to the system. Some of these, viewed broadly, are duties owed to the legal system as a whole, including the obligation of lawyers to respect and support the adversary system and not to act in ways that are prejudicial to the administration of justice. Viewed more narrowly, lawyers also have duties to the disciplinary regime the rules create. In this chapter, we consider some of these duties to the system.

A. THE DUTY TO REPORT: MODEL RULE 8.3(a)

You learn that a colleague is intentionally overbilling a client to support his cocaine habit. What must you do? You may have obligations to the client arising from your duty of loyalty. But, in addition, Rule 8.3 may require you to report the lawyer's behavior to "the appropriate professional authority."

Read Model Rule 8.3 carefully. Does it surprise you? Most jurisdictions have a reporting requirement; do you think you will find it easy to comply with one? While the duty to report on your colleagues (this is sometimes unflatteringly referred to as the "rat rule") seems expansive, note several constraints on the duty to report misconduct. First, you need not report every violation of the rules of professional responsibility, however trivial, to the authorities; you are required to report only a violation "that raises a substantial question as to that lawyer's honesty, trustworthiness or fitness as a lawyer in other respects." Second, the lawyer need not self-report; the rule applies only to "[a] lawyer who knows that *another* lawyer" has committed a violation of the requisite seriousness. Third, the rule requires knowledge of a violation; a mere rumor will not trigger the reporting duty. Fourth, the reporting requirement is trumped by the duty of confidentiality; the rule "does not require disclosure of information otherwise protected by Rule 1.6," though in such a situation, Comment [2] suggests that the lawyer should encourage the client to give the informed consent necessary to such disclosure. There is also an exception for information gained by a lawyer while "participating in an approved lawyers assistance program." What do you suppose an "approved lawyers assistance program" is, and why would participants in such a program be excused from the reporting requirement?

The Model Code, by contrast, required much more extensive reporting. Any lawyer "possessing unprivileged knowledge of a violation [of the disciplinary rules]" was required to report that knowledge to the appropriate disciplinary authority. The reporting requirement was not limited by the nature of the violation, and self-reporting was required. Why do you suppose the Model Rules moved from this broader requirement to a narrower rule which did not require self-reporting? Consider Comment [3] to Rule 8.3. Is widespread disregard of a rule a good reason to change it?

The requirement of reporting is widely adopted. Why? Consider the following case:

IN RE RIEHLMANN

891 So.2d 1239 (La. 2005)

PER CURIAM.

Respondent is a criminal defense attorney who was formerly employed as an Assistant District Attorney in the Orleans Parish District Attorney's Office. One evening in April 1994, respondent met his close friend and law school classmate, Gerry Deegan, at a bar near the Orleans Parish Criminal District Court. Like respondent, Mr. Deegan had been a prosecutor in the Orleans Parish District Attorney's Office before he "switched sides" in 1987. During their conversation in the bar, Mr. Deegan told respondent that he had that day learned he was dying of colon cancer. In the same conversation, Mr. Deegan confided to respondent that he had suppressed exculpatory blood evidence in a criminal case he prosecuted while at the District Attorney's Office. Respondent recalls that he was "surprised" and "shocked" by his friend's revelation, and that he urged Mr. Deegan to "remedy" the situation. It is undisputed that respondent did not report Mr. Deegan's disclosure to anyone at the time it was made. Mr. Deegan died in July 1994, having done nothing to "remedy" the situation of which he had spoken in the bar.

Nearly five years after Mr. Deegan's death, one of the defendants whom he had prosecuted in a 1985 armed robbery case was set to be executed by lethal injection on May 20, 1999. In April 1999, the lawyers for the defendant, John Thompson, discovered a crime lab report which contained the results of tests performed on a piece of pants leg and a tennis shoe that were stained with the perpetrator's blood during a scuffle with the victim of the robbery attempt. The crime lab report concluded that the robber had Type "B" blood. Because Mr. Thompson has Type "O" blood, the crime lab report proved he could not have committed the robbery; nevertheless, neither the crime lab report nor the blood-stained physical evidence had been disclosed to Mr. Thompson's defense counsel prior to or during trial. Respondent claims that when he heard about the inquiry of Mr. Thompson's lawyers, he immediately realized that this was the case to which Mr. Deegan had referred in their April 1994 conversation in the bar. On April 27, 1999, respondent executed an affidavit for Mr. Thompson in which he attested that during the 1994 conversation, "the late Gerry Deegan said to me that he had intentionally suppressed blood evidence in the armed robbery trial of John Thompson that in some way exculpated the defendant."

In May 1999, respondent reported Mr. Deegan's misconduct to the ODC [Office of Disciplinary Counsel]. In June 1999, respondent testified in a hearing on a motion for new trial in Mr. Thompson's armed robbery case. During the hearing, respondent testified that Mr. Deegan had told him that he "suppressed exculpatory evidence that was blood evidence, that seemed to have excluded Mr. Thompson as the perpetrator of an armed robbery." Respondent also admitted that he "should have reported" Mr. Deegan's misconduct, and that while he ultimately did so, "I should have reported it sooner, I guess."

On September 30, 1999, respondent gave a sworn statement to the ODC in which he was asked why he did not report Mr. Deegan's disclosure to anyone at the time it was made. Respondent replied:

> I think that under ordinary circumstances, I would have. I really honestly think I'm a very good person. And I think I do the right thing whenever I'm given the opportunity to choose. This was unquestionably the most difficult time of my life. Gerry, who was like a brother to me, was dying. And that was, to say distracting would be quite an understatement. I'd also left my wife just a few months before, with three kids, and was under the care of a psychiatrist, taking antidepressants. My youngest son was then about two and had just recently undergone open-heart surgery. I had a lot on my plate at the time. A great deal of it of my own making; there's no question about it. But, nonetheless, I was very, very distracted, and I simply did not give it the important consideration that it deserved. But it was a very trying time for me. And that's the only explanation I have, because, otherwise, I would have reported it immediately had I been in a better frame of mind.

DISCIPLINARY PROCEEDINGS

On January 4, 2001, the ODC filed one count of formal charges against respondent, alleging that his failure to report his unprivileged knowledge of Mr. Deegan's prosecutorial misconduct violated Rule 8.3(a) (reporting professional misconduct)....

On March 5, 2002, respondent answered the amended formal charges and admitted some of the factual allegations therein, but denied that his conduct violated the Rules of Professional Conduct. Specifically, respondent asserted that Rule 8.3(a) "merely requires that an attorney possessing unprivileged knowledge of a violation of this Code shall report such knowledge to the authority empowered to investigate such acts. It is undisputed that respondent did report his knowledge of Deegan's statements to Thompson's attorneys, with the clear understanding that this information would be reported to the District Attorney and the Court, undeniably authorities empowered to investigate Deegan's conduct." ...

In its report filed with the disciplinary board, the hearing committee concluded that respondent did not violate Rule 8.3(a), but that he should be publicly reprimanded for his violation of Rule 8.4(d)....

Based on its factual findings, the committee found that respondent did not violate Rule 8.3(a) because he did not have "knowledge of a violation" that obligated him to report Mr. Deegan to the ODC or to any other authority. The committee pointed out that it believed respondent's testimony that Mr. Deegan made equivocal statements in 1994 that did not rise to the level of a "confession" that Deegan had actually suppressed the crime lab report nine years earlier. The committee found Mr. Deegan qualified his statement that the evidence "might" have exculpated the defendant.... Consequently, the committee determined that respondent would have had no violation to report. The committee found Mr. Deegan's statements at most suggested a potential violation of the ethical rules, but the committee declined to construe Rule 8.3(a) to require a lawyer to report a potential violation of an ethical rule by another lawyer.

... In light of the mitigating factors present, and finding that a suspension would serve no useful purpose in this case, the committee recommended the imposition of a public reprimand.

Both respondent and the ODC filed objections to the hearing committee's recommendation.

The disciplinary board adopted the hearing committee's factual findings but rejected its application of Rule 8.3(a) of the Rules of Professional Conduct. The board determined that a finding of a violation of Rule 8.3(a) requires clear and convincing evidence that an attorney (1) possessed unprivileged knowledge of an ethical violation and (2) failed to report such knowledge to a tribunal or other authority empowered to investigate or act upon such violation. Concerning the knowledge requirement, the board considered various legal authorities interpreting both Louisiana Rule 8.3(a) and Model Rule 8.3(a), and determined that a lawyer's duty to report professional misconduct is triggered when, under the circumstances, a reasonable lawyer would have "a firm opinion that the conduct in question more likely than not occurred." The board explained that the requisite knowledge under Rule 8.3(a) is "more than a mere suspicion, but less than absolute or moral certainty."

Employing this analysis, the board concluded the committee erred in its finding that respondent had no duty to report because Mr. Deegan's statements were equivocal. The board found respondent must have understood from his 1994 conversation with Mr. Deegan that Mr. Deegan had suppressed evidence [which he was required by law to disclose]:

If Respondent did not understand from his conversation with Deegan that Deegan has suppressed evidence that he was obligated to produce, why was Respondent shocked and surprised? Why did Respondent tell Deegan that what he had done was "not right" and that Deegan had to "rectify" the situation? Respondent never changed his testimony in this respect. Obviously, if Respondent understood from his conversation with Deegan that Deegan had done nothing wrong, there would have been no occasion for Respondent to say that it was "not right" or that Deegan had to "rectify" what he had done. The Committee makes no attempt to explain these circumstances which are wholly inconsistent with the Committee's theory. This uncontradicted circumstantial evidence cannot be ignored. Indeed, if Deegan believed he had done nothing wrong, why did Deegan even bother to bring the matter up nearly ten years after Thompson was convicted? More importantly, why did he bring it up in the same conversation that he disclosed to Respondent that he had terminal colon cancer?

... Accordingly, the board found respondent had sufficient knowledge of misconduct by Mr. Deegan to trigger a duty to report the misconduct to the disciplinary authorities.

The board then turned to a discussion of whether respondent's failure to report Mr. Deegan's misconduct for more than five years after learning of it constituted a failure to report under Rule 8.3(a). The board acknowledged that Rule 8.3(a) does not provide any specific time limit or period within which the misconduct must be reported. Nevertheless, the board reasoned that Rule 8.3(a) serves no useful purpose unless it is read to require reporting to an appropriate authority within a reasonable time under the circumstances. Therefore, absent special circumstances, the board determined that a lawyer must report his knowledge of misconduct "promptly." Applying these principles to the instant case, the board determined respondent's disclosure in 1999 of misconduct he discovered in 1994 was not timely and did not satisfy the requirements of Rule 8.3(a).

... The board found respondent knowingly violated a duty owed to the profession, and that his actions resulted in both actual and potential injury to Mr. Thompson. The board noted that if respondent had taken further action in 1994, when Mr. Deegan made his confession, Mr. Thompson's innocence in connection with the armed robbery charge may have been established sooner. The board also observed that negative publicity attached to respondent's actions, thereby causing harm to the legal profession. The board determined the baseline sanction for respondent's conduct is a suspension from the practice of law....

DISCUSSION

In this matter we are presented for the first time with an opportunity to delineate the scope of an attorney's duty under Rule 8.3 to report the professional misconduct of a fellow member of the bar....

Louisiana's rule is based on ABA Model Rule 8.3; however, there are several differences between the Model Rule and the Louisiana Rule that was in effect in 2001, at the time the formal charges were filed in this case. Most significantly, Model Rule 8.3 requires a lawyer to report the misconduct of another lawyer only when the conduct in question "raises a substantial question" as to that lawyer's fitness to practice. Louisiana's version of Rule 8.3 imposed a substantially more expansive reporting requirement, in that our rule required a lawyer to report all unprivileged knowledge of any ethical violation by a lawyer, whether the violation was, in the reporting lawyer's view, flagrant and substantial or minor and technical. . . .

At the time the formal charges were filed in this case, Louisiana Rule 8.3(a) provided:

> A lawyer possessing unprivileged knowledge of a violation of this code shall report such knowledge to a tribunal or other authority empowered to investigate or act upon such violation.

Thus, the rule has three distinct requirements: (1) the lawyer must possess unprivileged knowledge of a violation of the Rules of Professional Conduct; (2) the lawyer must report that knowledge; and (3) the report must be made to a tribunal or other authority empowered to investigate or act on the violation. We will discuss each requirement in turn.

Knowledge

. . . [I]t is clear that absolute certainty of ethical misconduct is not required before the reporting requirement is triggered. The lawyer is not required to conduct an investigation and make a definitive decision that a violation has occurred before reporting; that responsibility belongs to the disciplinary system and this court. On the other hand, knowledge requires more than a mere suspicion of ethical misconduct. We hold that a lawyer will be found to have knowledge of reportable misconduct, and thus reporting is required, where the supporting evidence is such that a reasonable lawyer under the circumstances would form a firm belief that the conduct in question had more likely than not occurred. As such, knowledge is measured by an objective standard that is not tied to the subjective beliefs of the lawyer in question.

When to Report

Once the lawyer decides that a reportable offense has likely occurred, reporting should be made promptly. The need for prompt reporting flows from the need to safeguard the public and the profession against future wrongdoing by the offending lawyer. This purpose is not served unless Rule 8.3(a) is read to require timely reporting under the circumstances presented.

Appropriate Authority

Louisiana Rule 8.3(a) requires that the report be made to "a tribunal or other authority empowered to investigate or act upon such violation." The term "tribunal or other authority" is not specifically defined. However, as the comments to Model Rule 8.3(a) explain, the report generally should be made to the bar disciplinary authority. Therefore, a report of misconduct by a lawyer admitted to practice in Louisiana must be made to the Office of Disciplinary Counsel.

DETERMINATION OF RESPONDENT'S MISCONDUCT AND APPROPRIATE DISCIPLINE

Applying the principles set forth above to the conduct of respondent in the instant case, we find the ODC proved by clear and convincing evidence that respondent violated Rule 8.3(a). First, we find that respondent should have known that a reportable event occurred at the time of his 1994 barroom conversation with Mr. Deegan. Stated another way, respondent's conversation with Mr. Deegan at that time gave him sufficient information that a reasonable lawyer under the circumstances would have formed a firm opinion that the conduct in question more likely than not occurred. Regardless of the actual words Mr. Deegan said that night, and whether they were or were not "equivocal," respondent understood from the conversation that Mr. Deegan had done something wrong. Respondent admitted as much in his affidavit, during the hearing on the motion for new trial in the criminal case, during his sworn statement to the ODC, and during his testimony at the formal hearing.... The circumstances under which the conversation took place lend further support to this finding. On the same day that he learned he was dying of cancer, Mr. Deegan felt compelled to tell his best friend about something he had done in a trial that took place nine years earlier. It simply defies logic that respondent would now argue that he could not be sure that Mr. Deegan actually withheld *Brady* evidence [evidence which he was required by law to disclose] because his statements were vague and non-specific.

We also find that respondent failed to promptly report Mr. Deegan's misconduct to the disciplinary authorities. As respondent himself acknowledged, he should have reported Mr. Deegan's statements sooner than he did. There was no reason for respondent to have waited five years to tell the ODC about what his friend had done.

In his answer to the formal charges, respondent asserts that he did comply with the reporting requirement of Rule 8.3(a) because he promptly reported Mr. Deegan's misconduct to the District Attorney and the Criminal District Court through the attorneys for the criminal defendant, John Thompson. Respondent has misinterpreted Rule 8.3(a) in this regard. The word "tribunal" must be read in the context of the entire sentence in which it appears. The proper inquiry, therefore, is what authority is "empowered" to act upon a charge of attorney misconduct. In Louisiana, only this court possesses the authority to define and regulate the practice of law, including the discipline of attorneys. In turn, we have delegated to disciplinary counsel the authority to investigate and prosecute claims of attorney misconduct. Furthermore ... only this court may discipline an attorney found guilty of unethical behavior. Therefore, respondent is incorrect in arguing that he discharged his reporting duty under Rule 8.3(a) by reporting Mr. Deegan's misconduct to Mr. Thompson's attorneys, the District Attorney, and/or the Criminal District Court. It is undisputed that respondent did not report to the appropriate entity, the ODC, until 1999. That report came too late to be construed as "prompt."

.... Under all of the circumstances presented, we conclude that a public reprimand is the appropriate sanction.

Conclusion

Reporting another lawyer's misconduct to disciplinary authorities is an important duty of every lawyer. Lawyers are in the best position to observe professional misconduct and to assist the profession in sanctioning it. While a Louisiana lawyer is subject to discipline for not reporting misconduct, it is our hope that lawyers will comply with their reporting obligation primarily because they are ethical people who want to serve their clients and the public well. Moreover, the lawyer's duty to report professional misconduct is the foundation for the claim that we can be trusted to regulate ourselves as a profession. If we fail in our duty, we forfeit that trust and have no right to enjoy the privilege of self-regulation or the confidence and respect of the public.

[One dissenter would have imposed a harsher sanction.]

NOTES

1. Riehlmann reported Deegan's misconduct to the proper authorities in 1999. Was there anything strange about that?

2. The court concluded that the reporting requirement includes an implicit requirement of prompt reporting. Does that seem reasonable? If Riehlmann had waited till Deegan's death to report the matter, would that have been sufficiently prompt? Why or why not?

3. The court in its conclusion offered an explanation for the reporting requirement. Do you find it convincing? The facts in this case are, of course, troubling. What did Riehlmann's failure to disclose mean for Thompson?

4. The rule required that the lawyer have "knowledge" of a violation of the ethical rules to be required to report. How did the court define "knowledge"? Is this kind of "knowledge" the same as the "knowledge" that a client intends to give false testimony under Rule 3.3? If not, why not?

5. The dissenter would have imposed a more severe sanction on Riehlmann. The judge there might have been thinking about *In re Himmel*, 533 N.E.2d 790 (Ill. 1988), a case that stunned the Illinois bar. Attorney Himmel was approached by Forsberg, a client whose settlement in a personal injury case had been converted by her lawyer, Casey. Forsberg called the bar to complain about Casey; in addition, she retained Himmel to ask him to help her get her money back. Himmel did so, and ultimately secured some funds for Forsberg; he himself did not receive any fee for the work, though if Casey had paid more of the agreed-upon settlement, he would have. Himmel negotiated an agreement between Forsberg and Casey which provided that Forsberg would not

initiate an attorney disciplinary action against Casey. Himmel did not report Casey's wrongdoing to the state bar. Ultimately, Casey misappropriated the funds of several other clients besides Forsberg. Himmel was disciplined for failing to report Casey. While Himmel claimed that the information about Casey's theft of client funds was privileged and therefore that he was not required to report it, the court rejected that claim because Himmel's conversations with Forsberg had taken place while her mother and/or fiancé were present. Himmel's sanction was a year's suspension from the practice of law. Do you think the difference between the sanctions in *Riehlmann* and *Himmel* was justified? Should the fact that Himmel's client had already reported Casey to the bar authorities excuse his failure to report? Why or why not?

6.   Might imposing stringent discipline on Riehlmann for his violation have unintended consequences? Does that concern you?

7.   The failure to report is a disciplinary violation. Can it also create civil liability? Client retained Gavin to prepare her will and provide legal services to her estate after her death. Client then died, leaving behind a sizeable estate. Gavin rented space to another lawyer, Averna, and frequently referred work to him. After Gavin was diagnosed with terminal lung cancer, he began converting funds from Client's estate. Gavin died; after his death, the administrator for Client's estate learned that Gavin had stolen over $400,000 from the estate. Plaintiff, the estate, sued Averna, arguing that Averna had known of Gavin's behavior and that he had a legally enforceable duty to report Gavin's misconduct, which should create liability to Plaintiff. Should the claim be successful? *See Estate of Spencer v. Gavin*, 946 A.2d 1051 (N.J. Super. Ct. App. Div. 2008).

B. DUTIES OF SUPERVISORY AND SUBORDINATE LAWYERS

The reporting obligation may not appear to take adequate account of the precarious position in which it could place a junior lawyer. Suppose that you are an associate at a law firm; you conclude that a senior lawyer at your firm is engaged in billing fraud. Do you think you have an obligation to disclose that violation? The Rule 8.3 obligation is not delegable; it is possessed by any lawyer with the requisite knowledge. You cannot avoid your obligation merely by reporting your suspicions to someone at your firm. At the same time, you might be concerned that reporting a senior lawyer at your firm will cost you your job, or at the very least the good opinion of the firm's partners.

You might also be concerned about whether you are correct about your conclusion that the senior lawyer has violated the ethics rules. The stakes of being wrong seem disturbingly high. Does consulting a senior lawyer at the firm, and following her advice, provide a junior lawyer with any sort of safe harbor against disciplinary liability? This concern is not limited to the reporting rules, but might arise in any situation in which a junior lawyer is advised by a supervisory lawyer with regard to an ethics issue.

Model Rules 5.1 through 5.3 set out the governing principles with regard to the obligations of supervisory and subordinate lawyers. The Rules set out the obligations and responsibilities of supervisory lawyers, and the circumstances in which a lawyer can have vicarious liability for another person's violations of the rules of professional responsibility. They also address whether a subordinate lawyer can obey the direction of a supervisory lawyer and rely on that lawyer's assurances that the conduct in question is permissible under the ethics rules. What do these rules, and these cases, tell you about when a lawyer is responsible for another lawyer's violation of the rules, and when a lawyer can avoid discipline because she acted at another lawyer's direction?

1. VICARIOUS DISCIPLINARY LIABILITY AND SUPERVISORY RESPONSIBILITY

Who is responsible for violations of the ethical rules? We begin with the default rule: that each lawyer is responsible for his or her own ethics violations. *See* Model Rule 5.2(a). This raises two questions. First, are there ever circumstances in which a lawyer is responsible and sanctionable for ethics violations committed by another lawyer? Second, is there any exception to the default rule—is there any situation in which a lawyer will not be held responsible for his or her own violations of the ethics rules?

Model Rules 5.1 and 5.2 address both of these issues. Rule 5.1 creates several different categories of potential disciplinary liability. First, partners and managers must "make reasonable efforts" to assure that the lawyers in the firm conform to the Rules; any lawyer supervising another lawyer must "make reasonable efforts" to ensure that the subordinate lawyer complies with the rules. Second, Rule 5.1(c) sets out the rules for vicarious liability, under which a lawyer will be responsible for another lawyer's violation of the ethics rules. Such liability exists if the other lawyer orders the conduct, ratifies it, or is a partner or supervisor in the offending lawyer's firm and knows of the conduct when it can be avoided or mitigated but does not act. While the rule is captioned "Responsibilities of Partners, Managers, and Supervisory Lawyers," are the opportunities for vicarious liability under the rule limited to supervisory lawyers?

Supervisory derelictions are rarely the subject of discipline. Consider, however, the following case:

ATTORNEY GRIEVANCE COMMISSION OF MARYLAND v. KIMMEL

955 A.2d 269 (Md. 2008)

HARRELL, JUDGE.

These attorney disciplinary actions examine alleged shortfalls by partners in a law firm in supervision of a relatively-inexperienced associate that followed the establishment by their out-of-state law firm of a beachhead office in Maryland. . . .

Findings of Fact and Conclusions of Law

In her written opinion, Judge Cox made the following factual findings:

K & S handles Lemon Law cases as a high volume practice. The applicable fee shifting statutes provide an incentive to automotive manufacturers to settle, as does the desire to promote customer satisfaction. In the experience of both Kimmel and Silverman, approximately 99% of their cases settle, if handled properly. . . . The firm relies extensively on paralegals and its own mechanical experts to manage high volume attorney caseloads.

In 2004, K & S decided to expand into Maryland. Although Kimmel and Silverman considered associating with a Maryland practitioner with experience in the Lemon Law field, they were unable to find a suitable candidate. Therefore they decided to hire and train an attorney to start up their Maryland practice.

Robin Katz responded to a web site job posting by K & S. . . .

Katz was first admitted to practice in Maryland in December 1996. From 1996 through 2003, Katz handled social security disability cases for Health Management Associates ("HMA") in a non-adversarial administrative law setting. Katz was hired in 2003 by Health Education Resource Organization ("HERO") as a staff attorney. Katz remained at HERO for approximately nine months.

When Katz interviewed at K & S in June 2004, she had no civil trial experience. However Katz had high volume work experience, and she had handled uncontested administrative and masters hearings. Rapkin conducted an interview and followed up with reference checks, including contact with administrative judges before whom Katz had tried cases. Katz was described as competent, well organized, and capable of handling a large caseload. Her former employer at HMA described her as someone capable of managing her own office. Rapkin knew that Katz had no jury trial experience, although he was unaware that she also had not handled contested matters. Rapkin also knew that Katz had managed a caseload of 200 to 300 social security cases. Overall, he thought Katz appeared to be a nice and competent individual who was capable of handling the job.

Katz received and accepted an offer from K & S on the same day as her interview. She spent the next month in the K & S home office in Ambler, Pennsylvania, where she was trained to handle Lemon Law cases. During that time, Rapkin took Katz with him to a couple of depositions and arbitrations. He also assisted her to develop Maryland forms for basic pleadings. She was trained on the firm method for preparing and evaluating cases. . . .

K & S utilizes "Time Matters," which is a computerized calendaring/database system. K & S policy requires that time sensitive matters be entered into Time Matters when they are received, at which time the due dates for deadlines and responses are calendared. The Time Matters system sends automated reminders of deadlines to the responsible lawyers and paralegals. Additionally, it enables supervising attorneys to monitor to ensure that case deadlines are met. . . . Katz acknowledges that she was trained on the Time Matters system. She described it as a tickler or calendaring system. She was well aware of her responsibility to input matters she received into the calendaring system.

After the month training period, Katz returned to Maryland. Katz made arrangements to procure office space and open an office in Owings Mills. Katz was the only person in the office. She shared equipment and some common space with other unrelated entities. Additionally, she had the shared use of a receptionist to answer and transfer calls. Katz was responsible for all of her own clerical work.

Katz understood that she would not have a paralegal in Maryland at the outset. She knew, however, that she would have access to paralegal assistance through Pennsylvania. She was led to believe that K & S would hire a paralegal for the Maryland office once it had a sufficient caseload.

K & S had begun to accept Maryland cases while Katz was still training in Pennsylvania. It was her belief that there existed approximately fifty Maryland cases by the time she opened the office in Maryland. Katz immediately started drafting Maryland complaints based upon Pennsylvania forms that she adapted to Maryland law.

Testimony and exhibits clearly reflect that K & S operates a volume practice in a number-driven environment. The overt emphasis on attorney numbers and expectations is pervasive in communications, and seems essential in the firm culture.

Starting in early September, K & S gave Katz a weekly benchmark for complaints to be filed. She was initially expected to put ten cases a week in suit, although that number increased in January 2005 to fifteen cases per week. In addition to the filing expectations, a specific revenue target of $10,000 per week in attorneys fees from settlements was established. This was confirmed to Katz in a November 23, 2004 e-mail from Rapkin, who initially supervised her work.

Katz's ability to meet her revenue expectations was the subject of a series of email exchanges, all of which emphasized the importance of this objective. In a particularly blunt exchange on November 29, 2004 from Rapkin, with copies to Silverman, Kimmel and the Office Manager, Katz was told:

> This is not what I want to see. The report you gave me says you settled 1 case in the last 2 weeks, and you have 224 cases. Let me make it clear, first and foremost, you must make your number. The number you have is not set for fun, it has a very important purpose. Your number is the most important way we judge how to give raises, whether we can fund support staff for your office, and as a practical

matter if all your cases come up for trial at the same time b/c they are not settled you won't be able to handle them all. Therefore, no excuses, don't call, no need to talk, just get on it and only call me with good positive news of settlements, or demands you are going to make.

The revenue quota was also documented in a memorandum outlining performance expectations for Katz in order for her to have a positive employment review. As stated in the Memorandum:

> You have already been told our expectations of how much income we expect you to bring to the firm each week, *on a consistent basis*. Every weekly number is based upon 52 weeks a year. Each lawyer shall make certain that when he or she is on vacation or holiday, the settlements for the weeks before and after are not forgotten. The attorney must make up the missing week/days settlements so the average income per week is still expected.
>
> . . . Your weekly number starting the week of 01/03/05 is $10,000.00. So there is no confusion, we expect you to consistently bring to the firm $10,000.00 in attorney fee and cost receivables each week in order to have a positive review in June.

It is clear that Katz did not consistently meet her performance benchmarks. No adverse action was initiated by K & S. However the performance measures were a regular point of emphasis. In January 2005, Kimmel assumed supervisory responsibility over Katz. The emphasis on her numbers remained.

On February 8, 2005 and April 12, 2005, Silverman e-mailed Katz expressing concern that she was not settling cases with manufacturers other than Ford and Chrysler. On May 10, 2005, Kimmel followed up on this topic and instructed Katz: "To break the backlog, I've decided to help you along." Kimmel directed Katz to send at least ten substantive letters three days per week to opposing counsel, and that unless Kimmel agreed in advance, this was "to be done without fail as instructed." As Kimmel described:

> I do not want form letters or correspondence that clearly shows the file has not been reviewed. Each letter should have substantial detail and/or a demand that applies accurately to that particular case. While you may disagree with this routine, watch what happens as a result. You will blow through your numbers, be better prepared for arbitrations and be in more frequent contact with clients. As a consequence, we can add another attorney and at least one paralegal. I want YOU to head up MD and make it a well-oiled machine, but allowing all manufacturers but two to largely ignore you while waiting for trial is NOT the way. Do what I ask and you will reap ALL the rewards of that labor, in ways you will find very beneficial.

Katz dutifully started sending out thirty letters per week, with copies forwarded to Kimmel three times per week. This continued from June 1, 2005 through the end of Katz's employment, except during vacation periods. On June 3, 2005 Kimmel again emailed Katz questioning the fees generated in her settlements, which were almost always $2,500 per case. In response to Katz's claim that most settlements were pre-suit, and fees would be larger in other cases, Kimmel commented:

> I for example, review every file every month, and it takes me about 30–60 minutes to update myself. Each month, between .5 and 1.0 are added to the file for that alone. Then there are issues that come up, protracted discussions, consultations with the experts and client, etc. No two cases are identical and so I expect that settlement of fees would be similar across the board, but not identical as they have been.

At the time, Katz had between 200 and 300 cases that would need such monthly review to follow this directive.

The issue of paralegal support for Katz was also a subject of continuing discussion. As early as September 23, 2004, Kimmel indicated that he agreed with Katz that the firm needed a "full time professional paralegal down there." It is clear that Katz could and did avail herself of paralegal support from the Pennsylvania office. This was not always a smooth process. . . . In late December, Katz inquired of the Office Manager whether there was any news about hiring a paralegal for Maryland. In response, she was reminded of the need to file fifteen complaints per week. . . .

It is clear that Katz's workload steadily increased over her tenure with K & S. By September 27, 2004, she had 127 cases, with 45 in suit. Barely a week later, on October 2, 2004 she reported that she had 194 cases. By November 8, 2004, she had 203 cases, with approximately 100 in suit. As of December 6, 2004, the number had grown to 239 cases, with 125 in suit. During the period from September 2004 through August 2005, Katz filed 461 suits in Maryland. She was assigned over 500 total matters. . . .

While the practice of the firm is to move aggressively toward settlement, and to settle most cases early, Katz had a volume of cases in suit with active discovery. Unlike the practice in some other jurisdictions, Maryland did not require early arbitration, so cases did not get pushed as easily towards settlement. Therefore, in addition to discovery, Katz began to handle a steady array of motions and court appearances. In one e-mail in late April 2005 that discussed calendar matters that were scheduled in the next six weeks, Katz noted six motions hearings in a week period, together with multiple mediations. Additionally, she had matters in jurisdictions throughout the state.

Katz managed to meet various competing demands with one glaring omission. She failed to enter deadlines into Time Matters in forty-seven cases. These were all Nissan or Toyota cases that were aggressively litigated by the law firm of Piper Rudnick. The discovery filed in those cases was relatively routine. However Katz did not access, or even attempt to access, paralegal assistance with responses in those cases.

Although Katz was assigned a specific paralegal in the Pennsylvania office to work with in her early months with the firm, that system evolved. By the fall of 2004, K & S paralegals were assigned to specific manufacturers, so discovery was referred by lawyers to the paralegals in charge of that manufacturer. Although there was a K & S paralegal to assist with Nissan and Toyota matters, Katz seemed unaware of that assignment. Since Katz sought no assistance in these cases, and discovery and motions were never logged into Time Matters, no alerts were generated when responses were delinquent.

When timely responses were not filed, a series of Motions for Sanctions seeking dismissal were filed. Katz did not respond to those Motions. Rather, she undertook to prepare discovery responses. In twenty-eight cases, the Motions for Sanctions were treated as Motions to Compel, and a deadline was set to file belated discovery responses. In eighteen of those matters, no discovery was ever filed. In the remaining ten, answers were filed outside the extended deadline. Renewed Motions for Sanctions were filed, and all but three of those were not even answered. The first case dismissal occurred in May 2005. Ultimately, dismissals with prejudice were entered in all forty-seven cases.

Katz was overwhelmed by January 2005. While she claimed to use her best judgment in juggling competing demands, that judgment was seriously flawed. Rather than prioritize the overdue discovery and motion responses, Katz continued to focus on putting cases in suit and pushing for settlements, as those were the objective criteria being measured within the firm. By that time, Katz was also out of the office a lot with court appearances and depositions. Katz demonstrated no appreciation of the risk she ran by ignoring the motions or overdue discovery. She seemed genuinely unaware that matters could or would be dismissed because of the discovery lapses.

Katz acknowledged that she was afraid to disclose her lapses to Kimmel and Silverman. Katz felt the partners were not pleased with her and that her job was on the line. While this assessment was not completely accurate, it impacted her decisions. Since the discovery and motions in the dismissed cases were never logged in to Time Matters, the problem could not be detected through the firm's computerized system. However Katz also acted affirmatively to cover up her difficulties. In June and July 2005, Katz forwarded Kimmel copies of at least ten letters she purportedly sent to opposing counsel in cases that she knew had already been dismissed.

The Iweala case was the first dismissed case that came to light. [In that case, Katz missed a discovery deadline and the case was dismissed with prejudice.]

On June 29, 2005, the Iweala dismissal came to the attention of K & S, and the Office Manager immediately communicated with Katz seeking an explanation. Katz characterized the dismissal as inappropriate, as she claimed to have timely filed discovery. Katz also represented that a Motion to Reopen had been filed. That Motion was not actually docketed until July 6, 2005.

Silverman contacted Katz when he learned of the problem, and was initially assured that she believed the matter could be reinstated. When Katz later acknowledged that she had made a mistake and the case could not be reinstated, Silverman did not take any further action. Silverman was unaware of any other problems at that time, and felt Katz was generally doing a good job. . . .

Katz was scheduled for a one-week vacation in late July. She returned to two bins of mail and other matters that had piled up in her absence. By that point she was totally overwhelmed. She described herself as depressed, crying all the time, and she had lost twenty pounds. Although the firm finally hired a paralegal for the Maryland office during July, Katz had the added responsibility to train the person. Katz submitted her resignation by e-mail on August 10, 2005, and left immediately. While the firm asked her to stay for a period to help with transition, she refused, citing health concerns.

Silverman drove to the Maryland office and met with Katz on the day she resigned. This was his first visit to the Maryland office. He described Katz as looking "like a beaten dog." He was immediately concerned by stacks of documents in her office that were not filed. When he looked in file cabinets, he found other loose papers. K & S mobilized attorneys and paralegals to assist in assessing the problem. The firm immediately hired three Maryland lawyers, and Katz's cases were all reassigned within a two to four week period. [The firm promptly resolved all client claims fairly.]

Based on these factual findings, the hearing judge concluded that Respondents violated MRPC 5.1. . . . [W]e adopt her conclusions.

As basic components of a "reasonable effort to have in place measures giving reasonable assurance that all lawyers in the firm conform to the Maryland Rules of Professional Conduct," partners must establish policies and procedures that, *inter alia*, are "designed to . . . identify dates by which actions must be taken in pending matters . . . and ensure that inexperienced lawyers are properly supervised." . . .

In the present case, numerous warning or alert indicators should have informed the partners and managing attorneys of K & S of the need for more heightened supervision than was given Katz. . . . Among the foundational responsibilities when opening and operating a branch office in a new and unfamiliar jurisdiction is to address adequately practice distinctions between the existing office and the beachhead location. In this case, neither the founding partners nor the Maryland attorney they hired to manage the Maryland office ever had filed a case in a Maryland circuit court before the Owings Mills office opened its doors.

In the opening forays into its emerging Maryland practice, K & S filed cases in the venue closest to the Owings Mills office, as was done with regard to its Pennsylvania office for Pennsylvania cases, unaware that in Maryland ordinarily a case must be filed either in the county where the motor vehicle was purchased or where the purchaser resides. Several distinctions between Maryland and Pennsylvania practices profoundly influence the handling of automotive warranty claims. Basic familiarity with Maryland law and practice would have highlighted differences in fee-shifting and early settlement provisions. An understanding of Maryland procedure would have highlighted differences in venue, choice of forum based on dollar amount of the claim, challenges to expert witnesses, and the desirability of perhaps establishing relationships with credible Maryland experts. To protect prospective Maryland clients from the harm of incompetent representation, these differences should have been researched, appreciated, and resolved during the design of supervisory procedures for the new office, not in the midst of ongoing litigation. . . .

Next, a relatively low level of experience of an attorney should indicate that more elaborate supervision is in order. . . . [W]e have in this case a firm with offices in five states and where the firm's experienced attorneys carry caseloads of 1,000 clients or more. In this business model and practice setting, a relatively inexperienced attorney was stationed alone in an office physically remote from the critical mass of the firm and directed to begin filing numerous cases as rapidly as possible. Katz had no experience in the practice of automobile warranty or "lemon" law. She also was a novice in other critical areas, such as circuit court pleadings and practice, jury trials, and contested litigation generally. Supervisory procedures should have been designed deliberately to address the attorney's inexperience and to counterbalance her physical distance from the ready availability of steadying interaction with peers and managers.

. . . Respondents were obligated to determine if Katz, in fact, was trained and experienced sufficiently to act as the managing attorney of K & S's Maryland office. They had no basis to assume such competence. . . .

Physical isolation of an attorney from peers and supervisors also indicates a heightened need to adapt supervisory strategies to ensure compliance with the Rules, even in an internet-oriented society. In this case, Respondents essentially relied on an isolated, inexperienced attorney to supervise herself. . . . Katz's supervisors did not inform themselves through periodic audits or on-site visits. Her supervisors depended, to a great degree, on her self-disclosures to determine if delegated tasks were completed.

Requests for help, however generalized, especially from a physically remote staff attorney, warrant investigation to determine whether the employee's perception that her failures are attributable to objective factors is accurate or whether increased supervision, support, and guidance might avert or reform performance shortfalls. The record shows that Katz repeatedly brought to her supervisor's attention her desire for on-site staff support in the Maryland office. Her requests did not foster an investigation by her supervisors to see if client obligations in Maryland were going unfulfilled. Instead, the response was to encourage her to adhere to the existing procedures, and ironically, to create more work. Her complaints that the workload in Maryland already was overwhelming resulted in verbal and written reminders of her quotas.

Respondents point out that other attorneys within the firm, even those with larger caseloads, handled discovery adequately by adhering to the firm's established procedures. The fact that other lawyers might have handled Katz's workload more efficiently is not persuasive. The Comments to MRPC Rule 5.1 clearly contemplate the need to individuate supervision based on "the nature of the practice" and the experience of the attorney. Katz opened 461 new cases over the course of her 13–month employment at K & S. She actively managed 15 to 20 cases per week. All told, she was responsible for over 500 matters. Her weekly benchmarks were to generate $10,000 in settlements and file at least fifteen complaints. She was scheduled to appear in a number of different courts, slated to appear at a number of settlement negotiations, and expected to run the office. Unsurprisingly to us, she announced to her direct supervisor that she needed help.

"Help" came in the form of communications intended to motivate her to work harder. Presumably, those missives and exhortations were consistent with K & S's standard practices. No one came to the Maryland office to help catch up on filing or to check on the situation until significant lapses occurred and major damage control efforts were required. "To help with the backlog," her supervisor demanded that she create at least 30 demand letters each week and forward the letters for his personal review. . . . Katz was promised local support prospectively, but only if she generated more work. Her assessment that she needed help *now* was not given adequate analysis or credence by her direct or ultimate supervisors. . . .

Thus, numerous indicators alerted Respondents to the need for a heightened level of supervision. . . . In addition, Respondents neglected other basic components of a reasonable supervision effort. Foremost among these failures was failing to supervise the identification of pending deadlines. K & S had in place an adequate system for tracking deadlines once the deadline was identified; however, the procedure for initially identifying and entering the deadline into the system was defeated too easily by the sole employee in the physically remote office. Many incoming pleadings, motions, and inquiries were mailed directly to the Maryland office, where Katz was responsible for opening and sorting the notices and entering the relevant data into the computer system. She had singular power to override the firm's deadline identification system simply by ignoring it . . . .

Respondents assert that "no reasonable supervision could have avoided the conduct." Yet, Kimmel testified that the moment he set foot in Katz's office for the first time, over one year after she was hired, he knew that something severely was amiss. He observed that paperwork was piled in her office and that Katz looked "like a beaten dog." If, before then, Kimmel had supervised more closely the opening of the new branch in Maryland, he likely would have discovered the problems much sooner. . . .

Respondents stress that help was available to Katz, "if she had been honest about the status of the cases." Comment 3 to MRPC Rule 5.1, however, counsels explicitly that "[T]he partners may not assume that all lawyers associated with the firm will inevitably conform to the Rules." Respondents were not free to assume that the associate inevitably would disclose her mishandled cases or conform with procedures for entering deadlines into the firm's computerized case management system.…

Respondents urge, at most, a reprimand for any failure to supervise in violation of MRPC 5.1. Bar Counsel recommends an indefinite suspension.

In regard to mitigation here, the hearing judge noted the "unusual circumstances" and "extraordinary pressures" Respondents faced in the aftermath of Katz's abrupt resignation and their sudden realization of the scope of the problems she left behind. Judge Cox noted with approval the damage control efforts of Respondents.

… Moreover, we are not unmindful of the influence of our disposition here on any reciprocal discipline that may be imposed by other jurisdictions.… We conclude that indefinite suspension is the appropriate base sanction in this case.

Because of Respondents' intense, immediate, and largely effective recovery efforts, however, we ultimately conclude that they may apply for reinstatement no sooner than 90 days. We are persuaded that Respondents understand where they erred and are unlikely to repeat history.…

[A dissenting opinion would have imposed a more substantial sanction.]

NOTES

1. Attorney Katz agreed to a voluntary disbarment based on the allegations in this case. What were her failures? Are the firm's partners vicariously liable for them? If not, what is the basis for discipline here? Could she have done anything to avoid the situation in which she found herself?

2. Kimmel was not a member of the Maryland bar. What impact would discipline have on him in a jurisdiction where he was not even admitted to practice? Why would he even bother to participate in a disciplinary proceeding in Maryland? As the court mentions, discipline in one jurisdiction may result in the application of "reciprocal discipline" in other jurisdictions. Reciprocal discipline often permits the imposition of a sanction based on a sanction imposed in another jurisdiction, as long as the lawyer had a full and fair opportunity to litigate the underlying facts in the initial proceeding. Therefore, it is often important for the lawyer to address these issues fully in the first proceeding in which they are raised, even if that is not the jurisdiction in which he is admitted. These matters are considered further in Chapter 15.

3. Was the firm's quota of a set amount of settlements per week proper? Why or why not?

2. SAFE HARBORS AND JUNIOR LAWYERS

PEOPLE v. CASEY

948 P.2d 1014 (Colo. 1997)

PER CURIAM.

A hearing panel of the supreme court grievance committee approved the findings and the recommendation of a hearing board that the respondent in this lawyer discipline case be suspended for forty-five days from the practice of law and be ordered to take and pass the Multi–State Professional Responsibility Examination (MPRE). The respondent has excepted to the recommendation as too severe. We disagree, and we accept the recommendation of the hearing panel and hearing board.

I.

The respondent was licensed to practice law in Colorado in 1989. The complainant and the respondent entered into an unconditional stipulation which the hearing board accepted. Based on the stipulation and evidence presented at the hearing, the board made the following findings by clear and convincing evidence.

In December 1994, S.R., a teenager, and her mother, met with the senior partner at the law firm where the respondent was an associate. In August 1994, S.R. attended a party held in the home of third parties. The police were called and they cited several persons at the party with trespassing and underage drinking. S.R. gave the police a driver's license in her possession that had been issued to her friend, S.J. A criminal summons charging trespass was issued to S.R. in the name of her friend, S.J. Since she was not aware of the summons in her name, S.J. failed to attend the first court hearing and a bench warrant was issued in her name. S.R., posing as S.J., later appeared to reset the matter. S.R. was arrested, jailed, and later released under the name of S.J.

After being assigned the case by the senior partner, the respondent wrote to the Colorado Springs City Attorney's Office, and advised the City Attorney, falsely, that he represented S.J., when he actually represented S.R. He requested and obtained discovery using S.J.'s name. He also notified the court clerk of his entry of appearance in the S.J. case. The senior partner "consulted and advised" the respondent, but the hearing board did not make findings as to when this occurred or as to the details of the conversation.

On February 14, 1995, the respondent appeared at a pretrial conference scheduled for S.J. His client, S.R., waited outside during the hearing. Although he spoke with an assistant city attorney about the case, the respondent did not reveal his client's true identity. The assistant city attorney agreed to dismiss the S.J. matter. The respondent presented the city's motion to dismiss the case and the court entered an order of dismissal on February 14, 1995.

Prior to the pretrial conference, S.J. called the respondent about the case. The respondent told her that he intended to get the trespassing charge dismissed, but that S.J. would then have to petition on her own to get the criminal record sealed. He also told S.J. the date and time of the pretrial hearing.

After the case was dismissed, the respondent met with his client and her mother, and S.J. and her stepfather. S.J. was upset that the respondent had spoken with the assistant city attorney outside of S.J.'s presence and she wanted to know if her name had been cleared. The respondent took S.J. and her stepfather outside, and explained that the trespassing charge had been dismissed and that his client would pay the court costs. The respondent admitted that S.J. would nevertheless have a criminal record and that she would have to petition the court to have her criminal record sealed. S.J.'s stepfather subsequently called his lawyer who reported the events to the district attorney.

The respondent stipulated that the foregoing conduct violated Colo. RPC 1.2(d) (counseling a client to engage, or assisting a client, in conduct that the lawyer knows is criminal or fraudulent); Colo. RPC 3.3(a)(1) (knowingly making a false statement of material fact or law to a tribunal); Colo. RPC 3.3(a)(2) (failing to disclose a material fact to a tribunal when disclosure is necessary to avoid assisting a criminal or fraudulent act by the client); Colo. RPC 8.4(c) (engaging in conduct involving dishonesty, fraud, deceit or misrepresentation); and Colo. RPC 8.4(d) (engaging in conduct prejudicial to the administration of justice).

II.

The hearing panel approved the hearing board's recommendations that the respondent be suspended for forty-five days and be required to take and pass the MPRE. The respondent has excepted to the panel's action. . . .

The respondent portrays his situation as involving a close question between the loyalty he owed his client, and his duty to the court. He apparently seeks to invoke the status of a "subordinate lawyer," as addressed in Colo. RPC 5.2:

Rule 5.2. Responsibilities of a Subordinate Lawyer

(a) A lawyer is bound by the Rules of Professional Conduct notwithstanding that the lawyer acted at the direction of another person.

(b) *A subordinate lawyer does not violate the Rules of Professional Conduct if that lawyer acts in accordance with a supervisory lawyer's reasonable resolution of an arguable question of professional duty.*

(Emphasis added.) He asserts that before he succeeded in getting the trespass charge dismissed, he studied the applicable ethical rules. Colo. RPC 1.6 provides in part:

(a) A lawyer shall not reveal information relating to representation of a client unless the client consents after consultation, except for disclosures that are impliedly authorized in order to carry out the representation, and except as stated in paragraphs (b) and (c).

(b) A lawyer may reveal the intention of the lawyer's client to commit a crime and the information necessary to prevent the crime.

However, Colo. RPC 3.3, which the respondent admits to having violated, states:

Rule 3.3.   Candor Toward the Tribunal

(a) A lawyer shall not knowingly:

(1) make a false statement of material fact or law to a tribunal;

(2) fail to disclose a material fact to a tribunal when disclosure is necessary to avoid assisting a criminal or fraudulent act by the client. . . .

(b) *The duties stated in paragraph (a) continue to the conclusion of the proceeding, and apply even if compliance requires disclosure of information otherwise protected by Rule 1.6.*

(Emphasis added). Colo. RPC 3.3(a)(2) applies because of his initial appearance before the court in which he represented, falsely, that he was appearing on behalf of the named defendant, S.J. At the pretrial conference he presented the motion to dismiss to the court resulting in the case being dismissed. The respondent had the duty to disclose to the court that his client was impersonating S.J. in the criminal proceedings.

Further, Colo. RPC 3.3(b) clearly resolves the respondent's claimed dilemma in that it provides that the duty to be truthful to the court applies even if to do so requires disclosure of otherwise confidential information. It is not "arguable" that the respondent's duty to his client prevented him from fulfilling his duty to be truthful to the court. The protection afforded by Colo. RPC 5.2(b) for a subordinate who acts in accordance with a supervisory lawyer's direction is not available to the respondent. . . .

The hearing board found the following factors in mitigation: the absence of a prior disciplinary record; full and free disclosure to the board or a cooperative attitude in the disciplinary proceedings; inexperience in the practice of criminal law; and the expression of remorse.

While we have determined that Colo. RPC 5.2(b) does not entitle the respondent to immunity, an attempt to obtain guidance from a senior partner and a failure of a senior partner to suggest a reasonable and ethical course of conduct for the respondent could be a factor to be considered in mitigation. Here, the board's finding that the senior partner "consulted and advised" the respondent, without detail about the advice, if any, given is inadequate to allow us to conclude that the consultation is a mitigation factor.

We conclude that the respondent's misconduct is serious enough to warrant a short suspension. The respondent's professed confusion regarding his professional responsibilities confirms that he should be required to take and pass the MPRE. Accordingly, we accept the board's and panel's recommendations. However, three members of the court would impose a more severe sanction.

III.

It is hereby ordered that William M. Casey be suspended from the practice of law for forty-five days, effective thirty days after this opinion is released. The respondent is ordered to take and pass the Multi–State Professional Responsibility Examination within one year from the date of this opinion. The respondent is also ordered to pay the costs of this proceeding in the amount of $2,270.64. . . .

Notes

1.   What rules did Casey violate? How did he claim that Rule 5.2 protected him? Was his claim successful? If not, why not? What is required for a junior lawyer to take advantage of the "safe harbor" provision of Rule 5.2? What is the default rule if those conditions are not satisfied?

2.   Casey claimed to be confused about the conflict between his duty to maintain his client's confidential information and his duty to the court. If he was confused, why do you think he was? Do you think sentencing him to retake the MPRE is a fair sanction?

3.   Casey's claim that he relied upon the advice of senior lawyers was weak. What if it had not been? If his supervisor had unequivocally directed him to represent to the court that S.R. was S.J., would his claim have been successful?

Was attorney Howes' claim stronger than Casey's? Was it ultimately effective? Why or why not?

IN RE HOWES
940 P.2d 159 (N.M. 1997)

PER CURIAM.

FACTS

. . . In early August 1988, Billy Wilson (Wilson) was shot and killed in an apartment house in Washington, D.C. On August 23, 1988, Darryl Smith (defendant) was arrested for this murder and subsequently gave a lengthy videotaped statement to police, in which he admitted being at the scene of the murder but claimed that the murder had actually been committed by a Larry Epps.

Public Defender Jaime S. Gardner was appointed to represent defendant, and respondent, who was at all material times an attorney licensed by this Court, represented the United States. At the time of the events giving rise to the charges in this case (November 1988), respondent practiced law as an Assistant United States Attorney (AUSA) in the Superior Court of the District of Columbia. . . .

On August 24, 1988, defendant appeared in the Superior Court of the District of Columbia and was ordered held without bond until a preliminary hearing could be held. On September 6, 1988, respondent moved the court to release defendant on his own recognizance pending further investigation of the case. Prior to defendant's release, respondent indicated to the public defender that he would like to speak with defendant about the case; however, she refused permission unless respondent was willing to offer her client complete immunity, which he was not willing to offer.

Between September 26 and October 5, 1988, defendant contacted District of Columbia Metropolitan Police Detective Donald R. Gossage (detective) on several occasions and made statements to him about the Wilson murder and two other murders. The detective told respondent about these statements. Respondent had no personal experience with a defendant who contacted police to discuss his own case, but office policy permitted him to deal with witnesses who were represented by counsel in other cases without notifying their attorneys. Respondent discussed the situation with the chief of the felony section, who told him to advise the detective that if defendant were to initiate further contact with the detective, the detective could listen but that he was not to initiate contact with defendant. There was no discussion about whether to notify the public defender. Respondent relayed the message to the detective and told him as well to make notes of anything defendant might say, so that any inconsistent statements could be used for impeachment purposes.

The public defender first learned of these contacts with her client through testimony presented at his preliminary hearing on October 5, 1988. Probable cause was found to charge defendant with the murder of Wilson, and he was remanded to custody and ordered held without bond. Defendant's attorney complained in open court about the contacts with her client made without her knowledge and asked the court to issue a directive that there be no further contacts with defendant. Respondent stated that he expected no further contacts with defendant but added that "if he wants to call us, we will take his call." The court issued no directive but observed on the record that the public defender would undoubtedly instruct her client that such contacts were not in his best interest.

Between October 5 and November 1, 1988, however, defendant continued his efforts to contact the detective from the jail. He left messages for the detective on his beeper and even spoke with him on several occasions regarding the Wilson murder and the other two cases (wherein he was not charged and, therefore, not represented by counsel). Respondent was aware that defendant was talking about the Wilson murder to the detective but did not notify the public defender or obtain her permission for the detective to discuss the case with her client.

On November 18, 1988, the detective was in respondent's office working with him on the Wilson murder case when respondent himself received a call from defendant on his private line. Respondent had never given his private number to defendant, although he had given it to the detective. At respondent's request, the detective listened in on an extension. Although defendant was advised that he did not have to speak with [respondent] and the detective and that his lawyer would not be happy, he proceeded to talk about the Wilson case for approximately six minutes while respondent and the detective listened and took notes. Defendant called back about ten minutes later and spoke with respondent and the detective for another fifteen minutes, although he was again reminded that the public defender would be unhappy with him. At the conclusion of this call, the detective agreed to visit defendant at the jail. Although respondent's notes indicate that defendant now was focusing almost exclusively on the Wilson murder, the public defender was advised neither of the calls nor of the impending visit with her client.

The detective had been advised by respondent that because defendant was initiating the calls, the constitutionality and the voluntariness of the statements were established and that he should "let Darryl talk" but refrain from posing questions of his own. After the call to his own office and the appointment for the detective to visit personally with defendant, respondent consulted with the chief and deputy chief of the felony section, who advised him that the detective should take a partner with him to the jail and give defendant his Miranda warnings before proceeding with the interview.

While the deputy chief recalled that there may have been some discussion of the ethical proprieties of communicating directly with defendant, the chief of the felony section acknowledged in his testimony that his primary concern in advising respondent was whether the evidence would be constitutionally admissible. The deputy chief did not recollect that respondent advised either himself or the chief that he had personally spoken with defendant. It is also clear from the record that the chief's advice as to any ethical considerations was more directed at the contacts the detective was having with defendant rather than to any calls respondent might be receiving. The chief acknowledged that his understanding of the rules regarding professional responsibility would probably not have affected his advice, because he "didn't think the D.C. bar rules had much to say about how the police behaved."

On November 21, 1988, the detective and a partner visited with defendant at the jail and gave Miranda warnings, but defendant refused to sign the form because, he said, it would make his lawyer angry. The meeting was terminated.

On November 25 or 26, 1988, respondent received four more collect calls from defendant from the jail, all of which he accepted. He reminded defendant that his attorney had already complained to the court about his contacts with representatives of the government but permitted defendant to continue to speak with him nonetheless. Respondent asked no questions but listened to everything defendant had to say. While his notes again indicate that defendant was now speaking only of the Wilson murder, respondent did not advise defendant's attorney of these calls.

Defendant was indicted for the murder of Wilson on December 8, 1988. The public defender subsequently sought to have defendant's statements to respondent and the detective suppressed and/or the indictment dismissed on the basis of prosecutorial misconduct. The motion was denied by written order dated July 10, 1989, but the judge referred the matter of respondent's possible violation of DR 7–104 of the Code of Professional Responsibility[1] to the District of Columbia Board of Professional Responsibility.

The Board of Professional Responsibility for the District of Columbia at that time had disciplinary jurisdiction over any attorney who engaged in the practice of law in the District of Columbia on a *pro hac vice* basis, but in 1988 the relevant rule did not apply to an AUSA practicing pursuant to 28 USC § 517. For this reason, the case was referred to the office of New Mexico's disciplinary counsel in May 1990.

Rule 16–805, NMRA subjects a lawyer admitted to practice in New Mexico to the disciplinary authority of this Court, even though he or she may be engaged in practice elsewhere. Both respondent and his employer, the United States Department of Justice (DOJ), filed federal suits challenging this Court's jurisdiction to conduct this disciplinary proceeding. Both suits were resolved in favor of this court's jurisdiction. . . .

The hearing committee and the disciplinary board concluded that respondent had violated Rule 16–402 by directly communicating about the subject of the representation with a party he knew to be represented by another lawyer in the matter without the consent of the other lawyer and without authorization of law to do so. The committee and the board panel also concluded that respondent had violated Rule 16–804(A) by knowingly communicating with defendant through the detective and by knowingly assisting and inducing the detective to communicate with defendant. . . .

DISCUSSION

I. The applicability of Rule 16–502(B) to respondent's actions.

Respondent first argues that New Mexico's Rule 16–502(B) should control the resolution of this case. This rule states that "a subordinate lawyer does not violate the Rules of Professional Conduct if that lawyer acts in accordance with a supervisory lawyer's reasonable resolution of an arguable question of professional duty." It is respondent's contention that he was a "subordinate lawyer" within the meaning of this rule and that, as such, he was not only entitled but also obligated to rely upon the advice given to him by the chief and deputy chief of the felony section. . . .

---

1. At all relevant times, Rule 7–104(A)(1) of the Code of Professional Responsibility in the District of Columbia read as follows:

During the course of his representation of a client a lawyer shall not communicate or cause another to communicate on the subject of the representation with a party he knows to be represented by a lawyer in that matter unless he has the prior consent of the lawyer representing the other party or is authorized by law to do so. [New Mexico rule 16–402 was essentially identical, as the court noted.]

Consequently, he asserts, his actions must be excused. Respondent's position fails for several reasons.

First of all, Rule 16–502(B) must be read in connection with Rule 16–502(A), which directs that "a lawyer is bound by the Rules of Professional Conduct notwithstanding that the lawyer acted at the direction of another person." The ABA Comment to Model Rule 5.2 makes it clear that the rule, taken as a whole, is not meant to immunize attorneys from accountability for their misconduct.

Respondent has cited no cases, and we are aware of none, which hold for the proposition that an attorney may be exonerated from the consequences of his or her misconduct simply on the basis that the unethical acts were committed upon another's instructions or authorization. The few reported cases on this topic uphold the theory that an attorney is always answerable for his or her own actions . . . .

Even more compelling, however, is that in this instance there was no "arguable question of professional duty" needing resolution. Respondent has argued that various memoranda generated in-house at the Department of Justice prior to his actions took the position that federal prosecutors are not bound by state disciplinary rules prohibiting communication with represented persons and has submitted these documents as exhibits to the record. We are not persuaded that an attorney's employer, even though that employer may be an attorney or an arm of the United States government, can create an "arguable question of professional duty" within the meaning of Rule 16–502(B) by the simple mechanism of unilaterally declaring that a particular rule of conduct is burdensome and should not apply to its employees.

In further support of his position that such an arguable question exists, respondent has cited numerous articles on the subject of whether or not federal prosecutors should be bound by state ethical rules. While we recognize that a debate currently rages regarding the applicability of ABA Model Rule 4.2 to federal prosecutors, all of the articles cited by respondent were published between 1990 and 1996 and were no doubt occasioned in part by former Attorney General Richard Thornburgh's *Memorandum* of June 8, 1989, which discussed the applicability of Rule 4.2 to federal prosecutors and which itself was issued after respondent's acts of misconduct. Respondent's duty to refrain from communicating with a represented criminal defendant is not subject to argument. According to the ABA Comment to Model Rule 5.2, if a question of ethical duty can be answered in only one way, "the duty of both lawyers is clear and they are equally responsible for fulfilling it."

Even if one were to accept the premise that an arguable question of professional duty with respect to Rule 16–402 existed in November 1988, it is apparent from the record of these proceedings that the discussions respondent had with the chief of the felony section regarding defendant's calls bore only a tangential relationship to respondent's ethical duties. The chief testified under oath that his "primary concern as a supervisor was whether the evidence was constitutionally admissible" and that he "would have focused on the constitutional issues involved in contacts between a defendant and a law enforcement representative; that is, I would have been focusing on his Fifth Amendment right to be silent, his Sixth Amendment right to counsel." Additionally, it is not clear from the testimony of the chief and deputy chief that they were even aware that respondent himself was communicating with defendant. Clearly respondent was not seeking advice as to his ethical obligations to defendant and to the public defender; any passing consideration of these duties which may have arisen was secondary to the primary question of how to obtain admissible evidence from defendant.

Rule 16–502 cannot and does not excuse respondent's conduct. . . .

V. Appropriate Sanction.

Finally, respondent asserts that even if we reject his other arguments and find that he has in fact violated our Rules of Professional Conduct, which we have done, he should not be disciplined for his offenses. . . .

The duty violated in this instance involves an attorney's duty to the legal system not to communicate improperly with those who are represented by other attorneys, one of the most elementary premises of the adversary system. Respondent had inappropriate contacts with the defendant directly on at least six separate occasions and on numerous other occasions through an intermediary (the detective). Although defendant initiated the contacts, respondent's repeated willingness to accept defendant's calls and his statement in open court (after defendant's attorney had objected to contacts between defendant and the detective outside of her presence) to the effect that "If he [defendant] wants to call us, we will take his call" indicate that he encouraged and perpetuated the communications and that his actions were intentional rather than the result of negligence or ignorance.

There is no evidence that the contacts resulted in actual injury to either defendant or the legal process in general. The potential for injury, however, is obvious. . . .

While the fact that respondent does not have a prior disciplinary record may be considered as a mitigating factor, there are several factors in aggravation of his misconduct. Most notable is the fact that he refuses to this day to accept or even recognize the wrongful nature of his conduct. When asked at one point whether, if put in the same position again he would do the same thing, respondent replied in the negative. His answer, however, appears to have been based more upon his annoyance at having become the subject of disciplinary charges than upon any remorse for his actions, as he went on to say:

> I would never put myself in a position again to be a guinea pig, a test case, whether or not [the chief of the felony section] gave me the right directions, whether or not the Attorney General or the Thornburgh Memorandum, whether or not the District of Columbia Court of

Appeals two years later said what happened was—if it was constitutional, it was proper. I would never again put myself in a position where so many authorities would second-guess what I thought I had done reasonably and within the bounds of my professional responsibilities.

Respondent then proceeded to remove any remaining doubt about whether or not he acknowledges that his actions were improper:

[W]hen you asked me if I would ever do this again, my answer was not to say that what I did then was wrong. I believe I was ethical and proper under those circumstances. And I would, given the same circumstances today, without any other changes, if this happened again, I would do the same thing. I wouldn't change.

We believe respondent's comments indicate a lack of appreciation for the importance of the duty at issue. We are not persuaded that he "was simply caught in a dispute."

A second aggravating factor is that at the time of this incident, respondent had substantial experience in the practice of law. He had graduated from the University of Virginia School of Law in 1978 and had clerked for two Federal judges before joining the U.S. Attorney's Office in 1984. Both the hearing committee and the disciplinary board found that at the time of these actions respondent was "an accomplished, seasoned, and sophisticated attorney." His violations of Rules 16–402 and 16–804(A) were due neither to ignorance nor incompetence....

[Howes was publicly censured and ordered to reimburse the disciplinary board the costs of this disciplinary proceeding in the amount of $8,663.52.]

NOTES

1.   The dispute in this case about whether assistant U.S. attorneys, federal government lawyers who often practiced in a range of different jurisdictions, should be subjected to the disciplinary rules in the jurisdictions where they were practicing was protracted. The U.S. Department of Justice initially claimed that its lawyers were not subject to the disciplinary authority of the many state jurisdictions in which those lawyers engaged in practice. Initially, the so-called Thornburgh Memorandum purported to exempt federal prosecutors from state ethics regulation. Subsequent regulation was superseded by a federal statute, the McDade Act, 28 U.S.C. § 530B, which requires federal prosecutors to comply with state law and ethics rules. *See also* Comment [5] to Model Rule 4.2. Does the comment change the result in this case?

2.   The lawyer in this case claimed that he had acted at the direction of his supervisors. Why, then, was his claim for the "safe harbor" denied?

3.   Reported cases denying the "safe harbor" claim under Rule 5.2 are rare, but cases granting it are rarer still. Why do you think that might be? Does Rule 5.2 really solve the problems of a junior lawyer being pressed to engage in unethical conduct?

4. A junior lawyer is subject to the bar's regulation, and a lawyer can have vicarious liability for another lawyer's violation of the rules. *See* Model Rule 5.1(c). A nonlawyer employee (including a summer associate, paralegal, administrative assistant or private investigator), by contrast, is not subject to discipline for violating the rules of legal ethics. Can a lawyer have vicarious liability for the conduct of such individuals? *See* Model Rule 5.3. This rule, coupled with Rule 8.4(a), makes it very difficult for a lawyer to avoid disciplinary authority by having a nonlawyer act in his stead.

C. DUTIES TO THE LEGAL SYSTEM: TEMPERING ZEAL

Another category of duties to the system reflects the notion that lawyers have some affirmative duty not to corrupt the legal system simply to further the interests of their clients. One might think that the lawyer's obligation is simply to advance the client's cause at all costs; Comment [1] to Model Rule 1.3 states that "A lawyer must ... act with commitment and dedication to the interests of the client and with zeal in advocacy upon the client's behalf." That zeal to accomplish the client's stated objective must yield, at least in some circumstances, to other values.

1. THE DUTY NOT TO COUNSEL THE CLIENT TO COMMIT A CRIME OR FRAUD

A client who consults a lawyer to get advice about committing a crime or fraud and who uses the lawyer's advice in furtherance of that end forfeits the protections of the attorney-client privilege. That may ultimately be a problem for the client. But what about the lawyer? Model Rule 1.2(d) prohibits a lawyer from counseling a client to commit a crime or fraud, or assisting a client in doing so. This is, of course, a delicate balance. The legal ethics rules are premised on the notion that confidentiality and privilege encourage clients to make full and fair disclosure to their lawyers in order to decide upon a course of action. A client who asks about his obligations under the law may be doing so to ascertain how to comply with those obligations, or how best to ignore them. How can a lawyer tell the difference? *See* Comment [9] to Model Rule 1.2. While the application of the rule may be challenging in specific instances, its message is clear: even if committing a crime or fraud would help the client, the lawyer is prohibited from advising or assisting the client to do so.

Assisting a client to commit a crime or fraud is a disciplinary violation; it can also lead to civil or criminal liability for the lawyer. Consider the facts of *Chapman Lumber, Inc. v. Tager*, 952 A.2d 1 (Conn. 2008). Tager represented Scalzo, who was in financial difficulty. Scalzo owed Chapman Lumber over $43,000. In exchange for Chapman agreeing to forego collection of the debt, Scalzo agreed to give Chapman a mortgage on a property he jointly owned with Martino at Padanaram Road. Scalzo told Chapman that there was sufficient equity in the property to pay his debt, but before executing a mortgage on the property, Scalzo quitclaimed his interest in the Padnaram Road property to Martino. Nonetheless, a month later, Tager, who was aware that Scalzo no longer had any interest in the property, told Chapman's counsel that there was more than $100,000 of equity in the property and that Scalzo was in "pretty good shape financially." Tager directed Scalzo to execute the note and mortgage, even though he knew that Scalzo did not own the property. Scalzo testified that he asked Tager whether this was proper, and that Tager said "that that wasn't our responsibility to do the title search, it was theirs, so we were not doing anything wrong, you can go ahead and sign the deed, you know, knowing that I didn't own the property." Tager advised Scalzo "that it was just like selling the Brooklyn Bridge a few times." Subsequently, after the documents were executed, Tager called Chapman's counsel and told him that Scalzo was deeply in debt and had no intention of paying Chapman. Chapman sued Tager for fraud and won a jury verdict. Tager appealed, claiming that the verdict was contrary to public policy because it imposed on him duties to a nonclient. Do you think this argument was effective? Why or why not?

2. SPECIAL DUTIES OF THE PROSECUTOR

"A prosecutor," Comment [1] to Model Rule 3.8 begins, "has the responsibility of a minister of justice and not simply that of an advocate." That responsibility comes with extraordinary power, as [later Justice] Robert H. Jackson wrote when he was Attorney General of the United States:

> The prosecutor has more control over life, liberty, and reputation than any other person in America. His discretion is tremendous.... The prosecutor can order arrests, present cases to the grand jury in secret session, and on the basis of his one-sided presentation of the facts, can cause the citizen to be indicted and held for trial.... While the prosecutor at his best is one of the most beneficent forces in our society, when he acts from malice or other base motives, he is one of the worst.

Robert H. Jackson, The Federal Prosecutor (April 1, 1940). But, Jackson wrote to an audience of prosecutors, the prosecutor could also be the repository of "fair play and decency":

> Your positions are of such independence and importance that while you are being diligent, strict, and vigorous in law enforcement you can also afford to be just. Although the government technically loses its case, it has really won if justice has been done.... Any prosecutor who risks his day-to-day professional name for fair dealing to build up statistics of success has a perverted sense of practical values, as well as defects of character.... [H]e can have no better asset than to have his profession recognize that his attitude toward those who feel his power has been dispassionate, reasonable and just.... A sensitiveness

to fair play and sportsmanship is perhaps the best protection against the abuse of power, and the citizen's safety lies in the prosecutor who tempers zeal with human kindness, who seeks truth and not victims, who serves the law and not factional purposes, and who approaches his task with humility.

Id. Justice Jackson to the contrary, many would not recognize the contemporary prosecutor in this humanistic and humble description. In the case below, the prosecutor did not seem to comply with this lofty view of his obligations. Is the result satisfying?

NORTH CAROLINA STATE BAR v. NIFONG

Before the Disciplinary Hearing Commission of the North Carolina State Bar
Amended Findings of Fact, Conclusions of Law and Order of Discipline
July 31, 2007

FINDINGS OF FACT

Defendant, Michael B. Nifong, (hereinafter "Nifong"), was admitted to the North Carolina State Bar on August 19, 1978, and is, and was at all times referred to herein, an attorney at law licensed to practice in North Carolina. . . .

During all times relevant to this complaint, Nifong actively engaged in the practice of law in the State of North Carolina as District Attorney for the Fourteenth Prosecutorial District in Durham County, North Carolina.

Nifong was appointed District Attorney in 2005. In late March 2006, Nifong was engaged in a highly-contested political campaign to retain his office.

In the early morning hours of March 14, 2006, an exotic dancer named Crystal Mangum reported that she had been raped by three men during a party at 610 North Buchanan Boulevard in Durham.

Ms. Mangum asserted that she had been vaginally, rectally, and orally penetrated with no condom used during the assault and with at least some of the alleged perpetrators ejaculating.

Various pieces of evidence were collected for later DNA testing, including evidence commonly referred to as a "rape kit," which contained cheek scrapings, oral, vaginal, and rectal swabs, a pubic hair combing, and a pair of Ms. Mangum's underwear.

The Durham Police Department (DPD) initiated an investigation in what would come to be known as "the Duke Lacrosse case" and executed a search warrant on the house at 610 North Buchanan Boulevard on March 16, 2006. The investigation revealed that the residents of 610 North Buchanan were captains of the Duke University lacrosse team, and that a majority of the other attendees at the March 13, 2006, party were members of the team.

On March 16, 2006, the three residents of 610 North Buchanan voluntarily assisted DPD in executing a search warrant at their residence. During the search, numerous pieces of evidence were seized for later testing. The three residents also provided voluntary statements and voluntarily submitted DNA samples for comparison testing purposes. One of the three residents was David Evans, who was later indicted for the alleged attack on Ms. Mangum.

On March 22, 2006, Nifong's office assisted a DPD investigator in obtaining a Nontestimonial Identification Order (NTO) to compel the suspects in the case to be photographed and to provide DNA samples.

On March 23, 2006, DNA samples from all 46 Caucasian members of the Duke University 2006 Men's Lacrosse Team were obtained pursuant to the NTO.

When Nifong learned of the case on March 24, 2006, he immediately recognized that the case would garner significant media attention and decided to handle the case himself, rather than having it handled by the assistant district attorney in his office who would ordinarily handle such cases. . . .

On March 27, 2006, the rape kit items and DNA samples from the lacrosse players were delivered to the State Bureau of Investigation (SBI) lab for testing and examination, including DNA testing.

On March 27, 2006, Nifong was briefed by Sergeant Gottlieb and Investigator Himan of the DPD about the status of the investigation to date. Gottlieb and Himan discussed with Nifong a number of weaknesses in the case, including that Ms. Mangum had made inconsistent statements to the police and had changed her story several times, that the other dancer who was present at the party during the alleged attack disputed Ms. Mangum's story of an alleged assault, that Ms. Mangum had already viewed two photo arrays and had not identified any alleged attackers, and that the three team captains had voluntarily cooperated with police and had denied that the alleged attack occurred.

During or within a few days of the initial briefing by Gottlieb and Himan, Nifong acknowledged to Gottlieb and Himan that the Duke Lacrosse case would be a very hard case to win in court and said "you know, we're f***ed."

Beginning on March 27, within hours after he received the initial briefing from Gottlieb and Himan, Nifong made public comments and statements to representatives of the news media about the Duke Lacrosse case and participated in interviews with various newspapers and television stations and other representatives of news media.

Between March 27 and March 31, Nifong stated to a reporter for WRAL TV news that lacrosse team members denied the rape accusations, that team members admitted that there was underage drinking at the party, and that otherwise team members were not cooperating with authorities. . . .

Between March 27 and March 31, 2006, Nifong stated to a reporter for NBC 17 News that the lacrosse team members were standing together and refusing to talk with investigators and that he might bring aiding-and-abetting charges against some of the players who were not cooperating with the investigation. . . .

Between March 27 and March 31, 2006, Nifong made the following statements to Rene Syler of CBS News: "The lacrosse team, clearly, has not been fully cooperative" in the investigation; "The university, I believe, has done pretty much everything that they can under the circumstances. They, obviously, don't have a lot of control over whether or not the lacrosse team members actually speak to the police. I think that their silence is as a result of advice with counsel"; "If it's not the way it's been reported, then why are they so unwilling to tell us what, in their words, did take place that night?"; that he believed a crime occurred; that "the guilty will stand trial"; and "There's no doubt a sexual assault took place."

Between March 27 and March 31, 2006, Nifong made the following statements to a reporter for NBC 17 TV News: "The information that I have does lead me to conclude that a rape did occur"; "I'm making a statement to the Durham community and, as a citizen of Durham, I am making a statement for the Durham community. This is not the kind of activity we condone, and it must be dealt with quickly and harshly"; [and] "The circumstances of the rape indicated a deep racial motivation for some of the things that were done. It makes a crime that is by its nature one of the most offensive and invasive even more so.". . .

Between March 27 and March 31, 2006, Nifong stated to a reporter for ESPN, "And one would wonder why one needs an attorney if one was not charged and had not done anything wrong."

Between March 27 and March 31, 2006, Nifong stated to a reporter for CBS News that "the investigation at that time was certainly consistent with a sexual assault having taken place, as was the victim's demeanor at the time of the examination." . . .

Between March 27 and March 31, 2006, Nifong made the following statements to a reporter for ABC 11 TV News: "I don't think you can classify anything about what went on as a prank that got out of hand or drinking that took place by people who are underage"; "In this case, where you have the act of rape—essentially a gang rape—is bad enough in and of itself, but when it's made with racial epithets against the victim, I mean, it's just absolutely unconscionable"; and "The contempt that was shown for the victim, based on her race was totally abhorrent. It adds another layer of reprehensibleness, to a crime that is already reprehensible." . . .

On or after March 27, 2006, Nifong stated to a reporter for the Charlotte Observer newspaper, "I would not be surprised if condoms were used. Probably an exotic dancer would not be your first choice for unprotected sex." . . .

On March 30, 2006, the SBI notified Nifong that the SBI had examined the items from the rape kit and was unable to find any semen, blood, or saliva on any of those items. . . .

On April 4, 2006, DPD conducted a photographic identification procedure in which photographs of 46 members of the Duke Lacrosse team were shown to Ms. Mangum. Ms. Mangum was told at the beginning of the procedure that DPD had reason to believe all 46 of the men depicted in the photographs she would view were present at the party at which she contended the attack had occurred. The procedure followed in this photographic identification procedure was conceived and/or approved by Nifong. During the photographic identification procedure, Ms. Mangum identified Collin Finnerty and Reade Seligman as her attackers with "100% certainty" and identified David Evans as one of her attackers with "90% certainty." Ms. Mangum had previously viewed photographic identification procedures which included photographs of Reade Seligman and David Evans and not identified either of them in the prior procedures.

On April 5, 2006, Nifong's office sought and obtained an Order permitting transfer of the rape kit items from the SBI to a private company called DNA Security, Inc. ("DSI") for more sensitive DNA testing than the SBI could perform. The reference DNA specimens obtained from the lacrosse players pursuant to the NTO were also transferred to DSI for testing, as were reference specimens from several other individuals with whom Ms. Mangum acknowledged having consensual sexual relations, including her boyfriend. . . .

Between April 7 and April 10, 2006, DSI performed testing and analysis of DNA found on the rape kit items. Between April 7 and April 10, DSI found DNA from up to four different males on several items of evidence from the rape kit and found that the male DNA on the rape kit items was inconsistent with the profiles of the lacrosse team members.

During a meeting on April 10, 2006 among Nifong, two DPD officers and Dr. Brian Meehan, lab director for DSI, Dr. Meehan discussed with Nifong the results of the analyses performed by DSI to that point and explained that DSI had found DNA from up to four different males on several items of evidence from the rape kit and that the DNA on the rape kit items was inconsistent with the profiles of all lacrosse team members.

The evidence and information referred to above was evidence or information which tended to negate the guilt of the lacrosse team members identified as suspects in the NTO. . . .

After the April 10, 2006 meeting with Dr. Meehan, Nifong stated to a reporter for ABC 11 TV News that DNA testing other than that performed by the SBI had not yet come back and that there was other evidence, including the accuser being able to identify at least one of the alleged attackers.

While discussing DNA testing at a public forum at North Carolina Central University on April 11, 2006, in the presence of representatives of the news media, Nifong stated that if there was no DNA found "[i]t doesn't mean nothing happened. It just means nothing was left behind."

On April 17, 2006, Nifong sought and obtained indictments against Collin Finnerty and Reade Seligman for first-degree rape, first-degree sex offense, and kidnapping. (The indicted members of the Duke lacrosse team are referred to collectively herein as "the Duke Defendants").

Before April 17, 2006, Nifong refused offers from counsel for David Evans, who was eventually indicted, to consider evidence and information that they contended either provided an alibi or otherwise demonstrated that their client did not commit any crime.

On April 19, 2006, two days after being indicted, Duke Defendant Reade Seligman through counsel served Nifong with a request or motion for discovery material, including, *inter alia*, witness statements, the results of any tests, all DNA analysis, and any exculpatory information.

By April 20, 2006, DSI had performed additional DNA testing and analysis and found DNA from multiple males on at least one additional piece of evidence from the rape kit.

By April 20, 2006, from its testing and analysis, DSI had determined that all the lacrosse players, including the two who had already been indicted, were scientifically excluded as possible contributors of the DNA from multiple males found on several evidence items from the rape kit.

On April 21, 2006, Nifong again met with Dr. Meehan and the two DPD officers to discuss all of the results of the DNA testing and analyses performed by DSI to date. During this meeting, Dr. Meehan told Nifong that: (a) DNA from multiple males had been found on several items from the rape kit, and (b) all of the lacrosse players, including the two players against whom Nifong had already sought and obtained indictments, were excluded as possible contributors of this DNA because none of their DNA profiles matched or were consistent with any of the DNA found on the rape kit items.

The evidence and information referred to above was evidence or information which tended to negate the guilt of the Duke Defendants.

At the April 21 meeting, Dr. Meehan told Nifong that DSI's testing had revealed DNA on two fingernail specimens that were incomplete but were consistent with the DNA profiles of two un-indicted lacrosse players, including DNA on a fingernail found in David Evans' garbage can which [was] incomplete but which was consistent with David Evans' DNA profile, and DNA from the vaginal swab that was consistent with the DNA profile of Ms. Mangum's boyfriend.

During the April 21, 2006 meeting, Nifong notified Dr. Meehan that he would require a written report to be produced concerning DSI's testing that reflected the matches found between DNA on evidence items and known reference specimens. Nifong told Dr. Meehan he would let Dr. Meehan know when he needed the report.

Sometime between April 21 and May 12, Nifong notified Dr. Meehan that he would need for him to prepare the written report for an upcoming court proceeding. As requested by Nifong, Dr. Meehan prepared a report that reflected the matches found by DSI between DNA found on evidence items and known reference specimens. This written report did not reflect that DSI had found DNA on rape kit items from multiple males who had not provided reference specimens for comparison ("multiple unidentified males") and did not reflect that all 46 members of the lacrosse team had been scientifically excluded as possible contributors of the male DNA on the rape kit items.

In May, 2006, Nifong made the following statements to a reporter for WRAL TV News: "My guess is that there are many questions that many people are asking that they would not be asking if they saw the results"; "They're not things that the defense releases unless they unquestionably support their positions"; and "So, the fact that they're making statements about what the reports are saying, and not actually showing the reports, should in and of itself raise some red flags." . . .

On May 12, 2006, Nifong again met with Dr. Meehan and two DPD officers and discussed the results of DSI's testing to date. During that meeting, consistent with Nifong's prior request, Dr. Meehan provided Nifong a 10–page written report which set forth the results of DNA tests on only the three evidence specimens that contained DNA consistent with DNA profiles from several known reference specimens. The three items in DSI's written report concerned DNA profiles on two fingernail specimens that were incomplete but were consistent with the DNA profiles of two unindicted lacrosse players, including DNA on a fingernail found in David Evans' garbage can which was incomplete but was consistent with David Evans' DNA profile, and DNA from the vaginal swab that was consistent with the DNA profile of Ms. Mangum's boyfriend. DSI's written report did not disclose the existence of any of the multiple unidentified male DNA found on the rape kit items, although it did list the evidence items on which the unidentified DNA had been discovered.

Nifong personally received DSI's written report from Dr. Meehan on May 12, 2006, and later that day provided it to counsel for the two Duke Defendants who had been indicted and for David Evans, among others.

When he received DSI's written report and provided it to counsel for the Duke Defendants, Nifong was fully aware of the test results that were omitted from the written report, including the test results revealing the existence of DNA from multiple unidentified males on rape kit items.

Three days later, on May 15, 2006, Nifong sought and obtained an indictment against David Evans for first-degree rape, first-degree sex offense, and kidnapping.

On May 17, Duke Defendant Collin Finnerty served discovery requests on Nifong, which specifically asked that any expert witness "prepare, and furnish to the defendant, a report of the results of *any* (not only the ones about which the expert expects to testify) examinations or tests conducted by the expert."

On May 18, 2006, Nifong provided various discovery materials to all three Duke Defendants, including another copy of DSI's written report, in connection with a hearing in the case on that same day. The discovery materials Nifong provided on May 18 did not include any underlying data or information concerning DSI's testing and analysis. The materials Nifong provided also did not include any documentation or information indicating the presence of DNA from multiple unidentified males on the rape kit items. Nifong also did not provide in the discovery materials any written or recorded memorialization of the substance of Dr. Meehan's oral statements made during his meetings with Nifong in April and May 2006 concerning the results of all DSI's tests and examinations, including the existence of DNA from multiple unidentified males on the rape kit items.

DSI's tests and examinations revealing the existence of DNA from multiple unidentified males on rape kit items and Dr. Meehan's oral statements regarding the existence of that DNA were evidence that tended to negate the guilt of the accused, Collin Finnerty, Reade Seligman and David Evans. Accompanying the discovery materials, Nifong served and filed with the Court written responses to the Duke Defendants' discovery requests. In these responses, Nifong stated: "The State is not aware of any additional material or information which may be exculpatory in nature with respect to the Defendant." In his written discovery responses, Nifong also identified Dr. Meehan and R.W. Scales, another person at DSI, as expert witnesses reasonably expected to testify at the trial of the underlying criminal cases pursuant to N.C. Gen. Stat. § 15A–903(a)(2). Nifong also gave notice in the written discovery responses of the State's intent to introduce scientific data accompanied by expert testimony. Nifong represented in the written discovery responses that all of the reports of those experts had been provided to the Duke Defendants.

At the time he made these representations to the Court and to the Duke Defendants in his written discovery responses, Nifong was aware of the existence of DNA from multiple unidentified males on the rape kits items, was aware that DSI's written report did not reveal the existence of this evidence, and was aware that he had not provided the Duke Defendants with memorializations of Dr. Meehan's oral statements regarding the existence of this evidence.

The representations contained in Nifong's May 18 written discovery responses were intentional misrepresentations and intentional false statements of material fact to opposing counsel and to the Court.

At the May 18, 2006 hearing, the Honorable Ronald Stephens, Superior Court Judge presiding, asked Nifong if he had provided the Duke Defendants all discovery materials. In response to Judge Stephens' inquiry, Nifong stated: "I've turned over everything I have."

Nifong's response to Judge Stephens' question was a misrepresentation and a false statement of material fact. . . .

On June 19, 2006, counsel for the Duke Defendants requested various materials from Nifong, including a report or written statement of the meeting between Nifong and Dr. Meehan to discuss the DNA test results. This request was addressed at a hearing before Judge Stephens on June 22, 2006.

In response to the Duke Defendants' June 19 discovery request and in response to Judge Stephens' direct inquiry, Nifong stated in open court that, other than what was contained in DSI's written report, all of his communications with Dr. Meehan were privileged "work product." Nifong represented to Judge Stephens, "That's pretty much correct, your Honor. We received the reports, which [defense counsel] has received, and we talked about how we would likely use that, and that's what we did."

At the time Nifong made these representations to Judge Stephens on June 22, Nifong knew that he had discussed with Dr. Meehan on three occasions the existence of DNA from multiple unidentified males on the rape kits items, which evidence was not disclosed in DSI's written report, and knew that Dr. Meehan's statements to him revealing the existence of DNA from multiple unidentified males on the rape kits items were not privileged work product.

Nifong's representations to Judge Stephens at the June 22 hearing were intentional misrepresentations and intentional false statements of material fact to the Court and to opposing counsel.

During the June 22 hearing, Judge Stephens entered an Order directing Nifong to provide ... the Duke Defendants with, among other things, "results of tests and examinations, or any other matter or evidence obtained during the investigation of the offenses alleged to have been committed by the defendant" and statements of any witnesses taken during the investigation, with oral statements to be reduced to written or recorded form.

Nifong did not comply with Judge Stephens' June 22 Order.

[Subsequently, the Duke Defendants made a motion to compel the complete file on the DSI testing, which was heard by Judge Osmond W. Smith III.]

In response to a direct question from Judge Smith, Nifong represented that DSI's written report encompassed all tests performed by DSI and everything discussed at his meetings with Dr. Meehan in April and May 2006. The following exchange occurred immediately thereafter on the Duke Defendants' request for memorializations of Dr. Meehan's oral statements:

> Judge Smith: So you represent there are no other statements from Dr. Meehan?
> Mr. Nifong: No other statements. No other statements made to me.

Nifong's statements and responses to Judge Smith at the September 22 hearing were intentional misrepresentations and intentional false statements of material fact to the Court and to opposing counsel.

On October 27, 2006, Nifong provided 1,844 pages of underlying documents and materials from DSI to the Duke Defendants pursuant to the

Court's September 22, 2006 Order but did not provide the Duke Defendants a complete written report from DSI setting forth the results of all its tests and examinations, including the existence of DNA from multiple unidentified males on the rape kit items, and did not provide the Duke Defendants with any written or recorded memorializations of Dr. Meehan's oral statements.

After reviewing the underlying data provided to them on October 27 for between 60 and 100 hours, counsel for the Duke Defendants determined that DSI's written report did not include the results of all DNA tests performed by DSI and determined that DSI had found DNA from multiple unidentified males on the rape kit items and that such results were not included in DSI's written report.

On December 13, 2006, the Duke Defendants filed a Motion to Compel Discovery, detailing their discovery of the existence of DNA from multiple unidentified males on the rape kit items and explaining that this evidence had not been included in DSI's written report . . . [The motion to compel was addressed by Judge Smith at a hearing on December 15, 2006.]

At the December 15 hearing, both in chambers and again in open court, Nifong stated or implied to Judge Smith that he was unaware of the existence of DNA from multiple unidentified males on the rape kit items until he received the December 13 motion and/or was unaware that the results of any DNA testing performed by DSI had been excluded from DSI's written report. . . .

Nifong's representations that he was unaware of the existence of DNA from multiple unidentified males on the rape kit items and/or that he was unaware of the exclusion of such evidence from DSI's written report, were intentional misrepresentations and intentional false statements of material fact to the Court and to opposing counsel.

[Subsequently, Nifong recused himself from the prosecution. The state Attorney General declared the Duke Defendants innocent of the charges and the charges were dismissed on April 11, 2007. A disciplinary proceeding was then brought against Nifong. At the proceeding, Nifong represented that he did not realize that the existence of DNA from multiple unidentified males on the rape kit items was not included in DSI's report when he provided it to the Duke Defendants or thereafter. The court found this a false statement.]

Nifong was required by statute and by court order to disclose to the Duke Defendants that tests had been performed which revealed the existence of DNA from multiple unidentified males on the rape kit items. . . .

Nifong knew or reasonably should have known that his statements to representatives of the news media had a substantial likelihood of prejudicing the criminal adjudicative proceeding.

CONCLUSIONS OF LAW

By making statements to representatives of the news media including but not limited to those [set forth above], Nifong made extrajudicial statements he knew or reasonably should have known would be disseminated by means of public communication and would have a substantial likelihood of materially prejudicing an adjudicative proceeding in the matter, in violation of Rule 3.6(a), and made extrajudicial statements that had a substantial likelihood of heightening public condemnation of the accused, in violation of Rule 3.8(f).

By instructing Dr. Meehan to prepare a report containing positive matches, Nifong knowingly disobeyed an obligation under the rules of a tribunal in violation of Rule 3.4(c).

By not providing to the Duke Defendants prior to November 16, 2006, a complete report setting forth the results of all tests and examinations conducted by DSI, including the existence of DNA from multiple unidentified males on the rape kit items and including written or recorded memorializations of Dr. Meehan's oral statements, Nifong:

> did not, after a reasonably diligent inquiry, make timely disclosure to the defense of all evidence or information required to be disclosed by applicable law, rules of procedure, or court opinions, including all evidence or information known to him that tended to negate the guilt of the accused, in violation of Rule 3.8(d); and

> failed to make a reasonably diligent effort to comply with a legally proper discovery request in violation of Rule 3.4(d)(3).

By falsely representing to the Court and to counsel for the Duke Defendants that he had provided all discoverable material in his possession and that the substance of all Dr. Meehan's oral statements to him concerning the results of all examinations and tests conducted by DSI were included in DSI's written report, Nifong made false statements of fact or law to a tribunal in violation of Rule 3.3(a)(1), made false statements of material fact to a third person in the course of representing a client in violation of Rule 4.1, and engaged in conduct involving dishonesty, fraud, deceit or misrepresentation in violation of Rule 8.4(c)....

Each of the violations set forth above separately, and the pattern of conduct revealed when they are viewed together, constitutes conduct prejudicial to the administration of justice in violation of Rule 8.4(d).

Nifong's misconduct is aggravated by the following factors: dishonest or selfish motive; a pattern of misconduct; multiple offenses; refusal to acknowledge wrongful nature of conduct in connection with his handling of the DNA evidence; vulnerability of the victims; and substantial experience in the practice of law.

Nifong's misconduct is mitigated by the following factors: absence of a prior disciplinary record and good reputation.

The aggravating factors outweigh the mitigating factors.

Nifong's misconduct resulted in significant actual harm to Reade Seligman, Collin Finnerty, and David Evans and their families. Defendant's conduct was, at least, a major contributing factor in the exceptionally intense national and local media coverage the Duke Lacrosse case received and in the public condemnation heaped upon the Duke Defendants. As a result of Nifong's misconduct, these young men experienced heightened public scorn and loss of privacy while facing very serious criminal charges of which the Attorney General of North Carolina ultimately concluded they were innocent.

Nifong's misconduct resulted in significant actual harm to the legal profession. Nifong's conduct has created a perception among the public within and outside North Carolina that lawyers in general and prosecutors in particular cannot be trusted and can be expected to lie to the court and to opposing counsel. . . .

Nifong's misconduct resulted in prejudice to and significant actual harm to the justice system. Nifong has caused a perception among the public within and outside North Carolina that there is a systemic problem in the North Carolina justice system and that a criminal defendant can only get justice if he or she can afford to hire an expensive lawyer with unlimited resources to figure out what is being withheld by the prosecutor. . . .

This Hearing Committee has considered all alternatives and finds that no discipline other than disbarment will adequately protect the public, the judicial system and the profession. . . .

Michael B. Nifong is hereby DISBARRED from the practice of law.

NOTES

1. How did attorney Nifong get himself into this situation? What was he thinking? Some critics have suggested that *Nifong* is notable largely for its novelty, and contend that prosecutors who commit misconduct are rarely subjected to discipline for it. In that regard, consider the hearing committee's conclusion that Nifong had damaged the legal system by creating the perception that "a criminal defendant can only get justice if he or she can afford to hire an expensive lawyer with unlimited resources. . . ." Was that a false perception? Isn't that in fact what the Duke defendants had? Without extensive legal work, would Nifong's misconduct ever have come to light?

2. The consequences of prosecutorial misconduct can be profound. Consider the case of Timothy Masters. Masters was convicted in 1999 of a 1987 murder notwithstanding the fact that there was no physical evidence or witness testimony connecting him to the crime. Nine years later he was released, after advanced DNA testing demonstrated no evidence of his presence at the scene or participation in the crime (but suggested the presence of three other individuals). The prosecution failed to turn over multiple pieces of evidence, including lengthy notes of consultation with a forensic psychologist, and footprint casts found in a "drag trail" leading to the body of the victim, which did not belong to Masters. The prosecutors in the case—both of whom were judges by the time Masters' conviction was overturned—were censured. *See* P. Soloman Banda, *Did a psychological profile go too far?*, Prince George Citizen, April 6, 2008; *People v. Gilmore*, 2008 WL 4328245 (Colo. 2008); *People v.*

Blair, 2008 WL 4329012 (Colo. 2008). Is a censure sufficient punishment under the circumstances?

3. In some circumstances, prosecutorial misconduct can result in state liability. In 2003, Shih–Wei Su was released from prison when a federal appeals court ruled that the prosecutor in his case had knowingly elicited false testimony from a crucial prosecution witness, and then argued to the jury, notwithstanding her office's knowledge that the witness had lied, that the witness had testified truthfully. *Su v. Filion*, 335 F.3d 119 (2d Cir. 2003). Su filed a disciplinary complaint against the prosecutor; the prosecutor claimed that she did not know the testimony was false and that she had been "naive, inexperienced and, possibly, stupid." The prosecutor received a written admonition. Su brought suit. In 2008, the City of New York paid Su $3.5 million to compensate him for his wrongful incarceration. Jim Dwyer, *Prosecutor Misconduct, At A Cost of $3.5 Million*, New York Times, Oct. 22, 2008.

4. Is Rule 3.8 necessary, or does it simply reiterate obligations that are incumbent upon any attorney? Consider also Rule 3.6, which the Hearing Committee ruled that Nifong had violated. Does it apply only to prosecutors, or to all lawyers?

5. You might think that there is a potential First Amendment problem with limiting a lawyer's right to speak to the press, as Model Rules 3.6 and 3.8 do. The U.S. Supreme Court considered this issue in *Gentile v. State Bar of Nevada*, 501 U.S. 1030 (1991). Gentile represented Sanders, who owned Western Vault Corporation. Undercover police officers reported that four kilograms of cocaine and $300,000 in travelers' checks were missing from a vault at Western. Police investigation, reported extensively by the press, indicated that police officers who had had free access to the vault during the relevant time period were not suspects, but Sanders was; at one point, the police reported to the press that the two detectives with access to the vault had been "cleared" as possible suspects after passing lie detector tests. Hours after Sanders was indicted for the thefts, Gentile, concerned that the press reporting would poison the potential jury pool, called a press conference. There, he stated that his client was "an innocent person," that "the person that was in the most direct position to have stolen the drugs and money" was one of the police detectives, that his client was "being used as a scapegoat," and that some of the alleged victims were "known drug dealers and convicted money launderers and drug dealers." Sanders was acquitted at trial. Gentile was disciplined by the State Bar, on the ground that his statements had a "substantial likelihood of materially prejudicing" an adjudicative proceeding. Gentile challenged his discipline. In a complex and divided decision, the Supreme Court held that the Nevada rule imposed a permissible restraint on lawyer speech about pending cases. It nonetheless concluded that Gentile's discipline had been improper, because the rule was impermissibly vague; Gentile could reasonably have understood that his right under the rules to disclose the "general nature of the . . . defense" he intended to offer included the information he provided at the press conference. In response to *Gentile*, Model Rule 3.6 was amended in 1994 to add Model Rule 3.6(c), which permits a lawyer, notwithstanding the constraints of Model Rule 3.6(a), to "make a statement that a reasonable lawyer would believe is required to protect a client from the substantial undue prejudicial effect of recent publicity not

initiated by the lawyer or the lawyer's client," as long as the statement is "limited to such information as is necessary to mitigate the recent adverse publicity." Does this alleviate some of the chilling effect on speech that might have been a concern after *Gentile*?

6. Besides the ethics rules, caselaw and statutes create a separate set of obligations on a prosecutor to disclose exculpatory evidence to the defense.

D. DUTIES TO THE LEGAL SYSTEM: MAINTAINING THE PERCEPTION OF LEGITIMACY

The Model Rules impose on lawyers an obligation not to "engage in conduct that is prejudicial to the administration of justice." Model Rule 8.4(d). This is a broad term, and carries with it the potential for overenforcement. But in some cases it is not difficult to view a lawyer's conduct as "prejudicial to the administration of justice."

IN RE CURRY

880 N.E.2d 388 (Mass. 2008)

MARSHALL, C.J.

Attorney Kevin P. Curry contests an information filed in the county court by the Board of Bar Overseers (board) that unanimously recommends his disbarment for violating [*inter alia*, the Massachusetts equivalent of Model Rules 8.4(a), (c), and (d), Model Rule 1.2(d), and Model Rule 4.1, as well as a provision prohibiting a lawyer from engaging in "any other conduct that adversely reflects on his fitness to practice law."] The disciplinary proceedings against him arose from Curry's role in a scheme to impugn the integrity of a Superior Court judge in an ongoing matter by invading the confidential communications between the judge and her former law clerk in an attempt to affect the outcome of the case. . . . We accept the board's recommendation and remand the case to the county court where a judgment of disbarment shall enter. . . .

We turn now to the background of this case, whose factual complexity requires a lengthy summary.

1. *Background.*

a. *Demoulas litigation.* This bar disciplinary proceeding has its origins in the protracted legal warfare between the family of George Demoulas and the family of Telemachus Demoulas over interests in the family supermarket business. . . . Demoulas Super Markets, Inc. (DSM), and other entities jointly owned by the families of brothers George and Telemachus Demoulas were estimated to be worth approximately $1 billion. Two law suits filed in Superior Court in 1990 by George's family against Telemachus and his family would eventually determine ownership and control of the bulk of the Demoulas fortune. The first lawsuit alleged that the Telemachus Demoulas defendants had fraudulently transferred stock from

George's family to themselves, and that Telemachus's children had fraud-ulently received 400 shares of DSM stock belonging to George's family (stock transfer case). The second suit, brought by Arthur S. Demoulas, George's son, while the first case was pending, alleged that the Telema-chus branch of the family had diverted corporate opportunities from DSM to entities the defendants separately controlled (shareholder derivative case). Superior Court Judge Maria Lopez presided over both cases.

The stock transfer case was tried before a jury. Judge Lopez directed verdicts for Telemachus's children on certain counts. Subsequently, in May, 1994, the jury returned verdicts in favor of George's family against Telemachus and his family for breach of duty related to the fraudulent transfer of stock and other interests belonging to the plaintiffs. Judge Lopez reserved the issue of damages.

The shareholder derivative case was tried before Judge Lopez without a jury from December 12, 1994, through May 15, 1995. Her decision was entered on August 3, 1995. Judge Lopez's law clerk for the trial was then in his second year of clerkship for the Superior Court; he worked on the case from the fall of 1994 until the end of August, 1995, when his clerkship ended.

Both the stock transfer case and the shareholder derivative case took fateful turns in three decisions issued by Judge Lopez in August, 1995. [With those decisions] ... it was settled that Telemachus's branch of the family would lose much of their control of the Demoulas businesses and fortune. Not surprisingly, the Telemachus Demoulas defendants were alarmed at this prospect. They were disappointed in the group of attorneys and law firms to whom they had paid millions of dollars in legal fees, and they were convinced that Judge Lopez was biased against them. Their suspicions of Judge Lopez were heightened by some of these attorneys, who assured them that Judge Lopez was "too dumb" to have written the *Demoulas* decision.

We turn now to the events germane to this disciplinary proceeding. At the time of the conduct at issue in this matter, approximately August, 1995, through August, 1997, the Demoulas litigations were still ongoing....

b. *The initial meeting with the Demoulas family.* In 1995, Curry was a member in good standing of the Massachusetts bar, having gained admis-sion in 1968. Early in his career he spent five and one-half years as an assistant attorney general in the office of the Massachusetts Attorney General. Curry then entered private practice.

In August, 1995, approximately two weeks after Judge Lopez issued the *Demoulas* decision, Curry and Ernest Reid, a private investigator who had worked with Curry in the past, sent a letter to Telemachus proposing to meet with him concerning "a matter of importance and confidence."[1] As a result of this communication, Curry, Reid, and members of the Demoulas

---

1. Curry had no previous contact or relationship with any of the Demoulas family members. Curry testified before the special hearing officer that Reid instigated the idea of contacting Telemachus. The special hearing officer rejected Curry's version of events, in part because, "through the course of the hearing in this matter, I found Curry's testimony regarding his

family, including Telemachus and his son, Arthur T. Demoulas (Arthur T.), met at DSM headquarters in Tewksbury in early September, 1995. Curry told his hosts what they were apparently eager to hear: Judge Lopez had decided the shareholder derivative case against them before opening statements in the case. Specifically, he told them, among other things, that the case was "over before it began." He proceeded to make salacious and disparaging remarks about Judge Lopez's character on and off the bench, and also about the character of the plaintiffs' attorneys. Curry told Telemachus and the others that Judge Lopez had previously done a "big favor" for another individual in "a big case." Curry told them that their case was "fixed." However, at the time he made this presentation, Curry, in the words of the special hearing officer, "had no documentation to support any of his scurrilous charges."

Curry's aim was true. Telemachus was aghast that he had "been had." He asked Curry what could be done. Curry informed Telemachus and the others that they would need evidence of what Curry described as Judge Lopez's "prior corrupt acts" and "judicial misconduct" to take to this court and to the media. Curry volunteered himself and Reid to produce the evidence. A week after the meeting, Arthur T. asked Curry and Reid to investigate Judge Lopez.[2] In the ensuing twelve months, Reid mined public records for information on the personal and professional lives of Judge Lopez and of the attorneys who had worked on the Demoulas cases for George's family. In November, 1996, Curry reviewed Judge Lopez's written decisions to that date in an effort to determine whether the judge had written the *Demoulas* decision.

In November, 1996, Arthur T. gave Curry a resume that the law clerk, with Judge Lopez's permission, had sent to various Demoulas defense counsel in the fall of 1995 seeking employment. Reid and Curry deduced from the resume that the law clerk was interested in international commercial civil litigation. Together they decided to contact the law clerk under the guise of offering him lucrative employment in that field. In the words of the special hearing officer, they concocted the law clerk's "dream job."

c. *Initial meetings with the law clerk.* To further their plan, Reid gathered public documents relating to the law clerk, his neighbors, his parents, and their neighbors. In April 1997, Reid contacted the law clerk by telephone. Using his real name, Reid told the law clerk that he was a headhunter who wished to interview him about an "attractive opportunity" as an attorney at a law firm, at a salary of $90,000 per year. The law clerk was excited,[3] and Reid set up a meeting in the law clerk's home on April 9, 1997, to discuss the "opportunity."

---

involvement in the events at issue to be almost completely unreliable and not believable. I believed little of what Curry said, unless it was corroborated by a witness whom I found to be credible or was merely background information."

2. Curry asked for and received an initial payment of $25,000 for his services, and was eventually paid a total of about $130,000 to $140,000 by Arthur T.

3. The law clerk had had difficulty obtaining employment at the end of his first year of clerkship in the Superior Court, and again after his second year of clerkship ended in the fall of

At their first meeting, Reid slightly changed course. He told the law clerk (falsely) that his client was a corporation with offices in Bermuda, New York, and Boston, and that the corporation was looking for in-house counsel. Using the pretext that his client demanded a candidate with excellent writing skills, Reid then asked him if he had worked on any "cases of note" while clerking for the Superior Court. The law clerk promptly replied, "[W]e wrote the *Demoulas* decision." When asked to clarify, he said, "I wrote the decision." He also told Reid that Judge Lopez had read, but not edited, the decision. A general discussion ensued about Judge Lopez, her husband, and her husband's businesses. Reid left with a promise to be back in touch.

The next day, Reid met Curry in Forest Hills Cemetery, where they often met for confidential talks. Among other things, Reid recounted the law clerk's remarks about authoring the *Demoulas* decision, and told Curry that the law clerk had sent him a copy of the decision. Curry then telephoned Arthur T. to report what he had learned from Reid.

On May 4, 1997, Reid called the law clerk to tell him that the "client" was impressed with the writing samples, especially the *Demoulas* decision. Reid arranged another interview for May 7, 1997. At the second meeting, Reid again emphasized the lucrative and adventurous aspects of the fake in-house position and probed more deeply into the authorship of the *Demoulas* decision. Among other things, the law clerk claimed that, although he discussed the case with Judge Lopez during the lengthy trial, the legal conclusions were his. When Reid asked if the case were rightly decided, the law clerk replied, "The [Supreme Judicial Court] upheld me so what does it matter." Reid said the client would like to meet him either in New York or in Halifax, Nova Scotia, to which the law clerk agreed.

d. *The first sham interview (Halifax).* Reid subsequently reported to Curry that he did not have the "right vibes" from the law clerk at the second meeting and could not get what he "wanted" from him. The two decided on a third meeting with the law clerk, this time in Halifax, Nova Scotia. The special hearing officer did not credit Curry's testimony that Halifax was chosen because it was a place Reid had always wanted to visit. She concluded that Halifax was chosen because, unlike Massachusetts, Nova Scotia is a jurisdiction in which recording a conversation is legal so long as one party consents to the tape recording.

The preparations for the Halifax interview were substantial. The plan was for Curry to present himself to the law clerk as "Kevin Concave," an employee of a fictitious British Pacific Surplus Risks, Ltd. (British Pacific), an "international insurance underwriting business." Richard LaBonte, a private detective recommended by Reid, would also be present at the Halifax interview. LaBonte was to pose as "Richard LaBlanc," another British Pacific employee. Reid and Curry arranged for business cards to be printed with the aliases of Curry and LaBonte. The business cards listed

---

1995. Eventually he did so, with the assistance of Judge Lopez, and in the spring of 1997, when he was first contacted, he was employed at a Boston law firm.

an address for British Pacific that was an actual address in London, a
working facsimile number, and a telephone number that was answered by
a person with an English accent when the law clerk called, as he later did.
Curry and the two investigators also discussed whether the meeting with
the law clerk should be tape recorded. The special hearing officer found
that a decision not to tape record the interview was made during a
telephone conference among the three in Halifax prior to the interview.

Reid provided LaBonte with extensive documentation concerning the law
clerk. He scripted a set of interview questions. Some time before June 5,
1997, Curry gave Reid a round-trip airline ticket to Halifax and $300 in
cash, both of which Reid passed on to the law clerk. The money was
allegedly to compensate the law clerk for missing a day's work.[4]

On June 5, 1997, the law clerk flew to Halifax. At a meeting room in the
Citadel Hotel, he met "Kevin Concave" (Curry), who was introduced as
the director of operations at British Pacific, and "Richard LaBlanc"
(LaBonte), "the person who put out fires" for the company. As the
interview progressed from introductory generalities to specifics about the
supposed job, the law clerk began to stutter. "Concave" told the law clerk
that they knew he stuttered, and reassured him that they were interested
primarily in his writing skills. When he asked how they knew he stuttered, Curry produced a recommendation letter mentioning his stutter
that had been written by attorney Stephen Mulcahy in support of the law
clerk's application for admission to the Massachusetts bar. The law clerk
then volunteered that he did not personally know Mulcahy, but that
Mulcahy had written the required recommendation letter as a favor to a
mutual acquaintance, another attorney, who was unable to submit a
letter. The information about the bar recommendation letter was news to
Curry and LaBonte.

The interview then proceeded with Curry spinning tales about the worldwide reach of British Pacific and the "adventures" the law clerk would
have around the world in his work for the company. He told the law clerk
that he would be paid in excess of $90,000 per year, in part to compensate
him and his wife for lengthy stays they would be required to make in
different countries. Then followed a series of questions by Curry and
LaBonte that was, in the words of the special hearing officer, "unquestionably designed to inquire into . . . Judge Lopez's deliberative process in the
Demoulas decision, as well as to elicit potentially damaging personal
information about her." Curry emphasized that writing skills were extremely important for the job. He told the law clerk, falsely, that attorney
Robert Shaw was British Pacific's outside counsel, who had reviewed the
Demoulas decision and was very impressed. Curry then asked how the law
clerk could have written the entire decision, as he claimed. According to

---

4. The special hearing officer noted: "[The law clerk's] reaction to receiving the $300 was,
'Great.' He had heard about big firm recruitment where the prospects are 'taken to a concert or
some place special,' and he thought receiving the $300 was something similar. . . . His testimony
demonstrates how naive he was about the recruiting process. Had [the law clerk] been more
sophisticated, being handed $300 in cash for compensation for missing a day's work would have
set off warning bells."

the testimony of Curry and LaBonte, the law clerk told them that Judge Lopez was biased and predisposed to find for the plaintiffs, and that she had told him before the trial started who "the good guys and the bad guys" were, and who the "winner and losers" were going to be. Curry and LaBonte also testified that the law clerk made negative comments about Judge Lopez's work habits and deliberately downplayed her contributions to the decision. The law clerk, in turn, testified that he had not made the statements attributed to him about Judge Lopez's predisposition in the *Demoulas* case. The special hearing officer, who credited most of the law clerk's testimony, did not credit his testimony on this issue. She concluded that he had indeed made statements to LaBonte and Curry about Judge Lopez's alleged predisposition against the Telemachus Demoulas defendants. She also concluded that Curry exaggerated and misrepresented the nature of the law clerk's statements about Judge Lopez, both to Arthur T. and in this bar discipline proceeding. . . .

e. *The aftermath of the Halifax sham interview.* Back in Boston, Curry relayed to Arthur T., "I think we got him." On June 8, 1997, Arthur T., in turn, told Gary Crossen, one of the Telemachus Demoulas family defense counsel, about Curry and Reid and the Halifax sham. Crossen was unimpressed with the report that the law clerk claimed to have written the entire *Demoulas* decision. However, he believed that the information that Judge Lopez had prejudged the case to be both "troubling" and "significant."

The same day he met with Crossen, Arthur T. also met with Curry to suggest that Crossen draft Curry's affidavit about the interview. Curry took offense at this suggestion and drafted his own affidavit. In his statement, Curry swore that the law clerk had declared four times during the course of the interview that Judge Lopez was "predisposed to find for the Plaintiffs," and that she had told him who the "bad guys and the good guys were" and who the "winners were going to be before the case began." Curry also averred that the law clerk claimed to have written the entire *Demoulas* decision, and that his bar application contained a letter of recommendation from an attorney who did not know him.[5] Curry signed, but did not date, the affidavit, which he gave to Crossen.

LaBonte also drafted an affidavit . . . LaBonte signed and dated the affidavit and transmitted it by facsimile to Curry the next day.

On June 9, 1997, Curry met in Crossen's office with Arthur T. and Richard K. Donahue, another member of the defense team. The men discussed how best to make use of what Crossen considered the most important information from the Halifax sham interview, the information concerning Judge Lopez's alleged predisposition. Among other options,

---

5. The law clerk submitted an application for admission as an attorney to the Supreme Judicial Court in 1993. The application required submission of "two letters addressed to the Board of Bar Examiners stating facts relative to [the applicant's] character by persons who know [the applicant]." Applicants also were instructed to obtain the recommendation of "an attorney of the court of the Commonwealth of Massachusetts," who would "certify that the petitioner is of good moral character."

they considered filing the affidavits with the Commission on Judicial Conduct and verifying or further pursuing the Halifax information by continuing the ruse in New York or Bermuda, both one-party consent jurisdictions in which they might secretly tape record the law clerk's comments.

On or about June 11, 1997, Crossen determined that the best course of action would be to verify the Halifax information using his own investigators. He concluded that the best way to do this was to continue the job ruse and secretly tape record the law clerk's statements in New York. At a subsequent planning meeting for the New York "interview" attended by Crossen, three of his investigators, and Arthur T., Curry spoke about how the second interview should be conducted based on Curry's experiences with the law clerk.

The group ultimately decided that the law clerk would be told that the New York interview would be with a "decision maker" at British Pacific, a "Peter O'Hara." O'Hara's role was to be played by Peter Rush, a private investigator who previously had worked as a United States Secret Service special agent-in-charge in Boston. The planning group, which included Curry, also decided that LaBonte, whom the law clerk knew as "Richard LaBlanc" of British Pacific, should be present at the interview, and that Crossen and Stewart Henry, a private investigator, would go to New York to "monitor" the situation. . . . Curry was a reluctant supporter of the New York plan, arguing instead that his and LaBonte's affidavits were sufficient to proceed with action to have Judge Lopez removed from the case.

On the day of the interview, June 17, 1997, Curry arrived unexpectedly at the New York hotel suite where the interview was to take place to reiterate his opposition to the plan. Crossen disagreed. Curry remained at the hotel suite for approximately fifteen minutes, during which time he made a call from his cellular telephone and was heard to say, "Everything looks okay to me. It's all set. . . . Anything else you want. . . . Okay. I'm out of here." He was not present for the interview. Curry's fear of being displaced by the defendants' regular counsel had come to pass. For purposes of this bar disciplinary proceeding, his role in the law clerk matter was over.

2. *Bar disciplinary proceedings.* In January, 2002, the Office of Bar Counsel (bar counsel) filed a three-count petition for discipline against Curry, Crossen, and Donahue in connection with the law clerk matter. . . .

[T]he board designated a special hearing officer to take evidence and make findings of fact, conclusions, and recommendations. Over the next eighteen months, the special hearing officer heard twenty-four days of testimony involving twenty-one witnesses, accepted 177 documents in evidence, and made numerous evidentiary rulings. Her report issued on May 11, 2005, concluding that Curry's actions in connection with the law clerk matter violated all of the disciplinary rules under which he was charged, with one minor exception. The board unanimously adopted the special hearing officer's recommendation that Curry be disbarred. . . .

We now turn to Curry's challenges to the board's legal conclusions.

5. *Violations of the code of professional responsibility.* Curry claims that, contrary to the board's conclusions, his conduct in setting up the first interview in Halifax to "secure admissions" about "improper conduct" by Judge Lopez in the stockholder derivative case was "proper and ethical." The disciplinary rules, he says, do not prohibit "pretextual" interviews as a means of getting at the truth. Alternatively, Curry argues that, even if his conduct violated the rules, he acted reasonably and in good faith in an area where the rules were unclear. He further contends that the testimony of his expert, which the special hearing officer excluded, would have supported his defense of good faith. Finally, Curry asserts that, "where highly responsible attorneys differ about whether [Curry's] conduct was unethical, it is grossly unfair and unjust to disbar [him] in the case which announces a new rule." We reject each of these arguments for the reasons explained below.

The purpose of the disciplinary rules and accompanying proceedings is to protect the public and maintain its confidence in the integrity of the bar and the fairness and impartiality of our legal system. Without the public's trust that lawyers and judges act in good faith and strictly within the bounds of our laws and professional norms, the rule of law has little practical force. The record amply demonstrates that Curry violated the most basic ethical precepts of his profession and, in so doing, has harmed both the legal profession and the public's perception of our justice system.

a. *Dishonesty and false statements.* The admonitions of the disciplinary rules against "conduct involving dishonesty, fraud, deceit, or misrepresentation," and "[k]nowingly mak[ing] a false statement of law or fact," both of which are central to this case, are not aspirational. They are not obscure. They harbor no implicit exception. Nor are they limited to statements made in court or to interactions between the lawyer and the client.

Curry's conduct in this matter raised "dishonesty, fraud, deceit, or misrepresentation" and "false statement[s] of law or fact" to heady levels. His misconduct began with baseless insinuations to the Telemachus Demoulas family that he knew Judge Lopez was predisposed against them and that he could gather other evidence of the judge's misconduct. His chicanery then blossomed into the creation of an entirely false universe, complete with sham executives and a sham multinational enterprise with a verifiable London telephone number. In this fabricated world, designed to ensnare a judge in a pending case through the words of her former law clerk, Curry compounded his deceit by appearing as Kevin Concave, spinning lies about a nonexistent job opportunity to the law clerk in the hopes of mining "admissions" from the young man. . . . He participated in planning meetings to further the deception of the law clerk by means of another sham "job interview" in New York, which would be tape recorded without the law clerk's knowledge or permission for purposes of coercing the law clerk's sworn testimony against Judge Lopez in a motion to recuse in ongoing litigation. Curry's actions were not on the boundaries of ethical conduct, "about which reasonable [attorneys] differ."...

Curry argues, however, that his treatment of the law clerk was of a piece with instances in which lawyers employ undercover investigators to uncover discrimination in housing or employment or other violations of civil and criminal laws. It was not.... "Testing" involves deception of a particular kind: investigators pose as members of the public interested in procuring housing or employment, in order to determine whether they are being treated differently based on their race or sex. Their aim is to reproduce an existing pattern of illegal conduct....

Curry's scheme is different from such investigations not only in degree but in kind—as both the special hearing officer and the board rightly concluded. Unlike discrimination testers or investigators who pose as members of the public in order to reproduce pre-existing patterns of conduct, Curry built an elaborate fraudulent scheme whose purpose was to elicit or potentially threaten the law clerk into making statements that he otherwise would not have made. In particular, by leading the law clerk to believe that his "dream job" depended on the outcome of his interview, flying him to Nova Scotia, and paying him hundreds of dollars in cash, Curry created an artificial situation designed to cause the law clerk to make statements about Judge Lopez and the *Demoulas* decision that he would not have made absent such inducements. Curry further structured the ruse so as to elicit a particular set of answers to those questions: by emphasizing that the law clerk's future was riding on his writing skills, Curry pressured him to give an account of the process of writing the *Demoulas* decision in which the law clerk claimed Judge Lopez played little or no role....

Curry also makes an analogy between his conduct and that of government prosecutors. This analogy is even less apt than the analogy to testers and other private investigators.... [T]o suggest that government attorneys might engage in some forms of subterfuge and deception does nothing to excuse Curry's conduct, which unambiguously violates the ethical rules.

b. *Harm to the administration of justice.* Curry's conduct was self-evidently "prejudicial to the administration of justice," in violation of DR 1–102(A)(5), for at least two reasons. First, the purpose of Curry's project, and the basis on which he sought to insinuate himself into the Demoulas legal team, was to discredit and thereby disqualify Judge Lopez in an ongoing matter, even though he had no credible evidence of any kind to suspect Judge Lopez of a scintilla of bias against the defendants, or of any other judicial misconduct. He presented himself to the losing Demoulas side armed only with the belief—which turned out to be correct—that he could persuade them to pay him substantial legal fees by stoking their doubts about whether they had been fairly treated by the court. Put another way, Curry, who as an attorney is "an officer of the court," was willing to sacrifice the reputation of the court for his own personal financial gain. Because the administration of justice depends on a baseline of confidence in the integrity of the judicial system, Curry's self-generated, duplicitous project was "prejudicial to the administration of justice." At the time of Curry's conduct in this matter, Judge Lopez continued to preside over ongoing litigation in the *Demoulas* family disputes. "A system that permits an attorney without objective basis to challenge the integrity, and thereby the authority, of a judge presiding over a case elevates brazen and irresponsible conduct above competence and diligence, hallmarks of professional conduct."

Second, Curry's efforts to pierce the confidential communications of a former law clerk and a judge in a pending matter to benefit one of the litigants also constitute "conduct prejudicial to the administration of justice." Curry insists that his contact with the law clerk was proper because "[t]here is no privilege in Massachusetts protecting communications between a judge and her law clerk." Here Curry targets the wrong mark. Curry is correct that we have not explicitly recognized a privilege regarding communications between a judge and her law clerk, a matter we need not address here, for Curry's logic is flawed. That such a privilege has not been explicitly recognized does not mean that an attorney (or anyone else, for that matter) is free to induce or coerce a law clerk into revealing confidential communications between the clerk and the judge about an ongoing matter to benefit one of the litigants, in particular confidential communications that the law clerk otherwise would not have revealed. The administration of justice requires respect for the internal deliberations and processes that form the basis of judicial decisions, at very least while the matter is still pending. . . .

The disrespect Curry displayed to the court is, as well, disrespect to his chosen profession. Disciplinary Rule 1–102(A)(6) provides that a lawyer shall not "[e]ngage in any other conduct that adversely reflects on his fitness to practice law." This rule has been applied to a variety of categories of misconduct, any of which reflects adversely on the attorney's fitness to practice. Here, because Curry's misconduct was of a kind that calls into question his candor, motives, and respect for the legal system, we readily conclude that he "behaved in such a way that [he] is no longer worthy of the trust the courts and public must place in [his] representations, [his] conduct, and [his] character." . . .

c. *Client misconduct.* Disciplinary Rule 7–102(A)(7) provides that, in representing a client, a lawyer shall not "[c]ounsel or assist his client in conduct that the lawyer knows to be illegal or fraudulent." As we discussed above, Curry was the one who first reached out to Arthur T., and then not only encouraged, but prodded, his client to authorize, fund, and continue multiple attempts to pressure the law clerk by means of "dishonesty, fraud, deceit, [and] misrepresentation." Curry thereby violated DR 7–102(A)(7). . . .

d. *Use of agents.* Disciplinary Rule 1–102(A)(2) provides that an attorney shall not "[c]ircumvent a Disciplinary Rule through actions of another." In other words, an attorney may not delegate to another that which he himself is prohibited from doing. An investigator is "another" for purposes of this rule. Curry engaged in most of the conduct at issue in these proceedings in concert with his investigator Ernest Reid. When Reid and other investigators working with Curry engaged in conduct that would have violated disciplinary rules had Curry done it himself, Curry thereby violated DR 1–102(A)(2) as well. A lawyer's obligations of good faith to the tribunal and to others would mean little if the lawyer could use surrogates to achieve by deceit and falsehood that which he himself could not do. . . .

Curry argues that, even if he violated the disciplinary rules, disbarment is a disproportionately severe sanction. . . . Taken as a whole, Curry's conduct was sufficiently sustained and egregious to merit disbarment.

Curry's role as the instigator of the baseless plan to discredit Judge Lopez constitutes a significant aggravating factor. Unlike the existing lawyers representing the Telemachus Demoulas family, Curry had no reason to insinuate himself into the *Demoulas* litigation, and he did so only by positing salacious allegations against Judge Lopez for which he had no support. None of the misconduct in this case, by Curry or by the other attorneys who later became involved, would ever have happened had Curry's pecuniary motivations not overwhelmed any respect he might have felt for a sitting judge, her law clerk, their internal deliberations, their families, their character, and his own basic ethical obligations, all in the course of ongoing litigation.

NOTES

1. The story gets even more bizarre after Curry's involvement ended. After the "job interview" with the law clerk, attorney Crossen met with the clerk again, disclosed the ruse, and threatened him with disclosure of his false bar letter if he did not cooperate. The law clerk retained counsel, went to the FBI, and met with Crossen on more than one occasion while secretly taping the conversations with FBI authorization. Meanwhile, Crossen was having the law clerk kept under surveillance and his family watched and photographed. Ultimately, the FBI subpoenaed the lawyers and investigators; the reverse sting was disclosed by the law clerk and his lawyer at a press conference. The hearing officer characterized Crossen's behavior as "border[ing] on outright extortion"; Crossen, like Curry, was disbarred. *In re Crossen*, 880 N.E.2d 352 (Mass. 2008). Crossen argued that his conduct just reflected his zeal for his client's cause; the court responded "with the elementary observation that 'an attorney is not free to [do] anything and everything imaginable . . . under the pretext of protecting his client's right to a fair trial.'" 880 N.E.2d at 376.

2. If the facts stated by the law clerk were true, was there anything wrong with the law clerk's drafting the opinion for the judge? with the judge having largely predecided the case before trial? with the law clerk submitting a letter of reference from a reference who did not know him personally? What, if anything, was wrong with the way Curry sought to learn these facts?

3. In this case, it is easy to see why conduct that attempted to undermine a sitting judge in an ongoing matter was deemed "prejudicial to the administration of justice." But there is some line-drawing required in this regard. Does any criticism of a judge amount to conduct "prejudicial to the administration of justice"? Does the obligation of respect for the system sometimes interfere with a lawyer's ability to speak her mind? Consider the following case:

STANDING COMMITTEE ON DISCIPLINE OF THE UNITED STATES DISTRICT COURT FOR THE CENTRAL DISTRICT OF CALIFORNIA v. YAGMAN

55 F.3d 1430 (9th Cir. 1995)

KOZINSKI, CIRCUIT JUDGE.

Never far from the center of controversy, outspoken civil rights lawyer Stephen Yagman was suspended from practice before the United States District Court for the Central District of California for impugning the integrity of the court and interfering with the random selection of judges by making disparaging remarks about a judge of that court. We confront several new issues in reviewing this suspension order.

I

The convoluted history of this case begins in 1991 when Yagman filed a lawsuit pro se against several insurance companies. The case was assigned to Judge Manuel Real, then Chief Judge of the Central District. Yagman promptly sought to disqualify Judge Real on grounds of bias.[1] The disqualification motion was randomly assigned to Judge William Keller, who denied it and sanctioned Yagman for pursuing the matter in an "improper and frivolous manner."[2]

A few days after Judge Keller's sanctions order, Yagman was quoted as saying that Judge Keller "has a penchant for sanctioning Jewish lawyers: me, David Kenner and Hugh Manes. I find this to be evidence of anti-semitism." The district court found that Yagman also told the Daily Journal reporter that Judge Keller was "drunk on the bench," although this accusation wasn't published in the article.

Around this time, Yagman received a request from Prentice Hall, publisher of the much-fretted-about Almanac of the Federal Judiciary, for com-

---

1. As the basis for this claim, Yagman cited an earlier case where Judge Real had granted a directed verdict against Yagman's clients and thereafter sanctioned Yagman personally in the amount of $250,000. We reversed the sanctions and remanded for reassignment to another judge. *In re Yagman*, 796 F.2d 1165, 1188 (9th Cir.1986). Though we found no evidence that Judge Real harbored any personal animosity toward Yagman, we concluded that reassignment was necessary "to preserve the appearance of justice." *Id.* On remand, Judge Real challenged our authority to reassign the case, and Yagman successfully petitioned for a writ of mandamus. *See Brown v. Baden*, 815 F.2d 575, 576–77 (9th Cir.1987). The matter came to rest when the Supreme Court denied Judge Real's petition for certiorari.

2. The sanctions order harshly reprimanded Yagman, stating that "neither monetary sanctions nor suspension appear to be effective in deterring Yagman's pestiferous conduct," 137 F.R.D. at 318, and recommended that he be "disciplined appropriately" by the California State Bar, *id.* at 319. On appeal, we affirmed as to disqualification but reversed as to sanctions. *Yagman v. Republic Ins.*, 987 F.2d 622 (9th Cir.1993).

ments in connection with a profile of Judge Keller.[3] Yagman's response was less than complimentary.[4]

A few weeks later, Yagman placed an advertisement (on the stationary of his law firm) in the L.A. Daily Journal, asking lawyers who had been sanctioned by Judge Keller to contact Yagman's office.

Soon after these events, Yagman ran into Robert Steinberg, another attorney who practices in the Central District. According to Steinberg, Yagman told him that, by levelling public criticism at Judge Keller, Yagman hoped to get the judge to recuse himself in future cases. Believing that Yagman was committing misconduct, Steinberg described his conversation with Yagman in a letter to the Standing Committee on Discipline of the U.S. District Court for the Central District of California (the Standing Committee).

A few weeks later, the Standing Committee received a letter from Judge Keller describing Yagman's anti-Semitism charge, his inflammatory statements to Prentice Hall and the newspaper advertisement placed by Yagman's law firm. Judge Keller stated that "Mr. Yagman's campaign of harassment and intimidation challenges the integrity of the judicial system. Moreover, there is clear evidence that Mr. Yagman's attacks upon me are motivated by his desire to create a basis for recusing me in any future proceeding." Judge Keller suggested that "[t]he Standing Committee on Discipline should take action to protect the Court from further abuse."

After investigating the charges in the two letters, the Standing Committee issued a Petition for Issuance of an Order to Show Cause why Yagman should not be suspended from practice or otherwise disciplined. Pursuant to Central District Local Rule 2.6.4, the matter was then assigned to a panel of three Central District judges, which issued an Order to Show Cause and scheduled a hearing. Prior to the hearing, Yagman raised serious First Amendment objections to being disciplined for criticizing

---

3. The Almanac is a loose-leaf service consisting of profiles of federal judges. Each profile covers the judge's educational and professional background, noteworthy rulings, and anecdotal items of interest. One section—which many judges pretend to ignore but in fact read assiduously—is styled "Lawyers' Evaluation." Perhaps because the comments are published anonymously, they sometimes contain criticism more pungent than judges are accustomed to. Judges who believe the comments do not fairly portray their performance occasionally ask Prentice Hall to seek additional comments; Prentice Hall's letter to Yagman was sent pursuant to such a request. The updated survey indeed produced a more positive—and we believe more accurate—picture of Judge Keller than the original survey. *Compare* 1 Almanac of the Fed. Judiciary 48 (1991–1) *with* 1 Almanac of the Fed. Judiciary 49–50 (1991–2).

4. The portion of the letter relevant here reads as follows:

It is outrageous that the Judge wants his profile redone because he thinks it to be inaccurately harsh in portraying him in a poor light. It is an understatement to characterize the Judge as "the worst judge in the central district." It would be fairer to say that he is ignorant, dishonest, ill-tempered, and a bully, and probably is one of the worst judges in the United States. If television cameras ever were permitted in his courtroom, the other federal judges in the Country would be so embarrassed by this buffoon that they would run for cover. One might believe that some of the reason for this sub-standard human is the recent acrimonious divorce through which he recently went: but talking to attorneys who knew him years ago indicates that, if anything, he has mellowed. One other comment: his girlfriend ..., like the Judge, is a right-wing fanatic.

SER 316 (letter dated June 5, 1991). . . .

Judge Keller. Both sides requested an opportunity to brief the difficult free speech issues presented, but the district court never acted on these requests. The parties thus proceeded at the hearing without knowing the allocation of the burden of proof or the legal standard the court intended to apply.

During the two-day hearing, the Standing Committee and Yagman put on witnesses and introduced exhibits. In a published opinion issued several months after the hearing, the district court held that Yagman had committed sanctionable misconduct, and suspended him from practice in the Central District for two years.

II

[The Court rejected Yagman's argument that conflicts of interest of members of the Standing Committee deprived him of due process.]

III

Local Rule 2.5.2 contains two separate prohibitions. First, it enjoins attorneys from engaging in any conduct that "degrades or impugns the integrity of the Court." Second, it provides that "[n]o attorney shall engage in any conduct which ... interferes with the administration of justice." The district court concluded that Yagman violated both prongs of the rule. Because different First Amendment standards apply to these two provisions, we discuss the propriety of the sanction under each of them separately.

A

1.   We begin with the portion of Local Rule 2.5.2 prohibiting any conduct that "impugns the integrity of the Court." As the district court recognized, this provision is overbroad because it purports to punish a great deal of constitutionally protected speech, including all true statements reflecting adversely on the reputation or character of federal judges. A substantially overbroad restriction on protected speech will be declared facially invalid unless it is "fairly subject to a limiting construction."

To save the "impugn the integrity" portion of Rule 2.5.2, the district court read into it an "objective" version of the malice standard enunciated in *New York Times Co. v. Sullivan*, 376 U.S. 254 (1964). Relying on *United States Dist. Ct. v. Sandlin*, 12 F.3d 861 (9th Cir.1993), the court limited Rule 2.5.2 to prohibit only false statements made with either knowledge of their falsity or with reckless disregard as to their truth or falsity, judged from the standpoint of a "reasonable attorney."

Sandlin involved a First Amendment challenge to Washington Rule of Professional Conduct 8.2(a), which provided in part: "A lawyer shall not make a statement that the lawyer knows to be false or with reckless disregard as to its truth or falsity concerning the qualifications, integrity, or record of a judge." Though the language of the rule closely tracked the *New York Times* malice standard, we held that the purely subjective standard applicable in defamation cases is not suited to attorney disciplinary proceedings. Instead, we held that such proceedings are governed by an objective standard, pursuant to which the court must determine "what the reasonable attorney, considered in light of all his professional functions, would do in the same or similar circumstances." The inquiry focuses on whether the attorney had a reasonable factual basis for making the statements, considering their nature and the context in which they were made.

Yagman nonetheless urges application of the *New York Times* subjective malice standard in attorney disciplinary proceedings. *Sandlin* stands firmly in the way. In *Sandlin,* we held that there are significant differences between the interests served by defamation law and those served by rules of professional ethics. Defamation actions seek to remedy an essentially private wrong by compensating individuals for harm caused to their reputation and standing in the community. Ethical rules that prohibit false statements impugning the integrity of judges, by contrast, are not designed to shield judges from unpleasant or offensive criticism, but to preserve public confidence in the fairness and impartiality of our system of justice.

Though attorneys can play an important role in exposing problems with the judicial system, *false* statements impugning the integrity of a judge erode public confidence without serving to publicize problems that justifiably deserve attention. *Sandlin* held that an objective malice standard strikes a constitutionally permissible balance between an attorney's right to criticize the judiciary and the public's interest in preserving confidence in the judicial system: Lawyers may freely voice criticisms supported by a reasonable factual basis even if they turn out to be mistaken.

Attorneys who make statements impugning the integrity of a judge are, however, entitled to other First Amendment protections applicable in the defamation context. To begin with, attorneys may be sanctioned for impugning the integrity of a judge or the court only if their statements are false; truth is an absolute defense. Moreover, the disciplinary body bears the burden of proving falsity.

It follows that statements impugning the integrity of a judge may not be punished unless they are capable of being proved true or false; statements of opinion are protected by the First Amendment unless they "imply a false assertion of fact." Even statements that at first blush appear to be factual are protected by the First Amendment if they cannot reasonably be interpreted as stating actual facts about their target. Thus, statements of "rhetorical hyperbole" aren't sanctionable, nor are statements that use language in a "loose, figurative sense."

With these principles in mind, we examine the statements for which Yagman was disciplined.

2.   We first consider Yagman's statement in the Daily Journal that Judge Keller "has a penchant for sanctioning Jewish lawyers: me, David Kenner and Hugh Manes. I find this to be evidence of anti-semitism." Though the

district court viewed this entirely as an assertion of fact, we conclude that the statement contains both an assertion of fact and an expression of opinion.

Yagman's claim that he, Kenner and Manes are all Jewish and were sanctioned by Judge Keller is clearly a factual assertion: The words have specific, well-defined meanings and describe objectively verifiable matters. Nothing about the context in which the words appear suggests the use of loose, figurative language or "rhetorical hyperbole." Thus, had the Standing Committee proved that Yagman, Kenner or Manes were not sanctioned by Judge Keller, or were not Jewish, this assertion might have formed the basis for discipline. The committee, however, didn't claim that Yagman's factual assertion was false, and the district court made no finding to that effect. We proceed, therefore, on the assumption that this portion of Yagman's statement is true.

The remaining portion of Yagman's Daily Journal statement is best characterized as opinion; it conveys Yagman's personal belief that Judge Keller is anti-Semitic. As such, it may be the basis for sanctions only if it could reasonably be understood as declaring or implying actual facts capable of being proved true or false.

In applying this principle, we are guided by section 566 of the Restatement (Second) of Torts, which distinguishes between two kinds of opinion statements: those based on assumed or expressly stated facts, and those based on implied, undisclosed facts. The statement, "I think Jones is an alcoholic," for example, is an expression of opinion based on implied facts, because the statement "gives rise to the inference that there are undisclosed facts that justify the forming of the opinion." Readers of this statement will reasonably understand the author to be implying he knows facts supporting his view—*e.g.*, that Jones stops at a bar every night after work and has three martinis. If the speaker has no such factual basis for his assertion, the statement is actionable, even though phrased in terms of the author's personal belief.

A statement of opinion based on expressly stated facts, on the other hand, might take the following form: "[Jones] moved in six months ago. He works downtown, and I have seen him during that time only twice, in his backyard around 5:30 seated in a deck chair ... with a drink in his hand. I think he must be an alcoholic." This expression of opinion appears to disclose all the facts on which it is based, and does not imply that there are other, unstated facts supporting the belief that Jones is an alcoholic.

A statement of opinion based on fully disclosed facts can be punished only if the stated facts are themselves false and demeaning. The rationale behind this rule is straightforward: When the facts underlying a statement of opinion are disclosed, readers will understand they are getting the author's interpretation of the facts presented; they are therefore unlikely to construe the statement as insinuating the existence of additional, undisclosed facts. Moreover, "an opinion which is unfounded reveals its lack of merit when the opinion-holder discloses the factual basis for the idea''; readers are free to accept or reject the author's opinion based on their own independent evaluation of the facts. A statement of opinion of this sort doesn't "imply a false assertion of fact," and is thus entitled to full constitutional protection....

Yagman's Daily Journal remark is protected by the First Amendment as an expression of opinion based on stated facts.... Yagman disclosed the basis for his view that Judge Keller is anti-Semitic and has a penchant for sanctioning Jewish lawyers: that he, Kenner and Manes are all Jewish and had been sanctioned by Judge Keller. The statement did not imply the existence of additional, undisclosed facts; it was carefully phrased in terms of an inference drawn from the facts specified rather than a bald accusation of bias against Jews. Readers were "free to form another, perhaps contradictory opinion from the same facts," as no doubt they did.

3. The district court also disciplined Yagman for alleging that Judge Keller was "dishonest." This remark appears in the letter Yagman sent to Prentice Hall in connection with the profile of Judge Keller in the Almanac of the Federal Judiciary. The court concluded that this allegation was sanctionable because it "plainly impl[ies] past improprieties." Had Yagman accused Judge Keller of taking bribes, we would agree with the district court. Statements that "could reasonably be understood as imputing specific criminal or other wrongful acts" are not entitled to constitutional protection merely because they are phrased in the form of an opinion.

When considered in context, however, Yagman's statement cannot reasonably be interpreted as accusing Judge Keller of criminal misconduct. The term "dishonest" was one in a string of colorful adjectives Yagman used to convey the low esteem in which he held Judge Keller. The other terms he used—"ignorant," "ill-tempered," "buffoon," "sub-standard human," "right-wing fanatic," "a bully," "one of the worst judges in the United States"—all speak to competence and temperament rather than corruption; together they convey nothing more substantive than Yagman's contempt for Judge Keller. Viewed in context of these "lusty and imaginative expression[s]," the word "dishonest" cannot reasonably be construed as suggesting that Judge Keller had committed specific illegal acts. Yagman's remarks are thus statements of rhetorical hyperbole, incapable of being proved true or false....

Were we to find any substantive content in Yagman's use of the term "dishonest," we would, at most, construe it to mean "intellectually dishonest"—an accusation that Judge Keller's rulings were overly result-oriented. Intellectual dishonesty is a label lawyers frequently attach to decisions with which they disagree. An allegation that a judge is intellectually dishonest, however, cannot be proved true or false by reference to a "core of objective evidence." Because Yagman's allegation of "dishonesty" does not imply facts capable of objective verification, it is constitutionally immune from sanctions.

4.   Finally, the district court found sanctionable Yagman's allegation that Judge Keller was "drunk on the bench." Yagman contends that, like many of the terms he used in his letter to Prentice Hall, this phrase should be viewed as mere "rhetorical hyperbole." The statement wasn't a part of the string of invective in the Prentice Hall letter, however; it was a remark Yagman allegedly made to a newspaper reporter. Yagman identifies nothing relating to the context in which this statement was made that tends to negate the literal meaning of the words he used. We therefore conclude that Yagman's "drunk on the bench" statement could reasonably be interpreted as suggesting that Judge Keller had actually, on at least one occasion, taken the bench while intoxicated. Unlike Yagman's remarks in his letter to Prentice Hall, this statement implies actual facts that are capable of objective verification.

For Yagman's "drunk on the bench" allegation to serve as the basis for sanctions, however, the Standing Committee had to prove that the statement was false. This it failed to do; indeed, the committee introduced no evidence at all on the point. While we share the district court's inclination to presume, "[i]n the absence of supporting evidence," that the allegation is untrue, the fact remains that the Standing Committee bore the burden of proving Yagman had made a statement that falsely impugned the integrity of the court. By presuming falsity, the district court unconstitutionally relieved the Standing Committee of its duty to produce evidence on an element of its case. Without proof of falsity, Yagman's "drunk on the bench" allegation, like the statements discussed above, cannot support the imposition of sanctions for impugning the integrity of the court.

B

As an alternative basis for sanctioning Yagman, the district court concluded that Yagman's statements violated Local Rule 2.5.2's prohibition against engaging in conduct that "interferes with the administration of justice." The court found that Yagman made the statements discussed above in an attempt to "judge-shop"—i.e., to cause Judge Keller to recuse himself in cases where Yagman appeared as counsel.

The Supreme Court has held that speech otherwise entitled to full constitutional protection may nonetheless be sanctioned if it obstructs or prejudices the administration of justice. Given the significant burden this rule places on otherwise protected speech, however, the Court has held that prejudice to the administration of justice must be highly likely before speech may be punished.

In a trio of cases involving contempt sanctions imposed against newspapers, the Court articulated the constitutional standard to be applied in this context. Press statements relating to judicial matters may not be restricted, the Court held, unless they pose a "clear and present danger" to the administration of justice. The standard announced in these cases is a demanding one: Statements may be punished only if they "constitute an imminent, not merely a likely, threat to the administration of justice. The danger must not be remote or even probable; it must immediately imperil."... In an oft-quoted passage, the Court noted that "the law of contempt is not made for the protection of judges who may be sensitive to the winds of public opinion. Judges are supposed to be men of fortitude, able to thrive in a hardy climate."

More recently, the Court held that the "clear and present danger" standard does not apply to statements made by lawyers participating in pending cases. *Gentile*, 501 U.S. at 1075. In *Gentile,* the Court concluded that lawyers involved in pending cases may be punished if their out-of-court statements pose merely a "substantial likelihood" of materially prejudicing the fairness of the proceeding. The Court gave two principal reasons for adopting this lower threshold, one concerned with the identity of the speaker, the other with the timing of the speech. First, the Court noted, lawyers participating in pending cases have "special access to information through discovery and client communications." As a result, their statements pose a heightened threat to the fair administration of justice, "since [they] are likely to be received as especially authoritative." Second, statements made during the pendency of a case are "likely to influence the actual outcome of the trial" or "prejudice the jury venire, even if an untainted panel can ultimately be found." The Court also noted that restricting the speech of lawyers while they are involved in pending cases does not prohibit speech altogether but "merely postpones the attorneys' comments until after trial."...

The Court in *Gentile* thus focused on situations where public statements by lawyers impair the "fair trial rights" of litigants, and discussed at some length the strong governmental interest in limiting prejudicial comments in this context....

The special considerations identified by *Gentile* are of limited concern when no case is pending before the court. When lawyers speak out on matters unconnected to a pending case, there is no direct and immediate impact on the fair trial rights of litigants. Information the lawyers impart will not be viewed as coming from confidential sources, and will not have a direct impact on a particular jury venire. Moreover, a speech restriction that is not bounded by a particular trial or other judicial proceeding does far more than merely postpone speech; it permanently inhibits what lawyers may say about the court and its judges—whether their statements are true or false.... We conclude, therefore, that lawyers' statements unrelated to a matter pending before the court may be sanctioned only if they pose a clear and present danger to the administration of justice.

The district court found that Yagman's statements interfered with the administration of justice because they were aimed at forcing Judge Keller to recuse himself in cases where Yagman appears as counsel. Judge-shopping doubtless disrupts the proper functioning of the judicial system and may be disciplined. But after conducting an independent examination of the record to ensure that the district court's ruling "does not constitute a forbidden intrusion on the field of free expression," we conclude that the sanction imposed here cannot stand.

Yagman's criticism of Judge Keller was harsh and intemperate, and in no way to be condoned. It has long been established, however, that a party cannot force a judge to recuse himself by engaging in personal attacks on the judge. . . .

Criticism from a party's attorney creates an even remoter danger that a judge will disqualify himself because the federal recusal statutes, in all but the most extreme circumstances, require a showing that the judge is (or appears to be) biased or prejudiced against a party, not counsel. . . .

Notwithstanding this well-settled rule, judges occasionally do remove themselves voluntarily from cases as a result of harsh criticism from attorneys. As the district court recognized, then, a lawyer's vociferous criticism of a judge could interfere with the random assignment of judges. But a mere possibility—or even the probability—of harm does not amount to a clear and present danger: "The danger must not be remote or even probable; it must immediately imperil."

We conclude that "the danger under this record to fair judicial administration has not the clearness and immediacy necessary to close the door of permissible public comment." As noted above, firm and long-standing precedent establishes that unflattering remarks like Yagman's cannot force the disqualification of the judge at whom they are aimed. The question remains whether the possibility of voluntary recusal is so great as to amount to a clear and present danger. We believe it is not. Public criticism of judges and the decisions they make is not unusual, yet this seldom leads to judicial recusal. Judge Real, for example, despite receiving harsh criticism from Yagman, did not recuse himself in *Yagman v. Republic Ins.*, where Yagman was not merely the lawyer but also a party to the proceedings. Federal judges are well aware that "[s]ervice as a public official means that one may not be viewed favorably by every member of the public," and that they've been granted "the extraordinary protections of life tenure to shield them from such pressures." Because Yagman's statements do not pose a clear and present danger to the proper functioning of the courts, we conclude that the district court erred in sanctioning Yagman for interfering with the administration of justice.

NOTES

1.   Yagman's discipline was lifted. Does that provide comfort to lawyers who believe they have valid criticism of judges to offer? Here, a federal district court authorized a two-year suspension based on Yagman's conduct; it took a year and substantial amicus participation by a lengthy list of First Amendment experts to get the discipline reversed. Would you roll the dice on making such public comments, even if it turns out (as it did here) that they are constitutionally protected?

2.   One author argues that the First Amendment standards reflected in *Yagman* are ignored by most state courts, which routinely impose sanctions "for attorney speech that brings the judiciary into disrepute," often requiring

lawyers to bear the burden of proving the truth of their statements rather than imposing the burden of proving falsity on the disciplinary authority. Margaret Tarkington, *The Truth Be Damned: The First Amendment, Attorney Speech, and Judicial Reputation* (Sept. 18, 2008), *available at* http://ssrn.com/ abstract=1270268. Does shielding the judiciary from criticism really protect the integrity of the judicial process? Consider, for example, *In re Atanga*, 636 N.E.2d 1253 (Ind. 1994). Attorney Atanga was a sole practitioner who had been in practice for two years. He agreed to represent an indigent client in a criminal matter; the client had already been scheduled for a probation revocation hearing on December 6. Atanga and the prosecutor agreed to reschedule the hearing because Atanga had another commitment on December 6, but subsequently the prosecutor wanted to move the hearing back to December 6. The prosecutor, *ex parte*, got the court to reschedule the hearing to December 6. Atanga sought a continuance, which was denied, and told the court clerk that he could not attend the hearing because of his prior commitment. When Atanga did not appear on December 6, the judge held him in contempt and had him arrested. Atanga was held in the jail overnight, and required to come into court, in the presence of his client, wearing jail attire. Some time after the proceeding was over, a reporter for the local ACLU newsletter asked Atanga about the situation; Atanga said that he though the judge was "ignorant, insecure, and a racist." Atanga was charged with violating Rule 8.2(a). While the court agreed that the judge's behavior was "unusual," that *ex parte* communications between the prosecution and the court "should not be done as matter of course," and that jailing the attorney was a "questionable practice," it also found that Atanga's comments "clearly draw disfavor to the integrity of the court and there is no basis upon which to conclude that the comments were anything else but reckless." *Id*. at 1258. Atanga was suspended for thirty days. A dissenting judge noted that there was "an insufficient factual basis upon which to find that Mr. Atanga's remarks were made with 'reckless disregard as to [their] truth or falsity'" and noted that Mr. Atanga provided extraordinary service to the state's indigent criminal defendants and to the bar; he was at the time the president-elect of his county bar association. *Id*. at 1261.

3. Yagman's comments may have been protected, but the court variously terms them as "harsh" and "intemperate." Were his statements that the judge was "anti-semitic" and that he was "drunk on the bench" damaging to the justice system? If so, why was it improper to punish him? On the other hand, if judges are ignorant, insecure, or racist, why is it improper to say so? We do not ordinarily permit the law to suppress speech to preserve the public's good opinion of entities that deserve criticism. Do the ethics rules in effect, permit this with regard to the judiciary?

4. Model Rule 8.2 provides that "[A] lawyer shall not make a statement that the lawyer knows to be false or with reckless disregard as to its truth or falsity concerning the qualifications or integrity of a judge, adjudicatory officer or public legal officer, or of a candidate for election or appointment to judicial or legal office." Does the rule adequately address the constitutional questions involved? the policy questions?

5. Rules prohibiting conduct that "impugns the integrity of the Court" or "interferes with the administration of justice" seem vague enough. What

about a rule that prohibits "undignified or discourteous conduct toward the tribunal" or requires that a lawyer "treat with courtesy and respect all persons involved in the legal process"? In *Grievance Administrator v. Fieger*, 719 N.W.2d 123 (Mich. 2006), Geoffrey Fieger was reprimanded for violating these rules through the making of "uncontestedly discourteous, undignified, and disrespectful" statements about the appellate judges who had heard and decided his client's case. These statements, made on Fieger's radio show, included a suggestion that the judges "[k]iss [his] ass," that they were "jackass Court of Appeals judges," and that the judges had "changed their name from, you know, Adolf Hitler and Goebbels." The state court upheld the constitutionality of the rules and the imposition of discipline on Fieger, stating, "The rules are a call to discretion and civility, not to silence or censorship, and they do not even purport to prohibit criticism." In a subsequent decision, the Federal District Court for the Eastern District of Michigan struck down the rules (known as the "courtesy and civility provisions") as overly broad and vague. *Fieger v. Michigan Supreme Court*, 2007 WL 2571975 (E.D. Mich. 2007). Why shouldn't the disciplinary system be able to prevent the kind of offensive and scurrilous statements that Fieger made?

E. DUTIES TO THE LEGAL SYSTEM: THE DUTY TO PERFORM PRO BONO SERVICE

Model Rule 6.1 purports to create a duty "to provide legal services to those unable to pay." Read the rule carefully, however. Does the rule create an obligation, or just an aspirational goal? The states, for the most part, follow the Model Rules in this regard. Why? If pro bono service is important, why not require it? The demand for free legal services for indigent persons certainly exceeds the supply. Should practicing lawyers have an obligation to serve some of those unmet needs? Or would such a requirement simply facilitate what in some cases might be the provision of substandard legal services to those clients? Does suggesting that the legal service needs of the poor in our country should be met through the occasional volunteer efforts of otherwise-employed lawyers understate the problem and overvalue the solution? Even if the requirement were a mere drop in the bucket, it might make a significant difference to those clients served by it.

Some states have devised creative ways of encouraging pro bono service without mandating it. Florida, for example, treats pro bono service as "aspirational rather than mandatory," Florida Bar Rule 4–6.1(a), but requires admitted lawyers to report whether or not they have completed the "aspirational" pro bono expectation. Florida Bar Rule 4–6.1(d). While failing to perform pro bono service will not subject lawyers to discipline in Florida, failing to report whether or not they have performed that service will. A lawyer can satisfy the aspirational expectation through the performance of 20 hours of service annually, or by donating $350 per year to a legal aid organization. What do you think of that approach?

PROBLEMS

1.   Associate goes to the copy machine at the office and finds on it a letter from a client asking the firm's senior partner, Partner, to explain why the client's trust account was overdrawn. Must Associate report Partner to the bar? *See* Debra Cassens Weiss, *A Letter Left on a Copier Spurs an Associate's Ethical Response*, ABA Journal, June 17, 2008.

2.   When new evidence called into question the prior murder convictions of two individuals, Prosecutor was asked to reexamine the evidence. Prosecutor determined that the two men were not guilty, that their convictions should be overturned, and that they should not be retried. Prosecutor's supervisor disagreed and insisted that Prosecutor pursue the case. Prosecutor did so, but deliberately helped the other side to win. He told the defense lawyers what strategy to pursue, tracked down witnesses, and in other respects assisted the defense. Did Prosecutor act properly? *See* Benjamin Weiser, *Doubting Case, a Prosecutor Helped the Defense*, New York Times, June 23, 2008.

CHAPTER 13

DUTIES TO THE GUILD: REGULATION OF ADVERTISING AND SOLICITATION

■ ■ ■

Most of the rules that we have considered so far, and the duties that they impose on lawyers, reflect concerns about and obligations towards other parties: clients, the courts, or third persons. But some regulation of lawyers reflects more parochial concerns: some rules governing lawyers are meant to protect lawyers.

Constraints on advertising and solicitation are complex. Some regulation of advertising and solicitation by lawyers reflects the kind of client-centered concerns that motivate regulation in other contexts: protecting laypersons from lawyers' supposedly superior powers of persuasion, or avoiding situations in which overreaching or self-dealing by lawyers is likely to occur. But some regulation seems directed more at the protection of the profession (or certain sectors of the profession) than innocent third parties. Do we restrict and regulate attorney advertising because it is bad for potential clients, or because it is bad for lawyers? Is this regulation in the public interest, or in the profession's interest? Even if society were in agreement that advertising and solicitation by lawyers should be prohibited, such regulation of speech invokes constitutional values. How should those interests be accommodated?

A. ADVERTISING

For a long time, lawyers were forbidden to advertise. The 1908 Canons of Professional Ethics prohibited attorney advertising outright. Canon 27 provided: "The most worthy and effective advertisement possible, even for a young lawyer, is the establishment of a well-merited reputation for professional capacity and fidelity to trust.... [S]olicitation of business by circulars or advertisements, or by personal communications, or interviews not warranted by personal relations, is unprofessional." Regulations like this protected a particular vision of lawyers, in which lawyers traveled in the same social circles as their clients and obtained their clients through their reputations in their communities. That made entry into the profession for newcomers or outsiders extremely difficult. As Jerold S. Auerbach wrote in *Unequal Justice: Lawyers and Social Change in Modern America* 43 (1976),

The prohibition against advertising instructed lawyers that success flowed from their 'character and conduct,' not from aggressive solicitation. It thereby rewarded the lawyer whose law-firm partners and social contacts made advertising unnecessary at the same time that it attributed inferior character and unethical behavior to attorneys who could not afford to sit passively in their office awaiting clients. . . . The lower a fee a lawyer earned, and the less discreet he was in pursuit of it, the more likely it was that his 'money getting' activities would be scrutinized and criticized.

Early cases disciplining lawyers for advertising are consistent with this view. Consider, for example, *In re Schwarz*, 161 N.Y.S. 1079 (App. Div. 1916). Schwarz, who did collections work, used a variety of circulars, solicitation letters and advertisements to encourage potential clients to engage his services. The court described the advertisements in detail, and deemed them "typical of modern advertising business methods," but "utterly abhorrent to professional notions or standards." "Unless the ancient and honorable profession of the law, whose practitioners are officers of the court of the highest fiduciary character . . . is to be degraded to the rank of a quack medicine business enterprise, the advertising and business solicitation methods here under review must be emphatically and absolutely condemned." *Id.* at 1083. Schwarz was severely censured; a dissenting judge was of the view that nothing short of disbarment would be an appropriate punishment.[1]

These restrictions did not only affect isolated or powerless lawyers. In *In re Connelly*, 240 N.Y.S.2d 126 (App. Div. 1st Dep't 1963), several partners in a New York law firm were disciplined for cooperating in the preparation of an article in *Life* magazine that was a behind-the-scenes look at their firm. The article, the court scolded, had the "objectionable effect" of constituting "a portrayal of certain causes which the respondents' firm has been engaged in, the manner of conduct of the same, the magnitude of the interests involved, and the importance of its position in the practice of law." *Id.* at 136. "There can be no justification for the participation and acquiescence by an attorney in the development and publication of an article which, on its face, plainly amounts to a self-interest[ed] and unethical presentation of his achievements and capabilities." *Id.* at 138.

As long as advertising was not considered "speech," it had no constitutional protection and the profession was free to prohibit it. That changed after the following case:

BATES v. STATE BAR OF ARIZONA
433 U.S. 350 (1977)

MR. JUSTICE BLACKMUN delivered the opinion of the Court.

As part of its regulation of the Arizona Bar, the Supreme Court of that State has imposed and enforces a disciplinary rule that restricts advertis-

---

1. Attorney Schwarz's misadventures continued. He was again sanctioned for solicitation, and this time the Appellate Division, New York's intermediate appellate court, ordered him disbarred. *In re Schwarz*, 186 N.Y.S. 535 (App. Div. 1921). This order was affirmed over the dissent of three judges of the New York Court of Appeals, the state's highest court, including then-Judge Cardozo. 132 N.E. 921 (N.Y. 1921).

ing by attorneys. This case presents whether the operation of the rule violates the First Amendment, made applicable to the State through the Fourteenth.

I

Appellants John R. Bates and Van O'Steen are attorneys licensed to practice law in the State of Arizona. As such, they are members of the appellee, the State Bar of Arizona. After admission to the bar in 1972, appellants worked as attorneys with the Maricopa County Legal Aid Society.

In March 1974, appellants left the Society and opened a law office, which they call a 'legal clinic,' in Phoenix. Their aim was to provide legal services at modest fees to persons of moderate income who did not qualify for governmental legal aid. In order to achieve this end, they would accept only routine matters, such as uncontested divorces, uncontested adoptions, simple personal bankruptcies, and changes of name, for which costs could be kept down by extensive use of paralegals, automatic typewriting equipment, and standardized forms and office procedures. More complicated cases, such as contested divorces, would not be accepted. Because appellants set their prices so as to have a relatively low return on each case they handled, they depended on substantial volume.

After conducting their practice in this manner for two years, appellants concluded that their practice and clinical concept could not survive unless the availability of legal services at low cost was advertised and in particular, fees were advertised. Consequently, in order to generate the necessary flow of business, appellants on February 22, 1976, placed an advertisement in the Arizona Republic, a daily newspaper of general circulation in the Phoenix metropolitan area. [T]he advertisement stated that appellants were offering 'legal services at very reasonable fees,' and listed their fees for certain services.

Appellants concede that the advertisement constituted a clear violation of Disciplinary Rule 2–101(B). The disciplinary rule provides in part:

> (B) A lawyer shall not publicize himself, or his partner, or associate, or any other lawyer affiliated with him or his firm, as a lawyer through newspaper or magazine advertisements, radio or television announcements, display advertisements in the city or telephone directories or other means of commercial publicity, nor shall he authorize or permit others to do so in his behalf.

Upon the filing of a complaint initiated by the president of the State Bar, a hearing was held.... The committee recommended that each of the appellants be suspended from the practice of law for not less than six months. Upon further review by the Board of Governors of the State Bar

... the Board recommended only a one-week suspension for each appellant, the weeks to run consecutively.

Appellants ... then sought review in the Supreme Court of Arizona, arguing, among other things, that the ... rule infringed their First Amendment rights. The court rejected [the] claim....

Turning to the First Amendment issue, the plurality noted that restrictions on professional advertising have survived constitutional challenge in the past.... Although recognizing that *Virginia Pharmacy Board v. Virginia Consumer Council*, 425 U.S. 748 (1976), and *Bigelow v. Virginia*, 421 U.S. 809 (1975), held that commercial speech was entitled to certain protection under the First Amendment, the plurality focused on passages in those opinions acknowledging that special considerations might bear on the advertising of professional services by lawyers. The plurality apparently was of the view that the older decisions dealing with professional advertising survived these recent cases unscathed, and held that Disciplinary Rule 2–101(B) passed First Amendment muster....

We noted probable jurisdiction.

II

[In Part II, the court held that the Sherman Act did not preclude Arizona's advertising regulation.]

III

The First Amendment

A

Last Term, in *Virginia Pharmacy Board v. Virginia Consumer Council*, the Court considered the validity under the First Amendment of a Virginia statute declaring that a pharmacist was guilty of 'unprofessional conduct' if he advertised prescription drug prices. The pharmacist would then be subject to a monetary penalty or the suspension or revocation of his license. The statute thus effectively prevented the advertising of prescription drug price information. We recognized that the pharmacist who desired to advertise did not wish to report any particularly newsworthy fact or to comment on any cultural, philosophical, or political subject; his desired communication was characterized simply: "I will sell you the X prescription drug at the Y price." Nonetheless, we held that commercial speech of that kind was entitled to the protection of the First Amendment.

Our analysis began with the observation that our cases long have protected speech even though it is in the form of a paid advertisement.... [A] consideration of competing interests reinforced our view that such speech should not be withdrawn from protection merely because it proposed a mundane commercial transaction.... The listener's interest is substantial: the consumer's concern for the free flow of commercial speech often may be far keener than his concern for urgent political dialogue. Moreover, significant societal interests are served by such speech. Advertising, though entirely commercial, may often carry information of import to significant issues of the day. And commercial speech serves to inform the public of the availability, nature, and prices of products and services, and thus performs an indispensable role in the allocation of resources in a free enterprise system. In short, such speech serves individual and societal interests in assuring informed and reliable decisionmaking.

Arrayed against these substantial interests in the free flow of commercial speech were a number of proffered justifications for the advertising ban. Central among them were claims that the ban was essential to the maintenance of professionalism among licensed pharmacists. It was asserted that advertising would create price competition that might cause the pharmacist to economize at the customer's expense. He might reduce or eliminate the truly professional portions of his services: the maintenance and packaging of drugs so as to assure their effectiveness, and the supplementation on occasion of the prescribing physician's advice as to use. Moreover, it was said, advertising would cause consumers to price-shop, thereby undermining the pharmacist's effort to monitor the drug use of a regular customer so as to ensure that the prescribed drug would not provoke an allergic reaction or be incompatible with another substance the customer was consuming. Finally, it was argued that advertising would reduce the image of the pharmacist as a skilled and specialized craftsman, an image that was said to attract talent to the profession and to reinforce the good habits of those in it to that of a mere shopkeeper.

Although acknowledging that the State had a strong interest in maintaining professionalism among pharmacists, this Court concluded that the proffered justifications were inadequate to support the advertising ban.... And we observed that 'on close inspection it is seen that the State's protectiveness of its citizens rests in large measure on the advantages of their being kept in ignorance.' But we noted the presence of a potent alternative to this 'highly paternalistic' approach: 'That alternative is to assume that this information is not in itself harmful, that people will perceive their own best interests if only they are well enough informed, and that the best means to that end is to open the channels of communication rather than to close them.' The choice between the dangers of suppressing information and the dangers arising from its free flow was seen as precisely the choice 'that the First Amendment makes for us.'

We have set out this detailed summary of the *Pharmacy* opinion because the conclusion that Arizona's disciplinary rule is violative of the First Amendment might be said to flow a fortiori from it. Like the Virginia statutes, the disciplinary rule serves to inhibit the free flow of commercial information and to keep the public in ignorance. Because of the possibility, however, that the differences among professions might bring different constitutional considerations into play, we specifically reserved judgment as to other professions.

In the instant case we are confronted with the arguments directed explicitly toward the regulation of advertising by licensed attorneys.

B

The issue presently before us is a narrow one. First, we need not address the peculiar problems associated with advertising claims relating to the quality of legal services. Such claims probably are not susceptible of precise measurement or verification and, under some circumstances, might well be deceptive or misleading to the public, or even false. Appellee does not suggest, nor do we perceive, that appellants' advertisement contained claims, extravagant or otherwise, as to the quality of services. Accordingly, we leave that issue for another day. Second, we also need not resolve the problems associated with in-person solicitation of clients at the hospital room or the accident site, or in any other situation that breeds undue influence by attorneys or their agents or 'runners.' Activity of that kind might well pose dangers of overreaching and misrepresentation not encountered in newspaper announcement advertising. Hence, this issue also is not before us. Third, we note that appellee's criticism of advertising by attorneys does not apply with much force to some of the basic factual content of advertising: information as to the attorney's name, address, and telephone number, office hours, and the like. The American Bar Association itself has a provision in its current Code of Professional Responsibility that would allow the disclosure of such information, and more, in the classified section of the telephone directory. We recognize, however, that an advertising diet limited to such spartan fare would provide scant nourishment.

The heart of the dispute before us today is whether lawyers also may constitutionally advertise the prices at which certain routine services will be performed. Numerous justifications are proffered for the restriction of such price advertising. We consider each in turn:

1. The Adverse Effect on Professionalism. Appellee places particular emphasis on the adverse effects that it feels price advertising will have on the legal profession. The key to professionalism, it is argued, is the sense of pride that involvement in the discipline generates. It is claimed that price advertising will bring about commercialization, which will undermine the attorney's sense of dignity and self-worth. The hustle of the marketplace will adversely affect the profession's service orientation, and irreparably damage the delicate balance between the lawyer's need to earn and his obligation selflessly to serve. Advertising is also said to erode the client's trust in his attorney: Once the client perceives that the lawyer is motivated by profit, his confidence that the attorney is acting out of a commitment to the client's welfare is jeopardized. And advertising is said to tarnish the dignified public image of the profession.

We recognize, of course, and commend the spirit of public service with which the profession of law is practiced and to which it is dedicated. The present Members of this Court, licensed attorneys all, could not feel otherwise. And we would have reason to pause if we felt that our decision today would undercut that spirit. But we find the postulated connection between advertising and the erosion of true professionalism to be severely strained. At its core, the argument presumes that attorneys must conceal from themselves and from their clients the real-life fact that lawyers earn their livelihood at the bar. We suspect that few attorneys engage in such self-deception. And rare is the client, moreover, even one of the modest means, who enlists the aid of an attorney with the expectation that his services will be rendered free of charge. . . .

Moreover, the assertion that advertising will diminish the attorney's reputation in the community is open to question. Bankers and engineers advertise, and yet these professions are not regarded as undignified. In fact, it has been suggested that the failure of lawyers to advertise creates public disillusionment with the profession. The absence of advertising may be seen to reflect the profession's failure to reach out and serve the community: Studies reveal that many persons do not obtain counsel even when they perceive a need because of the feared price of services or because of an inability to locate a competent attorney. Indeed, cynicism with regard to the profession may be created by the fact that it long has publicly eschewed advertising, while condoning the actions of the attorney who structures his social or civic associations so as to provide contacts with potential clients.

It appears that the ban on advertising originated as a rule of etiquette and not as a rule of ethics. Early lawyers in Great Britain viewed the law as a form of public service, rather than as a means of earning a living, and they looked down on 'trade' as unseemly. Eventually, the attitude toward advertising fostered by this view evolved into an aspect of the ethics of the profession. But habit and tradition are not in themselves an adequate answer to a constitutional challenge. In this day, we do not belittle the person who earns his living by the strength of his arm or the force of his mind. Since the belief that lawyers are somehow 'above' trade has become an anachronism, the historical foundation for the advertising restraint has crumbled.

2. The Inherently Misleading Nature of Attorney Advertising. It is argued that advertising of legal services inevitably will be misleading (a) because such services are so individualized with regard to content and quality as to prevent informed comparison on the basis of an advertisement, (b) because the consumer of legal services is unable to determine in advance just what services he needs, and (c) because advertising by attorneys will highlight irrelevant factors and fail to show the relevant factor of skill.

We are not persuaded that restrained professional advertising by lawyers inevitably will be misleading. Although many services performed by attorneys are indeed unique, it is doubtful that any attorney would or could advertise fixed prices for services of that type. The only services that lend themselves to advertising are the routine ones: the uncontested divorce, the simple adoption, the uncontested personal bankruptcy, the change of name, and the like—the very services advertised by appellants. Although the precise service demanded in each task may vary slightly, and although legal services are not fungible, these facts do not make advertising misleading so long as the attorney does the necessary work at the advertised price. The argument that legal services are so unique that fixed rates cannot meaningfully be established is refuted by the record in this case: The appellee State Bar itself sponsors a Legal Services Program in which the participating attorneys agree to perform services like those advertised by the appellants at standardized rates.... We thus find of little force the assertion that advertising is misleading because of an inherent lack of standardization in legal services.

The second component of the argument that advertising ignores the diagnostic role fares little better. It is unlikely that many people go to an attorney merely to ascertain if they have a clean bill of legal health. Rather, attorneys are likely to be employed to perform specific tasks. Although the client may not know the detail involved in performing the task, he no doubt is able to identify the service he desires at the level of generality to which advertising lends itself.

The third component is not without merit: Advertising does not provide a complete foundation on which to select an attorney. But it seems peculiar to deny the consumer, on the ground that the information is incomplete, at least some of the relevant information needed to reach an informed decision. The alternative—the prohibition of advertising—serves only to restrict the information that flows to consumers. Moreover, the argument assumes that the public is not sophisticated enough to realize the limitations of advertising, and that the public is better kept in ignorance than trusted with correct but incomplete information. We suspect the argument rests on an underestimation of the public. In any event, we view as dubious any justification that is based on the benefits of public ignorance....

3. The Adverse Effect on the Administration of Justice. Advertising is said to have the undesirable effect of stirring up litigation. The judicial machinery is designed to serve those who feel sufficiently aggrieved to bring forward their claims. Advertising, it is argued, serves to encourage the assertion of legal rights in the courts, thereby undesirably unsettling societal repose....

But advertising by attorneys is not an unmitigated source of harm to the administration of justice. It may offer great benefits. Although advertising might increase the use of the judicial machinery, we cannot accept the notion that it is always better for a person to suffer a wrong silently than to redress it by legal action.... Advertising is the traditional mechanism in a free-market economy for a supplier to inform a potential purchaser of the availability and terms of exchange. The disciplinary rule at issue likely has served to burden access to legal services, particularly for the not-quite-poor and the unknowledgeable. A rule allowing restrained advertising would be in accord with the bar's obligation to 'facilitate the process of intelligent selection of lawyers, and to assist in making legal services fully available.' ABA Code of Professional Responsibility EC 2–1 (1976).

4. The Undesirable Economic Effects of Advertising. It is claimed that advertising will increase the overhead costs of the profession, and that these costs then will be passed along to consumers in the form of increased fees. Moreover, it is claimed that the additional cost of practice will create a substantial entry barrier, deterring or preventing young attorneys from penetrating the market and entrenching the position of the bar's established members.

These two arguments seem dubious at best. Neither distinguishes lawyers from others, and neither appears relevant to the First Amendment. The ban on advertising serves to increase the difficulty of discovering the lowest cost seller of acceptable ability. As a result, to this extent attorneys are isolated from competition, and the incentive to price competitively is reduced. Although it is true that the effect of advertising on the price of services has not been demonstrated, there is revealing evidence with regard to products; where consumers have the benefit of price advertising, retail prices often are dramatically lower than they would be without advertising. It is entirely possible that advertising will serve to reduce, not advance, the cost of legal services to the consumer.

The entry-barrier argument is equally unpersuasive. In the absence of advertising, an attorney must rely on his contacts with the community to generate a flow of business. In view of the time necessary to develop such contacts, the ban in fact serves to perpetuate the market position of established attorneys. Consideration of entry-barrier problems would urge that advertising be allowed so as to aid the new competitor in penetrating the market.

5. The Adverse Effect of Advertising on the Quality of Service. It is argued that the attorney may advertise a given 'package' of service at a set price, and will be inclined to provide, by indiscriminate use, the standard package regardless of whether it fits the client's needs.

Restraints on advertising, however, are an ineffective way of deterring shoddy work. An attorney who is inclined to cut quality will do so regardless of the rule on advertising. . . .

6. The Difficulties of Enforcement. Finally, it is argued that the wholesale restriction is justified by the problems of enforcement if any other course is taken. Because the public lacks sophistication in legal matters, it may be particularly susceptible to misleading or deceptive advertising by lawyers. . . .

It is at least somewhat incongruous for the opponents of advertising to extol the virtues and altruism of the legal profession at one point, and, at another, to assert that its members will seize the opportunity to mislead and distort. We suspect that, with advertising, most lawyers will behave as they always have: They will abide by their solemn oaths to uphold the integrity and honor of their profession and of the legal system. For every attorney who overreaches through advertising, there will be thousands of others who will be candid and honest and straightforward. And, of course, it will be in the latter's interest, as in other cases of misconduct at the bar, to assist in weeding out those few who abuse their trust.

In sum, we are not persuaded that any of the proffered justifications rise to the level of an acceptable reason for the suppression of all advertising by attorneys. . . .

IV

In holding that advertising by attorneys may not be subjected to blanket suppression, and that the advertisement at issue is protected, we, of course, do not hold that advertising by attorneys may not be regulated in any way. We mention some of the clearly permissible limitations on advertising not foreclosed by our holding.

Advertising that is false, deceptive, or misleading of course is subject to restraint. . . . In fact, because the public lacks sophistication concerning legal services, misstatements that might be overlooked or deemed unimportant in other advertising may be found quite inappropriate in legal advertising. For example, advertising claims as to the quality of services— a matter we do not address today—are not susceptible of measurement or verification; accordingly, such claims may be so likely to be misleading as to warrant restriction. Similar objections might justify restraints on in-person solicitation. We do not foreclose the possibility that some limited supplementation, by way of warning or disclaimer or the like, might be required of even an advertisement of the kind ruled upon today so as to assure that the consumer is not misled. In sum, we recognize that many of the problems in defining the boundary between deceptive and nondeceptive advertising remain to be resolved, and we expect that the bar will have a special role to play in assuring that advertising by attorneys flows both freely and cleanly.

. . . The constitutional issue in this case is only whether the State may prevent the publication in a newspaper of appellants' truthful advertisement concerning the availability and terms of routine legal services. We rule simply that the flow of such information may not be restrained, and we therefore hold the present application of the disciplinary rule against appellants to be violative of the First Amendment.

NOTES

1. *Bates* was the beginning of the Supreme Court's application of commercial speech doctrine to attorney advertising. While *Bates* restricted its holding to the advertising of prices for routine legal services, the cases following it applied the doctrine to overturn regulations restricting the mailing of announcements and the language used in advertisements, *In re RMJ*, 455 U.S. 191 (1982), the use of specialist designations, *Peel v. Attorney Registration and Disciplinary Comm'n of Illinois*, 496 U.S. 91 (1990), and newspaper advertisements targeted to clients in need of particular legal services, *Zauderer v. Office of Disciplinary Counsel*, 471 U.S. 626 (1985).

2. As the opinion reflects, regulation that prohibits false or misleading advertising is still permitted. Can a lawyer be disciplined for stating on his

letterhead that he has been "Published in Federal Reports, 3d Series," and for indicating on his website that he is "one of the elite percentage of attorneys to be published in Federal Law Reports—the large law books that contain the controlling caselaw of the United States"? *See North Carolina State Bar v. Culbertson*, 627 S.E.2d 644 (N.C.App. 2006). What about using the image of a pit bull wearing a spiked collar and the telephone number 1–800–PIT-BULL in television advertising? In *Florida Bar v. Pape*, 918 So.2d 240 (Fla. 2005), the court upheld discipline of the lawyers who used this tactic. The court concluded that the ad improperly characterized the quality of the lawyers' services, and provided depictions that are "deceptive, misleading or manipulative," because they suggested that the lawyers could engage in aggressive, vicious conduct prohibited by the rules of professional responsibility. It concluded that the advertisements "demean all lawyers and thereby harm both the legal profession and the public's trust and confidence in our system of justice." Did the court act properly?

Bates did not mean that states stopped trying to regulate attorney advertising. Far from it. Times also changed. The *Bates* vision of dispassionate advertisements in the print media providing relevant, if dull, consumer information contrasts vividly with contemporary television advertising by lawyers. Regulation of this advertising is difficult. Consider the following excerpts from the Iowa Rules of Professional Conduct. What is prohibited by these rules? Do you think they pass constitutional muster?

IOWA RULES OF PROFESSIONAL CONDUCT

Rule 32:7.1. Communications concerning a lawyer's services

(a) A lawyer shall not make a false or misleading communication about the lawyer or the lawyer's services. A communication is false or misleading if it contains a material misrepresentation of fact or law, or omits a fact necessary to make the statement considered as a whole not materially misleading.

(b) A lawyer shall not communicate with the public using statements that are unverifiable. In addition, advertising permitted under these rules shall not rely on emotional appeal or contain any statement or claim relating to the quality of the lawyer's legal services.

COMMENT

. . . [3] A lawyer should ensure that information contained in any advertising which the lawyer publishes, or causes to be published, is relevant, is dignified, is disseminated in an objective and understandable fashion, and would facilitate the prospective client's ability to make an informed choice about legal representation. A lawyer should strive to communicate such information without undue emphasis upon style and advertising stratagems that hinder rather than facilitate intelligent selection of counsel. Appeal should not be made to the prospective client's emotions, prejudices, or personal likes or dislikes. Care should be exercised to ensure that false hopes of success or undue expectations are not communicated. Only unambiguous information relevant to a layperson's decision regarding legal rights or the selection of counsel, provided in ways that comport with the dignity of the profession and do not demean the administration of justice, is appropriate in public communications.

New York State's recent attempt to regulate attorney advertising was challenged in the following case. What do you think of the advertisements the state was attempting to regulate here? What do you think of the regulatory attempt to address them?

ALEXANDER v. CAHILL
2007 WL 2120024 (N.D.N.Y. 2007)

SCULLIN, SENIOR JUDGE.

I. INTRODUCTION

Plaintiffs filed their Complaint on February 1, 2007, seeking a declaratory judgment that certain provisions of New York's amended rules on attorney advertising violate the First Amendment and requesting a permanent injunction prohibiting Defendants from enforcing those amendments.... [T]he parties further agreed to resolve their differences by way of summary judgment. The following constitutes the Court's written determination of these motions.

II. BACKGROUND

Plaintiff James L. Alexander is a New York-licensed attorney and managing partner of Plaintiff Alexander & Catalano LLC, which has offices in Syracuse and Rochester. Alexander & Catalano advertises its legal services through broadcast media, print advertisements, and other forms of public media. Prior to February 1, 2007, Alexander & Catalano's commercials often contained jingles and special effects, including wisps of smoke and blue electrical currents surrounding the firm's name. A number of the firm's commercials also contained fictional or comical scenes.

Plaintiff Alexander & Catalano believes that some of its previously-used advertising techniques may violate the amended rules. Since February 1, 2007, it has stopped running many of its advertisements and has altered other advertisements in an effort to assure that it was in compliance with the amended rules. Notably, it has stopped using its slogan "the heavy hitters." Additionally, the firm has stopped running advertisements portraying its attorneys as giants towering over downtown buildings, depicting its attorneys counseling space aliens concerning an insurance dispute, and representing its attorneys running as fast as blurs to reach a client in distress....

Defendants are the Chief Counsels or Acting Chief Counsels of various departmental or district disciplinary committees. In their official roles, they are collectively charged with initiating investigations into complaints concerning attorney misbehavior....

In June 2006, the four presiding justices approved several proposed amendments to the existing disciplinary rules governing attorney advertising. The presiding justices submitted the amendments for public comment. . . . On January 4, 2007, after further revision, the presiding justices adopted the final version of the amendments, which took effect on February 1, 2007.

The amendments effect a number of significant changes to the State's previous rules on law firm advertising. The first group of amendments addresses restrictions on potentially misleading advertisements and consists of several rules:

N.Y. Comp. Codes R. & Regs. tit. 22, § 1200.6:

    (c) An advertisement shall not:

        (1) include an endorsement of, or testimonial about, a lawyer or law firm from a client with respect to a matter still pending;

        * * *

        (3) include the portrayal of a judge, the portrayal of a fictitious law firm, the use of a fictitious name to refer to lawyers not associated together in a law firm, or otherwise imply that lawyers are associated in a law firm if that is not the case;

        * * *

        (5) rely on techniques to obtain attention that demonstrate a clear and intentional lack of relevance to the selection of counsel, including the portrayal of lawyers exhibiting characteristics clearly unrelated to legal competence;

        * * *

        (7) utilize a nickname, moniker, motto or trade name that implies an ability to obtain results in a matter.

. . .

III. DISCUSSION

. . . It is well-established that attorney advertising is commercial speech that enjoys some First Amendment protection. Moreover, there is a long line of cases applying the *Central Hudson* test to attorney-advertising rules. Accordingly, the Court will analyze the State's amended rules pursuant to the test in *Central Hudson*.

Under the *Central Hudson* test, Defendants must (1) assert that there is a substantial State interest to be achieved by the restriction; (2) demonstrate that the restriction materially advances the state interest; and (3) establish that the restriction is narrowly drawn. *See Central Hudson*, 447 U.S. at 564–66. "This burden is not satisfied by mere speculation or conjecture; rather, [the defendant] . . . must demonstrate that the harms it recites are real and that its restriction will in fact alleviate them to a material degree." Some form of empirical or anecdotal evidence is usually required.[1]

N.Y. Comp. Codes R. & Regs. tit. 22, § 1200.6(c)

As noted above, amendments to § 1200.6(c) prohibit attorney advertisements from containing endorsements and testimonials about matters still pending, portrayals of judges, techniques to obtain attention that lack relevance to selecting counsel, portrayals of attorneys with characteristics unrelated to legal competence, and use of a nickname, moniker, motto, or trade name that implies an ability to obtain results in a matter.

a. Does the State have a substantial interest?

Defendants assert that "[t]he State has a substantial interest in encouraging the clean flow of truthful, helpful, relevant, verifiable information about attorney services and, conversely, restricting the introduction of non-truthful, unhelpful, irrelevant material." In addition, Defendants contend that the State has an interest in maintaining attorney professionalism and respect for the bar. In response, Plaintiffs assert that the restrictions are impermissibly based on the State's desire to prohibit attorney advertisements that it finds offensive or distasteful.

Defendants' essential argument that the State has a substantial interest in protecting consumers from misleading attorney advertisements is well-supported. Moreover, the parties submitted a New York State Bar Association Task Force Report, dated October 21, 2005, indicating that the State genuinely held this asserted interest:

> The Committee identified a number of key issues and problems that exist under the current attorney advertising regime. These include: [f]alse, deceptive or misleading advertisements, in print, broadcast, and on-line advertisements.... [A]lthough a very small minority of advertisements could be categorized as false or deceptive on their face, about a third of them ... were found to be deceptive.

Accordingly, the Court finds that Defendants have established that the State has a substantial interest to ensure that attorney advertisements are not misleading and, therefore, have satisfied the first *Central Hudson* prong with respect to § 1200.6(c).

b. Do the amendments materially advance the State's interest?

In support of this prong of the *Central Hudson* test, Defendants submitted two short press releases which merely summarize the new restrictions, a

---

1. Defendants assert that they are entitled to rely on common sense, history, and consensus alone to support the State's restrictions in the absence of other evidence. However, the Court notes that this "evidence" alone has not sufficed in attorney-advertising cases. In *Florida Bar v. Went for It*, 515 U.S. 618 (1995), the State of Florida presented a two-year study of attorney advertising containing statistical evidence from a consumer survey and anecdotal evidence in the form of newspaper editorials and consumer complaints. See 515 U.S. at 626–27. Moreover, precedent from other circuits shows that the proponent of a restriction must present some actual evidence beyond the unsupported assertion that the state relied on common sense, history, or consensus.

DVD recording of a Monroe County Bar Association forum considering the scope of the amendments on August 17, 2006, at which former Presiding Justice Eugene F. Pigott was a panelist, and the New York State Bar Association Task Force Report. Defendants did not submit any statistical or anecdotal evidence of consumer problems with or complaints about misleading attorney advertising. Nor did they specifically identify any studies from other jurisdictions on which the State relied in implementing the amendments. [T]he record as to this issue in this case is notably lacking.

Notwithstanding, the Court finds that the Task Force Report, by itself, is sufficient to support a finding that the State's interests are materially advanced with respect to two amendments: § 1200.6(c)(3) (prohibition on the portrayal of judges in attorney advertisements) and § 1200.6(c)(7) (prohibition on the use of trade names that imply an ability to obtain results).

Task Force Report regarding judges:

> The following, if used in public communications or communications to a prospective client, are likely to be false, deceptive or misleading: ... a communication that states or implies that the lawyer has the ability to influence improperly a court, court officer, governmental agency or government official....

Task Force Report regarding trade names:

> The Committee endorsed COSAC's continuation of the ban on use of trade names, which is also in the current DR's, believing that trade names are far too likely to be false, deceptive and misleading to consumers of legal services.

Accordingly, the Court finds that Defendants have satisfied the second *Central Hudson* prong with respect to these specific amendments.

However, Defendants have not shown how the remaining amendments of § 1200.6(c) materially advance the State's interests. The Task Force Report, rather than providing support for their adoption, recommended a different approach. For instance, the Task Force recommended imposing new disclosure and review requirements along with bolstering enforcement of the existing rules instead of imposing new content-based restrictions.

Moreover, the Task Force recommended adopting guidelines such as those that the Monroe County Bar Association issued, which would seem contrary to much of § 1200.6(c) in that they permit dramatizations, pictures, and stylistic elements that might be prohibited under § 1200.6(c)(5). In contrast to the amended rules, the Monroe County Bar Association guidelines contemplate such advertising techniques while providing guidance as to their proper use rather than seeking their wholesale prohibition. The relevant sections of the Monroe County Bar Association guidelines provide as follows:

Advertising that recreates, dramatizes or simulates situations or persons should fairly represent the underlying facts and properly disclose that they have been staged.

* * *

Pictures and other stylistic elements should be used to reinforce traditional considerations, and should not unduly frighten, inflame or otherwise manipulate viewers into ignoring rational considerations. Lawyer advertising should not be likely to shock or offend a substantial segment of the community or to foster disrespect for the law, the legal profession or the judicial system.

Since Defendants have submitted no other evidence to support this requirement, the Court finds that Defendants have not satisfied their burden on the second *Central Hudson* prong, and, therefore, it GRANTS Plaintiffs' and DENIES Defendants' motion for summary judgment on Plaintiffs' claims concerning the following amendments:

§ 1200.6(c)(1) prohibiting endorsements and testimonials from a client about a pending matter;

the portions of § 1200.6(c)(3) prohibiting the portrayal of a fictitious law firm, the use of a fictitious name to refer to lawyers not associated in a firm, or otherwise implying that lawyers are associated in a firm if that is not the case;

§ 1200.6(c)(5) prohibiting the use of techniques to obtain attention that demonstrate a clear and intentional lack of relevance to the selection of counsel, including the portrayal of lawyers exhibiting characteristics clearly unrelated to legal competence; and

the portions of § 1200.6(c)(7) prohibiting the use of a nickname, moniker, or motto that implies an ability to obtain results.

c. *Are §§ 1200.6(c)(3) and (c)(7) narrowly tailored?*

As noted above, the Court finds that Defendants have adequately justified § 1200.6(c)(3), concerning the portrayal of judges, and § 1200.6(c)(7), concerning the use of trade names that imply an ability to obtain results, under the second *Central Hudson* prong.

Under the third *Central Hudson* prong, a restriction is not narrowly drawn if it is " ' "broader than reasonably necessary to prevent the" perceived evil.' " *Peel v. Attorney Registration & Disciplinary Comm'n,* 496 U.S. 91, 107 (1990). Therefore, recognizing the value of the free flow of commercial information, the Supreme Court has stated that a state may not impose a prophylactic ban on potentially misleading speech merely to spare itself the trouble of "distinguishing the truthful from the false, the helpful from the misleading, and the harmless from the harmful." *Zauderer v. Office of Disciplinary Counsel,* 471 U.S. 626, 646 (1985).

In *Zauderer,* the Supreme Court held that a state may not categorically ban illustrations in attorney advertisements. Although the Court recognized the convenience of a blanket ban, it concluded that, due to the possibility of case-by-case enforcement, a prophylactic rule was impermissible. *See id.*; *see also Peel*, 496 U.S. at 110 (noting the possibility of requiring a disclaimer in a case involving advertising an attorney's certification as a trial specialist). Finally, in both *Zauderer* and *Peel*, the Court required the proponent of the restriction to make a showing of the need for a blanket ban rather than less restrictive means.

As written, that portion of § 1200.6(c)(3) that prohibits the portrayal of judges and that portion of § 1200.6(c)(7) that prohibits the use of trade names that imply an ability to obtain results are categorical bans. Defendants have failed to produce any evidence that measures short of categorical bans would not have sufficed to remedy the perceived risks of such advertising being misleading. There is nothing in the record to suggest that a disclaimer would have been ineffective. For portrayals of judges, the State could have required a disclaimer similar to that required for a fictional scene, which is found in § 1200.6(c)(4). For trade names implying an ability to obtain results, there is no evidence that the existing disclaimer that "[p]rior results do not guarantee a similar outcome" in § 1200.6(e) or some other similar disclaimer would have been ineffective. Finally, and very importantly, Defendants have not given the Court any reason to believe that better enforcement of the then-existing rules on a case-by-case basis, as the Task Force Report recommended, would not accomplish the desired results. Accordingly, the Court finds that Defendants have not established that these amendments are narrowly tailored. Therefore, the Court GRANTS Plaintiffs' and DENIES Defendants' motion for summary judgment on Plaintiffs' claims concerning §§ 1200.6(c)(3) and (7)....

In sum, the Court notes that it is altogether appropriate for the Appellate Division of the State of New York, having been charged by law with the responsibility of overseeing the professional conduct of attorneys admitted to practice before the courts of New York, to be concerned with the issue of attorney advertising. Without question there has been a proliferation of tasteless, and at times obnoxious, methods of attorney advertising in recent years. As a result, among other things, the public perception of the legal profession has been greatly diminished. Although the Court finds it commendable that the Appellate Division of the State of New York and the disciplinary committees that function on its behalf pursue ways to regulate the manner and means by which attorneys who choose to advertise may do so, they must be mindful of the protections such advertising has been afforded and take the necessary steps to see that the regulation of such advertising is accomplished in a manner consistent with established First Amendment jurisprudence.

NOTES

1. What do you suppose the New York rulemakers intended with these provisions? Are they appropriate? This case is currently on appeal, so this is far from the last word on the constitutionality of attorney advertising restrictions. The analytical approach the court adopts here, however, is noncontro-

versial. How does the court analyze whether an advertising restriction is an unconstitutional restraint on protected commercial speech?

2.   Do you think the kind of advertising that the Alexander firm did is good for the profession? Bad for the profession? Should states be able to regulate advertising because the rulemakers believe that some lawyers employ trashy advertising that demeans the profession? Is protecting the good image of lawyers a substantial state interest?

3.   Model Rules 7.1–7.2 deal with advertising, but advertising is an area in which many states have opted to write their own unique rules. Some require preapproval of broadcast ads. Does preapproval seem a reasonable limit on a lawyer's ability to advertise?

4.   Advertising is regulated state-by-state, but advertisements regularly can be seen in multiple jurisdictions. How should such advertising be regulated? Florida's newly revised ethical rules provide that its advertising rules apply both to lawyers admitted to practice in Florida and to out-of-state lawyers, but only if they both have a permanent presence in Florida and advertise in Florida. Florida Rules of Professional Conduct 4–7.1(b) & (c). Does this mean that a lawyer from outside Florida airing an advertisement that will be televised within Florida—perhaps on a national cable channel—is not subject to Florida's advertising regulations? If you were a lawyer from a state with a relatively restrictive advertising rule, how would you feel about the prospect that you could be disciplined for violating the rule, but out-of-state attorneys could not? Is this a sensible way to regulate advertising?

5.   Needless to say, much attorney contact with prospective clients now takes place on the Internet. The Model Rules have very little to say about regulation of attorney web pages. Do they need to? Do the rules regarding print advertising and solicitation adequately deal with the current information environment? A deleted portion of the *Alexander* decision dealt briefly with New York's blanket prohibition on pop-up ads (which the court struck down) and its requirement that a domain name that does not include the name of the lawyer or law firm include the actual name of the lawyer, and not "imply an ability to obtain results" (which the court upheld).

6.   The propriety of advertising that includes client testimonials, the subject of one of the amendments to the New York disciplinary rules at issue in *Alexander*, remains a hotly disputed topic. Can a lawyer use a televised advertisement in which a client (perhaps a celebrity, perhaps just a satisfied customer) states that she was pleased with the services she received from the lawyer? Before the amendments to the disciplinary rules, a New York ethics opinion, *N.Y. State Bar Ethics Op. 792* (2006), had concluded that celebrity testimonials were permissible as long as they were not "false, deceptive or misleading" and the celebrity was not paid for the testimonial. *Compare* Arkansas Rule 7.1(d) (advertisement is false or misleading if it "contains a testimonial or endorsement").

B.   SOLICITATION OF CLIENTS

Advertising is one way to obtain clients, but it's far from the only way. Lawyers have tried a range of techniques to attract clients, including

in-person solicitation, mail solicitation, and, most recently, Internet solicitation. What concerns do you have about these various methods of
attracting clients? Are there dangers involved in them for potential
clients? Are there advantages as well? Should these methods of soliciting
clients be subject to strict regulation? Are these approaches enough like
advertising that the same constitutional concerns come into play?

1. IN–PERSON SOLICITATION

You learn that a person in your town has been in a car accident and
suffered serious injuries. You go to the hospital, locate the patient, and
from the bedside urge her to hire you to represent her in her personal
injury lawsuit. Have you behaved properly? *See* Model Rule 7.3.

Restrictions on in-person solicitation are ubiquitous. Does the following case suggest why?

OHRALIK v. OHIO STATE BAR ASSOCIATION
436 U.S. 447 (1978)

MR. JUSTICE POWELL delivered the opinion of the Court.

In *Bates v. State Bar of Arizona*, 433 U.S. 350 (1977), this Court held that
truthful advertising of "routine" legal services is protected by the First
and Fourteenth Amendments against blanket prohibition by a State. The
Court expressly reserved the question of the permissible scope of regulation of "in-person solicitation of clients—at the hospital room or the
accident site, or in any other situation that breeds undue influence—by
attorneys or their agents or 'runners.' " *Id.*, at 366. Today we answer part
of the question so reserved, and hold that the State—or the Bar acting
with state authorization—constitutionally may discipline a lawyer for
soliciting clients in person, for pecuniary gain, under circumstances likely
to pose dangers that the State has a right to prevent.

I

Appellant, a member of the Ohio Bar, lives in Montville, Ohio. Until
recently he practiced law in Montville and Cleveland. On February 13,
1974, while picking up his mail at the Montville Post Office, appellant
learned from the postmaster's brother about an automobile accident that
had taken place on February 2 in which Carol McClintock, a young woman
with whom appellant was casually acquainted, had been injured. Appellant
made a telephone call to Ms. McClintock's parents, who informed him that
their daughter was in the hospital. Appellant suggested that he might visit
Carol in the hospital. Mrs. McClintock assented to the idea, but requested
that appellant first stop by at her home.

During appellant's visit with the McClintocks, they explained that their
daughter had been driving the family automobile on a local road when she
was hit by an uninsured motorist. Both Carol and her passenger, Wanda
Lou Holbert, were injured and hospitalized. In response to the McClin-

tocks' expression of apprehension that they might be sued by Holbert, appellant explained that Ohio's guest statute would preclude such a suit. When appellant suggested to the McClintocks that they hire a lawyer, Mrs. McClintock retorted that such a decision would be up to Carol, who was 18 years old and would be the beneficiary of a successful claim.

Appellant proceeded to the hospital, where he found Carol lying in traction in her room. After a brief conversation about her condition, appellant told Carol he would represent her and asked her to sign an agreement. Carol said she would have to discuss the matter with her parents. She did not sign the agreement, but asked appellant to have her parents come to see her. Appellant also attempted to see Wanda Lou Holbert, but learned that she had just been released from the hospital. He then departed for another visit with the McClintocks.

On his way appellant detoured to the scene of the accident, where he took a set of photographs. He also picked up a tape recorder, which he concealed under his raincoat before arriving at the McClintocks' residence. Once there, he re-examined their automobile insurance policy, discussed with them the law applicable to passengers, and explained the consequences of the fact that the driver who struck Carol's car was an uninsured motorist. Appellant discovered that the McClintocks' insurance policy would provide benefits of up to $12,500 each for Carol and Wanda Lou under an uninsured-motorist clause. Mrs. McClintock acknowledged that both Carol and Wanda Lou could sue for their injuries, but recounted to appellant that "Wanda swore up and down she would not do it." The McClintocks also told appellant that Carol had phoned to say that appellant could "go ahead" with her representation. Two days later appellant returned to Carol's hospital room to have her sign a contract, which provided that he would receive one-third of her recovery.

In the meantime, appellant obtained Wanda Lou's name and address from the McClintocks after telling them he wanted to ask her some questions about the accident. He then visited Wanda Lou at her home, without having been invited. He again concealed his tape recorder and recorded most of the conversation with Wanda Lou. After a brief, unproductive inquiry about the facts of the accident, appellant told Wanda Lou that he was representing Carol and that he had a "little tip" for Wanda Lou: the McClintocks' insurance policy contained an uninsured-motorist clause which might provide her with a recovery of up to $12,500. The young woman, who was 18 years of age and not a high school graduate at the time, replied to appellant's query about whether she was going to file a claim by stating that she really did not understand what was going on. Appellant offered to represent her, also, for a contingent fee of one-third of any recovery, and Wanda Lou stated "O. K."

Wanda's mother attempted to repudiate her daughter's oral assent the following day, when appellant called on the telephone to speak to Wanda. Mrs. Holbert informed appellant that she and her daughter did not want to sue anyone or to have appellant represent them, and that if they decided to sue they would consult their own lawyer. Appellant insisted that Wanda had entered into a binding agreement. A month later Wanda confirmed in writing that she wanted neither to sue nor to be represented by appellant. She requested that appellant notify the insurance company that he was not her lawyer, as the company would not release a check to her until he did so. Carol also eventually discharged appellant. Although another lawyer represented her in concluding a settlement with the insurance company, she paid appellant one-third of her recovery in settlement of his lawsuit against her for breach of contract.

Both Carol McClintock and Wanda Lou Holbert filed complaints against appellant with the Grievance Committee of the Geauga County Bar Association. The County Bar Association referred the grievance to appellee, which filed a formal complaint with the Board of Commissioners on Grievances and Discipline of the Supreme Court of Ohio. After a hearing, the Board found that appellant had violated Disciplinary Rules (DR) 2–103(A) and 2–104(A) of the Ohio Code of Professional Responsibility. The Board rejected appellant's defense that his conduct was protected under the First and Fourteenth Amendments. The Supreme Court of Ohio adopted the findings of the Board, reiterated that appellant's conduct was not constitutionally protected, and increased the sanction of a public reprimand recommended by the Board to indefinite suspension.

DR 2–103(A) of the Ohio Code (1970) provides:

> A lawyer shall not recommend employment, as a private practitioner, of himself, his partner, or associate to a non-lawyer who has not sought his advice regarding employment of a lawyer.

DR 2–104(A) (1970) provides in relevant part:

> A lawyer who has given unsolicited advice to a layman that he should obtain counsel or take legal action shall not accept employment resulting from that advice, except that:
>
> > (1) A lawyer may accept employment by a close friend, relative, former client (if the advice is germane to the former employment), or one whom the lawyer reasonably believes to be a client.

The decision in *Bates* was handed down after the conclusion of proceedings in the Ohio Supreme Court. We noted probable jurisdiction in this case to consider the scope of protection of a form of commercial speech, and an aspect of the State's authority to regulate and discipline members of the bar, not considered in *Bates*. We now affirm the judgment of the Supreme Court of Ohio.

II

The solicitation of business by a lawyer through direct, in-person communication with the prospective client has long been viewed as inconsistent with the profession's ideal of the attorney-client relationship and as posing a significant potential for harm to the prospective client. It has been proscribed by the organized Bar for many years. Last Term the Court ruled that the justifications for prohibiting truthful, "restrained" advertising concerning "the availability and terms of routine legal services" are insufficient to override society's interest, safeguarded by the First and Fourteenth Amendments, in assuring the free flow of commercial information. *Bates*, 433 U.S., at 384. The balance struck in *Bates* does not predetermine the outcome in this case. The entitlement of in-person solicitation of clients to the protection of the First Amendment differs from that of the kind of advertising approved in *Bates*, as does the strength of the State's countervailing interest in prohibition.

A

Appellant contends that his solicitation of the two young women as clients is indistinguishable, for purposes of constitutional analysis, from the advertisement in *Bates*. Like that advertisement, his meetings with the prospective clients apprised them of their legal rights and of the availability of a lawyer to pursue their claims. According to appellant, such conduct is "presumptively an exercise of his free speech rights" which cannot be curtailed in the absence of proof that it actually caused a specific harm that the State has a compelling interest in preventing. But in-person solicitation of professional employment by a lawyer does not stand on a par with truthful advertising about the availability and terms of routine legal services, let alone with forms of speech more traditionally within the concern of the First Amendment.

Expression concerning purely commercial transactions has come within the ambit of the Amendment's protection only recently. In rejecting the notion that such speech "is wholly outside the protection of the First Amendment," *Virginia Pharmacy, supra*, at 761, we were careful not to hold "that it is wholly undifferentiable from other forms" of speech. We have not discarded the "common-sense" distinction between speech proposing a commercial transaction, which occurs in an area traditionally subject to government regulation, and other varieties of speech. To require a parity of constitutional protection for commercial and noncommercial speech alike could invite dilution, simply by a leveling process, of the force of the Amendment's guarantee with respect to the latter kind of speech. Rather than subject the First Amendment to such a devitalization, we instead have afforded commercial speech a limited measure of protection, commensurate with its subordinate position in the scale of First Amendment values, while allowing modes of regulation that might be impermissible in the realm of noncommercial expression.

Moreover, "it has never been deemed an abridgment of freedom of speech or press to make a course of conduct illegal merely because the conduct was in part initiated, evidenced, or carried out by means of language, either spoken, written, or printed." Numerous examples could be cited of communications that are regulated without offending the First Amendment.... [T]he State does not lose its power to regulate commercial activity deemed harmful to the public whenever speech is a component of that activity. Neither *Virginia Pharmacy* nor *Bates* purported to cast doubt on the permissibility of these kinds of commercial regulation.

In-person solicitation by a lawyer of remunerative employment is a business transaction in which speech is an essential but subordinate component. While this does not remove the speech from the protection of the First Amendment, as was held in *Bates* and *Virginia Pharmacy*, it lowers the level of appropriate judicial scrutiny.

As applied in this case, the Disciplinary Rules are said to have limited the communication of two kinds of information. First, appellant's solicitation imparted to Carol McClintock and Wanda Lou Holbert certain information about his availability and the terms of his proposed legal services. In this respect, in-person solicitation serves much the same function as the advertisement at issue in *Bates*. But there are significant differences as well. Unlike a public advertisement, which simply provides information and leaves the recipient free to act upon it or not, in-person solicitation may exert pressure and often demands an immediate response, without providing an opportunity for comparison or reflection. The aim and effect of in-person solicitation may be to provide a one-sided presentation and to encourage speedy and perhaps uninformed decisionmaking; there is no opportunity for intervention or counter-education by agencies of the Bar, supervisory authorities, or persons close to the solicited individual. The admonition that "the fitting remedy for evil counsels is good ones" is of little value when the circumstances provide no opportunity for any remedy at all. In-person solicitation is as likely as not to discourage persons needing counsel from engaging in a critical comparison of the "availability, nature, and prices" of legal services; it actually may disserve the individual and societal interest, identified in *Bates*, in facilitating "informed and reliable decisionmaking."

It also is argued that in-person solicitation may provide the solicited individual with information about his or her legal rights and remedies. In this case, appellant gave Wanda Lou a "tip" about the prospect of recovery based on the uninsured-motorist clause in the McClintocks' insurance policy, and he explained that clause and Ohio's guest statute to Carol McClintock's parents. But neither of the Disciplinary Rules here at issue prohibited appellant from communicating information to these young women about their legal rights and the prospects of obtaining a monetary recovery, or from recommending that they obtain counsel. DR 2–104(A) merely prohibited him from using the information as bait with which to obtain an agreement to represent them for a fee. The Rule does not prohibit a lawyer from giving unsolicited legal advice; it proscribes the acceptance of employment resulting from such advice.

Appellant does not contend, and on the facts of this case could not contend, that his approaches to the two young women involved political expression or an exercise of associational freedom, "employ[ing] constitutionally privileged means of expression to secure constitutionally guaranteed civil rights." A lawyer's procurement of remunerative employment is a subject only marginally affected with First Amendment concerns. It falls within the State's proper sphere of economic and professional regulation. While entitled to some constitutional protection, appellant's conduct is subject to regulation in furtherance of important state interests.

B

The state interests implicated in this case are particularly strong. In addition to its general interest in protecting consumers and regulating commercial transactions, the State bears a special responsibility for maintaining standards among members of the licensed professions. "The interest of the States in regulating lawyers is especially great since lawyers are essential to the primary governmental function of administering justice, and have historically been 'officers of the courts.'" While lawyers act in part as "self-employed businessmen," they also act "as trusted agents of their clients, and as assistants to the court in search of a just solution to disputes."

As is true with respect to advertising, it appears that the ban on solicitation by lawyers originated as a rule of professional etiquette rather than as a strictly ethical rule. But the fact that the original motivation behind the ban on solicitation today might be considered an insufficient justification for its perpetuation does not detract from the force of the other interests the ban continues to serve. . . .

The substantive evils of solicitation have been stated over the years in sweeping terms: stirring up litigation, assertion of fraudulent claims, debasing the legal profession, and potential harm to the solicited client in the form of overreaching, overcharging, underrepresentation, and misrepresentation. The American Bar Association, as *amicus curiae*, defends the rule against solicitation primarily on three broad grounds: It is said that the prohibitions embodied in DR2–103(A) and 2–104(A) serve to reduce the likelihood of overreaching and the exertion of undue influence on lay persons, to protect the privacy of individuals, and to avoid situations where the lawyer's exercise of judgment on behalf of the client will be clouded by his own pecuniary self-interest.

We need not discuss or evaluate each of these interests in detail as appellant has conceded that the State has a legitimate and indeed "compelling" interest in preventing those aspects of solicitation that involve fraud, undue influence, intimidation, overreaching, and other forms of "vexatious conduct." We agree that protection of the public from these aspects of solicitation is a legitimate and important state interest.

III

Appellant's concession that strong state interests justify regulation to prevent the evils he enumerates would end this case but for his insistence that none of those evils was found to be present in his acts of solicitation. He challenges what he characterizes as the "indiscriminate application" of the Rules to him and thus attacks the validity of DR 2–103(A) and DR 2–

104(A) not facially, but as applied to his acts of solicitation. And because no allegations or findings were made of the specific wrongs appellant concedes would justify disciplinary action, appellant terms his solicitation "pure," meaning "soliciting and obtaining agreements from Carol McClintock and Wanda Lou Holbert to represent each of them," without more. Appellant therefore argues that we must decide whether a State may discipline him for solicitation *per se* without offending the First and Fourteenth Amendments.

We agree that the appropriate focus is on appellant's conduct. And, as appellant urges, we must undertake an independent review of the record to determine whether that conduct was constitutionally protected. But appellant errs in assuming that the constitutional validity of the judgment below depends on proof that his conduct constituted actual overreaching or inflicted some specific injury on Wanda Holbert or Carol McClintock. His assumption flows from the premise that nothing less than actual proved harm to the solicited individual would be a sufficiently important state interest to justify disciplining the attorney who solicits employment in person for pecuniary gain.

Appellant's argument misconceives the nature of the State's interest. The Rules prohibiting solicitation are prophylactic measures whose objective is the prevention of harm before it occurs. The Rules were applied in this case to discipline a lawyer for soliciting employment for pecuniary gain under circumstances likely to result in the adverse consequences the State seeks to avert. In such a situation, which is inherently conducive to overreaching and other forms of misconduct, the State has a strong interest in adopting and enforcing rules of conduct designed to protect the public from harmful solicitation by lawyers whom it has licensed.

The State's perception of the potential for harm in circumstances such as those presented in this case is well founded. The detrimental aspects of face-to-face selling even of ordinary consumer products have been recognized and addressed by the Federal Trade Commission, and it hardly need be said that the potential for overreaching is significantly greater when a lawyer, a professional trained in the art of persuasion, personally solicits an unsophisticated, injured, or distressed lay person. Such an individual may place his trust in a lawyer, regardless of the latter's qualifications or the individual's actual need for legal representation, simply in response to persuasion under circumstances conducive to uninformed acquiescence. Although it is argued that personal solicitation is valuable because it may apprise a victim of misfortune of his legal rights, the very plight of that person not only makes him more vulnerable to influence but also may make advice all the more intrusive. Thus, under these adverse conditions the overtures of an uninvited lawyer may distress the solicited individual simply because of their obtrusiveness and the invasion of the individual's privacy, even when no other harm materializes. Under such circumstances, it is not unreasonable for the State to presume that in-person solicitation by lawyers more often than not will be injurious to the person solicited.

The efficacy of the State's effort to prevent such harm to prospective clients would be substantially diminished if, having proved a solicitation in circumstances like those of this case, the State were required in addition to prove actual injury. Unlike the advertising in *Bates*, in-person solicitation is not visible or otherwise open to public scrutiny. Often there is no witness other than the lawyer and the lay person whom he has solicited, rendering it difficult or impossible to obtain reliable proof of what actually took place. This would be especially true if the lay person were so distressed at the time of the solicitation that he could not recall specific details at a later date. If appellant's view were sustained, in-person solicitation would be virtually immune to effective oversight and regulation by the State or by the legal profession, in contravention of the State's strong interest in regulating members of the Bar in an effective, objective, and self-enforcing manner. It therefore is not unreasonable, or violative of the Constitution, for a State to respond with what in effect is a prophylactic rule.

On the basis of the undisputed facts, we conclude that the Disciplinary Rules constitutionally could be applied to appellant. He approached two young accident victims at a time when they were especially incapable of making informed judgments or of assessing and protecting their own interests. He solicited Carol McClintock in a hospital room where she lay in traction and sought out Wanda Lou Holbert on the day she came home from the hospital, knowing from his prior inquiries that she had just been released. Appellant urged his services upon the young women and used the information he had obtained from the McClintocks, and the fact of his agreement with Carol, to induce Wanda to say "O. K." in response to his solicitation. He employed a concealed tape recorder, seemingly to insure that he would have evidence of Wanda's oral assent to the representation. He emphasized that his fee would come out of the recovery, thereby tempting the young women with what sounded like a cost-free and therefore irresistible offer. He refused to withdraw when Mrs. Holbert requested him to do so only a day after the initial meeting between appellant and Wanda Lou and continued to represent himself to the insurance company as Wanda Holbert's lawyer....

The facts in this case present a striking example of the potential for overreaching that is inherent in a lawyer's in-person solicitation of professional employment. They also demonstrate the need for prophylactic regulation in furtherance of the State's interest in protecting the lay public. We hold that the application of DR2–103(A) and 2–104(A) to appellant does not offend the Constitution.

NOTES

1. The facts of *Ohralik* would make a great final exam question in a professional responsibility course. What rules of professional conduct did Ohralik violate in his interactions with McClintock and Holbert?

2. What is the standard the court applies to the "commercial speech" element inherent in in-person solicitation? How does the court resolve Ohralik's First Amendment claim?

3. Model Rule 7.3 precludes not only in-person solicitation, but solicitation through "live telephone or real-time electronic contact." Are the risks of these types of solicitation as problematic as the in-person variety?

4. Model Rule 7.3 prohibits in-person solicitation "from a prospective client where a significant motive for the lawyer's doing so is the lawyer's pecuniary gain." The source for this limit on the prohibition is *In re Primus*, 436 U.S. 412 (1978), decided the same day as *Ohralik*. Attorney Primus, a member of the South Carolina bar, was associated with the ACLU in Columbia, South Carolina. At the request of a local businessman in another town, Primus met with a group of women who had been sterilized or threatened with sterilization as a condition of receiving Medicaid. At the meeting, appellant advised the women of their legal rights and suggested the possibility of a lawsuit. She followed up with a letter to one of the women, letting her know that the ACLU had agreed to provide free legal representation for the women if they wished to bring suit. The letter was intercepted by one of the doctors accused of the sterilizations, and, based on the letter, a complaint was made about Primus to the South Carolina bar. Primus was disciplined for soliciting a client. The Supreme Court overturned the order of discipline.

The Court distinguished *Ohralik,* which involved "in-person solicitation for pecuniary gain," from Primus's offer of free representation. Moreover, Primus's "actions were undertaken to express personal political beliefs and to advance the civil-liberties objectives of the ACLU, rather than to derive financial gain." Primus's solicitation of litigants thus had an expressive and associational component and the communication to the potential client came "within the generous zone of First Amendment protection reserved for associational freedoms." This was the case even though the ACLU might subsequently seek an award of counsel fees if it achieved a successful outcome. The Court concluded that South Carolina's disciplinary action did not satisfy the "exacting scrutiny applicable to limitations on core First Amendment rights." "At bottom," it stated,

> the case against appellant rests on the proposition that a State may regulate in a prophylactic fashion all solicitation activities of lawyers because there may be some potential for overreaching, conflict of interest, or other substantive evils whenever a lawyer gives unsolicited advice and communicates an offer of representation to a layman. Under certain circumstances, that approach is appropriate in the case of speech that simply propose[s] a commercial transaction.... In the context of political expression and association, however, a State must regulate with significantly greater precision.

5. Lawyer calls a remote acquaintance, invites him to lunch and a round of golf at the country club, and suggests over lunch that the acquaintance throw some of his business's legal work Lawyer's way. Is this in-person solicitation? Why or why not? Does this pose some of the risks that concerned the Court in *Ohralik*? Do you suppose that lawyers are disciplined for this kind of solicitation? If not, is that because the prohibition on in-person solicitation contains

an implicit class distinction, or for some other reason? Does that seem fair to you?

2. TARGETED SOLICITATION LETTERS

Ohralik makes clear that the court will permit significant regulation of in-person solicitation of clients by lawyers when that solicitation does not include an expressive or associational component. What about written solicitation? Written solicitation has elements of both advertising and in-person solicitation inherent in it, and the court's differing approaches to these issues might suggest that this is a complex problem. There are also different types of written solicitation: casting a broad net to offer legal services to a wide variety of people, or targeting the offer of services to people who the lawyer might know for some reason are in particular need of the services to be offered. The latter—the so-called "targeted solicitation letter"—has been the subject of a changing legal landscape.

The Supreme Court's initial view was that solicitation letters were more like advertising than like in-person solicitation. In *Shapero v. Kentucky Bar Ass'n*, 486 U.S. 466 (1988), attorney Shapero sought to send out the following letter to solicit clients:

> It has come to my attention that your home is being foreclosed on. If this is true, you may be about to lose your home. Federal law may allow you to keep your home by *ORDERING* your creditor [*sic*] to *STOP* and give you more time to pay them.
>
> You may call my office anytime from 8:30 a.m. to 5:00 p.m. for *FREE* information on how you can keep your home.
>
> Call *NOW*, don't wait. It may surprise you what I may be able to do for you. Just call and tell me that you got this letter. Remember it is *FREE*, there is *NO* charge for calling.

The Kentucky authorities imposed a blanket prohibition on targeted written solicitations and refused to permit Shapero to send the letters. Shapero challenged the prohibition on First Amendment grounds.

The Supreme Court first noted that lawyer advertising was protected commercial speech, and that a written letter to the public at large would be indistinguishable from a permitted advertisement. It then concluded that the state could not penalize the use of the targeted letter simply because it was more efficient than the permissible, broader letter. "[T]he First Amendment does not permit a ban on certain speech merely because it is more efficient; the State may not constitutionally ban a particular letter on the theory that to mail it only to those whom it would most interest is somehow inherently objectionable."

The state bar argued that the case was simply " '*Ohralik* in writing.' " The Court rejected this characterization, stating that it "misses the mark.... In assessing the potential for overreaching and undue influence, the mode of communication makes all the difference." The reduced capacity for "overreaching, invasion of privacy, the exercise of undue influence, and outright fraud" in a written, as opposed to in-person solicitation, and the potential for oversight of written communications made *Shapero* very different from *Ohralik*. "Unlike the potential client with a badgering advocate breathing down his neck, the recipient of a letter and the 'reader of an advertisement ... can "effectively avoid further bombardment of [his] sensibilities simply by averting [his] eyes." ' " In dissent, Justice O'Connor argued that the analytical framework of the advertising cases should be reexamined.

One might have thought that *Shapero* resolved the question of the constitutionality of prohibitions on targeted solicitation letters. As the following case shows, that turned out not to be the case. Why?

FLORIDA BAR v. WENT FOR IT, INC.

515 U.S. 618 (1995)

JUSTICE O'CONNOR delivered the opinion of the Court.

Rules of the Florida Bar prohibit personal injury lawyers from sending targeted direct-mail solicitations to victims and their relatives for 30 days following an accident or disaster. This case asks us to consider whether such Rules violate the First and Fourteenth Amendments of the Constitution. We hold that in the circumstances presented here, they do not.

I

In 1989, the Florida Bar (Bar) completed a 2–year study of the effects of lawyer advertising on public opinion. After conducting hearings, commissioning surveys, and reviewing extensive public commentary, the Bar determined that several changes to its advertising rules were in order. In late 1990, the Florida Supreme Court adopted the Bar's proposed amendments with some modifications. Two of these amendments are at issue in this case. Rule 4–7.4(b)(1) provides that "[a] lawyer shall not send, or knowingly permit to be sent ... a written communication to a prospective client for the purpose of obtaining professional employment if: (A) the written communication concerns an action for personal injury or wrongful death or otherwise relates to an accident or disaster involving the person to whom the communication is addressed or a relative of that person, unless the accident or disaster occurred more than 30 days prior to the mailing of the communication." Rule 4–7.8(a) states that "[a] lawyer shall not accept referrals from a lawyer referral service unless the service: (1) engages in no communication with the public and in no direct contact with prospective clients in a manner that would violate the Rules of Professional Conduct if the communication or contact were made by the lawyer." Together, these Rules create a brief 30-day blackout period after an accident during which lawyers may not, directly or indirectly, single out accident victims or their relatives in order to solicit their business.

In March 1992, G. Stewart McHenry and his wholly owned lawyer referral service, Went For It, Inc., filed this action for declaratory and injunctive relief in the United States District Court for the Middle District of Florida challenging Rules 4–7.4(b)(1) and 4–7.8(a) as violative of the First and Fourteenth Amendments to the Constitution. McHenry alleged that he routinely sent targeted solicitations to accident victims or their survivors within 30 days after accidents and that he wished to continue doing so in the future. Went For It, Inc., represented that it wished to contact accident victims or their survivors within 30 days of accidents and to refer potential clients to participating Florida lawyers. In October 1992, McHenry was disbarred for reasons unrelated to this suit, *Florida Bar v. McHenry*, 605 So.2d 459 (Fla.1992). Another Florida lawyer, John T. Blakely, was substituted in his stead.

The District Court referred the parties' competing summary judgment motions to a Magistrate Judge, who concluded that the Bar had substantial government interests, predicated on a concern for professionalism, both in protecting the personal privacy and tranquility of recent accident victims and their relatives and in ensuring that these individuals do not fall prey to undue influence or overreaching. Citing the Bar's extensive study, the Magistrate Judge found that the Rules directly serve those interests and sweep no further than reasonably necessary. The Magistrate recommended that the District Court grant the Bar's motion for summary judgment on the ground that the Rules pass constitutional muster.

The District Court rejected the Magistrate Judge's report and recommendations and entered summary judgment for the plaintiffs. The Eleventh Circuit affirmed on similar grounds.... We granted certiorari, and now reverse.

II

A

Constitutional protection for attorney advertising, and for commercial speech generally, is of recent vintage. Until the mid–1970's, we adhered to the broad rule ... that ... "the Constitution imposes no such restraint on government as respects purely commercial advertising." In 1976, the Court changed course. In *Virginia Bd. of Pharmacy v. Virginia Citizens Consumer Council, Inc.*, 425 U.S. 748, we invalidated a state statute barring pharmacists from advertising prescription drug prices. At issue was speech that involved the idea that " 'I will sell you the X prescription drug at the Y price.' " Striking the ban as unconstitutional, we rejected the argument that such speech "is so removed from 'any exposition of ideas,' and from 'truth, science, morality, and arts in general, in its diffusion of liberal sentiments on the administration of Government,' that it lacks all protection."

In *Virginia Bd.*, the Court limited its holding to advertising by pharmacists, noting that "[p]hysicians and lawyers ... do not dispense standardized products; they render professional *services* of almost infinite variety and nature, with the consequent enhanced possibility for confusion and deception if they were to undertake certain kinds of advertising." One

year later, however, the Court applied the *Virginia Bd.* principles to invalidate a state rule prohibiting lawyers from advertising in newspapers and other media. In *Bates v. State Bar of Arizona*, the Court struck a ban on price advertising for what it deemed "routine" legal services: "the uncontested divorce, the simple adoption, the uncontested personal bankruptcy, the change of name, and the like." Expressing confidence that legal advertising would only be practicable for such simple, standardized services, the Court rejected the State's proffered justifications for regulation.

Nearly two decades of cases have built upon the foundation laid by *Bates.* It is now well established that lawyer advertising is commercial speech and, as such, is accorded a measure of First Amendment protection. Such First Amendment protection, of course, is not absolute. We have always been careful to distinguish commercial speech from speech at the First Amendment's core. " '[C]ommercial speech [enjoys] a limited measure of protection, commensurate with its subordinate position in the scale of First Amendment values,' and is subject to 'modes of regulation that might be impermissible in the realm of noncommercial expression.' " ...

Mindful of these concerns, we engage in "intermediate" scrutiny of restrictions on commercial speech, analyzing them under the framework set forth in *Central Hudson Gas & Elec. Corp. v. Public Serv. Comm'n of N.Y.*, 447 U.S. 557 (1980). Under *Central Hudson,* the government may freely regulate commercial speech that concerns unlawful activity or is misleading. Commercial speech that falls into neither of those categories, like the advertising at issue here, may be regulated if the government satisfies a test consisting of three related prongs: First, the government must assert a substantial interest in support of its regulation; second, the government must demonstrate that the restriction on commercial speech directly and materially advances that interest; and third, the regulation must be " 'narrowly drawn.' " *Id.* at 564–565.

B

... The Bar asserts that it has a substantial interest in protecting the privacy and tranquility of personal injury victims and their loved ones against intrusive, unsolicited contact by lawyers. This interest obviously factors into the Bar's paramount (and repeatedly professed) objective of curbing activities that "negatively affec[t] the administration of justice." *The Florida Bar: Petition to Amend the Rules Regulating the Florida Bar– Advertising Issues*, 571 So.2d at 455; see also Brief for Petitioner (describing Bar's effort "to preserve the integrity of the legal profession"). Because direct-mail solicitations in the wake of accidents are perceived by the public as intrusive, the Bar argues, the reputation of the legal profession in the eyes of Floridians has suffered commensurately. The regulation, then, is an effort to protect the flagging reputations of Florida lawyers by preventing them from engaging in conduct that, the Bar maintains, " 'is universally regarded as deplorable and beneath common decency because of its intrusion upon the special vulnerability and private grief of victims or their families.' "

We have little trouble crediting the Bar's interest as substantial. On various occasions we have accepted the proposition that "States have a compelling interest in the practice of professions within their boundaries, and ... as part of their power to protect the public health, safety, and other valid interests they have broad power to establish standards for licensing practitioners and regulating the practice of professions." Our precedents also leave no room for doubt that "the protection of potential clients' privacy is a substantial state interest."

Under *Central Hudson's* second prong, the State must demonstrate that the challenged regulation "advances the Government's interest 'in a direct and material way.' " That burden, we have explained, " 'is not satisfied by mere speculation or conjecture; rather, a governmental body seeking to sustain a restriction on commercial speech must demonstrate that the harms it recites are real and that its restriction will in fact alleviate them to a material degree....' "

The direct-mail solicitation regulation before us does not suffer from such infirmities. The Bar submitted a 106–page summary of its 2–year study of lawyer advertising and solicitation to the District Court. That summary contains data—both statistical and anecdotal—supporting the Bar's contentions that the Florida public views direct-mail solicitations in the immediate wake of accidents as an intrusion on privacy that reflects poorly upon the profession. As of June 1989, lawyers mailed 700,000 direct solicitations in Florida annually, 40% of which were aimed at accident victims or their survivors. A survey of Florida adults commissioned by the Bar indicated that Floridians "have negative feelings about those attorneys who use direct mail advertising." Fifty-four percent of the general population surveyed said that contacting persons concerning accidents or similar events is a violation of privacy. A random sampling of persons who received direct-mail advertising from lawyers in 1987 revealed that 45% believed that direct-mail solicitation is "designed to take advantage of gullible or unstable people"; 34% found such tactics "annoying or irritating"; 26% found it an "invasion of your privacy"; and 24% reported that it "made you angry." Significantly, 27% of direct-mail recipients reported that their regard for the legal profession and for the judicial process as a whole was "lower" as a result of receiving the direct mail.

The anecdotal record mustered by the Bar is noteworthy for its breadth and detail. With titles like "Scavenger Lawyers" (The Miami Herald, Sept. 29, 1987) and "Solicitors Out of Bounds" (St. Petersburg Times, Oct. 26, 1987), newspaper editorial pages in Florida have burgeoned with criticism of Florida lawyers who send targeted direct mail to victims shortly after accidents. The study summary also includes page upon page of excerpts from complaints of direct-mail recipients. For example, a Florida citizen described how he was " 'appalled and angered by the brazen attempt' " of a law firm to solicit him by letter shortly after he was injured and his fiancee was killed in an auto accident. Another found it " 'despicable and inexcusable' " that a Pensacola lawyer wrote to his mother three days after his father's funeral. Another described how she was " 'astounded' " and then " 'very angry' " when she received a solicitation following a minor accident. Still another described as " 'beyond comprehension' " a letter his nephew's family received the day of the nephew's funeral. One citizen wrote, " 'I consider the unsolicited contact from you after my child's accident to be of the rankest form of ambulance chasing and in incredibly poor taste. . . . I cannot begin to express with my limited vocabulary the utter contempt in which I hold you and your kind.' "

In light of this showing—which respondents at no time refuted—we conclude that the Bar has satisfied the second prong of the *Central Hudson* test. In dissent, Justice KENNEDY complains that we have before us few indications of the sample size or selection procedures employed by Magid Associates (a nationally renowned consulting firm) and no copies of the actual surveys employed. As stated, we believe the evidence adduced by the Bar is sufficient to meet the standard. . . . After scouring the record, we are satisfied that the ban on direct-mail solicitation in the immediate aftermath of accidents . . . targets a concrete, nonspeculative harm.

In reaching a contrary conclusion, the Court of Appeals determined that this case was governed squarely by *Shapero v. Kentucky Bar Assn.*, 486 U.S. 466 (1988). Making no mention of the Bar's study, the court concluded that " 'a targeted letter [does not] invade the recipient's privacy any more than does a substantively identical letter mailed at large. The invasion, if any, occurs when the lawyer discovers the recipient's legal affairs, not when he confronts the recipient with the discovery. . . .' "

While some of *Shapero*'s language might be read to support the Court of Appeals' interpretation, *Shapero* differs in several fundamental respects from the case before us. First and foremost, *Shapero*'s treatment of privacy was casual. Contrary to the dissent's suggestions, the State in *Shapero* did not seek to justify its regulation as a measure undertaken to prevent lawyers' invasions of privacy interests. Rather, the State focused exclusively on the special dangers of overreaching inhering in targeted solicitations. Second, in contrast to this case, *Shapero* dealt with a broad ban on *all* direct-mail solicitations, whatever the time frame and whoever the recipient. Finally, the State in *Shapero* assembled no evidence attempting to demonstrate any actual harm caused by targeted direct mail. The Court rejected the State's effort to justify a prophylactic ban on the basis of blanket, untested assertions of undue influence and overreaching. Because the State did not make a privacy-based argument at all, its empirical showing on that issue was similarly infirm.

We find the Court's perfunctory treatment of privacy in *Shapero* to be of little utility in assessing this ban on targeted solicitation of victims in the immediate aftermath of accidents. While it is undoubtedly true that many people find the image of lawyers sifting through accident and police reports in pursuit of prospective clients unpalatable and invasive, this case targets a different kind of intrusion. The Bar has argued, and the record reflects, that a principal purpose of the ban is "protecting the personal privacy and tranquility of [Florida's] citizens from crass commercial intrusion by attorneys upon their personal grief in times of trauma." The intrusion targeted by the Bar's regulation stems not from the fact that a lawyer has learned about an accident or disaster (as the Court of Appeals notes, in many instances a lawyer need only read the newspaper to glean this information), but from the lawyer's confrontation of victims or relatives with such information, while wounds are still open, in order to solicit their business. In this respect, an untargeted letter mailed to society at large is different in kind from a targeted solicitation; the untargeted letter involves no willful or knowing affront to or invasion of the tranquility of bereaved or injured individuals and simply does not cause the same kind of reputational harm to the profession unearthed by the Bar's study.

Nor do we find *Bolger v. Youngs Drug Products Corp.*, 463 U.S. 60 (1983), dispositive of the issue, despite any superficial resemblance. In *Bolger*, we rejected the Federal Government's paternalistic effort to ban potentially "offensive" and "intrusive" direct-mail advertisements for contraceptives. Minimizing the Government's allegations of harm, we reasoned that "[r]ecipients of objectionable mailings ... may ' "effectively avoid further bombardment of their sensibilities simply by averting their eyes." ' " We found that the " 'short, though regular, journey from mail box to trash can ... is an acceptable burden, at least so far as the Constitution is concerned.' " Concluding that citizens have at their disposal ample means of averting any substantial injury inhering in the delivery of objectionable contraceptive material, we deemed the State's intercession unnecessary and unduly restrictive.

Here, in contrast, the harm targeted by the Bar cannot be eliminated by a brief journey to the trash can. The purpose of the 30-day targeted direct-mail ban is to forestall the outrage and irritation with the state-licensed legal profession that the practice of direct solicitation only days after accidents has engendered. The Bar is concerned not with citizens' "offense" in the abstract, but with the demonstrable detrimental effects that such "offense" has on the profession it regulates. Moreover, the harm posited by the Bar is as much a function of simple receipt of targeted solicitations within days of accidents as it is a function of the letters' contents. Throwing the letter away shortly after opening it may minimize the latter intrusion, but it does little to combat the former....

Passing to *Central Hudson*'s third prong, we examine the relationship between the Bar's interests and the means chosen to serve them. With respect to this prong, the differences between commercial speech and noncommercial speech are manifest.... [T]he "least restrictive means" test has no role in the commercial speech context. "What our decisions require," instead, "is a 'fit' between the legislature's ends and the means chosen to accomplish those ends," a fit that is not necessarily perfect, but reasonable; that represents not necessarily the single best disposition but one whose scope is 'in proportion to the interest served,' that employs not necessarily the least restrictive means but ... a means narrowly tailored to achieve the desired objective."

Respondents levy a great deal of criticism at the scope of the Bar's restriction on targeted mail. "[B]y prohibiting written communications to all people, whatever their state of mind," respondents charge, the Rule "keeps useful information from those accident victims who are ready, willing and able to utilize a lawyer's advice." This criticism may be parsed into two components. First, the Rule does not distinguish between victims in terms of the severity of their injuries. According to respondents, the Rule is unconstitutionally overinclusive insofar as it bans targeted mailings even to citizens whose injuries or grief are relatively minor. Second, the Rule may prevent citizens from learning about their legal options, particularly at a time when other actors—opposing counsel and insurance adjusters—may be clamoring for victims' attentions. Any benefit arising from the Bar's regulation, respondents implicitly contend, is outweighed by these costs.

We are not persuaded by respondents' allegations of constitutional infirmity. We find little deficiency in the ban's failure to distinguish among injured Floridians by the severity of their pain or the intensity of their grief. Indeed, it is hard to imagine the contours of a regulation that might satisfy respondents on this score.... Unlike respondents, we do not see "numerous and obvious less-burdensome alternatives" to Florida's short temporal ban. The Bar's rule is reasonably well tailored to its stated objective of eliminating targeted mailings whose type and timing are a source of distress to Floridians, distress that has caused many of them to lose respect for the legal profession.

Respondents' second point would have force if the Bar's Rule were not limited to a brief period and if there were not many other ways for injured Floridians to learn about the availability of legal representation during that time. Our lawyer advertising cases have afforded lawyers a great deal of leeway to devise innovative ways to attract new business. Florida permits lawyers to advertise on prime-time television and radio as well as in newspapers and other media. They may rent space on billboards. They may send untargeted letters to the general population, or to discrete segments thereof. There are, of course, pages upon pages devoted to lawyers in the Yellow Pages of Florida telephone directories.... These ample alternative channels for receipt of information about the availability of legal representation during the 30-day period following accidents may explain why, despite the ample evidence, testimony, and commentary submitted by those favoring (as well as opposing) unrestricted direct-mail solicitation, respondents have not pointed to—and we have not independently found—a single example of an individual case in which immediate solicitation helped to avoid, or failure to solicit within 30 days brought about, the harms that concern the dissent. In fact, the record contains considerable empirical survey information suggesting that Floridians have little difficulty finding a lawyer when they need one. Finding no basis to question the commonsense conclusion that the many alternative channels for communicating necessary information about attorneys are sufficient, we see no defect in Florida's regulation.

III

... We believe that the Bar's 30-day restriction on targeted direct-mail solicitation of accident victims and their relatives withstands scrutiny under the three-pronged *Central Hudson* test that we have devised for this context. The Bar has substantial interest both in protecting injured Floridians from invasive conduct by lawyers and in preventing the erosion of confidence in the profession that such repeated invasions have engendered. The Bar's proffered study, unrebutted by respondents below, provides evidence indicating that the harms it targets are far from illusory. The palliative devised by the Bar to address these harms is narrow both in scope and in duration. The Constitution, in our view, requires nothing more.

JUSTICE KENNEDY, with whom JUSTICE STEVENS, JUSTICE SOUTER, and JUSTICE GINSBURG join, dissenting.

Attorneys who communicate their willingness to assist potential clients are engaged in speech protected by the First and Fourteenth Amendments. That principle has been understood since *Bates v. State Bar of Ariz.*, 433 U.S. 350 (1977). The Court today undercuts this guarantee in an important class of cases and unsettles leading First Amendment precedents, at the expense of those victims most in need of legal assistance. With all respect for the Court, in my view its solicitude for the privacy of victims and its concern for our profession are misplaced and self-defeating, even upon the Court's own premises.

I take it to be uncontroverted that when an accident results in death or injury, it is often urgent at once to investigate the occurrence, identify witnesses, and preserve evidence. Vital interests in speech and expression are, therefore, at stake when by law an attorney cannot direct a letter to the victim or the family explaining this simple fact and offering competent legal assistance. Meanwhile, represented and better informed parties, or parties who have been solicited in ways more sophisticated and indirect, may be at work. Indeed, these parties, either themselves or by their attorneys, investigators, and adjusters, are free to contact the unrepresented persons to gather evidence or offer settlement. This scheme makes little sense. As is often true when the law makes little sense, it is not first principles but their interpretation and application that have gone awry....

I

As the Court notes, the first of the *Central Hudson* factors to be considered is whether the interest the State pursues in enacting the speech restriction is a substantial one. The State says two different interests meet this standard. The first is the interest "in protecting the personal privacy and tranquility" of the victim and his or her family. As the Court notes, that interest has recognition in our decisions as a general matter; but it does not follow that the privacy interest in the cases the majority cites is applicable here. The problem the Court confronts, and cannot overcome, is our recent decision in *Shapero v. Kentucky Bar Assn.*, 486 U.S. 466 (1988). In assessing the importance of the interest in that solicitation case, we made an explicit distinction between direct, in-person solicitations and direct-mail solicitations. *Shapero*, like this case, involved a direct-mail solicitation, and there the State recited its fears of "overreaching and undue influence." We found, however, no such dangers presented by direct-mail advertising. We reasoned that "[a] letter, like a printed advertisement (but unlike a lawyer), can readily be put in a drawer to be considered later, ignored, or discarded." . . . In assessing the substantiality of the evils to be prevented, we concluded that "the mode of communication makes all the difference." The direct mail in *Shapero* did not present the justification for regulation of speech presented in *Ohralik v. Ohio State Bar Assn.*

To avoid the controlling effect of *Shapero* in the case before us, the Court seeks to declare that a different privacy interest is implicated. As it sees the matter, the substantial concern is that victims or their families will be offended by receiving a solicitation during their grief and trauma. But we do not allow restrictions on speech to be justified on the ground that the expression might offend the listener. On the contrary, we have said that these "are classically not justifications validating the suppression of expression protected by the First Amendment." And in *Zauderer v. Office of Disciplinary Counsel of Supreme Court of Ohio*, 471 U.S. 626 (1985), where we struck down a ban on attorney advertising, we held that "the mere possibility that some members of the population might find advertising . . . offensive cannot justify suppressing it.". . .

All the recipient of objectionable mailings need do is to take "the 'short, though regular, journey from mail box to trash can.'" As we have observed, this is "an acceptable burden, at least so far as the Constitution is concerned." If these cases forbidding restrictions on speech that might be offensive are to be overruled, the Court should say so.

In the face of these difficulties of logic and precedent, the State and the opinion of the Court turn to a second interest: protecting the reputation and dignity of the legal profession. The argument is, it seems fair to say, that all are demeaned by the crass behavior of a few. The argument takes a further step in the *amicus* brief filed by the Association of Trial Lawyers of America. There it is said that disrespect for the profession from this sort of solicitation (but presumably from no other sort of solicitation) results in lower jury verdicts. In a sense, of course, these arguments are circular. While disrespect will arise from an unethical or improper practice, the majority begs a most critical question by assuming that direct-mail solicitations constitute such a practice. The fact is, however, that direct solicitation may serve vital purposes and promote the administration of justice, and to the extent the bar seeks to protect lawyers' reputations by preventing them from engaging in speech some deem offensive, the State is doing nothing more (as *amicus* the Association of Trial Lawyers of America is at least candid enough to admit) than manipulating the public's opinion by suppressing speech that informs us how the legal system works. The disrespect argument thus proceeds from the very assumption it tries to prove, which is to say that solicitations within 30 days serve no legitimate purpose. This, of course, is censorship pure and simple; and censorship is antithetical to the first principles of free expression.

II

Even were the interests asserted substantial, the regulation here fails the second part of the *Central Hudson* test, which requires that the dangers the State seeks to eliminate be real and that a speech restriction or ban advance that asserted state interest in a direct and material way. The burden of demonstrating the reality of the asserted harm rests on the State.... Here, what the State has offered falls well short of demonstrating that the harms it is trying to redress are real, let alone that the regulation directly and materially advances the State's interests. The parties and the Court have used the term "Summary of Record" to describe a document prepared by the Florida Bar (Bar), one of the adverse parties, and submitted to the District Court in this case. This document includes no actual surveys, few indications of sample size or selection procedures, no explanations of methodology, and no discussion of excluded results. There is no description of the statistical universe or scientific framework that permits any productive use of the information the so-called Summary of Record contains. The majority describes this anecdotal matter as "noteworthy for its breadth and detail," but when examined, it is noteworthy for its incompetence. The selective synopses of unvalidated studies deal, for the most part, with television advertising and phone book listings, and not direct-mail solicitations.... The most generous reading of this document permits identification of 34 pages on which direct-mail solicitation is arguably discussed. Of these, only two are even a synopsis of a study of the attitudes of Floridians towards such solicitations. The bulk of the remaining pages include comments by lawyers about direct mail (some of them favorable), excerpts from citizen complaints about such solicitation, and a few excerpts from newspaper articles on the topic. Our cases require something more than a few pages of self-serving and unsupported statements by the State to demonstrate that a regulation directly and materially advances the elimination of a real harm when the State seeks to suppress truthful and nondeceptive speech.

It is telling that the essential thrust of all the material adduced to justify the State's interest is devoted to the reputational concerns of the Bar. It is not at all clear that this regulation advances the interest of protecting persons who are suffering trauma and grief, and we are cited to no material in the record for that claim. Indeed, when asked at oral argument what a "typical injured plaintiff get[s] in the mail," the Bar's lawyer replied: "That's not in the record ... and I don't know the answer to that question." Having declared that the privacy interest is one both substantial and served by the regulation, the Court ought not to be excused from justifying its conclusion.

III

... Were it appropriate to reach the third part of the *Central Hudson* test, it would be clear that the relationship between the Bar's interests and the means chosen to serve them is not a reasonable fit. The Bar's rule creates a flat ban that prohibits far more speech than necessary to serve the purported state interest. Even assuming that interest were legitimate, there is a wild disproportion between the harm supposed and the speech ban enforced....

To begin with, the ban applies with respect to all accidental injuries, whatever their gravity....

There is, moreover, simply no justification for assuming that in all or most cases an attorney's advice would be unwelcome or unnecessary when the survivors or the victim must at once begin assessing their legal and financial position in a rational manner. With regard to lesser injuries, there is little chance that for any period, much less 30 days, the victims will become distraught upon hearing from an attorney. It is, in fact, more likely a real risk that some victims might think no attorney will be interested enough to help them. It is at this precise time that sound legal advice may be necessary and most urgent.

Even as to more serious injuries, the State's argument fails, since it must be conceded that prompt legal representation is essential where death or injury results from accidents. The only seeming justification for the State's restriction is the one the Court itself offers, which is that attorneys can and do resort to other ways of communicating important legal information to potential clients. Quite aside from the latent protectionism for the established bar that the argument discloses, it fails for the more fundamental reason that it concedes the necessity for the very representation the attorneys solicit and the State seeks to ban. The accident victims who are prejudiced to vindicate the State's purported desire for more dignity in the legal profession will be the very persons who most need legal advice, for they are the victims who, because they lack education, linguistic ability, or familiarity with the legal system, are unable to seek out legal services.

The reasonableness of the State's chosen methods for redressing perceived evils can be evaluated, in part, by a commonsense consideration of other possible means of regulation that have not been tried. Here, the Court neglects the fact that this problem is largely self-policing: Potential clients will not hire lawyers who offend them.... The State's restriction deprives accident victims of information which may be critical to their right to make a claim for compensation for injuries. The telephone book and general advertisements may serve this purpose in part; but the direct solicitation ban will fall on those who most need legal representation: for those with minor injuries, the victims too ill informed to know an attorney may be interested in their cases; for those with serious injuries, the victims too ill informed to know that time is of the essence if counsel is to assemble evidence and warn them not to enter into settlement negotiations or evidentiary discussions with investigators for opposing parties.... The very fact that some 280,000 direct-mail solicitations are sent to accident victims and their survivors in Florida each year is some indication of the efficacy of this device. Nothing in the Court's opinion demonstrates that these efforts do not serve some beneficial role. A solicitation letter is not a contract. Nothing in the record shows that these communications do not at the least serve the purpose of informing the prospective client that he or she has a number of different attorneys from whom to choose, so that the decision to select counsel, after an interview with one or more interested attorneys, can be deliberate and informed. And if these communications reveal the social costs of the tort system as a whole, then efforts can be directed to reforming the operation of that system, not to suppressing information about how the system works. The Court's approach, however, does not seem to be the proper way to begin elevating the honor of the profession.

IV

It is most ironic that, for the first time since *Bates v. State Bar of Arizona*, the Court now orders a major retreat from the constitutional guarantees for commercial speech in order to shield its own profession from public criticism. Obscuring the financial aspect of the legal profession from public discussion through direct-mail solicitation, at the expense of the least sophisticated members of society, is not a laudable constitutional goal. There is no authority for the proposition that the Constitution permits the State to promote the public image of the legal profession by suppressing information about the profession's business aspects. If public respect for the profession erodes because solicitation distorts the idea of the law as most lawyers see it, it must be remembered that real progress begins with more rational speech, not less.... The image of the profession cannot be enhanced without improving the substance of its practice....

Today's opinion is a serious departure, not only from our prior decisions involving attorney advertising, but also from the principles that govern the transmission of commercial speech. The Court's opinion reflects a new-found and illegitimate confidence that it, along with the Supreme Court of Florida, knows what is best for the Bar and its clients. Self-assurance has always been the hallmark of a censor. That is why under the First Amendment the public, not the State, has the right and the power to decide what ideas and information are deserving of their adherence.... By validating Florida's rule, today's majority is complicit in the Bar's censorship. For these reasons, I dissent from the opinion of the Court and from its judgment.

NOTES

1.   What was the substantial governmental interest that justified the regulation here? Is protection of the reputation of the legal profession a substantial governmental interest?

2.   The Florida ban on targeted solicitation was only 30 days. Could a jurisdiction impose a permanent ban on targeted solicitation of accident victims? *See Revo v. Disciplinary Board of the Supreme Court for the State of New Mexico*, 106 F.3d 929 (10th Cir. 1997).

3.   While lawyers were prohibited from soliciting the business of these potential clients during the 30-day window, were others permitted to contact them? Is that a concern? Would Model Rule 4.3 permit a lawyer for a tortfeasor to settle a claim with an unrepresented plaintiff during the 30-day period during which the Florida statute prohibited the mailing of targeted solicitation letters? *See* Comment [2] to Model Rule 4.3. Would a lawyer for a tortfeasor be permitted to send an insurance adjuster or investigator to an unrepresented plaintiff to settle a potential claim during that time? *See* Model Rule 4.3, 8.4(a). Some suggest that if contact by plaintiffs' lawyers is prohibited during the 30-day period following an accident, contact by representatives for the other side should be as well. What do you think?

3.   OTHER SOLICITATION METHODS

In addition to in-person and targeted mail solicitation, what other methods might lawyers use to attract clients? One might be referrals—suggestions by others that potential clients employ the lawyer's services. Referrals can come from several different places, and the rules regulate these different sources differently.

First, referrals can come from other lawyers. Why might a lawyer choose to refer a case to another lawyer? Lawyers refer away cases and clients all the time, perhaps because the client seeks help in an area in which the lawyer lacks expertise or simply doesn't practice. Many of those referrals come with no strings attached. One can imagine, though, that if a potentially lucrative case walks in the door, a lawyer who refers the case to another lawyer—perhaps a specialist in the field—might like to claim a "referral fee" or a share of the fees that the lawyer who takes the case ultimately earns. Can the referring lawyer do so? *See* Model Rule 1.5(e). Can a lawyer have a standing agreement with another lawyer to refer all relevant matters to the other lawyer, something like "I'll send all my clients to you for estate planning if you send all your clients to me when they have personal injury claims"? Why might such an agreement be problematic? *See* Model Rule 7.2(b)(4) and Comment [8] to Model Rule 7.2.

Referrals can also come from non-lawyers. Can a lawyer agree to pay a non-lawyer, like a taxi driver or the desk clerk at the emergency room of a hospital, for handing out her business cards or recommending her to individuals in need of legal services? *See* Rule 7.2(b). Why is this impermissible? In lieu of paying a referral fee, can the lawyer simply agree to pay the non-lawyer a part of the fee he receives? *See* Rule 5.4(a).

Referrals can also come from referral services. The Rules permit lawyers to make payments to a referral service only if such a service "has been approved by an appropriate regulatory authority." Model Rule 7.2(b)(2). The theory is that potential clients will view referral services as "consumer-oriented organizations that provide unbiased referrals to lawyers with appropriate experience in the subject matter of the representation." Comment [6] to Model Rule 7.2. Therefore, lawyers should pay to participate only in those referral services that live up to those expectations.

The legitimacy of internet referral services to generate clients has produced some disputes. Can a lawyer pay a fee to register with a website, in exchange for which the website will forward inquiries from potential clients with appropriate types of legal problems? In *New York State Bar Ass'n Comm. on Prof'l Ethics Op. 799* (2006), the answer was no. The fee amounted to a prohibited payment to someone in exchange for recommending the lawyer, which was prohibited by the New York rules. While merely listing the lawyer's contact information would have been acceptable, the service did more. "[W]e find that the line is crossed ... when a website purports to recommend a particular lawyer or lawyers for the prospective client's problem, *based on an analysis of that problem.*" (emphasis in original).

PROBLEMS

1. Lawyer televised an advertisement depicting himself as an "experienced, aggressive personal injury lawyer who was prepared to take and had taken personal action on behalf of clients." Lawyer, however, had not actively been engaged in the practice of law in the state for nine years. His role in the law firm was as a "spokesperson," and the work was actually done by one or two attorneys and several paralegals. "In contrast to the image of respondent depicted in the commercials, respondent has never tried a case to its conclusion and has conducted approximately 10 depositions." Was it proper to discipline Lawyer based on his airing of this commercial? *See In re Shapiro,* 780 N.Y.S.2d 680 (App. Div. 4th Dep't 2004).

2. May a lawyer place in an advertisement a reference to his being designated a "Super Lawyer" by a media group? Does it matter how the group came to bestow the designation "Super Lawyer"? How about "Best Lawyer in America"? *See N.J. Ethics Op. 39* (2006); *Allen, Allen, Allen & Allen v. Williams,* 254 F.Supp.2d 614 (E.D. Va. 2003).

3. Organization operated a website which collected information about attorneys and, based on a formula devised by Organization, rated and displayed a comparative numerical ranking of lawyers. Lawyer complained that Organization's website used an inaccurate and invalid system for rating lawyers, and that Organization's scale unfairly rated him as "average," a 5.5 ranking on a

ten-point scale. Lawyer claimed that the rankings could harm his reputation, could cost him clients, and could mislead the public into bypassing him unfairly. He sought to enjoin Organization's publication of ratings on its website. Should Lawyer succeed? *See Browne v. Avvo, Inc.*, 525 F.Supp.2d 1249 (W.D. Wash. 2007).

4. The law firm of Keller & Keller televised an advertisement in which actors, purporting to be a senior insurance adjuster and a junior insurance adjuster, were discussing a claim. In the ad, the junior adjuster proposed denying and delaying in order to avoid paying the claim. The senior adjuster asked which lawyer was representing the victim, and upon hearing the firm was Keller & Keller, replied, "Keller & Keller? Let's settle this one." The state has a provision prohibiting advertisements which "contain a statement or opinion as to the quality of the services or contains a representation or implication regarding the quality of legal services." Does the firm's ad violate this rule? If so, does the rule violate the First Amendment? *See In re Keller*, 792 N.E.2d 865 (Ind. 2003). Is it misleading? *See Farrin v. Thigpen*, 173 F.Supp.2d 427 (M.D.N.C. 2001).

5. May a lawyer's advertisement include a coupon for dollars off the cost of legal services, or a coupon for a free initial consultation? Does this violate a prohibition on characterizing rates or fees as "cut-rate," "lowest," "give-away," "below cost," "discount," or "special," or is it more like characterizing fees as "reasonable" or "moderate"? *See Supreme Court of Ohio Board of Commissioners on Grievances and Discipline Opinion 2005–9* (2005); *cf. South Carolina Bar Ethics Advisory Committee 6–27* (1997).

6. On the internet, Lawyer located a chat room created for victims and families of a recent mass disaster. The purpose of the chat room was to provide emotional support to victims and their families. Lawyer monitored the conversation in the chat room for a while, then introduced herself as a lawyer and offered to answer any questions for persons in the chat room. Has Lawyer violated the professional responsibility rules? *See Cal. Eth. Op. 2004–166.*

7. Company contacted Lawyer to ask if he wanted to participate in Company's attorney-client matching service. Company described its services as follows: When a consumer seeking an attorney visits Company's website, the consumer fills out a questionnaire describing the services being sought. Company reviews the description and provides it to fee-paying participant lawyers practicing in the appropriate field and geographic area. Company takes on only a limited number of lawyers in each field and region. Attorneys who are interested in representing the potential client can respond directly to the consumer describing their relevant experience and their fee structures; consumers can then view the lawyer's profiles on Company's website, and if interested, the consumers can contact the lawyers directly. If Lawyer provides three reference letters to Company, he can attain "verified status," in which case clients would see a "verified" logo attached to Lawyer's online profile; the names of verified lawyers appear above other lawyers on the list the consumer receives, and use of a "verified" lawyer provides a very small money-back guarantee to consumers. Lawyer would pay a flat fee to Company. May Lawyer participate in the matching service? *See Washington State Bar Informal Op. 2106* (2006); *cf. Rhode Island Supreme Court Ethics Advisory Panel Op. No. 2005–01.*

CHAPTER 14

DUTIES TO THE GUILD: ADMISSION TO THE BAR AND UNAUTHORIZED PRACTICE

■ ■ ■

One of the duties of lawyers is to avoid the unauthorized practice of law. See Model Rule 5.5(a). Ordinarily, to be authorized to practice law, a lawyer must be admitted to practice in the jurisdiction. What does "admitted to practice" mean?

A. ADMISSION TO PRACTICE

Most jurisdictions require a lawyer to fulfill several requirements to be admitted to practice. This means that a lawyer is licensed to practice law. We often refer to this as being "admitted to the bar," shorthand for saying that the lawyer has satisfied all the requirements of licensure in the jurisdiction where he or she wishes to practice. Be careful: this is not the same as belonging to a bar association! In some jurisdictions, which have a so-called "integrated" bar, all lawyers admitted to practice in the jurisdiction are members of the bar association. In other jurisdictions, bar association membership is simply a voluntary affiliation, which lawyers can choose to take part in or not, as they wish.

1. EDUCATION

In most jurisdictions, a person seeking admission to practice must be a graduate of an accredited law school. Some states accredit their own law schools; many others do not. Those states rely instead on the accreditation procedures of the American Bar Association, which is recognized as the accrediting agency for law schools by the U.S. Department of Education.

A person who graduates from an ABA-accredited law school ordinarily has satisfied the educational requirements for bar admission in any state. A person who has graduated from a state-accredited law school will satisfy the educational requirements for admission to practice in that state, but other states may decide that such education does not satisfy the educational requirements for admission to practice. This may mean that the lawyer cannot be admitted to practice in another state, and that disqualification can be permanent. *See In re Doering*, 751 N.W.2d 123 (Neb. 2008). Doering graduated from a California law school which, at the time he attended it, was not ABA-accredited (though it was accredited in California and subsequently secured ABA accreditation). Twenty-five years later, he sought admission to the bar of the state of Nebraska. Although Doering had practiced in Georgia in good standing for ten years, the Nebraska Supreme Court declined to waive its requirement that applicants for admission to the state bar—even those with significant practice experience elsewhere—have attended an ABA-accredited law school. "Doering would have us evaluate nonaccredited U.S. law schools on a case-by-case basis to determine whether a particular school, at a certain point in time, provided a legal education that was substantially equivalent to that from an ABA-accredited law school. But such a case-by-case approach . . . would impose upon this court an unreasonable and unnecessary burden." *Id.* at 1010–11. Doering was not admitted to the Nebraska bar.

How does a law school secure—or retain—ABA accreditation? The ABA, through its Council of the Section of Legal Education and Admissions to the Bar, promulgates standards for approval of law schools, and initial accreditation and subsequent periodic "site visits" assess law schools' compliance with those standards. Site visitors delve into the quality of faculty, facilities, student services and libraries, inquire into budget and fiscal matters, and assess student retention, bar passage rates, and placement information, and report on these matters to the accreditors.

Some scholars have argued that the ABA's accreditation processes make legal education more expensive and ultimately less accessible, which in turn makes the profession less diverse. *See, e.g.,* George B. Shepherd, *No African–American Lawyers Allowed: The Inefficient Racism of the ABA's Accreditation of Law Schools,* 53 J. Legal Educ. 103 (2003); John Nussbaumer, *The Disturbing Correlation Between ABA Accreditation Review and Declining African–American Law School Enrollment,* 80 St. John's L. Rev. 991 (2006). How should the accreditation process take account of the need for diversity in and access to the profession?

Seven states permit some form of apprenticeship in lieu of law school. This very traditional route to the practice has declined substantially in importance, but remains available, subject to the structure and reporting requirements imposed by the jurisdiction. In Vermont, for example, a person who has completed three-quarters of the coursework required for an undergraduate degree may participate in the state's Law Office Study Program. A lawyer or judge admitted for at least three years must commit to supervising the candidate for four years, 25 hours per week. At the end of the apprenticeship, candidates must take and pass the bar examination. Do you think that such a procedure prepares candidates for law practice as well as law school? Better? Should more jurisdictions permit people to secure admission to practice this way? Why do you suppose that most jurisdictions do not? As the costs of legal education increase, should states provide alternative routes to legal practice? What are the advantages and disadvantages of "reading the law"?

2. EXAMINATION

In most jurisdictions, sitting for and passing the bar examination is required for new lawyers seeking admission to practice. Some would say that the bar examination assures the competency of new practitioners. Does the bar examination do that effectively? Are there aspects of the bar examination that are irrelevant to or inconsistent with competency? How do we guarantee the competency of already-existing lawyers?

The "pass rates" for bar examinations vary radically from state to state; in 2007 California's pass rate was 65%, while Minnesota's was 91%. Why? (It might be relevant to note that California is a state with a large number of state-accredited law schools. How might that affect the jurisdiction's pass rate? Why?) As a graduating law student, do you want to seek admission to practice in a state with a bar examination that has a high pass rate, or a low pass rate? Why? As a practicing lawyer, do you want to be in a state with a high pass rate or a low pass rate? Why might your answers to these two questions be different?

Some states permit lawyers admitted to practice in another jurisdiction with a certain amount of practice experience to be admitted to the bar without sitting for the bar exam. This is sometimes referred to as "waiving in" or "admission on motion." Some states have a reciprocal arrangement, granting these privileges only to states that will grant them in turn to their own lawyers. Are these "comity" provisions permissible? In *Morrison v. Board of Law Examiners of the State of North Carolina*, 453 F.3d 190 (4th Cir. 2006), Morrison claimed that North Carolina's rules on comity admission, which required that the lawyer's prior practice experience be in a state which had comity with North Carolina, violated the Privileges and Immunities Clause of Article IV, § 2 and the Fourteenth Amendment as well as the Equal Protection Clause. The court rejected the claim. "North Carolina is not discriminating against citizens of other States in favor of her own. The rule simply represents North Carolina's 'undertaking to secure for its citizens an advantage by offering that advantage to citizens of any other state on condition that the other state make a similar grant.'" *Id.* at 194.

Some states, however, are decidedly ungenerous about admitting lawyers from other jurisdictions without requiring them to sit for the bar exam. What do you suppose the justification is for a highly restrictive policy on admission of lawyers from other jurisdictions? Does this reflect concerns about competency, or about limiting the supply of lawyers? Why is it useful for lawyers to make it more difficult for others to enter the profession?

The bar examination is offered twice a year, in July and February. In many jurisdictions, it can take a long time for the examiners to score all the exams and release results. If you do not learn your results on the July bar examination until November, what does that mean for your ability to prepare for the February administration of the examination? Retaking the bar examination can also be expensive, because an applicant must pay fees to sit for the examination, because full-time study interferes with work, and because many consider a bar review course essential to success on the examination. The bar exam looms as a daunting and for some law graduates insurmountable obstacle to admission to practice.

The bar examination has been criticized on two major counts. One is that it tests very few of the skills that a practicing lawyer needs. The other is that it has a disparate impact on non-majority takers, resulting in a negative impact on the diversity of the profession. Kristin Booth Glen, *When and Where We Enter: Rethinking Admission to the Legal Profession*, 102 Colum. L. Rev. 1696 (2002). Then-Dean Glen proposed an alternative route to admission that would require applicants for bar admission to serve a three-month assignment as lawyers in the court system, with their work assessed by trained evaluators. Do you think some kind of practical assessment system is an appropriate alternative to the bar examination? Would you opt for it if given the choice?

3. FITNESS OR "GOOD MORAL CHARACTER"

Most jurisdictions impose some sort of character requirement for admission to the bar. Described, often, as a requirement of "good moral character," the requirement permits significant delving into the backgrounds and experiences of applicants to the bar and far-reaching inquiry into their histories. One rationale for the good moral character requirement is client protection; lawyers will be entrusted with clients' assets and their secrets, and the bar apparatus wishes to undertake some screening to determine who is worthy of that responsibility. Another rationale is that bar disciplinary enforcement is lax and underfunded in many jurisdictions; if it will be difficult to police applicants once they are admitted to practice, that might make it more important to ensure that no mistakes are made in the admissions phase. Aaron M. Clemens, *Facing the Klieg Lights: Understanding the 'Good Moral Character' Examination for Bar Applicants*, 40 Akron L. Rev. 255 (2007). Is it fair to apply a more stringent standard to those seeking admission to the practice than to those already in it?

According to the Supreme Court, "A State can require high standards of qualification, such as good moral character or proficiency in its law, before it admits an applicant to the bar, but any qualification must have a rational connection with the applicant's fitness or capacity to practice law." *Schware v. Board of Bar Examiners of New Mexico*, 353 U.S. 232, 239 (1957). In that case, the Court held that Mr. Schware's previous membership in the Communist Party and his work as a labor activist, including several arrests and the use of aliases to avoid bias, did not demonstrate his lack of good moral character. What rational connection is there between the various elements of the good moral character requirement, as expounded in the following cases, and the practice of law?

(A) CRIMINAL HISTORY

IN RE HAMM

123 P.3d 652 (Ariz. 2005)

McGREGOR, CHIEF JUSTICE.

James Hamm petitioned this Court to review the recommendation of the Committee on Character and Fitness (the Committee) that his application for admission to the State Bar of Arizona (the Bar) be denied. Having reviewed the record and the Committee's report, we conclude that James Hamm has failed to establish the good moral character necessary to be admitted to the practice of law in Arizona and deny his application.

I.

In September 1974, James Hamm was twenty-six years old and living on the streets of Tucson. Although he previously had attended divinity school and worked as a part-time pastor, Hamm describes his life in 1974 as reflecting a series of personal and social failures. In 1973, he had separated from his wife, with whom he had a son. Although he had no criminal record, he supported himself by selling small quantities of marijuana and, again according to Hamm, he used marijuana and other drugs and abused alcohol.

On September 6, 1974, Hamm met two young men who identified themselves as college students from Missouri. The two, Willard Morley and Zane Staples, came to Tucson to buy twenty pounds of marijuana. Hamm agreed to sell it to them, but apparently was unable to acquire that quantity of marijuana. Rather than call off the transaction, Hamm and two accomplices, Garland Wells and Bill Reeser, agreed to rob Staples and Morley of the money intended for the purchase. On September 7, Wells gave Hamm a gun to use during the robbery. Later that day, Wells and Hamm directed Morley and Staples to drive to the outskirts of Tucson, purportedly to complete the drug transaction; Reeser followed in another vehicle. Both Wells and Hamm carried guns; Morley and Staples were unarmed. Hamm sat behind Morley, the driver, and Wells sat behind Staples. At some point, Hamm detected that Staples was becoming suspicious. As Morley stopped the car, and without making any demand on the victims for money, Hamm shot Morley in the back of the head, killing him. At the same time, Wells shot Staples. Hamm then shot Staples in the back as he tried to escape and shot Morley once again. Wells also shot Morley, then pursued Staples, whom he ultimately killed outside of the car. Hamm and Wells took $1400.00 from the glove compartment, fled the scene in the van driven by Reeser, and left the bodies of Morley and Staples lying in the desert.

Hamm took his share of the money and visited his sister in California. At the hearing held to consider his application to the Bar, he told the Committee that he "was compelled to come back to Tucson", despite knowing he probably would be caught. Police officers arrested Hamm shortly after his return. While in custody, he told the police that Morley and Staples were killed in a gun battle during the drug deal. Initially charged with two counts of first-degree murder and two counts of armed robbery, Hamm pled guilty to one count of first-degree murder and was sentenced to life in prison, with no possibility of parole for twenty-five years.

Once in prison, Hamm began taking steps toward rehabilitation and became a model prisoner. After spending one year in maximum security, he applied for and received a job in a computer training program that allowed him to be transferred to medium security. Once in medium security, Hamm apparently took advantage of any and every educational opportunity the prison system had to offer. He completed certificates in yoga and meditation and, on his own, studied Jungian psychology. He helped fellow inmates learn to read and write and to take responsibility for their actions. He obtained a bachelor's degree in applied sociology, *summa cum laude,* from Northern Arizona University through a prison study program.

After Hamm completed six years in medium security, prison officials transferred him to minimum security, where he worked on paint and construction crews. He received a significant degree of freedom, which allowed him to live in a dormitory rather than in a cell and occasionally to drive unaccompanied to nearby towns. He testified that he was the only inmate permitted to head a work crew. Hamm reported to the Committee that he played an instrumental role on various prison committees, particularly the committee that developed a new grievance procedure within the Department of Corrections. In addition, he wrote grant proposals for libraries, for handicapped prisoners, and for obtaining greater legal assistance for prisoners.

While in prison, he met and married Donna Leone. She and Hamm founded Middle Ground Prison Reform (Middle Ground), a prisoner and prisoner family advocacy organization involved in lobbying for laws related to the criminal justice system and prisons. Middle Ground also provides public education about those topics.

In 1989, the Governor, acting on the recommendation of the Arizona Board of Pardons and Parole (the Board), commuted Hamm's sentence. When he had served nearly seventeen years, in July 1992, the Board released Hamm on parole, conditioned upon no use of alcohol or drugs, drug and alcohol testing, and fifteen hours of community service each month. In December 2001, the Arizona Board of Executive Clemency granted Hamm's third application for absolute discharge.

Between his release in August 1992 and his absolute discharge in December 2001, Hamm performed thousands of hours of community service. He advocated for prisoners' rights in various forums by writing position papers, appearing on radio programs, testifying in legislative hearings, and speaking at churches, schools, and civic organizations. He also appeared in a public service video encouraging children not to do drugs or join gangs. Hamm now works as the Director of Advocacy Services at Middle Ground Prison Reform.

While on parole, Hamm graduated from the Arizona State University College of Law. In July 1999, Hamm passed the Arizona bar examination and, in 2004, filed his Character and Fitness Report with the Committee.

II.

The Rules of the Supreme Court of Arizona establish the process through which the Committee and this Court evaluate applications for admission to the Bar, and prior case law clarifies the burden an applicant must satisfy to establish good moral character. We begin with a review of the rules.

A.

The Committee may recommend an applicant for admission only if that applicant, in addition to meeting other requirements, satisfies the Committee that he or she is of good moral character. The applicant bears the burden of establishing his or her good moral character. In determining whether an applicant's prior conduct indicates a lack of good moral character, the Committee must consider the following non-exhaustive list of factors:

A. The applicant's age, experience and general level of sophistication at the time of the conduct

B. The recency of the conduct

C. The reliability of the information concerning the conduct

D. The seriousness of the conduct

E. Consideration given by the applicant to relevant laws, rules and responsibilities at the time of the conduct

F. The factors underlying the conduct

G. The cumulative effect of the conduct

H. The evidence of rehabilitation

I. The applicant's positive social contributions since the conduct

J. The applicant's candor in the admissions process

K. The materiality of any omissions or misrepresentations by the applicant.

If the applicant fails to convince the Committee of his or her good moral character, the Committee has a *duty not to recommend* that person to this Court. After the Committee submits its report, an aggrieved applicant may petition this Court for review.

B.

... The ultimate question in cases such as this is whether the applicant has established good moral character, a concept with which we have wrestled as we have attempted to define its boundaries....

We agree with Hamm that, under the Rule applicable to Hamm's application, our concern must be with the applicant's present moral character.... Past misconduct, however, is not irrelevant. Rather, this Court must determine what past bad acts reveal about an applicant's current character.

III.

[T]he Committee conducted a formal hearing to consider Hamm's application.... Hamm, representing himself, and his wife presented extensive testimony. In addition, the Committee heard from three licensed attorneys who had worked with Hamm and who recommended his admission and also considered letters from those opposed to and in support of Hamm's application.... In its report, the Committee stated that, in reaching its conclusions, it considered the following:

> 1) Hamm's unlawful conduct, which included the commission of two violent "execution style" murders and his testimony as to the facts surrounding the murders.

> 2) Hamm's omissions on his Application and his testimony in explaining his failure to disclose all required information.

> 3) Hamm's neglect of his financial responsibilities and/or violation of a longstanding child support court order and his testimony as to his failure to comply with the court order.

> 4) Hamm's mental or emotional instability impairing his ability to perform the functions of an attorney including his testimony as to any diagnosis and treatment.

After reviewing all these factors, the Committee concluded that Hamm had not met his burden of establishing that he possesses the requisite character and fitness for admission to the Bar and accordingly recommended that his application be denied....

A.

The serious nature of Hamm's past criminal conduct is beyond dispute. Hamm acknowledges that no more serious criminal conduct exists than committing first-degree murder. Our society reserves its harshest punishment for those convicted of such conduct.

Hamm's past criminal conduct and the serious nature of that conduct affect the burden he must meet to establish good moral character. He must first establish rehabilitation from prior criminal conduct....

The added burden becomes greater as past unlawful conduct becomes more serious.... "[I]n the case of extremely damning past misconduct, a showing of rehabilitation may be virtually impossible to make." Indeed, we are aware of no instance in which a person convicted of first-degree murder has been admitted to the practice of law.

To show rehabilitation, Hamm must show that he has accepted responsibility for his criminal conduct. Hamm fully recognizes his need to make this showing. Indeed, he states that his rehabilitation could not have proceeded absent such acceptance. We recognize the Committee's concern that Hamm has not yet fully accepted responsibility for the two murders. Hamm *says* he has done so, repeatedly and strongly, but some of his other statements indicate to the contrary. The inconsistencies among his various statements related to accepting responsibility are most evident when he discusses Staples' murder. Although he *told* the Committee that he accepts responsibility for Staples' murder, in fact he consistently assigns that responsibility to his accomplice. His testimony revealed almost no attention to the commission or aftermath of Staples' murder. Hamm concedes that he has focused on his role in Morley's murder rather than on his role in Staples' murder. The difference in approach, he explains, resulted from one postcard written to him by Morley's grandmother and his decision to use his connection to Morley to provide motivation to overcome difficulties. We have no reason to doubt that Hamm's focus on Morley's murder aided him, using his words, in "accomplishing things that people have been telling me I can't do and we're [Hamm and Morley] still doing it today". That fact, however, does nothing to assure us that Hamm has taken responsibility for Staples' murder, as he must if he is to establish rehabilitation.

We also give serious consideration to the Committee's finding that Hamm was not completely forthright in his testimony about the murders. Hamm has insisted in his filings with this Court that he did not intend to kill, but only to rob, his victims. The agreed facts, however, lead directly to the inference that Hamm intended to kill. He conspired with his accomplices to rob the victims; he accepted the gun provided by Wells and took it with him in the car with the victims; he testified that, although he did not intend to kill the victims, he was "afraid" they would be killed when he got in the car; he shot Morley without ever attempting a robbery and shot him a second time to make certain he was dead; and he also shot Staples to prevent his escape. The Committee observed Hamm testify and was able to judge the credibility of his testimony in light of uncontested facts. We agree that the record shows that Hamm, despite his current protestations to the contrary, intended to kill the victims. His failure to confront the fact that these murders were intentional undermines his statements that he fully accepts responsibility for his actions.

As did the Committee, we give substantial weight to Hamm's attempts at rehabilitation.... Were rehabilitation the only showing Hamm must make to establish good moral character, we would weigh those factors tending to show rehabilitation against those tending to show a lack thereof. Under the facts of this case, however, we need not decide whether the facts of record establish rehabilitation.

When an applicant has committed first-degree murder, a crime that demonstrates an extreme lack of good moral character, that applicant must make an extraordinary showing of present good moral character to establish that he or she is qualified to be admitted to the practice of law. Even assuming that Hamm has established rehabilitation, showing rehabilitation from criminal conduct does not, in itself, establish good moral character.... An applicant must establish his current good moral character, independent of and in addition to, evidence of rehabilitation. We conclude that Hamm failed to make that showing.

B.

We share the Committee's deep concern about Hamm's longstanding failure to fulfill, or even address, his child support obligation to his son, born in 1969, four years before Hamm and his first wife separated. Not until he prepared his application for admission to the Bar in 2004 did Hamm make any effort to meet his responsibility to provide support for his son. During the Committee hearing, Hamm advanced several explanations for his failure to do so. Like the Committee, we find none of his explanations credible.

Although Hamm attempts to excuse his failure to pay child support by pointing out that he never received a copy of a final divorce decree, Hamm scarcely can claim that he lacked awareness of his obligation. A few months after he and his wife separated in 1973, Hamm was arrested on a misdemeanor charge of failing to pay child support.... Hamm made no effort to learn the extent of his financial obligation to his son from 1974, when Hamm was twenty-six years old, until 2004, when he was fifty-five. During those nearly thirty years, he gained sophistication and attended law school. He must have known, and certainly should have known, that he had long avoided a basic parental obligation.

Hamm also attempted to excuse his inattention to his obligation by explaining that he learned, first from a private investigator hired by his wife in 1988, and later from his son, that his former wife's new husband had adopted his son. His reliance on the private investigator's 1988 report to excuse his failure is surprising, given the fact that his son was only months from the age of majority when Hamm learned of the report; he provides no explanation for his lack of concern prior to that date.

Hamm further explained that only when he applied for admission to the Bar in 2004 did he discover that his son had not been adopted and then "calculated the child support payment [due] over the years." Hamm determined that he owed $10,000.00 and, even though the statute of limitations barred an action to recover past amounts due, contacted his son and set up a repayment schedule.

... Hamm's failure to meet his parental obligation for nearly thirty years makes it more difficult for him to make the required extraordinary showing that he "has conducted himself as a man ordinarily would, should, or does."

We also agree with the Committee that Hamm did not display honesty and candor in discussing his failure to pay child support with the Committee. Hamm testified both that his son told him personally that he had been adopted and that his son "adamantly refused" to accept interest payments on the unpaid child support.

Hamm's son testified, however, that he had never been adopted, that prior to his contact with Hamm he had changed his name himself, and that he had not told Hamm he had been adopted. Hamm's son also did not report adamantly refusing interest payments. In response to a question from the Committee about interest payments, he said:

> Discussions about interest? Seems like whenever we were talking about it, you know, he said it was a large amount, and it seems like the subject of interest did come up. I can't remember exactly, you know, what we said about it. But, you know, I didn't push the issue or anything, say, well, you know, you're going to pay me interest for this or what, or is there any interest. It wasn't really an issue or important to me.

We discern no reason that Hamm's son would have been other than forthright about these matters, while Hamm had every reason to present himself in the best possible light.[1] Like the Committee, we find the testimony of his son to be more credible.

C.

We further conclude that Hamm did not adequately explain his failure to disclose an incident involving him and his current wife, Donna, when he submitted his application to the Committee.

In 1996, Hamm and Donna engaged in a physical altercation outside a convenience store. Donna "yelled the word 'kidnap' out of the window" of the vehicle Hamm was driving, causing him to pull over and leave the vehicle. During their tussle, Donna tore Hamm's shirt. Both called the police, who arrested neither Hamm nor Donna. The incident and what Donna describes as her "embellishments" caused such great concern to the Hamms, particularly because Hamm was on parole, that Donna submitted to a polygraph administered by a private company to demonstrate that Hamm had not kidnapped her. The two also underwent marital counseling.

Nonetheless, when filling out his Character and Fitness Report, Hamm failed to disclose the incident to the Committee. Question 25 on the report asks specifically whether the applicant, among other things, has been "questioned" concerning any felony or misdemeanor. Hamm told the Committee that, in reading the application, he missed the word "ques-

---

1. Rather than acknowledge any inconsistencies between his testimony and that of his son, Hamm lashed out at the Committee's refusal to agree with Hamm's argument, which the Committee could accept only if it accepted Hamm's testimony on this issue as credible. Hamm accused the Committee of "totally ignor[ing] the content of [Hamm's Petition] to which it supposedly was responding."

tioned" in the list of encounters with law enforcement that Question 25 directs an applicant to report.

Hamm's explanation strains credulity. . . . [W]e infer from Hamm's knowledge of the law and his efforts in 1996 to document a defense for the domestic incident that he fully understood its importance and must have known that the incident would be of interest to the Committee. His failure to include it in his initial application further affects his ability to make the needed extraordinary showing of good moral character.

D.

Hamm's actions during these proceedings also raise questions about his fitness to practice law. The introduction to Hamm's petition before this Court begins:

> The consequences of this case for Petitioner take it out of the ordinary realm of civil cases. If the Committee's recommendation is followed, it will prevent him from earning a living through practicing law. This deprivation has consequences of the greatest import for Petitioner, who has invested years of study and a great deal of financial resources in preparing to be a lawyer. . . .

This language repeats nearly verbatim the language of the United States Supreme Court in *Konigsberg v. State Bar,* 353 U.S. 252 (1957). If an attorney submits work to a court that is not his own, his actions may violate the rules of professional conduct. We are concerned about Hamm's decision to quote from the Supreme Court's opinion without attribution and are equally troubled by his failure to acknowledge his error. When the Committee's response pointed to Hamm's failure to attribute this language to *Konigsberg,* he avoided the serious questions raised and refused to confront or apologize for his improper actions, asserting instead: "From Petitioner's perspective, any eloquence that might be found in the Petition does not derive from any prior case decided in any jurisdiction, but rather from the gradual development of his own potential through study, reflection, and devotion to the duty created by his commission of murder." Hamm apparently either does not regard his actions as improper or simply refuses to take responsibility. In either case, his actions here do not assist him in making the requisite showing of good moral character.

When Hamm committed first-degree murder in 1974, he demonstrated his extreme lack of good moral character. . . . [W]e agree with those jurisdictions that have held that an applicant with such a background must make an extraordinary showing of rehabilitation and present good moral character to be admitted to the practice of law. Perhaps such a showing is, in practical terms, a near impossibility. We need not decide that question today, however, because Hamm's lack of candor before the Committee and this Court, his failure to accept full responsibility for his serious criminal misconduct, and his failure to accept or fulfill, on a timely basis, his parental obligation of support for his son, all show that Hamm has not met the stringent standard that applies to an applicant in his position who seeks to show his present good moral character. . . .

Because James Hamm has failed to meet his burden of proving that he is of good moral character, we deny his application for admission to the State Bar of Arizona.

NOTES

1. Did the fact that Hamm had been convicted of first-degree murder mean that he lacked the present good moral character necessary to practice law? Can someone who has committed such a serious crime ever be sufficiently rehabilitated to warrant admission to practice?

2. Do you think the court treated the other issues in Hamm's petition the same way it would have had Hamm's prior conviction been less serious? Did it bend over backwards to find other problems with good moral character in his petition?

3. As you can see from this case, candor and attitude are critically important to admission. Why? Lawyers as a group are not known as humble, self-deprecating, or particularly straightforward about their shortcomings. Why is it necessary to act that way to get admitted to practice?

4. The Rules of Professional Conduct apply only to lawyers. If an applicant for admission is not truthful in the application process and is admitted, can she be disciplined for that failure? Model Rule 8.1 applies the obligation of candor to an applicant for admission, and Comment [1] suggests that false-hoods in the application are a basis for discipline if the attorney is admitted. This is the only Model Rule that permits discipline to be imposed for conduct that occurred prior to the lawyer's admission.

5. Do you think that Hamm can ever be admitted to practice in Arizona? Why or why not?

(B) FISCAL IRRESPONSIBILITY

FLORIDA BOARD OF BAR EXAMINERS EX REL. M.A.R.

755 So.2d 89 (Fla. 2000)

PER CURIAM.

Petitioner M.A.R. asks this Court to review the recommendations of the Florida Board of Bar Examiners. We have jurisdiction. For the reasons expressed below, we approve the Board's recommendation that M.A.R. be denied admission to The Florida Bar at this time.

Petitioner M.A.R. filed an application for admission to The Florida Bar on March 14, 1995. On December 23, 1996, the Florida Board of Bar Examiners filed formal specifications against him alleging several items of misconduct. After a formal hearing, the Board found that M.A.R. had violated a court order regarding child support and, although the record contains evidence of a far greater default, found that the amount in arrears was at least $17,000, as admitted by M.A.R. The Board found the fact that M.A.R.'s children did not suffer as a result of his non-payment did not mitigate the seriousness of the conduct, and that M.A.R.'s evidence regarding an agreement between M.A.R. and his former spouse relating to his non-payment of child support did not establish an affirmative defense to the proven allegations. The record is certainly subject to a reasonable interpretation that M.A.R. made a personal decision, and his ex-wife was simply forced to accept the consequences of that decision.

Additionally, the Board found that M.A.R. failed to timely file federal income tax returns and timely pay taxes in 1987, 1988, 1989, and 1990, and that since 1995, he has written over forty bad checks, the most recent being issued only one week prior to the formal hearing. The Board further found that M.A.R. gave a false oath on certain documents submitted to the Board by executing and having those documents notarized prior to filling in the information. M.A.R. admitted these actions, but at the formal hearing he testified that he did not appreciate the inappropriateness of his actions at the time the documents were notarized. The Board found this testimony unpersuasive in light of his testimony at his previous investigative hearing that his actions were motivated, in part, by a desire not to reveal unfavorable information to the notaries with whom he worked.

Next, the Board found that M.A.R. lied on his application for admission to law school with regard to his prior arrest and probation for DUI. Although M.A.R. testified that his statement on the application was not intentionally false and was due to his misreading of the question on the application, the Board rejected this explanation as unworthy of belief. Finally, the Board found that M.A.R. had falsely represented himself to be an attorney in a letter to a creditor.

At the formal hearing ... M.A.R. presented character testimony from an attorney friend and testimony from his mother. He also presented exhibits showing his child support payments, his law school application, a letter of recommendation from the associate dean of his law school, and a Certificate of Release of IRS tax lien. The Board found this presentation insufficient to establish a defense or to mitigate any of the proven misconduct and insufficient to establish rehabilitation. The Board concluded that M.A.R.'s violation of the child support order was individually disqualifying and that the remaining instances of misconduct were collectively disqualifying. Accordingly, it recommended that M.A.R. not be admitted to The Florida Bar. M.A.R. now seeks review of this recommendation.

Essentially, M.A.R. takes issue with the Board's conclusion that his misconduct is disqualifying for admission to the bar. As to his violation of the child support order, he argues that there were mitigating circumstances which sufficiently explain and excuse his actions. As to the remaining instances of misconduct, he argues that considering the surrounding circumstances, they are not serious enough to reflect negatively on his character and fitness to practice law.

We disagree and find that, when considered in the aggregate, the proven instances of misconduct are sufficient to justify nonadmission. This Court has set forth the test to be applied in determining character and fitness for admission to The Florida Bar: "First, are the facts in this case such that a reasonable [person] should have substantial doubts about the petitioner's honesty, fairness, and respect for the rights of others and for the laws of the state and nation? Second, is the conduct involved in this case rationally connected to the petitioner's fitness to practice law?"

. . . M.A.R.'s failure to pay child support shows a lack of respect for the rights of his children and his ex-wife and a lack of respect for the law and for the court order itself. The marital settlement agreement which was reflected in the child support order required M.A.R. to pay only $150 a week for three children, and while he may have paid some child support, there were several years during which he paid very little. For the years 1989 through 1992, according to his own account, he paid a total of only $2551.

. . . [R]egardless of his alleged ability to pay the amounts required, he still clearly violated and disregarded a court order. This conduct was based upon a personal decision which forced others to accept the consequences. Such misconduct is rationally connected to M.A.R.'s fitness to practice law. It is exceedingly important that potential members of the Bar respect and obey orders of the court and follow proper channels to seek modification of those orders, rather than simply ignoring them. One may always find excuses to present when conduct is in violation of a court order, but the citizens of Florida are entitled to more than excuses when we certify the character and fitness of our lawyers.

Moreover, M.A.R.'s failure to timely file and pay federal income taxes and his conduct in writing worthless checks show dishonesty, financial irresponsibility, and a lack of respect for the law and for the rights of others. M.A.R. admits to writing over forty worthless checks in the past four and a half years. Significantly, this misconduct occurred after M.A.R. had already graduated from law school, and he admits that it has continued until as late as one week prior to his formal hearing. This Court has characterized the practice of routinely writing worthless checks as "fundamentally dishonest" even if the checks are eventually made good, and has stated that such behavior is "inconsistent with fitness to practice law."

M.A.R.'s conduct in continuing to write worthless checks and failing to timely file and pay income taxes is rationally connected to his fitness to practice law because it not only demonstrates a total disregard for the law, it also calls into serious question his ability to properly handle client funds. . . . [E]conomic irresponsibility, as shown through chronic worthless check writing, "creates a potential danger to the public should [the applicant] be placed in a position of handling trust funds." Finally, M.A.R.'s conduct in having certain bar application documents notarized prior to completing the required information on the documents, his misrepresentation on his law school application, and his misrepresentation that he was an attorney also generates doubts as to his honesty and integrity. While M.A.R. attempts to minimize the significance of each of these instances with explanations and excuses for his conduct, when considered together and along with the other proven instances of misconduct, they simply tend to show a lack of candor. We must appreciate the rational distinction between valid and justified reasons for unacceptable conduct and excuses that are simply a facade, and we must be vigilant to make certain that our certification process not descend to the level of approving less than acceptable prior conduct by merely attaching a string of excuses and explanations.

Unquestionably, conduct showing dishonesty is rationally related to an applicant's fitness to practice law. This Court has placed special emphasis on truthfulness and candor as a requirement for those seeking admission to The Florida Bar.

Accordingly, we find that the proven specifications, when considered in the aggregate, are sufficient to justify nonadmission, and we approve the Board's recommendation that M.A.R. not be admitted to The Florida Bar at this time.

NOTES

1. Does this result seem unduly harsh to you? Do you suppose that admitted lawyers in Florida who write bad checks are disbarred? If not, is it fair to exclude M.A.R. from practice on a ground that would not cause him to lose his license if he were already admitted?

2. The court does not address whether M.A.R. was able to pay his child support obligation. Do you think ability to pay should be a relevant consideration?

(C) MENTAL HEALTH ISSUES

Is it proper for bar authorities to inquire into the mental health of applicants? In the past, authorities often inquired broadly into whether an applicant had ever received mental health treatment or help. Most courts, however, acknowledge that such broad inquiries into past circumstances are prohibited by the Americans with Disabilities Act. Is an inquiry into current mental health status relevant to an applicant's fitness to practice law? Why or why not?

Another concern is that admission to the bar is ordinarily permanent. If an applicant seeking admission currently satisfies the requirements, but has only recently been treated for chemical dependency or mental illness that resulted in conduct that would otherwise have rendered the applicant unfit to practice law, should the applicant be granted permanent admission? Admissions authorities might be required to choose between permanent admission or a denial of admission on the ground that the applicant's prior condition rendered the applicant unfit, both drastic choices and neither necessarily appropriate. The ABA's recent response was to suggest a third choice, by adopting the Model Rule on Conditional Admission to Practice Law in February 2008. The rule suggests the possibility that an individual who has recently recovered from a disqualifying condition could be admitted subject to conditions designed to monitor the applicant and assure that the lawyer continues to be fit to practice. According to the report accompanying the proposed rule, nineteen states and Puerto Rico had such a conditional admission rule at the time the model rule was drafted.

(D) OTHER ISSUES

HALE v. COMMITTEE ON CHARACTER AND FITNESS FOR THE STATE OF ILLINOIS

335 F.3d 678 (7th Cir. 2003)

Matthew Hale is a public advocate of white supremacy and the leader of an organization (formerly called the World Church of the Creator) dedicated to racism and anti-Semitism. He comes before us today because he seeks to be admitted to practice law in the state of Illinois. The Illinois State Bar requires applicants not only to demonstrate proficiency in the law on a written bar examination, but also to pass a character and fitness exam. Hale succeeded in satisfying the first of these hurdles, but not the second. His defeat came at the hands of the Committee on Character and Fitness (Committee) appointed by the Illinois Supreme Court, which found him unfit to practice law. Hale challenged that determination both before the Illinois Supreme Court and then the Supreme Court of the United States, claiming among other things that the Committee had violated his First Amendment rights by acting solely on the basis of his viewpoints. Unsuccessful in that effort, he then turned to the U.S. District Court for the Northern District of Illinois with a fresh lawsuit again raising his First Amendment claim.... This time he lost because the district court concluded, in part, that the *Rooker–Feldman* doctrine did not permit it to review the earlier decision of the Illinois Supreme Court.... [W]e find that Hale has had his day in the state courts, and that the district court correctly dismissed his suit.

I

Hale's avowed mission in life is to bring about the hegemony of the white race, the legal abolition of equal protection, and the deportation of non-white Americans by non-violent means. With these goals in mind, Hale attended Southern Illinois University School of Law, graduating with a J.D. and passing the Illinois bar exam in 1998. In his application for admission to the Illinois State Bar, Hale disclosed his active role in promoting racism and anti-Semitism.

Hale's application was referred to a single member of the Committee on Character and Fitness.... This member advised the Board that he was not prepared to recommend that Hale be admitted to practice law in Illinois.

... [T]he Chairperson of the Third District Committee assigned Hale's application to a three-person "Inquiry Panel" for further review. On December 18, 1998, in a 2–1 written decision, the Inquiry Panel recommended that the Committee refuse to approve Hale's admission to practice law in Illinois. The Committee rejected the argument that Hale was merely an applicant with distasteful views that were nonetheless protected under the First Amendment. Instead, it said, Hale's active commitment to bigotry under "any civilized standards of decency" demonstrated a "gross deficiency in moral character, particularly for lawyers who have a special responsibility to uphold the rule of law for all persons." In short, the Committee believed that Hale was likely to commit acts of various kinds in the future that were inconsistent with membership in the bar.

The Inquiry Panel's recommendation that Hale not be certified resulted in the automatic creation by the Committee of a five-member "Hearing Panel" to determine with finality whether Hale should be certified for admission to practice law. The Panel held a hearing on April 10, 1999, at which multiple witnesses testified that Hale possessed the requisite character and fitness to practice law. Hale himself testified before the Panel, and asserted that he was prepared to comply with the Rules of Professional Conduct. He also indicated, however, that he believed that the Rules applied only while he worked as an attorney, and not while he practiced his religion.

On June 30, 1999, the Hearing Panel denied Hale's application. It began by drawing a distinction between Hale's First Amendment right to express ideas and his right to become a member of the Illinois bar, commenting that the case was "not about Mr. Hale's First Amendment rights. The issue here is whether Mr. Hale possesses the requisite character and fitness for admission for the practice of law." The Hearing Panel based its decision that Hale had not satisfied his burden of proving that he possessed the requisite character and fitness on several findings. First, the Hearing Panel believed that Hale's outspoken intent to continue discriminating in his private life, especially taken together with negative character evidence such as academic probation, an order of protection, and a list of arrests (not convictions), was inconsistent with the Rules of Professional Conduct. The Hearing Panel was also concerned about Hale's refusal to repudiate a 1995 letter he wrote in response to published commentary in support of affirmative action, in which Hale [used a racial slur]. The letter, the Hearing Panel found, was insulting, inappropriate, and showed a "monumental lack of sound judgment" that would put Hale "on a collision course with the Rules of Professional Conduct." Finally, the Hearing Panel concluded that Hale was not candid and open with it during the hearing.

Hale petitioned the Illinois Supreme Court to reconsider the Committee's denial. Hale asked the Illinois Supreme Court to review the constitutionality of the Committee's decision, in addition to challenging the constitutionality of the disciplinary rule against discrimination (Rule 8.4(a)(5) of the Illinois Rules of Professional Conduct). Hale's complaint squarely raised the claim that the Committee had violated the First and Fourteenth Amendments when it arbitrarily denied his bar application, because it based its decision not on any conduct in which Hale may have engaged, but instead solely on its speculation about his likely future conduct and its distaste for his political and religious beliefs. The Committee filed a response.... It asked the Illinois Supreme Court to sustain its decision and to deny certification of Hale's bar application. On November 12, 1999, the Illinois Supreme Court denied Hale's petition for review—an action that had the effect of leaving the Committee's decision in place. Justice Heiple dissented from the court's refusal to conduct plenary proceedings in the case.

Hale then filed a petition for a writ of *certiorari* with the Supreme Court of the United States.... The Supreme Court of the United States denied his petition without comment.

Frustrated with what he perceived to be a total lack of access to a judicial body that would give him a full hearing on his First Amendment claims, Hale then turned to the district court and filed the present case.

... The district court dismissed the entire lawsuit for lack of subject matter jurisdiction and on grounds of *res judicata*. This appeal followed.

II

The central question we must decide is a procedural one: did the proceedings that culminated in the Illinois Supreme Court's decision to allow the Committee's rejection of Hale's application to stand qualify as "judicial proceedings," such that the doctrine that forbids lower federal courts to sit in review of state court decisions or the preclusion doctrines should apply? If the answer to that is yes, we are finished, because the Supreme Court of the United States has had an opportunity to consider whether the Illinois court's decision violated federal law, and it chose not to hear the case. If the answer to that question is no, however, then this case would have to be remanded to the district court for further proceedings on the merits of his claims.

... [T]he role of state courts in bar admissions does not present a new *Rooker–Feldman* issue. The *Feldman* case itself raised the question whether the U.S. District Court for the District of Columbia had jurisdiction to review decisions of the D.C. Court of Appeals in bar admission matters. The Court first decided that the proceedings before the D.C. Court of Appeals (the equivalent for this purpose to the Illinois Supreme Court in our case) in connection with the two petitions for waiver from a rule governing admission to the bar were judicial in nature, not legislative, ministerial, or administrative.... It followed that the federal court had no jurisdiction to review the D.C. Court of Appeals' decision denying the petitions for waiver....

The path Hale's case, and all others like it, took to the Illinois Supreme Court, began after the Committee had finished all of its proceedings—that is to say, after the Hearing Panel decided to deny Hale's application once and for all. At that point, the applicant must turn to Rule 708(e) of the Illinois Supreme Court Rules, which reads as follows:

> A law student registrant or applicant who has availed himself or herself of his or her full hearing rights before the Committee on Character and Fitness and who deems himself or herself aggrieved by the determination of the committee may ... petition the Supreme Court for review within 35 days after service of the Committee's decision upon the law student registrant or applicant....

Once the Rule 708 petition is before the Illinois Supreme Court, the court usually takes one of two actions: denial or plenary review. In the majority of cases, not surprisingly, the court denies the petition for review....

One of Hale's concerns is that this process does not allow him to present before the court serious constitutional challenges to the Committee's decision, such as his First Amendment claim....

Hale argues, the mere fact that the court *may* hear and consider a constitutional challenge does not mean that it has done so in every case. He analogizes the Illinois Supreme Court's role in Rule 708 petitions to ... the Supreme Court of the United States's role in ruling on petitions for a writ of certiorari.... [A] decision by the highest court not to take a case carries with it no implication at all about the court's view on the merits. It is simply a decision to refrain from accepting the case for review. If that were all that the Illinois Supreme Court did in Rule 708 petitions, Hale would have a much stronger case.

Justice Heiple's dissenting opinion suggests that the court was playing exactly this kind of passive role, but ... a dissent does not reflect the state of the law. The court itself has said that the final decision concerning the admission of an applicant to the bar rests with itself. Moreover, the fact that the court may decide a Rule 708 appeals on a paper record, as it did in Hale's case, does not mean that the court failed to decide the case on the merits. There is no rule that requires full briefing and oral argument in every case.... That is essentially what the Illinois Supreme Court does in its response to Rule 708 petitions, unless it thinks that expanded proceedings are necessary.

We therefore reject Hale's argument that he had no prior opportunity to litigate his constitutional challenges to the Illinois Supreme Court's decision not to override the Committee's recommendation to deny his admission to the bar. He did, and he was unsuccessful. His challenge to the Illinois Supreme Court's decision not to admit him to the bar has been adjudicated, and he must take any further complaints he has about the outcome of that adjudication to the state courts of Illinois.

The judgment of the district court dismissing Hale's action is hereby AFFIRMED.

Here is the dissent from the Illinois Supreme Court decision denying Hale's appeal:

IN RE MATTER OF MATTHEW F. HALE, PETITIONER

723 N.E.2d 206 (Ill. 1999)

JUSTICE HEIPLE, dissenting:

Petitioner Matthew F. Hale applied for admission to practice law in Illinois. The Committee on Character and Fitness concluded that his application should be denied. Petitioner now asks this court to review the Committee's decision. Thus, the question before the court at this juncture is not whether petitioner should be licensed to practice law. The question, rather, is whether the Supreme Court should consider his appeal. Because the petition raises questions of constitutional significance that should be resolved openly by this court, I dissent from the majority's refusal to hear this case.

The crux of the Committee's decision to deny petitioner's application to practice law is petitioner's open advocacy of racially obnoxious beliefs. The Hearing Panel found that petitioner's "publicly displayed views are diametrically opposed to the letter and spirit" of the Rules of Professional Conduct. The Inquiry Panel found that, in regulating the conduct of attorneys, certain "fundamental truths" of equality and nondiscrimination "must be preferred over the values found in the First Amendment." Petitioner contends that the Committee's use of his expressed views to justify the denial of his admission to the bar violates his constitutional rights to free speech. That constitutional question deserves explicit, reasoned resolution by this court. Instead, the court silently accepts the conclusion of the Committee, which asserted that "[t]his case is not about Mr. Hale's First Amendment rights." To the contrary, this case clearly impacts both the first amendment to the federal Constitution and article I, section 4, of the Illinois Constitution.

In addition, the Committee's ruling on petitioner's application presents a second important issue which this court should address. The Committee seems to hold that it may deny petitioner's application for admission to the bar without finding that petitioner has engaged in any specific conduct that would have violated a disciplinary rule if petitioner were already a lawyer. The Committee merely speculates that petitioner is "on a collision course with the Rules of Professional Conduct" and that, if admitted, he will *in the future* "find himself before the Attorney Registration and Disciplinary Commission." I believe this court should address whether it is appropriate for the Committee to base its assessment of an applicant's character and fitness on speculative predictions of future actionable misconduct.

The question also arises: If all of petitioner's statements identified by the Committee had been made after obtaining a license to practice law, would he then be subject to disbarment? That is to say, is there one standard for admission to practice and a different standard for continuing to practice? And, if the standard is the same, can already-licensed lawyers be disbarred for obnoxious speech?

The Illinois Supreme Court is the licensing authority for all Illinois lawyers. Its rules cover all aspects of admission to the bar and professional conduct thereafter. It has the power to license, regulate, and to disbar. The issues presented by Mr. Hale's petition are of such significant constitutional magnitude that they deserve a judicial review and determination by this court.

For the reasons given, I respectfully dissent from the denial of the petition for review.

NOTES

1.   Hale, a committed racist, wished to be admitted to the bar of the state of Illinois. Was the determination that, based on his beliefs, he lacked the necessary character and fitness to be a lawyer appropriate? Hale claimed that, in fact, he was more honest, and showed better moral character, than lawyers who were racist but who lied and concealed that in their dealings with the bar authorities. What do you think of his argument? Should lawyers who share Hale's views be disbarred? On what basis?

2.   Subsequently, Hale was charged with and convicted of soliciting the murder of a federal judge. In light of the other cases you have read in this chapter, do you think it likely that courts will once again need to deal with an application by Hale for admission to practice?

3.   The *Hale* case raised the issue whether an applicant's racist beliefs should preclude his admission to the practice of law. These issues have arisen more routinely in the context of political beliefs. The U.S. Supreme Court wrestled with these issues in two rounds of cases, one in the early 1960s and one in the early 1970s. While the analysis of the cases is complex and far from straightforward, the Court's conclusion ultimately was that mere membership in an organization or holding of particular beliefs was protected First Amendment conduct and that those beliefs or membership, standing alone, could not justify exclusion from the profession or be inquired into as part of the admission process. It was, however, permissible to inquire into an applicant's activities and beliefs if the answers reflected an inability to comply with the requirements of the profession, and to deny admission on that ground. A loyalty question was permissible, for example, if the jurisdiction would require an admitted lawyer to swear or affirm her willingness to uphold the Constitution. An inquiry could also be made into an applicant's specific intent to advance illegal goals, like overthrowing the government by illegal means. Does this distinction between protected beliefs or membership, on the one hand, and prohibited behavior, on the other, help us understand *Hale*?

4.   As the court mentioned, Illinois has a disciplinary rule prohibiting discrimination. Illinois RPC 8.4(a)(5) provides:

> A lawyer shall not ... engage in conduct that is prejudicial to the administration of justice. In relation thereto, a lawyer shall not engage in adverse discriminatory treatment of litigants, jurors, witnesses, lawyers, and others, based on race, sex, religion, national origin, disability, age, sexual orientation or socioeconomic status.

Another rule, Illinois RPC 8.4(a)(9)(A), makes violating an antidiscrimination statute a disciplinary offense if the conduct "reflects adversely on a lawyer's fitness as a lawyer." If the admissions authorities in Illinois were convinced that Hale would be unable to comply with these rules, would it be legitimate to decline to admit him on that basis?

Do the Model Rules prohibit discriminatory behavior? *See* Comment [3] to Model Rule 8.4. Does this Comment adequately address the problem of lawyers who engage in discriminatory behavior? Is it limited in ways that the Illinois rule is not? Should the Model Rules do a better job of addressing discriminatory conduct by lawyers?

B. UNAUTHORIZED PRACTICE OF LAW BY NONLAWYERS

As we have seen, the process of being admitted to practice law is lengthy, complex, demanding, and costly. When is it necessary to be admitted to practice law? Can someone who has the necessary skills to assist clients, but who is not a lawyer, engage in the business of providing services similar to those a lawyer provides?

One might imagine that some activities—like appearing on behalf of a client in court—are quintessentially the "practice of law" and that only a lawyer or someone authorized by law to act as a lawyer (like a law student under a student practice rule) may engage in them. But lawyers do all kinds of things that fall outside the realm of traditional, in-court activities. May a nonlawyer engage in those activities? Can a trained paralegal aid others in applying for immigration benefits? Can a lawyer's administrative assistant help people fill out the forms to obtain restraining orders or simple divorces? This is an easy question if those people work in a law office and under a lawyer's supervision. But what if they want to provide such services on their own? Can nonlawyers make a business out of using their skills and knowledge of law and the legal process to assist others? This was what the plaintiff tried to do in the following case. Why was that problematic?

BERGANTZEL v. MLYNARIK

619 N.W.2d 309 (Iowa 2000)

TERNUS, JUSTICE.

The appellee, Terri Bergantzel, brought a small claims action against the appellant, Jan Mlynarik, to recover a contingent fee based on Bergantzel's assistance in negotiating a settlement of Mlynarik's personal injury claim.

We granted discretionary review of the district court's affirmance of the small claims judgment allowing such a fee. Because Bergantzel is not a licensed attorney, we hold that the contingent fee contract is against public policy and may not be enforced. Accordingly, we reverse and remand for dismissal of Bergantzel's action. . . .

The defendant in this action, Jan Mlynarik, was seriously injured in a motor vehicle accident. He entered into a written contract with the plaintiff, Terri Bergantzel, under which Bergantzel was to "assist in the negotiation with the insurance companies and attorney, if necessary, in the settlement of [Mlynarik's] claim" resulting from the accident. In consideration for this assistance, Bergantzel was to receive fifteen percent of the amount recovered after payment of doctors' bills. The contract stated that Bergantzel was not an attorney and that the payment to her was to cover her expenses only. In the event that the services of an attorney were required, the contract provided that Bergantzel would "either pay for the consultation with an attorney or, if the attorney fees exceed the fifteen percent, [would] forfeit all claims to the settlement money."

It is undisputed that, pursuant to this agreement, Bergantzel negotiated a settlement with the tortfeasor's insurance carrier for the limits of the tortfeasor's policy—$100,000. Her work included locating witnesses, preparing affidavits, making long-distance phone calls, obtaining Mlynarik's medical and school records, obtaining a physician's opinion letter, and communicating with the insurance company. For her work, Mlynarik paid Bergantzel slightly over $12,000, which was fifteen percent of the recovery after medical expenses were deducted.

Bergantzel then undertook similar efforts to negotiate a settlement with Mlynarik's underinsured motorist (UIM) carrier. Bergantzel obtained a settlement offer from the insurance company for $35,000. She told Mlynarik that if he wanted a larger recovery, he would need to hire an attorney. Mlynarik decided to consult with an attorney and entered into a contingent fee agreement with attorney Randall Shanks. Shanks successfully negotiated a $65,000 settlement with Mlynarik's UIM carrier and received his contingent fee. Bergantzel was also paid her contingent fee, with the exception of $1,650. Bergantzel brought suit against Mlynarik for this sum.

At trial, Mlynarik urged that Bergantzel engaged in the unauthorized practice of law and, therefore, could not recover under their contract. The trial court rejected this defense, stating:

> Bergantzel did not represent Mlynarik in court, nor did she file any pleading on his behalf. The court concludes that her efforts to locate witnesses, prepare affidavits, obtain medical and school records, and talk with insurance companies did not involve "the art of exercising professional judgment" and [did] not constitute the unauthorized practice of law. Bergantzel did not give Mlynarik advice about his

rights under the law. She encouraged him to consult with an attorney. She did not hold herself out to be an attorney.

Based on these conclusions, the court entered judgment in favor of Bergantzel for $1,650 plus interest and court costs.

Mlynarik filed an appeal to the district court. The district court affirmed the decision of the small claims court. Mlynarik then sought discretionary review by this court, which was granted. . . .

There is no dispute in the case before us that Bergantzel seeks to recover payment under the contract for her services in negotiating a settlement with Mlynarik's UIM carrier. That leaves three issues for our consideration: (1) Was Bergantzel prohibited from negotiating this settlement because she was not a licensed attorney?; (2) If so, does the attorney licensing requirement have a regulatory purpose?; and (3) Is the interest in enforcement of a contingent fee contract for the performance of legal services by a nonlawyer clearly outweighed by the public policy underlying the attorney licensing requirement? We consider each question separately.

Was Bergantzel Prohibited From Negotiating a Settlement of Mlynarik's UIM Claim Because She Was Not a Licensed Attorney?

Iowa Code section 602.10101 states:

> The power to admit persons to practice as attorneys and counselors in the courts of this state, or any of them, is vested exclusively in the supreme court which shall adopt and promulgate rules to carry out the intent and purpose of this article.

Pursuant to this authority, the court has adopted rules pertaining to the practice of law, requiring that persons desiring to practice law in Iowa be admitted to the bar. There is no dispute that Bergantzel was not admitted to practice law in Iowa.

That brings us to the most problematic issue in this case: was Bergantzel's negotiation of a UIM settlement the practice of law? Like many other states, Iowa has found it difficult to articulate an "all-inclusive definition of the practice of law." . . .

We are not without guidance, however, in our endeavor to determine whether a particular activity is the practice of law. Such guidance is provided by Ethical Consideration 3–5 of the Iowa Code of Professional Responsibility:

> [T]he practice of law includes, but is not limited to, representing another before the courts; giving of legal advice and counsel to others relating to their rights and obligations under the law; and preparation or approval of the use of legal instruments by which legal rights of others are either obtained, secured or transferred even if such matters never become the subject of a court proceeding.
>
> *Functionally, the practice of law relates to the rendition of services for others that call for the professional judgment of a lawyer.*

The essence of the professional judgment of the lawyer is the educated ability to relate the general body and philosophy of law to a specific legal problem of a client; and thus, the public interest will be better served if only lawyers are permitted to act in matters involving professional judgment. Where this professional judgment is not involved, nonlawyers, such as court clerks, police officers, abstracters, and many governmental employees, may engage in occupations that require a special knowledge of law in certain areas.

But the services of a lawyer are essential in the public interest whenever the exercise of professional legal judgment is required.

Based on this ethical consideration, this court [has] concluded that the exercise of professional judgment was at the core of the practice of law. We distinguished a lawyer's ability to exercise professional judgment from a layperson's use of their knowledge of the law:

When lawyers use their educated ability to apply an area of the law to solve a specific problem of a client, they are exercising professional judgment.... [In law school, lawyers] learn to recognize issues first and then how to solve those issues in an ethical manner, using their knowledge of the law. See EC 3–2 ("Competent professional judgment is the product of a trained familiarity with law and legal processes, a disciplined, analytical approach to legal problems, and a firm ethical commitment."). The practice of law is no different: lawyers determine what the issues are and use their knowledge of the law to solve them in an ethical way. This is the art of exercising professional judgment.

In contrast, nonlawyers who use their knowledge of the law for informational purposes alone are not exercising a lawyer's professional judgment. For example, an abstracter must have knowledge of what constitutes a lien on real estate. An abstracter uses this knowledge, which is legal in nature, when the abstracter shows the lien in the abstract of title. In doing so, the abstracter is simply furnishing the title examiner—a lawyer—information that the lawyer needs in advising the client on the marketability of title. In this scenario, the abstracter is simply furnishing information; the title examiner is exercising professional judgment on a legal question. The abstracter is not practicing law; the title examiner is.

Thus, the definitive issue here is whether Bergantzel's actions required the exercise of professional judgment on a legal issue or question that affected the rights of a third party.

In reviewing Bergantzel's efforts on behalf of Mlynarik, we find her negotiations with the insurance companies of greatest concern. Whether the negotiation of a personal injury settlement is the practice of law is an issue of first impression in this jurisdiction. Therefore, we turn to cases from other states for guidance....

It appears from our review of the case law that courts considering this issue have concluded that the negotiation of a settlement on behalf of the injured party requires the exercise of professional judgment and is, therefore, the practice of law. . . .

In *Dauphin Co. Bar Ass'n v. Mazzacaro*, 351 A.2d 229 (Pa. 1976), a county bar association sought to enjoin a licensed casualty adjuster on the ground that the adjuster's representation of tort claimants constituted the unauthorized practice of law. The record showed that the adjuster only represented claimants where liability was undisputed. In such cases, for a contingent fee, the adjuster investigated the accident, estimated the amount of damages sustained, made a demand upon the tortfeasor or the tortfeasor's insurance company, and attempted to negotiate a settlement. Based on these facts, the district court granted the requested injunctive relief and the Pennsylvania Supreme Court affirmed. In rejecting the adjuster's argument that his actions did not require the exercise of any legal judgment on behalf of the injured party, the court stated:

> While the objective valuation of damages may in uncomplicated cases be accomplished by a skilled lay judgment, an assessment of the extent to which that valuation should be compromised in settlement negotiations cannot. Even when liability is not technically "contested," an assessment of the likelihood that liability can be established in a court of law is a crucial factor in weighing the strength of one's bargaining position. A negotiator cannot possibly know how large a settlement he can exact unless he can probe the degree of unwillingness of the other side to go to court. Such an assessment, however, involves an understanding of the applicable tort principles (including the elements of negligence and contributory negligence), a grasp of the rules of evidence, and an ability to evaluate the strengths and weaknesses of the client's case vis a vis that of the adversary. The acquisition of such knowledge is not within the ability of laypersons, but rather involves the application of abstract legal principles to the concrete facts of the given claim. As a consequence, it is inescapable that lay adjusters who undertake to negotiate settlements of the claims of third-party claimants must exercise legal judgments in so doing. . . .

> In sum, we conclude that such third-party claimant representation by lay adjusters constitutes the unauthorized practice of law.

In a similar early case from Louisiana, the Louisiana Court of Appeals held that a lay claims adjuster who undertook to investigate and settle a wrongful death claim was engaged in the unauthorized practice of law. *Meunier v. Bernich*, 170 So. 567, 572 (La. App. 1936). Like the agreement in the present case, the contract in *Meunier* stated that the adjuster was not a lawyer and, if the adjuster could not obtain a satisfactory settlement offer from the tortfeasor, the claimants were free to engage the services of an attorney. The lawsuit arose when the claimants refused to pay the adjuster the contingent fee upon which they had agreed. In rejecting the adjuster's claim that he was not engaged in the practice of law, the court stated:

> But, [the adjuster] does more than mere investigation work. He undertook, by contract, to enforce, secure, settle, adjust, or compromise whatever claim the Bernichs had arising out of the fatal accident. In this employment, it became necessary for him to examine the facts of the case, and to advise the Bernichs regarding the liability of the [railroad] in damages for the death of their child. Not only did he advise the defendants that liability existed, but he made a lawyer's demand on the railroad company, informing [it] that responsibility had attached to it for the negligent killing of the little girl.

> Thus, in the performance of his contract, [the adjuster] had to advise his client concerning the redress of a legal wrong, which advice he was not qualified to impart, because he does not possess the legal training exacted by the Supreme Court. . . . He is engaged in the business of settling and adjusting personal injury claims, and it is well established that the doing of these acts constitutes the practice of law.

We agree with the reasoning of these courts that the negotiation of a settlement of an injured party's claim for damages requires the exercise of professional judgment. Here, Bergantzel, in determining the amount of any settlement demand or counteroffer, was required to have "an understanding of the applicable tort [and underinsured motorist] principles . . . , a grasp of the rules of evidence, and an ability to evaluate the strengths and weaknesses of [Mlynarik's] case vis a vis that of the [UIM carrier]." . . . The mere process of negotiating with the insurance company involved legal assessments that required the exercise of professional judgment regardless of whether Bergantzel shared her assessments or evaluations with Mlynarik. By negotiating a settlement on Mlynarik's behalf, Bergantzel was indirectly advising Mlynarik on the settlement value of his claim. . . . We hold that Bergantzel engaged in the practice of law when she represented Mlynarik in negotiation of a settlement of Mlynarik's UIM claim.

This conclusion does not, however, end our inquiry. We must still determine whether Bergantzel's actions were unauthorized. That is because, in other areas, we have permitted nonlawyers to perform tasks that are arguably the practice of law; the preparation of tax returns by accountants is a good example. . . .

In considering Bergantzel's services from this perspective, we conclude that the public interest is not served by allowing laypersons to negotiate settlements on behalf of injured parties. Although the record shows that Bergantzel had experience as a private investigator, her skills as an investigator and her knowledge of the necessary information required to document a claim are far removed from the legal assessments necessary to an evaluation of that claim for purposes of determining a likely recovery from the tortfeasor or UIM carrier. The public is best served, we think, by requiring that licensed attorneys perform this service so that the benefits of their legal education, skills and experience can be used to negotiate a fair settlement with the tortfeasor or the tortfeasor's insurer. From a practical standpoint, we note that such services are readily available to the public from lawyers on a contingent fee basis; thus, there is no need to permit nonlawyers to perform these functions.

Consistent with our conclusions, we hold that Bergantzel was prohibited under Iowa law from rendering the negotiation services required by her contract with Mlynarik because she was not licensed to practice law in this state. We must now determine whether Iowa's attorney licensing requirement is regulatory in nature.

Does the Attorney Licensing Requirement Have a Regulatory Purpose?

Individuals licensed to practice law in Iowa must graduate from an accredited law school and must demonstrate proficiency in the practice of law, either by successfully passing the Iowa bar examination or by demonstrating five years of legal practice in another jurisdiction. In addition, licensed attorneys must complete fifteen hours of continuing legal education each year to maintain their law license. Finally, lawyers practicing in Iowa must comply with the Iowa Code of Professional Responsibility; their failure to do so may result in a reprimand, a suspension of their license, or a permanent revocation of their license. It is also significant that the underlying goal of the licensing and supervision of attorneys is to protect the public from the consequences of unqualified legal advisors.

These facts unquestionably demonstrate that the attorney licensing requirement has a regulatory purpose. We now determine whether "the interest in the enforcement of the [contract] is clearly outweighed by the public policy behind the [licensing] requirement."

Is the Interest in Enforcement of the Agreement Between Bergantzel and Mlynarik Clearly Outweighed by the Public Policy Behind the Attorney Licensing Requirement?

The Restatement has identified several factors to consider in balancing the competing interests implicated in the enforcement of a contract that violates public policy:

> (2) In weighing the interest in the enforcement of a term, account is taken of
>
>> (a) the parties' justified expectations,
>>
>> (b) any forfeiture that would result if enforcement were denied, and
>>
>> (c) any special public interest in the enforcement of the particular term.
>
> (3) In weighing a public policy against enforcement of a term, account is taken of
>
>> (a) the strength of that policy as manifested by legislation or judicial decisions,

(b) the likelihood that a refusal to enforce the term will further that policy,

(c) the seriousness of any misconduct involved and the extent to which it was deliberate, and

(d) the directness of the connection between that misconduct and the term.

Restatement 178(2)-(3), at 6–7.

First, under the available record, we cannot determine whether Bergantzel knew her negotiation of the settlements constituted the practice of law. Given the fact that she had performed under the contract, she certainly expected to be paid. For purposes of our analysis, we assume, without deciding, that this expectation was justified. Second, it appears that Bergantzel will suffer a forfeiture in that she has already rendered her performance and will be denied compensation for those services. As a final matter, there does not appear to be any ascertainable special public interest in the enforcement of this contract.... [W]here performance of an activity is illegal, the public interest weighs against enforcement.

Although the factors just discussed reveal some interest in enforcement, that interest is clearly outweighed by the factors militating against enforcement. The factors weighing against enforcement, as previously stated, include (1) the strength of the public policy against the unauthorized practice of law, (2) the likelihood that refusal to enforce the contract will further that policy, (3) the seriousness of any misconduct involved and the extent to which Bergantzel was culpable, and (4) the directness of the connection between the unauthorized conduct and the contract.

Our first step is to identify the public policy underlying the licensure requirement. We agree with the Minnesota Supreme Court's discussion of the rationale for regulating the practice of law:

> [The] purpose [for which lawyers are licensed as the exclusive occupants of their field] is to protect the public from the intolerable evils which are brought upon people by those who assume to practice law without having the proper qualifications....

As for the second factor against enforcement, we think that a refusal to enforce the contract will further the public policy evidenced by the attorney licensure provisions. "[T]aking the economic benefit out of contracts that violate [public policy] by holding them unenforceable 'very definitely would promote the public policy.'" Turning to the third factor, we find nothing in the record to suggest that Bergantzel knew her actions were unauthorized, yet deliberately proceeded. Nonetheless, it cannot be questioned that the unauthorized practice of law is a very serious matter. Both lawyers and nonlawyers are subject to severe sanctions for such conduct....

The fourth and final factor concerns the nexus between the lack of license and the contract at issue. In the present case, there is an undeniably direct connection. The performance for which Bergantzel seeks compensation is the unauthorized practice of law, conduct that she was prohibited by law from performing. In other words, the unlicensed conduct is not a collateral matter.

Weighing all the factors, we conclude that the interest in refusing to enforce the contract must prevail. The fact that Bergantzel has already performed and, in that sense, Mlynarik will receive a windfall, simply does not outweigh the strong public policy against the unauthorized practice of law. Accordingly, we conclude that the contract is unenforceable.

NOTES

1.   Why do you suppose Mlynarik consulted Bergantzel rather than an attorney? In the court's view, there was no need to permit nonlawyers to provide services like the ones Bergantzel provided, because lawyers were readily available to perform them on a contingent fee basis. Was that accurate? Would a lawyer have provided services on the same terms Bergantzel offered?

2.   Will Bergantzel provide these services again to other potential customers? Why or why not?

3.   Bergantzel appeared pro se before the state Supreme Court. Do you think she did a good job? What do you think of the work she did for Mlynarik? Did she earn her fees? What do you suppose Mlynarik did after this case was decided?

4.   States regulate the unauthorized practice of law in different ways. In the *Bergantzel* case, the claim that Bergantzel was engaged in unauthorized practice was asserted by a private party as a defense to a contract claim. Unauthorized practice is also a crime in some jurisdictions. In some states, an administrative entity is charged with policing the prohibition on unauthorized practice; such an entity has the power to seek to enjoin actors engaging in unauthorized practice from doing so, and to pursue contempt citations if those actors violate the injunctions.

5.   Unauthorized practice is the worst of both worlds for the person engaging in it. On the one hand, the contract for payment once the services have been provided is unenforceable; Bergantzel did the work and didn't get paid. On the other hand, a nonlawyer holding himself out as providing adequate legal services may be answerable in malpractice as a lawyer would be. *See Webb v. Pomeroy*, 655 P.2d 465 (Kan. App. 1982).

6.   One category of person who is particularly susceptible to an allegation of unauthorized practice restrictions is a disbarred or suspended lawyer. Such a person is effectively a nonlawyer, and is therefore subject to the same restrictions as a lay person, but because of the person's history and experience, he or she may be more likely than others to overreach. Many jurisdictions accordingly impose quite stringent constraints on what a disbarred lawyer can do in a law office. Pennsylvania, for example, prohibits a formerly admitted attorney from "performing any law-related activity" for any firm or lawyer that he or she worked for at the time of the conduct that resulted in disbarment or suspension. Can a suspended lawyer do accounting and billing

or IT work for his former law firm during his period of suspension? *See Philadelphia Bar Ass'n Ethics Op. 2007–3* (permitting the work as long as the "suspended attorney performs no legal or paralegal work or law related activities").

Which of these activities do you think constitutes the practice of law?

(a) Drafting a collective bargaining agreement on behalf of a union. Does it matter if the drafter uses a form or a prior contract and simply fills in the blanks? *Ohio State Bar Ass'n v. Burdzinski, Brinkman, Czarzasty & Landwehr, Inc.*, 858 N.E.2d 372 (Ohio 2006).

(b) Advising parents involved in child dependency and neglect cases, including drafting discovery documents for the parents to use *pro se*. Does it make a difference if the parents provided powers of attorney authorizing the nonlawyer to act as their agent? *People v. Shell*, 148 P.3d 162 (Colo. 2006).

(c) An insurance company distributing a pamphlet entitled "Do I Need an Attorney?" to people with claims for which the insurer might be liable. "The pamphlet allegedly aided claimants in processing their claims by providing them with information regarding whether they should hire an attorney before learning about any settlement offers by [the insurer] and fee arrangements the claimant should make should they decide to retain an attorney. The insurer did not distribute the pamphlet to claimants known to be represented by counsel." *Allstate Insurance Co. v. The West Virginia State Bar*, 233 F.3d 813 (4th Cir. 2000).

(d) Using a firm in India to do legal research and prepare strategy for a case in an area in which you have limited legal experience, when none of the attorneys at the firm in India are not admitted to practice in the United States. *San Diego County Bar Association Ethics Op. 2007–1*.

While Bergantzel was a freelancer, many established service providers who are not lawyers perform services that rely to some extent on legal knowledge. Accordingly, decisions about whether such work entails unauthorized practice can have significant consequences for both providers and users of such services. Consider the case below. What did it mean for title insurers? for lawyers? for buyers of real estate?

IN RE UPL ADVISORY OPINION 2003–2

588 S.E.2d 741 (Ga. 2003)

PER CURIAM.

We granted the State Bar of Georgia's petition for discretionary review to consider the opinion of the Standing Committee on the Unlicensed Practice of Law that the preparation and execution of a deed of conveyance on behalf of another and facilitation of its execution by anyone other than a duly licensed Georgia attorney constitutes the unauthorized practice of law. Because we agree with the UPL Standing Committee that only a licensed Georgia attorney may prepare or facilitate the execution of a deed of conveyance, we approve UPL Advisory Opinion No. 2003–2. It is well established that this Court has the inherent and exclusive authority to govern the practice of law in Georgia, including jurisdiction over the unlicensed practice of law. In this regard, we have issued formal advisory opinions which confirmed that a lawyer cannot delegate responsibility for the closing of a real estate transaction to a non-lawyer and required the physical presence of an attorney for the preparation and execution of a deed of conveyance (including, but not limited to, a warranty deed, limited warranty deed, quitclaim deed, security deed, and deed to secure debt). In other words, we have consistently held that it is the unauthorized practice of law for someone other than a duly-licensed Georgia attorney to close a real estate transaction or to prepare or facilitate the execution of such deed(s) for the benefit of a seller, borrower, or lender.

The proponents of lay conveyancing, or witness-only closings, urge this Court to overturn UPL Advisory Opinion No. 2003–2 because, they contend, requiring the services of Georgia lawyers for real estate closings and the execution of deeds of conveyances needlessly harms the public interest by increasing price and decreasing choice for consumers.... [W]e continue to believe that the public interest is best protected when a licensed Georgia attorney, trained to recognize the rights at issue during a property conveyance, oversees the entire transaction. If the attorney fails in his or her responsibility in the closing, the attorney may be held accountable through a malpractice or bar disciplinary action. In contrast, the public has little or no recourse if a non-lawyer fails to close the transaction properly. It is thus clear that true protection of the public interest in Georgia requires that an attorney licensed in Georgia participate in the real estate transaction.

Although it is within this Court's exclusive authority to determine the scope of the practice of law, we note that since at least 1932 it has been the statutory policy in the State of Georgia that only attorneys properly licensed in Georgia are authorized to close real estate transactions. Although the language of this statute does not control the practice of law in Georgia, we find it is consistent with our holding that only an attorney duly licensed in this State can prepare and facilitate the execution of a deed of conveyance. This policy was enacted and continues to exist for the benefit of the public and we are unpersuaded that the time has come to change the policy with regard to lay conveyances or witness-only closings. Accordingly, we hereby approve UPL Advisory Opinion No. 2003–2.

NOTES

1. There were several amicus curiae submissions to the court in this case, including briefs from the U.S. Department of Justice and the Federal Trade Commission, as well as title companies, real estate brokers, and notaries. Why do you suppose this case was so vigorously briefed?

2. The ABA at one point created a Task Force to consider the crafting of a model definition of the practice of law. After considerable time and effort and the preparation of a draft model definition, the Task Force instead recommended that each state devise its own definition of the practice of law. One

reason, perhaps, was the comment of the U.S. Department of Justice and the Federal Trade Commission in response to the draft, which opined that the proposed definition was "overbroad and could restrain competition between lawyers and nonlawyers to provide similar services to American consumers," and was "likely to raise costs for consumers and limit their competitive choices." One area of concern for the DOJ and FTC was restriction of nonlawyer competition in real estate closings and preparation of tax returns. Why might decisions like this one increase the price of those services?

3.   It should be clear that employing a person who is not a lawyer to do work that the courts deem to be the exclusive province of the lawyer can be problematic. What about using a library resource, like a book or a software product? Can that pose the same problems? Why or why not?

IN RE REYNOSO

477 F.3d 1117 (9th Cir. 2007)

BETTY B. FLETCHER, CIRCUIT JUDGE.

This appeal arises from an adversary proceeding initiated by the United States Trustee ("Trustee"), during the bankruptcy proceeding of Debtor Jayson Reynoso, against Henry Ihejirika, d/b/a Frankfort Digital Services, Ltd. and Ziinet.com (collectively, "Frankfort").

The United States Bankruptcy Court for the Northern District of California found that Frankfort, a seller of web-based software that prepares bankruptcy petitions, acted as a "bankruptcy petition preparer" within the meaning of 11 U.S.C. § 110 (2002) and violated the requirements thereof. The bankruptcy court concluded that Frankfort had committed fraudulent, unfair, or deceptive conduct, and had engaged in the unauthorized practice of law....

I.

During the relevant time period, Frankfort did business under a variety of names including Ziinet.com and 700law.com. The company is owned and operated by Henry Ihejirika. Ihejirika is not an attorney.

Frankfort sold access to websites where customers could access browser-based software for preparing bankruptcy petitions and schedules, as well as informational guides promising advice on various aspects of relevant bankruptcy law.

On January 30, 2002, debtor Jayson Reynoso accessed one of Frankfort's web sites—the "Ziinet Bankruptcy Engine". The site represented to potential customers, like Reynoso, that its software system offered expertise in bankruptcy law:

> Ziinet is an expert system and knows the law. Unlike most bankruptcy programs which are little more than customized word processors the Ziinet engine is an *expert system*. It knows bankruptcy laws right down to those applicable to the state in which you live. Now you no longer need to spend weeks studying bankruptcy laws.

It explained that its program would select bankruptcy exemptions for the debtor and would eliminate the debtor's "need to choose which schedule to use for each piece of information."

The site also offered customers access to the "Bankruptcy Vault"—a repository of information regarding "loopholes" and "stealth techniques." For example, according to the site, the Vault would explain how to hide a bankruptcy from credit bureaus and how to retain various types of property.

Reynoso paid $219 for a license to access the Ziinet Engine, including the Vault, for 60 days. The online software prompted Reynoso to enter his personal information, debts, income, assets, and other data into dialog boxes. The program then used the data to generate a complete set of bankruptcy forms.

As promised by the site, the software selected particular schedules and exemptions for Reynoso. For example, Reynoso's Schedule C ("Property Claimed as Exempt") specified that he claimed an exemption under § 703.140(B)(5) of the California Code of Civil Procedure. However, Reynoso testified that he did not type in this section number, and the bankruptcy court found that Reynoso "did not choose the exemptions that showed up on this schedule."

Where the bankruptcy forms provided a space for the signature and social security number of any non-attorney petition preparer, the software generated the response: "Not Applicable". Question #9 on the Statement of Financial Affairs required the debtor to "[l]ist all payments made [by] . . . debtor to any persons, including attorneys, for consultation concerning debt consolidation, relief under the bankruptcy law or preparation of a petition in bankruptcy within one year immediately preceding the commencement of this case". The software generated the following response:

> Realizing that this document is signed under penalty of perjury, I declare that I prepared my own bankruptcy by myself using a computer and that I was not assisted by an attorney, paralegal or bankruptcy preparer. I downloaded the software into my computer's browser as a web page, typed in my bankruptcy information and printed my bankruptcy documents on my printer in the privacy of my home without any human intervention other than mine. The software printed the official Federal bankruptcy forms with the information I typed in within a few seconds of my pressing the print button and no one other than myself inputted, edited or reviewed my bankruptcy information or handled my bankruptcy documents at any point in the process. The contents of my documents are based entirely on my own research and no one gave me legal advice or told me to include or omit any information from my documents.

The paragraph makes no mention of the fee that Reynoso paid to access Frankfort's software.

Reynoso printed the forms and filed his chapter 7 bankruptcy petition on February 28, 2002. During the first meeting with creditors, the chapter 7 trustee noticed errors in the petition and, upon questioning Reynoso, learned that he had paid for the assistance of an "online bankruptcy engine." Following further investigation, the Trustee commenced the instant adversary proceeding against Frankfort in October 2002.

On April 11, 2003, the bankruptcy court held that Frankfort was collaterally estopped from challenging its status as a bankruptcy petition preparer engaged in the unauthorized practice of law. Alternatively, the court considered the merits and found that Frankfort qualified as a bankruptcy petition preparer, had violated the requirements placed on such preparers by § 110, had committed fraudulent, unfair, or deceptive conduct, and had engaged in the unauthorized practice of law. . . .

III.

A.

Pursuant to 11 U.S.C. § 110(a)(1), a bankruptcy petition preparer is "a person, other than an attorney or an employee of an attorney, who prepares for compensation a document for filing."

Frankfort argues that the creation and ownership of a software program used by a licensee to prepare his or her bankruptcy forms is not preparation of a document for filing under the statute. Whether a software-provider may qualify as a bankruptcy petition preparer under 11 U.S.C. § 110(a)(1) is a question of first impression in the Ninth Circuit. We hold that the software at issue in this case qualifies as such.

Frankfort charged fees to permit customers to access web-based software. Frankfort's software solicited information from the customers. Critically, it then translated that information into responses to questions on the bankruptcy forms, and prepared the bankruptcy forms for filing using those responses. As the Bankruptcy Appellate Panel [BAP] noted, "The software did not simply place the debtors' answers, unedited and unmediated, into official forms where the debtors had typed them on a screen; rather, it took debtors' responses to questions, restated them, and determined where to place the revised text into official forms."

In sum, for a fee, Frankfort provided customers with completed bankruptcy petitions. Customers merely provided the data requested by the software and printed the finished forms. This is materially indistinguishable from other cases in which individuals or corporations[1] have been deemed bankruptcy petition preparers. It goes without saying that the customer must provide data to the preparer, and the customer's role in printing or otherwise reproducing the forms before filing does not alter the role of the preparer. Moreover, § 110 does not require that bankruptcy petition preparers have in-person interactions with their customers. The bankrupt-

---

1. The term "person" in the Bankruptcy Code includes corporations.

cy court and BAP did not err in concluding that Frankfort was a bankruptcy petition preparer.

B.

Having affirmed the determination that Frankfort was a bankruptcy petition preparer under 11 U.S.C. § 110, we now consider the propriety of the fines and other sanctions imposed by the bankruptcy court under the statute.

. . . . Section 110(i) permits a bankruptcy court, upon a finding that a bankruptcy petition preparer has engaged in a fraudulent, unfair, or deceptive act, to certify that fact to the district court for a determination of damages. Section 110(j)(2)(B) authorizes a bankruptcy court to enjoin a person from acting as a bankruptcy petition preparer upon a finding that she has continually engaged in, *inter alia,* violations of § 110 or any other fraudulent, unfair, or deceptive conduct.

The bankruptcy court found that Frankfort made false statements to the court and intentionally concealed its role as a preparer. Notably, the court found that Frankfort repeatedly and intentionally failed to disclose its identity as a bankruptcy petition preparer on the filings it prepared and failed to disclose the compensation it received for preparing the petitions as required by § 110(h). The bankruptcy court and BAP deemed these ongoing acts, as well as various representations by Frankfort (such as Frankfort's claim that it could show debtors how to "[f]ile bankruptcy and keep it off your credit report!" or to "keep 3, 4, or even 5 cars"), deceptive. We conclude that this finding was supported by sufficient evidence and was proper. Correspondingly, we affirm the bankruptcy court's certification to the district court and issuance of an injunction.

IV.

Since "bankruptcy petition" preparers are—by definition—not attorneys, they are prohibited from practicing law.

We look to state law for guidance in determining whether Frankfort has engaged in the unauthorized practice of law. The parties agree that California law applies.

California courts have long accepted that, in a general sense, "the practice of law . . . includes legal advice and counsel and the preparation of legal instruments and contracts." But they have recognized too that "ascertaining whether a particular activity falls within this general definition may be a formidable endeavor."

Determining whether particular assistance rendered in the preparation of legal forms constitutes the unauthorized practice is often especially challenging.

Several features of Frankfort's business, taken together, lead us to conclude that it engaged in the unauthorized practice of law. To begin, Frankfort held itself out as offering legal expertise. Its websites offered customers extensive advice on how to take advantage of so-called loopholes in the bankruptcy code, promised services comparable to those of a "top-notch bankruptcy lawyer," and described its software as "an expert system" that would do more than function as a "customized word processor[ ]."

The software did, indeed, go far beyond providing clerical services. It determined where (particularly, in which schedule) to place information provided by the debtor, selected exemptions for the debtor and supplied relevant legal citations. Providing such personalized guidance has been held to constitute the practice of law.

Frankfort's system touted its offering of legal advice and projected an aura of expertise concerning bankruptcy petitions; and, in that context, it offered personalized—albeit automated—counsel. We find that because this was the conduct of a non-attorney, it constituted the unauthorized practice of law. . . .

NOTES

1. How did the software product here engage in the unauthorized practice of law (UPL)?

2. Why do you suppose Reynoso chose to use Frankfort's software product instead of hiring a lawyer? Why does the court think that his choice should be impermissible?

3. This is not the only case in which a court has concluded that a software product engaged in unauthorized practice. In *Unauthorized Practice of Law Committee v. Parsons Technology, Inc.*, 1999 WL 47235 (N.D. Tex. 1999), the court concluded that a product sold by Parsons, the "Quicken Family Lawyer," violated Texas's prohibition on the unauthorized practice of law. The product offered legal forms, including employment agreements, leases, and wills, and claimed that it would "interview you in a logical order, tailoring documents to your situation." It also provided an "Ask Arthur Miller" feature, in which a law professor would pop up to offer videotaped answers to a series of general, predetermined legal questions. The court concluded that the product violated the unauthorized practice statute. Subsequently, the Texas legislature enacted an amendment to the unauthorized practice statute providing that the practice of law "does not include the design, creation, publication, distribution, display, or sale . . . [of] computer software, or similar products if the products clearly and conspicuously state that the products are not a substitute for the advice of an attorney." Why do you suppose the legislature acted? Does its addition to the statute solve the UPL problem with regard to products like the Quicken Family Lawyer?

C. UNAUTHORIZED PRACTICE OF LAW BY LAWYERS

As we've seen, the practice of law is jealously guarded by lawyers against encroachments by nonlawyers. There is a client protection component to these concerns. Is there also some protectionism at play?

You might think that the unauthorized practice restrictions would function primarily to distinguish between lawyers and nonlawyers, and between work that should be reserved to lawyers and work that others, besides lawyers, should be permitted to do. However, the "practice of law" constraint applies not only to nonlawyers practicing law, but to lawyers practicing law in jurisdictions where they are not admitted to practice. Practice by a licensed lawyer in a jurisdiction where he or she is not admitted to practice is, unless the rules of the jurisdiction permit it, unauthorized practice. Why should work by someone who is a lawyer, but who is not admitted to practice in the relevant jurisdiction, be treated as the equivalent of practice by someone with no legal education, skills, or training at all? The definition of "practice of law" not only defines what nonlawyers may not do, but what lawyers who are not admitted in the jurisdiction may not do. To some extent, the advantages of breadth in the definition of the practice of law in the context of nonlawyers come back to bite lawyers—at least, some lawyers—when the same definition is applied to lawyers' conduct outside their jurisdiction of admission. Which lawyers are likely to benefit from vigorous enforcement of prohibitions against UPL by non-admitted attorneys? Which lawyers are likely to resist, oppose, or ignore those rules?

There are exceptions to the rule that a lawyer may not engage in the practice of law in a jurisdiction where he or she is not admitted to practice. One is known as admission "pro hac vice"—meaning "for this one particular occasion." A lawyer may make an application to the court to be permitted to represent a client, in a particular litigation matter, in a jurisdiction where he or she is not admitted to practice. The pro hac vice rules may impose certain procedural requirements on the lawyer; most common is the requirement that the lawyer associate "local counsel," a lawyer admitted to practice in the jurisdiction who will assist the out-of-state lawyer. Some jurisdictions also limit the number of times in a year that a lawyer may seek pro hac vice admission. Why? What interests do such rules further?

Pro hac vice admission is only available to a lawyer seeking to litigate a matter in court, however. What if you wish to negotiate a transaction or conduct an arbitration in a jurisdiction where you are not admitted to practice? Traditionally, there was no mechanism for "just-this-once" approval of representation by an out-of-state lawyer in a nonlitigated matter. Lawyers in border towns and small practices were well aware of the constraints imposed on their work by the unauthorized practice rules. Lawyers in large national law firms often paid little attention to them, however, until the following case provided a very rude awakening.

BIRBROWER, MONTALBANO, CONDON & FRANK, P.C. v. SUPERIOR COURT

949 P.2d 1 (Cal. 1998)

CHIN, JUSTICE.

Business and Professions Code section 6125 states: "No person shall practice law in California unless the person is an active member of the State Bar." We must decide whether an out-of-state law firm, not licensed to practice law in this state, violated section 6125 when it performed legal services in California for a California-based client under a fee agreement stipulating that California law would govern all matters in the representation.

Although we are aware of the interstate nature of modern law practice and mindful of the reality that large firms often conduct activities and serve clients in several states, we do not believe these facts excuse law firms from complying with section 6125.... We therefore conclude that, to the extent defendant law firm Birbrower, Montalbano, Condon & Frank, P.C. (Birbrower), practiced law in California without a license, it engaged in the unauthorized practice of law in this state. We also conclude that Birbrower's fee agreement with real party in interest ESQ Business Services, Inc. (ESQ), is invalid to the extent it authorizes payment for the substantial legal services Birbrower performed in California. If, however, Birbrower can show it generated fees under its agreement for limited services it performed in New York, and it earned those fees under the otherwise invalid fee agreement, it may, on remand, present to the trial court evidence justifying its recovery of fees for those New York services. Conversely, ESQ will have an opportunity to produce contrary evidence. Accordingly, we affirm the Court of Appeal judgment in part and reverse it in part, remanding for further proceedings consistent with this opinion.

I. BACKGROUND

Birbrower is a professional law corporation incorporated in New York, with its principal place of business in New York. During 1992 and 1993, Birbrower attorneys, defendants Kevin F. Hobbs and Thomas A. Condon (Hobbs and Condon), performed substantial work in California relating to the law firm's representation of ESQ. Neither Hobbs nor Condon has ever been licensed to practice law in California. None of Birbrower's attorneys were licensed to practice law in California during Birbrower's ESQ representation.

ESQ is a California corporation with its principal place of business in Santa Clara County. In July 1992, the parties negotiated and executed the fee agreement in New York, providing that Birbrower would perform legal services for ESQ, including "All matters pertaining to the investigation of and prosecution of all claims and causes of action against TANDEM COMPUTERS INCORPORATED [Tandem]." The "claims and causes of action" against Tandem, a Delaware corporation with its principal place of business in Santa Clara County, California, related to a software development and marketing contract between Tandem and ESQ dated March 16, 1990 (Tandem Agreement). The Tandem Agreement stated that "The internal laws of the State of California (irrespective of its choice of law principles) shall govern the validity of this Agreement, the construction of its terms, and the interpretation and enforcement of the rights and duties of the parties hereto." Birbrower asserts, and ESQ disputes, that ESQ knew Birbrower was not licensed to practice law in California.

While representing ESQ, Hobbs and Condon traveled to California on several occasions. In August 1992, they met in California with ESQ and its accountants. During these meetings, Hobbs and Condon discussed various matters related to ESQ's dispute with Tandem and strategy for resolving the dispute. They made recommendations and gave advice. During this California trip, Hobbs and Condon also met with Tandem representatives on four or five occasions during a two-day period. At the meetings, Hobbs and Condon spoke on ESQ's behalf. Hobbs demanded that Tandem pay ESQ $15 million. Condon told Tandem he believed that damages would exceed $15 million if the parties litigated the dispute.

Around March or April 1993, Hobbs, Condon, and another Birbrower attorney visited California to interview potential arbitrators and to meet again with ESQ and its accountants. Birbrower had previously filed a demand for arbitration against Tandem with the San Francisco offices of the American Arbitration Association (AAA). In August 1993, Hobbs returned to California to assist ESQ in settling the Tandem matter. While in California, Hobbs met with ESQ and its accountants to discuss a proposed settlement agreement Tandem authored. Hobbs also met with Tandem representatives to discuss possible changes in the proposed agreement. Hobbs gave ESQ legal advice during this trip, including his opinion that ESQ should not settle with Tandem on the terms proposed.

ESQ eventually settled the Tandem dispute, and the matter never went to arbitration. But before the settlement, ESQ and Birbrower modified the contingency fee agreement. The modification changed the fee arrangement from contingency to fixed fee, providing that ESQ would pay Birbrower over $1 million. . . .

In January 1994, ESQ sued Birbrower for legal malpractice and related claims in Santa Clara County Superior Court. Birbrower removed the matter to federal court and filed a counterclaim, which included a claim for attorney fees for the work it performed in both California and New York. The matter was then remanded. . . . The court concluded that: (1) Birbrower was "not admitted to the practice of law in California"; (2) Birbrower "did not associate California counsel"; (3) Birbrower "provided legal services in this state"; and (4) "The law is clear that no one may recover compensation for services as an attorney in this state unless he or she was a member of the state bar at the time those services were performed." . . . .

The Court of Appeal affirmed the trial court's order, holding that Birbrower violated section 6125. The Court of Appeal also concluded that Birbrower's violation barred the firm from recovering its legal fees under the written fee agreement, including fees generated in New York by the attorneys when they were physically present in New York. . . .

We granted review to determine whether Birbrower's actions and services performed while representing ESQ in California constituted the unauthorized practice of law under section 6125 and, if so, whether a section 6125 violation rendered the fee agreement wholly unenforceable.

II. DISCUSSION

A.   The Unauthorized Practice of Law

. . . [A]lthough persons may represent themselves and their own interests regardless of State Bar membership, no one but an active member of the State Bar may practice law for another person in California. The prohibition against unauthorized law practice is within the state's police power and is designed to ensure that those performing legal services do so competently.

A violation of section 6125 is a misdemeanor. Moreover, "No one may recover compensation for services as an attorney at law in this state unless [the person] was at the time the services were performed a member of The State Bar."

Although the [State Bar] Act did not define the term "practice law," case law explained it as " 'the doing and performing services in a court of justice in any matter depending therein throughout its various stages and in conformity with the adopted rules of procedure.' " (*People ex rel. Lawyers' Institute of San Diego v. Merchants' Protective Corp.*, 209 P. 363 (1922) (*Merchants*).) *Merchants* included in its definition legal advice and legal instrument and contract preparation, whether or not these subjects were rendered in the course of litigation. . . .

In addition to not defining the term "practice law," the Act also did not define the meaning of "in California." In today's legal practice, questions often arise concerning whether the phrase refers to the nature of the legal services, or restricts the Act's application to those out-of-state attorneys who are physically present in the state.

Section 6125 has generated numerous opinions on the meaning of "practice law" but none on the meaning of "in California." In our view, the practice of law "in California" entails sufficient contact with the California client to render the nature of the legal service a clear legal representation. In addition to a quantitative analysis, we must consider the nature of the unlicensed lawyer's activities in the state. Mere fortuitous or attenuated contacts will not sustain a finding that the unlicensed lawyer practiced law "in California." The primary inquiry is whether the unlicensed lawyer engaged in sufficient activities in the state, or created a continuing relationship with the California client that included legal duties and obligations.

Our definition does not necessarily depend on or require the unlicensed lawyer's physical presence in the state. Physical presence here is one factor we may consider in deciding whether the unlicensed lawyer has violated section 6125, but it is by no means exclusive. For example, one may practice law in the state in violation of section 6125 although not physically present here by advising a California client on California law in connection with a California legal dispute by telephone, fax, computer, or other modern technological means. Conversely, although we decline to provide a comprehensive list of what activities constitute sufficient contact with the state, we do reject the notion that a person *automatically* practices law "in California" whenever that person practices California law anywhere, or "virtually" enters the state by telephone, fax, e-mail, or satellite.... We must decide each case on its individual facts.

This interpretation acknowledges the tension that exists between interjurisdictional practice and the need to have a state-regulated bar....

Exceptions to section 6125 do exist, but are generally limited.... [The court concluded that none applied in this case.]

B.   The Present Case

The undisputed facts here show that [no] definition of "practice law in California" would excuse Birbrower's extensive practice in this state. Nor would any of the limited statutory exceptions to section 6125 apply to Birbrower's California practice. As the Court of Appeal observed, Birbrower engaged in unauthorized law practice *in California* on more than a limited basis, and no firm attorney engaged in that practice was an active member of the California State Bar.... As the Court of Appeal concluded, "the Birbrower firm's in-state activities clearly constituted the [unauthorized] practice of law" *in California.*

Birbrower contends, however, that section 6125 is not meant to apply to *any* out-of-state *attorneys.* Instead, it argues that the statute is intended solely to prevent nonattorneys from practicing law. This contention is without merit because it contravenes the plain language of the statute. Section 6125 clearly states that *no person* shall practice law in California unless that person is a member of the State Bar. The statute does not differentiate between attorneys or nonattorneys, nor does it excuse a person who is a member of another state bar....

Birbrower next argues that we do not further the statute's intent and purpose—to protect California citizens from incompetent attorneys—by enforcing it against out-of-state attorneys. Birbrower argues that because out-of-state attorneys have been licensed to practice in other jurisdictions, they have already demonstrated sufficient competence to protect California clients. But Birbrower's argument overlooks the obvious fact that other states' laws may differ substantially from California law. Competence in one jurisdiction does not necessarily guarantee competence in another. By applying section 6125 to out-of-state attorneys who engage in the extensive practice of law in California without becoming licensed in our state, we serve the statute's goal of assuring the competence of all attorneys practicing law in this state.

California is not alone in regulating who practices law in its jurisdiction. Many states have substantially similar statutes that serve to protect their citizens from unlicensed attorneys who engage in unauthorized legal practice.... Whether an attorney is duly admitted in another state and is, in fact, competent to practice in California is irrelevant in the face of section 6125's language and purpose.... [A] decision to except out-of-state attorneys licensed in their own jurisdictions from section 6125 is more appropriately left to the California Legislature.

Assuming that section 6125 does apply to out-of-state attorneys not licensed here, Birbrower alternatively asks us to create an exception to section 6125 for work incidental to private arbitration or other alternative dispute resolution proceedings....

We decline Birbrower's invitation to craft an arbitration exception to section 6125's prohibition of the unlicensed practice of law in this state. Any exception for arbitration is best left to the Legislature....

Finally, Birbrower urges us to adopt an exception to section 6125 based on the unique circumstances of this case. Birbrower notes that "Multistate relationships are a common part of today's society and are to be dealt with in commonsense fashion." In many situations, strict adherence to rules prohibiting the unauthorized practice of law by out-of-state attorneys would be " 'grossly impractical and inefficient.' "

Although ... we recognize the need to acknowledge and, in certain cases, accommodate the multistate nature of law practice, the facts here show that Birbrower's extensive activities within California amounted to considerably more than any of our state's recognized exceptions to section 6125 would allow. Accordingly, we reject Birbrower's suggestion that we except the firm from section 6125's rule under the circumstances here.

C.   Compensation for Legal Services

Because Birbrower violated section 6125 when it engaged in the unlawful practice of law in California, the Court of Appeal found its fee agreement with ESQ unenforceable in its entirety. Without crediting Birbrower for some services performed in New York, for which fees were generated under the fee agreement, the court reasoned that the agreement was void and unenforceable because it included payment for services rendered to a California client in the state by an unlicensed out-of-state lawyer. The court opined that "When New York counsel decided to accept [the] representation, it should have researched California law, including the law governing the practice of law in this state." ... We agree with the Court of Appeal to the extent it barred Birbrower from recovering fees generated under the fee agreement for the unauthorized legal services it performed in California. We disagree with the same court to the extent it implicitly barred Birbrower from recovering fees generated under the fee agreement for the limited legal services the firm performed in New York.

It is a general rule that an attorney is barred from recovering compensation for services rendered in another state where the attorney was not admitted to the bar.... Because Birbrower practiced substantial law in this state in violation of section 6125, it cannot receive compensation under the fee agreement for any of the services it performed in California. Enforcing the fee agreement in its entirety would include payment for the unauthorized practice of law in California and would allow Birbrower to enforce an illegal contract.

Birbrower asserts that ... it should be permitted to recover fees for those limited services it performed exclusively *in New York* under the agreement. In short, Birbrower seeks to recover under its contract for those services it performed for ESQ in New York that did not involve the practice of law in California, including fee contract negotiations and some corporate case research. Birbrower thus alternatively seeks reversal of the Court of Appeal's judgment to the extent it implicitly precluded the firm from seeking fees generated in New York under the fee agreement.

We agree with Birbrower that it may be able to recover fees under the fee agreement for the limited legal services it performed for ESQ in New York to the extent they did not constitute practicing law in California, even though those services were performed for a California client.... Thus, although the general rule against compensation to out-of-state attorneys precludes Birbrower's recovery under the fee agreement for its actions in California, the severability doctrine may allow it to receive its New York fees generated under the fee agreement, if we conclude the illegal portions of the agreement pertaining to the practice of law in California may be severed from those parts regarding services Birbrower performed in New York....

Therefore, we conclude the Court of Appeal erred in determining that the fee agreement between the parties was entirely unenforceable.... Birbrower's statutory violation may require exclusion of the portion of the fee attributable to the substantial illegal services, but that violation does not necessarily entirely preclude its recovery under the fee agreement for the limited services it performed outside California.

[A dissenting justice would have held that the work done by Birbrower did not constitute the "practice of law".]

NOTES

1. Why do you suppose the Birbrower firm undertook to represent ESQ? Some additional facts may shed light on this matter. Beginning in 1986, Birbrower represented Kamal Sandhu, the sole shareholder of ESQ Business Services Inc., a New York corporation, of which his brother Iqbal Sandhu was the vice-president. In 1990, Kamal Sandhu asked Birbrower lawyer Kevin Hobbs to review a proposed software development and marketing agreement

between ESQ–NY and Tandem Computers Incorporated (hereafter Tandem). ESQ–NY and Tandem signed the agreement. Subsequently, a second corporation, also named ESQ Business Services, Inc., was incorporated in California, with Iqbal Sandhu as a principal shareholder. In 1992, ESQ–NY and ESQ–CAL jointly hired Birbrower to resolve the dispute with Tandem. At what point in this ongoing representation of an existing New York client should Birbrower have figured out that it was engaged in the unauthorized practice of law?

2.   Whether ESQ knew that Birbrower did not have any attorneys who were admitted to practice in California was a disputed question in this case. Did it make any difference? If ESQ had expressly signed a retainer agreement acknowledging that the Birbrower lawyers were not admitted to practice law in California, would the case have come out the same way? Why or why not?

3.   The opinion is clear that the law firm may not recover under the fee agreement for anything that constituted the practice of law "in California." What constitutes the practice of law "in California"? Could the Birbrower lawyers have avoided this problem by doing all the work from their offices in New York via fax, webcam, or teleconferencing? If not, how do we define the practice of law "in" a state?

4.   What does the court identify as the justification for the UPL statute? Are you convinced that it makes sense? In that regard, consider what happened after Hurricane Katrina. Several jurisdictions very quickly granted lawyers fleeing Alabama, Louisiana and Mississippi temporary rights to practice, though with different procedural requisites. Indiana, for example, gave such lawyers a "temporary provisional license," but required them to associate with local counsel. Ohio had a similar rule. Pennsylvania permitted lawyers fleeing Katrina to relocate in Pennsylvania for nine months, but required them to "limit their services to matters arising out of their home-state practice." Several states also expedited revisions to their ethics rules that expanded the right of out-of-state lawyers to practice in their jurisdiction, citing the need to do so in light of Katrina. Mississippi granted permission for lawyers from other jurisdictions to enter the state to provide pro bono legal assistance to Katrina's victims, as long as the help related to "rights, remedies, claims, defenses, injuries or damages resulting from Hurricane Katrina or its aftermath or evacuation." Does the speed with which the states eased up their unauthorized practice restrictions in the face of an emergency suggest that those restrictions are not really all that important?

5.   The consequences of UPL for lawyers can be dire, as this case shows. They can also be dire for clients. Consider *Preston v. University of Arkansas for Medical Sciences*, 128 S.W.3d 430 (Ark. 2003). Plaintiffs hired two lawyers to bring a medical malpractice claim. The lawyers were not admitted to practice in the state, and filed the complaint without first seeking admission pro hac vice. The court struck the pleading and, since the complaint was a nullity, concluded that the action had not been timely filed and dismissed the suit as time-barred. What is the plaintiffs' remedy?

6.   Engaging in unauthorized practice is also a violation of the ethical rules. Model Rule 5.5(a) provides: "A lawyer shall not practice law in a jurisdiction in violation of the regulation of the legal profession in that jurisdiction, or

assist another in doing so." The issue of assisting another sometimes arises in the context of employing disbarred or suspended lawyers. In a recent case, a New York lawyer was disciplined for permitting a disbarred attorney to work in his office and prepare court documents without any supervision by the lawyer. *See In re Hancock*, 863 N.Y.S.2d 804 (A.D. 2d Dep't 2008). The court concluded that Hancock "afforded so little regard to his law license as to allow a disbarred felon to use his name freely in court papers and to advertise himself as his paralegal." *Id.* at 806. The disbarred felon was Burton Pugach, who was famous for being disbarred after hiring thugs to throw caustic chemicals in the face of a former girlfriend.

7. Outsourcing may also create the potential for assisting another in unauthorized practice. *See ABA Ethics Op. 08–451.*

Birbrower sent shock waves through the profession; many law firms, like the Birbrower firm, performed services for clients wherever the client's matters took them and spent little time worrying about whether they were admitted to practice in those various jurisdictions. Lawyers with large national practices recognized that they were at a previously unrecognized risk of being unable to enforce their fee agreements.

The situation in which the Birbrower lawyers found themselves could not have been cured by pro hac vice admission, since that is ordinarily unavailable in alternative dispute resolution proceedings. Other categories of practitioner were at risk as well. One was in-house counsel. Imagine that you are a lawyer admitted to practice in Minnesota, working in a Minnesota law firm. A client, a corporation based in Illinois, asks you to join the company as in-house counsel and to move to Illinois to assume your post at the company's national headquarters. Even if you promptly seek admission to the bar in Illinois, that can take substantial time. Would you be engaging in unauthorized practice while you worked at your desk in Illinois, waiting for admission in the new state to which you have moved? Suppose that one day, as you sit in your office in Illinois, the vice-president of a Connecticut subsidiary calls you, asking for advice as to how the company should handle a problem under state law. Can you advise the Connecticut subsidiary? If you are in-house counsel for a company with nationwide or even global reach, you may be almost constantly giving legal advice to the client in ways that may tread dangerously close to unauthorized practice.

The ABA's response to the post-*Birbrower* furor was to revise Model Rule 5.5. Read the Rule and its comments at this point. The default rule is that a lawyer "shall not practice law in a jurisdiction in violation of the regulation of the legal profession in that jurisdiction, or assist another in doing so." Model Rule 5.5(a). Model Rule 5.5(c) creates a series of circumstances in which a lawyer may practice on a temporary basis in a jurisdiction in which he or she is not admitted to practice. If the representation is permitted by Rule 5.5(c), it does not violate Rule 5.5(a).

The Rule 5.5(c) exceptions permit temporary practice in a jurisdiction if a lawyer is admitted in another U.S. jurisdiction and is providing legal services if:

— the lawyer associates counsel, admitted to practice in the jurisdiction, who actively participates, Model Rule 5.5(c)(1);

— the work is "in or reasonably related to a pending or potential proceeding before a tribunal," if the lawyer is authorized to appear in that proceeding or expects to be, Model Rule 5.5(c)(2);

— the work relates to an alternative dispute resolution proceeding in which the lawyer is authorized to appear or expects to be, Model Rule 5.5(c)(3); or

— the services "arise out of or are reasonably related" to the lawyer's practice in a jurisdiction where the lawyer is admitted to practice, Model Rule 5.5(c)(4).

Would *Birbrower* have come out differently if Rule 5.5(c) had applied?

Model Rule 5.5(d) creates two other circumstances under which a lawyer not admitted in a jurisdiction may provide services there. One, 5.5(d)(1), is addressed to the in-house counsel problem. Do you think the resolution of the problem is satisfactory?

What is Model Rule 5.5(d)(2) about? Consider the following opinion:

PENNSYLVANIA BAR ASSOCIATION
ETHICS OPINION 2005–14
2005 WL 5544943 (Aug. 2005)

The inquirer received her law degree from a state university in the former USSR. This degree allowed her to practice law in all 15 republics of the former Soviet Union including Russia and Ukraine. Five years ago she received an LL.M. in Comparative Law degree from an ABA approved law school in the United States.

In 2004 the inquirer passed the bar exam in a state which has reciprocal admission with Pennsylvania. In addition, she passed the Multistate Professional Responsibility Exam. Her scores on both exams exceeded those required by Pennsylvania.

In 2005, the inquirer received a full unrestricted license to practice law in the state where she passed the bar exam. The license allows her to practice as an Attorney and Counselor at law in all the courts of the state. The inquirer's goal is to practice immigration law only, in Pennsylvania. The inquirer wants to know given her education and admission to the reciprocal state, whether she would be permitted ethically to practice immigration law in Pennsylvania from a law office in Pennsylvania. Furthermore she asks if this would be impacted by whether she is doing this as a sole practitioner or with a partner licensed in Pennsylvania.

A similar question was addressed in Committee opinion 2004–6. However, the circumstances there were slightly different in that the inquirer was eligible to take the Pennsylvania Bar Exam and was only going to be practicing in Pennsylvania with an out of state license for a temporary period of time. In the present inquiry there are two issues. First, whether given the inquirer's present qualifications, she is eligible to either take the Pennsylvania Bar Exam or eligible for admittance by waiver into Pennsylvania. Second, if she is not, whether Pennsylvania Rule of Professional Conduct 5.5 would nevertheless allow her to practice here.

Pennsylvania Bar Admission Rules [the B.A.R.s] govern both eligibility to take the bar exam as well as waiver into the bar from a reciprocal state. They also govern the licensing of an individual as a "foreign legal consultant."

B.A.R. 203 governs eligibility to sit for the Pennsylvania Bar Exam. The inquirer would not qualify to take the exam since she holds neither a Bachelor of Laws or Juris Doctor degree from an ABA accredited law school as required by B.A.R. 203(2). B.A.R. 205 governs admission to the Bar by foreign attorneys and graduates of foreign institutions. The inquirer would not qualify for admission under this B.A.R. because she can not meet the requirements of B.A.R. 205(b) in that she has not had 30 hours of education covering certain specific courses in an accredited American law school. B.A.R. 204 governs admission by waiver from a reciprocal state. Again, even though she is licensed in a reciprocal state the inquirer does not qualify for admission under this B.A.R. because she can not meet the educational requirements found in B.A.R. 204(1) nor the experience requirements found in B.A.R. 204(4).

The Committee notes that the inquirer might qualify to receive a license as a foreign legal consultant pursuant to B.A.R. 341 but this type of license would not permit her to practice the type of law in Pennsylvania about which she is asking.

The question thus becomes whether Rule 5.5 ... will permit an attorney licensed in another state, who is ineligible as presently educated to either sit for the Pennsylvania Bar Exam or waive into the Pennsylvania Bar, to nevertheless open an office in Pennsylvania for the limited practice of Immigration and Naturalization law. Provided that the inquirer is admitted to practice before the Immigration and Naturalization Court, based upon the provisions of Rule 5.5(d)(2), and the clarification of that rule provided by Comment 15, the answer is "yes." ...

Although the Comments to the Rules are not officially adopted by the Supreme Court they are included to further clarify and explain the Rules themselves. Comment 15 to Rule 5.5 is directly on point to this inquiry and provides that:

> Paragraph (d) identifies two circumstances in which a lawyer who is admitted to practice in another jurisdiction, and is not disbarred or suspended from practice in any jurisdiction, may establish an office or other systematic and continuous presence in this jurisdiction for the practice of law as well as provide legal services on a temporary basis. Except as provided in paragraphs (d)(1) and (d)(2), a lawyer who is

admitted to practice law in another jurisdiction and who establishes an office or other systematic or continuous presence in this jurisdiction must become admitted to practice law generally in this jurisdiction.

Since the inquirer's situation clearly fits within 5.5(d)(2) it becomes clear that [s]he is not required to be admitted to the Pennsylvania Bar in order to maintain an office here provided [s]he limits [her] practice to immigration work. This is true whether or not [s]he is in a partnership with a Pennsylvania admitted attorney.

There are several other issues to which the Committee would like to draw the inquirer's attention. Pursuant to Rule 5.5, Comment 19, "A lawyer who practices law in this jurisdiction pursuant to paragraph (c) or (d) or otherwise is subject to the disciplinary authority of this jurisdiction. See Rule 8.5(a)." Rule 8.5(a) provides in part that, " ... A lawyer not admitted in this jurisdiction is also subject to the disciplinary authority of this jurisdiction if the lawyer provides or offers to provide any legal services in this jurisdiction. A lawyer may be subject to the disciplinary authority of both this jurisdiction and another jurisdiction for the same conduct." Given the dual accountability provided by this Rule, the Committee urges the inquirer to also obtain an opinion from the appropriate body in the state to which she is admitted to practice to determine if her proposed conduct runs afoul of any of its ethics rules. Furthermore, the inquirer should understand that while her conduct in Pennsylvania while representing clients in Pennsylvania is subject to the Pennsylvania Rules (see Rule 8.5(b)(2)), it could also be subject to the Rules of the state in which she is admitted. . . .

The Committee notes that oftentimes state law issues, for example domestic relations law, will have an impact on representation in an immigration matter. The inquirer is required by Rule 1.1 (Competence), if dealing with any of these questions to have sufficient knowledge of such law in order to provide competent advice. However, the inquirer's involvement in such areas must be limited to advice and discussion on such matters as they impact the client's immigration matter and nothing further. Should the client request that the inquirer become more involved, to do so would place the inquirer in violation of Rule 5.5.

NOTES

1.   The trick with Rule 5.5 is to remember that it is the rules that govern the jurisdiction in which you wish to engage in temporary practice, not the rules of your jurisdiction of permanent admission, that determine whether temporary practice constitutes UPL. If you engage in unauthorized practice in a jurisdiction not your own, that violates Rule 5.5(a). So a lawyer who is found to have committed unauthorized practice in a jurisdiction where she is not entitled to practice may face discipline in the jurisdiction where she is admitted to practice, as well, conceivably, as discipline in the jurisdiction in which the UPL took place. Consider *In re Trester*, 172 P.3d 31 (Kan. 2007).

Trester was admitted to practice in Kansas in 1968, but never practiced there. He moved to California and took the bar examination four times, but did not pass it. Nonetheless, Trester practiced law in California for forty years. When California officials learned of this, he was charged with theft for taking retainers without a license to practice law. His convictions for theft and unauthorized practice were reported to Kansas, which imposed an indefinite suspension.

2.   The opinion makes clear that the lawyer in this case would be ineligible for admission to the Pennsylvania bar. This exception accordingly creates a permanent exception to the rule of admission when the lawyer limits her practice to an area of federal law in which she is otherwise permitted to practice. Why would the rules except federal practice from state regulation? Does the following case explain?

AUGUSTINE v. DEPARTMENT OF VETERANS AFFAIRS

429 F.3d 1334 (Fed. Cir. 2005)

DYK, CIRCUIT JUDGE.

Petitioner Cassandra Augustine was successful in her appeal to the Merit Systems Protection Board ("Board"). The Board held that the Department of Veterans' Affairs ("VA") violated Augustine's right to a veterans' preference under the Veterans' Preference Act, 5 U.S.C. § 3309, by not selecting her for a competitive civil service position. As the prevailing party, Augustine moved for attorney's fees under 5 U.S.C. § 3330c(b). The Board held that Augustine could not recover fees because her attorney was not licensed to practice in the state in which the services were rendered. We vacate the Board's decision and remand for further proceedings.

BACKGROUND

Many federal agencies, including the Board, permit both attorneys and non-attorneys to represent clients in administrative proceedings. Typically, non-attorney representatives are not entitled to an award of fees. Even when the private party is represented by an attorney, under the "American Rule," the prevailing party is generally responsible for his own attorney's fees. However, Congress has created several exceptions to this rule, allowing prevailing parties before federal courts or agencies to recover attorney's fees. The Veterans Employment Opportunities Act of 1998 ("VEOA") is such an exception. The VEOA provides that veterans who prevail in certain employment actions "shall be awarded reasonable attorney fees, expert witness fees, and other litigation expenses." 5 U.S.C. § 3330c(b) (2000). This case presents the question as to what, if any, role state law should play in determining who is an "attorney" for purposes of section 3330c(b).

The petitioner in this case, Augustine, filed a pro se appeal with the Board, arguing that the VA violated her right to a veterans' preference under the Veterans' Preference Act by not selecting her for the position of

"Veterans Service Representative." On March 14, 2000, the administrative judge ("AJ") rendered an initial decision concluding that the VA had violated the Veterans' Preference Act and ordering the VA to appoint Augustine to the Service Representative position retroactively and to compensate her for any loss of wages or benefits. The AJ also awarded liquidated damages for violations of the statute. The VA sought review by the full Board. The full Board then vacated the initial decision, and directed the parties to submit additional briefing to the full Board on various issues.

By August 13, 2001, Augustine retained an attorney, Wild Chang, to represent her. Augustine herself was a resident in California. Chang, who was also located in California, represented Augustine in the subsequent proceedings before the full Board as well as in a mediation conducted in August 2001. [Augustine, with Chang's assistance, prevailed before the Board.]

As the prevailing party, Augustine moved for attorney's fees and costs of $39,124.34 under the VEOA's attorney's fees provision. In an initial decision, the AJ agreed that the petitioner was a prevailing party but denied the fee request. Although Chang was licensed to practice law in both Massachusetts and New York, he was not licensed in California, where the services were performed. The AJ held that "although [Chang] could appear in the proceeding as a nonlawyer representative pursuant to Board regulations," he could not appear as an attorney unless California law permitted him to appear. The AJ reasoned that "[a]n attorney appearing before the Board, whether representing a private party or an agency, will be expected to conform to the applicable state rules governing attorney conduct." Concluding that "all services were evidently performed while counsel was in California," the AJ then determined that, as part of the rules governing attorney conduct in California, "a non-member of the California State Bar ... is [ ] forbidden to 'practice law in California,' " and may not "recover compensation for services as an attorney at law in California...."

While recognizing that the California prohibition had not applied to regulate practice in federal courts, the AJ explained that the Board was not a court.... Augustine then sought review by this court....

DISCUSSION

... The Board's decision here is not entirely clear. It could be read as holding that California law controls the right to practice as an attorney before the Board and the right to fees for performing such service. Alternatively, it could be read as holding that the federal attorney's fee statute incorporates state law. We conclude that neither ground for the decision is tenable.

I

We first address the theory that state law is controlling. Section 6125 of California Code provides that: "No person shall practice law in California unless the person is an active member of the State Bar."....

California courts have yet to fully articulate the scope of what constitutes "practicing law in California" under section 6125. They have made clear that section 6125 covers representation before California courts. *Birbrower*, 949 P.2d at 5. On the other hand, section 6125 "does not regulate practice before United States courts," and therefore does not restrict the receipt of attorney's fees for services related to federal court proceedings. . . .

Although the Ninth Circuit applied section 6125 to practice before state administrative agencies, our attention has not been directed to any instance in which section 6125 has been applied to restrict attorney practice before a *federal* administrative agency. To the contrary, a 1994 memorandum issued by the Office of Professional Competence, Planning & Development of the State Bar of California indicated that the bar at least does not view section 6125 as covering federal administrative proceedings:

> The State Bar takes the general position that where a non-member is permitted to practice before a federal court (district, appellate, admiralty) or a federal agency (INS, Patent Office), such individual is not engaged in the unauthorized practice of law while performing activities before such federal courts or agencies in California on behalf of clients.

The parties vigorously dispute whether the activities of petitioner's counsel violated California law. Whether or not California law applies, it is quite clear that state law purporting to govern practice before a federal administrative agency would be invalid. It is long established that any state or local law which attempts to impede or control the federal government or its instrumentalities is deemed presumptively invalid under the Supremacy Clause. . . .

So too state licensing requirements which purport to regulate private individuals who appear before a federal agency are invalid. In *Sperry v. Florida*, 373 U.S. 379 (1963), the Florida Bar attempted to enjoin a non-attorney from performing services in the state relating to a patent prosecution occurring before the United States Patent and Trademark Office ("PTO"). The Florida Bar argued that the non-attorney was engaged in the "unauthorized practice of law" because the Florida Bar had not licensed him. The Supreme Court held that a "State may not enforce licensing requirements which ... give the 'State's licensing board a virtual power of review over the federal determination' that a person or agency is qualified and entitled to perform certain functions," and found that the state's licensing requirements could not govern practice before the PTO.

Just as the states cannot regulate practice before the PTO, they cannot regulate practice before the Merit Systems Protection Board. Allowing state control would plainly impede the conduct of federal proceedings even though the Board does not have procedures for admitting counsel to practice before it. . . . California has no authority to require that attorneys practicing before the Board obtain a state license or to regulate the award of fees for work before federal agencies. To the extent that the Board held otherwise, that decision cannot stand. . . .

II

[The court rejected the theory that the federal law here incorporated state law.]

It seems to us axiomatic that the denial of fees to attorneys practicing before federal agencies would discourage such representation by attorneys. To allow attorneys to practice before federal agencies, while barring them from collecting fees under the attorney's fees statute, would, as a practical matter, bar such private representation entirely in many cases and limit representation to the few attorneys willing to serve without compensation. Under the government's theory it might even be impermissible for the attorney to receive compensation out of the client's own monetary recovery. A restrictive reading of the term "attorney" in the fee-shifting statute would thus naturally limit the opportunities that veterans would have in obtaining counsel.

Under these circumstances, the purposes of the fee-shifting statute can be served only by allowing fees for representatives who are licensed as attorneys in any state or federal jurisdiction, without regard to the state licensing requirements of the state in which services were rendered.

PROBLEMS

1. Moore was admitted to practice in Connecticut in 1975 and went to work at a collection agency. Within six months, his boss filed misconduct charges against him, alleging that he forged a court clerk's name on an execution of a nonexistent judgment and failed to remit funds to clients. Moore agreed to resign from the bar and the disciplinary matter was dropped. In 1981 he sought readmission to the bar in Connecticut but was denied; one relevant fact was that, during the pendency of his petition, he entered an appearance in court on behalf of a corporation in which he had an interest [corporations may not appear pro se, but only through counsel]. The court enjoined him from engaging in the unauthorized practice of law and fined him $750. In 1994, Moore sought admission to the bar of Massachusetts. The application he completed asked, "Have you ever been disbarred, suspended, reprimanded, censured, or otherwise disciplined or disqualified as an attorney?" Moore answered "No." He did not list his work at the collection agency on the form, though the application required him to list all employment he had held since his eighteenth birthday. He certified at the end of the form that his answers were "true, complete, and candid." Moore was admitted to practice in Massachusetts. Is he subject to discipline? If so, what discipline would be appropriate? *See In re Moore*, 812 N.E.2d 1197 (Mass. 2004); *see also In re Moore*, 866 N.E.2d 897 (Mass. 2007).

2. Lawyer was a partner in a Georgia law firm and was admitted to practice there. His firm was contacted by a North Carolina college, which asked the firm to investigate possible grade-fixing in the college's sports program.

Lawyer and a colleague visited the North Carolina campus, conducted an investigation, and prepared a report which criticized some university employees but largely cleared the university's president of wrongdoing related to the incident. Did Lawyer engage in the unauthorized practice of law? *See* Jonathan Ringel, *Ga. Lawyers Indicted for Advising N.C. College*, Fulton County Daily Report, April 8, 2004.

3.   Gould lived in Florida but was licensed as an attorney only in New York. He proposed to place an advertisement in a Florida publication that offered legal services "for New York legal matters only." Is this proper? What about an advertisement that said his Florida practice would be "limited to federal administrative law"? *See Gould v. Florida Bar*, 259 Fed. Appx. 208 (11th Cir. 2007).

4.   Plaintiffs obtained mortgages from two banks. The banks charged the plaintiffs "document preparation fees" of $50 and $150, respectively, for preparing documents, including promissory notes, deeds, and mortgages, relating to their mortgage loans. Plaintiffs claimed that the fees were impermissible because they constituted payment for document preparation by non-lawyers, which constituted the unauthorized practice of law. Should they get their money back? *See Goldberg v. Merrill Lynch Credit Corp.*, 981 So.2d 550 (Fla. App. 4th Dist. 2008).

CHAPTER 15

DISCIPLINARY JURISDICTION AND CHOICE OF LAW

■ ■ ■

Suppose there is an allegation that you have violated the rules of professional responsibility. Which jurisdiction has the authority to discipline you? And which rules of professional responsibility will be applied to you? These are two separate questions, and the answers to them may surprise you. If you are admitted to practice in a jurisdiction, never leave that jurisdiction, and practice exclusively the law of that jurisdiction for clients of that jurisdiction, the answer to these questions may seem obvious. But multijurisdictional activities and rules may make these issues more complex. Consider the following hypotheticals:

(1) You are admitted to practice in Jurisdiction A and while on vacation in Jurisdiction B you are arrested for shoplifting. Which jurisdiction[s] may subject you to discipline? *See* Rule 8.5(a).

(2) You are admitted to practice in Jurisdiction A and visit Jurisdiction B to meet with the client to discuss strategy in a case you are handling in A. Which jurisdiction[s] may subject you to discipline? *See* Comment [19] to Rule 5.5 and Rule 8.5(a).

(3) You are admitted to practice in Jurisdiction A. You disseminate an advertising flyer in Jurisdiction B that violates Jurisdiction B's rules of professional responsibility. Can B discipline you for your violation of its rules? Can A? Does it depend on whether the rules in the two jurisdictions are the same or different? *See* Rule 8.5(a) and 8.5(b)(2).

(4) You are admitted to practice in both Jurisdiction A and Jurisdiction B. You violate the trust account rules in Jurisdiction A. Can Jurisdiction A discipline you for your violation of its rules? Can B? Does it depend on whether the rules in the two jurisdictions are the same or different? *See* Rule 8.5(b)(2).

(5) You are admitted to practice in Jurisdiction A. You are asked to represent a client in a litigated matter pro hac vice in Jurisdiction B. You travel to Jurisdiction B and represent the client but in doing so you make a misrepresentation to the court in B. What rules will apply to your conduct in Jurisdiction B? *See* Rule 8.5(b)(1).

One thing these problems and Model Rule 8.5(a) suggest is that it is possible to be subject to the disciplinary authority of a jurisdiction where you are not admitted to practice. That might seem peculiar, because it is hard to imagine how sanctions from such a jurisdiction would effectively govern lawyer conduct. A jurisdiction in which you are admitted to practice has the power to take away your license to practice, by suspending or disbarring you. What can a jurisdiction in which you are not admitted to practice do? Consider the following case.

ATTORNEY GRIEVANCE COMMISSION OF MARYLAND v. BARNEYS

805 A.2d 1040 (Md. App. 2002)

HARRELL, JUDGE.

The Attorney Grievance Commission of Maryland, Petitioner, filed a Petition for Disciplinary Action against Bradford Jay Barneys, Respondent, charging him with misconduct in connection with his alleged unauthorized practice of law in Maryland. Specifically, the petition alleged that Respondent violated the following Maryland Rules of Professional Conduct ("MRPC"): 5.5(a) (Unauthorized practice of law); 7.5(a), (b), and (d) (Firm names and letterheads); 4.1 (Truthfulness in statements to others); 8.1(a) (Bar admission and disciplinary matters); and 8.4(b), (c), and (d) (Misconduct)....

I.

... Respondent, a member of the Bars of New York, Connecticut, and the District of Columbia, held himself out as a Maryland attorney beginning in August of 1996, when he opened an office at 7505 New Hampshire Avenue, Suite 301, Langley Park, Maryland. Without noting any jurisdictional limitation on the practice, Respondent used the name "Law Offices of Bradford J. Barneys, P.C." on his letterhead and business cards. The hearing court also found as a fact that, without being admitted to the Maryland Bar, Respondent engaged in the practice of law in Maryland during 1997 and 1998. The hearing court further determined that, despite the known pendency of Respondent's Maryland bar admission application, he nonetheless entered his appearance as counsel and otherwise represented clients in at least five cases in the District Court of Maryland, sitting in Prince George's County, and the Circuit Court for Prince George's County. In none of these cases had Respondent been either admitted to the Maryland Bar or admitted specially by the court.

The hearing judge further found that, of special note, Respondent engaged in the unauthorized practice of law in the case of State of Maryland v. Santiago Sanchez. There, Respondent entered his appearance and filed other papers. He also contacted Gates Bail Bonds to arrange for Mr. Sanchez's one hundred fifty thousand dollars bond. Specifically, Respondent proposed that Deborah Gates, on behalf of Gates Bail Bonds, "accept an assignment of Mr. Sanchez's worker's compensation settlement proceeds, promising future payment in the amount of Fifteen Thousand Dollars," because the settlement agreement already existed and the funds would be available within thirty days. When Ms. Gates agreed to the assignment, Respondent gave her a document printed on his letterhead and captioned, "Assignment of Settlement Proceeds," which was signed by Respondent and purportedly by Mr. Sanchez. In that document, Respondent committed "to observe all terms of [the assignment agreement] and . . . to withhold such funds from any settlement, judgment or verdict as may be necessary to adequately protect Gates Bail Bonds."

Furthermore, notwithstanding Respondent's agreement to withhold funds from the proceeds of Mr. Sanchez's worker's compensation case, Judge Whalen found that Martin Gerel, Esquire, not Respondent, represented Mr. Sanchez in that case. The hearing judge also determined that, although Respondent did not state affirmatively to Ms. Gates that he represented Mr. Sanchez in the worker's compensation case, Respondent lead her to believe that he did. In any event, Mr. Gerel, never having been informed by Respondent of the assignment, did not contact Ms. Gates before disbursing to Mr. Sanchez his share of the worker's compensation proceeds. Mr. Sanchez neither contacted Ms. Gates upon his release from jail nor appeared for trial. As a result, Gates Bail Bonds was not paid its fee and the bond posted by Gates Bail Bonds was forfeited.

Investigating Ms. Gates' complaint against Respondent, one of Petitioner's investigators, Mr. Peregoy, visited the building in which Respondent's office was located on 19 November 1998, finding a lobby sign describing Barneys as an "attorney at law" and "a law office sign in Respondent's name outside his suite." In response to Petitioner's subsequent letter apprising him of the Gates' complaint and threatening to seek an injunction unless he closed his Langley Park Office, Respondent agreed in a reply letter of 12 December to close his practice on New Hampshire Avenue, including removing the sign outside his suite door. The removal of the suite sign was confirmed by the investigator during a second visit to the building on 28 December 1998. Respondent later removed his business cards from open view and availability, although the lobby sign had not been removed, as of 22 January 1999, the date of the investigator's third visit to Respondent's Maryland office.

As indicated, on these findings, the hearing judge concluded that Respondent committed each of the rule violations charged. . . .

. . . The recommendation for sanction filed by Petitioner seeks Respondent's disbarment. In support of that recommendation, Petitioner reminds us of our decision in *Attorney Grievance Comm'n v. Harper and Kemp,* 737 A.2d 557, 566 (1999), where we stated that "unadmitted attorneys must be deterred from attempting to practice law in violation of the statutory prohibition against unauthorized practice." Petitioner asserts that there is "no reasonable basis" on which Respondent "could have thought that his conduct was lawful."

... Respondent filed a Recommendation for Sanctions asserting that the appropriate punishment for his conduct is a two-year prohibition against re-filing an application for admission to the Maryland Bar. Acknowledging that he engaged in the unauthorized practice of law, Respondent ... asserts that his violation of MRPC 5.5(a) was not a "deliberate and persistent" violation ...; rather, he now maintains, "even though [his] office was in Maryland, [he] primarily represented clients before the courts of the District of Columbia with the exception of the representation of five clients whom [he] represented in the Maryland Courts." ... Further, Respondent expresses his remorse, stating as follows:

> Respondent is deeply remorseful for his conduct in this case and has no prior disciplinary record in any jurisdiction. When Respondent opened his office in Maryland, Respondent was a new solo practitioner and was not aware of the prohibition of operating a law office in Maryland even where the primary law practice was in the District of Columbia. Respondent, however, was fully aware of the prohibition of entering his appearance in the Maryland Courts. For that, Respondent believes he should be punished. However, the appropriate sanction is not disbarment but rather an Order preventing Respondent from applying for admission to the Maryland Bar for a period of two years.

. . . .

II.

The purpose of the sanction imposed on an attorney following disciplinary proceedings is the same as for the proceedings themselves, which is well settled and often stated by this Court: to protect the public rather than to punish the attorney who engages in misconduct. As a result, this Court has firmly established the importance of sanctions in deterring attorneys from violating the disciplinary rules. As we explained in *Attorney Grievance Comm'n v. Garfield*, 797 A.2d 757, 764 (Md. 2002):

> [t]he public interest is served when this Court imposes a sanction which demonstrates to members of this legal profession the type of conduct that will not be tolerated. By imposing such a sanction, this Court fulfills its responsibility to insist upon the maintenance of the integrity of the Bar and to prevent the transgression of an individual lawyer from bringing its image into disrepute. Therefore, the public interest is served when sanctions designed to effect general and specific deterrence are imposed on an attorney who violates the disciplinary rules.

A.

Unauthorized Practice of Law (MRPC 5.5(a))—The Flagship Violation

Our research reveals six relatively recent cases dealing with attorneys whose flagship violations were of MRPC 5.5(a) (the prohibition against unauthorized practice of law). In five of those cases, the attorney was disbarred....

B.

Where Does Barneys' Case Fall on the Unauthorized Practice Continuum?

In four of the six unauthorized practice cases ... we expressly identified "deterrence" as one objective of the imposed sanctions. In Respondent's case, we would fail to achieve this goal, and be inconsistent with the clear majority of our prior cases, were we to adopt Respondent's proposed sanction or merely suspend him....

Respondent claims that he "has cooperated fully with the Attorney Grievance Commission" by voluntarily closing his Maryland office and operating from his office in the District of Columbia since approximately May 1999. The "voluntary" nature of Respondent's act is tempered, however, as he closed his office only after his involvement in the Sanchez case was discovered and he was threatened with an injunction action. Had his misconduct not been discovered then, there is nothing in the record to suggest Barneys would not have continued or even expanded his illegal activities. In our view, it seems that Respondent, at best, cooperated with the investigation (to the extent he did) only when he had little real choice to do otherwise. In addition, even if Respondent's ultimate termination of misconduct was viewed as voluntary, this alone would not warrant necessarily a sanction less than disbarment....

Although remorse and regret are recognized as mitigating factors, we find it impossible to parse with sufficient certainty whether Respondent's claimed remorse is sincere, mere lip service, or simply damage control....

Finally, suspending Barneys rather than disbarring him would give the impression that we view his conduct as more similar to the conduct of attorneys who violate MRPC 5.5(b), rather than 5.5(a). Respondent, however, did not assist another attorney in the unauthorized practice of law; he committed the violations directly and without valid excuse or justification.

Conclusion

Based on the Court's trend of disbarring attorneys for unauthorized practice violations under MRPC 5.5(a) violations, Respondent's multiple representation of clients in Maryland state courts, his deceptive conduct regarding the Sanchez/Gates Bail Bonds incident, the misrepresentations to Bar Counsel's investigator and on his Petition for admission, and the relative insubstantiality of any possibly mitigating circumstances, disbarment is the appropriate sanction.

NOTES

1.   What is the significance of being disbarred in a jurisdiction in which you were never admitted in the first place? In *In re Tonwe*, 929 A.2d 774 (Del. 2007), a Pennsylvania lawyer was found to have engaged in the unauthorized practice of law in Delaware. The disciplinary board in Delaware did not recommend disbarment, instead suggesting "a series of sanctions that effectively result in disbarment: 1. Respondent be declared permanently unfit for admission to the Delaware bar; 2. Immediate prohibition on Respondent's ability to appear in Delaware *pro hac vice;* 3. An Order directing Respondent to cease and desist from all practice of law in Delaware; and 4. Request and recommend disbarment by the Supreme Court of Pennsylvania." The court concluded that the board probably had not recommended disbarment because it did not think that it could, on the theory that "one has to be a member of the bar before one can be disbarred." The court rejected that conclusion. Instead it adopted the definition of disbarment for an unadmitted lawyer as "the unconditional exclusion from the admission to or the exercise of any privilege to practice law in this State." Based on that definition, the court disbarred Tonwe.

2.   Disbarment in a jurisdiction in which you are not admitted to practice thus will interfere with your ability to practice there. The most significant consequence of such a sanction, however, is probably reflected in what happened next to attorney Barneys:

IN RE BARNEYS

861 A.2d 1270 (D.C. 2004)

FARRELL, ASSOCIATE JUDGE:

The Board on Professional Responsibility (the Board) recommends imposition of reciprocal discipline on respondent (Barneys) in the form of disbarment, based upon a decision of the Court of Appeals of Maryland unconditionally excluding Barneys "from the admission to or exercise of any privilege to practice law in [Maryland]." Having made no appearance until now in these reciprocal discipline proceedings, Barneys argues for the first time that he may not be disciplined reciprocally in the circumstances of this case and that, in any event, the most he should receive is a nine-month suspension (combined with a fitness requirement) rather than disbarment—the latter a sanction, he contends, that is "significantly greater" than the exclusion from practice imposed by Maryland. We reject these arguments and accept the Board's recommendation.

I.

[The court described the facts found by the Maryland court.]

II.

[The court described the proceedings in the Maryland courts.]

On November 4, 2002, Bar Counsel for the District of Columbia sent a certified copy of the Maryland Court order to this court pursuant to D.C.

Bar R. XI, § 11(b). The Board also sent a notice to Barneys at his address last listed with the District of Columbia Bar, informing him of this proceeding and notifying him that the Board could recommend a sanction different from that imposed in Maryland, that is, either a greater or lesser sanction. On November 13, 2002, this court suspended Barneys pursuant to D.C. Bar R. XI, § 11(d), directed Bar Counsel to inform the Board of her position regarding reciprocal discipline, and ordered Barneys to show cause thereafter before the Board why identical, greater, or lesser discipline should not be imposed in the District. On December 13, 2002, Bar Counsel filed a statement arguing that none of the exceptions set forth in D.C. Bar R. XI, § 11(c) applied and urging the Board to recommend reciprocal discipline of disbarment. A copy of the statement of Bar Counsel was served by mail on Barneys at his primary address listed with the D.C. Bar. Barneys did not respond to the statement of Bar Counsel and did not otherwise participate in the proceedings before the Board. The Board now recommends disbarment.

III.

We have repeatedly held that "an attorney waives the right to contest the imposition of reciprocal discipline when he or she does not oppose the proposed discipline before the Board or fails to respond to the court's show cause order." In such circumstances, reciprocal discipline will be imposed unless doing so would lead to an "obvious miscarriage of justice." As Barneys failed to respond to the show cause order or participate in the proceedings before the Board, he may not challenge the imposition of reciprocal disbarment unless he can meet the "demanding" miscarriage of justice standard.

Barneys argues first, however, that he should not have to meet that standard because the Board lacked jurisdiction—what amounts to non-waivable subject matter jurisdiction—to discipline him reciprocally for unauthorized practice in Maryland. The argument appears to turn on the fact that, whereas in Maryland an attorney not a member of the state's Bar who engages in unauthorized practice there may be disciplined as an attorney (*i.e.*, by sanctions up to "disbarment"), the District of Columbia proceeds against such conduct—by anyone not licensed here, including a lawyer—through the court's Committee on Unauthorized Practice and court-imposed sanctions such as contempt, civil or criminal. Thus, Barneys asserts, his unauthorized practice would not be treated as "misconduct" by an attorney in this jurisdiction, hence was not reachable by reciprocal discipline. *See* D.C. Bar R. XI, § 11(c) ("Reciprocal discipline shall be imposed unless the attorney demonstrates . . . that: . . . (5) The misconduct elsewhere does not constitute misconduct in the District of Columbia.").

This argument is unpersuasive. . . . Barneys' actions in Maryland *were* misconduct within the meaning of this jurisdiction's ethical rules. *See* Rule 5.5 of the District of Columbia Rules of Professional Conduct ("A lawyer shall not: (a) practice law in a jurisdiction where doing so violates the regulation of the legal profession in that jurisdiction....''). As a lawyer admitted to practice in this jurisdiction, Barneys "is subject to the disciplinary authority of this jurisdiction, regardless of where [his] conduct occur[red]." Rule 8.5(a). Nothing in D.C. Bar Rule XI or any ethical rule he cites limits that jurisdiction, as he contends, to the initiation of an original disciplinary proceeding and not the imposition of reciprocal discipline.

There remains the question, then, of whether reciprocal disbarment of Barneys would amount to an "obvious miscarriage of justice." It arguably would do so if disbarment by Maryland of non-admitted attorneys such as Barneys meant, in practice, exclusion for a length of time much shorter than the five years applicable to attorneys disbarred in this jurisdiction. But Barneys has made no such showing. At the time of his conduct, "disbarment" in Maryland "when applied to an attorney not admitted by the Court of Appeals to practice law mean[t] *permanent* exclusion from exercising in any manner the privilege of practicing law in [Maryland]." As revised in 2001, Maryland's discipline rules still define "disbarment," as applied to an attorney not admitted to practice there, to mean "the unconditional exclusion from the admission to or the exercise of any privilege to practice law in this State." Barneys points to nothing in Maryland's rule governing reinstatement that envisions lifting of this unconditional exclusion substantially earlier than the five years provided by the District's rule.

... [W]e are satisfied that to impose here the same discipline that Maryland found necessary in this case yields no manifest injustice....

Accordingly, respondent Bradford J. Barneys is disbarred from the practice of law in the District of Columbia.

NOTES

1. What was lawyer Barneys disciplined for in the District of Columbia? What was the nature of his discipline?

2. You might have thought that "disbarment" meant a permanent loss of the license to practice. As this case shows, "disbarment" in many jurisdictions is not as permanent as popular opinion might suggest. Do you think this is wise?

3. It might seem as though participating in a disciplinary proceeding in a jurisdiction in which you are not admitted to practice is superfluous, since the jurisdiction is simply taking away a privilege you never had to begin with. Does the following case suggest that is an unwise course?

IN RE DEMOS
875 A.2d 636 (D.C. 2005)

TERRY, ASSOCIATE JUDGE:

[This case was originally scheduled for oral argument after having been postponed from an earlier date at respondent's request. When the case was called and respondent failed to appear in the courtroom, the court ordered the matter submitted without argument.]

The Board on Professional Responsibility ("the Board") recommends that we impose reciprocal, but not identical, discipline on respondent Demos for misconduct committed before the United States District Court for the District of Arizona (hereafter the "Arizona federal court"). On December 28, 1994, respondent was stricken from the Arizona federal court's roll of attorneys. The Board recommends that he be disbarred in the District of Columbia. We adopt the Board's recommendation and order respondent's disbarment.

I

Respondent passed the District of Columbia bar examination in 1983, but was not admitted to our bar at that time, for reasons explained in *In re Demos*, 579 A.2d 668 (D.C. 1990) (en banc).[1] Eventually, however, he was admitted on August 2, 1993.

In September of 1993, respondent applied for admission to the bar of the United States District Court for the Northern District of Texas. In his application he said he was a resident of Phoenix, Arizona, and practiced law with a firm in Tempe, Arizona. His application was approved, and respondent was admitted on October 4, 1993.

On October 25, 1993, respondent applied for admission to practice before the Arizona federal court. That court's Local Rule of Practice 1.5 provides that attorneys may be admitted to practice before the court if they are admitted "to any Federal Court" or admitted to practice in the state of Arizona. The rule further states, however, that attorneys who either reside in Arizona or have a principal office or practice in Arizona must be admitted to the bar of the State of Arizona. Therefore, according to the information he provided in his application to the Northern District of Texas, respondent needed to become a member of the Arizona bar before being admitted to practice before the Arizona federal court. Respondent sought to avoid this requirement by stating on his application for admission that he resided in an apartment in Albuquerque, New Mexico, and that his law firm was located in Washington, D.C.

Respondent was admitted to practice before the Arizona federal court by what that court later characterized as a "ministerial act," without appearing before a judicial officer. Soon thereafter, however, the Arizona federal court issued a show cause order "regarding the truth of the matters contained in his application." After a hearing, the Arizona federal court found that there were "numerous inconsistencies in connection with Mr. Demos' multiple application process." In particular, the District of Columbia address he listed for his law firm was merely "a mail drop address," and the "suite number" was a numbered mailbox rented from Mailboxes Etcetera. Likewise, there was no record that he had ever owned or rented

---

1. [While Demos was working as a law clerk for his father, he participated as an attorney in a deposition and lied to the court in a subsequent investigation of the matter. Ed.]

property at his stated address in Albuquerque. Additionally, the Arizona federal court noted that respondent said he expected to file his 1993 tax return in Arizona, leading the court to conclude "that his statement about the Arizona residence is more likely true than the Albuquerque residence statement contained on the application." The record also showed that respondent had an Arizona driver's license. Observing that there were "ample indicia that Arizona is indeed his place of residence," the Arizona federal court concluded that respondent "intentionally and knowingly misled [the court] in furnishing information on an application for admission," and that "his application to practice in the Northern District of Texas contained more accurate and truthful information regarding his residence, but would not have permitted him to be admitted under the Local Rule to practice in this District." As a result, respondent was stricken from the roll of attorneys in the Arizona federal court on December 28, 1994. Several months thereafter, in October 1995, his admission to the bar of the United States District Court for the Northern District of Texas was revoked.

On October 3, 2000, the District of Columbia Office of Bar Counsel reported to this court the actions of the courts in Arizona and Texas.[2] A week later ... this court suspended respondent, ordered him to show cause before the Board within ten days why identical, greater, or lesser discipline should not be imposed, and directed the Board to submit its recommendation. On November 7, 2000, Bar Counsel filed a statement with the Board asserting that the greater sanction of disbarment should be imposed. The Board, in its Report and Recommendation, agrees with Bar Counsel and recommends that respondent be disbarred in the District of Columbia.[3]

After the Board issued its report, respondent filed with this court on January 19, 2002, a "Statement of Exception" to the Board's recommendation. At no prior time did he respond to the court's show cause order, nor did he participate in the proceedings before the Board.

II

[The court concluded that respondent had not waived his right to contest greater discipline by failing to participate in the Board's proceedings.]

III

When an attorney is brought before our disciplinary system for misconduct occurring in another jurisdiction, the applicable rule states:

---

2. Respondent failed to notify Bar Counsel of these disciplinary actions, as he was required to do by D.C. Bar Rule XI, § 11(b). Bar Counsel discovered them during the investigation of an unrelated matter.

3. Disbarment is a greater sanction than merely being stricken from the roll of attorneys. In the District of Columbia a disbarred attorney must wait five years before applying for reinstatement, see D.C. Bar Rule XI, § 16(a), whereas the Rules of Practice of the Arizona federal court do not require that an attorney stricken from its rolls wait for any prescribed period of time before seeking readmission. Thus an attorney stricken from the rolls by the Arizona federal court could be reinstated within less than five years.

Reciprocal discipline shall be imposed unless the attorney demonstrates, by clear and convincing evidence, that:

(1) The procedure elsewhere was so lacking in notice or opportunity to be heard as to constitute a deprivation of due process; or

(2) There was such infirmity of proof establishing the misconduct as to give rise to the clear conviction that the Court could not, consistently with its duty, accept as final the conclusion on that subject; or

(3) The imposition of the same discipline by the Court would result in grave injustice; or

(4) The misconduct established warrants substantially different discipline in the District of Columbia; or

(5) The misconduct elsewhere does not constitute misconduct in the District of Columbia.

D.C. Bar Rule XI, § 11(c). This rule "creates a rebuttable presumption that the discipline will be the same in the District of Columbia as it was in the original disciplining jurisdiction." *In re Zilberberg,* 612 A.2d 832, 834 (D.C. 1992) (citation and footnote omitted). The purpose of the presumption is to avoid "an inconsistent disposition involving identical conduct by the same attorney."

Nevertheless, the authority of the Board to recommend greater discipline, and of this court to impose it, is well established. While one or more of the five exceptions listed in section 11(c) are typically cited by an attorney in urging that lesser discipline is warranted in the District of Columbia, the "substantially different discipline" exception in paragraph (4) can also be relied upon by Bar Counsel in arguing for greater discipline.

Determining whether the "substantially different discipline" exception warrants greater or lesser discipline involves a two-step inquiry. "First, we determine if the misconduct in question would not have resulted in the same punishment here as it did in the disciplining jurisdiction." "Same punishment" is defined as a sanction "within the range of sanctions that would be imposed for the same misconduct." Accordingly, the appropriate question for us to address is not whether Bar Counsel would have sought disbarment for respondent's misconduct if it had originally occurred here, but whether the original discipline elsewhere is within the range of sanctions possible here. . . . Second, if the discipline imposed in the District of Columbia would be different from that of the original disciplining court, we must then decide whether the difference is "substantial."

Being stricken from the rolls of attorneys in the Arizona federal court is the functional equivalent of an indefinite suspension, and an indefinite suspension is not one of the seven possible sanctions this court is authorized to impose. *See* D.C. Bar Rule XI, § 3(a)(2) (allowing suspension only for "an appropriate fixed period of time"). While ordinarily we would try to fashion a disciplinary sanction that is "functionally equivalent" to that imposed in the original jurisdiction, we will not do so here because disbarment not only is the norm, but typically has been the *only* sanction imposed by this court for intentional misrepresentations during the application process to the degree displayed by respondent.... The only analogous cases we have found that resulted in a sanction less than disbarment are distinguishable because they did not involve intentional false statements, such as those made here....

Thus we conclude that the discipline imposed by the Arizona federal court is not within the range of sanctions imposed (or available) in this jurisdiction. Because both parts of the "substantially different discipline" analysis are met, we hold that the greater sanction of disbarment is warranted under Rule XI, § 11(c)(4).

IV

Respondent ... claims "the record shows that [he] lacked the intent to mislead the court in his application." We interpret this claim as an invocation of the "infirmity of proof" exception under Rule XI, § 11(c)(2), thus raising the possibility that his misconduct would be met with something less than disbarment (assuming he is also arguing that his misrepresentations were reckless rather than intentional; *see In re Rosen,* 570 A.2d at 729–730 (nine-month suspension for reckless misrepresentation on bar application)). We reject any such assertion. "Unless there is a finding by the Board under [section 11(c)(2)] that is accepted by the Court, a final determination by a disciplining court outside the District of Columbia ... shall conclusively establish the misconduct for the purpose of a reciprocal disciplinary proceeding in this Court." Rule XI, § 11(c). The "infirmity of proof" exception is "not an invitation to the attorney to relitigate in the District of Columbia the adverse findings of another court in a procedurally fair proceeding." Because respondent was afforded an opportunity to present evidence on his own behalf at a proceeding in Arizona that appears from the record to have been fundamentally fair, we find no merit in this argument.

NOTES

1.   What do you suppose respondent wanted to claim about his misstatements in the Arizona district court? What precluded him from doing so?

2.   Do you think it is fair that lawyers in reciprocal discipline proceedings may not have the opportunity to relitigate the issues determined in the original proceeding? Why or why not?

3.   The D.C. rules on reciprocal discipline are similar, though not identical to, the reciprocal discipline rules contained in the ABA Model Rules for Lawyer Disciplinary Enforcement. Many jurisdictions have similar rules, which view another state's disciplinary proceeding as conclusively establishing the facts of the violation unless one of the exceptions applies. The exceptions are stingily recognized for the most part, and notwithstanding the invitation to do so, most courts applying reciprocal discipline conclude that the facts have been established by the foreign jurisdiction's determination in the matter.

PROBLEMS

1. Lawyer was admitted to practice in Kentucky. She was disbarred in Kentucky because she was convicted of a crime. Before her Kentucky indictment, Lawyer took and passed the Colorado bar examination. She did not disclose her subsequent conviction to the Colorado authorities, and she was admitted to practice in Colorado. When the Colorado authorities learned of Lawyer's failure to disclose in the admissions proceeding, she was suspended for one year. Five years later, Lawyer wanted to appear in a case in federal court in the District of Nevada. She sought court leave to be admitted pro hac vice. While the application for pro hac vice admission specifically inquired into prior discipline, Lawyer did not disclose her prior history. Subsequently, the Nevada court learned of Lawyer's misrepresentations and barred her from practicing in the District of Nevada for one year. What discipline, if any, in Colorado? *See People v. Mattox*, 862 P.2d 276 (Colo. 1993).

2. Chastain was a lawyer admitted to practice in both Colorado and South Carolina. He was disbarred in South Carolina for engaging in the unauthorized practice of law while under a suspension order. Based on the South Carolina disbarment, disciplinary proceedings were initiated against Chastain in Colorado. Chastain did not answer the allegations and did not appear in the proceeding. Can he be subjected to the same discipline in Colorado that he received in South Carolina? *See People v. Chastain*, 109 P.3d 1072 (Colo. O.P.D.J. 2005).

3. Gottesman was admitted to practice in Arizona and New Jersey. New Jersey imposed discipline on him; it found that he had worked with a private investigator with whom he divided attorney's fees and had assisted the investigator in the unauthorized practice of law. In the Arizona reciprocal discipline proceeding, Gottesman wanted to argue that he did not share fees with the investigator or assist him in the unauthorized practice of law. May he make those arguments before the Arizona court? *See In re Gottesman*, 834 P.2d 1266 (Ariz. 1992).

4. Lawyer was licensed to practice law in Texas and Oklahoma. The Texas disciplinary authorities initiated a discipline proceeding; Lawyer asked to be permitted to resign, and the court accepted his resignation. Oklahoma authorities then sought to impose reciprocal discipline on Lawyer based on his Texas resignation pending discipline. Under the Texas disciplinary rules, if the attorney moves to resign in lieu of discipline, disciplinary counsel submits a detailed description of the attorney's alleged conduct, and if the attorney does not withdraw the motion to resign, the allegations are deemed conclusively established. May Oklahoma impose reciprocal discipline? What should the punishment be? Does it matter if Lawyer claimed that he did not contest the Texas proceeding because he had already decided not to practice law in Texas any more? *See Oklahoma Bar Ass'n v. Heinen*, 60 P.3d 1018 (Ok. 2002).

5. Iulo was admitted to practice in New Jersey. He was convicted of misappropriating client funds (though the court described him as "an inept bookkeeper rather than a self-interested thief") and was permanently disbarred in 1989. Over several years, beginning in 1990, Iulo sought permission

to sit for the Pennsylvania bar examination. He disclosed his past disciplinary history and criminal conviction fully to the bar examiners. After several years, he was granted permission to sit for the bar examination; he passed it and was admitted to the Pennsylvania bar in July 1999. In December 1999, a proceeding for reciprocal disbarment was brought based on Iulo's New Jersey disbarment. Should he be subjected to reciprocal discipline? Is it relevant that in New Jersey, disbarment is for all intents and purposes permanent, with no realistic possibility for reinstatement? *See In re Iulo*, 766 A.2d 335 (Pa. 2001).

6.   Lawyer was disbarred in Florida for trust account violations. New York imposed reciprocal discipline on Lawyer and disbarred him based on the Florida disbarment. In New York, a disbarred lawyer is not eligible to apply for reinstatement until seven years from the date of disbarment. Florida permits a disbarred lawyer to apply for readmission five years after disbarment. Can Lawyer reapply in Florida after five years, or must he wait seven years? *See In re Simring*, 802 So.2d 1111 (Fla. 2000).

INDEX

References are to Pages

623

†